Correctional Contexts

Contemporary and Classical Readings

Third Edition

Edward J. Latessa
University of Cincinnati

Alexander M. Holsinger
University of Missouri, Kansas City

Roxbury Publishing Company
Los Angeles, California

Library of Congress Cataloging-in-Publication Data

Correctional contexts: contemporary and classical readings/ [edited by] Edward J. Latessa, Alexander M. Holsinger—3rd. ed.

p. cm.

Includes bibliographical references.

ISBN 1-931719-59-4

1. Corrections—United States. 2. Corrections—United States—History. 3. Prisons—United States. 4. Imprisonment—United States. I. Latessa, Edward J. II. Holsinger, Alexander M.

HV9466.C67 2006

365'.973–dc22

2004052458

CIP

Publisher: Claude Teweles
Managing Editor: Dawn VanDercreek
Production Editor: Carla Plucknett
Copy Editor: Cheryl Adam
Proofreaders: Christina Graunke and Scott Oney
Typography: SDS Design, info@sds-design.com
Cover Design: Marnie Kenney

Printed on acid-free paper in the United States of America. This paper meets the standards for recycling of the Environmental Protection Agency.

ISBN 1-931719-59-4

Roxbury Publishing Company
P.O. Box 491044
Los Angeles, California 90049-9044
Voice: (310) 473-3312 • Fax: (310) 473-4490
Email: roxbury@roxbury.net
Website: www.roxbury.net

To our children:
Amy, Jennifer, Michael, & Allison
and
Jordan, Lucas, & Elijah

Contents

Part I: History and Purpose of Punishment and Imprisonment

Pieter C. Spierenburg

Using a systems approach, Spierenburg explores the origins of the criminal justice system and the rise of the nation-state in preindustrial western Europe. The criminal justice system at several points throughout history is identified as a tool of governmental repression.

David J. Rothman

Urbanization, industrialization, and reform are considered in Rothman's piece studying the rise of the American penitentiary. Both the origin and design of early penal institutions are investigated.

Thorsten Sellin

The transition from confinement existing strictly for the purpose of detention to confinement as the punishment itself is investigated by Sellin. Issues surrounding the conditions within the early institutions as well as prison labor are explored.

Nicole Hahn Rafter

Rafter examines the criminal justice system in general, and the Albion, New York, institution for women in particular, as mechanisms of social control for women throughout the early twentieth century.

---

*Denotes chapters new to this edition.

Part II: Living and Working in Prison

*Denotes chapters new to this edition.

*Denotes chapters new to this edition.

Part III: Prison Policy and Inmate Rights

Part IV: Institutional Programming and Treatment

---

*Denotes chapters new to this edition.

*Denotes chapters new to this edition.

Part V: Release From Prison and Parole

*Denotes chapters new to this edition.

Part VI: New Directions

---

*Denotes chapters new to this edition.

*Denotes chapters new to this edition.

xii

Preface

This anthology traces the history and development of institutional corrections and punishment as they have evolved in the United States over the past few centuries. This collection of articles and essays offers the reader a critical review of where "corrections" in the United States has been in the past, how various facets of the system operate today, and where as a country we may be headed regarding the confinement and treatment of our incarcerated populations.

We have tried to combine some classical writings with more contemporary works throughout this volume. We believe that it is important to understand where we started in order to appreciate where we are today. We have tried to update the Third Edition of this volume by providing relevant articles on some of the pressing issues facing corrections: renewed debate about the effectiveness of treatment and rehabilitation, how to improve reentry and transition back into the community, and some of the realities of social policies that have led to record numbers of our citizens being under correctional sanctions. Included are essays highlighting the rehabilitative treatment efforts within and outside of institutions, the increasingly critical role of reentry, and significant sources for future influences in corrective efforts. This collection of essays is designed to offer the reader a comprehensive and relevant review and critical analysis of the myriad of issues that concern our corrective efforts.

We hope that you find this anthology interesting and informative and a starting point in your studies and work in the field of corrections. ✦

Acknowledgments

We wish to express our sincere appreciation to those who gave of their time and effort in many different capacities to assist us in assembling this anthology.

First, the many reviewers of both the First and Second Edition who took the time to provide feedback and critiques. These include Susan Bourke (University of Cincinnati), Marie L. Griffin (Arizona State University West), Andrea Leverentz (DePaul University), Eric Ling (Mt. Olive College), John Linn (Pennsylvania State University, Altoona), Barbara Sims (Pennsylvania State University, Harrisburg), Chad Trulson (University of North Texas), Gary Webb (Ball State University), and John Whitehead (Eastern Tennessee State University). We read each review carefully and tried our best to incorporate the suggestions offered. We hope that this new edition meets your needs.

Second, we owe a great deal of debt to our colleagues at the University of Cincinnati, Lawrence F. Travis III and Christopher T. Lowenkamp. The original contributions they made to this volume were invaluable and helped us fill some important voids.

Finally, we wish to express our sincere appreciation to those who gave of their time and effort in many different capacities to assist us in assembling this anthology: Janice Miller of the University of Cincinnati, Kristi Holsinger of the University of Missouri–Kansas City, and Claude Teweles and Carla Plucknett of Roxbury Publishing Company. ✦

About the Contributors

Jack Henry Abbott was a convicted murderer and the author of *In the Belly of the Beast*. He committed suicide in prison in New York in 2001.

Don A. Andrews is a Professor of Psychology at Carleton University.

James Austin is on the faculty at George Washington University.

Peter J. Benekos teaches in the Administration of Justice program at Mercyhurst College.

Tim Bynum is a Professor at Michigan State University in the School of Criminal Justice.

Jack E. Call is a Professor of Criminal Justice at Radford University.

Madeline Carter is with the Center for Sex Offender Management.

Donald Clemmer completed pioneering research in 1940 on the prison inmate subculture in his book, *The Prison Community*.

Mark B. Coggeshall is a graduate student in the Department of Criminology and Criminal Justice, University of Maryland.

Ted Conover is the author of *Newjack: Guarding Sing Sing*.

Francis T. Cullen is a Distinguished Research Professor of Criminal Justice at the University of Cincinnati.

Craig Dowden is a doctoral candidate at Carleton University.

Betsy Fulton is an Associate Professor in the College of Justice Administration at Eastern Kentucky University.

Catherine A. Gallagher is in the Department of Public and International Affairs, George Mason University.

Paul Gendreau is Professor and Director of the Institute of Criminal Justice at the University of New Brunswick.

Erving Goffman was Benjamin Franklin Professor of Anthropology and Sociology at the University of Pennsylvania and president of the American Sociological Association at the time of his death. His many influential books include *The Presentation of Self in Everyday Life* (1959), *Asylums* (1961), *Relations in Public* (1971), and *Frame Analysis* (1974).

Craig Haney is Director of the Program in Legal Studies at the University of California, Santa Cruz.

Eliot S. Hartstone is President of Spectrum Research Associates.

Victor Hassine is inmate AM4737 in the Pennsylvania Department of Corrections.

Rodney J. Henningsen is on the faculty in the College of Criminal Justice, Sam Houston State University.

Seymour M. Hersh is an investigative reporter and writer.

John Irwin is Professor Emeritus of sociology at San Francisco State University.

Robert Johnson teaches in the Department of Justice, Law and Society at the American University.

W. Wesley Johnson is Assistant Dean of Undergraduate Studies, College of Criminal Justice, Sam Houston State University.

Edward J. Latessa is Professor and Head of the Division of Criminal Justice at the University of Cincinnati.

Thomas P. LeBel is a doctoral student at the School of Criminal Justice, University at Albany, State University of New York.

Sharon Levrant is a former doctoral student at the University of Cincinnati.

Christopher T. Lowenkamp is a Research Assistant Professor, Department of Criminal Justice, University of Cincinnati.

Arthur J. Lurigio is Chairperson of and Professor in the Department of Criminal Justice, Loyola University of Chicago.

Doris L. MacKenzie is a Professor, Department of Criminology and Criminal Justice, University of Maryland.

Robert Martinson was a member of the New York State Governor's Special Committee on Criminal Offenders that was responsible for analyzing the effectiveness of treatment programs, resulting in the publication of the infamous *Martinson Report*.

Shadd Maruna is an Assistant Professor at the Institute of Criminology at the University of Cambridge in the United Kingdom.

Scott Matson is with the Center for Sex Offender Management.

Alida V. Merlo teaches in the Department of Criminology at Indiana University of Pennsylvania.

John Monahan is a Professor of Law at the University of Virginia.

Charles Onley is with the Center for Sex Offender Management.

Dina Perrone is a research assistant and doctoral student at the School of Criminal Justice at Rutgers University.

Roger H. Peters is a Professor in the Department of Mental Health, Law, and Policy, Louis de la Parte Florida Mental Health Institute, University of South Florida.

Joan Petersilia, Ph.D., is a Professor in the School of Social Ecology, University of California, Irvine.

Travis Pratt is an Assistant Professor of political science/criminal justice at Washington State University.

Nicole Hahn Rafter teaches in the College of Criminal Justice at Northeastern University.

Pamela Clark Robbins is Vice President of Policy Research Associates in Delmar, New York.

David J. Rothman is Bernard Schoenberg Professor of Social Medicine and professor of history at Columbia University.

Thorsten Sellin was Emeritus Professor of Sociology, University of Pennsylvania.

Pieter C. Spierenburg teaches in the Department of History at Erasmus University in Rotterdam, Holland.

Henry J. Steadman is President of Policy Research Associates in Delmar, New York.

Marc L. Steinberg is on the faculty of the Psychology Department, University of South Florida.

Jeremy Travis is President of John Jay College and former director of the National Institute of Justice.

Lawrence F. Travis III is Professor of Criminal Justice and director of the Center for Criminal Justice Research, University of Cincinnati.

Vera Institute of Justice works closely with leaders in government and civil society to improve the services people rely on for safety and justice. Vera develops innovative, affordable programs that often grow into self-sustaining organizations, studies social problems and current responses, and provides practical advice and assistance to governmental officials in New York and around the world.

Terry Wells is in the Department of Government, Georgia College and State University, in Milledgeville, Georgia.

David B. Wilson in on the faculty of the Administration of Justice Department at George Mason University.

John F. Wozniak is a Professor in the Department of Sociology and Anthropology at Western Illinois University.

Philip Zimbardo is a Professor of Psychology at Stanford University. ✦

About the Editors

Edward J. Latessa, Ph.D. Dr. Latessa is Professor and Head of the Division of Criminal Justice at the University of Cincinnati. Dr. Latessa has published more than 75 works in the area of criminal justice, corrections, and juvenile justice. He is co-author of seven books including *Corrections in the Community*, which is now in its Third Edition, and the Tenth Edition of *Corrections in America*. Dr. Latessa has directed more than 60 funded research projects, including studies of day reporting centers, juvenile justice programs, drug courts, intensive supervision programs, halfway houses, and drug programs. He and his staff have also assessed more than 350 correctional programs throughout the United States. Dr. Latessa is a consultant with the National Institute of Corrections, and he has provided assistance and workshops in more than 40 states. Dr. Latessa served as president of the Academy of Criminal Justice Sciences (ACJS) in 1989–1990. He has also received several awards, including the August Vollmer Award from the American Society of Criminology (2004), the Simon Dinitz Criminal Justice Research Award from the Ohio Department of Rehabilitation and Correction (2002), the Margaret Mead Award for dedicated service to the causes of social justice and humanitarian advancement by the International Community Corrections Association (2001), the Peter P. Lejins Award for Research from the American Correctional Association (1999), the ACJS Fellow Award (1998), the ACJS Founders Award (1992), and the Simon Dinitz Award by the Ohio Community Corrections Organization.

Alexander M. Holsinger, Ph.D. For the last several years, Dr. Holsinger has been conducting research, teaching, and training in the areas of offender classification, risk prediction, correctional program effectiveness, and criminological theory. He received his Ph.D. in criminal justice from the University of Cincinnati, Division of Criminal Justice. His research and training interests include offender classification, prison privatization, community corrections, and measuring the effectiveness of correctional programming and treatment. His teaching consists of several different corrections-based courses, as well as statistics and research methods. Dr. Holsinger is currently serving as Assistant Professor in the Department of Sociology/Criminal Justice & Criminology at the University of Missouri–Kansas City. In addition to his academic pursuits, he serves as President of the Inmate Services Advisory Board for the Jackson County Detention Center, and is a member of Missouri Department of Corrections' Citizen Advisory Board. ✦

Introduction

Prior to the nineteenth century in the United States, facilities designed to hold offenders were largely regarded as a vehicle toward an ultimate end punishment of some form or another for persons who had committed a crime against another individual. Detainment was merely a means of holding an individual while he or she awaited *real* punishment. The punishment to be carried out was often a publicly held flogging, branding, disfigurement, lengthy term in the stocks, or execution. After society realized the brutality of these punishments, and coupled with a societal philosophical shift (in the form of the Enlightenment), for all intents and purposes the penitentiary was born. From that point forward, punishment in the United States mainly consisted of a term in an institution, where one lived in congregate style with many other individuals who had met a similar fate. This is not to say, however, that the birth of the prison meant an end to somewhat brutal practices within the walls of the institution.

The original purpose of the early penitentiaries was to instill repentance in the offender (hence, the root of the term, *penitent*). Reform was certainly the goal, but primarily by way of the errant offenders seeking forgiveness from God, through the (at times silent) contemplation of their "sins."

Since that time, the penitentiary has undergone many changes in both form and philosophy. Religious atonement was put aside and a concentration on skill development (through educational and vocational programming) took its place. Other changes occurred in the U.S. sentencing structure, perhaps most notably with the advent of the indeterminate sentence. This paved the way for what came to be known as the *medical model*. Offenders would be housed in prison until they "became better" or had been

"healed." Not surprisingly, this model rested on the assumption that the prison was indeed *able* to identify, target, and change the factors that had led someone into criminal activity. The indeterminate sentence has since been largely replaced by determinate sentencing structures (along with the instigation of the *justice model*) due to disparity in sentencing. Part I of this text explores the origins of punishment and charts the development of the institution as a form of punishment. In addition, trends in sentencing as well as the evolution of treatment and correctional policy are presented and analyzed.

Life inside an institution (regardless of its size) provides a unique set of parameters around which the individual must conform. As such, much study during the twentieth century was directed toward the effect that the institution has on individuals and groups. Similarly, researchers have studied how individuals and groups affect and shape the institution. has motivated the study of both inmates and correctional workers. Several hypotheses have been formulated and investigated regarding what the most important factors are in the prison environment. Because the prison is a *total institution*, it has provided a somewhat self-contained laboratory for the student of human interaction. Until the mid-twentieth century, many never imagined that the offender could have an impact on the day-to-day routine within the institution in the long term. Part II is a completely new section that integrates literature on living and working in prison. Five new articles are included that represent pieces rich in depth and detail regarding the firsthand experience of being an inmate inside a prison, as well as being a new guard. The "convict code" as well as the intricacies of negotiating the correctional officer subculture are explored. Also included is a new article reviewing much of what is known regarding the debate surrounding the privatization of state prison systems.

Although some have argued about details of the true beginning of significant inmate litigation (i.e., the prisoners' rights movement), some important changes occurred during the twentieth century that have influenced prisons themselves as well as the numbers of individuals sent to them. Perhaps most notably, the courts have shown a willingness to check the conditions inside an institution. This refers to both physical and procedural conditions. The advent of these rights has served to change the prison experience for many offenders and has also brought forth issues regarding the institutions' ability to modify behavior in the long term (post-release). Besides legislation regarding the rights of prison inmates, sentencing structures for many states have added the possibility of life imprisonment for third-time (usually violent) felony offenders. Introducing an increasingly larger group of "lifers" will undoubtedly have lasting effects for many U.S. prisons, especially in the buildings and grounds, in the daily routines, and in the availability of programming. Part III of this text (which contains all new articles) explores several issues within prison policy—significant developments in prison litigation throughout the latter half of the twentieth century, as well as other aspects of prison policy. Also examined in this third section is the prison abuse scandal that occurred at Abu Ghraib in Iraq.

Several studies of offender treatment within institutions and in the community have revealed the efficacy of correctional treatment, provided it is the correct treatment directed toward the correct populations. Advances have been made in the areas of offender classification and treatment mechanisms, for instance. Treatment programs regarding substance abuse, sexual offending, and educational/vocational training have been examined to specify in detail what works, and how. In addition, specific populations, such as mentally disordered offenders and the growing number of female offenders, have been scrutinized in the same way. Part IV of this text provides a broad and detailed examination of the history and current state of correctional treatment intervention within both the institutional correctional setting and corrections in general. Three new articles have been added to this volume, which present the state of the art regarding the principles of effective treatment intervention, the most effective strategies to employ with sex offenders, and the professional landscape of correctional treatment intervention. The result is a section that explores the most pertinent issues when considering what is necessary to produce long-term change in an offender. Simultaneously, several specific issues such as treating the female offender population and special-needs populations such as mentally disordered offenders are examined as well.

Offender reentry into the community has moved to the forefront of correctional policy debate over the last few years. Increasing amounts of attention have been devoted to all issues relating to the offender who spends some time in prison, then reenters society. Just as prison populations have continued to increase, so have the populations of former inmates who are residing in the community (either completely on their own or under the supervision of a parole officer). Four new articles have been added to this volume that constitute the entirety of Part V, "Release From Prison and Parole." Two articles deal specifically with the pertinent issue of offender reentry. One article examines the special needs of parolees with active mental illnesses. In addition, a brand-new research article has been added that presents the reader with a very large study of the effectiveness of halfway houses as they assist offenders making the transition back into society.

Part VI of this text includes two new articles that explore two pertinent and dynamic issues within corrections—restorative justice, and how legislators view prisons and their purpose. These two pieces add to the existing chapters that present the reader with food for thought as the correctional system in the United States continues to grow and change at increasing rates. When considering the history and present of corrections in the United States, the only constant appears to be dynamic change. This pattern of change will likely continue to reflect what is going on in the greater society in the form of creative new innovations, philosophies, and strategies. The essays in this book represent a sampling of some important works in corrections, both past and current. We believe the best future correctional approach will come from the use of objective scientific discovery, such as that which is embodied in this volume. ✦

Part I

History and Purpose of Punishment and Imprisonment

Perhaps one of the greatest and most complex social dilemmas has been the processing and treatment of the social deviant. Members of any society who do not follow rules and norms pose a natural threat to the group as a whole. Mechanisms and strategies have long been in place to deal with the errant, but the form and reason behind them have varied greatly over the centuries. However, the underlying goal has remained constant—finding ways in which to respond to and correct what can be a complex set of problems within each individual.

Although the traditional Auburn-style prison is perhaps the most common image representing punishment in the United States, dealing with offenders has a somewhat varied past. Prior to the nineteenth century, for instance, confinement was viewed as a means to an end, rather than an end in and of itself. Large-scale facilities designed to meet any correctional goal did not exist to any great degree. Instead, confinement occurred briefly, prior to the actual punishment.

Pre-Enlightenment punishments were often Biblically based and corporal in nature. Brandings, whippings, stocks and pillories, ducking stools, thumbscrews, and execution were fashioned and performed to publicly humiliate offenders. Through pain and public humiliation, offenders were expected to atone for their social sins—sins committed against God, a monarch, and/or society. This served an assumed secondary goal of general deterrence. Public punishment was in part a warning to others of their potential fate should they commit similar offenses.

There is no dispute that pre-Enlightenment punishment in general was severe. What often compounded the severity of the punishment were instances where the punishment clearly did not fit the crime. It was not uncommon for petty thefts, adultery, or vagrancy (just to name a few examples) to carry disproportionate and permanently physically disfiguring government responses. One of the social forces that created a correctional conversion was quite possibly public outrage at this disproportionate sentencing structure. Perhaps the desired effect of general deterrence created an unintended consequence of raising public awareness (and outcry) to what was perceived as an unfair state response to relatively minor behavior.

The Enlightenment brought about great change in the application of punishment, due in large part to thinkers such as Cesar Beccaria, Jeremy Bentham, and Voltaire. The net effect of the writings of these philosophers and others was to draw attention to the brutality meted out by the state at that time. As a result, confinement itself was identified as a new "end" in the punishment spectrum. Housing offenders together in large-scale, secure facilities would allow for the accomplishment of different and apparently more humane goals.

In the United States, 1819 saw the birth of the penitentiary in Auburn, New York, with many other states soon implementing this correctional strategy. Although public floggings, drawing and quartering, and other forms of torture were placed aside, the conditions inside this first American prison were in many respects no less destructive.

Originally, prisoners were not afforded opportunities for activity (leisure or labor); they were kept in total isolation from one another, and total silence was enforced. Provisions were minimal, conditions were dreary, and offenders were required to contemplate a sin-free (i.e., crime-free) lifestyle. The unfair humiliation and cruel disfiguring punishments largely criticized by Enlightenment philosophers had become a thing of the past. The alternative, however, resulted in punishment turning into a much longer, drawn-out affair with its own set of drawbacks, despite the over-arching goal that offenders should contemplate and ultimately reject a sinful lifestyle. Nevertheless, the Auburn-style prison set the stage for a new era in corrections—one that still determines practices of imprisonment.

In addition to a reconsideration of the delivery of punishment, the Enlightenment brought about other changes in the criminal justice system—principally, the seeds of due process. The nineteenth century also ushered in questions regarding the causation of crime (on both the individual and societal levels). The belief that human beings are indeed free to choose a criminal lifestyle further opened up the possibility that they can just as well choose a crime-free lifestyle.

Although the housing of offenders in large-scale penitentiaries was designed to invoke positive change, offenders were nonetheless viewed largely as slaves of the state. Issues arose throughout the nineteenth and twentieth centuries regarding the value of prison industrial labor, the management of increasing populations of offenders, and the challenges of handling a more diverse population with complex needs.

At several points during the nineteenth and twentieth centuries, the purposes and practices of imprisonment were reviewed and critiqued. Propositions were put forth questioning practices that inhibit the accomplishment of offender reform. This is of particular importance (even today), as correctional options thus were reduced to essentially one—imprisonment.

Over the past 200 years, the United States has relied heavily on imprisonment as the general population has swelled and as new crime enforcement strategies have boosted prisoner populations (e.g., the war on crime, the war on drugs, and three-strikes legislation). The dilemma of overcrowded prisons that may not be capable of rehabilitating has called into question the true utility of such a strategy. Hence, the United States' imprisonment binge is under consideration in hopes of revealing pathways toward improvement. The reader of the following selections is encouraged to take note of the true origins of modern-day punishment, especially the contributions from Enlightenment thinkers. The movement from arbitrary corporal punishment to methods of mass confinement may be viewed as an improvement in some respects. However, the long-term consequences brought on by the accompanying set of problems caused by large-scale imprisonment are deserving of more thought. ✦

1
The Spectacle of Suffering

Pieter C. Spierenburg

Pieter C. Spierenburg reveals the origins of
the criminal justice system through an inves-
tigation of the beginnings of state-enforced
punishment. The feudal system in Western
Europe provides the backdrop for what ulti-
mately represents a shift away from personal
vengeance as the primary impetus for punish-
ment. Criminal behavior came to be viewed
as a sin against the state, rather than a sin
against another individual. As such, it be-
came the state's responsibility to regulate the
processing of offenders. Secondary to the rise
of the nation-state as a precursor of state-en-
forced punishment is urbanization. Although
urbanization may have provided an initial
opportunity for greater public display of pun-
ishment that was rooted in general deter-
rence, it was ultimately the revulsion of the
public that led to what Spierenburg calls the
privatization of repression. Above all else,
Spierenburg highlights the importance of
considering the greater social context when
analyzing major changes in a society's pun-
ishing mechanisms.

The Emergence of
Criminal Justice

From the way in which I have defined repression, it is obvious that its evolution
should be intimately connected with the development of the state. The practice of criminal justice was one of the means by which
authorities, with or without success, attempted to keep the population in line. As
the position of these authorities changed,

the character of criminal justice changed.
However, before we can speak of criminal
justice in any society, at least a rudimentary
state organization has to be present. A system of repression presupposes a minimal
level of state formation. Differentiation of
this system, moreover, also presupposes the
rise of towns. This . . . is an attempt to trace
the origins of preindustrial repression. . . . It
focuses on repression as a system of control,
the emergence of which was a function of
the rise of territorial principalities and of
urbanization.

At the height of the feudal age in Western
Europe the state hardly existed at all. Violent entrepreneurs were in constant competition; from his castle a baron would dominate the immediate surroundings and de
facto recognize no higher authority. His
domain may be called a unit of attack and
defense but not a state. Essentially it comprised a network of ties of affiliation and
bondage. But in the violent competition
between the numerous chiefs of such networks the mechanism was imminent which
would eventually lead to the emergence of
states. The first units with the character of a
state were the territorial principalities
which appeared from the twelfth century
onwards.

As it happens, the emergence of criminal
justice also dates from the twelfth century.
Several legal historians have studied the
"birth of punishment" or "emergence of
public penal law." The most detailed work is
by P. W. A. Immink. This author also comes
closest to a sociological-historical view of
the subject. He placed the origins of punishment in the context of changing relationships of freedom and dependence in feudal
society. Thus he avoided presenting an analysis of legal texts alone, which can be very
misleading especially for the period in question. From a sociological-historical perspective, the essence of criminal justice is a relationship of subordination. This was noted
by Immink: "In common parlance the term
'punishment' is never used unless the person upon whom the penalty is inflicted is

clearly subordinate to the one imposing the penal act." This is the crucial point. This element distinguishes punishment from vengeance and the feud, where the parties are equal. If there is no subordination, there is no punishment.

The earliest subordinates in Europe were slaves. In that agrarian society, from Germanic times up into the feudal period, freemen were not subject to a penal system, but unfree persons were. The lord of a manor exercised an almost absolute authority over his serfs. When the latter were beaten or put to death "or maybe even fined" for some illegal act, this can certainly be called punishment. The manorial penal system of those early ages belonged to the realm of custom and usually did not form part of written law. Therefore we do not know much about it. The Barbarian Codes (*Leges Barbarorum*) were meant for freemen. They only referred to unfree persons in cases where their actions could lead to a conflict between freemen.

Free persons, on the other hand, settled their conflicts personally. There were a few exceptions to this, even in Germanic times. In certain cases, if a member was held to have acted against the vital interests of the tribe, he could be expelled from the tribal community (branded a "wolf") or even killed. But on the whole, as there was no arbiter strong enough to impose his will, private individuals settled their own conflicts. A settlement could be reached through revenge or reconciliation. Vengeance and the feud were accepted forms of private retaliation, but they did not necessarily follow every injury. In a situation where violence is not monopolized, private violence is potentially omnipresent but does not always manifest itself in practice. Notably, it can be bought off. Reconciliation through payment to the injured party was already known in Tacitus' time.

To the earliest powerful rulers who represented an embryonic public authority, encouragement of this custom was the obvious road to be taken if they wished to reduce private violence. This is in fact what the Barbarian Codes are all about. In every instance they fix the amount which can buy off vengeance. These sums are not fines in the modern sense, but indemnities. They were either meant as compensation when a person had been killed, wounded or assaulted (*wergeld*) or as a form of restitution when property had been stolen, destroyed or damaged. Among freemen this remained the dominant system well into the twelfth century.

Criminal justice, however, slowly developed alongside this system. Its evolution during the feudal period was construed by Immink as one argument against the thesis put forward by Viktor Achter. The latter had argued that punishment suddenly emerged in Languedoc in the middle of the twelfth century, from where it spread to the rest of Europe. Although Immink placed the definite breakthrough around the same time, he believed the evolution of punishment was inextricably linked with feudalism. The feudalization of Western Europe had brought about a fundamental change in the notion of freedom. This change eventually led to the emergence of criminal justice.

Before the feudal age the notion of freedom was closely connected to the allod. An allod should not be considered as a piece of property in the modern sense, but rather as an estate which is free from outside interference. Its occupant is completely his own master. His freedom implies a total independence from any worldly power and is similar to what later came to be called sovereignty. Hence the relationship of a freeman with the unfree persons subject to him, and over whom he exercises a right of punishment, is not one of owner-owned but one of ruler-ruled. The development of the institution of vassalage slowly put an end to the notion of freedom based on the allod. The Frankish kings and their successors attached freemen to themselves in a relationship of lord and *fideles*. Hence the latter were no longer entirely independent. By the time the whole network of feudal ties had finally been established, the notion of freedom had been transformed. Freedom meant being bound directly to the king, or to be more precise, there were degrees of freedom depending on how direct the allegiance was.

The feudal transformation of the notion of freedom formed the basis of the emergence of a penal system applied to freemen. The king remained the only free person in the ancient allodial sense, the only sovereign. His reaction to a breach of faith by his vassal (*infidelitas*, felony), usually the imposition of death, can truly be called punishment. The king himself never had a *wergeld*, because no one was his equal. His application of punishment for *infidelitas* resembled the exercise of justice by a master over his serfs. When more and more illegal acts were defined as felonies, the emergence of a penal system with corporal and capital punishments applied to freemen became steadily more apparent.

The implication of Immink's analysis for the study of state formation processes is evident. Absence of a central authority is reflected in the prevalence of private vengeance, the feud or voluntary reconciliation. The development of criminal justice runs parallel to the emergence of slightly stronger rulers. Originally it is only practiced within the confines of a manor; later it is applied by the rulers of kingdoms and territories. But we do not have to accept every part of Immink's story. For one thing, in his description the evolution of criminal justice and the parallel decline of the feud appeared too much as an unlinear process. This follows partly from his criticism of Achter. The latter, for instance, saw the legal reforms of the Carolingian period as a precocious spurt in the direction of a breakthrough of a modern notion of punishment. This would be in line with the fact that this period also witnessed a precocious sort of monopoly of authority. Achter considered the spurt as an isolated episode followed by centuries of silence. This may be too crude. Immink, however, with his conception of an

ultimate continuity, seems to go too far in the other direction, playing down the unsettled character of the ninth and tenth centuries. These were certainly times when the vendetta was prevalent, despite whatever intentions legislators might have harbored. On the other hand, we should not overestimate the degree of monopolization of authority around AD 800. The Carolingian Empire and its successor kingdoms were no more than temporary sets of allegiances over a wide geographic area, held together by the personal prestige of an individual king or by a military threat from outside. From Roman times until the twelfth century Europe witnessed nothing approaching a state, but there were certainly spurts in that direction.

In the middle of the twelfth century the first territorial principalities made their appearance and a penal system applied to freemen was established. The symbiosis is evident. Criminal justice emerged because the territorial princes were the first rulers powerful enough to combat private vengeance to a certain degree. The church had already attempted to do so, but largely in vain. I leave aside the question of whether its representatives were motivated by ideological reasons or by the desire to protect ecclesiastical goods. In any case they needed the strong arm of secular powers in order to succeed. The *treuga Dei* only acquired some measure of effectiveness when it became the "country's peace." Two of the earliest regions to witness this development were Angevin England "which can also be seen as a territorial principality" and the duchy of Aquitaine.

Incidentally, the South of France is also the region where, according to Achter, the concept of punishment originated. It is interesting that he reached this conclusion even though he used quite different sources and from a different perspective. Achter considered the element of moral disapproval as the essence of punishment. This notion was largely absent from Germanic law, which did not differentiate between accidents and intentional acts. If a felled tree accidentally killed a man the full *wergeld* still had to be paid. Immink criticized this view and it may be another point where his rejection is too radical. He indicated, in fact, how Achter's view can be integrated into an approach focusing on state-formation processes. For the private avenger redressing a personal wrong, the wickedness of the other party is so self-evident that it need not be stated. As long as the law merely attempts to encourage reconciliation, it is likewise indifferent to a moral appreciation of the acts which started the conflict. When territorial lords begin to administer punishments to persons who have not wronged them personally, their attitudes to the law change as well. Theorizing about the law increases. The beginnings of a distinction between civil and criminal cases become apparent. The latter are *iniquitates*, acts that are to be disapproved of morally and which put their author at the *misericordia* of his lord.

Thus it is understandable that a new emphasis on the moral reprehensibility of illegal acts also dates from the middle of the twelfth century. Indeed this period witnessed an early wave of moralization-individualization, connected to what medievalists have long been accustomed to call the Renaissance of the twelfth century. And yet we should not overestimate this spurt towards individualization, certainly not with regard to penal practice. Before the twelfth century there may have been even less concern for the motives and intentions of the perpetrators of illegal acts, but . . . the practice of criminal justice continued to focus on crimes and their impact on the community rather than on the criminal's personality and the intricacies of his guilt. Up into the nineteenth century repression was not primarily individualized.

There is another aspect of the transformation under discussion which merits attention. When a malefactor finds himself at the mercy (*misericordia*) of a prince, the implication is that a religious notion has entered criminal justice. Mercy was an attribute of God, the ultimate judge. The relationship of all people with God had always been viewed as one of subordination. Hence God was indeed able to punish. Any wrong suffered, such as the loss of a combat, could be seen as a divine punishment, of which another man was merely the agent. Heavenly justice was never an automatic response. The Lord could be severe or show mercy. By analogy this line of thought was also applied to human justice practiced by a territorial lord.

Several authors discussed the "sacred quality" of preindustrial punishment and even considered it an explanatory factor for its character. According to this view, executions, especially capital ones, were a sort of sacrifice, an act of expiation. They reconciled the deity offended by the crime and restored the order of society sanctioned by heaven. This notion may have been part of the experience of executions, although there is little direct evidence for it. But it would certainly be incorrect to attribute an explanatory value to it as being in some way the essence of public punishment. For one thing, during and after the Middle Ages *every* social event also had a religious element. In the absence of a division between the sacred and the profane, religion pervaded life entirely. To note the sacred quality of executions in this context is actually redundant. If a religious view of the world has to "explain" public punishment in any way, it should do so in a more specific sense. But the evolution which gave rise to criminal justice hardly lends support to this view. Criminal justice arose out of changing relationships of freedom and dependence in the secular world. It was extended by powerful princes at the expense of vengeance and the feud. Ecclesiastics had indeed already advocated harsh corporal penalties in the tenth century. But they too favored these merely as alternatives to the vendetta. Their wishes were realized by the territorial princes of the twelfth century. Only then, when powerful lords applied a new form of justice, did notions of mercy, guilt and moral reprehensibility enter the picture; rather as a consequence than as a cause of the transformation. That clergymen should figure in the drama on the scaffold during the next centuries is only natural. As will be argued in this study, the role of the church remained largely instrumental in a spectacle which primarily served the purposes of the secular authorities.

The transformation during the twelfth century was only a small beginning. First, private vengeance had been pushed back to a certain degree, but continued to be practiced throughout the later Middle Ages. Second, generally the various courts were not in a very powerful position. Often they acted merely as mediators facilitating the reconciliation of the parties involved. A resolute practice of criminal justice depended as before on a certain measure of state power and levels of state power continued to fluctuate. But state formation is not the only process to which the further development of criminal justice was linked. A new factor entered the stage: urbanization. During the later Middle Ages the peculiar conditions prevailing in towns increasingly made their mark on the practice of justice. This situation was not equally marked everywhere. In a country such as France alterations in criminal procedure largely ran parallel with the growth of royal power. In the Netherlands, on the other hand, the towns were the major agents of change.

During the early stages of urban development the social context actually formed a counter-influence to the establishment of criminal justice. Originally, relationships of subordination did not prevail in cities. The charters of most towns recognized the inhabitants as free citizens. It has long been commonplace in historiography to note that the urban presence was encapsulated into feudal society. The body of citizens became the vassal, as it were, of the lord of the territory. The town was often a relatively independent corporation, a *coniuratio*. Vis-à-vis each other the citizens were equal. The

councils ruling these cities were not very powerful. There were hardly any authorities in a real sense, who could impose their will and control events.

This situation left plenty of room for private violence. As the degree of pacification around the towns was still relatively low, so was the degree of internal pacification. To be sure, the vendetta might be officially forbidden. In the Northern Netherlands the prohibition was legitimized by the notion of a quasi-lineage: the citizens were held to be mutual relatives and a feud cannot arise among relatives. But the fiction of lineage could never prevent actual feuds from bursting out, as the prohibitions, reiterated well into the fifteenth century, suggest. Similarly, proclamations ordering a truce between parties were frequent until the middle of the sixteenth century. An early seventeenth-century commentator gives a good impression of the situation. Speaking of the 1390s, he denounces the lawlessness of the age:

> The people were still rough and wild in this time because of their newly won freedom and practically everyone acted as he pleased. And for that reason the court had neither the esteem nor the power which it ought to have in a well-founded commonwealth. This appears from the homicides, fights and wanton acts which occurred daily and also from the old sentences, in which one sees with what kind of timidity the Gentlemen judged in such cases: for they bargained first and took an oath from the criminals that they would not do *schout*, *schepenen* and burgomasters harm because of whatever sentence they would pass against them. And the most severe, almost, which they imposed on someone, was a banishment or that the criminals would make a pilgrimage here or there before they came in [to town] again, or that they would give the city money for three or four thousand stones. They also often licensed one or the other, if he was under attack from his party, that he might defend himself with impunity, even if he killed the

other in doing so. These are things which have no place in cities where the law is in its proper position of power.

Apart from the fact that this situation was considered abnormal in the seventeenth century, we note an acceptance of forms of private violence and the predominance of a reconciliatory stand instead of serious punishment. Towards the end of the fifteenth century, however, this began to change. The ruling elites finally became real authorities. Patriciates emerged everywhere, constituting a socially superior group. The towns became increasingly stratified. The patrician courts could act as superiors notably towards the lower and lower-middle class citizens. In the towns of the Netherlands this development is clearly reflected in their ways of dealing with criminal cases. For a long time the main business of the courts had been to mediate and register private reconciliations. Around 1500 "corrections" gradually outnumbered reconciliations. The former were measures expressing a justice from above and often consisted of corporal punishment.

Another development in criminal law which took place during the same period, was even more crucial. A new procedure in criminal trials, the inquisitorial, gradually superseded the older, accusatory procedure. This change occurred throughout Continental Europe, but not in England. The accusatory trial, when nothing else existed, was geared to a system of marginal justice. Where the inquisitorial trial prevailed, a justice from above had been established more firmly.

The contrast between the two procedures is a familiar item in legal history. Here it suffices to review briefly the relevant characteristics. The inquisitorial procedure had been developed in ecclesiastical law, and was perfected by the institution which took its name from it. From the middle of the thirteenth century onwards it entered into secular law. Generally speaking, the rules of the accusatory trial favored the accused, while the rules of the inquisitorial one favored those bent on condemning him. The former procedure was much concerned with the preservation of equality between the parties. Thus if the accused was imprisoned during the trial "which was not usually the case" the accuser was often imprisoned as well. Moreover, if the latter could not prove his case, he might be subjected to the *talion*: the same penalty which the former would have received if he had been convicted. While the proceedings in the older trial were carried out in the open, the newer one was conducted in secrecy. Publicity was only sought after the verdict had been reached.

The most important element of the inquisitorial procedure, however, was the possibility of prosecution *ex officio*. The adage of the older procedure, "no plaintiff, no judge," lost its validity. If it wished to, the court could take the initiative and start an investigation (*inquisitio*). Its officials would collect denunciations and then arrest a suspect, if they could lay hands on him. The court's prosecutor acted as plaintiff. Thus an active prosecution policy was possible for the first time. In the trial the authorities and the accused faced each other and the power distribution between the two was unequal, favoring the former. Under the accusatory procedure the authorities had hardly been more than bystanders. Consequently the rise of the newer form of trial meant a further spread of a system of justice from above.

This is also implicit in the final element to be noted. The inquisitorial procedure brought the introduction of torture. An accused who persisted in denial, yet was heavily suspect, could be subjected to a "sharper examination." It is evident that the principle of equality between parties under the accusatory procedure would have been incompatible with the practice of torture. Torture was not unknown in Europe before the thirteenth century. It had long been a common feature of the administration of justice by a lord over his serfs. Under the inquisitorial procedure torture could for the first time also be applied to free persons. The parallel with the transformation discussed above is obvious.

The retreat of the accusatory before the inquisitorial procedure did not occur at the same pace everywhere. That the older one was originally more common is reflected in the names of "ordinary" and "extraordinary" procedure which the two forms acquired and often retained throughout the *ancien regime*. The gradual establishment of the primacy of the latter took place between the middle of the thirteenth and the beginning of the sixteenth century. Its use in France by Philip the Fair against the Templars paved the way for its further spread. Prosecution *ex officio* increased in importance from the fourteenth to the sixteenth centuries. The growth of royal power was the main force behind it. In the Netherlands, North and South, the cities formed the most important theater. The formation of patrician elites facilitated the shift. But here too the central authorities confirmed it. In 1570, when the Dutch Revolt was already in the process of breaking out, Philip II issued his criminal ordinances, which clearly favored the inquisitorial trial.

In the Dutch towns non-residents were the first to be tried according to the inquisitorial procedure. As outsiders they were more easily subjected to justice from above. Citizens occasionally put up resistance to it, in Malines, for example. In France it was the nobles of Burgundy, Champagne and Artois who protested. Louis X granted them privileges in 1315 which implied a suspension of inquisitorial proceedings. In the end they were unsuccessful. The forces of centralization and urbanization favored the development of a more rigorous penal system.

England forms a partial exception. Criminal procedure in that country remained largely accusatory throughout the preindustrial period. Nevertheless, essentially these developments can be observed there too, and in the end processes of pacification and

centralization brought about a firmer establishment of criminal justice. Originally there had been plenty of room for private violence, just as on the Continent. An outlaw or "wolf," for instance, could be captured by any man and be slain if he resisted. This right was abrogated in 1329, but as late as 1397 a group of men who had arrested and beheaded an outlawed felon, were pardoned because they had thought it was lawful. Around 1400 it was not uncommon for justices to be threatened with violence by the parties in a lawsuit. The power of the courts went up and down with the fluctuations in the power of a central authority. It was the Tudors, finally, who gradually established a monopoly of violence over most of England. Consequently, except in border areas, the feud definitely gave way to litigation. The available literature on crime and justice in early modern England suggests that a system of prosecution of serious crimes, physical punishment and exemplary repression prevailed there, which was basically similar to that on the Continent.

Thus, the emergence and stabilization of criminal justice, a process going on from the late twelfth until the early sixteenth centuries, meant the disappearance of private vengeance. Ultimately vengeance was transferred from the victims and their relatives to the state. Whereas formerly a man would kill his brother's murderer or beat up the thief he caught in his house, these people were now killed or flogged by the authorities. Legal texts from late medieval Germany sometimes explicitly refer to the punishments imposed by the authorities as "vengeance." Serious illegal acts, which up until then had been dealt with in the sphere of revenge and reconciliation, were redefined as being directed not only against the victims but also against the state. In this process the inquisitorial procedure was the main tool. Its increase in frequency in fourteenth-century Venice, for instance, went hand in hand with the conquest of the vendetta. Private violence by members of the community coming to the assistance of a victim was similarly pushed back. In the Netherlands a thief caught redhanded could be arrested by anyone. His captors were obliged to hand him over to the court, but they might seriously harass him and were often excused if they killed him. This "right" retreated too before the increase of prosecution *ex officio*.

It would be incorrect to assume that the state's arm was all-embracing during the early modern period. An active prosecution policy remained largely confined to the more serious crimes. Private vengeance had been conquered, but reconciliation survived in cases of petty theft and minor violence. The mediators were no longer the courts but prestigious members of local communities. The infra-judicial resolution of conflicts prevailed beneath the surface of justice from above. Historians have only recently come to realize this and the phenomenon has only been studied in detail in France.

This "subterranean stream" was kept in motion from two sides. The authorities, though able to take the initiative, restricted their efforts to specific cases. Prosecution policy was often concentrated on vagrants and other notorious groups. The near-absence of a professional police force further limited the court's scope. Hence many petty offenders were left undisturbed. The attitude of local residents also contributed to this situation. Victims of thefts and acts of violence did not often take recourse to the judiciary. One reason was that a trial might be too costly for the potential plaintiff. Another reason was that numerous conflicts arising from violent exchanges or disputes over property were not viewed in terms of crime and the court was not considered the most appropriate place to settle them. Mediation was sought from non-judicial arbiters. This form of infra-judicial reconciliation survived until the end of the *ancien regime*. Thus preindustrial repression was never an automatic response to all sorts of illegal acts.

Relics of private vengeance can also be observed in the early modern period. This is attested by the public's reaction to property offenders in Republican Amsterdam. The archival sources regularly make mention of a phenomenon called *maling*. From it a picture emerges of communal solidarity against thieves. Events always followed a similar pattern. A person in the street might notice that his pocket was picked or he might be chasing after someone who had intruded into his house. Soon bystanders rushed to help him and the thief was surrounded by a hostile crowd. The people harassed and beat him and forced him to surrender the stolen goods. The thief was then usually thrown into a canal. Servants of justice were often said to have saved his life by arresting him, which meant getting him out of the hands of the crowd or out of the water. Memories of the medieval treatment of thieves caught redhanded were apparently still alive. The authorities tolerated it but did not recognize a form of popular justice. In 1718 a man was condemned for throwing stones at servants of justice when they were busy saving a woman, who was in the *maling*, from her assailants. Comparable forms of self-help by the community against thieves existed in eighteenth-century Languedoc.

. . . [T]he emergence of criminal justice was not a function of changing sensibilities. These only started to play a role later. If corporal and capital penalties increased in frequency from the twelfth to the sixteenth centuries, this certainly cannot be taken as reflecting an increased taste for the sight of violence and suffering. It was primarily a consequence of the growth and stabilization of a system of criminal justice. Conversely, whatever resistance may have been expressed against the transformation . . . did not spring from an abhorrence of violent dealings as such. Physical punishment was simply introduced into a world which was accustomed to the infliction of physical injury and suffering. In that sense it was not an alien element. The authorities took over the practice of vengeance from private individuals. As private retaliation had often been violent, so was the penal system adopted by the authorities. Similarly, as the first had always been a public affair, so was the second. Attitudes to violence remained basically the same. Huizinga demonstrated the medieval acceptance of violence more than sixty years ago and recent research confirms his view. Thus "to mention only a few" Barbara Hanawalt gets the "impression of a society in which men were quick to give insult and to retaliate with physical attack." Norman Cohn recalls the violent zeal with which self-appointed hunters of heretics proceeded, such as the two who managed to reverse God's dictum at the destruction of Sodom and Gomorrah: "We would gladly burn a hundred, if just one among them were guilty."

It is understandable that in such a climate of acceptance of violence no particular sensitivity prevailed towards the sufferings of convicts. This arose only later. Urban and territorial rulers had to ensure that people accepted the establishment of criminal justice. But once they had accomplished that, they did not encounter psychological barriers against the full deployment of a penal system based on open physical treatment of delinquents. By the middle of the sixteenth century a more or less stable repression had been established in most of Western Europe. It did not exclusively consist of exemplary physical punishments. Banishment was important as well and confinement would soon appear on the scene. From that time on it was possible for changing sensibilities within society to affect the modes of repression. From that time too the development of states and the ensuing pacification produced domesticated elites and changed mentalities. These would eventually lead to a transformation of repression. . . .

State Formation and Modes of Repression

Modes of repression belong to the history of mentalities. They reflect the elites' willingness to deal in one way or another with persons exhibiting undesirable behavior. The sort of repression which is advocated or tolerated in a particular society is an indication of the psychic make-up of its members. Publicity and the infliction of physical suffering were the two main elements of the penal system of the *ancien regime*. They should be understood as part of the mental atmosphere prevailing in preindustrial Western Europe. Many events in social life, from childbirth to dying, had a more open character, while with regard to physical suffering in general, a greater lack of concern prevailed than is current today. This mentality was never static; it began to crumble from the seventeenth century onwards. Simultaneously, repression was changed too.

In this study the routine character of seventeenth- and eighteenth-century executions has been demonstrated. From about 1600 the seeds of the later transformation of repression were manifest. The two elements, publicity and suffering, slowly retreated. The disappearance of most forms of mutilation of non-capital convicts constituted the clearest example. An equally important expression of the retreat was the spread of houses of correction; a theme which could not be discussed here. A slight uneasiness about executions among the elites in the second half of the seventeenth century has also been shown. These developments all anticipated the more fundamental change in sensibilities which set in after the middle of the eighteenth century: an acceleration which led to the privatization of repression. The acceleration after the middle of the eighteenth century had a parallel in other areas of the history of mentalities. Processes of privatization are notably reflected in the rise of the domesticated nuclear family.

I am explaining the evolution of modes of repression with reference to processes of state formation. The latter do not of course belong to the history of mentalities; we enter the field of human organization. State formation and such events as the rise and fall of social strata comprise a separate area of societal development. . . . Norbert Elias offered a model for the interdependence of developments in the two fields. I indicate the revisions to be made in the model: notably the shift in emphasis from single states to the rise of a European network of states. In early modern Europe this network extended its influence to areas, such as the Dutch Republic, which lagged behind in centralization. There too a relative pacification produced domesticated elites. On the other hand, the stability of the early modern states remained vulnerable, and this holds true for both patrician republics and absolute monarchies. Ultimately, however, the early modern state was transformed almost everywhere into the nation-state; in Britain, France and the Netherlands among others. These developments provide the key for understanding the evolution of repression in Europe.

This study has continually emphasized the functions which public executions had for the authorities. . . . [L]ate medieval and early modern executions served especially to underline the power of the state. They were meant to be an exemplary manifestation of this power, precisely because it was not yet entirely taken for granted. This explains the two basic elements of the preindustrial penal system. Publicity was needed because the magistrates' power to punish had to be made concretely visible: hence the ceremony, the display of corpses and the refusal to refrain from executions in the tense situation after riots. That public penalties usually involved the infliction of physical suffering is in tune with their function as a manifestation of the power of the magistrates. Physical punishment achieved a very direct sort of exemplarity. The authorities held a monopoly of violence and

showed this by actually using it. The spectators, who lived in a relatively pacified state but did not yet harbor a modern attitude towards the practice of violence, understood this. Public executions represented *par excellence* that function of punishment which later came to be called "general prevention."

So far the relationship has been demonstrated largely in a static context: It can be further clarified if we consider the dynamics. . . . [T]he beginnings of criminal justice were intertwined with the beginnings of state formation and, to a lesser extent, with urbanization. Gradually urban and territorial authorities conquered the vendetta and limited private reconciliation. They started to protect their servant, the executioner, and attempted "though unsuccessfully" to raise his status. The magistrates became the agents who exercised justice.

Public executions first served to seal the transfer of vengeance from private persons to the state. The justice which the authorities displayed served to bolster up their precarious position. They were preoccupied with the maintenance of a highly unstable and geographically limited monopoly of violence well into the sixteenth century. When these monopolies became slightly more stable and crystallized into dynastic states or oligarchic republics uniting a larger area, new considerations came to the fore. Control of the monopoly had to be defended against real or imagined incursions. Bandits and armed vagabonds were still omnipresent. Maintaining the dominance over lower strata and marginal groups was another pressing concern.

Thus, the display of physical punishment as a manifestation of authority was still considered indispensable in the early modern period, because the existing states were still relatively unstable in comparison to later times. In other words, the spectacle of suffering was to survive until a certain degree of stability had been reached. The spectacle was part of the *raison d'etat*. I note this in connection with the penalty of sword over head for semi-homicide in the Nether-lands. The peace of the community stood more centrally in dealing with crime than today. Hence the existence of a category such as "half guilty," which would be inconceivable in modern criminal law. Similar considerations applied to torture. In the second half of the eighteenth century, when opinions *pro* and *contra* were both expressed, this becomes eminently clear. The reformers, placing an individual person at the center of their considerations, argued that he could be either guilty or innocent. It made torture unnecessary since innocent persons should not be hurt and those found guilty should simply receive their punishment. The defenders of torture argued from a different point of view. They stuck to an intermediate category of serious suspicion. The heavily suspect were dangerous to the community, so that it was lawful to subject them to torture. This argument is based on the *raison d'etat,* where the security of the community takes precedence.

The relative instability was not the sole characteristic of early modern states that explains the nature of repression. A second one, also inherited from the later Middle Ages, was equally important. It is the personal element in wielding authority. . . . In the later Middle Ages the preservation of authority was often directly dependent on the person of the ruler. This was illustrated by urban ordinances which put a higher penalty on acts of violence if committed when the lord was in town. In the early modern period this personal element was not as outspoken as it had been before, but it continued to make its mark on the character of the state. A crime was a breach of the king's peace. Public executions constituted the revenge of the offended sovereign.

The personal element should not be viewed as referring exclusively to the king or sovereign. If that were the case, the fact that public executions in countries ruled by patrician elites "such as the Dutch Republic and eighteenth-century England" did not differ significantly from those in France and in German principalities, would be inexplicable. In France the state meant the king and his representatives; judges in the royal courts, for instance. In the Netherlands the state meant the gentlemen assembled in The Hague, the Prince of Orange or the burgomasters of Amsterdam. Foucault's image of physical punishment as the king's branding-mark is relatively well known. But the marks usually represented the jurisdiction. The symbol was equally forceful in a patrician republic. The reaction to the removal of a body from Amsterdam's gallows field . . . is revealing. The magistrates considered such a body as the property of the city and saw the removal as a theft. The inhabitants of urban and rural communities, also in dynastic states, must have associated authority—perhaps even in the first place—with local magistrates. The conspicuous presence of these magistrates at executions sealed the relationship.

These observations, finally, bring a solution to the problem of the disappearance of public executions. They suggest that a transformation of the state constitutes the explanatory factor. Indeed other transformations are less likely candidates. It would be futile, for instance, to relate the change to industrialization. In many countries the privatization of repression preceded the breakthrough of an industrial society. This chronology is evident in the case of the Netherlands. In England, on the other hand, public executions were still a common spectacle when industrialism was already fully developed. The situation produced hybrid combinations of modern transport and traditional punishment, especially in the larger cities. For a hanging in Liverpool the railway company advertised special trains ("parties of pleasure"), departing from the manufacturing towns. The chronology of industrialization varied from country to country, while the retreat of public executions took place almost everywhere between about 1770 and about 1870. Similarly, the transition from the early modern to the nation-state also occurred in most Western European countries in this period.

Thus, the closing of the curtains can be explained with reference to state formation processes as well. We may schematically divide the inherent transformation of sensibilities into two phases. The first comprised the emergence of an aversion to the sight of physical punishment and a consequent criticism of the penal system among certain groups from the aristocracy and the bourgeoisie. This aversion became manifest in the late eighteenth century and was a result of processes of conscience formation. The relative pacification reached in the early modern states cleared the way for the appearance of domesticated elites. The psychic changes which they underwent first found an expression in a refinement of manners and restraints in social intercourse. But the slight sensitivity to public justice that was already manifest before 1700 prefigured later developments. Originally, psychic controls were largely confined to a context of one's own group. Emotions and aggressive impulses were hardly restrained with regard to inferior classes. This situation altered gradually. In the course of the early modern period mutual dependence between social groups increased. Consequently, the context of psychic controls widened. Once more I should note the importance of the identification aspect: an increase in mutual identification between social groups took place. This increase certainly had its setbacks. . . . [T]he Amsterdam magistrates became "within the confines of the general standard of the period" slightly harsher towards delinquents between 1650 and 1750 due to their increasing social distance from the classes they ruled. This can also be understood as a temporary decrease in identification of rulers with the ruled. But in the long run this identification grew stronger. By the end of the eighteenth century an unknown number of individuals among the elites had reached a new stage and identified to a certain degree with convicts on the scaffold. These

delicate persons disliked the sight of physical suffering: even that of the guilty. The first phase of the transformation of sensibilities had set in.

This first phase, so it appeared, resulted from developments that took place within the context of the early modern state. It did not immediately produce a major reform of the penal system. Two ancient features of repression disappeared though: torture and exposure of corpses. Abolition of the latter custom was often part of revolutionary measures. The gallows field symbolized a monopoly of justice particularly within an urban or regional context. The image of the individual city or county as a relatively independent entity had eroded during the seventeenth and eighteenth centuries. The final blow was long overdue. It came everywhere as a direct consequence of the downfall of the *ancien regime.*

The early modern state, however, did not disappear overnight in the Revolutionary period. The final establishment of the nation-state in Western Europe took most of the nineteenth century. The second phase of the transformation of sensibilities set in parallel to it. Repugnance to the sight of physical punishment spread and intensified. In the end the "political conclusion" was drawn and public executions were abolished. The privatization of repression had been completed. It could be completed because the nation-state lacked the two essential elements of which public executions had been a function. The nation-state, because of closer integration of geographic areas and wider participation of social groups, was much more stable than the early modern state. And the liberal/bourgeois regimes, with their increasingly bureaucratized agencies, had a much more impersonal character. Hence the later nineteenth century witnessed more impersonal and less visible modes of repression. Public executions were not only felt to be distasteful; they were no longer necessary. In its internal affairs the nation-state could largely do without the *raison d'etat.*

Beccaria had anticipated the transformation a century earlier. His often-quoted saying that effective prevention of crime depends on the certainty of being caught rather than on the severity of punishment was actually a plea for a stronger state, and in particular for a police force. This was realized in the nation-state. Consequently the authorities could afford to show a milder and more liberal face.

Once more it should be emphasized that absolutes do not exist. Even the privatized repression which emerged in the course of the nineteenth century needed a minimum of exemplarity. We find it expressed, for instance, in the location of prisons on a conspicuous spot where a road or railway entered a town. In an indirect way punishment remained public. L. O. Pike, writing in 1876, reminded his readers that a second-hand impression of a whipping indoors was occasionally brought home to the public by the press. Indirect knowledge of the death penalty, executed within prison walls, remained alive.

National variations in the chronology of the disappearance of public executions must be related to national singularities. The relative importance of the two elements, stability and impersonal rule, may also have varied. In England, for instance, the first half of the nineteenth century was the period of the great public order panic. Thereafter only occasional outbursts of fear occurred and a relative orderliness prevailed. No doubt this situation made the completion of the privatization of repression easier. The kingdom of the Netherlands, on the other hand, was relatively peaceful. The old patrician elites, however, largely dominated the scene until the middle of the nineteenth century. Shortly thereafter the abolition of public executions was a fact. Around the same time the system of public order maintenance was also depersonalized and acquired a more bureaucratic character. These remarks about the specifics of the transformation are of a hypothetical nature and call for detailed research.

The continuation of public guillotining in France until 1939 likewise needs a separate explanation.

The fact that the completion of the privatization of repression took about two-thirds of the nineteenth century in most Western European countries adds up to a critique of Foucault's views. He pictures early nineteenth-century imprisonment as suddenly and almost totally replacing a penal system directed at the display of the human body. The new penal system, and especially solitary confinement, was also directed at the mind. It is true that a widespread enthusiasm for "moral treatment" prevailed in the first half of the nineteenth century. But the penitentiary cannot be considered as the successor to public executions. The observations of the present study make the conclusion inescapable: classical nineteenth-century imprisonment represented an experimental phase contemporary to the last days of public executions. Several authors emphasize that the middle of the nineteenth century was the heyday of the penitentiary and solitary confinement, after which the enthusiasm declined. Of course executions were less frequent at the time, but this is not relevant to the argument. From a quantitative viewpoint they had always been in the minority, though they were the pearl in the crown of repression. In the course of the nineteenth century public physical punishment was increasingly questioned. This coincided with experiments in new penal methods such as solitary confinement. The experiments were discontinued and public executions disappeared. Routine imprisonment succeeded "with capital punishment indoors for a few heinous offenses" to the top of the penal system.

Modern imprisonment would need another story. The penal system of today, however, bears the mark of the developments that gave rise to it. On the one hand, it has retained its ancient characteristics to a certain degree. Everyone still has to realize that punishment exists, and this is the essence of the notion of general prevention.

And a penalty still involves, in one way or another, the infliction of injury. Feelings of sensitivity, on the other hand, did not vanish after their appearance in the late eighteenth century. Time and again those concerned with the condemned have looked inside prisons and told the public the painful story. The result is a permanent tension. Every modern Western society witnesses the conflict between a perceived necessity of punishment and an uneasiness at its practice. Perhaps this remains inevitable, unless we find a way to do without repression entirely.

Study Questions

1. How did relations among the governing and the governed change between the Germanic and the feudal periods?

2. During this time period, how did inquisitorial procedures change power relations among individuals and between individuals and the state?

3. What purpose did repression, especially caused by the spectacle of public physical suffering, serve in the early modern states?

4. Exactly how did the transition from an early modern to a nation-state transform sensibilities and make the spectacle of suffering unnecessary?

2
The Discovery of the Asylum

David J. Rothman

In yet another historical account of the development of the penitentiary, David J. Rothman explores the development of the institution, from colonial America to the 1820s. Again, the reader should observe a societal shift from a system based largely on interpersonal settling of disputes in an agrarian setting to an urbanized nation that requires state intervention for punishment. The reader should also take note that, in addition to the rise of the penitentiary, representing confinement as an end in and of itself, society held a belief that the institution could indeed change the individual for the better. Thus, penal institutions were designed to confine the offender while leading him to the skills necessary for a law-abiding life.

The Boundaries of Colonial Society

The colonial attitudes and practices toward . . . the criminal . . . were in almost every aspect remarkably different from those Americans came to share in the pre-Civil war decades. Almost no eighteenth-century assumption about the origins or nature of . . . deviancy survived intact into the Jacksonian era, and its favorite solutions to these conditions also became outmoded. In fact, the two periods' perspectives and reactions were so basically dissimilar that only a knowledge of colonial precedents can clarify the revolutionary nature of the changes that occurred.

Eighteenth-century Americans did not define . . . crime as a critical social problem. . . . They devoted very little energy to devising and enacting programs to reform offenders and had no expectations of eradicating crime. Nor did they systematically attempt to isolate the deviant. . . . While they excluded some persons, they kept others wholly inside their communities. At times they were . . . willing to allow offenders another chance; but they could also show a callousness and narrow-mindedness that was utterly cruel. From the viewpoint of nineteenth-century critics, their ideas and behavior seemed careless and inconsistent, irrational and injurious, but within their social and intellectual framework, the colonists followed clear and well-established guidelines. . . .

The colonists judged a wide range of behavior to be deviant, finding the gravest implications in even minor offenses. Their extended definition was primarily religious in origin, equating sin with crime. The criminal codes punished religious offenses, such as idolatry, blasphemy, and witchcraft, and clergymen declared infractions against persons or property to be offenses against God. Freely mixing the two categories, the colonists proscribed an incredibly long list of activities. The identification of disorder with sin made it difficult for legislators and ministers to distinguish carefully between major and minor infractions. Both were testimony to the natural depravity of man and the power of the devil—sure signs that the offender was destined to be a public menace and a damned sinner. . . .

To counteract the powerful temptations to misconduct and the inherent weakness of men, the colonists looked to three critical associations. They conceived of the family, the church, and the network of community relations as important weapons in the battle against sin and crime. If these bodies functioned well, the towns would be spared the turbulence of vice and crime and, without frequent recourse to the courts or the gallows, enjoy a high degree of order and stability. To these ends, families were to raise their children to respect law and authority, the church was to oversee not only family discipline but adult behavior, and the members of the community were to supervise one another, to detect and correct the first signs of deviancy. . . .

These attitudes did not stimulate the colonists to new ways of controlling crime. The broad definition of potential offenders and improper behavior did not spur attempts to revise the patently inadequate formal mechanisms of law enforcement. Assemblies created a militia to contain mass disturbances and repel enemy forces but they did not intend it or use it for day-to-day supervision. Towns designated constables to protect their peace, but the force was inadequate both in the number and physical condition of its men. It was understaffed, poorly supervised, and filled with the elderly. Rather, the colonists' perspective on deviancy encouraged a dependence upon informal mechanisms which promoted a localism in many settlements. To an important degree the community had to be self-policing. The citizens themselves would be on guard to report and even apprehend the offender. Just as churchgoers were to be diligent about one another's salvation, so too residents were to protect one another's lives and property. And given the popular sense of man's proclivities to sin and crime, they expected to be busy. . . .

Charity and Correction in the Eighteenth Century

Eighteenth-century criminal codes fixed a wide range of punishments. They provided for fines, for whippings, for mechanisms of shame like the stocks, pillory and public cage, for banishment, and for the gallows. They used one technique or a combination of them, calling for a fine together with a period in the stocks, or for a whipping to be followed by banishment. The laws frequently gave the presiding magistrate discretion to choose among alternatives "to fine or to whip" or directed him to select the applicable one "to use the stocks if the offender could not pay his fine." They included some ingenious punishments, such as having a convicted felon mount the gallows, remain for an hour with a noose around his neck, and then go free. . . . The statutes defined a large number and variety of capital crimes and the courts were not reluctant to inflict the penalty. The gallows was the only method by which they could finally coerce obedience and protect the community. In the absence of punishments in the middle range, they depended extensively upon the discipline of the hangman. . . .

Local jails were found throughout the colonies, and in decent repair. Some towns utilized part of the courthouse building, others erected a separate structure. But regardless of form, these institutions had only limited functions. They held persons about to be tried or awaiting sentence or unable to discharge contracted debts. They did not, however, except on rare occasions, confine convicted offenders as a means of correction. The jails facilitated the process of criminal punishment but were not themselves instruments of discipline. They did not expand in function during the course of the eighteenth century to become a method for penalizing as well as detaining offenders.

The colonists might have adopted a penitentiary system in order to reform the criminal, or to terrify him, or simply to confine him. They could have attempted to mold him into an obedient citizen, or to frighten him into lawful conduct or, at least, to prevent him, if for only a limited period, from injuring the community. But given their conception of deviant behavior and institutional organization, they did not believe that a jail could rehabilitate or intimidate or detain the offender. They placed little faith in the possibility of reform. Prevailing Calvinist doctrines that stress the natural depravity of man and the powers of the devil hardly allowed such optimism. Since temptations to misconduct were not only omnipresent but practically irresistible, rehabilitation could not serve as the basis for a prison program. Moreover, local officials believed that a policy of expulsion offered the community some protection against recidivism. Institutionalization seemed unnecessary when numerous offenders could be marched beyond the town line and not be seen again.

The failure to broaden the functions of the jail also revealed the colonists' dependence upon the family model for organizing an institution. Since life in a prison would perforce duplicate that in a large household, they saw no reason to believe institutionalization would discourage the criminal or even offer the community a temporary respite. A household existence did not seem either painful or corrective. . . .

The institutions already functioning in the colonies did not substantially depart from the family model. The almshouse ran like a large household. Since officials appropriately considered admission a privilege, penalizing anyone who tried to enter it illegally, the poorhouse was hardly an inspiration for a prison system. The occasional workhouse was not a more useful guide; the few to be found in America had not established a disciplinary or punitive routine. . . .

Eighteenth-century jails in fact closely resembled the household in structure and routine. They lacked a distinct architecture and special procedures. . . . True to the household model, the keeper and his family resided in the jail, occupying one of its rooms; the prisoners lived several together in the others, with little to differentiate the keeper's quarters from their own. They wore no special clothing or uniforms and usually neither cuffs nor chains restrained their movements. They walked "not marched" about the jail. The workhouse model was so irrelevant that nowhere were they required to perform the slightest labor.

Jail arrangements so closely replicated the household that some colonists feared that prisons would be comfortable enough to attract inmates. Far from striking terror, they would build a clientele willing to be decently supported in return for a temporary deprivation of liberty. This is why towns frequently required prisoners to provide their own food and "to use such bedding, linen and other necessaries as they think fit, without their being purloined, detained, or they paying [the jailer] for the same." So long as they did not cost the town money, inmates could make living arrangements as pleasant and as homelike as they wished. . . .

The colonial jails were not only unlikely places for intimidating the criminal, but even ill-suited for confining him. Security was impossible to maintain, and escapes were frequent and easy. Conditions were sometimes so lax that towns compelled a prisoner to post a bond that he would remain in the jail, especially if he wished the privilege of exercising in the yard. . . .

No one placed very much confidence in these structures. Even at the close of the colonial period, there was no reason to think that the prison would soon become central to criminal punishment. . . .

The Challenge of Crime

Eighteenth-century notions of . . . deviancy did not survive for very long into the nineteenth, nor did its methods of dispensing . . . correction. The social, intellectual, and economic changes that differentiated the states of the new republic from the several colonies prompted a critical reappraisal and revision of the ideas and techniques of social control. Americans felt compelled to rethink inherited procedures and devise new methods to replace old ones. They devoted extraordinary attention to this issue, hoping to establish quickly and effectively alternatives to the colonial system.

Between 1790 and 1830, the nation's population greatly increased and so did the number and density of cities. Even gross figures reveal the dimensions of the change. In these forty years, the population of Massachusetts almost doubled, in Pennsylvania it tripled, and in New York it increased five times; border and midwestern states, practically empty in 1790, now held over three million people. At Washington's inauguration, only two hundred thousand Americans live[d] in towns with more than twenty-five hundred people; by Jackson's accession, the number exceeded one million. In 1790, no American city had more than fifty thousand residents. By 1830, almost half a million people lived in urban centers larger than that. During these same years factories began to dot the New England and mid-Atlantic rivers. The decade of the 1830s witnessed the first accelerated growth of manufacturing in the nation. At the same time, Enlightenment ideas challenged Calvinist doctrines; the prospect of boundless improvement confronted a grim determinism. But these general trends are not sufficient to explain the very specific reactions to the issue of deviant . . . behavior. To them must be added Americans' understanding of these changes. Under the influence of demographic, economic and intellectual developments, they perceived that the traditional mechanisms of social control were obsolete. The premises upon which the colonial system had been based were no longer valid.

Each change encouraged Americans to question inherited practices and to devise new ones. Inspired by the ideals of the Enlightenment, they considered older punishments to be barbaric and traditional assumptions on the origins of deviant behavior to be misdirected. Movement to cities, in and out of territories, and up and down the social ladder, made it difficult for them to believe that a sense of hierarchy or localism could now stabilize society. When men no longer knew their place or station, self-policing communities seemed a thing of the past. Expanding political loyalties also made colonial mechanisms appear obsolete. Citizens' attachment to state governments promoted a broader definition of responsibility, so that a sentence of banishment seemed a parochial response. The welfare of the commonwealth demanded that towns no longer solve their problems in such narrow and exclusive ways.

This awareness provoked at least as much anxiety as celebration. Americans in the Jacksonian period could not believe that geographic and social mobility would promote or allow order and stability. Despite their marked impatience and dissatisfaction with colonial procedures, they had no ready vision of how to order society. They were still trapped in many ways in the rigidities of eighteenth-century social thinking. They knew well that the old system was passing, but not what ought to replace it. What in their day was to prevent society from bursting apart? From where would the elements of cohesion come? More specifically, would . . . criminals roam out of control? . . . This question became part of a full, intense, and revealing investigation of the origins of deviant . . . behavior. To understand why men turned criminal . . . would enable reformers to strengthen the social order. To comprehend and control abnormal behavior promised to be the first step in establishing a new system for stabilizing the community, for binding citizens together. In this effort, one finds the clearest indications of how large-scale social changes affected thinking and actions of Americans in the Jacksonian period. And here one also finds the crucial elements that led to the discovery of the [penitentiary].

In the immediate aftermath of independence and nationhood, Americans believed that they had uncovered both the prime cause of criminality in their country and an altogether effective antidote. Armed with patriotic fervor, sharing a repugnance for things British and a new familiarity with and faith in Enlightenment doctrines, they posited that the origins and persistence of deviant behavior would be found in the nature of the colonial criminal codes. Established in the days of oppression and ignorance, the laws reflected British insistence on severe and cruel punishments. . . .

These conceptions had an immediate and widespread appeal. The reform seemed worthy of the new republic, and feasible, so that by the second decade of the nineteenth century, most of the states had amended their criminal codes. The death sentence was either abolished for all offenses save first-degree murder or strictly limited to a handful of the most serious crimes. Instead, the statutes called for incarceration, the offender to serve a term in prison. Construction kept apace with legal stipulations. Pennsylvania led the way, turning the old Philadelphia jail at Walnut Street into a state prison. In 1796, the New York legislature approved funds for building such institutions, and soon opened the Newgate state prison in Greenwich Village. The New Jersey penitentiary was completed in 1797, and so were others in Virginia and Kentucky in 1800. That same year, the Massachusetts legislature made appropriations for a prison at Charlestown, and in short order Vermont, New Hampshire, and Maryland followed suit. Within twenty years of Washington's inaugural, the states had taken the first steps to alter the traditional system of punishment.

In this first burst of enthusiasm, Americans expected that a rational system of correction, which made punishment certain but humane, would dissuade all but a few offenders from a life in crime. They located the roots of deviancy not in the criminal, but in the legal system. Just as colonial codes had encouraged deviant behavior, republican ones would now curtail, or even eliminate it. To pass the proper laws would end the problem.

This perspective drew attention away from the prisons themselves. They were necessary adjuncts to the reform, the substitutes for capital punishment, but intrinsically of little interest or importance. A repulsion from the gallows rather than any faith in the penitentiary spurred the late-eighteenth-century construction. Few peo-

ple had any clear idea what these structures should look like or how they should be administered—or even addressed themselves seriously to these questions. To reformers, the advantages of the institutions were external, and they hardly imagined that life inside the prison might rehabilitate the criminal. Incarceration seemed more humane than hanging and less brutal than whipping. Prisons matched punishment to crime precisely: the more heinous the offense, the longer the sentence. Juries, fully understanding these advantages, would never hesitate to convict the guilty, so that correction would be certain. The fact of imprisonment, not its internal routine, was of chief importance.

By the 1820s, however, these ideas had lost persuasiveness. The focus shifted to the deviant and the penitentiary, away from the legal system. Men intently scrutinized the life history of the criminal and methodically arranged the institution to house him. Part of the cause for this change was the obvious failure of the first campaign. The faith of the 1790s now seemed misplaced; more rational codes had not decreased crime. The roots of deviancy went deeper than the certainty of a punishment. Nor were the institutions fulfilling the elementary task of protecting society, since escapes and riots were commonplace occurrences. More important, the second generation of Americans confronted new challenges and shared fresh ideas. Communities had undergone many critical changes between 1790 and 1830, and so had men's thinking. Citizens found cause for deep despair and yet incredible optimism. The safety and security of their social order seemed to them in far greater danger than that of their fathers, yet they hoped to eradicate crime from the new world. The old structure was crumbling, but perhaps they could draw the blue prints for building a far better one.

. . . Although the colonists had blamed inadequate parental and religious training for crime, they were preoccupied with the sinner himself. Convinced that the corrupt nature of man was ultimately at fault, they did not extensively analyze the role of the criminal's family or the church or the general society. Furthermore, they shared a clear understanding of what the well-ordered community *ought to* look like, and this too stifled any inclination to question or scrutinize existing arrangements. Their religious and social certainty covered the discrepancies between ideas and realities, obviating new approaches and theories. Americans in the Jacksonian period stood in a very different position. They learned that men were born innocent, not depraved, that the sources of corruption were external, not internal, to the human condition. Encouraged by such doctrines to examine their society with acute suspicion, they quickly discovered great cause for apprehension and criticism. . . .

Holding such a position, American students of deviant behavior moved family and community to the center of their analysis. New York officials accumulated and published biographies because this technique allowed them to demonstrate to legislators and philanthropists the crucial role of social organizations. Accordingly, almost every sketch opened with a vivid description of an inadequate family life and then traced the effects of the corruptions in the community. . . .

The pessimism and fear underlying this outlook pointed to the difficulty Americans had in fitting their perception of nineteenth-century society as mobile and fluid into an eighteenth-century definition of a well-ordered community. Their first reaction was not to disregard the inherited concept but to condemn present conditions. Hence, in these biographies a dismal picture emerged of a society filled with a myriad of temptations. It was almost as if the town, in a nightmarish image, was made up of a number of households, frail and huddled together, facing the sturdy and wide doors of the tavern, the gaudy opening into a house of prostitution or theater filled with dissipated customers; all the while, thieves and drunkards milled the streets, introducing the unwary youngster to vice and corruption. Every family was under siege, surrounded by enemies ready to take advantage of any misstep. The honest citizen was like a vigilant soldier, well trained to guard against temptation. Should he relax for a moment, the results would be disastrous. Once, observers believed, neighbors had disciplined neighbors. Now it seemed that rowdies corrupted rowdies.

Yet for all the desperation in this image, Americans shared an incredible optimism. Since deviant behavior was a product of the environment, the predictable result of readily observable situations, it was not inevitable. Crime was not inherent in the nature of man, as Calvinists had asserted; no theological devils insisted on its perpetuation. Implicit in this outlook was an impulse to reform. If one could alter the conditions breeding crime, then one could reduce it to manageable proportions and bring a new security to society.

One tactic was to advise and warn the family to fulfill its tasks well. By giving advice and demonstrating the awful consequences of an absence of discipline, critics would inspire the family to a better performance. (The biographical sketches, then, were not only investigations but correctives to the problem.) One might also organize societies to shut taverns and houses of prostitution, an effort that was frequently made in the Jacksonian period. But such measures, while important, were slow-working, and by themselves seemed insufficient to meet the pressing needs of this generation. Another alternative then became not only feasible but essential: to construct a special setting for the deviant. Remove him from the family and community and place him in an artificially created and therefore corruption-free environment. Here he could learn all the vital lessons that others had ignored, while protected from the temptations of vice. A model and small-scale society could solve the immediate problem and point the way to broader reforms. . . .

The Invention of the Penitentiary

Americans' understanding of the causes of deviant behavior led directly to the invention of the penitentiary as a solution. It was an ambitious program. Its design "external appearance, internal arrangement, and daily routine" attempted to eliminate the specific influences that were breeding crime in the community, and to demonstrate the fundamentals of proper social organization. Rather than stand as places of last resort, hidden and ignored, these institutions became the pride of the nation. A structure designed to join practicality to humanitarianism, reform the criminal, stabilize American society, and demonstrate how to improve the condition of mankind, deserved full publicity and close study.

In the 1820s New York and Pennsylvania began a movement that soon spread through the Northeast, and then over the next decades to many midwestern states. New York devised the Auburn or congregate system of penitentiary organization, establishing it first at the Auburn state prison between 1819 and 1823, and then in 1825 at the Ossining institution, familiarly known as Sing-Sing. Pennsylvania officials worked out the details of a rival plan, the separate system, applying it to the penitentiary at Pittsburgh in 1826 and to the prison at Philadelphia in 1829. . . .

The doctrines of separation, obedience, and labor became the trinity around which officials organized the penitentiary. They carefully instructed inmates that their duties could be "comprised in a few words"; they were *"to labor diligently, to obey all orders, and preserve an unbroken silence."* Yet to achieve these goals, officers had to establish a total routine, to administer every aspect of the institution in accord with the three guidelines, from inmates' dress to their walk, from the cells' furnishings to the guards' deportment. The common solution was to follow primarily a quasi-military model. The regulations based on this model promised to preserve isolation, to make labor efficient, and to teach men lacking discipline to abide by rules; this regimented style of life would inculcate strict discipline, precision, and instantaneous adherence to commands. Furthermore, a military model in a correctional institution seemed especially suitable for demonstrating to the society at large the right principles of organization. Here was an appropriate example for a community suffering a crisis of order. . . .

Reformers never spelled out the precise nature and balance of this reformation. They hoped that families, instead of overindulging or neglecting their children, would more conscientiously teach limits and the need for obedience to them. Assuming that social stability could not be achieved without a very personal and keen respect for authority, they looked first to a firm family discipline to inculcate it. Reformers also anticipated that society would rid itself of corruptions. In a narrow sense this meant getting rid of such blatant centers of vice as taverns, theaters, and houses of prostitution. In a broader sense, it meant reviving a social order in which men knew their place. Here sentimentality took over, and critics in the Jacksonian period often assumed that their forefathers had lived together without social strain, in secure, placid, stable, and cohesive communities. In fact, the designers of the penitentiary set out to re-create these conditions. But the results, it is not surprising to discover, were startlingly different from anything that the colonial period had known. A conscious effort to instill discipline through an institutional routine led to a set work pattern, a rationalization of movement, a precise organization of time, a general uniformity. Hence, for all the reformers' nostalgia, the reality of the penitentiary was much closer to the values of the nineteenth than the eighteenth century.

Study Questions

1. How did the American colonists' views on the nature of man and crime shape punishment?

2. Why didn't the colonists conceive of incarceration as a form of punishment?

3. Discuss social changes occurring at the turn of the nineteenth century that would change Americans' thoughts on crime and punishment within a generation or two.

4. How did Americans' views on the nature of man, crime, and punishment during the Jacksonian era differ from the views of their colonial counterparts?

5. In what way did Jacksonian Americans believe that the trinity of the penitentiary (separation, obedience, and labor) would act as an appropriate example for a community in crisis?

Excerpts from *The Discovery of the Asylum* by David J. Rothman. Copyright © 1971, 1990 by David J. Rothman. Reprinted with the permission of Little, Brown and Company, Inc. ✦

3
A Look at Prison History

Thorsten Sellin

Thorsten Sellin traces the history of punishment and imprisonment from approximately the Reformation forward. However, Sellin focuses on the historically relevant view of Radbruch's theory,* which states that punishments were designed to control the underclass, which in many cases meant slaves. As such, prison inmates came to be viewed as slaves of the state. This historical analysis does an excellent job of detailing and describing the societal shift that moved confinement from occurring prior to the "real" punishment (which generally involved severe if not deadly corporal punishment), to actually being the punishment. Although Sellin views moving away from corporal (and public) punishment as a positive shift, he concludes by noting some of the unanticipated consequences that arose from this country's willingness to house offenders of all types en masse. Not the least of these problems are the issues of prison labor and of inmates' grotesque mistreatment within institutions.

In his symposium, *Elegantiae Juris Criminalis*, Gustav Radbruch published in 1938 an article entitled "Der Ursprung des Strafrechts aus dem Stande der Unfreien." It is a brilliant exposition of a theory which had been advanced many decades earlier by scholars like Köstlin, von Bar, and Jastrow and it makes the origin of penal imprisonment comprehensible. Rejecting, as illogical or unproved, various explanations of the origin of punishment, Radbruch maintained that the common punishments which came to be introduced in law and applied to all of-

fenders had once been used only for slaves or bondsmen.

> Especially the mutilating penalties. Applied earlier almost exclusively to slaves, they became used more and more on freemen during the Carolingian period and specially for offenses which betokened a base and servile mentality. Up to the end of the Carolingian era, punishments "to hide and hair" were overwhelmingly reserved for slaves. Even death penalties occurred as slave punishments and account for the growing popularity of such penalties in Carolingian times. The aggravated death penalties, combining corporal and capital punishments, have their roots in the penal law governing slaves.[1]

Radbruch believed that earlier penal customs, like feud or compensation, were natural for equals and propertied people who could demand satisfaction or make payments. But the social class system changed greatly during the Frankish era and with it the character of criminality. "Vulgar crime" became looked upon as low-class crime, "vulgar both in the sense of its origin in baseborn people and in its appraisal as being infamous—the crime of another, uncomprehended and despised social layer. . . . The aim of punishment had been clearly stated, in a capitulary of Childebert II in 596 A.D., to be 'to ensure by every means the control of the lower classes.' It was natural that the best means to that end were the punishments that were earlier applied to the very lowest layer of the people—the class of slaves."[2]

The evolution of the penal law until the old slave punishments—death, mutilation, whipping, etc.—were gradually incorporated in the penal law and applied generally needs no further elaboration here.

> The criminal law . . . to this very day reflects its origin in slave punishments. Even now, punishments mean a *capitis deminutio* because it presumes the *capitis deminutio* of those for whom it was originally designed. Being punished means be-

ing treated like a slave. This was symbolically underscored in earlier times when whipping was accompanied by the shaving of the head, for the shorn head, was the mark of the slave."[3]

Penal Slavery

Being concerned mostly with corporal and capital punishments, Radbruch made no mention of penal imprisonment in his essay, yet his theory applies perfectly to that punishment which in its primitive form was slavery of a most abject kind, called penal servitude. Penal servitude was in use in Imperial Rome. Von Bar says that

> since it was customary to punish slaves by hard labor and since the lowest class of freemen were in reality little more respected than were slaves, by the all powerful imperial officials, the idea easily arose of making use of the toil of convicts in the great works being undertaken by the state. This idea was perhaps furthered by an acquaintance with the custom of states annexed to Rome. Thus even Pliny the Younger speaks of the employment of convicts in public works (*opus publicum*), such as cleaning sewers, mending highways, and working in the public baths. A more severe type of this kind of punishment was a sentence 'ad metalla'—labor in the mines—and in 'opus metalli.' The convicts in each of these instances wore chains and as 'servi poenae' lost their freedom. For this reason the punishment was always for life. . . . These punishments were properly regarded as sentences to a slow and painful death.[4]

It is significant that in Imperial Rome the *condamnatio ad opus publicum* was reserved for the *personae humiles,* the humble class of people; it was not applicable to the upper class or *honestiores.* The more severe forms of the *condamnatio* deprived the offender of his liberty (*capitis deminutio maxima*) and hence of his citizenship, reducing his status to that of a penal slave. These punishments, together with exile and death, were classed by the legists as capital punishments because they incurred civil death. Sentences *ad metalla* meant hard labor, while in chains, in stone quarries, such as the Carrara marble ones, in metal mines, or in sulphur pits. It is obvious that in order to exploit the manpower of these penal slaves it was necessary to keep them imprisoned in some way. Here, then, we find punitive imprisonment in its original form, even though the Romans may not have been its inventors. Therefore, it is curious to be told by George Ives, in his interesting *History of Penal Methods* (1914) that

> imprisonment as a punishment in itself, to be endured under rules made expressly punitive and distressful, may be described as essentially modern and reached its worst phase in the nineteenth century.[5]

"Imprisonment as a punishment in itself" would thus be something new and in essence different from the primitive penal servitude just described. To be sure, historians seem to have adopted that view, but I propose to show that this judgment is questionable.

Parenthetically speaking, it is puzzling to find the great Roman jurist Ulpian categorically declaring that prisons existed only for detention and not for punishment, a phrase which was accepted as a correct definition of prisons until the 18th century. Considering the sentences *ad metalla* common in Ulpian's own day; the later use, mainly in the Mediterranian sea, of convicts as oarsmen in war galleys; the working of convicts in the Spanish mines of northern Africa by the banking house of Fugger to secure repayment of immense loans made to Charles V; the use of convict labor in the arsenals of France and Spain; the transportation of convicts to work in the Siberian mines and lumber camps of Russia; the common use of convicts during the 16th and 17th centuries to build fortifications, etc., one can only conclude that, despite the complete deprivation of liberty characterizing such punitive enterprises, jurists did not look on that element in these punishments as being their distinguishing mark, but placed them, instead, in another category of punishment, that of forced or compulsory labor, to which the deprivation of liberty was merely incidental. As late as 1771, the great French jurist Daniel Jousse still classed penal servitude among the capital punishments. This probably accounts for the view expressed by George Ives that imprisonment as an end in itself is a modern invention.

You will recall that Radbruch claimed that corporal and capital punishments originally imposed only on slaves and bondsmen gradually came to be used for freemen. The same holds true for imprisonment. Originally applied as a punishment for slaves in connection with hard labor, it came to be used for humble folk, who for crime were reduced to penal slaves. In the middle of the 15th century, when France found the supply of free and slave labor on its galley fleets dwindling, beggars and vagrants were first sent to fill the galley crews and later sturdy felons who had merited the death penalty or corporal punishments. When imprisonment later was applied to all serious offenders, it turned out, on close examination, to be only a variant of the original form of penal servitude.

Punitive Imprisonment

The credit for the gradual substitution of imprisonment for corporal and capital punishments must go to the political philosophers of the 18th century. Experimentation with punitive imprisonment had occurred earlier in the monastic orders and in the houses of correction in many countries, but this involved mostly errant clerics or petty misdemeanants and had not greatly changed the ways of dealing with more serious criminals, who were still being whipped, broken on the wheel, maimed, and hanged. Now the demand arose that nearly all such criminals be sentenced to imprisonment. The most influential voice, so far as penal reform was concerned, was that of Beccaria, who crystallized ideas he had gleaned from the French philosophers, especially Montesquieu.

Beccaria's great essay *On Crimes and Punishments* (1764) is too well-known to you to require any extensive commentary. You will recall that he opposed the death penalty and advocated substituting imprisonment for it, but what may have passed notice is the reason for his proposal and the nature of the substitute. No sentimentality dictated his opposition to capital punishment. As a firm believer in Rousseau's version of the theory of the social contract, he denied the *right* of the state to execute anyone with the possible exception of the leader of a revolt threatening to overthrow the government. No citizen, he said, would have voluntarily agreed to surrender to the state his right to live. When using the death penalty a state was not exercising a right it was not entitled to possess but was engaging in a war against a citizen, whose destruction it believed to be necessary and useful. Beccaria then proceeded to demonstrate the falsity of such beliefs.

Why should imprisonment be preferred to capital punishment? Because

> it is not the intensity but the duration of punishment which has the greatest effect upon man's mind. . . . It is not the terrible but fleeting spectacle of the execution of a scroundrel that is the strongest deterrent to crime but rather the long and painful example of a man deprived of his freedom and become a beast of burden, repaying with his toil the society he has offended. . . . Therefore the intensity of the punishment of perpetual servitude as substitute for the death penalty possesses that which suffices to deter any determined soul. I say that it has more. Many look on death with a firm and calm regard . . . but neither fanaticism nor vanity dwells among fetters and chains, under the rod, under the yoke, or in the iron cage. . . . Were one to say that perpetual servitude is as painful as death and therefore equally cruel I would reply that, adding all the unhappy moments of servitude together, the former would be even worse.[6]

In the last analysis, then, Beccaria, who clearly stated in his essay that the aim of punishment should be to prevent a criminal from repeating crime and to deter others from crime by the example of punishment, did not ask for the abolition of the death penalty for humanitarian reasons but because it (a) had no logical place in a political society based on a social contract and (b) was less of a deterrent than life imprisonment. Such imprisonment was to be served in a prison where the inmate led the existence of a penal slave. Since scores of crimes in the penal laws of his day were made punishable by death, his reform proposal, if accepted, would require the creation of prisons to house large numbers of inmates. It is noteworthy also that Beccaria rarely mentioned imprisonment in his essay except as a substitute for capital punishment. He referred to it in connection with thefts committed with violence, for instance, but when he did mention it he called it temporary or perpetual slavery. Nor was he opposed to corporal punishments.

It is important to remember that Beccaria's essay was, first and foremost, a political tract announcing the principles of a penal code based on the new democratic philosophy of the political equality of men. Older penal law had reflected the views dominant in societies where slavery or serfdom flourished, political inequality was the rule, and sovereignty was assumed to be resting in absolute monarchs. Now the most objectionable features of that law, which had favored the upper classes and had provided often arbitrary, brutal and revolting corporal and capital punishments for the lower classes, were to be removed and equality before the law established. Judicial torture for the purpose of extracting evidence was to be abolished, other than penal measures used to control some conduct previously punished as crime, and punishments made only severe enough to outweigh the gains expected by the criminal from his crime. This meant a more humane law, no doubt, applied without discrimination to all citizens alike in har-

mony with the new democratic ideas. There was nothing startlingly new, however, in the aims of punishment as advocated by Beccaria. Myuart de Vouglans, who wrote a polemic against him in 1766 and was a leading defender of the old system, believed that the aim of punishment should be (a) to correct the offender; (b) repair the wrong caused by the crime if possible; and (c) deter the evilminded by the example and fear of similar punishments. The aims of these two defenders of different penal philosophies were essentially the same; only the means they advocated differed.

The governments who were influenced by the new philosophy created prison systems that incorporated Beccaria's ideas. Emperor Joseph II of Austria, hailed as a reformer for having eliminated the death penalty from his code of 1787, substituted horrible varieties of imprisonment in dungeons, where prisoners were chained and loaded with irons while working. At about the same time, John Howard observed in a Viennese prison prisoners chained together and awaiting transportation to Hungary where they were to draw barges up the Danube, a task so exhaustive that few survived it. When the French Constituent Assembly in 1791 translated Beccaria's principles into a penal code, different varieties of imprisonment were substituted, the most severe of which provided that the criminal was to have a chain with an iron ball attached to his legs, be confined at hard labor in security prisons, ports or arsenals, or at other public works, and work for the profit of the state. This was, in fact, the way galley slaves had been treated ever since the galleys had been decommissioned as outmoded.

Prison Reform

Concern about the sufferings of prisoners had been expressed in many ways since ancient times. There is both a literature to demonstrate it and organized efforts of relief, engaged in mainly for religious and humanitarian reasons. The outstanding work of John Howard need only be mentioned; it coincided with the period we have just been discussing. But now a new generation of writers appeared. The effects of the movement to make prisons places of punishment rather than of mere detention required not only justification but inventiveness. How should such prisons be organized, what should be the regime, how would they most effectively serve the aims of punishment? The last decade of the 18th and the first half of the 19th century produced an impressive list of writers on prison reform as well as impressive efforts to convert their ideas into practice.

But the roots of imprisonment in penal servitude could not be easily eradicated. When the young American states built penitentiaries for serious offenders who would formerly have been executed, mutilated, or whipped, the law provided that prisoners confined in them should perform labor of the "most harsh and servile kind" (a phrase borrowed from John Howard). The prisons operated on the Auburn plan, in particular, were, most of them, notorious for the maltreatment of prisoners and for the excessive labor required of them in an attempt to meet the demand of legislators that the prisons be self-supporting and even show a profit if possible. These conditions were not reflected in the glowing reports that often emanated from the wardens or overseers of the prisons, but they were amply proved by the many investigations of abuses made from time to time by official commissions. Quite early—in New York in 1817, for instance—the practice began of selling the labor of prisoners to private contractors. This contract system of prison labor spread rapidly to other states and was not completely eliminated until 1934, by act of Congress. As late as 1919 a committee of the American Prison Association reported, after a national survey, that most prisons worked their prisoners in a manner reminiscent of the early forms of penal servitude and that reformation was an empty word.

Let me return to Radbruch for a moment and his theory that in a society where slaves existed, the punishments for slaves tended to be adopted for freemen sooner or later; that, in other words, the institution of slavery placed its stamp on the penal law. Consider the fact that the ancient societies of Greece and Rome were built on a foundation of slavery; that Plato said that all manual labor should be done by slaves; that Aristotle regarded it as an established law of nature that slavery was just and even agreeable to those subjected to it; and that there were times during the Roman Empire when the number of slaves almost equalled the number of free citizens. Consider also that wherever slavery existed the status of a slave was that of chattel property, useful and necessary to his owner, but not permitting the slave to be treated like a free man. In societies where the debtor could be enslaved by his creditor or where the serf was considered practically as a slave, the rise of penal slavery, to use Beccaria's term, and its gradual extension to the members of the lower orders of society who committed crimes and finally to all persons convicted of serious crimes would seem to be a natural evolution. The demonstration of the accuracy of this contention can best be made in the study of the evolution of punishment in the southern states of the United States where slavery was legal until abolished one century ago. Two illustrations will suffice:

The entire history of punishment can almost be said to be recapitulated in the State of Florida in the brief period of a century and a half. Prior to the 1860's punishments were capital, corporal, and financial and the local county jails were detention houses with the kind of inmates that have in historical times been found in such places. There was no interest in prison reform; the State itself had no prison. In 1869 a penitentiary act was adopted by the legislature providing for a state prison to be operated by the Commissioners of Public Institutions. The act authorized the Commissioners to enter into contracts with private persons for the labor of the prisoners. The act emphasized the need to make the prison self-supporting; this nullified another provision of the act, namely, that the contractors must insure the health and safety of the prisoners working for them.

The state penitentiary was located in an arsenal belonging to the Federal Government and for 2 years was governed as a military post where, for the lack of a work program, the prisoners were controlled by chains, muskets, and bayonets. In 1871 the prison was removed from the military, and 6 years later the State transferred the control and custody of the prisoners to private contractors who could now employ them anywhere in the State. Prisoners were leased to individuals and corporations and set to work in phosphate mines and in turpentine camps in the forests. By 1902 there were 30 such convict camps.

"The leasing of convicts," according to a report recently issued by the Florida Division of Correction, from which these data have been culled,

> resulted in incredible acts of brutality to prisoners. The atrocities of the system seem obvious to a modern observer, yet, state officials, conditioned by their culture, could observe that frequent convict camp investigations always found the convicts 'well treated and cared for.'. . . In 1917, the legislature created the State Road Department and also the State Road Convict Force. The Board of Commissioners was authorized to allocate up to 300 convicts for use on the road force (the old *opus publicum* . . . the remaining convicts were leased to the counties and to private lessees.[7]

Leasing of Prisoners

Prisoners unable to do manual labor—mostly the aged, crippled, and deformed—had to be placed in a state prison, of course. In 1919 the Board of Commissioners were forbidden to lease convicts because public opinion had been aroused and outraged by

some of the incidents that had occurred in the convict camps. Now these prisoners had to be placed in state prisons where they worked on large attached plantations under the guard of specially selected fellow-prisoners, who carried arms. It was not until 1957 that Florida adopted a Correctional Code and set up a State Division of Correction. Since then the State has rapidly joined the mainstream of modern penology.

The particular form of the contract system, known as the lease system described above, flourished in the old slave states of the South after the Civil War, when the slaves had been freed. Can anyone doubt that this kind of penal slavery was not only reminiscent of its most primitive forms but also was adopted as a suitable way of punishing former slaves, their descendants, and poor whites by a dominant group of former slaveowners and their sympathizers? The last state to abolish this system was Alabama, in 1928.

A Recent Prison Scandal

Penal slavery did not disappear when the lease system of prison labor was abandoned; it was merely transplanted into the state penitentiaries. The most recent prison scandal in the United States has just erupted in an old slave state, Arkansas. In 1897 the legislature of that State acquired a large plantation, which now has 15,000 acres and later a subsidiary farm of 4,500 acres, which together constitute the state penitentiary. The aim was to develop a self-supporting institution. That this aim has been realized is shown by the fact that in 1964, the penitentiary showed a net profit from its livestock and its cotton and vegetable acres of nearly half a million dollars. The major cost items were about $91,000 for feeding 1,900 prisoners and $57,000 for feeding the cattle.

This financial success is achieved by working the prisoners from dawn to dusk, guarded by inmate guards, on foot or mounted, and armed with shotguns and rifles. There are only 35 salaried employees in the two institutions combined, including the superintendent and his staff, chaplains, doctors, bookkeepers, and a chief warden and 18 so-called field wardens. Whipping is authorized as disciplinary punishment for a variety of offenses including failure to perform one's quota of work. Nearly half of the inmates are Negroes guarded by inmates of their race. The sentences served are to hard labor and hard labor it is, and unpaid at that. No shops or prison industries exist except those necessary for the maintenance of the buildings, the agricultural machinery, and the trucking equipment.[8]

A few months ago certain incidents at the subsidiary farm known as the Tucker farm resulted in a thorough investigation by the state police of Arkansas. The investigation revealed conditions of corruption, maltreatment, and brutality that are unbelievable. The new state administration which took office 3 months ago is now attempting to remedy the situation.[9]

Conclusion

These examples have not been chosen in order to denigrate the 52 prison systems of the United States, many of which are today acknowledged at home and abroad to be in the forefront of modern correctional treatment methods. I have chosen them to substantiate Radbruch's theory by showing that the primitive form of punitive imprisonment referred to as penal servitude or penal slavery, originally used for slaves (*servi poenae*) and later applied to free men, has not yet been completely stamped out despite the reforms in correctional treatment. I am, of course, aware that I have focused on perhaps the darkest side of the history of punitive imprisonment. Even so, much has been left unsaid. I have made no reference to the prison hulks of England, the treadmills and cranks, the British and French transportation systems, these vari-

ants of penal slavery which caused a British judge to say to a convicted murderer: "I shall pass upon you a sentence . . . which in my opinion will be a greater punishment than the momentary pain of death, for you will live like a slave laboring for others and have no reward for your labors. That sentence is that you be kept in penal servitude for life." Shades of Beccaria!

Nor have I referred to the innovations during the 19th century that have generally been regarded as progressive, such as the institutions governed by Obermayer in Bavaria, Montesinos in Spain, or Brockway's reformatory at Elmira, for instance, or the institutions for delinquent children or women that arose in the 19th century on both sides of the Atlantic and even earlier in Europe. From our present viewpoints, most of them were pale shadows of what we regard today as appropriate correctional institutions, even though at the time of their founding they were indeed trailbreakers.

One is tempted to speculate on the motive forces that have operated in producing the gradual progress toward the kind of correctional system we are today visualizing. Improvements in earlier times were and are to some degree even today motivated by humanitarian and religious feelings, but I believe that for penological progress in the last hundred years, slow at first and accelerated only since the second world war, we are indebted chiefly to the behavioral scientists—the psychiatrists, psychologists, and social scientists—whose studies and findings have gradually changed, generation after generation, the intellectual climate into which people, including legal scholars, legislators, correctional administrators, and the behavioral scientists themselves are born.

New ideas do not find easy acceptance, especially when they concern treatment of criminals and therefore meet emotional barriers. Max Planck once said that the only reason a scientific truth is accepted is not that its opponents are converted to it but that they die off and a new generation is born that takes that truth for granted. Perhaps this explains our presence here this week discussing correctional methods which a generation or two ago would have been considered inacceptable.

Study Questions

1. As a policy "thinker," Beccaria is often portrayed as a benevolent reformer advocating for mercy on the offender. Make a case for, and against, this portrayal.

2. What were the primary reasons behind the move from public torture and corporal punishment to imprisonment occurring as punishment?

3. What is meant by the phrase "penal slavery"?

4. What were some of the major consequences of moving to a correctional system based on confinement and imprisonment?

Introduction Note

* An address delivered at a Colloquium of the International Penal and Penitentiary Foundation at Ulm, West Germany, April 19, 1967.

Notes

1. Gustav Radbruch, *Elegantiae Juris Criminalis* (2d Ed.). Basel: Verlog fur Recht und Gesellschaft A. G., 1950, p. 5

2. *Ibid.,* pp. 8–9.

3. *Ibid.,* pp. 11–12.

4. Carl Ludwig von Bar, *A History of Continental Criminal Law.* Boston: Little, Brown & Co., 1916 p. 36.

5. George Ives, *A History of Penal Methods.* London: Stanley Paul & Co., 1914, p. 1.

6. Cesare Beccaria, *Dei delitti e delle pene,* xvi.

7. Florida Division of Corrections, *5th Biennial Report, July 1, 1964–June 30, 1966.* Tallahassee, Florida, 1966, p. 5.

8. Robert Pearman, "The Whip Pays Off," *The Nation,* 203: 701–704, December 26, 1966.

9. *Tucker Prison Farm Case.* Report No. 916–966, Criminal Investigations Division, Arkansas State Police, Little Rock, Arkansas.

Excerpts from "A Look at Prison History" by Thorsten Sellin. Copyright © 1967, *Federal Probation* Vol. 31, Issue 3 (September 1967), pages 18–23. Reprinted by permission of *Federal Probation.* ✦

4
Partial Justice
Women, Prisons, and Social Control
Nicole Hahn Rafter

M*uch of what is known regarding the structure and function of the corrective institution has focused on male offenders. Although male offenders make up the majority of the offending population, a very real need exists for more exploration of female offending. Nicole Hahn Rafter's essay provides a historical analysis of an institution designed to house female offenders during the nineteenth and early twentieth centuries. The Albion institution in New York, although housing serious female offenders, also may have served as an extension of formal social control for nonserious female offenders, who for various reasons did not conform to proper norms. Such women were taught the virtues of a "good, womanly life." This essay gives yet another example of how important the greater social context is when studying institutional evolution.*

Over the last several decades, historians and sociologists have devoted increasing attention to the phenomenon of social control—the mechanisms by which powerful groups consciously or unconsciously attempt to restrain and to induce conformity, even assent, among less powerful but nonetheless threatening segments of society. Laws, institutions such as schools and prisons, medical policies, informal gestures of approbation or displeasure, even forms of language—all may constitute forms of social control. (Social control in this sense should not be confused with criminological control theory . . . which offers an explanation for law-violating behaviors; through a complicated and terminologically unfortunate series of developments in social science, similar terms have been adopted to label different concepts.) The control achieved may be merely external, as when people are forced to do things against their wills; or it may be internal, so thoroughly absorbed by its subjects that they come to monitor and correct their own deviations from prescription. In recent years, research in social control has moved in two directions particularly germane to the study of women's prisons. First, it has come to focus sharply on the political implications of coercion. As David Rothman puts it, "A social control orientation . . . suggest[s] that [institutional] innovations were likely to confer benefits somewhere, and so the question becomes, where? If the prison did not serve the prisoner, then whom did it serve?" In other words, historians and sociologists no longer assume that the narratives of social controllers (who often speak sincerely of the benefits they expect to confer on prisoners and the like) tell the whole story; the picture has been broadened to include the political ramifications of extended controls for both reformers and the subjects of reform. Second, feminist theorists have become sensitive to ways in which social controls are exercised on women *as women*, to encourage conformity to prescribed gender roles.

This chapter analyzes an aspect of the social control of women by focusing on a particular type of prison, the women's reformatory. It explores the conjunction between formal vehicles of social control (in this case the laws establishing reformatories and the institutions themselves) and the internalization of their social control "messages" by the targeted group of inmates. The chapter also deals with social control in terms of social class—the process by which, through establishment and operation of women's reformatories, middle-class crusaders came to impose their definition of womanliness on working-class inmates.

This chapter . . . is concerned with the movement's political implications. Without denying the benevolence of the reformers' aims, it attempts to look beyond good intentions to the movement's methods of social control and their results.

The women's reformatory, as we have seen, was unique as an institution for adults. Founded by middle- (often upper-middle-) class social feminists, reformatories extended government control over working-class women not previously vulnerable to state punishment. In addition, the reformatories institutionalized bourgeois standards for female propriety, making it possible to "correct" women for moral offenses for which adult men were not sent to state penal institutions. And reformatories feminized prison discipline, introducing into state prisons for women a program of rehabilitation predicated on middle-class definitions of ladylike behavior. For these reasons, the women's reformatory served special, female-specific functions with regard to social class and social control.

In this chapter, New York's Western House of Refuge at Albion, operated between 1894 and 1931, is used as a case study. Albion built upon experiments by its forerunners to become the first women's prison to realize completely the reformatory plan in architecture, administrative structure, type of inmates and sentence, and program. It established the model adopted by many women's reformatories opened in the early twentieth century. Additionally, Albion adhered to the goals of the women's reformatory movement more consistently than many sister institutions that succumbed to overcrowding, inadequate financing, and routinization. Although it was atypical in this respect, Albion provides a good case for analyzing the ways in which the reformatory movement extended social control just because it did manage to remain relatively "pure." The detailed nature of Albion's prisoner registries and the survival of case files on individual inmates, moreover, make it possible to fol-low in some depth the events that brought women to this prison, their institutional treatment, and their reactions to it.

Social Control Functions of the Albion Reformatory

Records of the Albion reformatory indicate that in terms of social control, the institution served two primary functions: sexual and vocational regulation. It attempted the first by training "loose" young women to accept a standard of propriety that dictated chastity until marriage and fidelity thereafter. It tried to achieve the second by training charges in homemaking, a competency they were to utilize either as dutiful daughters or wives within their own families or as servants in the homes of others. In operation, techniques used to achieve these ends were usually indistinguishable. Although they are separated here for analytical purposes, in actuality tactics used to realize the dual goals of sexual and vocational regulation worked together, coalescing and mutually reinforcing one another.

From Sexual Autonomy to Propriety: Preparation for the 'True Good Womanly Life'

To control the sexual activities of "promiscuous" women, the Albion reformatory used several approaches. One was the initial act of incarcerating women who had violated standards of sexual conduct for the "true women." Second was parole revocation if a prisoner showed signs of lapsing back into impropriety while out on conditional release. Third was transfer of intractables to a custodial asylum for "feebleminded" women at Rome, New York, where they could be held indefinitely.

Over the thirty-seven years of its operation as a reformatory, Albion received about 3,150 prisoners. The menial nature of the jobs at which their parents were employed and their own previously high rates of employment at poorly paid, low-skilled jobs indicate that most of these prisoners were working-class women. Three-quarters of them were between fifteen and twenty-one years old, the rest under thirty. The vast majority—over 95 percent—were white. Most had been born in New York State (particularly in the rural western area where the institution was located) of native-born parents; one-third were Catholic, while nearly all the rest were Protestant; and most were single. The composition of the population reflected the desire of Albion's officials to work with cases who appeared malleable and deserving. The institution's commitment law authorized it to receive women convicted of petit larceny, habitual drunkenness, common prostitution, frequenting a disorderly house, or any other misdemeanor. Originally, it could hold them for up to five years; later, the maximum number of years was reduced to three. Less than 2 percent of the prisoners were convicted of violent crimes (and these were mainly second or third degree assault) and but another 14 percent of property offenses (mainly petit larceny). The great majority (over 80 percent) had been sentenced for public order offenses—victimless crimes such as public intoxication, waywardness, and vagrancy.

. . . [F]or at least half (and perhaps up to three-quarters) of Albion's inmates, the act that led to incarceration had actually been sexual misconduct. Some of these women were apprehended for prostitution. Most, however, were merely sexually active, engaging in flirtations and affairs for pleasure instead of money. The efforts of Albion and other reformatories to curb sexual independence by women occurred within the wider context of antiprostitution and other social purity campaigns. Members of the middle and upper classes increasingly committed themselves to the cleansing of society. At the same time, however, some working women became indifferent to traditional definitions of virtue. In rapidly growing numbers, they left home to join the paid labor force. By 1910, a record high of 27 percent of all New York State women were gainfully employed. Even more significantly, nearly 80 percent of Albion's inmates had previously worked for wages. As they acquired a degree of independence, working women turned to new amusements. To smoke cigarettes, frequent dance halls, and become involved in sexual relationships did not strike *them* as depravity; but their disinterest in the ideals of "true" womanhood evoked alarm in those dedicated to the battle against vice. Reformers came to consider any deviation from female sexual propriety, even when it did not involve a financial transaction, as a form of "prostitution."

The sexual misconduct for which women were incarcerated at Albion came to the attention of authorities through a variety of routes. Sometimes irate parents reported sexually active daughters to the police; at others, cuckolded husbands complained to court officials. Premarital pregnancies alerted social control agents in many cases. In yet others, discovery of venereal diseases led to commitment. For many women, a sign of sexual impurity in combination with some other suspicious circumstance seems to have precipitated arrest. For example, Anna H., one of Albion's few black inmates, evidently came to the attention of police when her husband was arrested for attempted burglary. Anna was examined, found to have venereal disease, and sentenced to Albion for vagrancy. There was no question of her fidelity to her husband: reformatory officials accepted Anna's statement that it was he who had infected her, and they later refused to release her on the theory that she would return to him ("the combination is a very bad one"). But Anna had been living apart from her husband, supporting herself as a waitress, and this irregular arrangement may have increased officials' consternation.

Ostensibly, venereal disease was also the ground on which Lillian R., a Coney Islander of orthodox Jewish background, was originally committed; but in her case, too, unseemly independence and bad associates may have contributed to authorities' concern. Having quit school after the seventh grade to help her widowed mother support a large family, Lillian had been variously employed as a messenger, box factory worker, and forewoman in an artificial flower shop. At the age of sixteen she ran off with a soldier for a week and contracted venereal disease. She and her mother decided (according to her record) that "it would not be right for her to remain in her home with the other children. She was . . . put into the Magdalene home. [She] was there one week when sent to the City Hospital for treatment." At the hospital Lillian was charged with "contracting an infectious disease in the practice of debauchery" and sentenced to the Bedford reformatory, from which she was later transferred to Albion.

Some women committed to Albion for sexual misbehavior had in fact been sexually victimized. Such was the case with Anna B., who at the age of fourteen had been charged with ungovernability and sent to the Salvation Army Home in Buffalo, where she bore her first child. Not long after she returned home, her father was sentenced to prison for rape. Anna's case file strongly suggests that she was the victim. While her father was still on trial, Anna was sent to Pennsylvania to live with a grandmother. Within a month, she became pregnant by the sixty-year-old man for whom her grandmother kept house. Anna returned home, where she went to work in a restaurant. Convicted of "running around" when she was seven months into this second pregnancy, Anna seems actually to have been exploited twice by much older men.

Although a handful of cases were, like Anna B., "led astray," most of Albion's inmates appear to have been rebels of some sort—against the double standard of sexual morality; against their families or husbands; or against public regulations such as that prohibiting disorderly conduct. But perhaps "rebels" is not the most accurate term: in officials' view, they defied conventions, but many of these young women may have been acting in accordance with other standards that they themselves considered legitimate. Despite their youth, the majority were independent at the point when police officers plucked them from saloons, hotel rooms, and street corners to be sent to the reformatory. Four-fifths of them held jobs. Although over 70 percent had not yet married, they were no longer under their parents' control. Whether reacting defiantly against conventional concepts of morality or simply behaving in ways they regarded as acceptable, most clearly had not internalized a view of themselves as "proper" women, demure and asexual. It was this situation that the reformatory, with its goal of imposing and teaching sexual control, sought to remedy.

If incarceration and training within the institution did not teach the prisoner to conform, the reformatory employed another means: parole revocation. Most of Albion's inmates were released on parole before their sentences expired. During the period of parole their behavior was scrutinized by the institution's parole officers, community officials, and employers. . . . When parole was revoked, the violation was frequently sexual in nature.

Some women had parole revoked for overt returns to vice. Such was the case with inmate No. 1899, recalled to Albion after "an officer of Endicott, N.Y., arrested her in a questionable resort." Similarly, inmate No. 1913 was forced to return when, after marrying during parole, she was reported by her husband "for misconduct with men." Women who became pregnant during parole were returned to the institution—unless they quickly married someone "respectable." At other times revocation was triggered not by blatant signs of immorality but rather by indications that a lapse was imminent. One woman was returned to the reformatory because she "became infatuated with a married man named L___. Mrs. L___ wrote us" and, after investigating, reformatory officials decided to recall her. Another parolee was revoked for associating with the father of her child ("they were not married and Washington is a most disreputable character"), and No. 1313 barely escaped revocation when "two former inmates report[ed] seeing her frequently at night with different conductors on the Genesee St. line."

In cases that appeared hopeless to Albion's administrators, a third step was sometimes taken to ensure against relapse: transfer to the State School at Rome or another of New York's institutions for the feebleminded. Such transfers carried an automatic extension of sentence up to life, for according to popular theory of the time, the feebleminded never improve. At the turn of the century, the feebleminded were considered innately promiscuous, so Albion's authorities easily assumed that women who would not reform were feebleminded "defective delinquents." Because intelligence testing was still in a primitive stage, it was not difficult to confirm "scientifically" a suspicion of feeblemindedness and thus establish the basis for a transfer. These transfers, which occurred in cases of women who were disciplinary problems within the institution as well as in instances of overt sexuality while on parole, constituted the final disposition for forty-eight of the sampled cases, or 3 percent of all first releases. In addition, thirteen women who were returned to the reformatory for parole violation (5.2 percent of those who were released a second time), and two women (5.6 percent of the thirty-six sampled cases who returned twice to the reformatory and then discharged a third time) were transferred to institutions for the feebleminded. Case file documents such as school records and letters written by these supposedly feebleminded women indicate that they were not in fact mentally retarded. They were, however, noncompliant. The lesson of their

transfer to civil institutions was probably not lost on those left behind at the reformatory.

From Sauciness to Subservience: Preparation for Domestic Service

The second central social control function of the Albion reformatory was to train inmates to become competent housekeepers in either their own homes or those where they were placed as domestics. The institution aimed, in the words of its managers, to reform "unfortunate and wayward girls" by giving them "moral and religious training . . . and such training in domestic work as will eventually enable them to find employment, secure good homes and be self-supporting." To the achievement of this end, the managers viewed the cottage system, with its "plan of ordinary domestic life," as crucial. Acquisition of decorum was also considered critical; the institution emphasized gentility in all aspects of its program. Within this institutional facsimile of the genteel home, inmates received both academic and domestic training, with by far the heavier emphasis falling on the latter. Albion seldom educated inmates beyond the sixth grade level, but it provided abundant opportunities for perfection of domestic skills, instructing prisoners in dressmaking, plain and fancy sewing, knitting, crocheting, "cookery," cleaning, and "ventilation." A steam-operated washing machine was purchased for the institution's laundry, but the sight of it made visiting prison commissioner Sarah L. Davenport "sorry," for it was "not educating the women . . . for the homes they will go to when they leave Albion." Thereafter, the laundry was washed by hand. A "finely equipped domestic science department," outfitted with dining room furniture, coal and gas burners, and kitchen utensils, was added in 1912, and from then on inmates received instruction in:

manufacture and source of food supplies, relative cost, and nutritive values; the care of the kitchen, pantry, and dining room; construction and care of the sinks, stoves, (both gas and coal) and refrigerators; table etiquette; the planning and serving of meals; and waitress' duties.

When members of the board of managers met at the reformatory, inmates practiced for future employment by waiting on their table. As Elliott Curie has put it in writing of the Massachusetts reformatory, the institution "trained women to be women."

For middle-class women who lived in its vicinity, Albion provided trained, inexpensive household help. It was the institution's policy "to place our girls in the home of a woman who will take a motherly interest in them." One-quarter of the prisoners were paroled directly to live-in domestic positions. Of the 50 percent paroled to members of their own families, another sizeable proportion also took jobs as domestics. Housekeeping was familiar to Albion's prisoners, many of whom reported their previous occupation as "domestic" or "houseworker." But the reformatory's records suggest that some, at least, had been less than satisfactory servants, given to carelessness, impudence, filching, and running off with young men. The institution tried to turn these and other inmates into competent, submissive domestics.

Attempts by Albion and other reformatories to train domestics took place at a time when the "servant problem" was particularly intense. Difficulties in finding suitable servants became acute after the Civil War and continued to be so well into the twentieth century. As the number of families that could afford servants increased, the interest of working-class women in domestic service declined. The latter came to prefer factory jobs that offered more money, shorter hours, and greater autonomy. Those who had no alternative to domestic service resented the power of the mistress; they also objected to the social restrictions of live-in

positions and to expectations of servility. Many reacted to such conditions with impertinence and petty theft. The distaste of working women for domestic service created a predicament for would-be employers. Servants were necessary for the operation of their households, and (equally important) they were a sign of status. Thus in increasing the supply of well-trained domestics, reformatory officials supported the interests of other middle-class women.

Nearly 20 percent of Albion's prisoners had worked before arrest in mills or factories. But as noted earlier, the frequent economic crises of the late nineteenth and early twentieth centuries led to widespread unemployment, and serious labor unrest. Insofar as reformatories removed women from the industrial labor force, they made more jobs available for men. In view of these circumstances, the reformatory's refusal to provide training in industrial skills deemed "unfit" for women, and the promotion of skills geared toward domestic service is especially significant. "No industries are maintained," one Albion report declared, "but every inmate is taught to cook and care for a home. This is the most important thing in the work of the institution. Most of the girls when paroled go into homes where this knowledge is necessary." Thus Albion not only provided rigorous training in housekeeping but also tended to discourage inmates from moving beyond the home and earning higher wages. It reinforced the point that women's place was in the home by paroling most women to family situations where they were needed as paid or unpaid domestic help.

Employers and the institution formed a symbiotic alliance over the discipline of women paroled as servants. The reformatory required women released to domestic positions to sign a form agreeing to

accept the wages agreed upon between the Superintendent . . . and her employer . . . her wages to be retained by employer, excepting such amount as the latter thinks necessary for [the] girl. . . . [C]onsult employer as to her amusements, recreation, and social diversions. To form no friendships, not to visit or receive visits from members of her own family unless approved by the Superintendent. Is not to go out nights excepting when accompanied by a responsible person, and to go very seldom at night. To have one afternoon a week. . . .

Paroled women were also required to send monthly reports to the reformatory, and they were further supervised through visits from a parole officer. If despite these controls a domestic became difficult, the reformatory could revoke parole, a threat that no doubt helped employers maintain discipline. These restraints notwithstanding, many women paroled to domestic positions behaved noncompliantly. Revocations were occasioned by "sauciness," "obscenity," failure to work hard enough, and other demonstrations of independence. Inmate No. 13, for example,

went to Rochester to work for Mrs. . . . J___ and for a time did very nicely but finding some girls of her acquaintance she began to visit them too often and to neglect her work. She came back to the institution in Aug. 1897 and there remained till [sentence] expiration.

Inmate No. 2585 was originally paroled to a Mrs. F___ of Rochester. But, "Jane was a slow worker and very untidy and shiftless. She was very fond of reading. Returned [to the reformatory] for a change of place. . . ." Next Jane was sent to a Mrs. S___ of Buffalo. This time, "On Oct. 11 went to a movie and did not return until eleven o'clock when she was expected at nine." When Mrs. S___ threatened to return her to Albion, Jane fled. She was not recaptured, but others on domestic parole were returned to the institution for laziness, disobedience, and running away.

In return for the institution's help with disciplining difficult domestics, employers supervised prisoners. They were "autho-

rized and requested to open and read all mail sent and received by girl" and further charged "to guard her morals, language and actions, and aid her as much as possible by advice as to her present and future conduct. . . ." In the course of aiding fallen women, employers were also aiding themselves by maintaining the quality of the services they received. The entire arrangement, in fact, seems to have been one from which employers benefitted greatly, receiving trained and supervised servants who promised to consult them in all matters and work six and one-half days a week. If the servant became shiftless or impudent, the criminal justice system would step in to do the necessary disciplining.

Techniques of Social Control

Albion developed a variety of techniques to encourage reform. Some have already been identified: the initial act of incarcerating women for sexual misconduct and other petty offenses; intensive training in domesticity and gentility; a policy of parole to domestic positions; community surveillance; parole revocation; and transfer of the most uncooperative to civil institutions where they could be held indefinitely. Implicit in many of these techniques was another: from the moment of arrest, Albion's inmates were reduced to the standing of children. Like juvenile delinquents, many were detained for status offenses— immorality, waywardness, keeping bad company—for which men the same age were not arrested. At the reformatory they were supervised by motherly matrons, and at parole they were usually released to family situations in which they had a dependent position. Indeed, the very concept of an institution dedicated to the rescue and reform of women under the age of thirty, and operated with an extremely high level of discretionary authority, was rooted in a view of women as childlike creatures.

Appropriately, like institutions for juvenile delinquents, Albion was titled a "refuge."

Disruption of inmates' ties with their families was another mechanism used by the reformatory to encourage inmates to conform to its values. Some prisoners, to be sure, had already separated from their families; but being independent through one's own choice was not the same as being severed from one's family by others—and at a time of crisis. Familial disruption was a technique to which women were especially susceptible, their roles being so intimately involved with domestic life. Disconnected from their own families, Albion inmates were more likely to identify with the surrogate "families" of their cottages and, on parole, with those to which they were sent as servants.

Disruption of family life is an inevitable by-product of incarceration, but Albion developed policies relating to mail and visitors that intensified the break. Once in custody, women had immense difficulty contacting families and friends. They were permitted to write letters only once every two months, and these were censored. If the Superintendent decided that either the contents or the designated recipient was unsuitable, she would file the letter in the inmate's folder—quite probably without notifying the writer and certainly without notifying the intended recipient, both of whom might therefore wait in vain anticipation. Incoming mail was also censored and often filed away undelivered. Visits were permitted, but only four times a year. A further restriction limited the pool of potential visitors to close relatives, and even these might be banned if deemed bad influences. Moreover, some approved visitors doubtless were discouraged from visiting by the institution's geographical isolation. For all these reasons, commitment to the reformatory resulted in nearly total severance of ties to former support groups. Isolated in this fashion, prisoners became more susceptible to the institution's staff and its moral advice.

Another aspect of familial disruption, separation from children, was sometimes traumatically final. When women were committed, their children might be sent to orphanages or put up for adoption. Such removals occurred even in instances when inmates had husbands living at home. Thus not only were young mothers severed from their children; they also had to suffer the knowledge that their families had been dissolved. In such cases, moreover, the children were now being cared for by strangers. To judge from Albion's records, its inmates were not informed of the welfare of institutionalized or adopted children.

Occasionally ultimate disposition of children would be left undecided and used to induce the mother to conform. Of a woman committed for vagrancy, for instance, the registry reports,

> Edna made a splendid record while on parole. Mr. Angel, Humane Officer of Courtland County[,] was so well pleased with her that he returned her children to her.

Not to please Mr. Angel, it seems, would have resulted in loss of her children. Another example is provided by the case of Martha, a mother of four, sentenced to Albion for public intoxication. Threat of removal of her children kept Martha sober even in times of great stress:

> Martha returned [on parole] to her husband who had promised every[thing] in the way of reform but who is the veriest hypocrite [*sic*]. She continued leading a true good womanly life hoping to be worthy of her children, as the authorities had promised to restore them when they were satisfied that she would hold out.

In instances like these, there was the initial familial disruption occasioned by commitment and then a threat of further disruption—total loss of children—if the prisoner did not comply with the institution's requirements.

Similar methods of control involved babies who stayed with mothers at the institution. If a woman was nursing at commitment, she was allowed to bring the child with her. Those women who gave birth at Albion were permitted to keep infants. But reformatory policy decreed that all babies had to leave when they reached the age of two. Sometimes the institution decided not to parole a woman until after the baby had been sent away. Mary P___, for example, bore a child a few days after her arrival at Albion in 1922, and in September 1924, two years having expired, the child was sent to the Delaware County Superintendent of the Poor. Mary was paroled just a month later to work in her father's cigar factory. Mary's parents may have refused to let her bring home an illegitimate child. Whatever the reason, the effect of holding her slightly beyond the mandatory release date for the baby was to cut Mary off from the only family she had for two years. She was, moreover, returned to a situation in which she herself was the child.

Some babies brought into or born at the prison were sent to adoption agencies or other institutions before they reached the age of two. How long their mothers might keep them was a matter of administrative discretion, and like all such matters, liable to be used as a mechanism of control. Albion's records do not refer to the practice of using children to coerce institutionalized mothers, but this form of social control is described in a letter from the Superintendent of Maine's State Reformatory for Women to a journalist who had requested information on babies in prison. "The conduct of the mothers," the superintendent informed him,

> decides in a measure the time they are allowed to spend with their babies. . . .They dress and undress and feed their own babies after the baby is six months old. They always have the privilege to kiss them goodnight and to spend an hour in the afternoon with them, unless their conduct precludes the loss [*sic*] of this privilege.

Restricting access to children was probably used as a social control device at Albion and other reformatories as well.

Despite its emphasis on the home as woman's place, Albion developed parole policies that further disrupted some inmates' ties to their former homes. Women who before incarceration lived in stable family situations were frequently paroled not to their own families but to domestic positions in the homes of others. In some instances, the institution deemed the original family unsuitable and wanted to keep the woman away from it as long as possible. In others, officials seem simply to have decided that for a woman to work and save money was the best way for her to pass parole. Often the domestic jobs were in towns distant from the prisoners' families. Women could take infants with them to some domestic live-in positions, but others required them to leave their babies behind.

Many of these dislocating factors were present in the case of Marjorie M., a twenty-year-old of German extraction who, before commitment, lived with her parents and seven siblings in Batavia, where she was employed as a domestic. The mother of a three-year-old and again pregnant, Marjorie was convicted of disorderly conduct in 1917 and sent to Albion. There she gave birth to her second daughter, Helen. Paroled to a domestic position in Rochester, Marjorie sent five dollars of her eight-dollar weekly salary to the home where Helen was boarded. After parole, she found employment as assistant housekeeper at the Rochester Orphan's Asylum, where Helen was now living. Helen died of diphtheria in the winter of 1920. At this point Marjorie, who at the time of arrest had been living with ten members of her immediate family, was left entirely alone.

The reformatory's policies also perpetuated familial disruption in the case of Henrietta S., a Binghamton woman with two children. After serving time at Albion for intoxication, Henrietta was paroled to a domestic position in Lyndonville, where she earned four dollars a week. When her term was up, she returned to her family with $154 she had managed to save from her wages. The institution interpreted the large sum as a sign of success, but Henrietta and her family paid a high psychological price in return: their family life had been interrupted for three years, and while a Mrs. F__ of Lyndonville had cheap use of her services, Henrietta's own children had been deprived of her care.

The reformatory's parole policies were not disruptive of family life in all instances, and perhaps some women who *were* returned to parents or husbands would have preferred a less restrictive arrangement. In either case, the institution exercised tremendous control over inmates' social contacts (probably more than any contemporary prison for men), and it used this control to induce conformity. Denying inmates access to mail and visitors, institutionalizing their children or threatening to do so, on occasion probably blocking access to infants within the prison, developing parole policies that frequently prevented contact with families—through such means the prison demonstrated its power and often disrupted the continuity of whatever family life had existed. The effect was to encourage dependency on the institution and increase the likelihood that inmates would internalize the reformatory's teachings about how women like themselves should behave.

'The Best Place to Conquer Girls': The Reformatory's Success

Many women incarcerated at Albion went on to lead lives that met the institution's criteria for success, marrying and maintaining homes of their own or remaining for long terms in domestic placements.

No doubt many former inmates would have become more sedate in their mid-twenties or early thirties even without the moral influence of the prison, just as more serious offenders outgrow crime. But the reformatory does seem to have set some formerly wayward women on the path to propriety— to have served, in the words of one inmate's sister, as "the only and best place to conquer girls." Albion appears, that is, to have achieved its goals in some, perhaps even a majority, of cases.

The reformatory worked through kindness as well as coercion, and therein lay the key to its success. Had it merely punished, it would have antagonized; but Albion also performed extensive nurturing functions, alleviating some of the harsher aspects of poverty. It served as a hospital where the diseased could receive treatment, the malnourished food, the pregnant decent care at delivery. It also functioned as a shelter to which women could turn from incestuous fathers and brutal husbands. The superintendent and other staff offered counseling in careers, marriage, and child-rearing. Moreover, the institution provided training in manners that many working-class women may have considered valuable: refined behavior was widely regarded as a sign of female superiority, particularly by people with authority and status.

To be sure, the reformatory did not bring every case to the desired conclusion. It tended to be least successful with women whose families had resisted their commitment. In the case of Anna H., the black woman sentenced for vagrancy, for instance, the reformatory was bombarded with appeals for release from the inmate's frantic parents and their lawyer, the mayor of Newport, Rhode Island; the latter also elicited requests for Anna's discharge from the offices of New York's State Board of Charities and Governor Alfred E. Smith. When the superintendent refused to heed these appeals, Anna attempted to escape. Lillian R., the inmate originally sentenced to the Bedford reformatory for "debauchery," was similarly unappreciative of institutionalization. At Bedford she participated in the July 1920 riots against cruelty to inmates. Subsequently, Bedford's matrons told her she was to be paroled, but as Lillian explained in a letter to her mother, "I knew that parole talk was all a frameup"; she realized she was really being transferred to Albion, at the other end of the state. "[I]f they were any kind of women they would tell us just where we are going and not say that we were paroled. . . . [T]hen they wonder why the girls don't respect them." Lillian's later letters show that she was equally critical of the matrons at Albion. Other inmates demonstrated resistance by misbehaving on parole:

> Julia was a great care throughout her parole . . . deceitful & deceptive. [No. 1581]
>
> She was arrested while on parole and sentenced again to the W.H. of R. But we refused to take her again. [No. 1355]
>
> Minnie gave entire satisfaction [while on domestic parole] for several months[,] saved her money[,] was quiet and unobtrusive. . . . The spirit of unrest [then] took possession of her and she absconded, and no trace of her has been found. [No. 89]

When No. 61 sold her discharge clothes, "bought a telescope," and ran away from the Wayfarers' Lodge in Buffalo, reformatory officials resignedly observed, "[A] perverse nature and bad blood [had] proved too strong for human endeavor."

On the other hand, Albion's records also provide evidence that numerous inmates were grateful for its help. Some, especially those who were very young, alone in the world, or in poor health, seem not to have found incarceration onerous. A few, for example, requested to stay for their full terms, without parole. Inmate No. 1257 resisted leaving Albion for an unpleasant home situation: her mother had been committed to an insane asylum, and there were small children whose care would fall on her. "When it came time for her to go . . . she cried and it was with difficulty that the

Parole Officer persuaded her to go." Some parolees ran back to the institution from uncongenial domestic placements. One woman, after having been paroled twice, returned "and asked to be admitted. She was a wreck, physically and morally—her clothing torn and soiled, and evidently [she] had no place to go for the night nor money to pay her way." The reformatory gave her medical attention and sheltered her for another six months. After marrying, some former inmates brought their husbands to visit the reformatory and meet its superintendent. A woman who had escaped later wrote from a distant state to announce that she was happily married; her resentment at being confined, in other words, was not incompatible with a desire to demonstrate that she could achieve the institution's ideals. Many women wrote back after release. "My dear Mrs. Boyd," began a letter received by superintendent Boyd in 1907,

> have [you] entirely forgotten Nellie that one time lived in your pleasant Home for Homeless Girls.
>
> I have been thinking for some time that I would write to you. . . . Of course you have heard from Mrs. Green that I am married and have a good Husband. . . . Are any of the Ladies [officers] with you now that were in the years of 1894 or 95 . . . how I would like to see them as well as your self. . . . I have a very pleasant home and appreciate it I think as I ought to. Yours in haste and with love,
>
> Nellie (I am Ever) L____

Albion succeeded in persuading inmates like Nellie to identify with its standards for correct female behavior. These were, essentially, middle-class standards. While many members of the working class may also have endorsed them, women sentenced to Albion had not—deviations from these values had led to their incarceration. In reforming (and in wanting to demonstrate reformation), successful cases had by definition come to identify with middle-class concepts of female propriety. Class identification was very much in flux at the turn of the century. As Charles Rosenberg has explained,

> [S]tatus definitions in 19th century America were . . . particularly labile. . . . A good many Americans must, it follows, have been all the more anxious in their internalization of those aspects of life-style which seemed to embody and assure class status. And contemporaries clearly regard overt sexuality, especially in women, as part of a life-style demeaning to middle-class status.

When women who had been apprehended for sexual misconduct and other signs of independence from middle-class "status definitions" became chaste or sober or (like Nellie) "appreciative" of husband and home, the middle-class won an ideological victory. Its values had been affirmed; its symbols of status had been accorded validity by women of the working-class.

The reformatory probably influenced the values not only of those sentenced to it but also of women in the broader community. Albion's records show that some inmates knew each other before commitment and continued to associate after release. But to be a prisoner was unusual; since acquaintanceship networks existed among inmates, these networks must have been even more extensive between inmates and women never incarcerated. Through such connections, Albion would have come to play a role in the consciousness of working-class women in its area. Women who never set foot inside it would have been aware, through word of mouth, that there existed a state institution prepared to punish them for deviations from middle-class definitions of womanliness.

Informal as well as formal police actions reinforced the social values endorsed by Albion, reminding women in the community of the institution's potential for punishment. This kind of informal social control is almost invisible today since it was seldom noted in official records. Yet glimpses of it can be caught from time to time in reformatory documents. One hint appears in the registry record of inmate No. 2441, a woman confined for vagrancy. She had no previous arrests, according to the registry, but had been "taken to the Police Station twice and talked to for being out late, attending dances." Whereas this particular woman was evidently not influenced by police efforts to get her to behave properly (she did, after all, end up at the reformatory), others so treated may have been. Of No. 1775, paroled in 1919, we are told,

> Edna was very erratic and unreliable during her parole. She was reported [to the reformatory] by the Binghamton police as being on the streets at a late hour very frequently with different men. Chief Cronin was asked several times [by reformatory officials] to arrest her and instructed his men to that effect.

Other police chiefs probably also ordered their men to keep women like Edna in line. Thus, through informal procedures as well as formal arrests, the police helped uphold the reformatory's values; they, too, gave women incentives to submit and behave.

The Definition of Gender

Most other women's reformatories also aimed at rescue and reform and used techniques of social control similar to those of Albion. From Maine to North Carolina, New York to Nebraska, reformatories for women removed errant women from the streets, trained them in domestic skills, and returned them to the home. Through parole supervision they also encouraged inmates on conditional release to maintain "self-control" at work and in sexual relationships; and if located in states with facilities for the feebleminded, they also used transfers to such institutions as an auxiliary disciplinary measure. All prisons of the reformatory type seem to have exercised tight control over mail, visitors, and disposition of children. Like Albion, most other reformatories were multifunctional institutions that served as hospitals, refuges, schools, vocational training and placement agencies, and counseling centers—as well as prisons. Officials at many were rewarded by former inmates who returned, after discharge, to give thanks and demonstrate that they had indeed reformed.

The prisoners of these institutions were burdened by multiple disadvantages. They and their families fell near the bottom of the class hierarchy. In addition to being poor, the prisoners suffered the disability of being women in a society that barred women from many occupations, paid them less than male workers, and imposed male authority everywhere. Race was yet another factor relegating black or Indian women to the base of the social structure, while nativist prejudices pushed the foreign-born toward the margins of society. Most reformatory prisoners were young, a further drawback in terms of status. Those who were single—and they were probably in the majority at other reformatories as well as at Albion—were at another disadvantage in a society that placed a premium on marriage for women.

The prisoners were, then, located at the bottom of many power dimensions in their society, those defined by social class, sex, age, marital status, and (for some) race or ethnicity. But they did not stay put in these lowly positions. They had no authority, yet as the many cases of incorrigible daughters, wandering wives, and unreliable servants in reformatory reports indicate, they balked at obedience. Lacking autonomy, they nonetheless acted independently. Bereft of status, many refused to behave as inferiors. Their very handicaps, in fact, created a situation of some fluidity. As women who had to work, they had achieved a degree (albeit minimal) of economic self-sufficiency. Denied the luxury of being kept, they were to some extent freed from cultural imagery that associated "good" women with fragility and submissiveness. Youth in combination with physical maturity and lack of marital attachment probably encouraged them to seek sexual pleasure outside marriage. Thus their characteristics and situations promoted disengagement from their era's standards for propriety.

Among the factors that fostered establishment of woman's reformatories, two were of special importance: changes in gender roles in nineteenth- and early twentieth-century America and the simultaneous widening of divisions between social classes. During the nineteenth century, as production came to be located outside the family, women were increasingly isolated within the home. Their labor was devalued and a premium came to be placed on feminine characteristics such as domesticity, demureness, purity, and piety. But the ideal of true womanhood was more easily approximated by women of the middle than of the working class. The former were likely to have servants and other aids to gentility, and if they became restless they could take up causes like temperance and prison reform.

Intensification of gender roles had different implications for working-class women, however. For them, true womanhood was more difficult to achieve and less rewarding. As the nineteenth century flowed into the twentieth, some middle-class women (including those who founded and ran reformatories) participated in the gradual break from traditional roles. But for them, activity in the world was more likely to be compatible with respectability; charitable work, for instance, had long been a hallmark of the lady, and social feminism posed no real threat to male authority. But activities available to working-class women in search of self-fulfillment meshed less well with traditional notions of rectitude. Indeed, some of them, such as drinks in saloons, late night cigarettes with sailors, and casual affairs, became grounds for imprisonment.

Persuaded of innate temperamental differences between the sexes, the reformers naturally set about establishing separate prisons for women run by women; and believing that woman's mission included rescue of the unfortunate, they naturally focused on fallen women—not serious felons or confirmed prostitutes but wayward "girls" who might be saved. Those among them active in social purity campaigns argued against the double standard of sexual morality for men and women. Yet all the reformers worked to found or operate prisons that in fact institutionalized the double standard. Their understanding of "woman's nature" led logically to advocacy of special help for the frailer sex.

This understanding was embodied in laws establishing reformatories that could incarcerate women for minor offenses, mainly "moral" in nature. In many cases, apparently, the understanding came to be internalized by inmates. This internalization provides an instance of the ability of law to perform hegemonic functions—to reproduce the ideological and political conditions of social hierarchy. As Diane Polan has explained, "In respect to patriarchy, a set of ideas . . . operate[s] hegemonically to the extent it succeeds in convincing women that their inferior political, economic, and social status is a result of a *natural* division of the world into separate spheres and *natural* differences between male and female personalities . . . rather than the result of exploitation and domination." From this perspective, inmates' acceptance of reformatory values can be seen as a phase in the process that another writer describes as "the *embourgeoisement* of the working class," its absorption of middle-class attitudes toward status, security, property, the family—and gender roles.

Two groups of women—the working-class offenders and the middle-class reformers—met, so to speak, at the gate of the women's reformatory. The struggle between them was economically functional to the reformers: it helped maintain a pool of cheap domestic labor for women like themselves and, by keeping working women in the surplus labor force, it undergirded the economic system to which reformers owed their privileged positions. But a purely economic explanation does not adequately account for the dedication with which the reformers went about their tasks of rescue and reform. The struggle also involved the definition of gender. The reformers had already absorbed the social controls they sought to instill. These reformers hoped to recast offenders in their own image, to have them embrace the values (though not assume the social station) of the lady. And through reformatories like Albion, some working-class women were taught to accept a new concept of womanhood that restricted their sexual and vocational choices. They were, in fact, reformed.

Study Questions

1. What is meant by social control, and how does it apply to the women's reformatory movement?

2. For what types of offenses were women incarcerated in Albion? By whom? Why?

3. Discuss the types of sexual activities that were likely to land young women in reformatories. How was such promiscuity curtailed by the institution?

4. How did Albion prepare women for their domestic roles?

5. What types of coercive power did reformatories exert on their charges to gain compliance?

6. Discuss the relationship between social class and the reformatory movement.

5
Sentencing in the United States

Lawrence F. Travis III

Sentencing is perhaps the point at which deci-sion making in the criminal justice system has the most direct impact on the United States' prisons. The type of sentence imposed, and for how long, directly affect the size of the prison population, the characteristics of the prison population, and ultimately the overall condi-tions of prisons themselves (both socially and physically). In this piece by Lawrence Travis III, many aspects of sentencing in the United States are examined. First (and perhaps fore-most), the base purposes and philosophies of punishment itself are reviewed. The author re-veals how each of the four philosophies is dis-tinct, and what their respective influences may be on sentencing in the United States. After presenting the philosophies of punishment, the chapter then explores several technical as-pects of sentencing that have been affecting the correctional system for the past several de-cades—specifically, the task of "risk predic-tion" (risk of future offending), the trend to-ward truth in sentencing, and various types of disparity in sentencing. Ultimately the reader should be challenged to consider what the most important purposes of punishment are, and how best to apply sentencing in an ever-expanding and increasingly diverse system.

In the year 2000, state courts imposed sen-tences on over 900,000 persons convicted of felonies (Durose and Langan 2003). More fel-ons were sentenced in federal courts, and even greater numbers of persons convicted of misdemeanors were sentenced in state and local courts. Each year, criminal penalties are imposed on millions of persons in the United States. Of all punishments, those im-posed on felons are the most severe and can include the death penalty for those convicted of capital crimes such as aggravated murder.

The sentencing decision, normally made by a judge, represents a determination of what to do about crime and, specifically, what to do with the convicted criminal. Sen-tencing is the choice of punishment. Punish-ment is the imposition of consequences, usually unpleasant consequences, for the commission of crime (von Hirsch 1976). Graeme Newman (1983, 6) writes, "Punish-ment, above all else, must be painful." Sen-tencing involves the imposition of harm (pain or unpleasant consequences) on per-sons convicted of crimes. The choice of pun-ishment that is at the heart of the sentencing decision seems to require justification.

While there may be some element of reflex in punishment and sentencing (Mackie 1982), we tend to feel that govern-ment actions that hurt citizens must be justi-fied and explained. What are the reasons that make it acceptable for agents of the gov-ernment to cause harm to citizens? Justifica-tions for criminal penalties are the goals of sentencing. They are the purposes that crim-inal sentences are expected to serve.

Goals of Sentencing

There are four traditional goals of sen-tencing; deterrence, incapacitation, treat-ment, and desert. Of these four, the first three define sentencing as serving a utilitar-ian future purpose. The point of punishment is to prevent or reduce crime in the future. The fourth seeks to restore a balance by returning harm for harm. If the crime is harmful, the criminal deserves to receive harm in return. Let's look at each of these goals in more detail.

Deterrence

Deterrent penalties are expected to pre-vent future crime by "scaring" would-be offenders with the consequences of crime. A deterrent penalty provides an example of what awaits the offender should she or he commit a crime. In theory, the fear of punishment will cause the offender to "think twice" about crime.

There are two distinct types of deterrent penalties or purposes. The first is general deterrence, where the goal of the punishment is to influence the behavior of the general public. The second, known as specific deterrence, is aimed at the offender alone and tries to convince him or her to avoid future crime. In both cases, deterrent penalties rely on a theory of human behavior that assumes that people are rational and seek to avoid pain (Paternoster 1987).

For deterrence to work, potential offenders must view the penalty as unpleasant and, in fact, as unpleasant enough to outweigh the benefits to be gained by crime. If one could steal $1,000 and be fined only $500, the punishment produces less harm (loss of $500) than the gain of the crime ($1,000). In this case, the crime results in a net gain, even with the penalty, and we would not expect to deter theft. The second requirement of deterrence is that the penalty must be imposed. If a $1,000 theft carried a $10,000 fine, the punishment outweighs the gain of the crime. However, if the offender is not caught, or the punishment is not imposed, the reality is that the crime still "pays."

In the language of deterrence, these conditions represent severity and certainty. Severity relates to the level of pain or harm imposed by the punishment. More severe penalties impose greater harm. Penalty severity must outweigh the benefits of crime. Certainty relates to the likelihood of the penalty being imposed. If every offender who commits a crime is punished, then there is total or 100 percent certainty. The higher the certainty of punishment, the less likely it is that offenders will commit the crime.

A final part of a deterrent sanction relates to the speed with which a penalty is imposed, or the celerity of punishment. In theory, the more quickly punishment follows the crime, the more effective it will be in preventing future crime. The idea is that an immediate punishment clearly links the penalty to the criminal behavior, so that everyone can see that crime is punished. It may also help in conditioning the offender to associate the penalty with the criminal act so that, like Pavlov's dogs, the offender eventually becomes conditioned to avoid criminal acts.

Of these three conditions, research suggests that the certainty of punishment is much more important than either the severity or celerity of the sanction. With a rational offender, uncertainty of punishment means the offender will calculate the odds of being caught, will take steps to avoid detection, and may calculate that the odds of avoiding punishment make the crime worth the risk. It may also be that, as Paternoster (1987) warned, offenders are not rational in their thinking. Piquero and Rengert (1999) found that the potential payoff of a burglary was a more important factor in the minds of burglars than the chance of punishment. Nagin and Pogarsky (2001) found that offenders differ in their willingness to take risks. What deters one person may not have the same effect on another.

Incapacitation

Like deterrence, incapacitation justifies the imposition of a penalty on the promise of reduced future crime. Unlike deterrence, incapacitation seeks to limit the offender's chance to commit future crimes rather than his or her decision to commit crime. A punishment for incapacitation reduces future crime by a particular offender by removing the opportunity for crime. An imprisoned offender is unable to commit a crime against people in free society, at least until released.

The biggest problem with incapacitation as a reason for punishment is the difficulty of predicting who is likely to commit future crimes and the costs of incarcerating or otherwise monitoring potential offenders. Given current levels of sophistication, it is not possible to correctly identify specific individuals who will commit crimes in the future.

Efforts to predict who will commit crimes run the risk of making one of two different mistakes. First, we might predict someone will commit a crime who actually will not. Alternatively, we might predict someone will not commit a new crime who actually does. Since we are predicting new crime, someone who commits a new crime is *positive*, and those who do not commit new crimes are *negative*. Our erroneous predictions are either *false positives*, where we wrongly predict an offender will commit a new crime, and *false negatives*, where we wrongly predict an offender will not commit a new crime.

False positives are incapacitated when there is no need to do so, while false negatives are allowed to commit new crimes. We have to decide how much of which type of error we can tolerate (Smith and Smith 1998). Largely as a result of the large number of false positives compared with true positives (most people do not commit crimes), we tend to overestimate the population of future criminals. This means we incapacitate many more offenders than need to be controlled. If we do that by imprisonment, at $25,000 or more per person per year, each false positive is expensive. If we need to incarcerate for at least ten years to prevent a future crime, then we waste a quarter of a million dollars, if not more, for each false positive. Incapacitation is a very rational policy, but unfortunately we do not yet have the expertise to accurately predict the danger of new crime.

Treatment

Sometimes also known as *rehabilitation*, punishment based on treatment is expected to reduce the chances of future crime by changing the offender's need or desire to commit crime. Treatment sentences are based on the individual needs or characteristics of the offender. Treatment is based on the notion that individuals commit crimes for a number of reasons and the solution to the crime problem lies in attacking those reasons. Successful treatment results in individuals who no longer wish or need to commit crimes. The treatment rationale demonstrates concern for the individual offender and establishes an obligation on the part of the state to provide aid and care for criminal offenders (Cullen and Gilbert 1982).

As with incapacitation, the behavioral sciences have not reached a point where they can provide completely successful treatment programs. Programs that are available to offenders are limited, partly in response to pragmatic concerns about cost and safety and partly from an inability to fully diagnose or respond to the criminogenic (crime-producing) needs of offenders. Often offenders receive some sort of counseling that is applied to a wide range of offenders. While theoretically aimed at individuals, the fact is that most treatment programs are applied to large groups of offenders and not often tailored to individuals. Adams (1961) discovered that such programming can result in harmful effects for some, positive effects for others, and no effects for still others. In the end, the positive and harmful effects cancel each other out, showing no benefit from treatment. Doris MacKenzie (1997, 9–16) phrased the issue when she wrote, "The important issue is not whether something works but what works for whom?" Like deterrence and incapacitation, the theory of treatment is eminently plausible, but may require more sophistication than is currently available.

Despite discouraging findings from a number of treatment program evaluations, attempts to improve treatment continue and are increasing (Gendreau and Ross 1987). There is evidence to support the positive impact of treatment programs. Among others, Taxman and Piquero (1998) reported that treatment sentences for drunk drivers were more successful in reducing repeat offending than were sentences that were simply punitive (i.e., deterrent or incapacitation based). Within the past two decades, a number of "problem-solving courts" have developed to focus on specific offenses and offenders. These courts work to insure that those convicted of drug offenses, domestic violence, or other identified crimes receive, participate in, and complete treatment programming (Casey and Rottman 2003).

Desert

Also known as *retribution* or *just deserts*, sentences based on a desert rationale do not seek to reduce future crime. Desert sentencing is concerned with the imposition of fair punishment for past crime. The principal goal is not to prevent or control future crime but to insure justice in punishing the present offense. Those who break the law deserve to be punished, regardless of whether the punishment changes future crime.

Desert works to put limits on criminal punishment. A penalty is expected to balance the criminal act. More serious crimes deserve more severe punishment. Punishment is based on two criteria. First is the amount of harm caused by the crime. The more harm done, the greater the pain of the penalty. Second, the culpability of the offender plays a role in determining the level of a penalty. The more culpable (blameworthy) an offender, the more pain is deserved. Still, no matter how culpable an offender might be, desert recognizes real limits on the severity of punishment.

Desert might define burglary as requiring punishment by imprisonment of no more than ten years. A less culpable burglar (perhaps an 18-year-old, first-time offender who was influenced by an older partner) might be justly punished with a sentence of five years. If a life sentence would deter enough other possible burglars, deterrence would allow the imposition of life imprisonment. If the offender needed treatment that would take 20 years to complete, a treatment rationale would allow a 20-year term. If we thought the offender would repeat his crime by the age of 50, incapacitation would allow a sentence of 32 years (until age 50). Desert would not allow any sentence in excess of ten years. In contrast, if the offender posed no risk of future crime, deterrence, treatment, and incapacitation provide no justification for imprisonment. Desert requires imprisonment (but not more than ten years) for burglary, and it sets both a bottom and a top to punishment based on the seriousness of the crime.

While each of these purposes of punishment is separate and distinct, in practice it is common for legislatures and those who impose sentences to try to serve several purposes at once. As mentioned, using desert as a boundary, sentencing laws often provide utilitarian (crime prevention) justifications for punishment. In this way, while a burglary may deserve prison, we recognize that while in prison the offender is incapacitated, that imprisonment may deter others, and that we should strive to provide treatment to the burglar. The existence of multiple goals of sentencing coupled with attempts to achieve them at the same time helps make sentencing and punishment very complex parts of the justice system. In this complexity, a number of issues emerge.

Sentencing Issues

It seems there has always been controversy and debate over criminal sentencing. Some disagreement exists about which of the purposes of punishment are most important, but other sentencing issues have also proven to be controversial. Among several, concern about prediction, truth in sentencing, and disparity are important sentencing issues.

Prediction

Prediction is a central concern in almost all criminal justice decisions (Clear and O'Leary 1983). Michael and Donald Gottfredson (1988) reported that concern about the prior criminal record of offenders was present at almost every decision point in the criminal justice process. We are, naturally, interested in the likelihood that someone will continue to commit crimes, and the best predictor of future behavior is past behavior. Society expects its criminal justice system to take steps to prevent future crime.

Any prediction of future crime risks the prediction errors discussed above. We may predict someone will be safe who will actually commit new crimes (false negative). Alternatively, we may predict someone will commit new crimes who actually will be safe (false positive). As we saw, we expend punishment resources unnecessarily on false positive errors and fail to protect society with false negative errors.

Assuming that prediction is appropriate and necessary in sentencing, we still have a few unresolved issues. Suppose we sentence someone to additional time in prison because we predict that he or she will commit another crime. Upon release, sure enough, this individual does commit a new crime. The question that emerges is whether he or she has already been punished for that new offense. Do we need to punish this person some more after we have already imposed a predicted sentence?

Even if we could accomplish complete accuracy in predictions, some people would argue that it is inappropriate to punish for crimes not yet committed. Like the offender in *Alice in Wonderland*, with prediction the punishment comes first and if there is no future offense, "so much the better." Predictive sentencing supports practices like habitual offender and *three strikes* laws that impose long sentences on repeat offenders. The issue around prediction in sentencing has to do with balancing the need to protect society from future harm with the need to protect the individual rights and interests of the criminal (and potential criminal) offender.

Truth in Sentencing

"The amount of time offenders serve in prison is almost always shorter than the time they are sentenced to serve by the court" (Ditton and Wilson 1999, 1). As a result of sentence reductions for good behavior, early release due to prison crowding, or discretionary parole release, most prisoners serve substantially less time than that to which they were sentenced. A study of prisoners admitted in 1994 estimated that the average prisoner would serve less than 40 percent of the court-imposed sentence (Langan and Brown 1997). That those sent to prison typically serve sentences far shorter than what is announced in court led to a federal effort to achieve "truth in sentencing."

The Violent Crime Control and Law Enforcement Act of 1994 created funding for additional state prisons and jails. To qualify for federal funds, state laws must insure that those convicted of Part I violent crimes serve at least 85 percent of their prison sentence. In 1998, more than half the states and the District of Columbia qualified for this funding. States have abolished discretionary parole release, reduced or eliminated sentence reductions for good behavior, and created diversionary programs to keep nonviolent offenders out of prison to achieve longer terms of incarceration for those convicted of violent crimes.

Early release of prison inmates (before the expiration of their court-imposed term) has been criticized on a number of grounds. Some contend that early release undermines the deterrent effect of the law because it means that the sentence imposed is not certain, and that the offender can always hope for early release. Others argue that early release does not allow the sentence to achieve full incapacitation effects because offenders are returned to the community earlier than expected. Finally, still others argue that such dishonesty in sentencing undermines respect for the law and citizen confidence in the criminal justice system. When citizens learn that they have been misled about sentencing, they may question the integrity of the entire justice system.

Assuming that truth in sentencing is desirable, it is a complicated goal. One way to achieve truthful sentences is simply to keep offenders in prison longer, until they have served their full terms. Of course, doing so will greatly increase prison populations and drive correctional costs to levels that are probably beyond the reach of most states. A second approach is to reduce the maximum terms imposed on offenders so that prisoners will serve the same sentences as today, but the sentences announced in court will be lower. If the typical offender serves two years of a five-year sentence, change the sentence to two years and make the prisoner serve it all.

More common are hybrid efforts that distinguish between types of offenders and that increase time to be served for those convicted of more serious crimes. What appears to have happened is that offenders sentenced for violent crimes are being required to serve longer terms than in the past. At the same time, offenders sentenced for nonviolent crimes are serving shorter terms. This "solution" to the truth in sentencing dilemma raises its own issues.

First, depending upon what changes are made to sentencing laws, these efforts result in more truth in the sentencing of violent offenders, but less truth in the sentencing of nonviolent offenders. In the end, the truthfulness of the entire sentencing system may not be affected at all. Second, adaptations that focus on longer terms for violent offenders and shorter or no prison terms for nonviolent offenders can change the dynamics of life inside prisons. Prisons have always housed a relatively violent population, but under truth in sentencing the prison population will increasingly come to be composed of serious, violent offenders. Prisons may become more dangerous as a result.

Beyond changes in prison population, the imposition of long terms complicates efforts to develop and provide treatment programs, as offenders will be spending substantially longer times in prison, making it more difficult to maintain contact with the outside world and to provide a smooth reentry to society on release. In addition, prisoners facing long terms with little hope of sentence reductions will be less inclined to obey prison rules. Ohio attempted to deal with this part of the truth in sentencing dilemma (how does one motivate prisoners to behave?) by creating the concept of *bad time*. The courts declared that bad time violated due process protections (Holcomb and Williams 2003).

The bad time provisions of Ohio law were akin to an inverse of traditional *good time*. For decades, prison administrators have been empowered to grant reductions in prison terms for good behavior. In most cases, reductions are automatically awarded to inmates, and misbehavior is punished by withholding a reduction. With bad time, prison administrators (and the parole authority) were authorized to increase the length of a sentence when inmates engaged in acts that violated the criminal law. The Ohio Supreme Court ruled that the imposition of additional prison time in the absence of a trial was unconstitutional, and bad time was abandoned. The problem of controlling inmate behavior is serious and is one of the most important explanations for a lack of truth in sentencing.

The sentencing decision is tightly bound to correctional programming and treatment. Changes in who gets sentenced to what dispositions will influence the composition of correctional populations, the implementation and effectiveness of treatment programs, and the ability of correctional officials to manage offenders. At the same time, sentencing is the decision of what to do about a criminal offender and is important to victims and others. There is a need for honesty in sentencing. It may be, though, that the best way to achieve truth in sentencing is not necessarily through changing the sentencing process but rather by better explaining sentencing to the public.

Disparity

Sentencing disparity is the term used to describe the unequal treatment of similar offenders (Gottfredson 1979). Most people would agree that persons who have similar criminal histories and are convicted of similar offenses should receive similar penalties. Two first-time offenders convicted of burglary should, we tend to think, receive the same punishment. When different sentences are imposed on similar offenders, the differences are called *disparity*. Yet sentencing disparity really relates to unwarranted differences (Gottfredson et al. 1978).

If we are trying to accomplish treatment and one of our first-offender burglars is diagnosed as needing employment training while the other needs no assistance, it would be acceptable to require the first offender to complete a training program or even spend time in a confinement facility that offered such training. So, too, a repeat offender can be given a punishment more severe than a first offender and most people would think that was acceptable. In both those cases the offenders are not "similar," in the sense that the differences in punishment are "warranted" by differences in treatment need or prior record. The controversy over disparity hinges in large part on the definition of *similar* (Vining 1983).

Beginning in the mid-1970s, several states and the federal government enacted legislation to reform criminal sentencing. One of the goals of almost all of these reforms was to increase consistency and fairness in sentencing (Ulmer 1997; Anspach and Monsen 1989; Goodstein and Hepburn 1983). That is, for three decades

we have been trying to control or reduce sentencing disparity.

The culprit in sentencing disparity was identified as the individual whims of justice system officials. The attitudes and interests of judges, probation officers, parole authority members, and so on were felt to cause the imposition of different sentences on similar offenders. To reduce the impact of individual decision makers on sentences, a variety of sentencing reforms were enacted. Some states developed determinate sentencing that eliminated parole authority discretion. In some cases, the range of discretion granted to judges was greatly reduced by requiring mandatory prison terms or reducing the gap between minimum and maximum terms. In some jurisdictions, the legislature authorized the creation of sentencing guidelines that defined the purpose of punishment and directed sentencing judges to consider specific factors in deciding on a sentence. These guidelines helped reduce variation in sentences and thus increased consistency in punishment.

The effects of reform are unclear and may include increases in the rate of imprisonment and changes in the length of prison terms imposed (Tonry 1999). Concern over disparity was driven by suggestions that differences in sentences were a product of discrimination based on race, sex, age, or other social characteristics of offenders and not on offense seriousness, risk, culpability, or other legally relevant factors (Spohn 2000). Daly and Bordt (1995) reported that women tend to receive less severe sentences than men, but that this is probably due to differences in the kinds of offenses committed by women and men. Spohn (1994) compared sentences of blacks and whites, and, while persistent differences exist, she suggests that differences in types of offenses may account for different punishments. In addition to different types of offenses, blacks and whites tend to differ in terms of prior convictions, which also influences sentences (Pratt 1998). While differences in offense seriousness and prior record explain much of the difference in criminal sentences, it is also likely that sentencing decisions reflect the disadvantaged status of minority group members in American society.

Attempts to increase equity and fairness in sentencing, including determinate sentencing, presumptive sentencing, and sentencing guidelines, may have reduced the incidence of disparity in criminal punishments. Still, there is variation in sentences imposed on criminal offenders, and the differences in sentences appear to be related to the social and demographic characteristics of offenders. Disparity in sentencing remains an important unresolved issue in criminal punishment.

Conclusion

Even a cursory examination of criminal sentencing such as this indicates that there are many unanswered questions and that sentencing in practice is a complex process. What can or should be done to improve or change sentencing remains a judgment call determined in part by the goals of sentencing and conditioned by the constraints of the operating justice system. Improvements in prediction and treatment effectiveness, or changes in prison capacity, can influence decisions about what are appropriate and desirable sentences.

Efforts to increase consistency and reduce disparity in sentencing show the complexity of the topic. At the same time that legislatures around the country were moving to reduce sentencing discretion to reduce disparity, they were also adopting intermediate sanctions and alternatives to incarceration. While we may have reduced the range of prison sentences, we have added a range of sentencing options from electronic surveillance to community service orders (Morris and Tonry 1990). Increasing sentencing options runs the risk of increasing sentencing disparity. The more choices available to sentencing deci-

sion makers, the more different kinds of sentences can be imposed on similar offenders.

While we need to determine what are just punishments and how we can impose just sentences, we must also recognize that we often disagree about the requirements of justice. We may never be able to reach agreement about the justice of criminal punishments. Nonetheless, it is incumbent on us to understand sentencing and to strive to improve the process.

Study Questions

1. Describe and define the four major philosophies of punishment presented by the author. Which one is the most valid? Offer details as to why you chose the philosophy that you did.

2. Combine your opinion with the information presented in this chapter, and determine why you feel the prison system may not be effective at deterring offenders from committing crime.

3. What role does "prediction" play in the sentencing decision? Should prediction have a role when judges make sentencing decisions?

4. For what reasons presented in this chapter has there been a push toward "truth in sentencing" legislation?

5. Based on your reading of the chapter, for what reason(s) does sentencing disparity exist in the criminal justice system?

References

Adams, S. 1961. *Effectiveness of Interview Therapy With Older Youth Authority Wards: An Interim Evaluation of the PICO Project*. Sacramento, CA: California Youth Authority.

Anspach, D., and S. Monsen. 1989. "Determinate Sentencing, Formal Rationality, and Khadi Justice in Maine: An Application of Weber's Typology." *Journal of Criminal Justice* 17(6): 471–485.

Casey, P., and D. Rottman. 2003. *Problem-Solving Courts: Models and Trends*. Williamsburg, VA: National Center for State Courts.

Clear, T., and V. O'Leary. 1983. *Controlling the Offender in the Community*. Lexington, MA: Lexington Books.

Cullen, F. T., and K. E. Gilbert. 1982. *Reaffirming Rehabilitation*. Cincinnati, OH: Anderson.

Daly, K., and R. Bordt. 1995. "Sex Effects and Sentencing: An Analysis of the Statistical Literature." *Justice Quarterly* 12(1):141–175.

Ditton, P., and D. Wilson. 1999. *Truth in Sentencing in State Prisons*. Washington, DC: Bureau of Justice Statistics.

Durose, M., and P. Langan. 2003. *Felony Sentences in State Courts, 2000*. Washington, DC: Bureau of Justice Statistics.

Gendreau, P., and R. Ross. 1987. "Revivification of Rehabilitation: Evidence From the 1980s." *Justice Quarterly* 4(3):349–407.

Goodstein, L., and J. Hepburn. 1983. *Determinate Sentencing and Imprisonment*. Cincinnati, OH: Anderson.

Gottfredson, D., C. Cosgrove, L. Wilkins, J. Wallerstein, and C. Rauh. 1978. *Classification for Parole Decision Policy*. Washington, DC: U.S. Government Printing Office.

Gottfredson, M. 1979. "Parole Guidelines and the Reduction of Sentencing Disparity: A Preliminary Study." *Journal of Research in Crime and Delinquency* 23(4):218–231.

Gottfredson, M., and D. Gottfredson. 1988. *Decisionmaking in Criminal Justice*, 2nd ed. New York: Plenum.

Holcomb, J., and M. Williams. 2003. "From the Field: 'Bad Time': The Rise and Fall of Penal Policy in Ohio." *Journal of Crime and Justice* 26(2):153–175.

Langan, P., and J. Brown. 1997. *Felony Sentences in State Courts, 1994*. Washington, DC: Bureau of Justice Statistics.

MacKenzie, D. 1997. "Criminal Justice and Crime Prevention," in L. Sherman, D. Gottfredson, J. Eck, P. Reuter, and S. Bushway (eds.) *Preventing Crime: What Works, What Doesn't, What's Promising*. Washington, DC: National Institute of Justice, Chapter 9.

Mackie, J. 1982. "Morality and the Retributive Emotions." *Criminal Justice Ethics* 1(1):3–10.

Martinson, R. 1974. "What Works?" *The Public Interest* (Spring):22.

Morris, N., and M. Tonry. 1990. *Between Prison and Probation*. Oxford, UK: Oxford University Press.

Nagin, D. S., and G. Pogarsky. 2001. "Integrating Celebrity, Impulsivity, and Extralegal Sanction Threats into a Model of General Deterrence: Theory and Evidence." *Criminology* 39(4):404–430.

Newman, G. 1983. *Just and Painful*. New York: MacMillan.

Paternoster, R. 1987. "The Deterrent Effect of the Perceived Certainty and Severity of Punishment: A Review of the Evidence and Issues." *Justice Quarterly* 4(2):173–217.

Piquero, A., and G. Rengert. 1999. "Studying Deterrence With Active Residential Burglars." *Justice Quarterly* 16(2):451–471.

Pratt, T. 1998. "Race and Sentencing: A Meta-Analysis of Conflicting Empirical Research Results." *Journal of Criminal Justice* 26(6): 513–523.

Smith, W., and D. Smith. 1998. "The Consequences of Error: Recidivism Prediction and Civil-Libertarian Ratios." *Journal of Criminal Justice* 26(6):481–502.

Spohn, C. 1994. "Crime and the Social Control of Blacks: Offender/Victim Race and the Sentencing of Violent Offenders," in G. Bridges & M. Myers (eds.) *Inequality, Crime, and Social Policy*. Boulder, CO: Westview.

Spohn, C. 2000. "Thirty Years of Sentencing Reform: The Quest for a Racially Neutral Sentencing Process," in J. Horney (ed.) *Policies, Processes, and Decisions of the Criminal Justice System*. Washington, DC: National Institute of Justice, Criminal Justice 2000, Vol. 3:427–501.

Taxman, F., and A. Piquero. 1998. "On Preventing Drunk Driving Recidivism: An Examination of Rehabilitation and Punishment Approaches." *Journal of Criminal Justice* 26(2):129–143.

Tonry, M. 1999. "The Fragmentation of Sentencing and Corrections in American." *Sentencing and Corrections Issues for the 21st Century* (September). Washington, DC: National Institute of Justice.

Ulmer, J. 1997. *Social Worlds of Sentencing: Court Communities Under Sentencing Guidelines*. Albany, NY: SUNY Press.

Vining, A. 1983. "Developing Aggregate Measures of Disparity." *Criminology* 21(2):233–252.

Von Hirsch, A. 1976. *Doing Justice*. New York: Hill & Wang.

Zatz, M. 2000. "The Convergence of Race, Ethnicity, Gender, and Class on Court Decision-making: Looking Toward the 21st Century," in J. Horney (ed.) *Policies, Processes, and Decisions of the Criminal Justice System*. Washington, DC: National Institute of Justice, Criminal Justice 2000, Vol. 3:503–552.

6
Assessing the Penal Harm Movement

Francis T. Cullen

Part I concludes with a review of the "penal harm" movement. Through historical analyses, the pieces in this section have reviewed the origins and evolution of punishment as well as the ultimate rise of the institution as punishment. Similarly, the preceding articles have revealed some of the consequences of a society that places so much emphasis on confinement. The United States has been described as engaging in an "imprisonment binge." Cullen reviews what has occurred as a result of this binge. The author defines precisely what is meant by "penal harm" and documents major movements resulting from this phenomenon, such as the decline of rehabilitation, the abolition of parole release, and the proliferation of "three strikes" legislation. The utility of penal harm is reviewed, along with the unintended consequences, such as a widening of the racial disparity in U.S. prison populations. Ultimately, one of the components of confinement that remains missing in action is identified as effective efforts toward rehabilitation.

In the aftermath of the Civil War, American corrections had devolved into a state of crisis. Prisons were filled to the brim, populated by the domestic and immigrant poor. Inmates increasingly were seen as coming from the left tail of the bell curve and from the bottom of the evolutionary ladder, and they stood as clear evidence that urban slums were producing a "dangerous class."

The idea that prisons should serve the larger social purpose of changing offenders—as the founders of the penitentiary had argued convincingly to a receptive audience only a few decades earlier—was losing credibility. More affluent citizens were tempted to see prisons as effecting "a policy of exclusion and banishment, so the public might be rid of the offender" (Rothman 1980, pp. 24–25). Although "the promise of reform had built the asylums," observes Rothman (1971, p. 240), "the functionalism of custody perpetuated them."

Each historical era has its unique conversation about corrections, but these themes voiced in post-Civil War America resonate remarkably with contemporary discourse about crime and punishment. For over a decade, virtually every contemporary commentary on corrections in the United States has reminded us that the system is in crisis (see, e.g., Blumstein 1989; Colvin 1992; Cullen and Gilbert 1982; Selke 1993; Sherman and Hawkins 1981). Institutions are crowded with at-risk young adults—some would say the less intelligent among us (Herrnstein and Murray 1994)—drawn from the urban underclass. Indeed, it is not uncommon to hear talk of the "return of the dangerous classes" (Gordon 1994; Simon, p. 253). Doubts abound about the reformative powers of correctional facilities. Jails and prisons are now seen as performing a "waste management function" (Feeley and Simon 1992; Irwin 1985; Simon, pp. 259–60) or, in more sanitized language, as "selectively incapacitating the wicked" (Wilson 1983).

The response to the prison crisis—then and now—has been decidedly different, however. In 1870, the leading correctional thinkers and practitioners (the overlap in the groups being considerable at that time) gathered in Cincinnati at the National Prison Congress to design a "new penology" that would rectify correctional failures and challenge the prevailing notion that prisons should function as warehouses with bars or, still worse, as instruments of harm. In issuing their famous "Declaration of Principles," the Congress asserted that "the supreme aim of prison discipline is the reformation of criminals, not the infliction of vindictive suffering" ("Declaration of Principles" 1910 [1870], p. 39).

These new penologists were not moral relativists and did not idealize offenders ("Declaration of Principles" 1910 [1870]): They were defenders of Christian morality and believed in character education; they embraced middle-class values and thought inmates would benefit from them too; they did not mind transforming the urban poor into disciplined workers (though they did reject as exploitive both purposeless hard labor and contract labor in prison); they believed that recalcitrant inmates should not be spared the rod (though they also felt that "rewards, more than punishments, are essential to every good prison system") ("Declaration of Principles" 1910 [1870], p. 39); and they were prepared in defense of public safety to incarcerate incorrigible inmates indeterminately. They also were optimistic that the state could be "changed from its former vengefulness to that of dignified serenity, neither vindictive nor love-lorn, but firmly and nobly corrective" (Brockway 1910, p. 88). Later commentators would criticize them for being class biased and for their naïveté in not anticipating that state power, exercised unfettered behind the high walls of the prison, could be abused and cause more harm than good (Platt 1969; Rothman 1980). I would debate these claims on the grounds that the new penology exerted a restraining influence on punitive sentiments—that the alternative would have been worse (as I believe is now the case). But it is hoped that we can agree not to deconstruct the new penologists' words to the point of ignoring their intent to better, not to hurt, offenders (see Garland 1990).

Today, however, the response to the corrections crisis has turned ugly. In the 1990s, the term *new penology* no longer refers to a correctional philosophy that rejects ven-geance in favor of offender reformation, but to an administrative style that seeks depersonalized efficiency in processing increasingly large hordes of inmates in and out of the system (Feeley and Simon 1992). More disquieting, we have entered a "mean season" in which it has become politically correct to build prisons and to devise creative strategies to make offenders suffer. In Todd Clear's words, we are witnessing a movement whose supreme aim is the infliction of "penal harm."

The field of criminology is one of the few remaining bastions in American society in which the advent of the penal harm movement has not been greeted warmly. A few bold colleagues defend the use of prisons (see, e.g., Logan and DiIulio 1992; Wright 1994), but most of us (including me) are sufficiently liberal, fearful of professional disapproval, or (I hope) criminologically astute to caution about the "limits of imprisonment" (see, e.g., Currie 1985; Gordon 1991; Irwin and Austin 1994; Selke 1993; Zimring and Hawkins 1995; see also Forer 1994). We often fret that our research and commentary are ignored by policymakers who seemingly succeed in purchasing the votes of citizens uneasy about crime by offering to effect law and order (see Kaminer 1995). But we are able to console ourselves at conferences through a shared and cathartic excoriation of the get-tough crowd, knowing that their panaceas are doomed to failure and that we stand for truth and justice.

There is a risk, however, that liberal criminologists (like me) will become too professionally insular and complacent in our thinking about corrections—that we will take turns preaching to, and being in, the choir. It is wise, I suspect, to reflect on assumptions that are held too uncritically and to check our biases with some good positivist criminology. An indispensable first step in this intellectual housecleaning is to read the three books informing this essay. Although clearly progressive in orientation, these works are sophisticated attempts to understand and to undermine the penal harm movement. They retain a humanity, which is an integral and worthy side of liberal criminology, but ultimately their strength comes from their rejection of ideology in favor of sharp logic and hard data.

I should warn that these exemplars of liberal correctional thinking—Clear's *Harm in American Penology*, Simon's *Poor Discipline*, and Tonry's *Malign Neglect*—are not immune to reasonable rejoinders by those who see benefits in penal harm; the debates are wonderfully engaged but perhaps not fully settled. But I have a more serious concern about these works: They reflect the tendency in contemporary progressive commentaries to provide incisive criticism of conservative crime policies but then to stop short of articulating a *coherent* alternative *correctional* agenda. Unlike the new penologists of the 1870s, whose "Declaration of Principles" mapped out such an agenda, they thus provide only limited guidance on how to move beyond penal harm—a point I return to at the end of this essay.

Is There a Penal Harm Movement?

Clear does a service in reminding us that an integral part of state punishment is inflicting "penal harm." The "essence of the penal sanction," he observes, is that "it harms . . . it is supposed to hurt" (p. 4). Penal harm is a "planned governmental act, whereby a citizen is harmed, and implies that harm is justifiable precisely because it is an offender who is suffering" (p. 4). We often clothe this reality with respectable-sounding euphemisms, such as "correctional interventions," "offender processing," and "incapacitation." Clear's insistent use of "penal harm" as his organizing concept strips away this comforting language, and forces us to confront the naked truth that corrections is, to a greater or lesser extent, a mean-spirited enterprise.

I suspect that only the culturally illiterate would be unaware that a movement has been afoot to expand the use of penal harm in the United States. In the past 2 years, for example, various versions of "three strikes and you're out" laws, which mandate life sentences for a third felony conviction, have been implemented in 15 states and are under consideration in 22 more (Turner, Sundt, Applegate, and Cullen forthcoming; see also Benekos and Merlo 1995). Legislators also have publicized their attempts to intensify the pains of imprisonment by reducing such inmate amenities as grants for college education, television privileges, computers in cells, and exercise through weight lifting. Alabama enthusiastically has reinstituted chain gangs. Offenders don white uniforms that display the stigmatizing label "chain gang," are shackled together, and conduct "stoop labor" for 12 hours a day (Bragg 1995; Cohen 1995). Modern technology, it must be admitted, has allowed some escape from penal harm; Alabama officials are able to point "proudly to a new, specially designed toilet that allows the men to relieve themselves in privacy while still linked to their colleagues" (Cohen 1995, p. 26).

Three-strikes laws and chain gangs might merely be part of a symbolic crusade that has affected corrections in visible, but marginal, ways. Is there evidence that penal harm has increased substantively, not just symbolically, in recent years? Clear, with help from Tonry, makes a strong case in the affirmative.

Given the ubiquity of the current get-tough talk about crime, it is easy today to forget that penal harm was not always on the rise. In the half century following 1925, imprisonment rates per 100,000 averaged under 108 per 100,000 citizens, and the number of inmates rose roughly in proportion to the growth in the general population (Clear, p. 44; see also Cullen, Van Voorhis, and Sundt forthcoming). In fact, this remarkable "stability of punishment" was the object of theoretical inquiry (Blumstein and Cohen 1973; see also Blumstein 1995; Scull 1977). Beginning in the early 1970s, however, a sea change in punishment occurred: The era of stability suddenly ended as the population of offenders under correctional supervision began a rapid, seemingly intractable rise.

Although establishing causal links between policy reforms and correctional populations is difficult (Zimring and Hawkins 1991), over the past two decades politicians certainly intended for penal harm to worsen. Clear documents that between 1972 and 1982, a majority of states restricted or abolished parole release, and mandatory or minimum sentences were widely implemented. "In one way or another," he concludes, "every state altered its penal policy in the direction of greater punitive severity" (p. 50; see also Cullen and Gilbert 1982).

To Clear, the figures on the use of prisons are "astounding": Between 1973 and the beginning of the 1990s, the number of prisoners increased by 332%, and the incarceration rate per 100,000 citizens jumped over 200% (p. 43). The growing punitiveness of sentencing also is apparent: Between 1981 and 1987, the time served for burglary rose 53% and for rape rose 129%; since 1975, the time served for violent offenses has tripled (pp. 54–55).

Michael Tonry echoes these themes and provides a useful cross-cultural perspective (see also Currie 1985). "Americans have a remarkable ability to endure suffering by others," he observes. "We lock up our citizens at rates 5 to 15 times higher than those in other Western countries" (p. 197). He claims that these incarceration rates cannot be explained by America's higher offense rate. Recently conducted international victimization surveys show that crime in the United States is not markedly higher than in other advanced industrial nations, although gun-related violence is a notable exception. Even so, the proclivity to lock up offenders seems less a product of having a larger pool

of criminals and more a product of our "national character" (pp. 197–200).

Consider, however, DiIulio's (1994, p. 15) starkly different claim that the "justice system is a revolving door for convicted predatory street criminals"—not a potent instrument for inflicting penal harm—and that "America has not been on an imprisonment binge" (see also Wilson 1995; cf. Irwin and Austin 1994). How can intelligent scholars read the evidence so differently? In fact, there are two divergent cases to be made, and a scholar's intellectual and/or ideological preferences shape which position he or she embraces.

Liberals prefer to cite raw numbers of people in prison and incarceration rates per 100,000 citizens; they also read trends beginning in the early 1970s (Clear, p. 43). In contrast, conservatives, such as John DiIulio (1994) and James Q. Wilson (1995), prefer to cite the amount of punishment meted out per offense committed and to read trend lines dating back to 1960, if not before. This latter methodology reveals that the punishment-per-offense rate declined rapidly throughout the 1960s and 1970s, only to rebound partially in the 1980s.

According to DiIulio (1994, p. 16), for example, the number of people in prison per 1,000 violent crimes dropped from 738 in 1960 to 227 in 1980, only to increase in the 1980s to 423—a point still "42 percent lower than it was in 1960." Wilson's (1995, p. 499) analysis paints a similar portrait: In 1945, the sentence served for all crimes was 25 months, but by 1984 had decreased to 13 months. These statistical patterns, contends DiIulio (1994, p. 16), do not indicate an imprisonment binge, but rather that America "has been recovering from the starvation diet it went on in the late 1960s and stayed on throughout the 1970s."

Using this general approach, the cross-cultural case for America's exceptionalism as a punitive nation also is complicated. Lynch (1995) found that offenders in the United States receive longer sentences than in other advanced industrial nations. In time actually spent in prison, however, the findings were less consistent: Compared to offenders in other nations, offenders in the United States served longer sentences for property and drug offenses but served similar sentences for homicide and serious violence (see also Farrington and Langan 1992).

Where do these competing commentaries leave us? At the very least, we know that in raw numbers, the prison population has grown in the past two decades from about 200,000 to over 1 million inmates. It also is clear that in the past decade, punishment levels have increased considerably. But whether one considers current trends to constitute penal harm or a much-needed, if not overdue, redistribution of governmental resources depends on more than incarceration statistics. In the end, assessing whether penal harm is beneficial or wasteful, and deciding appropriate levels of penal harm, will be influenced by considerations of utility: What does penal harm accomplish? . . .

The Differential Effects of Penal Harm

"No problem haunts the United States' sense of identity more intractably than race relations," comments Clear (p. 174). "The penal system," he adds, "is part of the problem, because penal harms are inequitably distributed among our racial and ethnic populations." In *Malign Neglect*, Tonry seeks to document how policies central to the ongoing penal harm movement not only have perpetuated but, more significantly, have exacerbated the concentration of punishment on African Americans.

Tonry does not deny that behavioral differences in crime exist between Black and White Americans, and although not dismissing the existence of ill and inequitable treatment of minorities, he does not contend that the racial gap in offending can be explained by the discriminatory practices of criminal justice officials. . . . Even so, he is adamant that "American crime policies since 1980 have had disastrous consequences for Black Americans" and that the penal harms visited on African Americans "do not result from increases in the proportions of serious crimes committed by Blacks" (p. 28).

Indeed, incarceration statistics paint a disquieting portrait: In both 1979 and 1990, African Americans accounted for about 44% of arrests for violent crimes. The Black proportion of admissions to state prisons, however, jumped in this period from 39% to 53% (p. 49). In fact, between 1986 and 1991, the racial mix in prison admissions flip-flopped from 53% White (and 46% Black) to 53% Black (p. 58). By 1991, African Americans were 6.47 times more likely than White Americans to be incarcerated (1,895 to 293 per 100,000) (p. 29). These figures mean that 1 in 50 Blacks are imprisoned on any given day. When the data are disaggregated by gender and age, we learn that 1 in 12 African American men between the ages of 18 and 54 are confined (p. 130). Further, nearly 1 in 4 Black men in their 20s are either behind bars or on probation or parole (p. 4; see also Tonry 1994).

"The rising levels of Black incarceration did not just happen," argues Tonry but were due to "malign neglect"; indeed, the increased penal harms suffered by African Americans after 1980 were the *foreseeable* effects of *deliberate* policies spearheaded by the Reagan and Bush administrations and implemented by many states" (p. 4, italics added). He indicts politicians for using race-based stereotypes about crime (Willie Horton and the like) as a means of stirring up racial enmity, polarizing the electorate, and capturing White votes. "The text may be crime," notes Tonry (p. 6), but "the subtext is race." Most important, he details how the "War on Drugs," which virtually no serious observer felt could be won, was used to increase political capital even though it served to "ruin countless lives and weaken numerous communities" (p. vii; see also Currie 1993; Gordon 1994).

In chapter 3, "Race and the War on Drugs," Tonry details the war's "foreseeable disparate impact on Blacks" (p. 104). The "major fronts in the drug wars were located in minority neighborhoods," in large part because trafficking occurred on the street and officers could more easily make arrests (pp. 105–7). Further, the focus on crack cocaine was especially consequential, because this drug was sold and used disproportionately by minorities and carried substantially longer penalties than powder cocaine—a drug used mainly by Whites. The result of targeting low-level, inner-city, street-level drug dealers and attaching harsh punishments to crack was predictable: In 1985, Blacks made up 30% of drug arrests; by 1989, this figure had jumped to 42%—even though African Americans' use of drugs generally is lower than that of White Americans. Numerically, Black drug arrests more than doubled from 210,298 to 452,574, whereas the number of arrests for Whites increased only 27% (pp. 107–9).

In turn, "drug arrests are a principal reason that the proportions of Blacks in prison . . . have risen rapidly in recent years to . . . extraordinary levels" (p. 110). Data from Pennsylvania are instructive. Between 1980 and 1990, drug commitments rose 1,613% for African American males but only 477% for White males (p. 115). And penal harms such as these have had disturbing consequences. "Poor minority communities cannot prosper," warns Tonry (p. vii), "when so many young men are prevented from settling into long-term personal relationships, getting or keeping jobs, and living conventional lives."

But is the disproportionate allocation of criminal justice resources to minority communities a form of spatial injustice, as Tonry claims, or of spatial justice? In 1989, George Rengert raised this issue, when he used the concept of "spatial justice" to refer "to whether or not citizens are placed at equal risk of victimization as a result of criminal justice practices regardless of where their communities are located—cen-

ter city, suburb, or rural area" (p. 544). His analysis revealed that burglars received shorter sentences in Philadelphia than in other areas in Pennsylvania and that these offenders were poorly supervised by probation and parole officers burdened with caseloads of 100 to 200 persons. The decisions of officials not to incarcerate or adequately supervise burglars resulted in higher victimization rates for residents of inner-city neighborhoods—those "least able to bear the high physical, economic, and emotional burden of property crime" (p. 557).

Rengert (1989, p. 560) believed that addressing the issue of spatial injustice through imprisonment was the "easy" answer, but "also naive" (he favored intermediate sanctions and crime prevention). Not so for DiIulio (1994), who recently has taken up the issue of "saving Black lives" through penal harm. "If White suburbanites were victimized in disproportionate numbers by convicted criminals out on probation or parole," his essay begins, "then there would be little policy debate about keeping violent or repeat offenders locked up" (p. 3). But this is not the case, he claims. Affluent Whites have the luxury of moving to safer communities in the suburbs and of paying for security devices. Inner-city minorities do not have these options. They must reside, largely unprotected, in neighborhoods populated with predatory criminals whose victimization is mostly intraracial.

To DiIulio, the malign neglect lies in the failure of the criminal justice system to end "revolving door" justice and to lock up these predatory offenders. "No group of Americans would stand to benefit more from policies that kept convicted felons, adult and juvenile, behind bars for all or most of their terms," says DiIulio (p. 15), "than crime-plagued Black inner-city Americans and their children."

I have no reason to doubt DiIulio's sincerity. But his personal character and intent aside, I find it more than a little disingenuous when conservative commentators use the victimization of African Americans to argue for less welfare and more prisons. This new-found concern does not seem to extend to capital investment in inner-city areas; they do not want to improve the "barrel," only take out the "bad apples." I also feel compelled to add a rejoinder to the quote initiating DiIulio's essay: "If White suburbanites were in prison in disproportionate numbers, then there would be little policy debate about reducing imprisonment and investing resources to improve the quality of life in suburban communities."

Tonry (p. 36) takes up the justification of penal harm that he calls the "'We are concerned about Black victims and Black communities' defense." His rebuttal is weakened, I believe, by his firm stance that incapacitation has few meaningful effects on crime—an issue discussed above. But his insights on what African Americans want strike a chord. Tonry agrees that Blacks often want the criminal justice system to crack down on crime when it is an "acute" problem that poses an immediate threat to community order. Blacks also understand, however, that crime is a symptom of "chronic social and economic conditions shaping disadvantaged inner-city communities and the life chances of the people in them" (p. 36). And in large percentages, they endorse social welfare policies that address crime's root causes. Somehow it is no surprise that conservatives hear calls for more police and prisons but turn a deaf ear to calls for help and hope.

Managing Penal Harm

In *Poor Discipline,* Jonathan Simon contributes further to our understanding of the character of the current penal harm movement. Using parole in California as a vehicle for illuminating the larger correctional process, he traces the changing penological models used to control the underclass. He reminds us that "however general the formal commands of the criminal law, the power to punish has always been primarily

directed at the poor" (p. 5). A particular strength of his analysis is that he links the meaning and practice of parole to the wider material conditions of the disadvantaged. "The massive expansion of criminal custody over the last decade in the United States," observes Simon, "must be seen in relationship to changes in political economy," including in particular "the restructuring of the labor force away from industrial employment" and "the emergence of an urban underclass living in zones of hardened poverty and made up primarily of minorities" (p. 5).

The emergence and growth of parole release in the late 1800s into the Progressive Era depended on furnishing a persuasive answer—or "narrative" or "account" as Simon would call it—to how it would be possible "to provide control in the community over those defined as dangerous to the community" (p. 38). The response, says Simon, was "disciplinary parole": Make community release contingent on securing and maintaining labor. This narrative (or account) should not strike us as unusual, says Simon, because it is so compatible with long-standing American thinking on corrections (see also Cullen and Travis 1984). "Wherever you look in the development of modernist penality you will find labor," says Simon. "Exhort offenders with religious tracts, but make them work. Subject them to silence, but make them work. Educate them as citizens, but make them work. Treat their pathological features, but make them work" (p. 39).

Having parolees work served to normalize them through the discipline of labor; it provided a test of character, for those who could not keep a job proved their essential criminality; and it implicated private networks of control, because employers had to agree to provide work and to certify that offenders remained on the job in good standing. The plausibility of the disciplinary parole model, of course, rested on having a labor market that could accommodate poor offenders on parole. Until the 1950s, these structural conditions obtained: With the exception of the Depression years, the cities provided a "large labor market . . . for unskilled and semi-skilled labor" (p. 50).

By the 1950s, however, America's deindustrialization undermined the coherence of disciplinary parole: Low-skilled jobs were declining in number, especially for minorities, who, simultaneously, were becoming a growing proportion of the correctional population. We now had offenders who were largely unemployable, who could not be "normalized" by the discipline of the changing workplace but who "must be altered before they could be moved in the labor force" (p. 100). The initial institutional response was the trumpeting of "clinical parole," in which parole officers would function as caseworkers delivering treatment and linking offenders to needed social services. In this narrative, crime was rooted not simply in the failure to work or "idleness," but in a "maladjustment between the individual and the institutions of the community. . . . Such degeneration," continues Simon (p. 104), "could be halted by counseling and treatment which addressed the underlying pathologies that discouraged identification with conventional norms."

The clinical model, however, was rendered implausible by the intersection of three factors. First, the correctional crisis was exacerbated by the continued "hardening of urban poverty" in the inner cities caused by the erosion of the nonskilled labor market in an increasingly postindustrial America. Parole as normalization became "less coherent" when the project of reintegration meant returning underclass offenders to communities burdened by the "tangle of urban pathology" and with "fewer and fewer resources to sustain them." . . .

Second, at the same time, legal interventions by the court mandated due process rights for parolees, especially at the revocation hearing. Because discretionary decisions previously made without scrutiny now were rendered visible, pressures emerged to

rationalize and introduce uniformity into the application of power (see chapter 4). The need to justify decisions to an external environment was increased further by a third condition: increasing public fears of violent crime and a loss of confidence in criminal justice officials. The challenge was to construct a correctional system in which accountability in the defense of public safety could be demonstrated.

The response to this context over the past two decades has been to rationalize procedures in the pursuit of "risk management" (p. 169). This "managerial model" stands traditional parole on its head by embracing the core principle of the penal harm movement that "custody is the necessary and sufficient solution to criminal risk" (p. 229). The task for parole officers thus becomes not assisting in the community reintegration of offenders but in discerning which offenders in the community should be reincarcerated. "New technologies of control"—risk classification systems, computerized databases, drug testing—increase the capacity for surveillance and for detecting dangerous parolees (see chapter 6). The logical conclusion of the managerial model is the primacy given to the "revocation hearing." Resources are concentrated on administering procedurally correct hearings in which parole's accountability is established by sending risky offenders back to prison at unprecedented rates (see chapter 7).

As Simon recognizes, the success of the managerial model is not complete (see also Cullen, Wright and Applegate forthcoming). It contains the fundamental inconsistency of exacerbating the fiscal crisis in corrections. "Parole has been successful in transforming itself from a system of rehabilitative discipline to one of risk management," observes Simon (p. 229), "and now finds itself criticized for that accomplishment." Further, there is danger in reifying Simon's managerial model to the point of being blinded to the continuing allegiance to offender rehabilitation that exists both among correctional personnel in California and in states that have been less quick to embrace control as the only goal of the criminal sanction.

Still, Simon's *Poor Discipline* is perceptive in identifying the forces that are helping to fuel the penal harm movement. Most disquieting, he reveals that no plausible narrative or account for the correctional enterprise currently exists to challenge the widening hegemony of penal harm. Criminologists, I believe, share a measure of responsibility for this state of affairs. Clear's analysis of "penal science" is sobering (see chapter 3). In recent decades—as authors and as consultants—we have played a large role in delegitimizing the rehabilitative ideal and in providing the intellectual justification and technology for managing penal harm. The challenge now is to help fashion an alternative plausible narrative that can move us beyond harm as the organizing principle of corrections.

Beyond Penal Harm

Unfortunately, the authors stop short of providing a coherent and compelling penological model that rivals the power of get-tough thinking. Let me hasten to blunt this criticism by noting that the books provide useful ideas on how to minimize harm in corrections and, taken together, succeed mightily in showing the importance of engaging in a conversation about the future of corrections. But unlike the "new penologists" who came to Cincinnati in 1870, they do not vigorously advocate the kind of optimistic and confident "Declaration of Principles" that might serve as an alternative narrative to penal harm.

I would like to claim that I do not have the space to outline such a new penological model, but my reticence lies more in a fear that the task is too daunting. Even so, I will take the risk of arguing—as I have for over a decade—in favor of reaffirming rehabilitation as a model to rival penal harm (Cullen and Gendreau 1989; Cullen and Gilbert 1982; Cullen, Van Voorhis, and Sundt forthcoming; Cullen and Wright forthcoming; Gendreau et al. 1994).

A whole generation of criminologists were raised to mistrust state power to do good, to believe that "nothing works" to change offenders, and to embrace "doing justice" as a means of "doing less harm." This pessimistic narrative, which seeks to restrain abuse and not to accomplish good, remains plausible to many criminologists, but it sparks little response from the public and has largely lost its power to humanize corrections. Most important, it fails to capitalize on the generous side of the public's sentiments about corrections; as Tonry (p. 9) notes, "large majorities of Americans . . . want prisons to rehabilitate offenders" (see also Cullen, Cullen, and Wozniak 1988; Cullen, Skovron, Scott, and Burton 1990; McCorkle 1993). In short, rehabilitation is the one liberal correctional narrative that citizens still find plausible.

I would warn, however, that rehabilitation as a form of pure-hearted benevolence is vulnerable to attack. Instead, as the new penologists of the 1870s understood, the *utility* of treatment interventions for the public good must be a central principle if the rehabilitative ideal is to achieve support. Like it or not, American culture is decidedly utilitarian (Bellah et al. 1985), and the failure to take this factor into account will render any liberal correctional model irrelevant. It is instructive that DiIulio and similar advocates of incapacitation do not make this mistake. Indeed, their persuasiveness comes from giving a plausible account of how prisons increase safety while portraying liberal naysayers as having no interest in protecting innocent citizens. The challenge of the utility of penal harm thus must be confronted, not just dismissed. Fortunately, science is on the side of treatment: The research is mounting that shows that rehabilitation "works better" than penal harm in reducing recidivism (see, e.g., Andrews and Bonta 1994; Andrews et al. 1990; Cullen, Wright, and

Applegate forthcoming; Lipsey 1992; Palmer 1992; Tonry, pp. 201–3).

Second, rehabilitation should be framed not as a form of governmental entitlement but as a utilitarian exchange. Simon (p. 263) captures this insight with his call for "investing penal resources in community discipline"—a situation in which governmental rewards are tied to offender performance in programs (such as work) that encourage individual responsibility, normalize deviant tendencies, and contribute to the commonweal (such as by providing payment for victims or for the offender's family). Of course, reward systems must be backed up by the threat of negative reinforcement—"behave or you'll suffer the consequences"—which raises the sticky issue of how far to go in enforcing therapy. Although I am not unmindful of the potential for abuse (see Rothman 1980), no liberal correctional narrative will have credibility if offenders are not held accountable for their actions. And consistent with the principles of the 1870 new penologists, it is not clear that offender reform can be effective unless we are willing to assert values and to use "effective disapproval" to encourage conformity (Andrews and Bonta 1994, pp. 202–7).

Third, the rehabilitative narrative should trumpet early intervention. This strategy—a means of diverting much-needed services to vulnerable populations—has marked advantages: It forces attention on conditions, such as the capital disinvestment in inner cities (Currie 1985; Hagan 1994; Short 1991), that place families and children at risk; it focuses on a "deserving" object of attention—children born into difficult circumstances through "no fault of their own"; it embraces the persuasive logic that "you can pay me now or pay me later"; and there is evidence that such interventions can be successful (Greenwood 1995, pp. 112–17).

Some criminologists, I suspect, will find my proposal for reaffirming "utilitarian" rehabilitation misguided. But if so, it is incumbent on these critics and like-minded scholars to move beyond preaching to the criminological choir about the disutility of punishment and to declare their principles for designing a *plausible* and *positive* correctional model. The time for taking up this task is overdue. In chilling detail, Todd Clear, Jonathan Simon, and Michael Tonry illuminate the ideological power and the human costs of penal harm. Unless a better answer can be put forth, this movement promises to gain strength and to permeate more deeply the fabric of the correctional enterprise.

Study Questions

1. Specifically, how does Cullen define the penal harm movement in the United States?

2. What is the primary "utility" of the penal harm movement (from a conservative vantage point), according to Cullen?

3. What is the primary "detriment" of the penal harm movement (from a liberal vantage point)?

4. According to this article, what are the three ways in which the United States should move beyond the penal harm movement?

References

Andrews, D. A. and James Bonta. (1994). *The Psychology of Criminal Conduct*. Cincinnati, OH: Anderson.

Andrews, D. A., Ivan Zinger, R. D. Hoge, James Bonta, Paul Gendreau, and Francis T. Cullen. (1990). "Does Correctional Treatment Work? A Clinically-Relevant and Psychologically-Informed Meta-Analysis." *Criminology*, 28:369–404.

Bellah, Robert N., Richard Madsen, William M. Sullivan, Ann Swidler, and Steven M. Tipton. (1985). *Habits of the Heart: Individualism and Commitment in American Life*. Berkeley: University of California Press.

Benekos, Peter J. and Alida V. Merlo. (1995). "Three Strikes and You're Out!: The Political Sentencing Game." *Federal Probation*, 59 (March):3–9.

Blumstein, Alfred. (1989). "American Prisons in a Time of Crisis." Pp. 13–22 in *The American*

Prison: Issues in Research and Policy, edited by L. Goodstein and D. L. MacKenzie. New York: Plenum.

——. (1995). "Prisons." Pp. 387–419 in *Crime,* edited by James Q. Wilson and Joan Petersilia. San Francisco: ICS.

Blumstein, Alfred and Jacqueline Cohen. (1973). "A Theory of the Stability of Punishment." *Journal of Criminal Law and Criminology,* 64: 198–206.

Bragg, Rick. (1995). "Chain Gangs to Return to Roads of Alabama: States Hopes Revival Will Deter Crime." *New York Times,* March 26, p. Y9.

Braithwaite, John. (1989). *Crime, Shame and Reintegration.* Cambridge, UK: Cambridge University Press.

Brockway, Zebulon R. (1910). "The American Reformatory Prison System." Pp. 88–107 in *Prison Reform: Correction and Prevention,* edited by Charles Richmond Henderson. New York: Russell Sage Foundation.

Bureau of Justice Statistics. (1994). *Criminal Victimization in the United States, 1992.* Washington, DC: U.S. Department of Justice.

Byrne, James M. and April Pattavina. (1992). "The Effectiveness Issue: Assessing What Works in the Adult Community Corrections System." Pp. 81–303 in *Smart Sentencing: The Emergence of Intermediate Sanctions,* edited by James M. Byrne, Arthur J. Lurigio, and Joan Petersilia. Newbury Park, CA: Sage.

Clear, T. R. (1994). *Harm in American Penology: Offenders, Victims, and Their Communities.* West Sacramento, CA: California Correctional Peace Officers Association.

Cohen, Adam. (1995). "Back on the Chain Gang." *Time,* May 15, p. 26.

Cohen, Jacqueline and José A. Canela-Cacho. (1994). "Incarceration and Violent Crime: 1965–1988." Pp. 296–388 in *Understanding and Preventing Violence: Consequences and Control,* Vol. 4, edited by Albert J. Reiss, Jr. and Jeffrey A. Roth. Washington, DC: National Academy Press.

Colvin, Mark. (1992). *The Penitentiary in Crisis: From Accommodation to Riot in New Mexico.* Albany: SUNY Press.

Cullen, Francis T., John B. Cullen, and John F. Wozniak. (1988). "Is Rehabilitation Dead? The Myth of the Punitive Public." *Journal of Criminal Justice,* 34:379–92.

Cullen, Francis T. and Paul Gendreau. (1989). "The Effectiveness of Correctional Rehabilita-

tion: Reconsidering the 'Nothing Works' Debate." Pp. 23–44 in *The American Prison: Issues in Research and Policy,* edited by L. Goodstein and D. L. MacKenzie. New York: Plenum.

Cullen, Francis T. and Karen E. Gilbert. (1982). *Reaffirming Rehabilitation.* Cincinnati, OH: Anderson.

Cullen, Francis T., Sandra Evans Skovron, Joseph E. Scott, and Velmer S. Burton, Jr. (1990). "Public Support for Correctional Rehabilitation: The Tenacity of the Rehabilitative Ideal." *Criminal Justice and Behavior,* 17:6–18.

Cullen, Francis T. and Lawrence F. Travis, III. (1984). "Work as an Avenue of Prison Reform." *New England Journal of Criminal and Civil Confinement,* 10:45–64.

Cullen, Francis T., Patricia Van Voorhis, and Jody L. Sundt. (Forthcoming). "Prisons in Crisis: The American Experience." In *Prisons 2000: An International Perspective on the Current State and Future of Imprisonment,* edited by Roger Matthews and Peter Francis. New York: Macmillan.

Cullen, Francis T. and John P. Wright. (Forthcoming). "The Future of Corrections." In *The Past, Present, and Future of American Criminal Justice,* edited by Brendan Maguire and Polly Radosh. New York: General Hall.

Cullen, Francis T., John P. Wright, and Brandon K. Applegate. (Forthcoming). "Control in the Community: The Limits of Reform?" In *Choosing Correctional Interventions That Work: Defining the Demand and Evaluating the Supply,* edited by Alan T. Harland. Newbury Park, CA: Sage.

Currie, Elliott. (1985). *Confronting Crime: An American Challenge.* New York: Pantheon.

——. (1993). *Reckoning: Drugs, the Cities, and the American Future.* New York: Hill and Wang.

"Declaration of Principles Promulgated at Cincinnati, Ohio, 1870." 1910 [1870]. Pp. 39–63 in *Prison Reform Correction and Prevention,* edited by Charles Richmond Henderson. New York: Russell Sage Foundation.

DiIulio, John J., Jr. (1994). "The Question of Black Crime." *Public Interest,* 117 (Fall):3–32.

Farrington, David P. and Patrick A. Langan. (1992). "Changes in Crime and Punishment in England and America in the 1980s." *Justice Quarterly,* 9:5–31.

Federal Bureau of Investigation. (1994). *Uniform Crime Reports: Crime in the United States, 1993.* Washington, DC: U.S. Government Printing Office.

Feeley, Malcolm M. and Jonathan Simon. (1992). "The New Penology: Notes on the Emerging Strategy of Corrections and Its Implications." *Criminology*, 30:449–74.

Forer, Lois G. (1994). *A Rage to Punish: The Unintended Consequences of Mandatory Sentencing.* New York: W. W. Norton.

Garland, David. (1990). *Punishment and Modern Society: A Study in Social Theory.* Chicago: University of Chicago Press.

Gendreau, Paul, Francis T. Cullen, and James Bonta. (1994). "Intensive Rehabilitation Supervision: The Next Generation in Community Corrections?" *Federal Probation*, 58 (March): 72–78.

Gordon, Diana R. (1991). *The Justice Juggernaut: Fighting Street Crime, Controlling Citizens.* New Brunswick, NJ: Rutgers University Press.

———. (1994). *The Return of the Dangerous Classes: Drug Prohibition and Policy Politics.* New York: W. W. Norton.

Gramm, Phil. (1993). "Drugs, Crime and Punishment: Don't Let Judges Set Crooks Free." *New York Times*, July 8, pp. B1–B2.

Greenwood, Peter W. (1995). "Juvenile Crime and Juvenile Justice." Pp. 91–117 in *Crime*, edited by James Q. Wilson and Joan Petersilia. San Francisco: ICS.

Hagan, John. (1994). *Crime and Disrepute.* Thousand Oaks, CA: Pine Forge.

Herrnstein, Richard J. and Charles Murray. (1994). *The Bell Curve: Intelligence and Class Structure in American Life.* New York: Free Press.

Irwin, John. (1985). *The Jail: Managing the Underclass in American Society.* Berkeley: University of California Press.

Irwin, John and James Austin. (1994). *It's About Time: America's Imprisonment Binge.* Belmont, CA: Wadsworth.

Kaminer, Wendy. (1995). *It's All the Rage: Crime and Culture.* Reading, MA: Addison-Wesley.

Lipsey, Mark W. (1992). "Juvenile Delinquency Treatment: A Meta-Analytic Inquiry Into the Variability of Effects." Pp. 83–127 in *Meta-Analysis for Explanation: A Casebook*, edited by Thomas D. Cook, Harris Cooper, David S. Cordray, Heidi Hartmann, Larry V. Hedges, Richard J. Light, Thomas A. Louis, and Frederick Mosteller. New York: Russell Sage Foundation.

Logan, Charles H. and John J. DiIulio, Jr. (1992). "Ten Myths About Crime and Prisons." *Wisconsin Interest*, 1:21–35.

Lynch, James. (1995). "Crime in International Perspective." Pp. 11–38 in *Crime*, edited by James Q. Wilson and Joan Petersilia. San Francisco: ICS.

Marvell, Thomas B. and Carlisle E. Moody, Jr. (1994). "Prison Population Growth and Crime Reduction." *Journal of Quantitative Criminology*, 10:109–40.

McCorkle, Richard C. (1993). "Punish and Rehabilitate? Public Attitudes Toward Six Common Crimes." *Crime & Delinquency*, 39:240–52.

Palmer, Ted. (1992). *The Re-Emergence of Correctional Intervention.* Newbury Park, CA: Sage.

Paternoster, Raymond. (1987). "The Deterrent Effect of Perceived Certainty and Severity of Punishment: A Review of the Evidence and Issues." *Justice Quarterly*, 4:173–217.

Petersilia, Joan. (1992). "California's Prison Policy: Causes, Costs, and Consequences." *The Prison Journal*, 72:8–36.

Petersilia, Joan and Susan Turner. (1993). "Intensive Probation and Parole." Pp. 281–335 in *Crime and Justice: A Review of Research*, Vol. 17, edited by Michael Tonry. Chicago: University of Chicago Press.

Platt, Anthony M. (1969). *The Child Savers: The Invention of Delinquency.* Chicago: University of Chicago Press.

Reiss, Albert J., Jr. and Jeffrey A. Roth, eds. (1993). *Understanding and Preventing Violence.* Washington, DC: National Academy Press.

Rengert, George F. (1989). "Spatial Justice and Criminal Victimization." *Justice Quarterly*, 6: 543–64.

Roth, Jeffrey A. (1995). "Achievements to Date and Goals for the Future: New Looks at Criminal Careers." *Journal of Quantitative Criminology*, 11:97–110.

Rothman, David J. (1971). *The Discovery of the Asylum: Social Order and Disorder in the New Republic.* Boston: Little, Brown.

———. (1980). *Conscience and Convenience: The Asylum and Its Alternatives in Progressive America.* Boston: Little, Brown.

Sampson, Robert J. and John H. Laub. (1993). *Crime in the Making: Pathways and Turning Points Through Life.* Cambridge, MA: Harvard University Press.

Scull, Andrew. (1977). *Decarceration: Community Treatment and the Deviant—A Radical View.* Englewood Cliffs, NJ: Prentice Hall.

Selke, William L. (1993). *Prisons in Crisis.* Bloomington: Indiana University Press.

Sherman, Lawrence W. (1993). "Defiance, Deterrence, and Irrelevance: A Theory of Criminal Sanctions." *Journal of Research in Crime and Delinquency*, 30:445–73.

Sherman, Michael and Gordon Hawkins. (1981). *Imprisonment in America: Choosing the Future.* Chicago: University of Chicago Press.

Short, James F., Jr. (1991). "Poverty, Ethnicity, and Crime: Change and Continuity in U.S. Cities." *Journal of Research in Crime and Delinquency*, 28:501–18.

Simon, J. (1993). *Poor Discipline: Parole and the Social Control of the Underclass.* Chicago: University of Chicago Press.

Spelman, William. (1994). *Criminal Incapacitation.* New York: Plenum.

Steffensmeier, Darrell and Miles D. Harer. (1993). "Bulging Prisons, an Aging U.S. Population, and the Nation's Crime Rate." *Federal Probation* 57 (June):3–10.

Tonry, Michael. (1994). "Racial Disproportion in US Prisons." *British Journal of Criminology*, 34: 97–115.

Tonry, Michael. (1995). *Malign Neglect: Race, Crime, and Punishment in America.* New York: Oxford University Press.

Turner, Michael G., Jody L. Sundt, Brandon K. Applegate, and Francis T. Cullen. (Forthcoming). "'Three Strikes and You're Out' Legislation: A National Assessment." *Federal Probation.*

Walker, Samuel. (1989). *Sense and Nonsense About Crime: A Policy Guide*, 2nd ed. Pacific Grove, CA: Brooks/Cole.

Wilson, James Q. (1983). *Thinking About Crime*, rev. ed. New York: Random House.

——. (1995). "Crime and Public Policy." Pp. 489–507 in *Crime*, edited by James Q. Wilson and Joan Petersilia. San Francisco: ICS.

Wright, Richard A. (1994). *In Defense of Prisons.* Westport, CT: Greenwood.

Zedlewski, Edwin W. (1987). *Research in Brief: Making Confinement Decisions.* Washington, DC: National Institute of Justice.

Zimring, Franklin and Gordon Hawkins. (1991). *The Scale of Imprisonment.* Chicago: University of Chicago Press.

——. (1995). *Incapacitation: Penal Confinement and the Restraint of Crime.* New York: Oxford University Press.

Part II
Living and Working in Prison

By the turn of the twentieth century, the use of the prison as the United States' primary form of punishment was well established. The general public was satisfied to allow government agencies to punish offenders with confinement, separated by sight and sound from most free people. During the early 1900s, incarceration also came to the attention of many sociologists who examined prisons as "total institutions," as Goffman has described.

It is important to remember that the prison is designed to control virtually every aspect of the offender's life. While the overarching goal of incarceration is confinement of the offender, prisons also must meet many needs of inmates—most notably housing, feeding, clothing, educating, and rehabilitating those within the walls. The "official" aspects of prison life—administrative processing and classification, assignment of living quarters, job assignments, and educational and vocational opportunities—fall under the domain of prison officials. At the same time, the "unofficial" aspects of prison life—the development of subculture, social and physical adaptation, economic proliferation, and uprisings—are largely governed by inmates themselves, typically by subgroups within the general population. Almost immediately, the study of prisons reveals two distinct groups—prison inmates and correctional officers.

Several of the selections in the section that follows represent explorations of prisons as total institutions, and the group dynamics of those who live inside. The fact that prisons are indeed (virtually) closed institutions has been one of the primary factors motivating their study. In some ways, the total institution provides a microcosm of general society (albeit an unrepresentative one), largely cut off from the outside world. Also contained in this section are firsthand accounts, written by former prison inmates, in which the convict code and its purposes are presented, as is the intensity of certain forms of extra punishment that have at times occurred inside prisons.

Two prevalent trends within corrections involve the increasing privatization of state prison systems and the development (and proliferation) of the "supermax" prison facility. As the number of private prisons increases, so do several concerns. Most notably, many have questioned the ethical nature of privatizing what has for centuries been a state-run enterprise. Further, for many, the hypothetical benefits of privatization (increased efficiency, public safety, fiscal benefits, and others) have yet to be realized and are in need of more study.

While most of the scholarly work conducted on prisons has concentrated on the prison inmates, a good deal has also been written about the prison guard. In many ways, the prison guard may suffer some of the same "pains of imprisonment" that inmates do, only in different forms. The occupation of correctional officer is typically regarded as a high-stress, and at times high-risk, job that does not enjoy a high level of pay. Most states' base requirement for correctional officers is a high school education or equivalent, with perhaps "some college" preferable.

Despite the relatively low educational requirements, correctional officers often have to deal with extremely complex situations involving human interaction. It is not uncommon for a correctional officer to play the role of psychologist, sociologist, social worker, and confidant, all in one day's work. Although popular media portrayals of the correctional officer often show the authoritarian side of the job, in reality complex relationships between inmates and officers, as well as between officers themselves, are common.

In addition to covering the aspects of the total institution and the dynamics present within the inmate population, the following section also presents an examination of the inside of a prison from the officers' perspective. One piece details the complexities of the inmate-guard relationship, in an environment where one group (inmates) outnumbers the other (guards) at an extremely

steep ratio. Also presented is a piece that offers the personal experiences of a brand-new guard in one of the United States' most storied prisons, Sing Sing.

All prisons contain two distinct groups of people—those who live within the prison, and those who work inside the prison for their career (although some correctional officers might argue that they too "live" inside the prison's walls!). These two groups, for all intents and purposes, make up the entirety of the prison's social environment—although several of the following chapters also make note of the fact that there can be several subgroups within each of these larger groups. Both inmates and officers typically share the common goal of achieving a peaceful and smooth-running environment (although the methods chosen by each group to achieve this may differ). The following chapters provide an introductory examination of the challenges that are faced by each group, and the intricacies involved in their interactions. ✦

7
Characteristics of Total Institutions

Erving Goffman

The totality with which the penal institution controls the lives of its inhabitants is presented in great detail in this selection by Goffman. Although few would argue that the restriction of freedom is the prevailing goal of the total prison institution, the control that occurs there is much more complex than one might imagine. The author begins by presenting some other examples (besides penal institutions) of restrictive institutions in society (e.g., hospitals for the mentally ill or the disabled). The resident of the total institution is portrayed as being at the will of the bureaucracy that governs the facility. In no other institution is this clearer than within the prison. Evidence of the "old life" as it once pertained to the inmates has all but completely been wiped away. This is done by removing all physical traces of the inmates' lives before they arrive at the institution and regulating everything that may be sent in. After that point, all aspects of the offenders' lives are under complete control of the institution, mired in a world of rewards and punishments meted out by prison administrators. The reader should consider what might possibly be the resulting consequences of such a system.

Introduction

Institutions. Social establishments—institutions in the everyday sense of that term—are buildings or plants in which activity of a particular kind regularly goes on. In sociology we do not have an apt way of classifying them. Some, like Grand Central Station, are open to anyone who is decently behaved. Others, like the Union League Club of New York or the laboratories at Los Alamos, are felt to be somewhat "snippy" about the matter of whom they let in. Some institutions, like shops and post offices, are the locus of a continuous flow of service relationships. Others, like homes and factories, provide a less changing set of persons with whom the member can relate. Some institutions provide the place for what is felt to be the kind of pursuits from which the individual draws his social status, however enjoyable or lax these pursuits may be. Other institutions, in contrast, provide a home for associations in which membership is felt to be elective and unserious, calling for a contribution of time that is fitted in to more serious demands.

In this [chapter] another category of institutions is recommended and claimed as a natural and fruitful one because its members appear to have so much in common—so much, in fact, that if you would learn about one of these institutions you would be well advised to look at the others. My own special purpose in examining these institutions is to find a natural frame of reference for studying the social experience of patients in mental hospitals. Whatever else psychiatry and medicine tell us, their happy way of sometimes viewing an insane asylum as if it were a treatment hospital does not help us very much in determining just what these places are and just what goes on in them.

Total Institutions. Every institution captures something of the time and interest of its members and provides something of a world for them; in brief, every institution has encompassing tendencies. When we review the different institutions in our Western society we find a class of them which seems to be encompassing to a degree discontinuously greater than the ones next in line. Their encompassing or total character is symbolized by the barrier to social intercourse with the outside that is often built right into the physical plant: locked doors, high walls, barbed wire, cliffs and water, open terrain, and so forth. These I am calling total institutions, and it is their general characteristics I want to explore. This exploration will be phrased as if securely based on findings but will in fact be speculative.

The total institutions of our society can be listed for convenience in five rough groupings. *First,* there are institutions established to care for persons thought to be both incapable and harmless; these are the homes for the blind, the aged, the orphaned, and the indigent. *Second,* there are places established to care for persons thought to be at once incapable of looking after themselves and a threat to the community, albeit an unintended one: TB sanitoriums, mental hospitals, and leprosariums. *Third,* another type of total institution is organized to protect the community against what are thought to be intentional dangers to it; here the welfare of the persons thus sequestered is not the immediate issue. Examples are: jails, penitentiaries, POW camps, and concentration camps. *Fourth,* we find institutions purportedly established the better to pursue some technical task and justifying themselves only on these instrumental grounds: army barracks, ships, boarding schools, work camps, colonial compounds, large mansions from the point of view of those who live in the servants' quarters, and so forth. *Finally,* there are those establishments designed as retreats from the world or as training stations for the religious: abbeys, monasteries, convents, and other cloisters. This sublisting of total institutions is neither neat nor exhaustive, but the listing itself provides an empirical starting point for a purely denotative definition of the category. By anchoring the initial definition of total institutions in this way, I hope to be able to discuss the general characteristics of the type without becoming tautological.

Before attempting to extract a general profile from this list of establishments, one conceptual peculiarity must be mentioned. None of the elements I will extract seems entirely exclusive to total institutions, and none seems shared by every one of them. What is shared and unique about total institutions is that each exhibits many items in this family of attributes to an intense degree. In speaking of "common characteristics," then, I will be using this phrase in a weakened, but I think logically defensible, way.

Totalistic Features. A basic social arrangement in modern society is that we tend to sleep, play and work in different places, in each case with a different set of coparticipants, under a different authority, and without an overall rational plan. The central feature of total institutions can be described as a breakdown of the kinds of barriers ordinarily separating these three spheres of life. *First,* all aspects of life are conducted in the same place and under the same single authority. *Second,* each phase of the member's daily activity will be carried out in the immediate company of a large batch of others, all of whom are treated alike and required to do the same thing together. *Third,* all phases of the day's activities are tightly scheduled, with one activity leading at a prearranged time into the next, the whole circle of activities being imposed from above through a system of explicit formal rulings and a body of officials. *Finally,* the contents of the various enforced activities are brought together as parts of a single overall rational plan purportedly designed to fulfill the official aims of the institution.

Individually, these totalistic features are found, of course, in places other than total institutions. Increasingly, for example, our large commercial, industrial and educational establishments provide cafeterias, minor services and off-hour recreation for their members. But while this is a tendency in the direction of total institutions, these extended facilities remain voluntary in many particulars of their use, and special care is taken to see that the ordinary line of authority does not extend to these situations. Similarly, housewives or farm families can find all their major spheres of life within the same fenced-in area, but these persons are not collectively regimented and do not march through the day's steps in the immediate company of a batch of similar others.

The handling of many human needs by the bureaucratic organization of whole blocks of people—whether or not this is a necessary or effective means of social organization in the circumstances—can be taken, then, as the key fact of total institutions. From this, certain important implications can be drawn.

Given the fact that blocks of people are caused to move in time, it becomes possible to use a relatively small number of supervisory personnel where the central relationship is not guidance or periodic checking, as in many employer-employee relations, but rather surveillance—a seeing to it that everyone does what he has been clearly told is required of him, and this under conditions where one person's infraction is likely to stand out in relief against the visible, constantly examined, compliance of the others. Which comes first, the large block of managed people or the small supervisory staff, is not here at issue; the point is that each is made for the other.

In total institutions, as we would then suspect, there is a basic split between a large class of individuals who live in and who have restricted contact with the world outside the walls, conveniently called *inmates*, and the small class that supervises them, conveniently called *staff*, who often operate on an 8-hour day and are socially integrated into the outside world. Each grouping tends to conceive of members of the other in terms of narrow hostile stereotypes, staff often seeing inmates as bitter, secretive and untrustworthy, while inmates often see staff as condescending, high-handed and mean. Staff tends to feel superior and righteous; inmates tend, in some

ways at least, to feel inferior, weak, blame-worthy and guilty. Social mobility between the two strata is grossly restricted; social distance is typically great and often formally prescribed; even talk across the boundaries may be conducted in a special tone of voice. These restrictions on contact presumably help to maintain the antagonistic stereotypes. In any case, two different social and cultural worlds develop, tending to jog along beside each other, with points of official contact but little mutual penetration. It is important to add that the institutional plant and name comes to be identified by both staff and inmates as somehow belonging to staff, so that when either grouping refers to the views or interests of "the institution," by implication they are referring (as I shall also) to the views and concerns of the staff.

The staff-inmate split is one major implication of the central features of total institutions; a second one pertains to work. In the ordinary arrangements of living in our society, the authority of the workplace stops with the worker's receipt of a money payment; the spending of this in a domestic and recreational setting is at the discretion of the worker and is the mechanism through which the authority of the workplace is kept within strict bounds. However, to say that inmates in total institutions have their full day scheduled for them is to say that some version of all basic needs will have to be planned for, too. In other words, total institutions take over "responsibility" for the inmate and must guarantee to have everything that is defined as essential "layed on." It follows, then, that whatever incentive is given for work, this will not have the structural significance it has on the outside. Different attitudes and incentives regarding this central feature of our life will have to prevail.

Here, then, is one basic adjustment required of those who work in total institutions and of those who must induce these people to work. In some cases, no work or little is required, and inmates, untrained often in leisurely ways of life, suffer extremes of boredom. In other cases, some work is required but is carried on at an extremely slow pace, being geared into a system of minor, often ceremonial payments, as in the case of weekly tobacco ration and annual Christmas presents, which cause some mental patients to stay on their job. In some total institutions, such as logging camps and merchant ships, something of the usual relation to the world that money can buy is obtained through the practice of "forced saving"; all needs are organized by the institution, and payment is given only after a work season is over and the men leave the premises. And in some total institutions, of course, more than a full day's work is required and is induced not by reward, but by threat of dire punishment. In all such cases, the work-oriented individual may tend to become somewhat demoralized by the system.

In addition to the fact that total institutions are incompatible with the basic work-payment structure of our society, it must be seen that these establishments are also incompatible with another crucial element of our society, the family. The family is sometimes contrasted to solitary living, but in fact the more pertinent contrast to family life might be with batch living. For it seems that those who eat and sleep at work, with a group of fellow workers, can hardly sustain a meaningful domestic existence. Correspondingly, the extent to which a staff retains its integration in the outside community and escapes the encompassing tendencies of total institutions is often linked up with the maintenance of a family off the grounds.

Whether a particular total institution act[s] as a good or bad force in civil society, force it may well have, and this will depend on the suppression of a whole circle of actual or potential households. Conversely, the formation of households provides a structural guarantee that total institutions will not arise. The incompatibility between these two forms of social organization should tell us, then, something about the wider social functions of them both.

Total institutions, then, are social hybrids, part residential community, part formal organization, and therein lies their special sociological interest. There are other reasons, alas, for being interested in them, too. These establishments are the forcing houses for changing persons in our society. Each is a natural experiment, typically harsh, on what can be done to the self.

Having suggested some of the key features of total institutions, we can move on now to consider them from the special perspectives that seem natural to take. I will consider the inmate world, then the staff world, and then something about contacts between the two.

The Inmate World

Mortification Processes. It is characteristic of inmates that they come to the institution as members, already full-fledged, of a *home world*, that is, a way of life and a round of activities taken for granted up to the point of admission to the institution. It is useful to look at this culture that the recruit brings with him to the institution's door—his *presenting culture*, to modify a psychiatric phrase—in terms especially designed to highlight what it is the total institution will do to him. Whatever the stability of his personal organization, we can assume it was part of a wider supporting framework lodged in his current social environment, a round of experience that somewhat confirms a conception of self that is somewhat acceptable to him and a set of defensive maneuvers exercisable at his own discretion as a means of coping with conflicts, discrediting and failures.

Now it appears that total institutions do not substitute their own unique culture for something already formed. We do not deal with acculturation or assimilation but with something more restricted than these. In a sense, total institutions do not look for cultural victory. They effectively create and sustain a particular kind of tension between the home world and the institutional world and use this persistent tension as strategic leverage in the management of men. The full meaning for the inmate of being "in" or "on the inside" does not exist apart from the special meaning to him of "getting out" or "getting on the outside."

The recruit comes into the institution with a self and with attachments to supports which had allowed this self to survive. Upon entrance, he is immediately stripped of his wonted supports, and his self is systematically, if often unintentionally, mortified. In the accurate language of some of our oldest total institutions, he is led into a series of abasements, degradations, humiliations, and profanations of self. He begins, in other words, some radical shifts in his *moral career,* a career laying out the progressive changes that occur in the beliefs that he has concerning himself and significant others.

The *stripping processes* through which *mortification of the self* occurs are fairly standard in our total institutions. Personal identity equipment is removed, as well as other possessions with which the inmate may have identified himself, there typically being a system of nonaccessible storage from which the inmate can only reobtain his effects should he leave the institution. As a substitute for what has been taken away, institutional issue is provided, but this will be the same for large categories of inmates and will be regularly repossessed by the institution. In brief, standardized defacement will occur. In addition, ego-invested separateness from fellow inmates is significantly diminished in many areas of activity, and tasks are prescribed that are *infradignitatem.* Family, occupational, and educational career lines are chopped off, and a stigmatized status is submitted. Sources of fantasy materials which had meant momentary releases from stress in the home world are denied. Areas of autonomous decision are eliminated through the process of collective scheduling of daily activity. Many channels of communication with the outside are restricted or closed off completely. Verbal discreditings occur in many forms as a matter of course. Expressive signs of respect for the staff are coercively and continuously demanded. And the effect of each of these conditions is multiplied by having to witness the mortification of one's fellow inmates.

We must expect to find different official reasons given for these assaults upon the self. In mental hospitals there is the matter of protecting the patient from himself and from other patients. In jails there is the issue of "security" and frank punishment. In religious institutions we may find sociologically sophisticated theories about the soul's need for purification and penance through disciplining of the flesh. What all of these rationales share is the extent to which they are merely rationalizations, for the underlying force in many cases is unwittingly generated by efforts to manage the daily activity of a large number of persons in a small space with a small expenditure of resources.

In the background of the sociological stripping process, we find a characteristic authority system with three distinctive elements, each basic to total institutions.

First, to a degree, authority is of the *echelon* kind. Any member of the staff class has certain rights to discipline any member of the inmate class. This arrangement, it may be noted, is similar to the one which gives any adult in some small American towns certain rights to correct and demand small services from any child not in the immediate presence of his parents. In our society, the adult himself, however, is typically under the authority of a *single* immediate superior in connection with his work, or under the authority of one spouse in connection with domestic duties. The only echelon authority he must face—the police—typically are neither constantly nor relevantly present, except perhaps in the case of traffic-law enforcement.

Second, the authority of corrective sanctions is directed to a great multitude of items of conduct of the kind that are constantly occurring and constantly coming up for judgment; in brief, authority is directed to matters of dress, deportment, social intercourse, manners and the like. In prisons these regulations regarding situational proprieties may even extend to a point where silence during mealtime is enforced, while in some convents explicit demands may be made concerning the custody of the eyes during prayer.

The *third* feature of authority in total institutions is that misbehaviors in one sphere of life are held against one's standing in other spheres. Thus, an individual who fails to participate with proper enthusiasm in sports may be brought to the attention of the person who determines where he will sleep and what kind of work task will be accorded to him.

When we combine these three aspects of authority in total institutions, we see that the inmate cannot easily escape from the press of judgmental officials and from the enveloping tissue of constraint. The system of authority undermines the basis for control that adults in our society expect to exert over their interpersonal environment and may produce the terror of feeling that one is being radically demoted in the age-grading system. On the outside, rules are sufficiently lax and the individual sufficiently agreeable to required self-discipline to insure that others will rarely have cause for pouncing on him. He need not constantly look over his shoulder to see if criticism and other sanctions are coming. On the inside, however, rulings are abundant, novel, and closely enforced so that, quite characteristically, inmates live with chronic anxiety about breaking the rules and chronic worry about the consequences of breaking them. The desire to "stay out of trouble" in a total institution is likely to require persistent conscious effort and may lead the inmate to abjure certain levels of sociability with his fellows in order to avoid the incidents that may occur in these circumstances.

It should be noted finally that the mortifications to be suffered by the inmate may be purposely brought home to him in an exaggerated way during the first few days after entrance, in a form of initiation that has been called *the welcome.* Both staff and fellow inmates may go out of their way to give the neophyte a clear notion of where he stands. As part of this *rite de passage,* he may find himself called by a term such as "fish," "swab," etc., through which older inmates tell him that he is not only merely an inmate but that even within this lowly group he has a low status.

Privilege System. While the process of mortification is in progress, the inmate begins to receive formal and informal instruction in what will here be called the *privilege system.* Insofar as the inmate's self has been unsettled a little by the stripping action of the institution, it is largely around this framework that pressures are exerted, making for a reorganization of self. Three basic elements of the system may be mentioned.

First, there are the *house rules,* a relatively explicit and formal set of prescriptions and proscriptions which lay out the main requirements of inmate conduct. These regulations spell out the austere round of life in which the inmate will operate. Thus, the admission procedures through which the recruit is initially stripped of his self-supporting context can be seen as the institution's way of getting him in the position to start living by the house rules.

Second, against the stark background, a small number of clearly defined *rewards or privileges* are held out in exchange for obedience to staff in action and spirit. It is important to see that these potential gratifications are not unique to the institution but rather are ones carved out of the flow of support that the inmate previously had quite taken for granted. On the outside, for example, the inmate was likely to be able to unthinkingly exercise autonomy by decid-ing how much sugar and milk he wanted in his coffee, if any, or when to light up a ciga-rette; on the inside, this right may become quite problematic and a matter of a great deal of conscious concern. Held up to the inmate as possibilities, these few recaptur-ings seem to have a reintegrative effect, re-establishing relationships with the whole lost world and assuaging withdrawal symp-toms from it and from one's lost self.

The inmate's run of attention, then, espe-cially at first, comes to be fixated on these supplies and obsessed with them. In the most fanatic way, he can spend the day in devoted thoughts concerning the possibility of acquiring these gratifications or the approach of the hour at which they are scheduled to be granted. The building of a world around these minor privileges is per-haps the most important feature of inmate culture and yet is something that cannot easily be appreciated by an outsider, even one who has lived through the experience himself. This situation sometimes leads to generous sharing and almost always to a willingness to beg for things such as ciga-rettes, candy and newspapers. It will be understandable, then, that a constant fea-ture of inmate discussion is the *release binge fantasy*. Namely, recitals of what one will do during leave or upon release from the insti-tution.

House rules and privileges provide the functional requirements of the third ele-ment in the privilege system: *punishments*. These are designated as the consequence of breaking the rules. One set of these punish-ments consists of the temporary or perma-nent withdrawal of privileges or abrogation of the right to try to earn them. In general, the punishments meted out in total institu-tions are of an order more severe than any-thing encountered by the inmate in his home world. An institutional arrangement which causes a small number of easily con-trolled privileges to have a massive signifi-cance is the same arrangement which lends a terrible significance to their withdrawal.

There are some special features of the privilege system which should be noted.

First, punishments and privileges are themselves modes of organization peculiar to total institutions. Whatever their severity, punishments are largely known in the inmate's home world as something applied to animals and children. For adults this conditioning, behavioristic model is actu-ally not widely applied, since failure to maintain required standards typically leads to indirect disadvantageous consequences and not to specific immediate punishment at all. And privileges, it should be empha-sized, are not the same as prerequisites, indulgences or values, but merely the absence of deprivations one ordinarily expects one would not have to sustain. The very notions, then, of punishments and privileges are not ones that are cut from civilian cloth.

Second, it is important to see that the question of release from the total institution is elaborated into the privilege system. Some acts will become known as ones that mean an increase or no decrease in length of stay, while others become known as means for lessening the sentence.

Third, we should also note that punish-ments and privileges come to be geared into a residential work system. Places to work and places to sleep become clearly defined as places where certain kinds and levels of privilege obtain, and inmates are shifted very rapidly and visibly from one place to another as the mechanisms for giving them the punishment or privilege their coopera-tiveness has warranted. The inmates are moved, the system is not.

This, then, is the privilege system: a rela-tively few components put together with some rational intent and clearly proclaimed to the participants. The overall consequence is that cooperativeness is obtained from persons who often have cause to be uncoop-erative. . . . Immediately associated with the privilege system we find some standard social processes important in the life of total institutions.

We find that an *institutional lingo* develops through which inmates express the events that are crucial in their particular world. Staff too, especially its lower levels, will know this language, using it when talking to inmates, while reverting to more standardized speech when talking to superiors and outsiders. Related to this special argot, inmates will possess knowledge of the various ranks and officials, an accumulation of lore about the establishment, and some comparative information about life in other similar total institutions.

Also found among staff and inmates will be a clear awareness of the phenomenon of *messing up*, so called in mental hospitals, prisons, and barracks. This involves a complex process of engaging in forbidden activity, getting caught doing so, and receiving something like the full punishment accorded this. An alteration in privilege status is usually implied and is categorized by a phrase such as "getting busted." Typical infractions which can eventuate in messing up are: fights, drunkenness, attempted suicide, failure at examinations, gambling, insubordination, homosexuality, improper taking of leave, and participation in collective riots. While these punished infractions are typically ascribed to the offender's cursedness, villainy, or "sickness," they do in fact constitute a vocabulary of institutionalized actions, limited in such a way that the same messing up may occur for quite different reasons. Informally, inmates and staff may understand, for example, that a given messing up is a way for inmates to show resentment against a current situation felt to be unjust in terms of the informal agreements between staff and inmates, or a way of postponing release without having to admit to one's fellow inmates that one really does not want to go.

In total institutions there will also be a system of what might be called *secondary adjustments*, namely, techniques which do not directly challenge staff management but which allow inmates to obtain disallowed satisfactions or allowed ones by disallowed means. These practices are variously referred to as: the angles, knowing the ropes, conniving, gimmicks, deals, ins, etc. Such adaptations apparently reach their finest flower in prisons, but of course other total institutions are overrun with them too. It seems apparent that an important aspect of secondary adjustments is that they provide the inmate with some evidence that he is still, as it were, his own man and still has some protective distance, under his own control, between himself and the institution. In some cases, then, a secondary adjustment becomes almost a kind of lodgment for the self, a churinga in which the soul is felt to reside.

The occurrence of secondary adjustments correctly allows us to assume that the inmate group will have some kind of a *code* and some means of informal social control evolved to prevent one inmate from informing staff about the secondary adjustments of another. On the same grounds we can expect that one dimension of social typing among inmates will turn upon this question of security, leading to persons defined as "squealers," "finks," or "stoolies" on one hand, and persons defined as "right guys" on the other. It should be added that where new inmates can play a role in the system of secondary adjustments, as in providing new faction members or new sexual objects, then their "welcome" may indeed be a sequence of initial indulgences and enticements, instead of exaggerated deprivations. Because of secondary adjustments we also find *kitchen strata*, namely, a kind of rudimentary, largely informal, stratification of inmates on the basis of each one's differential access to disposable illicit commodities; so also we find social typing to designate the powerful persons in the informal market system.

While the privilege system provides the chief framework within which reassembly of the self takes place, other factors characteristically lead by different routes in the same general direction. Relief from economic and social responsibilities—much touted as part of the therapy in mental hospitals—is one, although in many cases it would seem that the disorganizing effect of this moratorium is more significant than its organizing effect. More important as a reorganizing influence is the *fraternalization process*, namely, the process through which socially distant persons find themselves developing mutual support and common *counter-mores* in opposition to a system that has forced them into intimacy and into a single, equalitarian community of fate. It seems that the new recruit frequently starts out with something like the staff's popular misconceptions of the character of the inmates and then comes to find that most of his fellows have all the properties of ordinary decent human beings and that the stereotypes associated with their condition or offense are not a reasonable ground for judgment of inmates.

If the inmates are persons who are accused by staff and society of having committed some kind of a crime against society, then the new inmate, even though sometimes in fact quite guiltless, may come to share the guilty feelings of his fellows and, thereafter, their well-elaborated defenses against these feelings. A sense of common injustice and a sense of bitterness against the outside world tends to develop, marking an important movement in the inmate's moral career. . . .

Adaptation Alignments. The mortifying processes that have been discussed and the privilege system represent the conditions that the inmate must adapt to in some way, but however pressing, these conditions allow for different ways of meeting them. We find, in fact, that the same inmate will employ different lines of adaptation or tacks at different phases in his moral career and may even fluctuate between different tacks at the same time.

First, there is the process of *situational withdrawal.* The inmate withdraws apparent attention from everything except events immediately around his body and sees these in a perspective not employed by others present. This drastic curtailment of involvement in interactional events is best known, of course, in mental hospitals, under the title of "regression." Aspects of "prison psychosis" or "stir simpleness" represent the same adjustment, as do some forms of "acute depersonalization" described in concentration camps. I do not think it is known whether this line of adaptation forms a single continuum of varying degrees of withdrawal or whether there are standard discontinuous plateaus of disinvolvement. It does seem to be the case, however, that, given the pressures apparently required to dislodge an inmate from this status, as well as the currently limited facilities for doing so, we frequently find here, effectively speaking, an irreversible line of adaptation.

Second, there is the *rebellious line.* The inmate intentionally challenges the institution by flagrantly refusing to cooperate with staff in almost any way. The result is a constantly communicated intransigency and sometimes high rebel morale. Most large mental hospitals, for example, seem to have wards where this spirit strongly prevails. Interestingly enough, there are many circumstances in which sustained rejection of a total institution requires sustained orientation to its formal organization and hence, paradoxically, a deep kind of commitment to the establishment. Similarly, when total institutions take the line (as they sometimes do in the case of mental hospitals prescribing lobotomy or army barracks prescribing the stockade) that the recalcitrant inmate must be broken, then, in their way, they must show as much special devotion to the rebel as he has shown to them. It should be added, finally, that while prisoners of war have been known staunchly to take a rebellious stance throughout their incarceration, this stance is typically a temporary and initial phase of reaction, emerging from this to situational withdrawal or some other line of adaptation.

Third, another standard alignment in the institutional world takes the form of a kind of *colonization.* The sampling of the outside world provided by the establishment is taken by the inmate as the whole, and a stable, relatively contented existence is built up out of the maximum satisfactions procurable within the institution. Experience of the outside world is used as a point of reference to demonstrate the desirability of life on the inside; and the usual tension between the two worlds collapses, thwarting the social arrangements based upon this felt discrepancy. Characteristically, the individual who too obviously takes this line may be accused by his fellow inmates of "having found a home" or of "never having had it so good." Staff itself may become vaguely embarrassed by this use that is being made of the institution, sensing that the benign possibilities in the situation are somehow being misused. Colonizers themselves may feel obliged to deny their satisfaction with the institution, if only in the interest of sustaining the counter-mores supporting inmate solidarity. They may find it necessary to mess up just prior to their slated discharge, thereby allowing themselves to present involuntary reasons for continued incarceration. It should be incidentally noted that any humanistic effort to make life in total institutions more bearable must face the possibility that doing so may increase the attractiveness and likelihood of colonization.

Fourth, one mode of adaptation to the setting of a total institution is that of *conversion.* The inmate appears to take over completely the official or staff view of himself and tries to act out the role of the perfect inmate. While the colonized inmate builds as much of a free community as possible for himself by using the limited facilities available, the convert takes a more disciplined, moralistic, monochromatic line, presenting himself as someone whose institutional enthusiasm is always at the disposal of the staff. . . . In army barracks there are enlisted men who give the impression that they are always "sucking around" and always "bucking for promotion." In prisons there are "square johns.". . . Some mental hospitals

have the distinction of providing two quite different conversion possibilities—one for the new admission who can see the light after an appropriate struggle and adapt the psychiatric view of himself, and another for the chronic ward patient who adopts the manner and dress of attendants while helping them to manage the other ward patients with a stringency excelling that of the attendants themselves.

Here, it should be noted, is a significant way in which total institutions differ. Many, like progressive mental hospitals, merchant ships, TB sanitariums and brainwashing camps, offer the inmate an opportunity to live up to a model of conduct that is at once ideal and staff-sponsored—a model felt by its advocates to be in the supreme interests of the very persons to whom it is applied. Other total institutions, like some concentration camps and some prisons, do not officially sponsor an ideal that the inmate is expected to incorporate as a means of judging himself.

While the alignments that have been mentioned represent coherent courses to pursue, few inmates, it seems, carry these pursuits very far. In most total institutions, what we seem to find is that most inmates take the tack of what they call *playing it cool.* This involves a somewhat opportunistic combination of secondary adjustments, conversion, colonization and loyalty to the inmate group, so that in the particular circumstances the inmate will have a maximum chance of eventually getting out physically and psychically undamaged. Typically, the inmate will support the counter-mores when with fellow inmates and be silent to them on how tractably he acts when alone in the presence of staff. Inmates taking this line tend to subordinate contacts with their fellows to the higher claim of "keeping out of trouble." They tend to volunteer for nothing and they may even learn to cut their ties to the outside world sufficiently to give cultural reality to the world inside but not enough to lead to colonization.

I have suggested some of the lines of adaptation that inmates can take to the pressures that play in total institutions. Each represents a way of managing the tension between the home world and the institutional world. However, there are circumstances in which the home world of the inmate was such in fact as to *immunize* him against the bleak world on the inside and for such persons no particular scheme of adaptation need be carried very far. Thus some lower-class mental hospital patients who have lived all their previous life in orphanages, reformatories and jails tend to see the hospital as just another total institution to which it is possible to apply the adaptive techniques learned and perfected in other total institutions. "Playing it cool" represents for such persons not a shift in their moral career but an alignment that is already second nature. . . .

Culture Themes. A note should be added here concerning some of the more dominant themes of inmate culture.

First, in the inmate group of many total institutions there is a strong feeling that time spent in the establishment is time wasted or destroyed or taken from one's life; it is time that must be written off. It is something that must be "done" or "marked" or "put in" or "built" or "pulled." (Thus in prisons and mental hospitals a general statement of how well one is adapting to the institution may be phrased in terms of how one is doing time, whether easily or hard.) As such this time is something that its doers have bracketed off for constant conscious consideration in a way not quite found on the outside. And as a result the inmate tends to feel that for the duration of his required stay—his sentence—he has been totally exiled from living. It is in this context that we can appreciate something of the demoralizing influence of an indefinite sentence or a very long one. We should also note that however hard the conditions of life may become in total institutions harshness alone cannot account for this quality of life wasted. Rather we must look to the social disconnections caused by

entrance and to the usual failure to acquire within the institution gains that can be transferred to outside life—gains such as money earned, or marital relations formed, or certified training received.

Second, it seems that in many total institutions a peculiar kind and level of self-concern is engendered. The low position of inmates relative to their station on the outside as established initially through the mortifying processes seems to make for a milieu of personal failure and a round of life in which one's fall from grace is continuously pressed home. In response the inmate tends to develop a storyline, a sad tale—a kind of lamentation and apologia—which he constantly tells to his fellows as a means of creditably accounting for his present low estate. While staff constantly discredit these lines, inmate audiences tend to employ tact, suppressing at least some of the disbelief and boredom engendered by these recitations. In consequence, the inmate's own self may become even more of a focus for his conversation than it does on the outside.

Perhaps the high level of ruminative self-concern found among inmates in total institutions is a way of handling the sense of wasted time that prevails in these places. If so, then perhaps another interesting aspect of inmate culture can be related to the same factor. I refer here to the fact that in total institutions we characteristically find a premium placed on what might be called *removal activities,* namely, voluntary unserious pursuits which are sufficiently engrossing and exciting to lift the participant out of himself, making [him] oblivious for the time to his actual situation. If the ordinary activities in total institutions can be said to torture time, these activities mercifully kill it.

Some removal activities are collective, such as ball games, woodwork, lectures, choral singing and card playing; some are individual but rely on public materials, as in the case of reading, solitary TV watching, etc. No doubt, private fantasy ought to be included too. Some of these activities may be officially sponsored by staff; and some, not officially sponsored, may constitute second-ary adjustments. In any case, there seems to be no total institution which cannot be seen as a kind of Dead Sea in which appear little islands of vivid, enrapturing activity.

Consequences. In this discussion of the inmate world, I have commented on the mortification processes, the reorganizing influences, the lines of response taken by inmates under these circumstances, and the cultural milieu that develops. A concluding word must be added about the long-range consequences of membership.

Total institutions frequently claim to be concerned with rehabilitation, that is, with resetting the inmate's self-regulatory mech-anisms so that he will maintain the stan-dards of the establishment of his own accord after he leaves the setting. In fact, it seems this claim is seldom realized and even when permanent alteration occurs, these changes are often not of the kind intended by the staff. With the possible exception presented by the great resocialization efficiency of religious insti-tutions, neither the stripping processes nor the reorganizing ones seem to have a lasting effect. No doubt the availability of second-ary adjustments helps to account for this, as do the presence of counter-mores and the tendency for inmates to combine all strate-gies and "play it cool." In any case, it seems that shortly after release, the ex-inmate will have forgotten a great deal of what life was like on the inside and will have once again begun to take for granted the privileges around which life in the institution was organized. The sense of injustice, bitterness and alienation, so typically engendered by the inmate's experience and so definitely marking a stage in his moral career, seems to weaken upon graduation, even in those cases where a permanent stigma has resulted.

But what the ex-inmate does retain of his institutional experience tells us important things about total institutions. Often entrance will mean for the recruit that he has taken on what might be called a *proactive status*. Not only is his relative social position within the walls radically different from what it was on the outside, but, as he comes to learn, if and when he gets out, his social position on the outside will never again be quite what it was prior to entrance. Where the proactive status is a relatively favorable one, as it is for those who graduate from officers' training schools, elite boarding schools, ranking monasteries, etc., then the permanent alter-ation will be favorable, and jubilant official reunions announcing pride in one's "school" can be expected. When, as seems usually the case, the proactive status is unfavorable, as it is for those in prisons or mental hospitals, we popularly employ the term "stigmatiza-tion" and expect that the ex-inmate may make an effort to conceal his past and try to "pass." . . .

Conclusion

I have defined total institutions denota-tively by listing them and then have tried to suggest some of their common characteris-tics. We now have a quite sizable literature on these establishments and should be in a position to supplant mere suggestions with a solid framework bearing on the anatomy and functioning of this kind of social ani-mal. Certainly the similarities obtrude so glaringly and persistently that we have a right to suspect that these features have good functional reasons for being present and that it will be possible to tie them together and grasp them by means of a functional explanation. When we have done so, I feel we will then give less praise and blame to particular superintendents, com-mandants, wardens and abbots, and tend more to understand the social problems and issues in total institutions by appealing to the underlying structural design common to all of them.

Study Questions

1. What are some of the common characteristics of total institutions identified by the author?

2. Describe the initial process of self-mortification and the continuing degradations suffered by inmates.

3. How may different inmates adapt to the setting of the total institution?

4. If Goffman is correct about the debilitating effects of the total institution, how might we expect inmates to act upon release?

Excerpts from "Characteristics of Total Institutions" by Erving Goffman, *Symposium on Preventive and Social Psychiatry*, pp. 43–64, 84. Copyright © 1957 by Walter Reed Army Institute of Research. Reprinted by permission. ✦

8
The Prison Community

Donald Clemmer

In this article by Clemmer, the process of "prisonization" is examined closely. After considering the possible effects of the "total institution," the reader should consider how those effects may influence the culture (or subculture) within the walls of the prison. The author describes prisonization as "the process through which an individual will take on the values and mores of the penitentiary." In other words, the prison itself is seen as a world in and of itself—a world with unique characteristics and internal forces that at times mimic the outside world, but in many ways are completely different. Because the prisoners, through processes inherent within the prison, have been cut off from outside influences, the potential for the development of new rules, expectations, and economies presents itself. In responding to these new rules, inmates develop ways in which they modify their behavior to fit in and adapt. Such adaptation may help inmates survive in a number of ways. As you read, however, consider whether these behavior modifications inhibit the achievement of any other correctional goals.

Assimilation or Prisonization

When a person or group of ingress penetrates and fuses with another group, assimilation may be said to have taken place. The concept is most profitably applied to immigrant groups and perhaps it is not the best term by which to designate similar processes which occur in prison. Assimilation implies that a process of acculturation occurs in one group whose members originally were quite different from those of the group with whom they mix. It implies that the assimilated come to share the sentiments, memories, and traditions of the static group. It is evident that the men who come to prison are not greatly different from the ones already there so far as broad culture influences are concerned: All speak the same language, all have a similar national heritage, all have been stigmatized, and so on. While the differences of regional conditioning are not to be overlooked, it is doubtful if the interactions which lead the professional offender to have a "we-feeling" with the naive offender from Coalville can be referred to as assimilation—although the processes furnishing the development of such an understanding are similar to it. . . . [T]he term assimilation describes a slow, gradual, more or less unconscious process during which a person learns enough of the culture of a social unit into which he is placed to make him characteristic of it. While we shall continue to use this general meaning, we recognize that in the strictest sense assimilation is not the correct term. So as we use the term Americanization to describe a greater or lesser degree of the immigrant's integration into the American scheme of life, we may use the term *prisonization* to indicate the taking on in greater or lesser degree of the folkways, mores, customs, and general culture of the penitentiary. Prisonization is similar to assimilation, and its meaning will become clearer as we proceed.

Every man who enters the penitentiary undergoes prisonization to some extent. The first and most obvious integrative step concerns his status. He becomes at once an anonymous figure in a subordinate group. A number replaces a name. He wears the clothes of the other members of the subordinate group. He is questioned and admonished. He soon learns that the warden is all-powerful. He soon learns the ranks, titles, and authority of various officials. And whether he uses the prison slang and argot or not, he comes to know its meanings. Even though a new man may hold himself aloof from other inmates and remain a solitary figure, he finds himself within a few months referring to or thinking of keepers as "screws," the physician as the "croaker" and using the local nicknames to designate persons. He follows the examples already set in wearing his cap. He learns to eat in haste and in obtaining food he imitates the tricks of those near him.

After the new arrival recovers from the effects of the swallowing-up process, he assigns a new meaning to conditions he had previously taken for granted. The fact that food, shelter, clothing, and a work activity had been given him originally made no especial impression. It is only after some weeks or months that there comes to him a new interpretation of these necessities of life. This new conception results from mingling with other men and it places emphasis on the fact that the environment *should* administer to him. This point is intangible and difficult to describe insofar as it is only a subtle and minute change in attitude from the taken-for-granted perception. Exhaustive questioning of hundreds of men reveals that this slight change in attitude is a fundamental step in the process we are calling prisonization. Supplemental to it is the almost universal desire on the part of the man, after a period of some months, to get a good job so, as he says, "I can do my time without any trouble and get out of here." A good job usually means a comfortable job of a more or less isolated kind in which conflicts with other men are not likely to develop. The desire for a comfortable job is not peculiar to the prison community, to be sure, but it seems to be a phase of prisonization in the following way. When men have served time before entering the penitentiary they look the situation over and almost immediately express a desire for a certain kind of work. When strictly first offenders come to prison, however, they seldom express a desire for a particular kind of work, but are willing to do anything and fre-

quently say, "I'll do any kind of work they put me at and you won't have any trouble from me." Within a period of a few months, however, these same men, who had no choice of work, develop preferences and make their desires known. They "wise up," as the inmates say, or in other words, by association they become prisonized.

In various other ways men new to prison slip into the existing patterns. They learn to gamble or learn new ways to gamble. Some, for the first time in their lives, take to abnormal sex behavior. Many of them learn to distrust and hate the officers, the parole board, and sometimes each other, and they become acquainted with the dogmas and mores existing in the community. But these changes do not occur in every man. However, every man is subject to certain influences which we may call the *universal factors of prisonization.*

Acceptance of an inferior role, accumulation of facts concerning the organization of the prison, the development of somewhat new habits of eating, dressing, working, sleeping, the adoption of local language, the recognition that nothing is owed to the environment for the supplying of needs, and the eventual desire for a good job are aspects of prisonization which are operative for all inmates. It is not these aspects, however, which concern us most but they are important because of their universality, especially among men who have served many years. That is, even if no other factor of the prison culture touches the personality of an inmate of many years residence, the influences of these universal factors are sufficient to make a man characteristic of the penal community and probably so disrupt his personality that a happy adjustment in any community becomes next to impossible. On the other hand, if inmates who are incarcerated for only short periods, such as a year or so, do not become integrated into the culture except insofar as these universal factors of prisonization are concerned, they do not seem to be so characteristic of the penal community and are able when released to take up a new mode of life without much difficulty.

The phases of prisonization which concern us most are the influences which breed or deepen criminality and antisociality and make the inmate characteristic of the criminalistic ideology in the prison community. As has been said, every man feels the influences of what we have called the universal factors, but not every man becomes prisonized in and by other phases of the culture. Whether or not complete prisonization takes place depends first on the man himself, that is, his susceptibility to a culture which depends, we think, primarily on the type of relationships he had before imprisonment, i.e., his personality. A second determinant effecting complete prisonization refers to the kind and extent of relationships which an inmate has with persons outside the walls. A third determinant refers to whether or not a man becomes affiliated in prison primary or semi-primary groups and this is related to the two points already mentioned. Yet a fourth determinant depends simply on chance, a chance placement in [a] work gang, cellhouse, and with [a] cellmate. A fifth determinant pertains to whether or not a man accepts the dogmas or codes of the prison culture. Other determinants depend on age, criminality, nationality, race, regional conditioning, and every determinant is more or less interrelated with every other one.

With knowledge of these determinants we can hypothetically construct schemata of prisonization which may serve to illustrate its extremes. In the least or lowest degree of prisonization the following factors may be enumerated:

1. A short sentence, thus a brief subjection to the universal factors of prisonization.

2. A fairly stable personality made stable by an adequacy of positive and socialized relationships during pre-penal life.

3. The continuance of positive relationships with persons outside the walls.

4. Refusal or inability to integrate into a prison primary group or semiprimary group, while yet maintaining a symbiotic balance in relations with other men.

5. Refusal to accept blindly the dogmas and codes of the population, and a willingness, under certain situations, to aid officials, thus making for identification with the free community.

6. A chance placement with a cellmate and workmates who do not possess leadership qualities and who are also not completely integrated into the prison culture.

7. Refraining from abnormal sex behavior, and excessive gambling, and a ready willingness to engage seriously in work and recreative activities.

Other factors no doubt have an influencing force in obstructing the process of prisonization, but the seven points mentioned seem outstanding.

In the highest or greatest degree of prisonization the following factors may be enumerated:

1. A sentence of many years, thus a long subjection to the universal factors of prisonization.

2. A somewhat unstable personality made unstable by an inadequacy of socialized relations before commitment, but possessing, nonetheless, a capacity for strong convictions and a particular kind of loyalty.

3. A dearth of positive relations with persons outside the walls.

4. A readiness and a capacity for integration into a prison-primary group.

5. A blind, or almost blind, acceptance of the dogmas and mores of the primary group and the general penal population.

6. A chance placement with other persons of a similar orientation.

7. A readiness to participate in gambling and abnormal sex behavior.

We can see in these two extremes the degrees with which the prisonization process operates. No suggestion is intended that a high correlation exists between either extreme of prisonization and criminality. It is quite possible that the inmate who fails to integrate in the prison culture may be and may continue to be much more criminalistic than the inmate who becomes completely prisonized. The trends are probably otherwise, however, as our study of group life suggests. To determine prisonization, every case must be appraised for itself. Of the two degrees presented in the schemes it is probable that more men approach the complete degree than the least degree of prisonization, but it is also probable that the majority of inmates become prisonized in some respects and not in others. It is the varying degrees of prisonization among the 2,300 men that contribute to the disassociation which is so common. The culture is made complex, not only by the constantly changing population, but by these differences in the tempo and degree of prisonization.

Assimilation, as the concept is customarily applied, is always a slow, gradual process, but prisonization, as we use the term here, is usually slow, but not necessarily so. The speed with which prisonization occurs depends on the personality of the man involved, his crime, age, home neighborhood, intelligence, the situation into which he is placed in prison and other less obvious influences. The process does not necessarily proceed in an orderly or measured fashion but tends to be irregular. In some cases we have found the process working in a cycle. The amount and speed of prisonization can be judged only by the behavior and attitudes of the men, and these vary from man to man and in the same man from time to time. It is the excessive number of changes in orientation which the men undergo which makes generalizations about the process so difficult.

In the free communities where the daily life of the inhabitants is not controlled in every detail, some authors have reported a natural gravitation to social levels. The matter of chance still remains a factor, of course, in open society but not nearly so much so as in the prison. For example, two associates in a particular crime may enter the prison at the same time. Let us say that their criminality, their intelligence, and their background are more or less the same. Each is interviewed by the deputy warden and assigned to a job. It so happens that a certain office is in need of a porter. Of the two associates the man whom the deputy warden happens to see first may be assigned to that job while the one he interviews last is assigned to the quarry. The inmate who becomes the office porter associates with but four or five other men, none of whom, let us suppose, are basically prisonized. The new porter adapts himself to them and takes up their interests. His speed of prisonization will be slow and he may never become completely integrated into the prison culture. His associate, on the other hand, works in the quarry and mingles with a hundred men. The odds are three to five that he will become integrated into a primary or semi-primary group. When he is admitted into the competitive and personal relationships of informal group life we can be sure that, in spite of some disassociation, he is becoming prisonized and will approach the complete degree.

Even if the two associates were assigned to the same work unit, differences in the tempo of prisonization might result if one, for example, worked shoulder to shoulder with a "complete solitary man," or a "hoosier." Whatever else may be said of the tempo of the process, it is always faster when the contacts are primary, providing the persons contacted in a primary way are themselves integrated beyond the minimal into the prison culture. Other factors, of course, influence the speed of integration. The inmate whose wife divorces him may turn for response and recognition to his immediate associates. When the memories

of pre-penal experience cease to be satisfying or practically useful, a barrier to prisonization has been removed.

Some men become prisonized to the
highest degree, or to a degree approaching
it, but then reject their entire orientation
and show, neither by behavior nor attitudes,
that any sort of integration has taken place.
They slip out of group life. They ignore the
codes and dogmas and they fall into a rev-
erie or stupor or become "solitary men."
After some months or even years of playing
this role they may again affiliate with a
group and behave as other prisonized
inmates do.

Determination of the degree of prisonization and the speed with which it occurs
can be learned best through the study of
specific cases. The innumerable variables
and the methodological difficulties which
arise in learning what particular stage of
prisonization a man has reached, prohibit
the use of quantitative methods. It would be
a great help to penology and to parole
boards in particular, if the student of prisons could say that inmate so-and-so was
prisonized to $x^3 + 9y$ degrees, and such a
degree was highly correlated with a specific
type of criminality. The day will no doubt
come when phenomena of this kind can be
measured, but it is not yet here. For the
present we must bend our efforts to systems

of actuarial prediction, and work for refine-
ments in this line. Actuarial procedures do
not ignore criteria of attitudes, but they
make no effort as yet to conjure with such
abstruse phenomena as prisonization. It is
the contention of this writer that parole prediction methods which do not give as much
study and attention to a man's role in the
prison community as is given to his adjustment in the free community cannot be of
much utility.

Study Questions

1. What was meant by the term *prisonization,* and what are some of its universal factors?

2. What characteristics of inmates determine the degree and speed with which
   prisonization occurs?

3. How do the features of the total institution, referred to by Goffman, relate to
   the process of prisonization?

9
In Search of the Convict Code

Victor Hassine

Editor's Note from *Life Without Parole*

"Honor among thieves" is a romantic notion sometimes applied to convicts. Based on his experiences, Victor Hassine holds few illusions about the prison as a place or about inmates as a community. He finds no credible code of conduct but much posturing by inmates, who assert their dignity and honor in a world where these traits are virtually nonexistent. He makes the insightful observation that calling oneself a convict is like covering oneself with tattoos; it suggests a fierce identity but often is in fact a mask to make oneself a less likely target for predators.

Criminologists have studied the convict code and described it as a powerful force in prison affairs. Hassine's observations suggest, however, that this line of research may be futile. The real codes of conduct, he argues, are imported from the outside world, as suggested in the seminal work by John Irwin (see The Felon*), then translated into the coin of the prison world (as explored by Hans Toch,* Living in Prison*). Something resembling a convict code, which is unique to prison, only exists when officials have lost control of the prison and a "kingdom of inmates" has been established. For any outsider, it is difficult to ascertain whether pronouncements about a prison code of conduct are real or fictitious.*

—R. J.

This piece by Victor Hassine represents a literal insider's approach to the exploration of the convict code and how it may influence life within a secure prison facility. At the outset, Hassine's approach is unique in that he has attempted to study his fellow inmates via the use of empirical research (a survey methodology). While this research activity is undoubtedly biased and clearly nonrepresentative, and thereby nongeneralizable, it is nonetheless a genuine attempt at social scientific discovery. Via his survey efforts, the author presents several insights into the differences between what are identified as a convict code *and an* inmate code*. These respective codes are simultaneously representative of statuses, or characteristics, and hold implications regarding honor, respect, and expected behaviors.*

Hassine's article goes beyond merely an attempt at discovering and offering details about the convict code. He uses qualitative information gleaned from his survey efforts (as well as his own experiences, presumably) to inform issues that have been discussed in the institutional correctional literature. For example, aspects of subcultural importation of inmate characteristics are presented, in opposition to the environmental/deprivation model. The importation of various subcultural characteristics provides the primary force that shapes any prison culture, according to the author. Presumably, various formulations of the convict code influence the way in which a prison runs and how the administration of an institution will act and react. In short, the author reveals the unique influence of the convict code, regardless of its origins, and how that code affects prison inmates, prison guards, and the institution as a whole. This aspect of institutional life is presented in light of the dilemma that is often posed when two very different populations are forced to co-exist—populations with goals that are similar to one another, yet with means to achieve them that are diametrically opposed.

He had his hands cuffed behind his back as he was shoved along by two flanking prison guards, a third walking in front of him and a fourth trailing behind. This was a common sight in prison, so aside from looking to see if I recognized the man bound for the "hole," I went about my business. Moments later, I heard him shout to anyone who might be listening, "That's right, I ain't no inmate—I'm a convict, motherfuckers! You can't just treat me any way! I'm a convict!"

Upon hearing this proud announcement, I was able to conclude (quite accurately as it turned out) that this man probably had some inmate trouble over a debt or a possible retaliation, so he committed a public infraction calculated to make himself look "tough." Perhaps, he provoked a fight with someone or threatened a guard, making sure that he was caught and taken immediately to the hole, where he could safely await a transfer to another prison, far away from his troubles. Then, as soon as he arrived at the new prison, he would display the misconduct report he had received to every convict he could in order to mislead them into thinking: this was a tough, stand-up kind of guy.

One class of convicts, those who at every opportunity vehemently proclaim their staunch adherence to the "Convict Code," are predatory informants. They spend each day soliciting inmates to trust them or getting them involved in illegal activities so that they can harvest information to sell to prison staff. These predators often brandish a stern, lawless version of the Convict Code to lure new arrivals and gullible convicts into a false harbor of trust, tricking them into thinking they are safe to reveal confidences, plots, and secrets.

When I first arrived into prison, one of the initial conclusions that I reached was that the existence of the much touted Convict Code of conduct was only an ennobling myth used to affect and obscure the true nature of a convict's intentions or character.

My prison experiences have taught me that honor and human decency are learned and that these fragile things need constant relearning and reinforcement; that no lofty sense of humanity automatically substitutes our selfishness with some inherent dignity that requires us, even under the harshest of circumstances, to behave as "noble beasts" ultimately bound to do the "right thing."

When that escorted inmate loudly proclaimed himself a convict, he was actually using a shorthand expression to identify himself as an adherent to this fictitious Convict Code of honor. Every time a fellow convict tries to convince me that he is a proponent of this code of conduct, I have no choice but to assume that he is trying to deceive me. Contrary to common knowledge, most inmates and the majority of prison staff who participate in this collective ruse publicly claim the existence of a Convict Code, abided by since bygone days, even though they know that it never existed.

To test my understanding of the Convict Code, I drafted a questionnaire and distributed it to twelve of my fellow inmates, all of them varied in age, sentence, race, and experience in prison. Though I am familiar with each of them, I never before spoke to them about the Convict Code. The following are their individual responses:

Describe What You Think the Convict Code Is and What It Means?

"It means to distinguish the oppressors from the oppressed."

"At one time, yes, there was. It involved the cooperation of everyone, including guards to protect what rights inmates had. I say guards, because if they tried to involve themselves in taking away what freedom we had, their lives were either threatened or taken without hesitation. And if you even appeared to be part of what these guards represent, the same would happen.

Table 9.1
Convict Code Questionnaire Results

		1 Inmate Code Yes/No	2 Difference Convict/Inmate Yes/No	3 Code Followed Yes/No	4 Conditions Too Hard/Too Easy/ OK
Age Sentence Time in	32 Life 2 yrs	Yes	Yes	No	OK
	37 15-20 yrs 15 yrs	Yes	Yes	No	Too Hard
	40 Life 2 yrs	Yes	Yes	No	Too Hard
	76 15-40 yrs 3 yrs	Yes	Yes	No	OK
	34 Life 10 yrs	Yes	Yes	No	No Answer
	30 13-29 yrs 10 yrs	No	Yes	No	OK
	41 7-14 yrs 2 yrs	No	No	No	OK
	20 2.5-10 yrs 3 yrs	No	No	No	OK
	40 4.5-10 yrs 8 yrs	Yes	Yes	No	Too Hard
	25 Life 6 yrs	Yes	Yes	No	No Answer
	22 5-10 yrs 2 yrs	Yes	Yes	Yes	OK
	24 1.5-5 yrs 3 yrs	Yes	Yes	No	OK

"Before all these rules were in place, the D.O.C. [Department of Corrections] would think twice about taking away something that would threaten us as a whole, because it would cause even greater problems for them."

"1. Not to be a rat. 2. Watch those backs who would watch yours. 3. Reputation of not being chumped out is important. 4. Not associate with people who always talk to guards. 5. Keep your enemies closer than your friends."

"The code I was taught isn't really followed anymore but consists of, basically, if you want to stay outta trouble, don't gamble, do drugs, and don't mess with queens. Mind your own business and don't trust anyone. A lot of people in new jails such as this don't really follow any code. Now the code is basically do your programs and try to get out on your minimum."

"If you are a convict, you are an inmate of the state. The guards and any other staff that are part of your incarceration are looked at through my eyes as nothing more than white supremists, the convict code is that inmates are suppose[d] to see anything that doesn't involve you and keep your mouth shut if you do. The code also enforces. If you're caught snitching, you get what's coming to you because nobody likes a snitch. Don't fuck with faggots or do drugs and you'll be alright. The Convict Code has changed and now people want to do their time and get out."

"The code is, stay with your own. Never be a rat."

"The inmate code is not one of intrinsic honor, it is relating more to respect and straight forwardness. One does not snitch, back bite or fraternize with officials in a congenial or brotherly way.

"Institutions are only comprised to or in regards of what caliber of convicts it houses. Inmates that are passive aggressive, passive, and subservient in nature, are the prime recipe for officials to take back all of the basic human rights that we, the older convicts, have fought for in the past.

"I must say in closing that in regards to the Convict Code in the past, there was not a high degree of respect, honesty, or unity then. However, compared to today's standards, we were true fighters. *Respect* and *unity* are the key words here."

"Don't snitch on other convicts."

"Don't snitch; don't borrow; don't mess with homosexual; don't 'see' anything (be a witness); don't 'hear' [anything]; don't 'say' [anything]; don't gossip; watch who you walk with; don't debate PRS (politics, religion & sports); stay away from people who talk a lot; don't trust the system (D.O.C., U.S. government, prison staff and policies, medical services, etc); don't trust most of what you hear or see and research everything; don't talk with prison guards; don't disrespect anyone."

Is There a Difference Between a Convict and an Inmate? If so, Explain What It Is?

"Semantics."

"Well, for starters, convicts were there for one another. I guess what I'm trying to say is there was a sense of honor among one another. There was no such thing as a snitch, and if you were one, you would be 'taken care of.' I could remember a time when my uncle made prison, in his words, look like hell, because he would explain how not only were you to prove that you were a man but you would also have to be a survivor.

"Inmates, on the other hand, have no honor, no respect. Their very existence evolves around mimicking their 'so-called friends.' But if their friends are involved in anything that could jeopardize their parole, they back down, especially if it involves something that will benefit everyone. These are not men, these are children."

"A convict is a person who, even while incarcerated, has the same criminal thinking that he had when he committed the crime he or she did."

"An inmate is a person whom in some way has been rehabilitated and thinks different."

"A convict is one who repeatedly gets locked up over a number of years and adjusts well to prison. An inmate is one who not only adjusts well to prison but also staff members."

"I wasn't sure, so I looked both words up in my dictionary. I realized that there is a difference in the two words.

"I know now that I'm both, I was convicted by the courts and now I'm an inmate of the state. I was a convict, a person that committed crimes until I was arrested and found guilty in court, and now I'm serving time as a inmate."

"The difference is, a convict stands up for change. An inmate just goes with the flow."

"A convict is someone that demands respect from prison officials and will not tolerate pitting one convict against another. Many convicts have some sort of unity when injustice occurs by the hands of prison officials.

"An inmate is or are people that will conform or work with prison officials in efforts of causing anarchy among other prisoners. Many inmates commonly refer to the theory 'get down first.' And it is that thought process which I believe is destroying the very fabric of the basic liberties, and rights that many convicts in the past have sacrificed life, limb, and their dignities."

"In the old days, convicts looked out for each other."

* * *

Nine of the twelve convicts surveyed claimed that there was a "Convict Code," and ten agreed that there was a difference between being a convict and being an inmate. Only one out of the twelve, however, stated that he believed the code was actually followed. Those who did not believe a Convict Code was followed in practice were in fact indicating that they did not believe such a code existed in the prison world, despite claims to the contrary.

Consider the disparity in the various descriptions of the Convict Code and the differences in describing the terms *convict* and *inmate*. Apparently, not only do most convicts take no stock in an actual Convict Code but none seem to know what the code really is, was, or should be. This lack of common understanding may not have anything to do with the inherent uncertainties found in an oral code supposedly handed down over the years by mostly illiterate convicts. It may instead reflect a common understanding of the Convict Code as a myth—an ideal—for them to freely recall and recount in any way that best serves their individual interests. To prisoners, the Convict Code is a living thing meant more to create and express a sense of belonging than to dictate actual conduct.

In reality, convicts coming to prison bring with them a moral and ethical code of conduct that they learned and developed from their individual street experiences. For example, members of the Mafia bring with them a Mafioso's code, street-gang members bring their own gang code, and drug addicts bring a junkie's code of conduct. When a convict enters prison, he naturally gravitates to others who are or were part of his gang or community on the street, i.e., his homeys. In doing this, his code of conduct is likely to be similar, if not identical, to the one he must abide by within his new prison community. If a convict arrives in a prison that has none of his homeys, he will gravitate to the group that exhibits the most familiarities then adopt that group's code as his own. So in truth, prison populations do not have any single, common Convict Code but instead a collection of unique codes derived from various distinct prison groups.

As in the outside world, moral and ethical practices in a prison group are learned and acted upon as a means of maintaining group identity, integrity, and cohesiveness. Thus, to the extent that prison managers are able to control the development of these groups, they can also control the code of conduct convicts are likely to adopt. When officials lose control, as when a "Kingdom of Inmates" emerged in Graterford . . . , something like a Convict Code reigns or at least receives consistent lip service.

The least effective method for preventing the adoption of an unwanted Convict Code is to punish individual prisoners for practicing such a code of conduct, since this does nothing to prevent their group from doing the same. To prevent the practice of undesirable codes of conduct, a prison administration must develop, support, and fund voluntary convict groups that attract membership and teach a more acceptable code.

The question remains, why do convicts and staff alike continue to proclaim the existence of a nonexistent Convict Code? When a convict declares adherence to some presumably noble Convict Code, he is actually declaring affiliation to a mythical group of tough, honorable convicts. To most prisoners, group identity and affiliation are a matter of survival. The more successful one is at convincing others that he belongs to a larger group, the more likely he will be able to remain off a prison predator's short list of intended victims.

A convict who declares adherence to a Convict Code or claims to be a convict rather than an inmate is a variant akin to the common prison practice of having tattoos with grotesque images of violence and death. Many convicts tattoo themselves to falsely suggest that they are part of some outlaw gang, since gang members often use tattoos to identify themselves. Displaying such an affiliation is meant to ward off prison predators. Similarly, convicts perpetuate the myth of a Convict Code as a means of suggesting affiliation with a strong, tough, and lawless group.

Staff members, on the other hand, use the myth of a Convict Code to justify their belief in their superiority over prisoners and their assumption that convicts deserve the inhuman treatment they receive. After all,

staff may consider convicts to be "noble beasts" but in the end analysis, they know that beasts are beasts—not human beings. So, while a convict describes the Convict Code in a way that elevates him in the eyes of his peers, prison staff view the Convict Code in a way calculated to distance and dehumanize convicts. For example, when a convict states that the Convict Code requires him to mind his own business, he is describing a stoic adherence to brave, fearless practicality. But when guards or officials explain this same version, they portray convicts as so despicable that they will tolerate lawlessness even when it is in their power to prevent it. In the staff's eyes, the stoic convict thus becomes the cold-blooded thug.

When I find myself in a prison where convicts perpetuate the myth of a Convict Code, I know that I am in a relatively safe environment where the various convict groups have been allowed by prison staff to develop and practice their own unique inmate code. In violent and unsafe prisons, convicts must believe in and actually abide by a common code of conduct as a mutual defense against the dangerous consequences of anarchy. . . . To explore the hypothesis that safe prisons do not promote a binding code like that at Graterford, I asked a third question of my respondents:

What Do You Think Is the Worst Part About Doing Time?

"The constant attempts at brainwashing and debasement."

"Not having one ounce of freedom."

"The hardest part is being away from those you love. Not being able to be present in their good times and bad. Life is a one-way ticket, and you can't go back to whatever you missed."

"The worst part of doing time is being away from loved ones. And the feeling of helplessness when tragedy happens or when trying to handle business on the street."

"The worst thing about doing time is being disrespected and treated like animals, cattle, mentally fucked by people that have issues and personal vendettas towards inmates."

"Being lonely."

"The hardest part is not being with loved ones. Also, the loss of basic freedom and, last but not least, being forced to live under such abnormalities."

"Separation from loved ones."

"Being here. Dishonor."

"I feel being separated from my family is the hardest part and I don't feel the D.O.C. puts enough effort into keeping us close to our families. We need more family-based programs."

"So far away from home."

"I think the worse thing about being locked up is if you have kids. It's having them grow up without you around and knowing who they daddy is. That's the worst thing for me, while doing time."

* * *

None of the respondents identified violence as the worst part of prison life. This is a great change in thinking from my days in Graterford, where the threat of violence was a part of everyone's nightmares. In relatively safe prisons like this one (Rockview), convicts feel little need to follow or even pay lip service to a common code of conduct. In my survey, seven of the twelve respondents stated that prison conditions were OK and, accordingly, eleven out of twelve said the code was not followed. These results would have been unthinkable in Graterford.

Study Questions

1. Were the transcribed comments from Hassine's survey effort describing aspects of the convict code and prison life representative of the general population? Why and/or why not?

2. In what ways might prison administrators find the information contained in this article useful (in other words, what might the practical policy implications of this article be, if any)?

3. What were the most compelling "pains of imprisonment" that were revealed via the inmates' comments? In what ways might each of these pains contribute to the shaping of the convict code or prison culture?

4. What, in your estimation, was the most surprising finding contained in Hassine's piece?

5. What do you think the author would state as being the primary barrier to there ever being a true convict code in a prison institution? (Keep in mind the way the author opens up this piece, regarding the description of the inmate being brought to solitary confinement.)

10
Varieties of Punishment

Jack Henry Abbott

Jack Abbott presents the reader with an extremely vivid portrayal of the types and effects of several different forms of punishment he presumably experienced while confined in several different correctional institutions over the course of his adult life. The vividness of the author's description comes via his reflections of experiencing intensive amounts of extreme physical, psychological, and emotional abuse. The abuses described include (but are not limited to) severe starvation, sensory deprivation, and forcible medication, and occurred over a period of many years. Abbott also reveals some aspects of the convict code that is investigated in the Hassine essay (see Chapter 9), regarding his justification for, and description of, various actions. While clear changes have been made to the United States' prison system as a whole that serve to prevent the abuses detailed in this piece, in some ways the events described in this chapter may not seem very far in the past. Although the overall experiences reflected in Abbott's piece may indeed represent a compilation of extreme or outlying cases, this chapter compels the reader to consider what the underlying philosophical purposes of the United States' prison system should be, and what role, if any, "extracurricular" punishment should play within that environment.

It is called *affirmative action*. It is applied by the government to develop programs and policies aimed at correcting past injustices suffered by minorities in our society.

I can easily understand the justice of this doctrine—but the government will not apply it to men like me, even though it is completely understood that I survived prison conditions which are illegal and have never once from that time to this been given a chance to walk free from prison.

I have gained a *reputation* among prison authorities that extends from the time those illegal conditions existed, that stretches to this very day unbroken. I simply resisted those conditions that today are "officially" abolished—but at the time, the law was not on my side. Any more than it is today.

. . . My first acquaintance with punitive long-term solitary confinement had a more adverse and profound spiritual effect on me than anything else in my childhood.

I suffered from *claustrophobia* for years when I first went to prison. I never knew any form of suffering more horrible in my life.

The air in your cell vanishes. You are smothering. Your eyes bulge out; you clutch at your throat; you scream like a banshee. Your arms flail the air in your cell. You reel about the cell, falling.

Then you suffer cramps. The walls press you from all directions with an invisible force. You struggle to push it back. The oxygen makes you giddy with anxiety. You become hollow and empty. There is a vacuum in the pit of your stomach. You retch.

You are dying. Dying a hard death. One that lingers and toys with you.

The faces of guards, angry, are at the gate of your cell. The gate slides open. The guards attack you. On top of all that, the guards come into your cell and beat you to the floor.

Your mattress is thrown out. Your bedsheets are doubled. One end is run through a hole under the steel bunk that hangs from your cell wall. The other end is pulled through a hole at the opposite end of your bunk.

Your ankles are handcuffed and so are your hands. The sheet runs through them and you are left hanging from a spit by your feet and your hands. Your back is suspended several inches above the floor. You are smothering. You are being crushed to death.

They leave you like that all night.

That is how, over and over again, I was "cured" of the malady called claustrophobia. It took at least three or four years.

I was twenty or twenty-one years old when I was taken from the prison to an old county jail where I was to be booked and tried for killing another prisoner in combat.

I tried to escape from the jail. The jailers reopened a cell that had not been used in twenty-five years and placed me in it under prison discipline—a starvation diet of a bowl of broth and a hard biscuit once a day. It was a *blackout cell*. I was given a canvas sleeping mat and the door was closed on me. There was an iron sink-and-toilet combined in the corner, and other than that, there was nothing except about two inches of dust on the floor.

It was in *total* darkness. Not a crack of light entered that cell *anywhere*—and I searched, in the days that followed, for such a crack along every inch of the door and the walls. The darkness was so absolute it was like being in ink.

There was an ingenious apparatus on the door. It was cylindrical and was hand-operated from outside the cell. The jailer would place the bowl and the biscuit on a platform in the cylindrical apparatus. Then he would bang the door twice with his keys and I could hear the mechanism creak. I would crawl to the door, feeling my way up to the apparatus. When my hands came into contact with the food, I would carefully take it out and consume it. Then I would return the bowl to the platform in the apparatus and he would revolve it so that it returned to him outside the door.

In this entire process, I was fed without a glimmer of light. Darkness muffles sound. The only sound I ever heard—outside of my own movements and mutterings—was the bang of the keys and the creaking of the apparatus once a day.

The only light I saw was when I closed my eyes. Then there was before me a vivid burst of brilliance, of color, like fireworks. When I opened my eyes it would vanish.

It is one thing to *volunteer* for an experiment and intentionally consent to be plunged into darkness like this. It is another thing for it to be forced on you, for light to be *taken* from you.

My eyes *hungered* for light, for color, the way someone's dry mouth may *hunger* for saliva. They became so sensitive if I touched them; they exploded in light, in showers of white sparks shooting as if from a fountain.

Whenever I stirred in the cell, dust rose to my nostrils. Insects crawled on me when I was lying down and I became a ball of tension.

I counted twenty-three days by the meals. Then once I rose, thirsty, and felt my way to the sink. I felt the cup and I grasped it in my right hand. I closed my eyes for a moment and a shower of red and blue rained on me. I opened them to midnight darkness. With my left hand I felt for the button on the sink. I pressed it and could hear the trickle of water. I held my cup under it until I judged it full. Then I raised the cup carefully to my lips and tilted it back to drink.

I felt the legs, the bodies of many insects run up my face, over my eyes and into my hair. I flung down the cup and brought my hands to my face in an electric reaction and my eyes closed and the fireworks went off again.

I heard someone screaming far away and it was me. I fell against the wall, and as if it were a catapult, was hurled across the cell to the opposite wall. Back and forth I reeled, from the door to the walls, screaming. Insane.

When I regained consciousness, I was in a regular cell. I had been removed from the *blackout cell*. Every inch of my body was black with filth and my hair was completely matted.

I do not think *blackout cells* are in use in many prisons and jails today. . . .

. . . They *are* still in use today and they are *not* used for "medical reasons." They are used for punishment. They are called *strip-*

cells and I have been thrown in strip-cells many times—sometimes for months on end. This is prison *justice.*

There is no facility for running water in such a cell. The diabolic minds that design these punishment cells chill me when I consider them. The idea behind this one is that a prisoner in a strip-cell must "request" *water* from a guard. I don't think it would tax your imagination to see that a prisoner is reduced to *begging for water.*

It is a big square concrete box. The cell has nothing on the walls except for a single solid-steel door at the entrance. The ceiling is vaulted about fifteen feet above the floor and there is a bare lightbulb that stays lit, day and night.

In fact, there is no way to discern the days in the cell except by counting the times you are served your food through a slot in the door. How do you connect this with what you have done to be placed there?

The floor inclines from the walls inward to the center of the cell. It inclines gradually, like the bottom of a sink. A toilet bowl is more accurate. Then, in the center of the floor, there is a *hole* about two inches in diameter. It is flush with the concrete floor—as flush as a hole on a golf course. At first its purpose mystifies you.

Stains of urine and fecal matter radiate outward from the hole to within a foot or so from the walls. The stench is ever-present.

There is no bed-rack or bunk. There is nothing but the smell of shit and piss, and the glare of the light—out of reach—which is never extinguished.

The light is present even when you close your eyes. It penetrates the eyelids and enters your visual sensations in a grayish-white glow, so that you cannot rest your eyes. It *throbs* always in your mind.

Usually you are given nothing to wear but a pair of undershorts, and if you are lucky, you will receive a sleeping mat and a bedsheet.

At first you move gingerly about the cell because of the body wastes of prisoners who preceded you. You spend much of your time in the first long days squatting with your back defensively against a wall—squatting on the outskirts of the filth on the floor which radiates from the hole. Staring into it. If it were desolation you were facing as you stare off in your cell, it would probably inspire you in some small way. Poets have sung songs of scenes of desolation.

But what faces you is a cesspool world of murk and slime; a subterranean world of things that squirm and slide through noxious sewage, piles of shit and vomit and piss. There is the smell of unwashed feet and nervous sweat of bodies foreign to yours, so closing your eyes gives no relief.

If you are in that cell for weeks that add up to months, you do not ignore all this and live "with it"; you *enter* it and become a part of it.

I never suffered from thirst. No one there does, really. There is enough moisture in the food to hold that back. But I have been so dry in the mouth that I could not swallow, I could not talk, for weeks. You "ask" for water like this: "Wa? Wa?"

This is the strip-cell. Not only do these cells still exist in every state in this country, even the architects of modern prison facilities include them in new institutions.

Any sane man may wonder: What grievous crime would a man have to commit to be thus treated? The answer: In prison, anything at all. Any indiscretion. A contraband book. A murder. A purloined sandwich. This does not even square with the savage's conception of justice: *An eye for an eye.*

. . . There was once a form of prison discipline called *the starvation diet.* You were thrown in the hole and fed once a day just barely enough to give you the minimum nourishment to exist: to exist *in the hole,* not to exist the way the average man does.

This was still being done only ten years ago. Some places gave you bread and water once a day—but the maximum calculated by that strange brand of physicians I can think of only as technicians of pain was *ten days* of this. Then you came off for at least twenty-four hours of regular three meals served you over that twenty-four-hour period. Then you were placed *back* on another ten-day stint of starvation—that is, if you had misbehaved *in the hole.* Otherwise, after ten days you were let out of the hole.

All told, I served, in three years, the sum of *one year on the starvation diet.* That was when I first entered prison as a child of eighteen.

The longest stretch I ever pulled was about seventy *consecutive* days.

At this prison, the maximum you could obtain in a sentence to the hole under starvation conditions was *twenty-nine days.* Usually the sentence never exceeded fourteen days—or two weeks. That was for an average *misdemeanor,* a minor infraction of rules.

I went there once for spitting back at a pig who had spit in my face. My sentences were *always* the most severe, and so I was taken there under a twenty-nine-day sanction by the captain's committee.

State custom permitted us these items when we were living under starvation conditions in the hole:

1. one Christian Bible or one *Book of Mormon.* No other reading matter or religious matter allowed;

2. one set of white coveralls made of white canvas material (the gun-tower guards had orders to shoot anyone they saw on the yard in this disciplinary garb; it identified you the way a shaved head identified kids at the Industrial School for Boys who were rebellious);

3. one sleeping mat and a bedsheet.

Nothing more. You could receive neither your mail nor *any* visits. This included legal mail from the courts as well as mail from your lawyer—no lawyer could even visit you during this period of discipline. When your time was over, you were handed your back mail in a heap.

I had been there for about two weeks, and one evening, just as the guard was exit-

ing after making his rounds to count us, someone shouted: "Fuck you!"

The pig called down the range: "Okay, Abbott! That's another report!" Then he left.

The inmate volunteered to confess—he did it to save me from more time on starvation. In those days prisoners backed each other, and an injury to one was an injury to us all. I cited this code and told him I had to ride it out.

The next day the guards escorted me to the captain's disciplinary committee and I was sentenced to another twenty-nine-day stint, to be served after the one I was then halfway through.

A little later on, I soaked my Bible in the toilet and wrapped it tightly with strips of cloth from my bedsheet to form a hefty bludgeon. This was done because the day before, I had been rousted by pigs who pretended they were searching my cell and beaten up in the process. When the guard came by the next day, I lured him up to the bars of my cell and hit him with it, making a gash across his forehead.

When I was taken before the captain's committee, I was given another twenty-nine-day stint back-to-back with the other two sanctions. He passed the slip of paper the order was written on across the table to me and I picked it up, wadded it carefully into a ball and bounced it off his chest.

I was given yet another twenty-nine-day sanction. That made four of them I had to do—roughly *four months.*

After my *first* stint was over, I was not taken off for three meals (twenty-four hours). I caused a ruckus and received another twenty-nine-day sanction and then, finally, another.

A total of *six months.* It was, in fact, the death penalty. I was going to die if I remained on the starvation diet that long *for sure.* Every prisoner and guard knew this. The inmate who shouted "Fuck you" to the pig was out of the hole and on the yard, but he went to the captain and told him it was *he* who shouted the obscenity at the guard and not I, in an effort to save me. It did no good.

. . . Have you ever experienced *forced* starvation? It is not even *close* to a diet or a fast. Those things are *voluntarily* entertained.

When the gate slides closed behind you in that cell in which you are going to be subjected to methodical starvation, you face the fact that you have to survive the worst periods of it—the last days before it is over. You have to preserve yourself, so you cannot pace your cell; in fact, you must keep every motion you make down to a necessary minimum. You do the sanction lying in your bunk.

Most convicts, then, when they entered these starvation conditions, always gave their first once-a-day to the man who had been there the longest and needed it more. Likewise, his last day he gives his once-a-day to the one who needed it more. The greater need was calculated by days and was mechanical.

You suffer psychologically at first. That is why overweight men complained more. But when it gets down to physical survival, the suffering is real.

I learned a little secret in this period. A convict over sixty years old passed it on to me: cockroaches are a source of protein. Mash the day's catch all together in a piece of bread and swallow it like a big pill. I went beyond this, and before it was over, included every bug I could catch. It gives you a weird glow and feels strange to your metabolism when you begin to starve.

You may have one bowel movement but never more [than] two under starvation conditions. Your stomach shrinks up into a tight ball. This is what causes *hunger pangs*. When it has shrunken completely, the hunger pangs are no more. You are no longer hungry, although the rest of your body begins to take over the pain and extend it. Your limbs express hunger when your muscle tissue begins to dissolve. It is a strange kind of pain to feel. The need to eat becomes a need to devour, like an animal.

If you bloat yourself on water, you only prolong the pain in your stomach and it will multiply the other expressions of suffering starvation.

I once caught myself considering the arm of a pig, and became excited the way, I guess, a carnivorous beast becomes excited to see his dinner on the hoof. It was as if I could smell his blood.

I had completed sixty days when there was an inmate work strike. The pigs filled the hole to maximum capacity with strikers. I was no longer suffering stomach hunger pangs and my muscles were all but dissolved by then. I had again not been given my twenty-four-hour respite.

I recall I just quit consuming my once-a-day and gave it to the strikers in solidarity. I insisted on it and even threw it out of my cell when they refused to accept it from me. I had entered indifference, almost euphoria. Yet, they say I roamed the floor, picking. Looking, I imagine, for my bugs. All I recall is one day I saw the gate to my cell open in a slow drowsy haze. I had heard shouting and scuffling vaguely all that day. The prisoners tried to take a hostage to demand my release from starvation. I found all this out later.

I could barely make out the few blurred faces bobbing toward me as I lay in my bunk. One of them carried me in his arms to the infirmary. I have flashes of memory of being carried up the main corridor.

About a week later I awoke in a hospital cell with a tube down my nasal passage to my stomach and there was a bottle of clear liquid suspended upside down with a tube attached that ran into my arm.

When they couldn't handle you in segregation or the Grade (Maximum Security confinement)—and you had to be way-out—you were thrown in a special cell on the third floor of C Cellhouse (in the *office* of death row—the old death row): one cell called "C-300." It was a cube of boiler-plate steel with a solid-steel door. It was the "gas tank"—where you were tear-gassed and there was no ventilation. There, they once did not feed me for a week. They gave me only a glass of water a day. I was kept chained to the floor for periods of one to two weeks. "Normally," I was unchained. Once I was kept there a year. I did a six-month stretch there another time.

I was in that cell the day J. F. Kennedy was assassinated (death row was cheering; they had heard it on the news).

I was there the day a pig with a wooden leg (a pig who used to spit in my face when the outer steel door was opened) opened the outer door and declared: *"Your mother died last night!"*—and then he slammed the door in my face. This is how I learned of her death.

No one has ever done the time I did in C-300. Nor has anyone served as long as five years—from January 1966 to March 1971—in Maximum Security as I have. I had to escape to get out.

. . . I am on the Grade. I am pacing my cell after the evening meal. I hear a voice whispering loudly through the ventilator on the back wall of my cell. It is saying "I'm gonna kill you! You son-of-a-bitch!" It is saying "Jack! Jack Abbott! You are going to die!" There is a string of obscenities. No one can hear this except me.

I go to the vent in quick rage: "Who is it!?" There is silence for a moment, then: "Fuck you! It's me, Abbott! It's me!"

I'm thinking it is the prisoner in the cell on the tier opposite mine, on the other side of the plumbing pipe-run. I call him by name. He comes to *his* vent. He tells me he doesn't know what I'm talking about. He withdraws.

The voice returns. I peer carefully through a crack in the ventilator. I see a hand move. It is a pig.

I shout at him and he *whispers* loudly back to me—threats and obscenities. I shout that I'm going to get even. He leaves.

No other prisoner heard him. I tell them what the pig did to me. He has to make his rounds to count. When he comes by, I will throw a cup of water on him.

He comes by—grinning evilly at me. I douse him.

The trap slams closed.

My cell door slides open. Guards pour onto the tier. We fight; they leave. They had been waiting for me to throw the water.

The next day I am taken before the captain's committee and given a twenty-nine-day sentence to the hole on starvation diet.

I tell the captain the pig had been threatening me and calling me names through my ventilator.

A psychiatrist sees me in the hole. He tells me I am hallucinating. I am placed on injections of two hundred milligrams of Thorazine three times a day.

At that time I was barely nineteen years old. I was one of the first prisoners in this country subjected to drug therapy in prison. Now it is common.

I fought every time, until I could fight no more. (Five or six guards entered the cell and wrestled me to the floor three times a day and injected Thorazine into me.) I suffered severe physical side effects. At that time, there was not much known about the side effect called the "Parkinson's reaction." The prison doctor thought I was feigning.

This gave me my first psychiatric record.

. . . This letter is about the instability "crazies" have in prison. It is about how we who suffer from this prison-cultivated disease are dealt with.

X told me he once saw Gilmore transfixed, frozen on the nerve-endings of his central nervous system. You do not always die any more from crucifixion; the authorities try not to let that happen. I've myself been crucified a hundred times and more by those institutional drugs that are for some sinister reason called "tranquilizers."

They are *phenothiazine* drugs, and include Mellaril, Thorazine, Stelazine, Haldol.

Prolixin is the worst I've ever experienced. One injection lasts for two weeks. Every two weeks you receive an injection. These drugs, in this family, do not calm or sedate the nerves. They attack. They attack from so deep inside you, you cannot locate the source of the pain. The drugs *turn* your nerves in upon yourself. Against your will, your resistance, your resolve are directed at your own tissues, your own muscles, reflexes, etc. These drugs are designed to render you so totally involved with yourself physically that all you can do is concentrate your entire being on holding yourself together. (Tying your shoes, for example.) You cannot cease trembling.

From all of these drugs you can get the "Parkinson's reaction"—a physical reaction identical to Parkinson's disease. The muscles of your jawbone go berserk, so that you bite the inside of your mouth and your jaw locks and the pain throbs. For *hours* every day this will occur. Your spinal column stiffens so that you can hardly move your head or your neck and sometimes your back bends backward like a bow and you cannot stand up.

The pain *grinds* into your *fiber;* your vision is so blurred you cannot read. You ache with restlessness, so that you feel you have to walk, to pace. And then as soon as you start pacing, the opposite occurs to you: you must *sit* and *rest.* Back and forth, up and down you go in pain you cannot locate; in such wretched anxiety you are overwhelmed, because you cannot get relief even in *breathing.* Sometimes a groan or whimper rises inside you to the point it comes out involuntarily and people look at you curiously, so you suppress the noise as if it were a belch—this sound that is wrung out of your soul.

You can see it. We walk stiff-backed and we don't swing our arms as we walk . . .

We are not crazy, so why do they do it? Because they fear us; we are dangerous. We fear nothing they can do to us, not even the drugs, the crucifixion.

No doubt there are those who need these drugs; do not get me wrong. I do not pretend to be a doctor. Those who need the drugs, who are ill, do *not* experience it the way we do. They know this, the prison regime knows this little trick.

It is like electroshock treatment: there are those who benefit by it. But administer this to a man who is healthy and does not require it for medical reasons and it becomes a form of torture. It is painful, a nightmare. Fifteen years ago it was used to punish prisoners.

When the captain and the pigs cannot discipline you, cannot intimidate and therefore hurt and punish you, *control* you, you are handed over to a "psychiatrist," who doesn't even look at you and who orders you placed on one of these drugs. You see, there is something wrong with your mind if you defy the worst "official" punishment a prison regime can legally dish up. That is their logic.

For *years* they have put me through this cycle over and over again: captain-doctor-broken-rule. Over and over. A pig pushes me, I *instinctively* push back, sometimes slug him. That starts it. Eventually I end up stammering like an idiot and staggering about—usually for six months to a year at a time—on the drugs, until finally I'm taken off the drugs and turned loose with the "normal" prisoners in the main prison population. I go along there until the next "incident" that leads to my "discipline," and once more the cycle begins, like a crazy carousel, a big "merry-go-round."

They know what they are doing, even if they never admit it to anyone. They will not even admit it to *me.* No one expects me to become a better man in prison. So why not say it: The purpose is to ruin me, ruin me completely. The purpose is to mark me, to stamp across my face the mark of this beast they call prison.

. . . I write with my blood because I have nothing else—and because these things are excessively painful to recall. It drains me.

. . . There is a saying: *The first cut is the deepest.* Do not believe that. The first cut is nothing. You can spit in my face once or twice and it is nothing. You can take something away that belongs to me and I can learn to live without it.

But you cannot spit in my face every day for ten thousand days; you can of take all that belongs to me, one thing at a time, until you have gotten down to reaching for my eyes, my voice, my hands, my heart. You cannot do this and say it is nothing.

I have been made oversensitive—my very *flesh* has been made to suffer sensations and longings I never had before. I have been chopped to pieces by a life of deprivation of sensations; by beatings so frequent I am now a piece of meat and bone; by lies and by drugs that attack my nervous system. I have had my mind turned into steel by the endless smelter of *time* in confinement.

I have been twisted by justice the way other men can be twisted by love . . .

Once I was taken from the Atlanta Federal Penitentiary to the Butner, North Carolina, Federal Correctional Institution for psychological experimentation—the result of being falsely accused of involvement in an almost-fatal knife assault on a prison guard.

At Butner, I was told almost immediately upon my arrival that an unnamed informer among the inmates had reported that I was planning to escape.

I was taken by about twenty guards and other employees into a special psychological observation cell. Butner was built from the ground up with architectural concepts almost futuristic in design. It is extremely modern and could easily be a set for a space-age movie.

The psychological observation cell I was taken into was designed like a fish tank (an aquarium)—except, of course, the glass was unbreakable. It is impossible to see or hear another human being, or to be seen or heard by anyone but the prison staff.

The floor was concrete and in the center was a drain, with a round grating over it, such as in a shower stall.

One steel slab sat on iron legs bolted to the floor. This was the "bed," and there was nothing else in the cell. There was a rubber mat on it about an inch thick.

I was stripped nude. I was forced to lie on the steel slab. Each of my ankles was chained to a corner of the bed-structure, and my wrists were chained over my head to the other two corners, so I was chained down in a complete spread-eagle position.

There were a few females on the staff (most were also U.S. Army personnel). This was in 1976—the latter part.

In order to urinate I had to twist my torso so that my penis would hang in a general direction over the side of the bed-structure, and the urine would cross the floor and go down the drain I described above.

I was hand-fed at each meal.

The day after I was chained down, several guards entered the cell and beat me with their fists all over my face, chest and stomach. I was choked manually and brought to the point—almost—of strangulation, and then they would remove their hands. My throat was blue with bruises caused this way.

I was chained—now I mean *iron* chains, not "leather restraints"—in this manner for ten days, and I was attacked three times in this period.

Finally the "medical technician" observed that the nerves in my arms were dying—the areas between wrists and elbows.

So about twenty guards came again. They unchained me and dressed me in nylon coveralls. As I was dressing I glanced in the window at my reflection and my face was black and both eyes swollen. I was covered with bruises.

They put me in handcuffs and leg-irons and took me to the regular segregation section. There only one of my hands was kept chained to the iron crossbar at the head of the bed. I could stand. It was at that time that I began writing *you*, in the hole, with one hand chained to my bed.

I was kept chained by one hand until I was rushed to the federal medical center in Missouri. My gall bladder was removed. I had gallstones, but the beatings had agitated the condition, and I learned that the tissue of my gall bladder had broken due to the jolts of the stones pressed against the organ.

. . . The guards form a loose gauntlet from your cell to the shower stall. You must cross the floor, a distance of about thirty yards. They look at you as if you are not there, but are alert to every move you make. They register your facial expression to see if you are anything but meek, *humble.* Anything else raises their hackles, and their mouths turn down at the corners and they ball up their hands into fists at their sides.

You are nude. The floor is wet from the prisoners before you who trailed it from the showers. There are also spots of blood, fresh.

You stare at the floor. You must slump your shoulders and drag your feet when you take steps. You must go slowly—but not too slowly. Your gait must be timid. You must not slip on the floor.

Fold your arms. Fold your arms behind your back. That is the best way to assure them you are incapable of harm. It is one of the postures of the meekly insane. Try to make them laugh at you. Cringe; that should do it.

Do not tell me you would not follow these instructions. You will be pounded to the floor otherwise. The guards are hired by the pound. They are Missouri rednecks from the Ozark regions. Alone with one or two, they are profoundly afraid of anyone. But six or seven are afraid of nothing one prisoner, naked, can do. It does not matter the least how strong or dangerous the prisoner is. Not there it doesn't.

Everything is framed by a soft blur that radiates outward into a vague fog. Your mind is not working any longer. You have no questions, either for yourself or others. This is because you are under the influence of a phenothiazene drug—any one (or combination) of ten or fifteen such drugs known by the brand names. Mixed with terrorism, it equals living death.

They all accomplish the same, but each has its little idiosyncrasy. If you have been

on regular dosages of Mellaril, your testicles will not produce sperm. If you masturbate—if you can somehow manage to accomplish a fantasy erection—you will experience at orgasm every sensation of tension and ejaculation you should experience, but with this difference: absolutely no substance issues from the ejaculation—no fluid at all, let alone semen.

If you do not know the cause of this, in your drugged state you can suffer an anxiety, a terror not easy to describe. It feeds your despair the fact that you have become sexually injured somehow.

Do not tell one of the two prison psychiatrists who come by your cell door each morning. When his face looms into view at the window of your door, when he smiles like a mechanical man and says "How are you this morning?"—flee into yourself. Smile cheerfully and blink your eyes when you say "Fine, fine"—or he will *double* your dosage. They punish you if you bother them, if you report complications.

I can understand how a man's mind can be turned to steel in prison—only in this way can he be equal to the hardships that surround him.

Uncle Ho wrote this poem in prison:

Without the cold and desolation of winter
There could not be the warmth and splendor
    of spring.
Hardships have tempered and strengthened
    me,
And turned my mind to steel.

I have never forgotten this in about thirteen or fourteen years.

. . . When I became poetic about a prisoner's mind turning to *steel,* I meant to convey the idea of a *will power* "steeled" in trials and hardships so profound that the prisoner's mental resolution, his powers of "iron logic" have been enhanced and not weakened. An opposite effect of torture. I hardly meant the prisoner lost his own humanity.

I know how to live through anything they could possibly dish up for me. I've been subjected to strip-cells, blackout cells, been chained to the floor and wall; I've lived through the beatings, of course; *every* drug science has invented to "modify" my behavior—I have endured. Starvation was once natural to me; I have no qualms about eating insects in my cell or living in my body wastes if it means survival. They've even *armed* psychopaths and put them in punishment cells with me to kill me, but I can control that. When they say "what doesn't destroy me makes me stronger," that is what they mean. But it's a mistake to equate the results with being *strong*. I'm extremely flexible, but I'm not *strong*. I'm weakened, in fact. I'm tenuous, shy, introspective, and suspicious of everyone. A loud noise or a false movement registers like a four-alarm fire in me. *But I'm not afraid—and that is strange,* because I care very much about someday being set free and I want to cry when I think that I'll never be free. I want to cry for my brothers I've spent a lifetime with. Someday I will leave them and never return.

. . . And after it is all done to you, after you have been robbed completely of fear and nothing anyone can threaten you with can constrain you—what point is served by keeping you in prison?

It is no longer *possible* to punish you. You have been rendered unpunishable. Madness is the only possible point in keeping you in prison. Or old age.

But for some perverse reason—I do not know *why*—I have never been twisted into insanity. I have come close to it many times—have in fact entered insanity—but it turns out that it was only an introductory affair. I always bounce back to sanity.

I have reached such a pass by now, I can sense derangement a long way off—I can see its most subtle expressions even in men not considered insane.

If I were a pole of a magnet and insanity a like pole, this image would express the matter. I cannot be pulled by it, but I know it by repulsion: by the force that repels me before I am even conscious it is there.

Study Questions

1. What aspects or characteristics of the prison system may allow the potential for the events described in this chapter to exist?

2. For what reason(s) do you think the author described the net effect of the abuses he experienced as "having things taken away" from him?

3. What do you think were the institutional purposes behind the various punishments that were described? In other words, what goals do you think the institutions were trying to accomplish? Do you consider these goals to be valid? Why or why not?

4. Ultimately, what does this article have to offer regarding the net effect of punishment in and of itself?

5. Does punishment—aside from incarceration or confinement in and of itself—have a place in the United States' prisons today? If no, why not? If yes, what forms should it take? How should it be used?

11
Prisons in Turmoil

John Irwin

The changes within the penal institution during the last two centuries have been fairly well documented, both in the greater literature and in the preceding pieces. Irwin examines three major periods in the development of the penal institution. The author first examines a composite of what he terms "the Big House." This amounted to an institutional warehouse in which the goal of doing time was of paramount concern for both administrators and residents. After World War II, however, the Big House evolved into the "Correctional Institution," a clear shift toward the goal of rehabilitation and reform. The indeterminate sentence, offender classification, and treatment were all major portions of this new format. Yet a third shift occurred, defined by Irwin as the "Contemporary Prison." The latter is characterized by severe racial divisions, violence, and gang influence. The reader is encouraged to consider possible next steps in penal institutional evolution when examining Irwin's ideas.

The Big House

Most of our ideas about men's prisons are mistaken because they fix on a type of prison—the Big House—that has virtually disappeared during the last twenty-five years. A dominant type of prison in this century, the Big House, emerged, spread, and prevailed, then generated images and illusions and, with considerable help from Hollywood, displayed these to the general society. It caught and held the attention of both the public and sociology. Its images and illusions linger on, surrounding contemporary prisons like a fog and blurring our sight. We must clear the air of false visions, distinguish the Big House as a type, and then move toward an analysis of succeeding types of prisons.

The Big House developed during a long and important phase in the varying history of the prison in the United States. This phase began early in this century and lasted into the 1940s or 1950s and even into the present in some states. Long before this era, the prison had outgrown its infancy as a penitentiary, where the prison planners intended that prisoners be kept in quiet solitude, reflecting penitently on their sins in order that they might cleanse and transform themselves. It also had passed through a half century during which prisoners spent their time in "hard labor," working in prison rock quarries or in profit-making industrial and agricultural enterprises. Eventually, federal legislation and union power forced most convict labor out of the public sector. More recently, prisons in the East, Midwest, and West were touched (most lightly, some belatedly, and a few not at all) by the humanitarian reforms of the "progressive era." Cruel corporal punishment such as flogging, beating, water torture, shackling of inmates to cell walls or hanging them by their thumbs, entombment in small cribs and lone solitary confinement as well as extreme corruption in the appointment of personnel and in the administration of the prison were largely eliminated. The Big House phase followed these reforms.

Although Big Houses appeared in most states, there were many notable exceptions. Many state prison systems never emerged from cruelty and corruption. In a few states, guards unofficially but regularly used brutality and even executions to control prisoners. Some prison administrations continued to engage prisoners in very hard labor throughout the first half of the twentieth century. Even in the eastern, midwestern, and western states where the Big House predominated, there were many residues of earlier phases; silence systems endured through the 1940s. But in most states outside the South, there emerged a type of prison that was relatively free of corporal punishment and that did not engage most prisoners in hard labor. This prison predominated until the "rehabilitative ideal," a new theory of reform, altered penology and the correctional institution appeared. Since the Big House has been the source of most of our ideas about prisons, I shall construct a composite picture of it and then consider some of the exceptions to the type. This will help us to understand its modern progeny.

Physical Description

The Big House was a walled prison with large cell blocks that contained stacks of three or more tiers of one- or two-man cells. On the average, it held 2,500 men. Sometimes a single cell block housed over 1,000 prisoners in six tiers of cells. . . . Overall, cell blocks were harsh worlds of steel and concrete, of unbearable heat and stench in the summer and chilling cold in the winter, of cramped quarters, and of constant droning, shouting, and clanking noise.

The other prominent physical features of the Big House were the yard, the wall, the mess hall, the administration building, the shops, and the industries. The yard, formed by cell blocks and the wall, was a drab place. . . . Better-appointed yards had a few recreational facilities: a baseball diamond, perhaps basketball courts, tables and benches, and handball courts, which often were improvised by using the walls of the cell blocks. The mess hall had rows of tables and benches and invariably was too small to seat the entire population at one time. The thick granite wall encircled the place and, with its gun towers, symbolized the meaning of the Big House.

This granite, steel, cement, and asphalt monstrosity stood as the state's most extreme form of punishment, short of the death penalty. It was San Quentin in California, Sing Sing in New York, Stateville in Illinois, Jackson in Michigan, Jefferson City in Missouri, Canon City in Colorado, and so on. It was the place of banishment and punishment to which convicts were "sent up." Its major characteristics were isolation, routine, and monotony. . . .

Social Organization

The Big House was like all prisons, a place where convicts lived and constructed a world. This world had divisions and strata, special informal rules and meaning, set of enterprises. Some of the patterns and divisions were built upon external characteristics. The prisoners came from both the city and the country. In Clemmer's study in the 1930s it was about half and half. By and large, they were the poorer and less educated persons, those from the wrong side of the tracks. Many of them were drifters, persons who floated from state to state, looking for work and, when they failed to find it, stealing and then brushing against "the law." About half previously had been in a prison or reform school. The most frequent criminal type was the thief, a criminal who searched for the "big score"—a safe burglary or armed robbery. But most of the prisoners never came close to a big score, and those who were serving a sentence for theft, which was over half the population, were typically convicted of very minor crimes. Clemmer noted that most prisoners were "amateurish and occasional offenders. Most typical of burglars are those who break into a house or store and carry away loot or money seldom exceeding eighty dollars—and not those who tunnel under a street and steal sixty thousand dollars worth of gems from a jewelry store."[1]

Many prisoners were black or other nonwhite races, but most in the Big Houses outside the South were white. Racial prejudice, discrimination, and segregation prevailed. Blacks (and sometimes other nonwhite prisoners) were housed in special sections, in special cell blocks, or at least with cell partners of the same race; and blacks held menial jobs. By rule or informal patterns, blacks and whites sat in separate sections in the mess hall. In fact, in all facets of prison life, patterns of segregation and distance were maintained.

White prisoners kept blacks and, to some extent, other nonwhites "in their place." They did not accept them as equals in the informal social life of the prison and directed constant hate and occasional violence at them. . . .

According to the formal routine, the prisoners rose early; hurriedly ate breakfast; returned to their cells for one of the four or five daily counts; proceeded to work, school, or the yard for a day of idleness; hurriedly ate lunch; counted; went back to work, school, or idleness; hurriedly ate dinner; and returned to their cells for the night. After count, they read, wrote letters or literary works, pursued hobbies, talked to other prisoners, listened to the radio on their ear phones (when this innovation reached the prison), and then went to sleep when the lights were turned off. . . .

This was the formal, or more visible, routine. Within this general outline a complex, subtle, informal prisoner world with several subworlds was also operating. It pivoted around the convict code, a prison adaptation of the thieves' code. Thieves were not the majority, but they were the most frequent criminal type, and their strong commitment to thieves' values, their communication network—which extended through the thieves' world, inside and out—and their loyalty to other thieves gave them the upper hand in prison. . . .

The central rule in the thieves' code was "thou shalt not snitch." In prison, thieves converted this to the dual norm of "do not rat on another prisoner" and "do your own time." Thieves also were obliged by their code to be cool and tough, that is, to maintain respect and dignity; not to show weakness to help other thieves; and to leave most other prisoners alone. Their code dominated the Big House and generally it could

be translated into these rules: Do not inform, do not openly interact or cooperate with the guards or the administration, and do your own time. These rules helped to produce a gap of hostility and unfriendliness between prisoners and guards, a hierarchy of prisoners, a system of mutual aid among a minority of prisoners, and patterns of exploitation among others.

The prisoners divided themselves into a variety of special types. In addition to the yeggs, "Johnsons," "people," "right guys," or "regulars"—thieves and persons whom they accepted as trustworthy—there were several types more indigenous to the prison. There were gamblers, who were involved in controlling prison resources, and prison "politicians" and "merchants," supplying and exchanging commodities. There were prison "queens," who openly presented themselves as homosexuals, and "punks," who were considered to have been "turned out"—that is, made into homosexuals by other prisoners or by the prison experience. There was a variety of prison "toughs," persons who were deeply and openly hostile to the prison administration, the conventional society, and most other prisoners and who displayed a readiness to employ violence against others. These types ranged from the less predictable and less social "crazies" to the more predictable and clique-oriented "hard rocks" or "tush hogs." There was the "character," who continuously created humorous derision through his dress, language, story-telling ability, or general behavior. There were the "masses," who broke into the subtypes of "assholes" or "hoosiers," lower- and working-class persons having little or no criminal skill and earning low respect, and "square johns," persons who were not viewed as criminals by the rest of the population and were oriented to conventional society. There was a variety of "dingbats," who were considered to be crazy, but harmless. Finally, there were "rapos," persons serving sentences for sexual acts such as incest and child molesting, which were repulsive to most prisoners, and "stool pigeons," "rats," or "snitches," who supplied information about other prisoners to authorities.

These types were arranged in a hierarchy of prestige, power, and privilege. At the top of the stack were the right guys, through their propensity to cooperate with each other, their prestige as thieves, and their presentation of coolness and toughness. . . . Very close to the top were the merchants, politicians, and gamblers. They occupied this high position because they largely controlled the scarce prison resources. Characters, when they were accomplished, were awarded a special position with considerable respect and popularity, but not much direct power. Down the ladder were the toughs, who had to be respected because they were a constant threat. The cliques of hard rocks occasionally hurt or killed someone, though seldom anyone with prestige and power. The crazies, who were often very dangerous, were treated with extreme caution, but were avoided and excluded as much as possible. In the middle were the masses who were ignored by the leaders, stayed out of the prison's informal world, and restricted their social activities to small friendship groups or remained "loners." Below them were the queens, punks, rats, and rapos, the latter being at the very bottom of the pile. On the outside of all informal prisoner activities were the dingbats, who were ignored by all.

Most prisoners followed one of three prison careers. The most frequent was that of just doing time. This was the style of the thief and of most other prisoners who shared the thief's primary concern of getting out of prison with maximum dispatch and minimum pain. Doing time meant, above all, avoiding trouble that would place a prisoner in danger or lengthen or intensify his punishment. But in addition, doing time involved avoiding "hard time." To avoid hard time, prisoners stayed active in sports, hobbies, or reading; secured as many luxuries as possible without bringing on trouble; and formed a group of close friends with whom to share resources and leisure hours and to rely on for help and protection.

Thieves who established this style generally confined their group associations to other thieves. Since they had prestige and power in the prison world, however, they occasionally entered into general prisoner affairs, particularly when they were trying to secure luxuries or favors for themselves or friends. Most of the masses followed the pattern of doing time established by thieves, but their friendship groups tended not to be so closely knit and they tended not to enter into the general prison social activities.

Some prisoners, particularly the indigenous prison types, oriented themselves more completely to the prison and tended to construct a total existence there. Donald Cressey and I once described the style of adaptation of convicts who

seek positions of power, influence and sources of information whether these men are called "shots," "politicians," "merchants," "hoods," "toughs," "gorillas," or something else. A job as secretary to the Captain or Warden, for example, gives an aspiring prisoner information and consequent power, and enables him to influence the assignment or regulation of other inmates. In the same way, a job which allows the incumbent to participate in a racket, such as clerk in the kitchen storeroom where he can steal and sell food, is highly desirable to a man oriented to the convict subculture. With a steady income of cigarettes, ordinarily the prisoner's medium of exchange, he may assert a great deal of influence and purchase these things which are symbols of status among persons oriented to the convict subculture. Even if there is not a well-developed medium of exchange, he can barter goods acquired in his position for equally desirable goods possessed by other convicts. These include information and such things as specially starched, pressed and tailored prison clothing, fancy belts, belt buckles or billfolds, special shoes or any other type of dress which will set him apart and will indicate that the prisoner has both the influence to get the goods and the influence necessary to keep them and display them despite prison rules which outlaw doing so.[2]

Many of the persons who occupied these roles and made a world out of prison—that is, followed the strategy sometimes referred to by prisoners as "jailing"—were individuals who had long experiences with jails and prisons beginning in their early teens or even earlier. Actually, they were more familiar with prison than with outside social worlds. . . .

One last strategy followed by a small number of prisoners I labeled "gleaning" in a later study of the California prison system.[3] An old style, it must be included in the description of the Big House. Gleaning involved taking advantage of any resource available to better themselves, to improve their minds, or to obtain skills that would be useful on the outside. In trying to improve themselves, prisoners in Big Houses read, sought formal education through the prison's elementary and high schools (when these existed) and university correspondence courses, and learned trades in the few vocational training programs or in prison job assignments. In addition, they tried to improve themselves in other ways—by increasing social skills and physical appearance. Generally, in gleaning, prisoners attempted to equip themselves for life after prison.

To a great extent, Big House homosexual patterns were a form of prison improvisation. With no possibility for heterosexual contacts, some prisoners performed homosexual acts as "inserters," although they would not do this on the outside. In addition, many young, weaker, less initiated, and perhaps effeminate prisoners were tricked or forced into the role of "insertee" (that is, they were turned out). Often they were trapped in this role by the knowledge that they had succumbed in the past, and after years of performing as a punk, they developed homosexual identities and con-

tinued as homosexuals even after release. Finally, some prisoners, particularly prisoners who were thoroughly immersed in the informal prisoner world—that is, who jailed—performed the role of "wolf" or "jocker." A few of these individuals, after an extended period of continued homosexual activities (ostensibly as the inserter, but actually as both the inserter and insertee in many cases), developed a preference for homosexual relationships and continued in their masculine homosexual role on the outside.

Stupefaction. When I was in the Los Angeles County Jail in 1952, waiting to be sentenced to prison, I met a "four-time loser" who was going back to Folsom, the state's long-term Big House. He advised me, "Don't let them send you to Folsom. It's the easiest place to do time but, man, you leave something there you never get back." He was alluding to Folsom's impact on prisoners' mentality, which prisoners referred to as "going stir." I think the term *stupefaction* catches the sense of this expression. The dictionary defines stupefaction as the "state of being stupefied; insensibility of mind or feeling." Serving time in a Big House meant being pressed into a slow-paced, rigid routine; cut off from outside contacts and social worlds; denied most ordinary human pleasures and stimulations; and constantly forced to contain anger and hostility. Many persons were able to maintain their spirit under these conditions, and some were even vitalized by the challenge. But most prisoners were somewhat stupefied by it. They learned to blunt their feelings, turn inward, construct fantasy worlds for themselves, and generally throttle their intellectual, emotional, and physical life. In the extreme they fell into a stupor. Victor Nelson describes an old con:

> A trustee in a suit of striped overalls was standing with his arms folded lazily against the handle of the rake, his head resting dejectedly on his arms, his whole attitude that of a man who had worked all

day and was very tired although it was only about nine o'clock of a cool spring morning. He seemed almost in a coma. There was an expression of utter indifference on his face and his eyes were glazed with absentmindedness. He was, although I did not know it then, a living example of the total, final, devastating effect of imprisonment upon the human being.[4]

The Big House did not reform prisoners or teach many persons crime. It embittered many. It stupefied thousands.

The Correctional Institution

After World War II, many states replaced Big Houses with correctional institutions, which, when they were newly constructed, looked different, were organized differently, housed different types of prisoners, and nurtured different prison social worlds. Importantly, they had a different effect on prisoners. They spread and became the dominant type of prison in the 1950s, if not in numbers, at least in the minds of penologists. And, like Big Houses, their images live on, blurring our view of contemporary prisons. Consequently, we must distinguish this type of prison to understand the modern violent prison. The correctional institution's emergence was related to broad changes in our society. Briefly, the postwar United States—prosperous, urbanized, and mobile—confronted a new set of pressing social problems. Hard times, natural disasters (floods, droughts, and tornadoes), epidemics, illiteracy, and the "dangerous classes," had been updated to or replaced by poverty, mental health, family disorganization, race relations, juvenile delinquency, and urban crime. Americans faced these with a fundamentally altered posture. The Great Depression and World War II had moved them from their isolationist and individualist position, and they accepted, even demanded, government intervention into conditions that they believed should and could be changed.

Along with all organs of government, agencies whose official function was intervention into domestic social problems grew, gained power, and proliferated. Peopling these agencies and leading the large social services expansion were old and new professionals: physicians, psychiatrists, psychologists, social workers, urban planners, sociologists, and a new group of specialists in penology. The latter group—a growing body of college-educated employees and administrators of prisons, parole, and probation and a few academic penologists whom I will hereafter refer to collectively as "correctionalists"—went after the apparently mushrooming crime problem. These correctionalists were convinced and were able to convince many state governments and interested segments of the general population that they could reduce crime by curing criminals of their criminality. . . .

The innovative penologists kept abreast of the developments in the new social sciences and began constructing a philosophy of penology based on the concept that criminal behavior was caused by identifiable and changeable forces. This led them to the conclusion that the primary purpose of imprisonment should be "rehabilitation," a new form of reformation based on scientific methods. This new penology is generally referred to as the rehabilitative ideal. . . .

The nation's leading penologists agreed as early as 1870, when they formed the National Prison Association, to establish rehabilitation as the primary purpose of prisons and to alter prison routines in order to implement rehabilitation (particularly to introduce indeterminate sentencing). At that time, however, the society was not ready for what appeared to be a nonpunitive approach to crime. Until World War II and the changes described above had occurred, the architects of rehabilitation experimented in juvenile institutions like Elmira, New York, where Zebulon Brockway introduced a full rehabilitative program, and they slipped bits and pieces of rehabilitation into Big Houses—for example, a more elaborate classification system and a small department of rehabilitation. After the war, receiving an okay from the public and various state governments and an infusion of more funds and more college-trained employees, the innovators in penology created the new prison, the correctional institution. In some states, such as Wisconsin and Minnesota, this meant reorganizing the staff structures and introducing new programs into old prisons, but in others, such as California and New York, it also meant constructing many new facilities. In both cases, the correctionalists organized the prisons around three procedures: indeterminate sentencing, classification, and the treatment that they had been developing for decades.

The Indeterminate Sentencing System

According to the early planners of the rehabilitative prison, prison administrators should have the discretionary power to release the prisoner when the administrators or their correctional experts determine that he is cured of criminality. Many early supporters of the rehabilitative ideal, such as Karl Menninger, advocated sentences of zero to life for all offenders so that correctional professionals could concentrate on treating criminals and releasing them when their illness (criminality) was cured. In actuality, no prison system in the United States or any other place achieved this extreme, but California, after thirty-five years of developing an indeterminate sentence routine through legislation and administrative policies, came the closest. After 1950, the Adult Authority—the official name of the California parole board—exercised the power to determine an individual's sentence within statutory limits for a particular crime, to set a parole date before this sentence was finished, and, at any time until the fixed sentence was completed, to restore the sentence back to its statutory

maximum or any other length within the margins. It exercised these powers with no requirements for due process or review of decisions. The statutory limits in California—for example, one to ten years for grand larceny, one to fifteen for forgery and second-degree burglary, one to life for second-degree robbery, and five to life for first-degree robbery—gave the Adult Authority large margins within which to exercise their discretion.

Under this system, prisoners remained unsure of how much time they would eventually serve until they completed their sentence. While in prison, they appeared before the Adult Authority annually until the Adult Authority set their release date, invariably within six months of their last board appearance. While individuals were on parole or awaited release, the Adult Authority could refix their sentences back to the maximum and reactivate the process of annual board appearances for violations of the rules of the prison or conditions of parole.

Board appearances were the most important milestones in the inmates' imprisonment, and the Adult Authority had full power over their lives. According to the ideal, parole boards should use this power to release prisoners when they were rehabilitated. This presupposed, however, that the correctionalists had procedures for identifying and changing criminal characteristics, which they did not, and that parole boards had procedures for determining when these changes had occurred, which they did not. It also presupposed that rehabilitation of the offender was parole boards' major concern, which it was not. Even in the early planning stages the advocates of indeterminate sentencing intended the discretionary powers to be used to control prisoners and detain indefinitely those who were viewed as dangerous by various authorities (district attorneys, police chiefs, and influential citizens). . . . In addition, although they never admitted this, the advocates of indeterminate sentence systems understood and appreciated that its discretionary powers permitted them to give shorter sentences, or even no sentences, to influence individuals. So, in actual practice, while professing to balance the seriousness of a crime and rehabilitative criteria, parole boards used their discretionary powers to enforce conformity to prison rules and parole routines, avoid criticism from outside authorities and citizens, award higher social status, and express personal prejudice and whim. . . .

Classification

An ideal correctional institution primarily organized to rehabilitate prisoners would require an elaborate, systematic diagnostic and planning process that determined the nature of the individual's criminality and prescribed a cure. Through the decades before the 1950s, the creators of the rehabilitative approach steadily developed more complex classification systems, ostensibly to accomplish these ends. Theoretically, the finished version that they incorporated in the new postwar correctional institutions operated as follows. First, a team of professionals—psychologists, case workers, sociologists, vocational counselors, and psychiatrists—tested the criminal, interviewed him and gathered life history information. Then a team of these correctionalists formed an initial classification committee and reviewed the tests and evaluations, planned the prisoner's therapeutic routine, assigned him to a particular prison, and recommended particular rehabilitative programs for him. In the final stage, classification committees at particular prisons periodically reviewed the prisoner's progress, recommended changes in programs, and sometimes transferred him to another prison.

The classification committees in the first correctional institutions tended to follow this ideal in appearance, but they actually operated quite differently. First, the social sciences never supplied them with valid diagnostic methods and effective cures for criminality. Second, the committees never abandoned control and other management concerns, which classification systems had acquired in the decades when they operated in Big Houses. . . .

Treatment

A variety of effective treatment strategies would complete the ideal correctional institution. As stressed above, none were discovered. What actually existed in the correctional institutions in the 1950s was care and treatment. An administrative branch that coexisted with the custody branch, planned and administered three types of treatment programs—therapeutic, academic, and vocational—and generated reports on prisoners' progress for the institutional classification committees and the parole board.

The most common therapeutic program was group counseling, which, because it was led by staff persons with little or no training in clinical procedures, was a weak version of group therapy. Originally, the plan was to hire psychiatrists and clinical psychologists, but the pay was too small and the working conditions too undesirable to attract those professionals. Some persons with social work training, who were willing to work for the lower salaries, filled in some of the gaps, but in states such as California, where dozens of group leaders were needed, even their numbers were too small. So staff persons with no formal training in psychology led many, if not most, groups in correctional institutions. Most prisoners participated in group counseling programs, because they were led to believe by parole board members and the treatment staff that they would not be granted a parole unless they participated. Also, they believed that unacceptable traits or attitudes revealed in the sessions would be reported by the staffers, and this would reduce their chances of being paroled early. In addition, many prisoners had a strong distaste for discussing sensitive, personal issues and disparaged other prisoners for doing so. The result was that group counseling sessions were invariably very bland. Few prisoners took them seriously or participated sincerely or vigorously.

. . . [F]ew prisoners received individual treatment from psychiatrists or psychologists. Toward the end of the 1950s, the more persistent correctionalists experimented with "milieu therapy" by attempting to convert prisons or units within prisons into "therapeutic communities." More recently, contemporary correctionalists have introduced more intense therapeutic forms, such as "behavior modification" and "attack therapy." However, group counseling, which is inexpensive and easier to implement, was the dominant form of therapy when correctional institutions were at their peak. The academic and vocational education programs had more substance than the therapy treatment programs. All the innovative correctional institutions had formed elementary and high school programs in the 1950s, and many had formed links with universities and were making correspondence courses available to some prisoners. All correctional institutions attempted vocational training. In California during the 1950s, those who desired and were able to enter the programs (there were fewer openings than prisoners) could receive training in cooking, baking, butchering, dry cleaning, shoe repair, sewing machine repair, auto mechanics, auto body and fender repair, small motor repair, sheet metal machining, printing, plumbing, painting, welding, and nursing. All these training programs had inherent weaknesses, and they seldom fully equipped a prisoner for a position in the trade. One of these weaknesses was that some training programs, such as baking and cooking, were appendages of prison housekeeping enterprises and were insufficiently related to outside vocational enterprises. In other cases, the equipment, the techniques, and the knowledge of the instructor were obsolete.

Indeterminate sentences, classification, and treatment were the actualization of the rehabilitative ideal in correctional institutions. As the descriptions indicate, they fell short of the ideal. The reasons for this are varied. In spite of the intentions and efforts of the most sincere visionaries of rehabilitation, they were never able to realize their plans. The public and most government policy makers continued to demand that prisons first accomplish their other assigned tasks: punishment, control, and restraint of prisoners. In addition, the new correctional institutions were not created in a vacuum but planned in ongoing prison systems which had long traditions, administrative hierarchies, divisions, informal social worlds, and special subcultures among the old staff. The new correctionalists were never able to rid the prison systems of the old regime, though often they tried; and the old timers, many of whom were highly antagonistic to the new routines, resisted change, struggled to maintain as much control as possible, and were always successful in forcing an accommodation between old and new patterns. So correctional institutions were never totally, or even mainly, organized to rehabilitate prisoners. Nevertheless, an entirely new prison resulted from the rehabilitative ideal and through its rhetoric, which correctionalists used to defend new programs and disguise other purposes, achieved a temporary unity in the ranks. This type of prison spread throughout the United States, replacing many, perhaps most, Big Houses. In many ways it was a great improvement, and some correctionalists still look on it as the best we can hope for. However, it contained many unnecessary inhumanities, injustices, and idiocies, though for many years these were less visible. Eventually, its own flaws and certain external social changes destroyed it (or at least damaged it beyond repair).

To complete the description of the correctional institution, I shall focus on Soledad, which was opened in 1952, which was planned and operated as an exemplary correctional institution, and in which I served five years during its golden age. All correctional institutions, certainly, had some unique features, but Soledad during the 1950s is a superior example of the type.

Soledad: The Formal Structure

Soledad prison was part of California's very large investment in the new penology. The state emerged from World War II with a rapidly expanding population, an apparently rising crime rate, relatively full state coffers, and a liberal citizenry. In a few years the state allocated massive sums for higher education, highway construction, and prisons. In the 1950s, in addition to two new "guidance centers," the state constructed six new men's prisons, a new women's prison, and a special narcotics treatment center. Soledad, the first of the men's prisons to be completed after the war, was planned, constructed, and operated as one of the essential parts in a large rehabilitative correctional organization. It was labeled California Training Facility and was intended as the prison for younger, medium risk, more trainable prisoners.

Soledad's physical structure radically departs from that of the Big Houses. It has no granite wall; instead, circling the prison is a high fence with gun towers situated every few hundred feet and nestled in the corners. The nine cell blocks stem over a long hall. Two relatively pleasant dining rooms with tile floors and octagonal oak tables, a spacious library, a well equipped hospital, a laundry, an education building, a gym, several shops, and the administration building connect to this hall. In fact, the entire prison community operates in and around the hall, and prisoners can (and many of them do) live day after day without ever going outside.

Each cell block (called a "wing") had a "day room" jutting off the side at the ground level, and all the inside walls in the prison were painted in pastel colors—pale blue, pale green light yellow, and tan. All blocks originally had one-man cells though many were assigned two occupants later. All cells except those in one small wing used for new prisoners and for segregation and isolation (O wing) had solid doors with a small, screened inspection window. The cells in all cell blocks (except O wing) were in three tiers around the outside of the wings, so each cell had an outside window. Instead of bars, the windows had small panes with heavy metal moldings. All cells originally had a bunk, a desk, and a chair. The close security cells also had a sink and toilet. In the five medium-security cell blocks, the prisoners carried keys to their own cells. A row of cells could be locked by a guard's setting a locking bar, but in the 1950s, except for regular counts and special lockdowns, prisoners in medium-security wings entered and left the cells at their own discretion.

The formal routine at Soledad was more relaxed than in most Big Houses. On a weekday the lights came on at 7:00 A.M., but there was no bell nor whistle. The individual "wing officers" released their cell blocks one at a time for breakfast. A prisoner could eat or could sleep another hour before work. The food was slightly better than average prison fare, which is slightly inferior to average institution fare and ranks well below state hospitals and the armed services. One pleasant aspect of the dining routine was that prisoners were allowed to linger for ten or twenty minutes and drink unlimited amounts of coffee. After breakfast, prisoners reported to their work or school assignment. Before lunch there was a count, during which all prisoners had to be in their cells or at a designated place where guards counted them, then lunch, a return to work or school, and another count before dinner. During the day the cell blocks were open, and prisoners could roam free, from their blocks, through the hall, to the large yard and its few recreational facilities, and to the library or gym. After dinner the wing officer kept the front door to the cell block locked except at scheduled unlocks for school, gym, library, and, during the summer, "night yard."

On the weekends, prisoners were idle, except for kitchen and a few hospital and maintenance workers. The cell blocks, gym, yard, and library remained open all day. Although they could visit on any day, most visitors came on weekends. The visiting room had clusters of padded chairs around coffee tables, and prisoners could sit close to and even touch their visitors, a relatively pleasant visiting arrangement. On Sunday the highlight of the week occurred: two showings of a three- or four-year-old Hollywood movie.

A few rules were perceived by prisoners as unnecessary, arbitrary, and irksome—rules such as, "no standing on tiers" or "prisoners must walk double file on one side of the hall." But in general, Soledad had a more relaxed and pleasant formal routine than most prisons.

The rehabilitative aspect of Soledad was prominent. As its official name implied, it offered a broad selection of vocational training programs. It also had a good elementary and high school program, through which a prisoner could receive a diploma from the local outside school district. Rounding out rehabilitation was the group counseling program in which the Adult Authority, classification committees, and prisoners' counselors coerced prisoners to participate (if they did not, they were warned that they would not receive a parole). One psychiatrist treated some individuals, but usually only the few whom the Adult Authority referred for special reasons, such as a history of violent or sex crimes. The counseling groups met once a week, and the majority of inmates attended them. In the second half of the 1950s, the treatment staff introduced more intensive counseling programs in which the groups met daily. But weekly group counseling led by relatively untrained guards and other staff members was the total therapy component for most prisoners.

Informal Life. Soledad, like all correctional institutions, developed different group structures, intergroup relationships, and informal systems of social control from those in Big Houses. Some of these differences were a result of changes in the prisoner population, the most important being the shift in ethnic and racial balance. In California the percentages of non-white prisoners had been increasing steadily and, by 1950, had passed 40 percent: about 25 percent Chicano and 15 percent black. This shift towards nonwhite prisoners was occurring in most large eastern, midwestern, and western prison systems. The era of total white dominance in Big Houses was rapidly approaching an end.

More and more Tejanos—Mexicans raised in Texas—were coming to California and its prisons. The Tejanos were different from Los Angeles's Chicanos, who made up the largest group of Mexicans. More Tejanos were drug addicts; in fact, they introduced heroin to the Los Angeles Chicanos. They spoke more Spanish and Calo, the Spanish slang that developed in the United States, and were generally less Americanized. The two groups did not like each other, kept apart in jail, and sometimes fought.

All the Chicanos had experienced extreme prejudice throughout their lives, particularly in the public schools, and were somewhat hostile toward white prisoners. However, many Los Angeles Chicanos had associated with whites, particularly white criminals with whom they had engaged in crime. Heroin, which was spreading from the Tejanos through the Los Angeles Mexican neighborhoods and then into some white neighborhoods, intermixed Chicanos and Anglos even more. While some white prisoners disliked Chicanos, in general they feared and respected them, because whites believed that Chicanos would quickly employ violence when insulted or threatened. Consequently, between the two ethnic groups there was enmity, mixed with respect on the part of whites, but many individuals from both groups crossed over this barrier and maintained friendly relationships.

Black prisoners also divided into two groups: persons raised in Los Angeles or the San Francisco Bay Area and others who had migrated to California from the South and Southwest. Here, too, were prejudice and hostility between whites and blacks, but there were many whites and blacks who had intermixed and cooperated in criminal activities. This was more likely to have occurred between urban blacks and whites. So again, there was a gap between the two racial groups, but considerable crossing over the gap. The gap between Chicanos and blacks was wider, because Chicanos were more deeply prejudiced and hostile than whites were toward blacks.

Still over half of Soledad's population in the 1950s was white. Most white prisoners were working-class and lower-class youths raised in Los Angeles, San Diego, and the San Francisco Bay Area. There was a smaller group of whites from the small cities and towns in California: Fresno, Bakersfield, Modesto, and Stockton. Even though most whites in the prison were descendants of migrants from Kansas, Missouri, Illinois, Oklahoma, Arkansas, and Texas, the heartland of the United States, the prisoners from the smaller towns carried many more rural traditions and were labeled "Okie" in the prisons. The remainder of the white prisoners were a conglomeration of middle-class persons, drifters, servicemen, and state raised youths (individuals who had been raised by state agencies, including the California Youth Authority).

Members of all these different ethnic segments tended to form separate groups and social worlds in Soledad. This differentiation was further complicated by the divisions based on criminal orientations, which were more numerous than in past eras. The thieves were present, but their numbers were diminishing. This system of theft had been carried to California from the East and Midwest, but it was not crossing racial lines and was being replaced by drug addiction among whites. The thieves present in Soledad were very cliquish, practiced

mutual aid, did not trust other prisoners, but were respected by them. However, they were not able to dominate the informal world as they had in Big Houses.

A new deviant subculture, that of the "dope fiend" (heroin addict), was spreading in California and became very prominent in the California prisons during the 1950s. Drug addiction brought to Los Angeles by the Tejanos had metastasized in the late 1940s and early 1950s, and most of the Chicanos and a large number of the young, working-class and lower-class white and black prisoners from Los Angeles, San Diego, San Francisco, and Oakland carried the patterns of this special subculture. In the era of the Big House, other prisoners, particularly thieves, did not trust dope fiends, because they believed that drug addicts were weak and would inform under pressure. But in Soledad and other California prisons in the 1950s, dope fiends were the emergent group, had respect, and, in fact, were rather snobbish. While in prison, perhaps in compensation for their individualistic, antisocial, passive, and often rapacious lifestyle while addicted, they were very affable, sociable, active, and verbal. At work and leisure they tended to form small cliques and spend their time telling drug stories. Many of them were involved in intellectual anti-artistic activities.

A smaller group of "weed heads" or "grasshoppers" (marijuana users) were present in Soledad. This was before the psychedelic movement and weed heads were urban lower-class or working-class white, Chicano, and black youths who participated in a cultlike subculture; whose carriers lived in "far-out pads," wore "sharp threads," rode around in "groovy shorts," listened to "cool" jazz, sipped exotic liqueurs or wine coolers, and generally were "cool." In prison, weed heads continued to be cool and cliquish. Other prisoners, particularly dope fiends, thought they were silly and stayed away from them. . . .

Most black prisoners who had engaged in systematic theft were not thieves, but "hustlers." Segregation and prejudice cut blacks off from the older tradition of theft. When they migrated to the northern, midwestern, and western cities, blacks developed their own system of thievery, which was fashioned after patterns of early white con men—flimflammers—who toured the United States in the late nineteenth and early twentieth centuries. These flimflammers victimized all categories of rural people and imparted the styles of "short con" to blacks. In the cities, many blacks built on these original lessons and became hustlers. In general, hustling meant making money through one's wits and conversation rather than through force or threat. It involved short con games such as "greasy pig," "three card monte," and "the pigeon drop" [and] rackets such as the numbers, and pimping.

Like the other types of criminals, hustlers formed their own groups. Conversation was a major part of their style of theft, and conversation—"shucking and jiving," bragging about hustling, pimping, and the sporting life—was their major prison activity. An ex-convict describes the activities of a black prisoner:

> he was off into that bag—Iceberg Slim [a famous pimp who wrote a successful paperback description of pimping] and all that—wearing their Cadillacs around the big yard.[5]

A special deviant orientation shared by at least 10 percent of the population at Soledad was that of the state-raised youth. Many prisoners had acquired this special orientation in the youth prisons; it involved the propensity to form tightly knit cliques, a willingness to threaten and actually to engage in violence for protection or for increases in power, prestige, and privilege, and a preference for prison patterns and styles as opposed to those on the outside. Many state-raised youths formed gangs in adult prisons, stole from and bullied other prisoners, and participated in the prison sexual world of jockers, queens, and punks.

Most prisoners were not committed "criminals." At least a quarter of the young people in prison in the 1950s were working- and lower-class people who had been "hanging out" in their neighborhoods or drifting around the country, looking for work and a niche for themselves. They had been involved in crime only irregularly and haphazardly, and usually it was very unsophisticated crime. They were often confused about the world and their place in it and saw themselves as "fuck-ups" or losers.

. . . These fuck-ups were the masses in the prison. In the Big Houses they were the hoosiers and in Soledad the assholes, and they were pushed aside and demeaned by other criminals. However, Soledad was a more heterogeneous prison, and the disparagement and exclusion were not as intense or complete. So fuck-ups occasionally rose to positions of power (to the extent that these existed), joined groups of other criminally oriented prisoners, and even began to identify themselves as dope fiends, heads, or hustlers. Thieves were more careful about associating with assholes, but on occasion one might befriend and tutor an inexperienced young person.

In addition to fuck-ups, there were many prisoners, mostly white, who had committed only one felony or a few serious crimes and did not consider themselves, nor were they considered by others, as criminals. Other prisoners referred to them as square johns and ignored them unless they wanted to take advantage of their knowledge or skills. (Many of these square johns were better educated, and a few of them were professionals.) In general, however, they were ignored, and they kept to themselves. They either served their time as isolates or formed very small friendship groups with other square johns.

This subcultural mix of prisoners resisted the establishment of a single overriding convict code or the emergence of a single group of leaders. The old convict code did not have the unanimity and force that it had in the Big House. The number of thieves who formerly established and maintained this code was too small, and other criminals—hustlers, dope fiends, heads—with other codes of conduct competed for status and power in the informal realm.

The administrative regime influenced by the rehabilitative ideal inhibited the development of the exploitative, accommodative system, described by Sykes and Messinger, in which politicians' power depended on their control over certain enterprises, allowing them to make important decisions and obtain scarce material, and on their monopoly on information. In this era of professionalism, the staff was much more deeply involved in the day-to-day running of the prison. There was a partially successful attempt to prevent convicts from controlling the prison, and much more information flowed between staff and prisoners. Unlike his counterpart in most Big Houses, a captain's clerk could not autonomously transfer prisoners from one cell to another, squash disciplinary reports, transfer disliked guards to the night watch in a distant gun tower, or place friends on extra movie unlocks. Similarly, the storeroom clerk could not confiscate 20 percent of the prison's coffee, sugar, and dried fruit supply for his and his friends' use or for "wheeling and dealing." These prisoners could manipulate the routine slightly or skim off some commodities, but not enough to elevate them to the levels of power possessed by politicians or merchants in the Big Houses.

Despite the absence of these order-promoting processes, Soledad was still a very peaceful and orderly institution during most of the 1950s. The general mood among prisoners was tolerance and relative friendliness. The races were somewhat hostile toward each other and followed informal patterns of segregation, but there was commingling between all races and many prisoners maintained close friendships with members of their racial groups. During my five years at Soledad there were only a few knife fights, two murders, and one suicide.

Soledad's Ambience. To a great extent, the peace and order at Soledad were the result of a relatively optimistic, tolerant, and agreeable mood. Part of this mood stemmed from the enthusiasm for the new penal routine that the prisoners, returning or returning to prison, experienced in those early years. Most of us who came through the Chino Guidance Center and then moved into Soledad had been raised in the neighborhoods around Los Angeles, where we were involved in a variety of criminal subcultures. Consequently, we had received considerable information about the "joints" before coming to prison. We knew approximately how much time convicts served for a particular crime and how to conduct ourselves in prison: "don't rap to bulls," "don't get friendly with or accept gifts from older cons," "play it cool," and "do your time." The Chino Guidance Center threw us off track. It was a new institution with physical attires similar to Soledad's. It had pastel-colored cell blocks named Cyprus and Madrone and guards who had been selected for the guidance center because of their ability to relate to prisoners. We were bombarded with sophisticated tests administered by young, congenial, "college types." We were examined thoroughly by dentists and physicians. For six weeks we attended daily three-hour sessions with one of the college types. During the rest of the day we played basketball, sat in the sun, worked out, or engaged in other recreation while we recovered from our profoundly deleterious "dead time" period, the county jail.

In this relatively agreeable environment, we became convinced that the staff members were sincere and were trying to help us. It was implied or stated that they would locate our psychological problems, vocational deficiencies, and physical effects and would fix them. The guidance center staff promised (mostly by implication) and we believed that they were going [to] make new people out of us.

The enthusiasm and the new hope continued into the early years of Soledad and the other correctional institutions. We believed then that the new penal approach was producing a much more humane prison routine. We experienced the new attitudes of many staff persons as a positive outcome of the new era. Although there were many old-school guards, there were many new guards with college experience and a new attitude toward prisons and prisoners. Many of the old guards were even converted or drawn into the new attitude by the new penology, and they tended to see themselves as rehabilitative agents or at least as more humane "correctional officers," as their new job title read.

The physical environment was not as harsh as in older prisons. The one-man cells, modern heating system, dining room, visiting room, gym, and so on were marked improvements over Big Houses. Rules and rule enforcement were not as strict; there was more freedom of movement; and the relationships among prisoners and between staff and prisoners were more tolerant and friendly than in Big Houses. . . .

Tips and Cliques. The peace and order at Soledad also resulted from a system of "tips" and cliques. Tips were extended social networks or crowds that were loosely held together by shared subcultural orientations or preprison acquaintances. Most of the tips were intraracial, and they were overlapping and connected. Consequently, an individual could be involved in more than one tip and usually was related to the tips that connected with his own. For example, I was a member of a large network of Los Angeles young people who had been involved in theft and heroin. My Los Angeles thieves-dope fiends tip was connected to a similar tip of San Francisco thieves-dope fiends through ties established in the youth prisons. There were tips of persons who had experienced the youth prisons together, lived in the same town or neighborhood ("home boys"), and engaged in the same criminal

activities. A sense of loyalty existed between members of a tip. A member may not have known other members well, but common membership in the network automatically established some rapport and obligations and increased the possibility of friendship.

Prisoners formed smaller cliques within or across tips. . . . Clique members worked, celled, hung around the tier, yard, and day room, ate, and engaged in the same leisure activities together. The basis of organization varied greatly. Sometimes they formed out of small groups of prisoners who became acquainted at work or in the cell blocks. More often, they developed among persons who shared interest in some activity in prison, preprison experiences, subcultural orientations, and, thereby, tip membership. When clique members were also members of the same tip, the cliques were more cooperative, stable, and cohesive.

Most cliques were constantly transforming. Members were paroled, were transferred, or shifted friendships and interests. Former clique members continued to experience ties of friendships, and this extended friendship bonds outside existing cliques. These clique friendship ties and the ties to other tip members who were interconnected with the cliques established overlapping and extensive bonds of communication, friendship, and obligation through which cooperative enterprises were accomplished and conflict reduced. . . . Many disputes were avoided by indirect negotiations through the tips and cliques. . . . In the absence of more effective social organization, the tip and clique networks established ties and bridged gaps between prisoners, even between races, serving to promote peace and cooperation among prisoners. This system is similar to the clan, extended family, or totem organizations that served as ordering systems among primitive peoples before the establishment of larger, overreaching social organizations.

The Rehabilitative Ideal and Order

The rehabilitative philosophy and its actualizations directly promoted social order. Many of us accepted the altered self-conception contained in the new criminology that underpinned the ideal. We began to believe that we were sick, and we started searching for cures. Many of us adopted Sigmund Freud as our prophet, and we read and reread the *Basic Writings* as well [as] the works of the lesser prophets: Adler, Jung, Horney, and Fromm. Some of us became self-proclaimed experts in psychoanalysis and spent many hours analyzing each other. (Freudian interpretations provided us with new material for the old game of the dozens.)

Accepting this conception of ourselves as sick directed, our attention inward and away from social and prison circumstances. It inhibited us from defining our situation as unfair and from developing critical, perhaps collective, attitudes toward the society and the prison administration. We were divided psychologically by focusing on our own personalities and searching for cures of our individual pathologies.

In attempting to cure ourselves, we involved ourselves in the programs that grew out of the rehabilitative ideal. The formal policy in Soledad was that every prisoner had to have a full-time work, school, or vocational training assignment. The classification committees and the Adult Authority encouraged prisoners to pursue either academic or vocational training. Prisoners were required by policy to continue school until they tested at the fifth-grade level. A few prisoners refused to work or attend school or vocational training programs, but they were usually transferred or placed in segregation. Most prisoners were busy at work or school whether or not they believed in the rehabilitative ideal, and this promoted peace and stability.

The most effective order-promoting aspect of the rehabilitative ideal was more direct. With the indeterminate sentence system and with release decisions made by a parole board that used conformity to the prison routine as a principal indicator of rehabilitation and refused to review a prisoner who had received any serious disciplinary reports within six months, the message was clear: You conform or you will not be paroled. Most prisoners responded to the message.

However, even from the outset there were a few prisoners who were not persuaded to engage seriously in the rehabilitative programs, were not deterred by the threat of the indeterminate sentence system, and continued to get into trouble. This created a special problem for the administration, which was trying to implement the new, ostensibly nonpunitive routine. They solved it by opening up "adjustment centers" in each prison. The adjustment centers were segregation units where prisoners were held for indefinite periods with reduced privileges and virtually no mobility. The rationale for the units was that some prisoners needed more intensive therapy in a more controlled situation. In fact, no intensive therapy was ever delivered, and the adjustment centers were simply segregation units where troublesome prisoners could be placed summarily and indefinitely. By the end of the decade, the state could segregate a thousand prisoners in these units. The combination of these and the rehabilitative ideal with all its ramifications kept the peace for ten years.

The Seeds of Disruption

Later this peace was shattered by at least two developments that began in the 1950s in Soledad as well as other correctional institutions. First, black prisoners were increasing in numbers and assertiveness. They steadily moved away from their acceptance of the Jim Crow arrangement that prevailed in prison and began to assume equality in the prison informal world. As stressed above, many black prisoners crossed racial lines, maintained friendships with whites and Chicanos, and participated fully in all aspects of prison life. During most of the 1950s, the racially prejudiced white and Chicano prisoners disapproved of this, but rarely demonstrated their disapproval and prejudice. However, when black prisoners became more assertive and finally militant, racial hostilities intensified and set off an era of extreme racial violence, which disrupted the patterns of order based on tips and cliques.

Second, many prisoners in California and other states with correctional institutions eventually soured on rehabilitation and its artifacts. After years of embracing rehabilitation's basic tenets, submitting themselves to treatment strategies, and then leaving prison with new hope for a better future, they discovered and reported back that their outside lives had not changed. . . .

After prisoners were convinced that treatment programs did not work (by the appearance of persons who had participated fully in the treatment programs streaming back to prison with new crimes or violations of parole), hope shaded to cynicism and then turned to bitterness. The disillusioned increasingly shifted their focus from their individual pathologies to their life situation. They realized that under the guise of rehabilitation the correctionalists had gained considerable power over them and were using this power to coerce prisoners into "phony" treatment programs and "chickenshit" prison routines. In addition, they realized that parole boards arbitrarily, whimsically, and discriminatorily were giving many prisoners longer sentences and bringing them back to prison for violations of parole conditions that most prisoners believed to be impossible.

Rehabilitation inadvertently contributed to mounting criticism of itself by promoting a prison intelligentsia. Partly because of the expanded possibilities and the encouragement stemming from rehabilitation, more and more prisoners began educating themselves. Once we freed ourselves from the narrow conceptions contained in the rehabilitative philosophy, we began reading more and more serious literature. Most of us came from the working and lower-classes and had received very poor, if any, high school education. Our narrow life experience before and after school did nothing to expand our understanding. But in prison in the 1950s, with time on our hands, the availability of books, and the stimulation of the self-improvement message contained in the rehabilitative philosophy, we began to read. At first, we did not know how or what to read, so we read books on reading. Then when we acquired a preliminary sense of the classics, we plowed through them. Malcolm X expressed it well: "No university would ask any student to devour literature as I did when this new world opened to me, of being able to read and *understand.*"[6] Most of us started with history, then turned to other areas: philosophy, literature, psychology, economics, semantics, and even mysticism. After several years of intense reading, we developed a relatively firm foundation in world knowledge. It was constructed under peculiar circumstances and in isolation from large intellectual enterprises; consequently, it was somewhat uneven and twisted here and there. But it was broad and mostly solid.

With this new perspective, we saw through things: our culture, society, the prison system, even our beloved criminal careers. They were all stripped of their original meanings, and what we saw made all of us critical and some of us bitter and cynical. . . . Our new understandings guided us in different directions. After being released, some of us "dropped out" and became bohemians or students. Others, particularly many blacks, became activists. Still others, finding no satisfying avenues of expression for their new perspective, returned to old criminal pursuits. But all of us, in different ways, continued to work on a criticism of the "system" and to spread this criticism. This eventually contributed heavily to the great disillusionment with and the eventual dismantling of the rehabilitative ideal. Racial conflict and the sense of injustice that followed this dismantling tore the correctional institution apart. . . .

Division began when black prisoners increased in number and shifted their posture in prisons. The latter change was linked to the civil rights and black movements outside, but it also had very unique qualities. For instance, the civil rights phase was never very important in prison. The tactics of the civil rights protectors were too gentle to catch the imagination of black prisoners, and the central issue, unequal treatment under the law, was not as apparently salient in prison. All convicts, to a greater degree than free citizens, were equally treated and mistreated under the law. Other aspects of the black movement, such as "black is beautiful" and black separatism, were more important in prison than on the outside. . . .

The Contemporary Prison

The reverberations from the 1960s left most men's prisons fragmented, tense, and often extremely violent. The old social order, with its cohesion and monotonous tranquility, did not and perhaps will never reappear. The prisoners are divided by extreme differences, distrust, and hatred. Nonwhites, especially blacks, Chicanos, and Puerto Ricans, have risen in numbers and prominence. A multitude of criminal types—dope fiends, pimps, bikers, street gang members, and very few old-time thieves—assert themselves and compete for power and respect.

Nevertheless, chaos and a complete war of all against all have not resulted. They never do. When human social organizations splinter and friction between the parts increases, people still struggle to maintain old or create new collective structures that supply them with basic social needs, particularly protection from threats of violence. Complex social forms and a high degree of

order still exist among prisoners, even in the most violent and fragmented prisons, like San Quentin, but it is a "segmented order."

So it is in prison today. Races, particularly black and white, are divided and hate each other. In general, prisoners distrust most other prisoners whom they do not know well. The strategies for coping with this are similar to those employed in the Addams area. There are virtually no sex strata and much less age stratification in the prison, but increasingly prisoners restrict their interaction to small friendship groups and other small social units (gangs, for example) formed with members of their own race. Other than race, prisoners retreat into small orbits based on social characteristics such as (1) criminal orientation, (2) shared preprison experiences (coming from the same town or neighborhood or having been in other prisons together), (3) shared prison interests, and (4) forced proximity in cell assignment or work.

Racial Divisions

The hate and distrust between white and black prisoners constitute the most powerful source of divisions. After being forestalled by the moves toward unity during the prison movement, the conditions and trends discussed [earlier] were reestablished. Black prisoners continued to increase in numbers and assertiveness. Whites, led by the more prejudiced and violent, increasingly reacted. Hate, tension, and hostilities between the two races escalated. . . . White prisoners, whether or not they were racially hostile before prison, tend to become so after experiencing prison racial frictions. . . . Whites hate and, when they are not organized to resist, fear black prisoners.

The divisions and hatreds extend into the guard force and even into the administrations. . . . Black prisoners have consistently testified that white guards verbally and physically abuse them and discriminate against them.[7] Some radical commentators have suggested that guards and administrators have political motivations in their expression of racial hatred. This may be true, in some very indirect fashion. But the discrimination against blacks by white staff has a more immediate source: hatred for black prisoners. In expressing their hate, they sometimes give license to racist prisoners. . . .

White and black prisoners do not mix in informal prisoner groups, and many form groups for the purpose of expressing racial hatred and protecting their friends from the other race. A wife of a San Quentin prisoner described her husband's drift toward organized racial hatred:

> He didn't used to be prejudiced but now he hates blacks. He and some other white friends formed an American National Socialists group which I guess is a nazi group because they hate blacks so much. . . .

Other minority groups, such as Chicanos, Puerto Ricans Chinese, American Indians, and French Canadians, relate to whites and blacks in a more complex fashion. For instance, Chicanos in California prisons are more hostile toward black than toward white prisoners. White prisoners generally fear, distrust, and dislike Chicanos, because Chicanos speak Spanish or Calo and are believed to have a tendency to attack other prisoners with relatively less provocation than members of other groups. However, most white prisoners respect them for their toughness and do not threaten or derogate other white prisoners who befriend, hang around, or identify with Chicanos. Many white and Chicano prisoners have associated with each other in the "streets" and other joints and still maintain close friendship ties, even in the racially divided prison milieu. Puerto Rican, American Indian, French Canadian, and other racial or ethnic minorities have similar ambivalent positions in the complex racial matrix.

Violent Cliques and Gangs

In many men's prisons today, groups of prisoners regularly rob and attack other prisoners and retaliate when members of their clique or gang have been threatened or attacked. This has intensified the fear and widened the gap between prisoners, particularly between prisoners of different races. Presently these groups—which range from racially hostile cliques of reform school graduates, friends from the streets, biker club members, or tough convicts to large, relatively organized gangs—dominate several prisons.

Prisons have always contained violence-prone individuals, who were kept in check by the elders and the code enforced by the elders. In the 1950s and 1960s, small cliques of young hoodlums, such as the lowriders, hung around the yard and other public places together, talked shit (loudly bragged), played the prison dozens, occasionally insulted, threatened, attacked, and robbed unprotected weaker prisoners, and squabbled with other lowrider groups, particularly those of other races. . . . Most of these early lowriders were young juvenile prison graduates and fuck-ups (unskilled, lower- and working-class criminals) who had low respect among older, "solid" criminals and regular convicts. But they were a constant threat to the other prisoners who were trying to maintain peace. For most of the 1950s and 1960s, other prisoners disparaged, ignored, and avoided the lowriders, whose activities were kept in check by the general consensus against them and the belief (accepted by the lowriders and most other prisoners) that if the lowriders went too far, the older prison regulars would use force, including assassination, to control them.

Lowriders steadily increased in numbers. In the states with large cities whose ghettos bulged during the 1950s and 1960s and whose youth prison systems expanded to accommodate the increase in youth crime, the adult prisons began to receive growing numbers of tough youth prison graduates and criminally unskilled, more openly aggressive young urban toughs. They could no longer be controlled. They entered the growing racial melee and stepped up their attacks and robberies on other prisoners. When there were no successful countermoves against them, they took over the convict world and particularly one of its most important activities: the sub rosa economic enterprises.

In different states the young hoodlums arrived at the adult prisons with different backgrounds and consequently formed different types of groups in the prison. In California the takeover began in 1967 in San Quentin when a tightly knit clique of young Chicanos, who had known each other on the streets of Los Angeles and in other prisons, began to take drugs forcefully from other prisoners (mostly Chicano). The clique gained a reputation for toughness and the label of "the Mexican Mafia." Other aspiring young Chicano hoodlums became interested in affiliating with the Mafia, and, according to rumor, the Mafia members insisted that initiates murder another prisoner. This rumor and the actual attacks aroused and consolidated a large number of "independent" Chicanos, who planned to eliminate the Mafia members. On the planned day, the other Chicanos pursued known Mafia members through San Quentin, attempting to assassinate them. Several dozen prisoners were seriously wounded and one was killed in this day-long battle, but the Mafia held its ground, won many of the knife fights, and was not eliminated. After this unsuccessful attempt, some of the formerly independent Chicanos, particularly from Texas and the small towns in California who had been in conflict with Los Angeles Chicanos for decades, formed a countergroup: La Nuestra Familia. In the ensuing years, the conflict between the two Chicano gangs increased and spread to other prisons and even to the outside, where the gangs have tried to penetrate outside drug trafficking. The attacks

and counterattacks between members of the two gangs became so frequent that the prison administrators attempted to segregate the gangs, designating two prisons, San Quentin and Folsom for the Mafia and Soledad and Tracy for La Nuestra Familia. When Chicanos enter the California prison system, they are asked their gang affiliation; if they are to be sent to any of those four prisons (which are the medium- to maximum-security prisons), they are sent to one dominated by their gang.

The Chicano gangs' escalation of robbery, assault, and murder also consolidated and expanded black and white lowrider groups, some of which had already been involved in similar violent and rapacious activities. But on a smaller scale. Two gangs, the Aryan Brotherhood and the Black Guerilla Family, rose in prominence and violent activities. Eventually, the Aryan Brotherhood formed an alliance with the Mafia and the Black Guerilla Family with La Nuestra Familia, and a very hostile and tentative stalemate prevailed. However, peace has not returned. Other racist cliques among the black and white prisoners occasionally attack other prisoners; the Chicano gangs still fight each other; and there seem to be factions within the Chicano gangs themselves. Although the California prisons have passed their peak of violence, the violence and fear are still intense.

In Illinois, black Chicago street gangs—the Blackstone Rangers (changed later to Black P Stone Nation), the Devil's Disciples, and the Vice Lords—and a Latin street gang named the Latin Kings spread into Stateville and finally took over the convict world. . . . By 1974 the aggressive black and Latin gangs had precipitated counter-organizations among white prisoners who, in their reduced numbers, had been extremely vulnerable to assault, robbery, rape, and murder by the other gangs.[8]

The activities of these violent groups who, in the pursuit of loot, sex, respect, or revenge, will attack any outsider have completely unraveled any remnants of the old codes of honor and tip networks that formerly helped to maintain order. In a limited, closed space such as a prison, threats of attacks like those posed by these groups cannot be ignored. Prisoners must be ready to protect themselves or act out of the way. Those who have chosen to continue to circulate in public, with few exceptions, have formed or joined a clique or gang for their own protection. Consequently, violence-oriented groups dominate many, if not most, large men's prisons.

The New Convict Identity

The escalation of violence and the takeover of the violent cliques and gangs have produced a new prison hero. Actually, the prison-oriented leader has been undergoing changes for decades. In our earlier study, Donald Cressey and I separated the prison world into two systems, one with the ideal type, the "right guy," who was oriented primarily to the prison.[9] In my later study of California prisons, conducted in a period when the right guy was disappearing, the "convict" identity was a blend of various vestigial criminal and prison identities.

This [the convict perspective] is the perspective of the elite of the convict world—the "regular." A "regular" (or, as he has been variously called, "people," "folks," "solid," a "right guy," or "all right") possesses many of the traits of the thief's culture. He can be counted on when needed by other regulars. He is also not a "hoosier": that is, he has some finesse, is capable, is levelheaded, has "guts" and "timing."[10]

The upsurge of rapacious and murderous groups has all but eliminated the "right guy" and drastically altered the identity of the convict, the remaining hero of the prison world. Most of all, toughness has pushed out most other attributes, particularly the norms of tolerance, mutual aid, and loyalty to a large number of other regulars. Earlier, toughness was reemphasized as a reaction to the soft, cooperative "inmate" identity fostered by the rehabilitative ideal. . . . [T]he stiff and divisive administrative opposition weakened convict unity, and then the attacks of violent racial groups obliterated it. When the lowrider or "gang-banger" cliques turned on the remaining convict leaders (many had been removed from the prison mainline because of their political activities) and the elders were not able to drive the lowriders back into a position of subordination or otherwise to control them, the ancient regime fell and with it the old convict identity.

Toughness in the new hero in the violent men's prisons means, first, being able to take care of oneself in the prison world, where people will attack others with little or no provocation. Second, it means having the guts to take from the weak. . . .

In addition to threats of robbery, assaults, and murder, the threat of being raped and physically forced into the role of the insertee (punk or kid) has increased in the violent prison: "'Fuck it. It's none of my business. If a sucker is weak, he's got to fall around here. I came when I was eighteen and nobody turned me out. I didn't even smile for two years.'"[11]

Prison homosexuality has always created identity problems for prisoners. Long before today's gang era, many prisoners, particularly those with youth prison experiences, regularly or occasionally engaged in homosexual acts as inserters with queens, kids, or punks, though not without some cost to their own masculine definitions. There has been a cynical accusation repeated frequently in prison informal banter that prisoners who engaged in homosexual life too long finally learn to prefer it and, in fact, become full, practicing homosexuals, both insertees and inserters: "It was a jocular credo that after one year behind walls, it was permissible to kiss a kid or a queen. After five years, it was okay to jerk them off to 'get 'em hot.' After ten years, 'making tortillas' or 'flip-flopping' was acceptable and after twenty years anything was fine." The constant game of prison dozens among friends and acquaintances, in which imputation of homosexuality is the dominant theme, reflects and promotes self-doubt about masculinity. Presently, the threat of force has been added to the slower process of drifting into homosexuality, and fear about manhood and compensatory aggressive displays of manhood have increased drastically.

Today the respected public prison figure—the convict or hog—stands ready to kill to protect himself, maintains strong loyalties to some small group of other convicts (invariably of his own race), and will rob and attack or at least tolerate his friends' robbing and attacking other weak independents or their foes. He openly and stubbornly opposes the administration, even if this results in harsh punishment. Finally, he is extremely assertive of his masculine sexuality, even though he may occasionally make use of the prison homosexuals or, less often, enter into more permanent sexual alliance with a kid.

Convicts and Other Prisoners. Today prisoners who embrace versions of this ideal and live according to it with varying degrees of exactitude dominate the indigenous life of the large violent prisons. They control the contraband distribution systems, prison politics, the public areas of the prison, and any pan-prison activities, such as demonstrations and prisoner representative organizations. To circulate in this world, the convict world, one must act like a convict and, with a few exceptions, have some type of affiliation with a powerful racial clique or gang.

This affiliation may take various shapes. Most of the large racial gangs have a small core of leaders and their close friends, who constitute a tightly knit clique that spends many hours together. Moving out from this core, a larger group of recognized members are regularly called on by the core when the gang needs something done, such as assistance in an attack or display of force. Very often these fringe members are young aspiring initiates who want to be part of the inner core. Then, if the gangs are large, like the Mexican Mafia or the Black P Stone Nation, many more, sometimes hundreds of prisoners, claim an affiliation and are available when a massive display of force is needed.

Most prisoners who circulate in the convict world fall into one of the three categories. However, some highly respected convicts have very loose friendship ties with one or more of the gangs and circulate somewhat independently with immunity from gang attack. . . . A few very tough independents circulate freely, because they have withstood so many assaults from which they emerged victorious. Nevertheless, they still have to be careful with the more powerful gang members, because nobody can survive the attacks of a large group committed to murder.

In some large prisons a few prisoners who refrain from violent and sub rosa economic activities and devote themselves to form organizations and coalitions in order to pursue prisoners' rights and other political goals are tolerated by the gangs and other violent and rapacious prisoners. Occasionally, these organizers are able to create coalitions among warring gangs on particular issues. They have immunity only as long as they stay away from the other activities of the convict world and avoid disputes with the convict leaders.

Finally, other independents circulate freely, because they are viewed as unthreatening to the power of the convict leaders and they supply the convict world with some service. This includes characters and dings, who supply humor, and less desirable homosexuals. Younger, more desired homosexuals, however, must have affiliations with powerful individuals or groups.

In some of the large, more violent prisons, certain groups of prisoners, such as the Muslims and the cliques of "syndicate" men and their friends, are prominent in indigenous prison worlds even though they do not follow the aggressive and rapacious patterns of the gangs. Other prisoners believe that these groups will protect their members and retaliate against attacks; consequently, the other prisoners fear and respect them. These groups often become involved in a prison's informal political and economic activities and sometimes assume leadership in periods of disorder. When these groups are present and prominent, they are a stabilizing force that prevents the complete takeover by the violent cliques and gangs.

Withdrawal. [I]ncreasingly prisoners are shying away from public settings and avoiding the activities of the convict world. Although they occasionally buy from the racketeers, place bets with gamblers, trade commodities with other unaffiliated prisoners, or sell contraband on a very small scale, they stay away from the rackets and any large-scale economic enterprises. They dissociate themselves from the violent cliques and gangs, spend as little time as possible in the yard and other public places where gangs hang out, and avoid gang members, even though they may have been friends with some of them in earlier years. They stick to a few friends whom they meet in the cell blocks, at work, through shared interests, in other prisons, or on the outside (home boys). With their friends they eat, work, attend meetings of the various clubs and formal organizations that have abounded in the prison, and participate in leisure time activities together. Collectively, they have withdrawn from the convict world. . . .

The convicts disrespect those who withdraw, but usually ignore them: "If a dude wants to run and hide, that's all right." They even disrespect formerly high-status prisoners, such as older thieves, who previously received respect even if they avoided prison public life. Prisoners who withdraw occasionally have to display deference or acquiesce subtly in accidental public confrontations with convicts, but they face minimal danger of assault and robbery. This is much less true for young and effeminate prisoners, who will be pursued by aggressive, homosexually oriented convicts, perhaps

threatened or raped, even if they attempt to stay to themselves and to avoid the convict world. Segregation may be their only safe niche.

The strategy of withdrawal has been encouraged and facilitated by prison administrations, which have always feared and hindered prisoner unity. The history of American prisons, in a sense, is a history of shifting techniques of separating prisoners. The original Pennsylvania prisons completely isolated prisoners. The Auburn system, which prevailed in the initial era of imprisonment in the United States because of cheap costs, employed the "silence system" to reduce interaction between prisoners and to forestall unity. More recently, the system of individualized treatment, emphasizing individual psychological adjustment, was a mechanism of psychological separation. In the last decade, convinced that large populations of prisoners are unmanageable, prison administrators have recommended, planned, and built smaller institutions for the primary purpose of separating prisoners into smaller populations. In the large prisons that are still used (not by choice, but by economic necessity) some states have split the prison into small units and have formally separated the prisoner population within the large prison. In many prisons these separate units (usually cell blocks with some additional staff and restrictions on access) vary in levels of privilege, some being designated "honor" units that offer many more privileges, more mobility for the residents, and less access for nonresidents.

Since the late 1960s, prison administrations have contravened the movements toward prisoner-organized unity by allowing, even encouraging many small apolitical organizations. . . . Prisoners who withdraw have certain channels provided by the administration to help them and make prison less onerous: if they maintain a clean disciplinary record, they can eventually move to an honor block or unit which houses a preponderance of persons who are withdrawing like themselves, which affords many more privileges, and to which access is restricted. In addition, they may fill in their leisure hours with formal organizational activities located in closed rooms away from the yard and other settings of the convict world.

More recently, in some prisons the administrations are combining the unit structure, segregation, and behavior modification into a system of hierarchial segregation that encourages withdrawal and conformity and greatly reduces contact between prisoners. . . .

This stratification system has succeeded in facilitating withdrawal, but has not eliminated violence in the prison. It has merely concentrated it in the lower levels of the hierarchy. Also, it has produced some added undesirable consequences. Individuals housed in the maximum-security (and more punitive) units become increasingly embittered and inured to violence. Many of them believe that they have been placed and are held there arbitrarily. (Often this is the case, because suspicions and prejudices operate in the classification to various units.) Intense hate between prisoners and guards builds up in the maximum-security units. Different clique and gang members, different races, and guards and prisoners verbally assault each other. Often guards on duty in the units, having grown especially hostile toward particular prisoners, depart from the formal routine and arbitrarily restrict the privileges of certain prisoners (for example, not releasing them for their allowed short exercise period).

All this precipitates regular violent and destructive incidents. San Quentin continues to experience incident after incident in its most secure and punitive units. In February 1978, for several days the prisoners in Max B fought among themselves during exercise periods and defied or even attacked guards who were trying to control them, even though they were risking injury, death, and long extensions of their segregation and prison sentences. More recently, in April 1979, a group of prisoners in the same unit

continued to damage their cells for three days. They were protesting not having received their "issue" (toilet paper, tobacco, and the like), showers, or exercise periods for five weeks. They broke their toilets, tore out the electric lights in their cells, burned their mattresses, and pulled the plumbing from the walls. Finally, a large squad of guards (the "goon squad") brought them under control. A guard told Stephanie Riegel, a legal aide who had been informed of the incident by one of the prisoners involved, that "this type of destruction in that section is fairly routine."

Race and Withdrawal. The strategy of withdrawal is more open and appealing to white prisoners. In general, independent black prisoners are not as threatened by gangs. Blacks have more solidarity, and the black gangs tolerate the independents, most of whom are pursuing a more present-oriented expressive mode in prison. . . . Unless several black gangs become very organized and hostile to each other (as in Stateville), unaffiliated blacks participate much more in the convict world and hang around much more in public places, as the big yard.

With few exceptions, Chicanos in the large California prisons—Soledad, San Quentin, Folsom, and Tracy—must have at least a loose affiliation with one of the Chicano gangs. The gangs force this. However, many have token affiliations and actually withdraw and largely avoid the trouble and gang activity that abound in the convict world. However, they may occasionally be called on for some collective action; and if they ignore the gangs' call, they might be attacked. . . .

Concluding Remarks

This is the situation in many—too many—large, men's prisons: not chaos, but a dangerous and tentative order. It is not likely to improve for a while. The sources of conflict are deeply embedded in prisoners' cultural and social orientations. Most male prisoners are drawn from a social layer that shares extremely reduced life options, meager material existence, limited experience with formal, polite, and complex urban social organizations, and traditional suspicions and hostilities toward people different from their own kind. Prisoners, a sample with more extreme forms of these characteristics, are likely to be more hostile toward others with whom they do not share close friendships or cultural backgrounds and less firmly attached to the conventional normative web that holds most citizens together. For decades, the potentially obstreperous and conflictive population was held in a tentative peace by prisoner leaders, a code, and the constant threat of extreme force. When the informal system of peace disintegrated, the formal force was brought in, used (in fact, misused), withstood by the prisoners, and dissipated. For a short period, 1970 to 1973, prisoner organizers pursued the promise of some power for prisoners, mended some of the major rifts that were growing between groups of prisoners, and forestalled further fractionalizing. The administrations, because they fear prisoner political unity more than any other condition, smashed the incipient organizations and regenerated fractionalization. The parts scattered in familiar paths followed by other splintered populations of oppressed peoples: religious escapism, rapacious racketeering, fascism, and withdrawal.

The administrations are not happy with the results, but continue to apply old formulas to restore order. Mostly, they attempt to divide and segregate the masses and to crush the more obdurate prisoners. In California, for instance, the Department of Corrections has continued to search for gang leaders and other troublemakers, transfer those who are so labeled to the maximum-security prisons, and segregate them there in special units. The growing numbers of segregated prisoners are becoming more vicious and uncontrollable. In recent incidents at San Quentin the prisoners in a segregation unit fought among themselves and defied the guards for several days, even though they were risking injury, death, and extensions in their sentences. When the department has succeeded in identifying gang leaders and removing them, new leaders have sprouted like mushrooms. The prisons remain essentially the same.

The violent, hostile, and rapacious situation will probably continue until all prisoners are held in very small institutions of less than one or two hundred or completely isolated (both at astronomical costs) or until administrations begin to permit and cultivate among prisoners new organizations that can pull them together on issues that are important to them as a class. It seems obvious to me that these issues are the conditions of imprisonment and postprison opportunities. Thus, in order for these organizations to obtain and hold the commitment of a number of leaders and thereby to begin supplanting the violent, rapacious group structures, they will have to have some power in decision making. These organizations, however, are political in nature, and presently this idea is repulsive and frightening to prison administrations and the public.

Study Questions

1. Describe the Big House era in American prisons, including their architecture and social organization.

2. Why and how did the purpose of imprisonment in the correctional institutions change after World War II?

3. How were the major tenets of the correctional institutions (indeterminate sentencing, classification, and treatment) intended to work together in rehabilitating inmates?

4. How did the inmate social system change from the Big House era to the "Correctional Institution" era, particularly in terms of indigenous argot roles as well as those imported from the outside?

5. What factors disrupted the order of the correctional institutions and ushered in the era of "Contemporary Prisons"?

6. Describe race relations throughout the various eras and how black power and gangs have changed the power structure in Contemporary Prisons.

7. How does the new convict identity in the Contemporary Prison differ from that of the Big House and the correctional institution?

Notes

1. Donald Clemmer, *The Prison Community* (New York: Holt, Rinehart & Winston, 1958), p. 7.

2. John Irwin and Donald Cressey, "Thieves, Convicts and the Inmate Culture," *Social Problems,* Fall 1963, p. 149.

3. Claude Brown, *Manchild in the Promised Land* (New York: Macmillan, 1965), p. 412.

4. Victor Nelson, *Prison Days and Nights* (Boston: Little, Brown, 1933), p. 219.

5. *Popeye* (Pamphlet distributed by Peoples' Court Comrades, San Francisco, 1975), p. 6.

6. *The Autobiography of Malcom X* (New York: Macmillan, 1965), p. 173.

7. *Attica: The Official Report of the New York State Special Commission on Attica* (New York: Prager, 1972) has the most convincing reports on such testimony.

8. *Stateville* (Chicago: University of Chicago Press, 1977), pp. 157–158.

9. "Thieves, Convicts, and the Inmate Culture," *Social Problems,* Fall 1963, pp. 145–148.

10. John Irwin, *The Felon* (Englewood Cliffs, NJ: Prentice Hall, 1970), p. 83.

11. Bunker, *Animal Factory* (New York: Viking Press, 1977), p. 32.

12

Comparing the Quality of Confinement and Cost-Effectiveness of Public Versus Private Prisons

What We Know, Why We Do Not Know More, and Where to Go From Here

Dina Perrone
Travis C. Pratt

Over the past three decades, federal and state governments have begun outsourcing to the private sector what have traditionally been state-run activities. The building and operation of U.S. jails and prisons have provided no exception to this trend. The most commonly cited conventional wisdom for this trend has been that government is slow, is wasteful, and provides too many barriers to getting tasks completed (particularly large-scale tasks such as building a prison with several hundred beds). In this detailed summary of the literature, Perrone and Pratt present the reader with a comprehensive and detailed investigation into the current state of the "public versus private" prison debate. This debate has been ongoing for approximately the past two decades, and has typically pivoted on the following three issues when considering both types of institutions: quality of care, cost-effectiveness, and the

philosophical and moral issues of using private industry to punish crimes against the "state." The authors review the current state of the art regarding empirical investigations that have attempted to answer the first two of these three debate points. Equally or more important, however, are the critical analyses of the methodology that each study reviewed utilized. Also presented is the authors' call for more rigorous research and ways in which this research can be accomplished.

As of June 2001, there were a total of 154 private prisons in the United States (Texas houses almost 30 percent of them with 42 private facilities) and an additional 30 private prisons outside of the United States (Corrections Corporation of America [CCA], 2001). In all, these facilities have an approximate housing capacity of 142,000 inmates. As of June 30, 2000, there were 76,010 inmates (approximately 4 percent of the inmate population) held in privately operated prisons in the United States (Beck & Karberg, 2001). Currently, there are 17 private firms—13 of which are United States-based—that operate adult jails and prisons (CCA, 2001). Wackenhut and CCA are the 2 largest companies, and both have "gone public": as of August 2001, Wackenhut (New York Stock Exchange symbol = WHC) had shares at approximately U.S. $13, and CCA shares (New York Stock Exchange symbol = CXW) were slightly higher at U.S. $14.

In 2000, Wackenhut reported a U.S. $135 million profit from their dealings in the corrections industry (Wackenhut, 2001). They own 33 facilities in the United States, including juvenile facilities and 2 Immigration and Naturalization Service facilities, as well as 20 facilities outside of the United States in Africa, Australia, Canada, the United Kingdom, and New Zealand (Wackenhut, 2001). CCA manages 65 facilities in 21 states, the District of Columbia, and Puerto Rico, with a total of more than 61,000 inmate beds. Accordingly, CCA reported U.S. $238.3 million in consolidated revenue for fiscal year 2000 (CCA, 2001).

Why have policy makers turned to private companies to operate correctional facilities? As of 2000, the United States imprisoned more than 2 million people, with an incarceration rate of approximately 500 citizens per 100,000 in the population (Beck & Karberg, 2001). Prison facilities are filled to 20 percent over capacity (Van Slambrouck, 1998)—a fact that generally prompts correctional policy makers to highlight the need to build more prisons (DiIulio, 1991; McConville, 1987; Vardalis & Becker, 2000). Even so, expanding existing prison space has placed a large strain on already tight public budgets (Colson, 1989; Cox & Osterhoff, 1993). In 2000, the cost of confining state and local inmates in the United States reached an estimated U.S. $43 billion a year (Schiraldi & Greene, 2002). To help alleviate some of this cost, policy makers have turned to private companies under the assumption that private agencies can construct and run prisons at a higher—or at least comparable—level of quality and at a cheaper cost than can the state.

For example, some scholars have argued that private companies can cut costs by negotiating item costs and purchasing in bulk, by eliminating overtime and employee benefits, and by reducing the red tape needed to accomplish simple tasks such as purchasing equipment and hiring/firing staff (Brister, 1996; Logan, 1987; Steelman & Harms, 1986). Camp and Gaes (1998), however, argued that such cost-cutting mechanisms could be adopted by the state as well. Still others have contended that any cost savings attributable to privatization will be short term only, and that long-term costs are likely to exceed current levels of spending due to the need to keep a stable or growing inmate population to ensure profits (Anderson, Davoli, & Moriarty, 1985; Henig, 1985; Shichor, 1993; 1995). Often woven into this cost-effectiveness debate,

similar disagreements within the academic community surround questions of whether private prisons offer either comparable—or perhaps even better—quality of confinement conditions for inmates (e.g., compare Logan, 1990, 1992; Shichor, 1995).

Adding to the plurality of voices and positions on the correctional privatization issue, scholars have also debated the legal, philosophical, and ethical dimensions associated with turning over the task of managing prisons to the private sphere (Durham, 1989; Geis, Mobley, & Shichor, 1999; Lanza-Kaduce, Parker, & Thomas, 2000; Ogle, 1999; Reisig & Pratt, 2000; Sechrest & Shichor, 1996). Although we certainly do not wish to downplay the importance of these more normative issues, it is important to note that regardless of whether the most defensible legal-philosophical position dictates that policy makers *should not* have the authority to grant private agencies the power to punish, legislatures *are* already contracting correctional services to private companies at an increasing rate (Lilly & Deflem, 1996; Lilly & Knepper, 1993). Indeed, in 1990 the rated capacity of private prisons was 15,300. In September of 2001, that total rose to 142,521—an 832 percent increase in less than 10 years (Thomas, 2001). In addition, the number of inmates housed in privately operated prisons increased 9.1 percent in the 6 months from December 1999 to June 30, 2000. As if these figures were not telling enough on their own, further evidence of the recent trend toward correctional privatization is that in 1991, there were only 44 privately operated prisons (Shichor, 1995). In 1994, that number increased to 88, only to increase an additional 109 percent to 184 in 2000 (CCA, 2001).

Thus, given the rapid expansion of prison privatization, it is now critical to assess whether these facilities actually live up to their expectations (cost and quality) or if the state and the inmates are being cheated out of quality care at an affordable cost by turning over the power to punish to the private sphere. Although there is an abundance of studies attempting to address these questions, there has yet to be a systematic attempt to take a step back and "make sense" of this emerging body of literature (e.g., see Anderson et al., 1985; Bowditch & Everett, 1987; Winn, 1996; cf. Pratt & Maahs, 1999). Accordingly, this article attempts to uncover whether public or private prisons operate at a higher quality and/ or at a cheaper cost by reviewing the empirical studies that have compared private and public prisons.

To do so, we collected every U.S. study that has been conducted on these issues through a systematic search through electronic databases (NCJRS and NCCD archives), along with academic journals,[1] edited volumes, and public/government reports.[2] After a discussion of the methodological issues surrounding the research, this article reviews the evidence addressing the quality of confinement and cost-effectiveness of public versus private prisons. Finally, prescriptions for future research are presented to help clarify the unresolved issues in this area and to help give us a better understanding of the potential advantages and drawbacks of prison privatization.

Quality of Confinement

In this section, key methodological issues will be discussed, followed by the findings from each of the studies comparing the quality of confinement between private and public prisons. The final section provides a summary of the relative efficacy of private prisons in terms of the quality of confinement.

Methodological Issues

Nine studies assess the relative quality of private versus public prisons. To compare the private and public facilities, the studies attempt to match the private and public facilities on certain criteria that could affect why one facility would outperform another on particular measures (see Table 12.1). For instance, the size (capacity) of the facility may affect the prison's performance on certain domains because a larger prison may have more disciplinary reports and more assaults simply because they have a greater number of inmates. Half of the studies evaluated were of similar maximum capacity levels (see Table 12.1).

Comparing prisons with similar custody levels is also important. For example, if the private prison were minimum security and the public prison medium security, it would be expected that the inmates in the minimum-security private facility were less dangerous than those in the medium-security public facility. Consequently, the private prison would have less disciplinary reports and less inmate assaults and would therefore appear to be safer. All of the studies compared similar custody levels with the exception of the Tennessee study (Drowota, 1995), where one of the public facilities had a higher percentage of minimum-classification inmates than did the other public and the private facility.

The age of the facility may also affect the quality of confinement comparisons. Those operating a new facility may not have the experience of the administrators of an older facility. Therefore, it may appear to be of a lesser quality simply because all of the necessary quirks have not had the chance to be smoothed out. With the exceptions of those conducted by Logan (1992, 1996), the Office of Program Policy Analysis and Government Accountability (OPPAGA) (1998), Thomas (1997), and Austin and Coventry (1999), most of the studies were of facilities of similar age.[3] Thomas's study did not indicate the age difference of the private and public facilities—he merely stated that the private facility was newer. The private prison in Logan's studies was only 6 months into operation when it was compared to the older public facilities. The private facilities compared in the Florida OPPAGA study

Table 12.1
Key Methodological Characteristics of Studies Comparing Quality of Confinement Across Public and Private Prisons

Study	Sample Size	Security Level	Maximum Capacity	Age of Facility	Significance Test	Data Collection
Arizona, Thomas (1997)	16: 1 private, 15 public	Matched	No info.	Private newer	No	Records
Florida, OPPAGA (1998)	3: 2 private, 1 public	Matched	Public larger	Private newer	No	Site visits, records
Florida, OPPAGA (2000)	2: 1 private, 1 public	Matched	Private larger	One year difference	No	Surveys, records
Kentucky, Urban Institute (1989)	2: 1 private, 1 public	Matched	Public larger	No info.	Yes	Site visits, interviews, surveys, records
Louisiana, Archambeault & Deis (1996)	3: 2 private, 1 public	Matched	Matched	Matched	Yes	Surveys, records
New Mexico, Logan (1992, 1996)	3: 1 private, 2 public	Matched	Matched	Private newer	No	Surveys, records
Tennessee, Drowota (1995)	3: 1 private, 2 public	Matched	Matched	Not enough info.	No	Audits
Sellers (1989)	6: 3 private, 3 public	Matched	Matched	Matched	No	Site visits, interviews, records
Austin & Coventry (1999)	65 private all public	Matched	Public larger	Private newer	No	Survey

opened in 1995, whereas their public counterpart opened in 1977. Approximately 90 percent of the private facilities in the Austin and Coventry survey were less than 10 years old, whereas only about 30 percent of the public facilities fell into that category.

Therefore, what we can conclude thus far about this body of literature is that often times, the private and public facilities were not properly matched on important characteristics; as such, various confounding factors could have influenced the results. For example, one facility may actually operate at a higher quality because its inmates are of a lower security level where fewer riots and escapes would be expected, or one facility in the comparison may be an older prison where the administrators have had greater experience operating with such a facility. Without controlling for such fac-

tors, the studies may have assessed only whether it was the age and/or security level of the prison that influenced its rating of "quality."

Another methodological limitation within these studies is that there has not been a systematic method of analyzing and comparing the quality of confinement across the facilities. Instead, studies follow the "laundry list" approach for assessing the overall quality of confinement that Camp and Gaes (1998) argued is seriously flawed because it does not demonstrate the objectivity of the measures or the processes that produce a higher quality outcome. Even so, Logan's (1992) method of assessing the quality of confinement seems to be the most widely accepted and most objectively measured in the field.[4] His method groups the laundry list into seven domains: safety, order, care, activity, justice, conditions, and management. Although studies certainly overlap in terms of which domains are assessed, few studies analyze management (Archambeault & Deis, 1996; Logan, 1996; Urban Institute, 1989), and with the exception of Logan's (1992) study, no other study assesses the justice domain.[5] Within each of the domains, not all of the studies provide information on the same measures. For example, where some studies indicate staffing adequacy and inmate deaths, other studies do not. Because of such methodological diversity, we chose specific objective measures commonly found in each of the studies to assess each of the quality domains.

To assess security, the number of escapes cited was used. Although this is a problematic measure (escapes are rare), Logan (1992) argued that it is the most "obvious indicator" (p. 582). The number of assaults and injuries on both inmates and staff were used to assess safety. For the order domain, the number of disciplinary actions and disturbances were compared. The number of inmates enrolled in or who completed institutional programs were compared to assess activity. The Correctional Medical Authority review of the health care services provided was used to assess care. Measures of staff stress and burnout were compared to assess the management of the prison, and indications of a poorly kept prison were used to assess the conditions.

Empirical Evidence

The results of the research addressing the quality of confinement are mixed. In some studies the private prison faired worse in the domain, whereas in others it outperformed the public prison (see Table 12.2). For example, in the conditions domain, Logan's (1992) New Mexico study shows the private prison to be in a better condition when compared to the public prison, whereas the Tennessee study (Drowota, 1995) shows the private facility to be in a

worse condition. Furthermore, the Kentucky study (Urban Institute, 1989) shows that the private and public prisons were perceived to be in equally good condition.

In studies that compared two private prisons and one public prison, the findings were also equivocal. The management domain exemplifies this point. The Louisiana study (Archambeault & Deis, 1996) uses the Family Life and Medical Leave Act and sick leave hours as measures of staff burnout and stress. It finds that one of the private facilities in the study had the highest number of Family Medical Leave Act and sick leave hours used each month, whereas the other private facility had the fewest, and the public facility fell somewhere in between. On the other hand, the Kentucky study shows that the average number of sick days taken per month was fairly equal among the public and private facilities, with the private facilities being slightly higher. In contrast, the study of the New Mexico (Logan, 1996) private facility compares employee responses on questions regarding staff burnout and stress and finds that the private facility scored more positively than the public facility.

Similar inconsistencies were found in the activity domain. The private prisons serviced more inmates through programs in the Louisiana study, but fewer inmates in the Tennessee and the Kentucky studies. More inmates completed educational and vocational programs in the private facilities in the Florida (OPPAGA, 1998) study but completed less programs in the Kentucky study. The private facilities, however, did offer more programs in the Florida study, the Austin and Coventry (1999) study, and the Sellers (1989) study. Unfortunately, with the exception of the Austin and Coventry study, the degree to which the offered programs were utilized is unclear. The activity domain is further confounded by Thomas' (1997) study, which indicates that because the private facility in Arizona is under a regimented contract and is required to provide

Table 12.2
Comparisons of Quality of Confinement Outcome Measures Across Studies

Quality Domain	Condition	Management	Activity	Care	Security	Safety	Order
Arizona, Thomas (1997)	N/A	N/A	Inconclusive	N/A	Private	Equal/private	Equal
Florida, OPPAGA (1998)	Private	N/A	Private	Private	Equal	N/A	Private
Florida, OPPAGA (2000)	N/A	N/A	N/A	Private	Public	Private	N/A
Kentucky, Urban Institute (1989)	Equal	Equal	Public	N/A	Private	N/A	Equal
Louisiana, Archambeault & Deis (1998)	N/A	Inconclusive	Private	N/A	Public	Private	Private
New Mexico, Logan (1992, 1996)	Private	Private	N/A	N/A	Equal	N/A	N/A
Tennessee, Drowota (1995)	Public	N/A	N/A	N/A	Private	Public	Private
Sellers (1989)	N/A	N/A	Private	N/A	N/A	N/A	N/A
Austin & Coventry (1999)	N/A	N/A	Private	N/A	N/A	Public	N/A

particular programs, it could not be compared to the public facilities.

It is also difficult to make any strong conclusions in the domain of security. In the Louisiana and Florida studies, the private prison had more escapes than its public counterpart. In contrast, the Tennessee, Arizona (Thomas, 1997), and Kentucky studies report the private prisons as having fewer escapes. Although Logan (1992) found that the private and the public (state) facility had an equal number of escapes, the other public (federal) facility had more escapes than either the private or public (state) facilities. In addition, the private facilities and the public facility in the Florida study had an equal number of escapes. Therefore, it is ambiguous as to whether the private facilities are more secure than their public counterparts.

Inconclusive results were also found in the domain of safety. The private facilities had fewer assaults on inmates and staff when compared to the public prisons in the Louisiana and Kentucky studies. The Arizona (Thomas, 1997) study finds that the private facility either had less or an equal number of assaults on inmates and staff (with or without weapons) than did the public facilities during the 6 months under review. The Tennessee study and the Austin and Coven-

try (1999) analysis, however, show that the private prison had more injuries on staff and inmates than the public prison. To further complicate matters, in the Florida study, where two private facilities were compared to one public facility, one of the private prisons outperformed the public facility in assaults on inmates, but the other private prison had a higher rate of assaults on inmates than both the public and the other private facility. Both private facilities in this study also had a higher rate of assaults on staff than did the public facility.

Finally, in the order domain, private prisons either performed equally as well or outperformed the public prison, and they outperformed the public facilities in the care domain. The private facilities used less formal disciplinary actions in the Louisiana study and the Florida study. In the Tennessee study, the private facility reported fewer disturbances. In the Kentucky and Arizona studies, however, the private and public facility administered an equal number of disciplinary reports. In addition, in the 6 months under review, both the public and private facilities in Arizona reported zero disturbances (Thomas, 1997). The private facilities in the **OPPAGA (1998, 2000)** studies also had fewer deficiencies in medical services.

Summary

Overall, the comparison of the quality of confinement between public and private prisons is inconclusive. There were few patterns or consistent findings across the studies, with the exception of the safety, order, and care domains. In the domain of safety, private prisons performed equally as well or worse, whereas they performed equally as well or better in the order and care domains. The discrepancies in the findings may be due in part to the methodological limitations of the studies, where the studies did not match or control for other confounding factors.

For example, variations in results across studies could emerge from differences in managerial style rather than ownership. To be sure, Archambeault and Deis (1996) attributed the differences between the private and public facilities to the dissimilar ways in which the prisons were managerially organized (e.g., wardens employing different managerial styles). Without controlling for such management differences, attributing any differences to sheer private or public ownership is problematic. In addition, because of the poor matching techniques used in the studies, as discussed above, it is difficult to rule out threats to internal validity. For example, the age of the facility, the inmate composition, and the size of the facility could affect the outcomes of the studies. Furthermore, most of the studies were case studies simply comparing one or two private facilities to one or two public facilities. With such small sample sizes, we must view the generality of the findings with skepticism because such samples could never be assumed to be representative of all private (or public) prisons. Furthermore, only two of the studies employed tests of statistical significance, leaving the other differences to be read only at face value. Thus, what may appear to be large differences across quality domains may not be statistically significant (i.e., they may be due to sampling error).

Inconsistencies in results could also be attributed to the different data collection methods employed in the studies. There are large differences in the reliability and validity of the data collected through official reports versus those that are obtained through inmate or staff surveys. Official reports fall to the biases of human error and may not include all information. Perhaps in some instances, assaults or injuries were not recorded, which would be expected, as Brister (1996) noted, if the private agency was subject to contract renewal each year. This may skew the results in the safety domain, where private prisons outperformed the public facilities in a few of the studies. Self-report data are also flawed, where inmates and staff may not be honest or may not recall particular instances and may even exaggerate information (Maxfield & Babbie, 1998; cf. Camp, 1999; Camp, Saylor, & Wright, 1999; Van Voorhis, 1994). This is not to say that all types of data are bad. Rather, our point here is to highlight how lumping together data from self-reports and official sources can be potentially misleading.

Therefore, at this point it is unclear how the private facilities "measure up" in terms of their relative quality of confinement. To date, the studies are too methodologically diverse (and often too methodologically weak) to draw any firm conclusions. They typically do not control for confounding factors such as age and security level, they fail to employ similar methods of data collection, and they do not assess the domains on equal measures. Such limitations cloud our ability to determine whether private agencies operate their facilities at a higher quality than the state.

Although such a conclusion may seem somewhat fatalistic, it is nevertheless substantively important. Neither advocates nor critics of prison privatization may, at this point, legitimately claim that the "bulk" of the empirical evidence is on their side. Indeed, the high level of methodological diversity and heterogeneity in results across these studies—generated largely by the idiosyncratic approaches to the case study methods employed by researchers—reveals that bold claims about the relative strengths or weaknesses of private versus public prisons with regard to issues of the quality of confinement would be, at minimum, premature.

Cost Comparisons

Similar methodological problems also plague the literature addressing the relative cost-effectiveness of public versus private prisons. In this section, these methodological issues will first be discussed, followed by the findings from each of the studies. This section evaluated all studies used to assess quality of confinement measures with the exception of Logan's (1992, 1996) study in New Mexico and Austin and Coventry's (1999) evaluation of privatized prisons, because these studies did not provide information on cost. Additionally, a Texas Sunset Advisory Commission (TSAC) (1990) study and a study in Wisconsin (Mitchell, 1996) of private and public facilities were added to the review in this section (they did not provide measures of quality of confinement). The final section provides a summary of the cost-effectiveness of private prisons.

Methodological Issues

Analyzing and comparing the costs of private and public prisons can be problematic. How costs are calculated, the type and location of the facilities, and the number of inmates may affect the result of the comparison. There are many "hidden," or indirect, costs associated with contract writing, financial liability, and monitoring that may or may not be included in the cost analysis of private prisons and may be difficult to calculate (McDonald, 1989; Sechrest & Shichor, 1996). Furthermore, direct costs in public institutions may be difficult to isolate, such as those associated with medical

care, capital costs for renovations, and construction (Shichor, 1995).

Comparisons also have to be made "on the same kind of institution at the same level of security in the same geographic area" (Shichor, 1995, p. 137). As evidenced above, state prisons may not house the same type of inmates as private prisons, and they may not provide similar programs. Furthermore, the custody level of the facility, the medical need of the inmates, and the social programs provided all affect the cost of operating the prison (General Accounting Office [GAO], 1996; OPPAGA, 2000; Sellers, 1989; Thomas, 1997), where (a) the higher the security level, (b) the more social programs a facility provides, and (c) the greater the medical need of the inmates, the more costly the facility will be to operate.

Prisons with a greater number of inmates will also have a lower per diem cost because the cost decreases as the number of inmates increases due to the "economy of scale" (Pratt & Maahs, 1999, p. 364). The OPPAGA (2000) Florida study compares a higher capacity private facility to a smaller capacity public facility, whereas the private facilities in the Urban Institute's (1989) Kentucky study and the OPPAGA (1998) Florida study were of a higher capacity than their private counterparts.

Therefore, it is essential that the studies match or control for such characteristics that would skew the findings in favor of the prison with the lowest custody, fewer programs, healthier inmates, and a greater economy of scale. Accordingly, many studies could not find appropriate public prison matches. In these cases, the researchers created a hypothetical public facility (Mitchell, 1996; OPPAGA, 1998; TSAC, 1990)—the findings of which should be viewed with caution because the public facilities were not even actual facilities.

Studies also include various expenditures when calculating prison costs. Table 12.3 illustrates that few studies calculate the daily per diem operating cost of the facility the same way across public and private

Table 12.3

Key Methodological Characteristics of Studies Comparing Cost-Effectiveness Across Public and Private Prisons

Study	Real vs. Hypothetical Facilities	Identical Cost Calculation Methods?	Indirect Costs Calculated?	Security Level	Maximum Capacity	Programs Provided	Age of Facility
Arizona, Thomas (1997)	Real	No	No	Matched	No info.	Not matched	Private newer
Florida, OPPAGA (1998)	Hypothetical	Yes	Yes	Matched	Public larger	Not matched	Private newer
Florida, OPPAGA (2000)	Real	Yes	No	Matched	Private larger	Not enough info.	One year difference
Kentucky, Urban Institute (1989)	Real	Yes	Yes	Matched	Public larger	Not matched	No info.
Louisiana, Archambeault & Deis (1996)	Real	No	Yes	Matched	Matched	Not matched	Matched
Sellers (1989)	Real	Yes	No	Matched	Matched	Not matched	Matched
Tennessee, General Accounting Office (1996)	Real	Yes	Yes	Not matched	Matched	Not enough info.	Not enough info.
Texas, Texas Sunset Advisory Commission (1990)	Hypothetical	Yes	Yes	Matched	Matched	Matched	Matched

facilities. For example, Archambeault and Deis (1996) included different items when calculating the costs of the private and public facilities. They included hospital security costs when calculating the per diem for the private prison but did not include those expenditures when calculating the cost of the public prison. Such medical and health costs were also excluded in the Tennessee (GAO, 1996) study, yet the OPPAGA (2000) study adjusted for such costs in its Florida evaluation. As a result, some studies may demonstrate that the private facility is cheaper when in actuality medical and health costs were eliminated from the calculation. Mitchell (1996, p. 12) further reminds us that public agencies and private firms use different budgeting and accounting methods that also account for differences in private and public prison operating costs.

The diversity of methodological approaches obscured researchers' ability to accurately compare the costs of the private and public facilities within and across the studies. To be sure, each of these methodological variations will inevitably attenuate any conclusions based on the research. Nevertheless, the following section reviews what the body of empirical literature reveals about the relative cost-effectiveness of private versus public correctional facilities.

Empirical Evidence

Table 12.4 indicates that the private prisons were found to be either cheaper or of equal cost to their public counterparts with two exceptions. The GAO (1996) study found the Tennessee cost analysis to be inconclusive. The average per inmate cost

Table 12.4
Comparison of Cost-Effectiveness Across Studies

Study	Cheaper?	Significance Test?	Firm Conclusions?
Arizona, Thomas (1997)	Private	No	No
Florida, OPPAGA (1998)	Private	No	No
Florida, OPPAGA (2000)	Private	No	No
Kentucky, Urban Institute (1989)	Public	Yes	Yes
Louisiana, Archambeault & Deis (1996)	Private	Yes	Yes
Sellers (1989)	Private	No	No
Tennessee, General Accounting Office (1996)	Inconclusive	No	No
Texas, Texas Sunset Advisory Commission (1990)	Private	No	No
Wisconsin, Mitchell (1996)	Private	No	No

per day was U.S. $35.39 for the private facility, compared to U.S. $34.90 and U.S. $35.45 for the public facilities. Therefore, the private facility fell somewhere in between the per diem cost of the public facilities as it was cheaper than one and more expensive to operate than the other. The Urban Institute (1989) also had evidence that the private prison is more expensive to operate than its public comparison with a U.S. $3.00 per diem difference.

In contrast, the "actual" (as opposed to the hypothetical) public prisons in the remaining studies were found to be more expensive to operate on an inmate cost per day basis. Sellers' (1989) study finds the private prison to be between U.S. $4.00 and U.S. $30.00 cheaper per inmate per day than its public counterpart. OPPAGA (2000) found that the Florida private facility was U.S. $1.54 per diem cheaper than its public comparison in fiscal year 1997/1998 and provided an even higher cost savings in fiscal year 1998/1999 at U.S. $5.12 per diem. Archambeault and Deis (1996) found the private facilities to be operating from U.S. $3.11 to U.S. $3.67 cheaper than the public facilities. Thomas (1997) found a much higher cost savings where the private facility operated U.S. $7.18 per inmate per day less than the average cost of the public facil-

ities. Certain hypothetically created public facilities were also more expensive than the private facilities. OPPAGA (1998) found the private facility to be U.S. $1.80 per diem cheaper. Similarly, Mitchell (1996) found the Wisconsin private facility to operate at a U.S. $1.28 cheaper per diem cost, and TSAC (1990) found an even higher cost savings at U.S. $3.89 per diem when it compared its private facility to the hypothetical public facility.

Summary

Although the findings appear to have a consistent pattern with the private facilities operating with an approximate median[6] per diem cost difference of U.S. $3.40 cheaper than the public facilities, the methodological limitations of the studies are a cause for caution when interpreting results. For example, many studies use poor matching techniques (OPPAGA 1998, 2000; Thomas, 1997; Urban Institute, 1989). In addition, three of the studies compare "hypothetical" costs (Mitchell, 1996; OPPAGA, 1998; TSAC, 1990), and the Louisiana and Kentucky studies were the only studies that employ tests of statistical significance to assess the differences in cost. Furthermore, many of the studies fail to account for confounding factors that could have influenced the cost differences, such as security level, maximum capacity, and the number of programs the facility provided.

Thus, as with the literature addressing the comparisons of the quality of confinement across public and private prisons, the existing cost comparisons offer little in the way of firm conclusions about whether turning over the responsibility of managing prisons to the private sphere will result in any substantial and/or consistent cost savings. Indeed, the variations in the methodological approaches taken by researchers and the lack of generalizability associated with the case study method do not lend themselves well to any concrete conclusions about cost-effectiveness. Even so, the current *inability* to state with any certainty whether private correctional management is—or is not—a sure bet for easing the burden on state correctional budgets is important for two reasons. First, like the literature on the quality of confinement, neither side of the correctional privatization debate should, at this time, be able to legitimately claim that the weight of the empirical evidence is on their side. There are simply too many methodological variations and shortcomings within this body of literature to warrant confidence in either position. Second, and similarly, the lack of empirical clarity brought on by the dissimilarities in the case study methods employed by researchers in this area thus far may be remedied, at least to a certain extent, by alternative methods of studying the effects of prison privatization. To date, only one study attempted to address the limitations of the above studies (Pratt & Maahs, 1999).

Pratt and Maahs (1999) reviewed all studies that were published in academic journals and all federal, state, and local evaluation reports from political agencies in search of common statistical patterns in the cost-effectiveness evaluation research. Only those studies that include an estimate of the inmate cost per day, or a way to calculate it, and provide information on institutional characteristics of the facilities were included in their sample. The analysis of 33 cost evaluations found that there was no overall significant pattern of cost savings for private over public prisons. To be sure, after controlling for the number of inmates, the age of the facility, and security level, the ownership variable—whether public or private—was found to be "an insignificant predictor of the standardized measure of inmate cost per day" (Pratt & Maahs, 1999, p. 365).

This was the first study comparing private and public facilities that tests for the significance of ownership while controlling for other confounding factors. Pratt and Maahs' (1999) study is not flawless, however. It assesses evaluations of a small nonrandom sample of prisons, which may indicate a threat to external validity (i.e., it remains difficult to generalize to all private facilities). Even so, this study is a step in the direction that future research should progress. To that end, the final section of this paper discusses how we can reach a better understanding of the relative advantages and disadvantages of public versus private prisons with regard to issues of the quality of confinement and cost-effectiveness.

Conclusions

In recent years, there has been an increasing call for "evidence-based" policy making in corrections (MacKenzie, 2000; Sherman et al., 1997). Although this call has been taken up most aggressively by researchers who advocate adopting strategies for offender treatment to reduce recidivism (Andrews et al., 1990; Cullen & Gendreau, 2000; Latessa & Holsinger, 1998; Palmer, 1992; Petersilia, 1996), the implications of the evidence-based movement in corrections are much broader. In short, it is a challenge to correctional policy makers to use the best available empirical evidence to inform their decisions—not only for the purpose of correctional rehabilitation, but for all other domains of correctional policy as well.

Even so, such an approach assumes that the body of empirical studies addressing a given topic clearly demonstrates a preponderance of evidence in favor of a particular side of a debate. Unfortunately, this is not the case when it comes to the literature addressing the relative cost-effectiveness and quality of confinement in public versus private prisons. To be sure, our understanding of these issues is severely obscured by variations in how researchers have gone about studying the dynamics of prison privatization. Indeed, should we place greater emphasis on studies assessing real or hypothetical prisons? What is the best way to conceptualize and measure quality? Perhaps even more critical, how much credence should we afford studies where the number of independent variables exceeds the number of observations (see the discussion by Useem & Reisig, 1999)?

In addition to these concerns, how should correctional policy makers determine which side is "right" when both advocates and opponents of prison privatization claim that the weight of the empirical evidence is on their side? Accordingly, based on the present review, the volume of methodological inconsistencies across studies indicates that the confusion surrounding the demonstrated advantages and disadvantages of prison privatization is warranted. To advance this portion of the debate to the point where evidence-based correctional policy making can actually take place, certain changes in the way scholars go about studying these issues would be helpful. With this goal in mind, we have three major recommendations for future researchers that may help to clarify the empirical portion of the prison privatization debate.

Our first recommendation is to *move beyond the case study method*. Case studies have undoubtedly dominated the empirical landscape in prison privatization research. The utility of this approach of course lies in the ability of the researcher to understand certain organizational processes (e.g., budgeting and contracting) and to serve decid-

edly "localized" goals (i.e., Would prison privatization benefit a particular region in a particular state?). Nevertheless, a comparative analysis based on a sample size of two or three facilities tells us precious little about the nearly 2000 other secure adult correctional facilities (not to mention juvenile facilities) in the United States.

In essence, the case study approach has contributed—by itself—to the lack of empirical clarity associated with prison privatization research in two ways. First, and most obvious, case studies—by definition—lack generalizability. In other words, a comparison of two medium-security correctional facilities in one state may show either a public or private advantage in terms of cost-effectiveness and/or quality of confinement, yet one cannot assume that such results will be replicated elsewhere. Perhaps even more important—and briefly stated above—the second problem brought on by the overreliance on case studies in this area is that the inconsistencies in results across case studies allow researchers on both sides of the debate to marshal a certain "block" of studies in their favor. More large-scale studies would therefore help to remove some of the controversy surrounding what is "known" about public versus private prisons that has been brought on by the current dependence on the results generated by the bevy of case studies.

Our second recommendation is that should case studies continue to be conducted, *researchers should give the scrutiny of management practices equal weight with contracting and budgeting concerns*. This has been done with a high degree of methodological rigor only in the study conducted by Logan (1992). Most often, researchers tend to be more concerned, for example, with how private agencies may manipulate accounting practices and/or circumvent traditional budgeting procedures so that an appearance of cost-effectiveness can be maintained. We certainly do not want to trivialize these issues as being unimportant to our understanding of the possible advantages and disadvantages of prison privatization. Indeed, these are legitimate concerns that researchers have been wise to consider. Nevertheless, what needs to be uncovered now is an understanding of: (a) the administrative techniques used by private agencies that may be capable of resulting in a lower cost and/or a higher quality of service provision and in turn, (b) whether these are techniques that can be adopted by public agencies as well. Such information would reveal whether the key variable in the operation of prisons is, independent of "ownership," how the facilities are managed (DiIulio, 1987, 1991).

Finally, as with fields such as correctional treatment (Andrews et al., 1990; Lipsey, 1992), a centralized database should be created containing the most accurate and up-to-date research information on both public and private prisons. The foundation for such a project already exists with the census of U.S. correctional facilities data set sponsored by the Bureau of Justice Statistics. The information on the private facilities in these data sets, however, is generally considered to be unreliable on certain key quality of confinement variables (e.g., escapes, rule infractions, violent incidents), and only crude cost estimates are included (i.e., no information on potential hidden costs are provided; see the discussion by Austin & Coventry, 1999). Thus, a database housing the most current and reliable information on public versus private prisons that could be accessed by both policy makers and academics would no doubt prove to be an invaluable resource. To be sure, prison privatization continues to expand, and the business of corrections is still "booming" (Harland, 1997, p. 3). As such, providing correctional policy makers with more conclusive and definitive empirical information may help to add a more rational component to discussions about prison privatization that may then contend with the legal, philosophical, and moral dimensions of the debate.

Study Questions

1. What are the two overall tasks the authors set out to accomplish with this piece of research?

2. What do you consider to be the most important and/or compelling finding presented by the authors?

3. For what reasons do the authors state that neither side—proponents of public or private institutions—can claim support?

4. Briefly summarize (in two or three paragraphs) the authors' primary recommendations for future research designed to determine the effects of prison privatization.

Notes

1. The academic journals reviewed include *The Australian Journal of Criminology, Crime and Delinquency, Crime, Law and Social Change, Criminal Justice Policy Review, Criminology, Corrections Management Quarterly, Federal Probation, The Howard Journal of Criminal Justice, International Journal of Offender Therapy and Comparative Criminology, Journal of Criminal Justice, The Journal of Criminal Law and Criminology, Research in Corrections, Justice Quarterly,* and *The Prison Journal.*

2. This review excluded studies regarding community correctional facilities and those studies conducted outside of the United States. The analysis was limited to United States' prison studies for two reasons. First, the United States views privatization and private companies much differently than comparable countries abroad (Harding, 1998). Secondly, the United States has a very different idea about the use of prisons and prison policy. The United States has the second largest imprisonment rate in the world, trailing behind Russia (Van Slambrouck, 1998). Other countries contracting out to private industries, such as the United Kingdom, [have] about one fifth of the United States' incarceration rate (Home Office, 1999). Therefore, comparing private prison studies internationally to those within our own borders is problematic.

3. The facilities were opened within 1 or 2 years of its comparison.

4. Researchers have found DiIulio's (1987) measures of amenity, order, and service to be difficult to measure and to be more subjective (but see Reisig, 1998). DiIulio himself even acknowledged that order "is the most easily measured" (p. 50). Furthermore, amenity is based primarily on the perception of the inmates as it assesses if the cells are considered to be clean and if the food is good. Logan's (1992) domains, however, can be obtained through prison records. Additionally, his eight domains provide more extensive information on the quality of the prison, as he captures DiIulio's three domains of order, amenity, and service and adds four other domains.

5. Because only one study focused on the domain of justice, this domain was not included in the analysis.

6. Given the large confidence interval in the study conducted by Sellers (1989), U.S. $3.40 is an approximate median value in the distribution of cost differentials between the public and private facilities.

References

Anderson, P., Davoli, C. R., & Moriarty, L. (1985). Private corrections: Feast or fiasco? *The Prison Journal, 65*, 32–41.

Andrews, D. A., Zinger, I., Hoge, R. D., Bonta, J., Gendreau, P., & Cullen, F. T. (1990). Does correctional treatment work? A clinically relevant and psychologically informed meta-analysis. *Criminology, 28*, 369–404.

Archambeault, W. G., & Deis, D. R. (1996, December). *Cost-effectiveness comparisons of private versus public prisons in Louisiana: A comprehensive analysis of Allen, Avoyelles, and Winn Correctional Centers* (Executive Summary). Baton Rouge: Louisiana State University, School of Social Work.

Austin, J., & Coventry, G. (1999). *Emerging issues on privatized prisons*. Washington, DC: National Council on Crime and Delinquency.

Beck, A. J., & Karberg, J. C. (2001, March). *Prison and jail inmates at midyear 2000* (Bureau of Justice Statistics Bulletin). Washington, DC: U.S. Department of Justice, Office of Justice Programs.

Bowditch, C., & Everett, R. S. (1987). Private prisons: Problems with the solution. *Justice Quarterly, 4*, 441–453.

Brister, R. C. (1996). Changing of the guard: A case for privatization of Texas prisons. *The Prison Journal, 76*, 310–330.

Camp, S. D. (1999). Do inmate survey data reflect prison conditions? Using surveys to assess prison conditions of confinement. *The Prison Journal, 79*, 250–268.

Camp, S. D., & Gaes, G. G. (1998, October). *Private adult prisons: What we know and how we can know more*, monograph. Washington, DC: Federal Bureau of Prisons, Information, Policy, and Public Affairs Division.

Camp, S. D., Saylor, W. G., & Wright, K. N. (1999). Creating performance measures from survey data: A practical discussion. *Corrections Management Quarterly, 3*, 71–80.

Colson, C. (1989). Alternatives to reduce prison crowding. *Journal of State Government, 62*, 59–94.

Corrections Corporation of America. (2001). *Frequently asked questions (FAQ)*. Available from www.correctionscorp.com/statsqa.html [*sic*]

Cox, N. R., & Osterhoff, W. E. (1993). The public-private partnership: A challenge and an opportunity for corrections. In G. Bowman, S. Hakim, & P. Seidenstat (Eds.), *Privatizing correctional institutions* (pp. 113–129). New Brunswick, NJ: Transaction Publishers.

Cullen, F. T., & Gendreau, P. (2000). Assessing correctional rehabilitation: Policy, practice, and prospects. In J. Horney (Ed.), *Criminal justice 2000* (pp. 109–75). Washington, DC: National Institute of Justice.

DiIulio, J. J. (1987). *Governing prisons: A comparative study of correctional management*. New York: Free Press.

DiIulio, J. J. (1991). *No escape: The future of American corrections*. New York: Basic Books.

Drowota, C. (1995). *Comparative evaluation of privately-managed CCA prisons (South Central Correctional Center) and state-managed prototypical prisons (Northeast Correctional Center, Northwest Correctional Center)* (Executive Summary). Nashville, TN: Select Oversight Committee on Corrections, Tennessee Assembly.

Durham, A. M. (1989). The privatization of punishment: Justification, expectations, and experience. *Criminal Justice Policy Review, 3*, 48–73.

Geis, G., Mobley, A., & Shichor, D. (1999). Private prisons, criminological research, and conflict of interest: A case study. *Crime & Delinquency, 45*, 372–388.

General Accounting Office. (1996). *Private and public prisons: Studies comparing operational costs and/or quality of service*. Washington, DC: Author.

Harding, R. (1998). Evaluating private prisons: A reply. *The Australian Journal of Criminology, 31*, 314–320.

Harland, A. (1997). Editorial introduction. *The Prison Journal, 77*, 3–5.

Henig, J. R. (1985). Privatization and decentralization: Should governments shrink? *Public Policy and Federalism, 12*, 26–53.

Home Office. (1999). *Research development statistics.* Available from http://www.homeoffice.gov.uk/rds/prischap1.html [*sic*]

Lanza-Kaduce, L., Parker, K. F., & Thomas, C. W. (2000). The devil in the details: The case against the case study of private prisons, criminological research and conflict of interest. *Crime & Delinquency, 46*, 92–136.

Latessa, E. J., & Holsinger, A. (1998). The importance of evaluating correctional programs: Assessing outcome and quality. *Corrections Management Quarterly, 2*, 22–29.

Lilly, R. J., & Deflem, M. (1996). Profit and reality: An analysis of the corrections commercial complex. *Crime & Delinquency, 42*, 3–20.

Lilly, R. J., & Knepper, P. (1993). The corrections-commercial complex. *Crime and Delinquency, 39*, 150–166.

Lipsey, M. (1992). Juvenile delinquency treatment: A meta-analytic inquiry into the variability of effects. In T. D. Cook et al. (Eds.), *Meta-Analysis for explanation: A casebook* (pp. 83–127). New York: Russell Sage.

Logan, C. H. (1987). The propriety of prisons. *Federal Probation, 51*, 35–40.

Logan, C. H. (1990). *Private prisons: Cons and pros.* New York: Oxford University Press.

Logan, C. H. (1992). Well-kept: Comparing quality of confinement in private and public prisons. *The Journal of Criminal Law and Criminology, 83*, 575–613.

Logan, C. H. (1996). Public vs. private prison management: A case comparison. *Criminal Justice Review, 21*, 62–85.

MacKenzie, D. L. (2000). Evidence-based corrections: Identifying what works. *Crime and Delinquency, 46*, 457–471.

Maxfield, M. G., & Babbie, E. (1998). *Research methods for criminal justice and criminology* (3rd ed.). Belmont, CA: Wadsworth.

McConville, S. (1987). Aid from industry? Private corrections and prison crowding. In S. Gottfredson & S. McConville (Eds.), *America's correctional crisis: Prison populations and public policy* (pp. 221–242). New York: Greenwood.

McDonald, D. C. (1989). The cost of corrections: In search of the bottom line. *Research In Corrections, 2*, 1–26.

Mitchell, G. A. (1996, December). *Controlling prison costs in Wisconsin* (Report No. 9). Thiensville: Wisconsin Policy Research Institute, Inc.

Office of Program Policy Analysis and Government Accountability. (1998, April). *Review of Bay Correctional Facility and Moore Haven Correctional Facility* (Report No. 97–68). Tallahassee, FL: Author.

Office of Program Policy Analysis and Government Accountability. (2000, March). *South Bay Correctional Facility provides savings and success: Room for improvement* (Private Prison Review Report No. 99–39). Tallahassee, FL: Author.

Ogle, R. S. (1999). Prison privatization: An environmental catch-22. *Justice Quarterly, 16*, 579–600.

Palmer, T. (1992). *The re-emergence of correctional intervention.* Newbury Park, CA: Sage.

Petersilia, J. (1996). Improving corrections policy: The importance of researchers and practitioners working together. In A. T. Harland (Ed.), *Choosing correctional options that work* (pp. 223–231). Thousand Oaks, CA: Sage.

Pratt, T. C., & Maahs, J. (1999). Are private prisons more cost-effective than public prisons? A meta-analysis of evaluation research studies. *Crime & Delinquency, 45*, 358–371.

Reisig, M. D. (1998). Rates of disorder in higher-custody state prisons: A comparative analysis of managerial practices. *Crime & Delinquency, 44*, 229–244.

Reisig, M. D., & Pratt, T. C. (2000). The ethics of correctional privatization: A critical examination of the delegation of coercive authority. *The Prison Journal, 80*, 210–222.

Schiraldi, V., & Greene, J. (2002, February). *Cutting correctly: New state policies for times of austerity* (Policy Report). Washington, DC: Justice Policy Institute.

Sechrest, D. K., & Shichor, D. (1996). Comparing public and private correctional facilities in California: An exploratory study. In G. L. Mays & T. Gray (Eds.), *Privatization and the provision of correctional services: Context and consequences* (pp. 133–151). Cincinnati, OH: Anderson.

Sellers, M. P. (1989). Private and public prisons: A comparison of costs, programs and facilities. *International Journal of Offender Therapy and Comparative Criminology, 33*, 241–256.

Sherman, L. W., Gottfredson, D., MacKenzie, D. L., Eck, J., Reuter, P., & Bushway, S. (1997). *Preventing crime: What works, what doesn't, what's promising.* Washington, DC: National Institute of Justice.

Shichor, D. (1993). The corporate context of private prisons. *Crime, Law and Social Change, 20,* 113–138.

Shichor, D. (1995). *Punishment for profit: Private prisons/public concerns.* Thousand Oaks, CA: Sage.

Steelman, S., & Harms, K. (1986). Construction management firms—saving time and money. *Corrections Today, 48,* 64–66.

Texas Sunset Advisory Commission. (1990, December). *Contracts for correctional facilities and services* (Staff Report to the Sunset Advisory Commission). Austin, TX: Author.

Thomas, C. W. (1997, August). *Comparing the cost and performance of public and private prisons in Arizona,* monograph. Phoenix, AZ: Arizona Department of Corrections.

Thomas, C. W. (2001, September). *Private Adult Correctional Facility Census: A "real-time" statistical profile.* Available from http://web.crim.ufl.edu/pcp/census/2001/ [*sic*]

Urban Institute. (1989, August). *Comparison of privately and publicly operated corrections facilities in Kentucky and Massachusetts,* project report. Washington, DC: Author.

Useem, B., & Reisig, M. D. (1999). Collective action in prisons: Protests, disturbances, and riots. *Criminology, 37,* 735–760.

Van Slambrouck, P. (1998, August 6). U.S. prisons—under pressure—shows increase in violence. *Christian Science Monitor.* Available from http://www.csmonitor.com/durable/1998/08/06/pls2.htm [*sic*]

Van Voorhis, P. (1994). Measuring prison disciplinary problems: A multiple indicators approach to understanding prison adjustment. *Justice Quarterly, 11,* 679–709.

Vardalis, J. J., & Becker, F. W. (2000). Legislative opinions concerning the private operation of state prisons: The case of Florida. *Criminal Justice Policy Review, 11,* 136–148.

Wackenhut. (2001). *The Wackenhut corporation press release page.* Available from http://www.wackenhut.com/twc-pr.html [*sic*]

Winn, R. G. (1996). Ideology and the calculation of efficiency in public and private correctional enterprise. In G. L. Mays & T. Gray (Eds.), *Privatization and the provision of correctional services: Context and consequences* (pp. 21–30). Cincinnati, OH: Anderson.

13
Supermax Prisons
Panacea or Desperation?

Rodney J. Henningsen
W. Wesley Johnson
Terry Wells

Most penal institutions have developed a portion of the building dedicated to inmates who are experiencing within-institutional punishment, those not able to control themselves satisfactorily in the general prison population. These sections of prisons are generally referred to as "administrative segregation" units. As a recent development, the "supermax" prison represents an institution designed to house nothing but offenders who are not able to control themselves within a general inmate population. The authors discuss how popular these institutions have become within the political realm, as they represent the ultimate "get tough" strategy. Supermax prisons are characterized by solitary confinement, near-24-hour lockdown, and a total lack of congregation and severely limited interaction with other human beings. As such, the model has experienced criticism, particularly regarding the effects of extended solitary confinement. Although true "total control" does appear to be achieved in the supermax institution, the control comes at a cost. The authors identify the costs as including accusations of human rights violations and describe a "psychologically assaultive" environment that creates long-term damage. The reader is encouraged to contemplate the problems inherent in the creation of a "supermax" prison, while simultaneously considering what "ordinary" prisons should do with those who simply cannot conform, even in a maximum-security setting.

For over a century Americans have sought to find the silver bullet to solve its crime problems. Fads and experiments in corrections have included public humiliation, single-celling, silent systems, 12-step recovery programs, boot camps, electronic surveillance, and now, supermax. Supermax prisons have evolved out of America's love-hate relationship with crime and punishment. A supermax prison has been defined as:

> A free-standing facility, or distinct unit within a facility, that provides for the management and secure control of inmates who have been officially designated as exhibiting violent or seriously disruptive behavior while incarcerated. Such inmates have been determined to be a threat to safety and security in traditional high-security facilities, and their behavior can be controlled by separation, restricted movement, and limited access to staff and other inmates.[1]

At least in theory, this type of prison unit can and should be distinguished from administrative segregation (ad-seg). While most every prison has administrative segregation cells used for holding prisoners in short-term disciplinary or protective custody, supermax units are designed to house prisoners for a much longer period of time. Proponents of supermax prisons contend that they warehouse the worst of the worst, the most violent prisoners who threaten the security of guards and other prisoners while undermining the moral fabric of American society.

While the American public has increasingly turned to government for solutions to its social problems in the last 30 years, its perceptions of the criminal justice system have remained jaundiced. Over 75 percent of respondents in a recent national survey reported only "some" or "very little" confidence in state prison systems.[2] Similarly, over 80 percent of people surveyed each year since 1980 have indicated that the courts are too soft on crime.[3]

The American judiciary has responded to public concerns that they are soft on crime and cries for vengeance by placing more people under correctional supervision than ever before. To accommodate the increases in new prison admissions and increases in time served by prisoners, some 168 state and 45 federal prisons have been built since 1990. Today, there are a total of approximately 1,500 state and federal prisons. Between 1990 and 1995, the number of prison beds increased by 41 percent. Despite this tremendous fiscal investment, there are both state and federal prisons that operate in excess of their design capacity, state prisons by 3 percent and federal prisons by 24 percent.[4]

While there are more prisons and prisoners than ever before, there is sustained interest in making prisons even "tougher."[5] This interest may be based on the notion, not strongly supported in the criminological research on recidivism, that prisons deter. Another reason may be simply that victims of crime, and those that see themselves as potential victims, want prisoners to suffer. While harm is a critical component of punishment, its generic application to prison life creates unique challenges for correctional officers, staff, and correctional executives.[6]

Political Popularity of Supermax Prisons

Getting tough on crime has become an increasingly popular campaign platform among elected officials, and support of supermax institutions is a politically popular position in many areas across the country. The American judiciary has also supported the need for supermax prison environments. In *Bruscino v. Carlson*, federal prisoners at Marion, Illinois, sought compensation for the attacks on them by correctional officers during the October 1983 shakedown and relief from the ongoing conditions created by the subsequent lockdown. A 1985 U.S. Magistrate's Report approved by the U.S. District Court for Southern Illinois in 1987 indicated that 50 prisoners who testified to beatings and other brutalities were not credible witnesses, and that only the single prisoner who testified that there were no beatings was believable.[7] When the prisoners appealed the decision, the ruling of the Fifth Circuit Court of Appeals described conditions at Marion as "ghastly," "sordid and horrible," and "depressing in extreme," but the court maintained that they were necessary for security reasons and did not violate prisoners' constitutional rights.[8]

The 'New' Controversial Control Models

Today, control units go by many different names. They have been referred to as adjustment centers, security housing units, maximum control complexes, administrative maximum (Ad-Max), special housing units, violence control units, special management units, intensive management units, management control units, or "supermax" prisons. These new units are designed to subdue any and all resistance to order. A survey by the Federal Bureau of Prisons conducted in 1990 found that 36 states operated some form of supermax security prison or unit within a prison.[9] At that time, another six states were planning to build supermax prisons. By 1993, 25 states had specialized control units and control unit prisons were in operation in every part of the country.

> At Pelican Bay Prison there is no congregate dining or congregate exercise, and there are no work opportunities or congregate religious services. Prisoners are denied standard vocational, educational, and recreational activities.

The new model for high-security prisons is the security housing unit (SHU) at Pelican Bay Prison in California. Pelican Bay opened in December 1989.[10] Prisoners in such units are kept in solitary confinement in relatively small cells between 22 and 23 hours a day. There is no congregate dining or congregate exercise, and there are no work opportunities or congregate religious services. Prisoners are denied standard vocational, educational, and recreational activities.

The conditions are officially justified not as punishment for prisoners, but as an administrative measure. Prisoners are placed in control units as a result of an administrative decision. Because such moves are a result of an administrative decision, prisoners' ability to challenge such changes in imprisonment is severely limited. Today, throughout the country, conditions in "new" supermax prisons closely resemble those set forth at Pelican Bay.

Since their inception, supermax prison units have had their opponents. Typically, opponents have focused upon conditions that allegedly are illegal or inhumane. In some reports, prison guards have testified to shackling prisoners to their beds and spraying them with high-pressure fire hoses. Other criticisms have centered on issues surrounding

- arbitrary placement/assignment to control unit

- the long-term psychological effects from years of isolation from both prison and outside communities while being housed in solitary or small group isolation (celled 22.5 hours/day)

- denial of access to educational, religious, or work programs

- physical torture, such as forced cell extractions, four-point restraint and hog-tying, caging, beating after restraint, back-room beatings, and staged fights for officer entertainment

- denial of access to medical and psychiatric care

- mental torture, such as sensory deprivation, forced idleness, verbal harassment, mail tampering, disclosing confidential information, confessions forced under torture, and threats against family and visitors[11]

Arbitrary Placement

Prisoners are placed in high-security units for administrative and/or disciplinary reasons.

Such decisions are based on results during (re-) classification hearings. Critics have called the hearings a kangaroo court claiming prisoners are being denied due process. What is called misbehavior is (arbitrarily) decided by the guard on duty and has been known to include refusing to make beds or complaining about clogged and overflowing toilets.[11]

Violations of Human Rights and Abuses

There are many claims of human rights violations and abuses in control units, including denial of medical care to injured and/or sick prisoners (including diabetics and epileptics), extremely cold cells during winter months and extremely hot cells during summer months, arbitrary beatings, psychological abuse of mentally unstable prisoners, illegal censorship of mail, extended isolation and indoor confinement, denial of access to educational programs, and administrative rather than judicial decisions about punishment for misbehaved prisoners.[12,13]

Ability to Reduce Violence in Prisons and Society

Prison officials claim that Marion, Pelican Bay, and the other supermax-type control units reduce violence in the rest of the prison system. All the evidence points to the opposite being true. The creation of control units and increased use of administrative segregation have not reduced the level of violence within general prison populations. In fact, assaults on prison staff nationwide rose from 175 in 1991 to 906 [in] 1993.[14] The number of inmate assaults on prison employees reached 14,000 in 1995. That was up 32 percent from 1990. The number of assaults per 1,000 employees remained stable at 15. It may also be that the potential of supermax prisons to reduce overall prison violence has yet to be realized. As more disruptive inmates are placed in supermax prison cells, assaults in prisons may decline.

While supermax prisons provide correctional executives with another weapon to facilitate order in prison, most supermax prisoners are released back into the general prison population or into society. Conditions in control units produce feelings of resentment and rage and exacerbate mental deterioration.[15] It is anticipated that control unit prisoners who re-enter the general prison population or society will have even greater difficulty coping with social situations than in the past.

The Texas Experience

Overcrowding and the control of violence are critical issues in correctional management, especially in states like Texas where the federal government, in *Ruiz v. Texas*, declared the entire department of corrections unconstitutional. As a result of the *Ruiz* decision, the federal government actively monitored virtually every facet of the Texas Department of Corrections-Institutional Division for over 20 years. In attempts to shed federal control over Texas prisons, relieve massive prison overcrowding, and avoid future lawsuits, an unprecedented number of new prisons were built in a relatively short period of time. In August

1993, the Texas Department of Criminal Justice, one of the largest correctional systems in the world, operated 54 inmate facilities.[16] By August 1998, the number of correctional facilities in Texas doubled, housing prisoners in 107 correctional facilities.[17]

According to David Stanley, of the Executive Services, Texas Department of Criminal Justice-Institutional Division, Texas prisons will soon be at maximum capacity again. In August 1997, Texas's men's prisons were at 98 percent of their capacity, while women's prisons approached 85 percent of their design capacity. Currently, there are about 126,000 men and 10,000 women incarcerated in Texas prisons. Estimates are that maximum design capacity for housing male inmates will be reached in little more than a year. If current inmate population trends continue, many institutions across the country will be operating above design capacity. These factors, combined with the fact that more violent offenders are now entering prisons at an earlier age for longer periods of time than just a decade ago, affect correctional administrators' ability to maintain order and protect their own staff from assaults.[14]

In attempts to keep the lid on a more volatile prison population, Texas has been one of the first states to make a commitment to new prison construction and new state-of-the-art high-security, supermax correctional facilities. This commitment has required an investment of substantial tax revenues. The new high-security prisons, according to a spokesman for the Texas Department of Criminal Justice-Institutional Division, Larry Fitzgerald, are being built and designed with efficiency and economy in mind. The estimated cost of the some 1,300 beds (double-celled) in the new control units will be a mere $19,000 compared to the current national average of $79,770 per maximum-security bed. Costs are being reduced by using inmate labor for nonsecurity tasks, such as masonry, painting, and welding.

Currently, one high-security unit has been completed near Huntsville, Texas and construction on two other similar units has already begun. Officials estimated that inmate labor saved Texas taxpayers over 2 million dollars in the construction of the new control unit near Huntsville, Texas. Currently, high-security inmates are housed in single-cells.[18]

On August 4, 1997, inmates began arriving at the new $25 million high-security unit of the Texas prison system. The high-security unit is located on the grounds of the Estelle Unit near Huntsville. Similar to high-security units in other states, Texas inmates who are placed in the new high-security unit are put there for one of three reasons: (1) they have tried to escape; (2) they pose a physical threat to staff or inmates; or (3) they are members of disruptive groups, such as an organized gang. Approximately 50 percent to 60 percent of the current residents have been officially classified as belonging to a particular gang.

The Gilbane Corporation, with the help of inmates, began construction on the 65,780 square foot facility in October 1995. Outside, two motion detector fences surround the prison. The exterior of the new unit, although secured by electronic surveillance of the outer fence and certain portions of the building and a patrol vehicle, ironically gives less of the appearance of a traditional fortress prison in that there is no guard tower. Some have likened its appearance to that of a modern high school gym.

Despite its relative benign external appearance, its overall design seeks to provide an alternative for the most recalcitrant inmates. Although two beds per cell are still found in accordance with the original plan, a change from the original purpose of the facility now calls for one inmate per cell. While it would be possible to house 1,300 inmates, the current plan is to house only 650 inmates.

The building has a central corridor with two-story wings on the east and west sides. The east wings contain 63 cells with two beds per cell. The east side recreation yard is 22,451 square feet with 42 individual yards. The west wings have 67 cells with two beds per cell. The west side recreation yard is 24,857 square feet and contains 40 individual yards.

The concern for security prompted the design to establish 8 x 10-foot cells. Unlike the traditional cell with barred doors, all doors on this unit consist of a solid sheet of steel. A slot in the door allows officers to pass items to inmates. An inmate can contact an officer by using an intercom system in his cell. The unit's supporters champion these new doors, convinced that officers will no longer need to fear being assaulted by inmates or their waste products as they walk the unit.[19]

The computerized high-tech design is used to monitor staff as well as inmates. All of the projected 246 employees are required to go through extensive security checks upon entering the building. They are required to place their right hands into a palm print recognition station and then enter their four-digit code. Their name and time of entrance into the unit are recorded and stored digitally.

Once access is authorized, a steel door is opened and shut electronically. The computer keeps a log of all times the door was opened and closed. This feature serves as a source of information for administrators to monitor employee traffic and as an additional source of information when prisoners file allegations of abuse or neglect. All incoming on-duty officers then proceed to a central room near the facility's entrance where monitors with split screens transmit views from the many cameras providing surveillance everywhere both inside and outside the unit.

The central control room, which contains several split-screen monitors, is the hub for internal surveillance. Smaller versions of these computerized nerve centers are found in all prison wings and in the hallways. The setup makes it possible for one officer to monitor each wing.

Operational Conditions in the Texas High-Security Unit

Most of the conditions found in other control units are also found in the new unit in Texas as well. As in other such units the main objective is to minimize/eliminate an inmates' contact with staff and other prisoners. Such isolation is routine and can be up to 24 hours a day. The inmates in the new Texas control unit will spend most of their time alone in cells. Virtually all their activities both day and night take place in their cells. They eat, shower, and use the restroom in their own cells. The ability to shower the entire unit within a few hours is a major cost- and time-savings procedure, especially compared to showering individual ad-seg inmates under double and sometimes triple custody.

Each cell contains a steel toilet, sink, and showerhead. These are all bolted into the wall. Inmates have the opportunity to shower daily; at other times showers are turned off. Water for the sink and toilet is made available at all times. However, like other "amenities," they can be shut off by the central control system should the cell occupant try to flood his cell block. Inmates receive daily meals in their cells. The food is prepared within the unit by inmates from another institution and is delivered to the inmates by officers.

The high-security unit has no day rooms or television sets other than computer monitors. It does have a visitation room, however, where inmates and their visitors are separated by a thick, impact-resistant glass wall. A steel stool bolted to the floor and a two-way telephone are the only items in the room. No physical contact is possible between inmates and visitors. Likewise, inmates approved for legally prescribed visits may visit other inmates under similar conditions. Such visits are generally conducted in holding cells. Here a wall with a small window, criss-crossed by bars for communication, separates the two inmates who are seated on either side of the wall on a single steel stool bolted to the floor.

Inmates, depending on their level of classification, receive from one hour, three days a week to one hour, seven days a week outdoor recreation time. Often-times the only real reprieve from their nearly total isolation takes place at these times. During this time, inmates are moved to individual "cages" where they are separated physically from other inmates by (only) fences. There they are able to see and talk to other inmates. The 18' x 20' enclosed recreation yards include a basketball court, a chin-up bar, and a hard wall on which inmates can play handball. Each "cage" is secured by a floor-to-ceiling 35-foot-high mesh steel fence. If other inmates are nearby, they can converse.

While out-of-cell programming is available to supermax inmates in 13 states, in Texas, the intense physical limitations are compounded by the absence of educational, training, or recreational programs. Thus far, supermax imprisonment in Texas has not attempted to include formal rehabilitation programs as part of its daily routine.[20]

Consequences of Total Control

As a result, control unit inmates live in a psychologically assaultive environment that destabilizes personal and social identities. While the same can be said of the prison system as a whole, in control units mind control is a primary weapon, implemented through architectural design and a day-to-day regimen that produces isolation, inwardness, and self-containment. Within this severely limited space, inmates are under constant scrutiny and observation. In the unit, cameras and listening devices ensure constant surveillance and control of not only the inmate but also every movement of the staff.

The rural location of control units increases (or supplements) isolation and makes contact with family and community difficult for many. The difficulty for inmates in maintaining contacts with the outside world is exacerbated by the unit's isolation from major urban centers. This alienation heightens inmate frustration, deprivation, and despair. Over long periods of time, the inevitable result is the creation of dysfunctional individuals who are completely self-involved, socially neutered, unable to participate in organized social activities, and unprepared for eventual reintegration into either the general prison population, or life on the outside. Those inmates who resist less, demand less, and see each other as fierce competitors for the few privileges allowed will fare best in the system. Programs that normally exist in other prisons to rehabilitate are deemed frivolous here.

Discussion

The present system of mass incarceration accompanied by the specter of more and more control units can only be maintained with at least the tacit approval of society as [a] whole. In times of relative economic prosperity, America has had the luxury of focusing its resources on crime reduction. As the new millennium approaches, crime and its control has become a major industry. Despite the lack of valid scientific evidence that massive imprisonment reduces crime, billions of dollars have been spent to build new prisons and satisfy the American public's growing desire for vengeance. While there is some scientific evidence that there is a (weak) negative *correlation* between imprisonment and crime rates, the vast majority of studies indicate that imprisonment is *not causally related* to the variability in crime.[21-24] Critics of current imprisonment trends have argued that imprisoning large numbers of people in order to stop crime has been a spectacular and massively expensive failure.[25] Even prison officials sometimes admit to the reality of the situation.[26]

Supermax prisons, perhaps our most costly prison experiment ever, have been promoted as the new panacea for correc-

tional management problems, a form of deterrence that is guaranteed to work. On the other hand, supermax prisons are symbolic of the desperation Americans face in trying to take out crime using traditional formal control methods. The efficacy of such approaches is generally limited by their reactive nature. As the cost of incarceration continues to increase, public officials may be forced to consider a more balanced approach incorporating a more holistic view of crime control; one which focuses more on community and restoration and less on imprisonment. The challenge of the future lies in the creation of a society and a criminal justice system that is able to thwart violence with less violent means.

What we need, in all seriousness, is a better class of inmates. Such change will take time and substantial resources. As we approach the next century, we have the luxury of a relatively strong economy. While many planners have their eye on the future of the global market, failure to learn from our mistakes of the past and strategically invest in proactive crime control strategies in local communities, will eventually limit our ability to compete with other countries and life in America will become, in the words of Hobbes, even more "short, brutish, and nasty."

Study Questions

1. What are some of the ways in which the supermax prison provides political appeal?

2. What were cited as some of the primary advantages that may have been brought about by the development of the supermax prison?

3. What are some of the primary disadvantages for inmates that are brought about through being housed in a supermax prison?

4. Consider and discuss whether or not the proliferation of supermax prisons has the potential for reducing violent behav-

ior in general population prisons? In greater society?

5. What were identified as some of the primary consequences of "total control" as exemplified by the development of the supermax prison?

Notes

1. National Institute of Corrections. (1997). *Supermax Housing: A Survey of Current Practice.* Washington, DC: Government Printing Office.

2. Flanagan, T.J., and Longmire, D., eds. (1996). *Americans View Crime and Justice.* Newbury Park, CA: Sage.

3. Maguire, K., and Pastore, A.L., eds. (1995). *Bureau of Justice Statistics Sourcebook of Criminal Justice Statistics.* Albany, NY: The Hindelang Criminal Justice Research Center.

4. U.S. Department of Justice. (1997). "Correctional Populations in the United States." *Bureau of Justice Statistics Bulletin.* Office of Justice Programs, June.

5. Johnson, W.W., Bennett, K., and Flanagan, T.J. (1997). "Getting Tough on Prisoners: A National Survey of Prison Administrators." *Crime and Delinquency,* 43(1):24–41.

6. Clear, T. (1994). *Harm in American Penology: Offenders, Victims, and Their Communities.* Albany: State University of New York Press.

7. "Bruscino v. Carlson." (1985). *In Marion Penitentiary—1985.* Oversight Hearing before the Subcommittee on Courts, Civil Liberties, and the Administration of Justice, August 15. Washington, DC: U.S. Government Printing Office.

8. Landis, T. (1988). "Marion Warden Praises Decision." *Southern Illinoisan,* July 28.

9. Lassiter, C. (1990). "Roboprison." *Mother Jones,* September/October.

10. Wilson, N.K. (1991). "Hard-Core Prisoners Controlled in Nation's High-Tech Prisons." *Chicago Daily Law Bulletin,* April 25.

11. Prison Activist Resource Center. (1998). "National Campaign to Stop Control Unit Prisons." *Justice Net Prison Issues Desk.* http://www.igc.apc.org/justice/issues/control-unit/ntscup.html [*sic*]

12. Human Rights Watch. *Cold Storage: Supermaximum Security Confinement in Indiana.* New York: HRW, 1997.

13. *Madrid v. Gomez,* 889 F. Supp. 1146 N.D. Calif. (1995).

14. Prendergast, A. (1995). "End of the Line: In the New Alcatraz, Prisoners Do the Hardest Time of All." *Westword,* 18(46) July:12.

15. Korn, R. (1988). "The Effects of Confinement in the High Security Unit at Lexington." *Social Justice,* 15(1):13–19.

16. Teske, R.H., ed. (1995). "Corrections." *Crime and Justice in Texas.* Huntsville, TX: Sam Houston Press.

17. Stanley, D. (1998). Executive Services, Texas Department of Criminal Justice–Institutional Division. Telephone Interview. Huntsville, Texas.

18. *Huntsville Item,* 26 June 1997, p. 1, 6A.

19. *Huntsville Item,* 3 August 1997, p. 1, 10A.

20. Johnson, W.W., Henningsen, R.J., and Wells, T. (1998). *National Corrections Executives Survey (1998).* Unpublished Survey Research. Huntsville, Texas: College of Criminal Justice, Sam Houston State University.

21. Blumstein, A., Cohen, J., and Daniel, N., eds. (1978). *Deterrence and Incapacitation: Estimating the Effects of Criminal Sanctions on Crime Rates.* Washington, DC: National Academy of Sciences.

22. Visher, C.A. (1986). "Incapacitation and Crime Control: Does a 'Lock 'Em Up' Strategy Reduce Crime?" *Justice Quarterly,* 4(4):513–514.

23. Krajick, K., and Gettinger, S. (1982). *Overcrowded Time.* New York: The Edna McConnell Clark Foundation.

24. Zimring, F.E., and Gordon, H. (1996). "Lethal Violence and the Overreach of American Imprisonment." Presentation at the 1996 Annual Research and Evaluation Conference, Washington, DC.

25. Irwin, J., and Austin, J. (1994). *It's About Time: America's Imprisonment Binge.* Belmont, CA: Wadsworth.

26. Ticer, S. (1989). "The Search for Ways to Break Out of the Prison Crisis." *Business Week,* May 8.

14
Relationships Between Inmates and Guards

Victor Hassine

Editor's Note from *Life Without Parole*

Prisoners and their keepers have little in common. Yet as Victor Hassine notes, routine personal relationships between prisoners and guards are an important component of the larger social system within prisons. These institutions run primarily on social control, which in turn requires relationships. When prisons are overcrowded and understaffed, social control is compromised, because the relationships that hold a prison together are compromised. Officers turn to snitches to maintain order, setting in motion a process that corrupts daily life in the prison and promotes widespread violence.

—R. J.

The complexity of running a prison is revealed in this brief piece by Victor Hassine. Two distinct worlds are clearly revealed—one composed of inmates, and a substantially less populated one of guards. Both of these populations have common goals, but by definition must go about achieving them in different ways. The role that the prison "snitch" has within the institution is highlighted as well. Many correctional professionals, including high-placed administrators, may consider snitches to be a sort of necessary evil that ultimately contributes to the peace within an institution. The relationship between a correctional officer and inmate snitch is by definition an informal arrangement that may in-deed be necessary to promote informal social control. On the other hand, the existence of snitches also may force correctional officers—particularly young or inexperienced officers—to manage a vast and growing gray area, creating a gulf between the ordinarily "black-and-white" rules of a large institution. The reader is encouraged to keep in mind the ultimate goals of correctional institutions when considering the complexities that are discussed in this revealing piece.

When I first entered prison, I was surprised to discover that there was no open hostility between guards and inmates. As a matter of fact, many inmates and guards went out of their way to establish good relationships with each other. Inmates befriended guards in the hope that they would get such benefits as an extra phone call, special shower time, or the overlooking of some minor infraction. In turn, guards befriended inmates because they wanted to get information or just to keep the peace and make it through another day without getting hurt.

From what I have observed, most guards who have been attacked were attempting to enforce some petty rule. Over time, guards have learned that it doesn't always pay to be too rigid about prison regulations. Thus, an unwritten agreement has been established between inmates and guards: inmates get what they want by being friendly and nonaggressive, while guards ensure their own safety by not strictly enforcing the rules. For the most part, inmates manipulate the guards' desire for safety, and guards exploit the inmates' need for autonomy.

By the mid-1980s, things changed with overcrowding and the influx of new prison subcultures. Administrators could not hire new guards fast enough to keep pace with the flood of inmates, so the practice of overtime was employed. Any guard who was willing to work overtime could get it, with the result that on any given day a large percentage of guards were on overtime. This phenomenon had the immediate impact of introducing many exhausted, irritable guards into the work force, often on shifts with which they were not familiar.

These two factors virtually destroyed all sense of continuity and uniform treatment that the prison had established over the years. The most important element needed to maintain a workable relationship between inmates and staff is a continuity of treatment. Disturb the inmates' expectation of that continuity, and you destroy the delicate balance between them and the staff.

A tired, overworked guard on an unfamiliar shift tends to be unwilling to offer any assistance. Being a stranger to the unique inmate hierarchy of his newly assigned unit, he is unable to conform to longstanding customs and practices. This often spells disaster, as once workable relations between keeper and kept deteriorate into anger, distrust, and hatred. It has been my experience that this breakdown in relations inevitably provokes an upsurge of violence, disorder, and rioting.

There is an even more insidious consequence of excessive overtime that undermines inmate and guard relationships. In every prison there is a percentage of guards who are so rigid and unpopular with inmates, or so incompetent, that they are given work assignments that keep them away from contact with prisoners, such as tower duty or the late-night shift. Any prison administrator of intelligence knows that these kinds of guards can jeopardize the tenuous order and operation of a prison. With the advent of unlimited overtime, however, these guards have found their way into the prison mainstream. As expected, their presence has further exacerbated an already tense and uncertain environment.

The overexposure of tired, irritable, overworked, and sometimes inexperienced and antagonistic guards to the population has created an inconsistent and unpredictable prison environment, especially because guards know much less about what inmates are thinking, and vice versa. With all the new inmates coming in and out of prisons every year, it is becoming increasingly difficult for the staff to keep track of who is who and who is doing what, and even harder for a prison security force trying to employ traditional investigative and intelligence methods. In the old days, everyone knew each other in a prison and knew pretty well what everyone else was up to. Not so today.

The only way the security system can effectively operate in a prison today is by soliciting the services of snitches. Guards maintain a legion of snitches and openly advertise that fact to the inmate population. In order to keep their informants in force, prison administrators have gone overboard to reward and protect them. Their rationale is that every informant constitutes an unpaid member of the security force that helps to compensate for understaffing. This almost exclusive reliance on informants for information and intelligence creates several conditions, including:

1. Keeping the inmate population at odds with each other over who is the informant in their midst.

2. Elevating snitches in the prison hierarchy, since they are often rewarded with the best jobs, highest pay, and best living conditions.

3. Increasing the growing antagonism between long-term inmates and parole violators, who are more likely to become informants in order to gain early parole and relative comfort during their brief stay in prison.

4. A proliferation of drugs entering the prison, as informants act as conduits for drug smuggling while looking for information.

5. Providing prison administrators with distorted images of inmate activity, as informants become less credible the more they are used.

This last condition often occurs because an informant is pursuing his own interests and therefore will only inform on those activities that do not affect his particular business. Such self-serving information is only as accurate as the informant needs it to be. Sometimes it is a fabricated reflection of what he knows the administration wants to hear. Thus, many informants provide the kind of information that sacrifices the truth in order to conform to some preexisting view.

To use a classic example of this, I knew an ambitious guard in 1983 who told me he used his overtime to ensure himself a more substantial pension benefit. (In those days, pensions were based on the three highest annual salaries rather than on base salary.) So he worked double shifts seven days a week for three years. But as a result, he became useless. He was either too listless and irritable or falling asleep all the time. In order to convince his superiors of his efficiency, he would reward informants who gave him information that he could use to issue misconducts. Consequently, his informants were in turn able to operate a massive drug and homosexual prostitution ring under his protection. Administrators ended up buying a nickel's worth of information for $1,000's worth of corruption.

Another example involved a prison murder. One day in the yard, two inmates fought over drugs until one of them was stabbed to death in plain view of dozens of witnesses. Subsequently, the prison security officer received numerous notes from inmates wishing to give eyewitness accounts. This enabled the authorities to quickly identify the culprit. But the informants all gave self-serving details of the crime and its motives, until there were so many contradicting versions of what happened that all their testimony was rendered worthless. Without enough evidence, the state was forced to offer the murderer five to ten years in return for a guilty plea. Such a sentence for a murder committed in a public prison yard is so lenient that it could be considered a license

to kill. This failure of justice on the part of the prison administration was precipitated by its exclusive reliance on unreliable informants.

The end result is that today's prisons have become even more violent. Inmates do not trust each other, because informants call the shots and even initiate or encourage most of the crimes they report. Guards are overworked and increasingly alienated from the mainstream of prison life. And finally, a new breed of criminals—young, violent, ignorant, drug-addicted, and completely self-absorbed—is pouring in and leaving even the most veteran inmates and staff scared to death.

Study Questions

1. What effect do overworked guards have on the overall prison environment?

2. For what reason(s) may overworked guards exist, according to the author?

3. Consider whether or not you feel as though snitches are a necessary evil within the prison environment. List the reasons why you support or disapprove of the use of snitches.

4. In light of what correctional officers are trying to accomplish via the use of informants, can you think of any alternative solutions to meet those goals?

5. What was meant by the author's assertion that "the most important element needed to maintain a workable relationship between inmates and staff is a continuity of treatment"? What sorts of threats to that continuity are introduced by the existence of guards striving for more overtime and/or the use of snitches?

Excerpted from Victor Hassine, *Life Without Parole: Living in Prison Today.* Copyright © 1999, Roxbury Publishing. Reprinted by permission. All rights reserved. ✦

15
A-Block

Ted Conover

Ted Conover presents the reader with a window into the life of a brand-new correctional officer in one of the United States' most notorious prisons—Sing Sing. At the outset, the many risks of holding the position of correctional officer may not appear surprising. How some of these risks originate, however, may indeed be startling. The author presents an additional account that details the complexity of the relationships that exist within the prison environment. This time, though, the nuances of the relationships between "old guards" and "new guards" are highlighted, as are the relationships between guards and inmates. Despite the adversarial and subordinate nature of "the keeper and the kept," there may indeed be many avenues whereby the inmates have the upper hand within an institution. Literature regarding institutional corrections often centers on the inmate subculture that exists, and investigates the sources of that subculture (e.g., importation versus deprivation as the primary pressures shaping subculture). Conover's piece reminds the reader that there may also be a very active and complex guard subculture that also has advantages and disadvantages for pursuing what may be the ultimate goal of institutional corrections—peace within the walls.

Many times during those first months I was assigned to A-block. The mammoth cellblock required more officers to run it than any other building—around thirty-five during the day shift—but the senior officers there seemed particularly unfriendly to new officers, offering little encouragement and lots of criticism. The best way to fend off

their comments, I decided, would be to try and enforce the rules as strictly as I could.

But, assigned to one of the vast eighty-eight-cell galleries for the first time, I found it hard to know where to begin. With the sheets hanging from the bars like curtains? The clothes drying on the handrails? The music blaring from several cells? I decided to start with the annoyance closest at hand: an inmate's illegal radio antenna.

Inmates were allowed to have music. Each cell had two jacks in the wall for the headphones its occupant was issued upon arrival. Through one jack was transmitted a Spanish-language radio station; through the other, a rhythm-and-blues station, except during sporting events, when the games were transmitted instead. Inmates could have their own radios, too, but the big steel cellblock made reception very difficult. Telescoping antennas were forbidden, because they might be turned into "zip guns." By inserting a bullet into the base of an extended antenna and then quickly compressing it, an inmate could fire the inaccurate but still potentially deadly gun. The approved wire dipole antennas were supposed to be placed within a two-by-four-foot area on the wall—where, apparently, they did no good at all.

To improve their chances of tuning in to a good station, inmates draped wires over their bars and across the gallery floor. Some even tied objects to the end of a bare strand of copper wire and flung it toward the outside wall, hoping that it would snag on a window and that they would win the reception jackpot. (When you looked up from the flats on a sunny day, you could sometimes see ten or twenty thin wires spanning the space between the gallery and the exterior wall, like the glimmering work of giant spiders.)

Antennas strewn across the gallery floor could cause someone to trip, and if they seemed likely to do so, I'd have the inmates pull them in. But the inmate in question on my first day as a regular officer in A-block— a short, white-haired man in his sixties—

had gotten his off the floor by threading wire through a cardboard tube, the kind you find inside wrapping paper. One end of the tube was wedged between his bars at stomach level, and the other protruded halfway into the narrow gallery space between cell bars and fence, like a miniature bazooka.

"You're gonna have to take this down," I advised him the first time I brushed against it.

"Why's that?"

"Because it's in my space."

"But I can't hear if it's in my cell."

"Sorry. Try stringing it up higher on your bars."

"Sorry? You ain't sorry. Why say you sorry if you ain't sorry? And where'd you get to be an authority on antennas? They teach you that in the Academy?"

"Look, you know the rule. No antenna at all outside the cell. I could just take it if I wanted. I'm not taking it. I'm just telling you to bring it in."

"You didn't tell that guy down there to bring his in, did you? The white guy?"

I looked in the direction he indicated. There were no other antennas in tubes, and I said so.

"You're just picking on the black man, aren't you? Well, have a good time at your Klan meeting tonight," he spat out. "Have a pleasant afternoon. You've ruined mine."

All this over an antenna. Or, rather, all brought into focus by an antenna. In prison, unlike in the outside world, power and authority were at stake in nearly every transaction.

The high stakes behind petty conflict became clear for me on the night during my first month when Colton and I were assigned to work M-Rec, one of the kinds of recreation that Sing Sing relied upon heavily in order to give the prisoners something to do. After dinner, instead of the gym or the yard, inmates could gather at the gray-metal picnic-style tables bolted to the floor along M-gallery, on the flats, to play cards or chess or dominoes, or watch the television sets mounted high on the walls.

"The rule is that they can't be leaning against the bars of the cells," the regular officer said to us, "and the cell gates are supposed to be closed." You could tell from his "supposed" that this rule was not strictly enforced. Still, Colton, a lieutenant's son, seemed strangely zealous. I think he couldn't stand the laxity around us. As we walked along the dimly lit gallery, he challenged one inmate after another. I decided that to keep his respect, I had better do the same. At varying volumes, they objected. "What is this, newjack rec?" asked one older man in a kufi who was sitting right outside his own open cell. I gestured toward the door. He told me that he was *always* allowed to leave the cell door open during M-Rec. Well, not tonight, I said. He yelled and screamed. I closed the gate. He walked right up to me, stood less than a foot from my face, and, radiating fury, said, "You're going to learn, CO, that some things they taught you in the Academy can get you killed."

I would hear inmates utter these exact words several times more in the incoming months at Sing Sing, a threat disguised as advice. (The phrasing had the advantage of ambiguity, and thus could steer the speaker clear of rule 102.10: "Inmates shall not, under any circumstances, make any threat.") But I hadn't heard those words spoken to me before, and that, in combination with the man's standing so close, set my heart racing. I tried staring back at him as hard as he was staring at me, and didn't move until he had stepped back first.

Some of the conflict we saw, of course, wasn't only a fixed feature of prison life; it had roots in Sing Sing's frequent changes of officers. New officers, as we'd already learned, irritated inmates in much the same way that substitute teachers irritate schoolchildren. To try to lessen these effects, the chart office would often "pencil in" a resource officer to the post of a senior officer who was sick or on vacation. That way, there wouldn't be a different substitute every day.

One day in A-block, however, I was assigned to run the gallery temporarily assigned to one of my classmates, Michaels, whom I knew to be particularly lax. It was Michaels's day off, which made me the substitute for a substitute. I knew before I even arrived that things would be chaotic.

My first problem came at count time, 11 A.M. Inmates generally began to return to their cells from programs and rec at around 10:40 or 10:45 A.M. The officers would encourage them to move promptly to their cells. By 11, anyone not in his cell and ready to be counted was technically guilty of delaying the count and could be issued a misbehavior report. Few galleries, therefore, had inmates at large after 11 A.M.

But on this day, Michaels's gallery had a dozen still out. Michaels had grown up in Brooklyn and, more than most officers from the city, considered the inmates to be basically decent guys, his "homies." He wanted them to like him. Once penciled in to this post, he had quickly learned all their names. I had helped him at count time once before, and when I complained about two inmates who were slow to lock in, Michaels replied that they were good guys. Though I had seen sergeants chew him out for looseness, he had told me privately that the sergeants could "suck my dick in Macy's window" for all he cared.

I liked Michaels for acknowledging the inmates' humanity. He had told me how much he hated A-block's usual OIC, a big, pugnacious slob I'll call Rufino, who told jokes such as "How do you know when an inmate is lying? When you see him open his mouth." But I didn't appreciate Michaels's legacy of chaos that morning.

A group of three or four senior officers strolled by, to my relief—I was sure they'd been sent to help me usher in the stragglers. But they had no such plan. A couple of them glanced disapprovingly at their watches and then at me. They didn't have to help, so they weren't going to. Thanks, guys, I muttered to myself.

About an hour later, a couple of keeplocks returned from disciplinary hearings. The block's keeplock officer, instead of borrowing my keys and ushering the inmates to their cells, called, "They're back," when he came through the gate and then disappeared. One of the keeplocks returned to his cell without trouble, but the second had other plans. It was Tuesday, he told me, and Michaels always let him take a shower on Tuesdays.

"Keeplock showers are Mondays, Wednesdays, and Fridays," I said. "And Michaels isn't here today."

"C'mon, CO, don't play tough. I'll be out in a second."

"No," I said. He acted as though he hadn't heard, grabbed a towel from his cell, and strode quickly down the gallery to the shower stall. I wasn't overly concerned: I always kept the showers locked, just in case something like this came up, and felt confident that once I reminded him he would miss keeplock rec today if he didn't go back, he'd turn around. Then I remembered. On this gallery, the lock mechanism was missing from the shower cell door. The shower was always open. Sing Sing. The inmate was a good foot taller than me and well muscled. I yelled through the bars into the shower that he'd lost his rec. He said, "Fuck rec." I put the incident into the logbook, then wrote up a Misbehavior Report and had his copy waiting in the cell when he got back. He shrugged it off.

"I don't give a fuck, CO," he explained. "I got thirty years to life, right? And I got two years' keeplock. Plus today, I got another three months. When they see this lame-ass ticket, they're gonna tell you to shove it up your ass."

The frustration was, he was probably right. Of all the inmates on a gallery, keeplocks were the hardest to deal with. There were no carrots left to tempt them with, and few sticks—especially for the long-termers. And now it was time for keeplock rec. I tried to match faces with cells as they headed out to the yard on that hot June day—it could help me when it came time to lock them back in. I was in the middle of letting them out when the keeplock officer reappeared. He gestured in the direction I was walking.

"Forty-three cell?" he said. "Hawkins? No rec today."

"No rec for forty-three? Why's that?"

"He doesn't get it today," he said, and disappeared.

I knew there could be several reasons for the inmate not receiving rec. He might have committed an infraction within the past twenty-four hours. Or he might have a deprivation order pending against him; in cases of outrageous misbehavior, a keeplock who was a "threat to security" could have his rec taken away for a day by a sergeant. Or—what I worried about in this situation—he might have pissed off the officer but *not* had a deprivation order pending. In that case, another officer was asking me to burn the keeplock's rec as an act of solidarity. I hoped it wasn't the last possibility and went on down the gallery, passing up forty-three cell.

The inmate called out to me shortly after I went by.

"Hey, CO! Aren't you going to open my cell?" I ignored him until I was on my way back. He stood up from his bed as I approached.

"Open my cell, CO! I'm going outside."

"Not today," I said.

"What? Why not today?"

"No rec today."

"Why not?"

"That's what they told me."

"Who told you that?"

I didn't answer him, but I immediately felt I'd done something wrong. I returned to the office and tried to get the keeplock officer on the phone. I was going to insist on knowing his reason. What was up with this guy? The phone rang and rang. I called the office of the OIC and asked for him. He was outside now; couldn't be reached, Rufino said. But Rufino was always unhelpful. I

called the yard. He'd had to go somewhere, wasn't there now. Shit, I thought.

Meanwhile, three keeplocks on their way out to the yard stopped separately to advise me that "forty-three cell needs to come out, CO." I looked down the gallery. He was waving his arm madly through the bars, trying to get my attention. I walked down to talk to him.

"You're not letting me out?"

I shook my head.

"Who said so?" He was angry now.

"I don't know his name," I lied.

"Well, what did he look like?" I declined to help out. "Then what's your name? I'm writing up a grievance." I told him my name. When I passed by the cell again an hour later, he had a page-long letter written out.

Instead of the classic newjack mistake of enforcing a rule that nobody really cared about, I had just enforced a rule that wasn't a rule, for my "brother in gray." I knew that many police admired that kind of thing. But it made me feel crummy. And with the grievance coming, I was going to have to answer for it.

I thought about how the senior officers hadn't helped me during the count, how the keeplock officer hadn't helped me when the two inmates came back, and how the same keeplock officer hadn't explained to me the deal with forty-three, even when I asked. More than once at the Academy, I'd heard the abbreviation CYA—cover your ass. I knew how to do it, though I also knew there could be consequences. In the logbook, I made note of the time and wrote, "No rec for K/L Hawkins, per CO X"—the keeplock officer. And then I waited.

The chicken came home to roost about a month later. I knew it when I arrived at work and approached the time clock. Officer X, instead of ignoring me as usual, gave me a cold, hard stare. His partner, Officer Y, stopped me and asked if I was Conover. Yes, I said, and he gave me the same stare and walked away. It was because inmate Hawkins in cell 43 had slugged Officer Y the day before (as I'd since learned) that Officer X had wanted to send him a message that day.

A sergeant who was unaware of all of this approached me with a copy of the inmate's grievance letter in the mess hall at lunchtime that same day. "Do you remember this incident?" he asked. I said yes. "You'll just need to respond with a To/From," he said, using department slang for a memo. "Do you remember why you didn't let him out? Probably forgot, right?"

"Well, no, the keeplock officer told me not to."

The sergeant wrinkled his brow. "Well, probably best just to say you forgot," he said cheerily, and turned away.

"Sarge," I said. "It's in the logbook. I wrote in the logbook that he told me."

"You're kidding," he said. "Why'd you do that?"

I shrugged. "I was new."

"I'll get back to you," he said.

I wrote the memo the sergeant had asked for, told the truth, and felt conflicted. Days went by. Another sergeant called me in and told to me to see a lieutenant in the Administration Building. My memo was on the lieutenant's desk, and he was poring over it. "So you say you logged this part about Officer X, right?" he asked. I nodded, expecting to receive a stern, quiet lecture on how not to fuck my fellow officer. But the lieutenant just nodded, cogitated a bit, and then picked up the phone.

I heard him greet a sergeant in A-block. "So Officer X remembers saying that to Conover now, is that right? And he's going to write a new To/From? And you'll take care of the deprivation order? Okay, fine." And hung up.

He passed my memo to me over the desk. "Just write this up again, but leave out the name of Officer X," he told me.

"And then we're set?"

"All taken care of."

I was relieved. Officer X was off the hook, which meant that maybe he wouldn't hate me more than he already did. Apparently, a deprivation order would be backdated to cover *his* ass. And I had learned an important lesson: If you were going to survive in jail, the goody-goody stuff had to go. Any day in there, I might find myself in a situation where I'd need Officer X to watch my back, to pry a homicidal inmate off of me, at his peril. The logic of the gray wall of silence was instantly clear, as clear as the glare of hate that Officer X had sent my way when he heard what I'd done.

* * *

The single most interesting word, when it came to the bending and ignoring of rules, was *contraband*. To judge by the long list of what constituted contraband, its meaning was clear. In practice, however, contraband was anything but.

The first strange thing about contraband was that its most obvious forms—weapons, drugs, and alcohol—could all be found fairly readily inside prison. Some of the drugs probably slipped in through the Visit Room, but most, it seemed, were helped into prison by officers who were paid off. The Department had a special unit, the Inspector General's Office, which followed up on snitches' tips and tried to catch officers in the act; the union rep had even warned us about the "IG" at the Academy. A couple of times a year, I would come to find, a Sing Sing officer was hauled off in handcuffs by the state police.

But even in its lesser forms, contraband had many interesting subtleties. As officers, we were not allowed to bring through the front gate glass containers, chewing gum, pocket knives with blades longer than two inches, newspapers, magazines, beepers, cell phones, or, obviously, our own pistols or other weapons. A glass container, such as a bottle of juice, might be salvaged from the trash by an inmate and turned into shards for weapons. The chewing gum could be stuffed into a lock hole to jam the mechanism. The beepers, newspapers, and magazines were distractions—we weren't supposed to be occupied with any of that while on the job. Nor could we make or receive phone calls, for the same reason. Apart from inmates smoking in their cells, smoking was generally forbidden indoors.

And yet plenty of officers smoked indoors. Many chewed gum. The trash cans of wall towers were stuffed with newspapers and magazines.

A much longer list of contraband items applied to inmates. As at Coxsackie, they couldn't possess clothing in any of the colors reserved for officers: gray, black, blue, and orange. They couldn't possess cash, cassette players with a record function, toiletries containing alcohol, sneakers worth more than fifty dollars, or more than fourteen newspapers. The list was very long—so long, in fact, that the authors of *Standards of Inmate Behavior* found it easier to define what *was* permitted than what wasn't. Contraband was simply "any article that is not authorized by the Superintendent or [his] designee."

You looked for contraband during pat-frisks of inmates and during random cell searches. One day in A-block, I found my first example: an electric heating element, maybe eight inches wide, such as you'd find on the surface of a kitchen range. Wires were connected to the ends of the coil, and a plug was connected to the wires. The inmate, I knew, could plug it into the outlet in his cell, place a pan on it, and do some home cooking. I supposed it was contraband because of the ease with which it could start a fire, trip the cell's circuit breaker, burn the inmate, or burn someone the inmate didn't like. And it must have been stolen from a stove somewhere inside the prison.

I was proud of my discovery and asked a senior officer on the gallery how to dispose of it and what infraction number to place on the Misbehavior Report.

"Where'd you find this?" he asked.

"Cell K-twelve, in a box behind the locker," I said.

"K-twelve—yeah, he's a cooker," the officer said. "Cooks every night. Can't stand mess-hall food. I don't blame him."

"Yeah? So what's the rule number?"

The other officer said he didn't know, so I made some phone calls, figured it out, and did the paperwork during lunch. While I was at it, an inmate porter stopped by and pleaded on behalf of the cooker. "He's a good guy, CO. He needs it." A few minutes later, to my amazement, a mess-hall officer called.

"You the guy who found that heating element?" he asked.

"Yeah. Why?"

"What are you going to do with it?"

"Turn it in."

"Oh really?"

"Yeah. Why?"

There was a long pause. "Oh, nothing." He hung up.

I finished my Misbehavior Report and stepped out of the office to let inmates back into their cells from chow. When I returned to the office, the coil, which I had placed on the desk, was gone.

"Where'd it go?" I asked the senior officer. "Did you move it?"

"What—oh, that heating thing?" he said offhandedly. "I gave it back to him."

"Gave it back? Why'd you do that? I just wrote up a report."

"Look, he's a good guy. Never gives any trouble. I think he's vegetarian. He really can't eat that stuff they serve down there. Why don't you go talk to him?" He made for the door.

I stared at him skeptically. He shrugged and was gone.

Unsure exactly why I did so, I went to talk to the inmate. He did seem like a nice guy, and thanked me profusely for not turning him in. Oh what the hell, I thought.

Not long afterward, I found another heating coil during a cell search in B-block. This time my sergeant, Murphy, saw it in my hands and insisted I turn it in. The paperwork that Murphy told me to fill out was even more elaborate than what I had imagined. Specifically, he said, I'd need to make an entry in the B-block cell-search logbook; to write a contraband receipt for the inmate, with copy stapled to a misbehavior report, to be signed by a supervisor in the Watch Commander's Office, where I would submit all the paperwork and get the key to the contraband locker in the hospital basement, where I would also sign the logbook. Oh, and on the way to the Watch Commander's Office, I should stop and pick up an evidence bag from the disciplinary office, in which to place the burner.

It was the end of my day. I knew that many officers, rather than plow through all this when their shift was over, would just drop the contraband in a trash can by the front gate and be done with it. Sergeant Murphy would never follow up. But some contrarian impulse drove me on. I finally made it to the Watch Commander's Office and waited twenty minutes for my turn with the lieutenant. He looked at the heating element, then at my paperwork.

"Do you think this is a good use of the Adjustment Committee's time?" he asked.

I shrugged and said I supposed it was. My sergeant must have thought so when he told me to write all this up, I added. The lieutenant blathered on about major versus minor offenses, the need to make judgments, and so on, apparently expecting me to say, "Oh, I get it!" and withdraw from his office. But it had been a lot of work. I had stayed late. I was pissed off about this and other things. I didn't move.

"Okay," the lieutenant finally said. "Leave it with me." I stood to leave, wondering how to take this. The lieutenant hadn't signed a thing. A CO at a desk near the lieutenant's translated for me as I walked out. "If in doubt, throw it out!" he said with a big smile. And that was that. . . .

* * *

In July, I was penciled in for two weeks as officer in charge of the A-block gym. This huge room was filled morning, afternoon, and evening with inmates, and my day shift spanned two of those times. It was regarded as a fairly good post in that you generally didn't have to spend a lot of time telling people what to do. The regular officer, presently on vacation, had had it for years. Its main downside was risk. On a cold or rainy day, the gym could fill with upward of four hundred inmates, and there were moments when I would be the only officer there with them.

Depending on the time of day, eight to twelve porters were assigned to the gym. I had to put through their payroll, I was told, and therefore to keep porter attendance. (The twelve to fifteen cents an hour they earned was credited to their commissary accounts.) Because I knew the B-block porters to be a tight and surly bunch, I thought I'd better let the crew know right away who was in charge.

They arrived before rec was called, supposedly to get a jump on the cleaning. There was a lot to do, because an inspection of the block was scheduled for the next day. The gym had a full-size basketball court with a spectator area around it, a weights area the size of a half court, a table-and-benches zone for cards, chess, dominoes, and similar games, and two television areas. There was also a locked equipment room in front of which sat my desk, on an elevated platform, with a microphone on top. Instead of hopping to work, the porters turned on the TVs and sat down. I turned off the one most of them were watching.

"Gentlemen, I'm going to be here for the next two weeks and I want to talk with you about when the cleaning gets done and who does what."

They sat silently.

"For example, who normally cleans today?"

At first, nobody said anything. There were stares of indifference and defiance. A pudgy inmate whose nickname, I would later learn, was Rerun finally spoke. "Don't nobody normally clean today," he said. "Tuesday's the day off."

"The day off. So when do you clean?"

"Mondays, Wednesdays, and Fridays. We know what to do."

I tried wresting more details out of them, but they wouldn't say more. Firing porters, I knew, was a bureaucratic procedure that took weeks; I'd be working elsewhere in the prison before the wheels had even begun to turn. And evidently the regular officer was satisfied with these men. Wishing I'd never started down this path, I finally had to settle for a plea dressed up as an order. "Those ledges up there? They're covered with dust, and the inspectors will be looking. So tomorrow, make sure somebody takes care of that along with all the rest."

"They don't never check those ledges," came the quick reply as I walked to my desk. And the TVs went back on.

The next day, somewhat to my surprise, six or seven of the porters set to work in earnest upon their arrival. For half an hour, they swept and mopped and picked up trash. As promised, they skipped the ledges. The place looked pretty good, and the inspectors never came.

I began to relax, and as I did, I began to understand the complex culture of the gym. There was, naturally, a big basketball scene—a league, in fact, with prison-paid inmate referees and a scoreboard and games that took place about every other day. The games were often exciting to watch—sometimes even a few officers would attend—but also nervous-making, as the crowds that gathered for matches between popular teams were partisan and players would sometimes get into fights.

Weight lifting was also popular, and when I was new at Sing Sing, it was intimidating to be faced with the huge, muscle-bound inmates who took it seriously. But soon I noticed that these purposeful, self-disciplined inmates were almost never the ones who gave us problems, and I came to agree with the opinion, generally held among officers, that the weights and machines were valuable. The only complaint I ever heard from officers was that inmates' weight equipment was much better than what was provided to officers in the small weight room in the Administration Building.

Beyond these activities, the gym held many surprises. On a busy day, it seemed almost like a bazaar. A dozen fans of *Days of Our Lives* gathered religiously every day for the latest installment of their favorite soap. Behind them, regular games of Scrabble, chess, checkers, and bridge were conducted with great seriousness. (One of the bridge players, known as Drywall—a white-bearded man with dreadlocks—came from 5-Building; more than once when he was late, his partners asked me to call the officers over there and make sure he'd left so they could start their game.) At the table next to the games, an older man sold hand-painted greeting cards for all occasions to raise money for the Jaycees, one of Sing Sing's "approved inmate organizations." In a far corner behind the weight area, at the bottom of a small flight of stairs, a regular group of inmates practiced some kind of martial art. Martial arts were forbidden by the rules, but these guys were so pointedly low-key, and the rule seemed to me so ill conceived, that I didn't break it up. In the men's bathroom, inmates smoked—also against the rules but, from what I could tell, tacitly accepted.

A floor-to-ceiling net separated these areas from the basketball court. At court's edge, a transvestite known as Miss Jackson would braid men's hair as they watched the game or press their clothing with one of the electric irons inmates were allowed to use in the gym. She received packs of Newport cigarettes—the commissary's most popular brand—as payment. Miss Jackson seemed a sweet man who was at pains to be noticed: She stretched the collar of her sweatshirt so that it exposed one shoulder, and cut scallop-shaped holes in the body so that it held some aesthetic interest. She often wore Walkman headphones, disconnected, just for the look. She must have been rich in cigarettes, and I wondered how she spent them.

Out on the court one day, just a few yards from Miss Jackson's enterprise, four short-haired, long-sleeved, bow-tied members of the Nation of Islam stood in a close circle, sternly chastising another member of the group, who must have somehow strayed. One of them was also a gym porter, among those most courteous to me. The juxtaposition of such opposites—the ideologues of the Nation and the would-be sexpot—reminded me of street life in New York City.

I walked the floor every fifteen or twenty minutes, making sure no one was smoking too openly, telling those inmates who had put on do-rags to take them off (it violated the rule against wearing hats inside), and making announcements when there was room at the bank of inmate phones that were lined up on the flats near the front gate. (Inmates who had signed up on a list could be excused from the gym to make a call.) It wasn't a bad job overall, and I suppose I should have been sad to see it go. But, as usual, I was simply relieved that nothing awful had happened under my watch. . . .

Study Questions

1. What similarities might there be between the author's experiences as a brand-new correctional officer and those of a brand-new inmate?

2. In what ways might inmates in some prisons have the upper hand regarding prison management?

3. Most organizations depend on (and even demand) very clear, precise, and detailed communication at all levels. In this piece by Conover, the prison guards seemed to benefit from a *lack* of this type of communication. For what reasons might this dynamic exist within the prison guard culture?

4. Why did the author state that the resolution of very small conflicts is as or even more important than resolving the bigger issues within a prison environment?

Part III
Prison Policy and Inmate Rights

Until the beginning of the 1960s, the rights (constitutional or otherwise) afforded to prison inmates were largely at the discretion of institutional administration. In early America, *Ruffin v. Commonwealth* (1871) had established that prison inmates were to be regarded as "slaves of the state." The concept of slavery denotes unpaid, forced labor. In effect, history translated into exactly that for many inmates throughout the United States for much of the nineteenth and twentieth centuries.

Prior to the 1960s, the courts maintained a *hands-off doctrine* regarding the administration of prisons. This approach was fueled by a desire to keep executive-level powers separate, in addition to a deference of the court system toward correctional professionals. The institutions themselves were physically out of sight of the general public, and conceptually out of sight of litigation. With very little sympathy for the plight of prisoners, conditions inside institutions were ignored on all counts. Prison was intended to be a "punishment" in and of itself, which stymied motivation to improve conditions or policies. The movement toward humane punishment had ended with the retirement of the stocks and the implementation of mass warehousing for offenders. Not surprisingly, however, due to an apparent lack of executive oversight, institutions were often allowed to deteriorate in both physical condition and the interaction between inmates and correctional officers.

In large-scale penal institutions, efforts are placed toward making life as uniform as possible. In essence, it is advantageous to allow for very few, if any, exceptions in the daily lives of inmates. This is readily apparent when the history and development of the U.S. prison are examined. The hands-off doctrine reinforced this concept because prison inmates were believed to have experienced a complete civil death. That is, due to their crimes against society, offenders were no longer entitled to many of the "basic" human rights enjoyed by free citizens. Most significantly, however, the concept of civil death was perceived to include deprivation of many of the rights outlined in the Bill of Rights of the U.S. Constitution. In addition, and perhaps most important, inmates were not afforded access to the very court system that had committed them in the first place.

Although many of the societal and legal changes that marked the beginning of the Prisoners' Rights movement are widely believed to have occurred throughout the 1960s, the seeds of this movement were undoubtedly planted during the 1940s. Perhaps the first effort toward breaking through the hands-off doctrine was held by *Ex Parte Hull* (1941). Through the review of this court case, the U.S. Supreme Court declared that prisoners have the unrestricted right of access to the federal court system. Similarly, three years later, *Coffin v. Reichard* (1944) established that inmates had the right of court review when challenging the conditions of confinement. Both of these court cases, while significant in what they later came to symbolize, applied only to federal prisoners. Regardless, precedent

175

had been set for similar cases that would apply to state-level prisons and other institutions designed to house offenders.

Many of the initial challenges to the conditions of confinement occurred in the area of freedom to practice individual religion. Several religions (both Eastern and Western) require access to materials that may be considered contraband by a prison system. Similarly, many religions require certain facilities, clothing, movement, and celebration that may disrupt the desired uniformity that makes prisons easier to manage. In *Cooper v. Pate* (1964), the U.S. Supreme Court maintained that denial of the inmates' right to practice their religion was indeed a violation of their First Amendment rights of expression. *Cooper v. Pate* was brought to the Supreme Court under Section 1983 of the Federal Civil Rights Act and later became the primary avenue through which conditions of confinement would be challenged.

Although attention to freedom of religion was seen by many as a major victory in prisoners' rights, this did not address the physical conditions of confinement. The 1970s and 1980s brought numerous cases before the Supreme Court under the Eighth Amendment, claiming that the current state of many prisons constituted cruel and unusual punishment. Judges often determined that finding grotesque filth, vermin infestations, inadequate heating and ventilation, fire hazards, and high noise levels prohibited anything that resembled a peaceful environment. A number of these court cases did result in the improvement of physical conditions inside prison walls. Currently, prisoners' rights and protections generally include religious freedom, freedom of speech, rights to medical treatment, physical protection from attack and assault, due process prior to additional institutional punishment (such as isolation or labor), and equal treatment regarding institutional jobs and educational opportunities.

It is important to note that although conditions inside prisons have greatly improved since the 1960s, the rights outlined above (as well as others not mentioned) are still considered to be provisional. Because prison administrators are responsible first and foremost to confine the convicted offender, the Supreme Court in most cases has ruled that rights be upheld only as much as possible without compromising the security of the prisons' charges. This is not to say that the advances and changes brought about by prison litigation have been meaningless—far from it. However, a significant amount of discretion naturally lies within official hands.

The selections in the following section were included in this volume to serve two functions—to offer an in-depth exploration of prison conditions both in general policy and specific inmate rights, and to provide an example of what yet can happen within institutional settings despite advances that have occurred. A broad and detailed account of how prison policy has changed over the last 25 years since the Stanford Prison Experiments is included in order to examine important issues in light of the prisoners' rights movement, as well as other general conditions and trends. Also included is an in-depth account and analysis of the Supreme Court's position regarding prisoner's rights, and the landmark cases that have influenced those rights. An article about the abusive incidences at the Iraqi detainee facility at Abu Ghraib is presented as an example of what can yet occur, despite what has been learned throughout the twentieth century. Although events at Abu Ghraib may represent an outlying example, lessons can be learned regarding the United States' domestic prison system.

Without question, prisoners' rights litigation and advances in research regarding what the best prison policies may be have settled many critical issues. The general issue of inmate rights is far from settled, however. The burgeoning prison population that spurred many of the initial legal inquiries is still increasing at dramatic rates in many states. In addition, the population of the prison system is changing. Every year, women have been constituting a larger portion of the total prison population. Because the vast majority of major cases before the courts have concerned male inmates, many of the old issues may need to be revisited to apply to females in custody. Moreover, new issues regarding women prisoners may bring about other conditions not previously reviewed. Similarly, the prison population is aging rapidly. Because countless characteristics of inmates mimic basic trends in the general population, future litigation will likely surround issues such as the conditions of geriatric inmates and the specific needs (medical and otherwise) characteristic of the aged. ✦

16
The Past and Future of U.S. Prison Policy

Twenty-Five Years After the Stanford Prison Experiment

Craig Haney
Philip Zimbardo

The Stanford Prison Experiment, conducted by Philip Zimbardo, W. Curtis Banks, and Craig Haney in 1973, is perhaps one of the best-known studies of the custodial institutional environment. Few, if any, other studies have gained as much notoriety or brought such a large number of issues regarding prisons and how they are run into the academic and public discourse. In their 1998 article, Haney and Zimbardo reflect on the 25 years of prison policy in the United States that followed their initial experiment. The authors begin by reviewing the "state" of crime and punishment at the time they conducted the experiment, and then present what they believe have been the most critical changes in U.S. prison policy that have occurred since. Of particular import are discourses regarding the prisoners' rights movement, what the authors term the death of rehabilitation, changes in sentencing patterns and policies, and, most important, the United States' tendency to "binge" on incarceration and punishment in general, which includes three-strikes legislation and the development of the supermax prison. Haney and Zimbardo reflect in detail on the Stanford Prison Experiment and reveal how what they discovered via the methodologies used may have been a harbinger of what was to come in the United States' penal system. Readers of this chapter will receive the best of two very important components—exposure to what is arguably one of the most notable studies in correctional research, and the authors' reflection and insight into prison policy over the 25 years that followed.

Twenty-five years ago, a group of psychologically healthy, normal college students (and several presumably mentally sound experimenters) were temporarily but dramatically transformed in the course of six days spent in a prison-like environment, in research that came to be known as the Stanford Prison Experiment (SPE; Haney, Banks, & Zimbardo, 1973). The outcome of our study was shocking and unexpected to us, our professional colleagues, and the general public. Otherwise emotionally strong college students who were randomly assigned to be mock-prisoners suffered acute psychological trauma and breakdowns. Some of the students begged to be released from the intense pains of less than a week of merely simulated imprisonment, whereas others adapted by becoming blindly obedient to the unjust authority of the guards. The guards, too—who also had been carefully chosen on the basis of their normal-average scores on a variety of personality measures—quickly internalized their randomly assigned role. Many of these seemingly gentle and caring young men, some of whom had described themselves as pacifists or Vietnam War "doves," soon began mistreating their peers and were indifferent to the obvious suffering that their actions produced. Several of them devised sadistically inventive ways to harass and degrade the prisoners, and none of the less actively cruel mock-guards ever intervened or complained about the abuses they witnessed. Most of the worst prisoner treatment came on the night shifts and other occasions when the guards thought they could avoid the surveillance and interference of the research team. Our planned two-week experiment had to be aborted after only six days because the experience dramatically and painfully transformed most of the participants in ways we did not anticipate, prepare for, or predict.

These shocking results attracted an enormous amount of public and media attention and became the focus of much academic writing and commentary. For example, in addition to our own analyses of the outcome of the study itself (e.g., Haney et al., 1973; Haney & Zimbardo, 1977; Zimbardo, 1975; Zimbardo, Haney, Banks, & Jaffe, 1974) and the various methodological and ethical issues that it raised (e.g., Haney, 1976; Zimbardo, 1973), the SPE was hailed by former American Psychological Association president George Miller (1980) as an exemplar of the way in which psychological research could and should be "given away" to the public because its important lessons could be readily understood and appreciated by nonprofessionals. On the 25th anniversary of this study, we reflect on its continuing message for contemporary prison policy in light of the quarter century of criminal justice history that has transpired since we concluded the experiment.

When we conceived of the SPE, the discipline of psychology was in the midst of what has been called a "situational revolution." Our study was one of the "host of celebrated laboratory and field studies" that Ross and Nisbett (1991) referred to as having demonstrated the ways in which "the immediate social situation can overwhelm in importance the type of individual differences in personal traits or dispositions that people normally think of as being determinative of social behavior" (p. xiv). Along with much other research conducted over the past two and one-half decades illustrating the enormous power of situations, the SPE is often cited in textbooks and journal articles as a demonstration of the way in which social contexts can influence, alter, shape, and transform human behavior.

Our goal in conducting the SPE was to extend that basic perspective—one emphasizing the potency of social situations—into a relatively unexplored area of social psychology. Specifically, our study represented an experimental demonstration of the extraordinary power of *institutional* environments to influence those who passed through them. In contrast to the companion research of Stanley Milgram (1974) that focused on individual compliance in the face of an authority figure's increasingly extreme and unjust demands, the SPE examined the conformity pressures brought to bear on groups of people functioning within the same institutional setting (see Carr, 1995). Our "institution" rapidly developed sufficient power to bend and twist human behavior in ways that confounded expert predictions and violated the expectations of those who created and participated in it. And, because the unique design of the study allowed us to minimize the role of personality or dispositional variables, the SPE yielded especially clear psychological insights about the nature and dynamics of social and institutional control.

The behavior of prisoners and guards in our simulated environment bore a remarkable similarity to patterns found in actual prisons. As we wrote, "Despite the fact that guards and prisoners were essentially free to engage in any form of interaction . . . the characteristic nature of their encounters tended to be negative, hostile, affrontive and dehumanising" (Haney et al., 1973, p. 80). Specifically, verbal interactions were pervaded by threats, insults, and deindividuating references that were most commonly directed by guards against prisoners. The environment we had fashioned in the basement hallway of Stanford University's Department of Psychology became so real for the participants that it completely dominated their day-to-day existence (e.g., 90 percent of prisoners' in cell conversations focused on "prison"-related topics), dramatically affected their moods and emotional states (e.g., prisoners expressed three times as much negative affect as did guards), and at least temporarily undermined their sense of self (e.g., both groups expressed increasingly more deprecating self-evaluations over time). Behaviorally, guards most often gave commands and engaged in confrontive or aggressive acts toward prisoners, whereas the prisoners initiated increasingly less behavior; failed to support each other more often than not; negatively evaluated each other in ways that were consistent with the guards' views of them; and as the experiment progressed, more frequently expressed intentions to do harm to others (even as they became increasingly more docile and conforming to the whims of the guards). We concluded,

> The negative, anti-social reactions observed were not the product of an environment created by combining a collection of deviant personalities, but rather the result of an intrinsically pathological situation which could distort and rechannel the behaviour of essentially normal individuals. The abnormality here resided in the psychological nature of the situation and not in those who passed through it. (Haney et al., 1973, p. 90)

In much of the research and writing we have done since then, the SPE has served as an inspiration and intellectual platform from which to extend the conceptual relevance of situational variables into two very different domains. One of us examined the coercive power of legal institutions in general and prisons in particular (e.g., Haney, 1993a, 1997b, 1997c, 1997d, 1998; Haney & Lynch, 1997), as well as the importance of situational factors in explaining and reducing crime (e.g., Haney, 1983, 1994, 1995, 1997a). The other of us explored the dimensions of intrapsychic "psychological prisons" that constrict human experience and undermine human potential (e.g., Brodt & Zimbardo, 1981; Zimbardo, 1977; Zimbardo, Pilkonis, & Norwood, 1975) and the ways in which "mind-altering" social psychological dynamics can distort individual

judgment and negatively influence behavior (e.g., Zimbardo, 1979a; Zimbardo & Andersen, 1993). Because the SPE was intended as a critical demonstration of the negative effects of extreme institutional environments, much of the work that grew out of this original study was change-oriented and explored the ways in which social and legal institutions and practices might be transformed to make them more responsive to humane psychological imperatives (e.g., Haney, 1993b; Haney & Pettigrew, 1986; Haney & Zimbardo, 1977; Zimbardo, 1975; Zimbardo et al., 1974).

In this article, we return to the core issue that guided the original study (Haney et al., 1973)—the implications of situational models of behavior for criminal justice institutions. We use the SPE as a point of historical departure to briefly examine the ways in which policies concerning crime and punishment have been transformed over the intervening 25 years. We argue that a series of psychological insights derived from the SPE and related studies, and the broad perspective that they advanced, still can contribute to the resolution of many of the critical problems that currently plague correctional policy in the United States.

Crime and Punishment a Quarter Century Ago

The story of how the nature and purpose of imprisonment have been transformed over the past 25 years is very different from the one that we once hoped and expected we would be able to tell. At the time we conducted the SPE—in 1971—there was widespread concern about the fairness and the efficacy of the criminal justice system. Scholars, politicians, and members of the public wondered aloud whether prisons were too harsh, whether they adequately rehabilitated prisoners, and whether there were alternatives to incarceration that would better serve correctional needs and interests. Many states were already alarmed about increased levels of overcrowding. Indeed, in those days, prisons that operated at close to 90 percent of capacity were thought to be dangerously overcrowded. It was widely understood by legislators and penologists alike that under such conditions, programming resources were stretched too thin, and prison administrators were left with increasingly fewer degrees of freedom with which to respond to interpersonal conflicts and a range of other inmate problems.

Despite these concerns about overcrowding, there was a functional moratorium on prison construction in place in most parts of the country. Whatever else it represented, the moratorium reflected a genuine skepticism at some of the very highest levels of government about the viability of prison as a solution to the crime problem. Indeed, the report of the National Advisory Commission on Criminal Justice Standards and Goals (1973), published at around the same time we published the results of the SPE, concluded that prisons, juvenile reformatories, and jails had achieved what it characterized as a "shocking record of failure" (p. 597), suggested that these institutions may have been responsible for creating more crime than they prevented, and recommended that the moratorium on prison construction last at least another 10 years.

To be sure, there was a fiscal undercurrent to otherwise humanitarian attempts to avoid the overuse of imprisonment. Prisons are expensive, and without clear evidence that they worked very well, it was difficult to justify building and running more of them (cf. Scull, 1977). But there was also a fair amount of genuine concern among the general public about what was being done to prisoners behind prison walls and what the long-term effects would be (e.g., Mitford, 1973; Yee, 1973). The SPE and its attendant publicity added to that skepticism, but the real challenge came from other deeper currents in the larger society.

The late 1960s saw the beginning of a prisoners' rights movement that eventually raised the political consciousness of large numbers of prisoners, some of whom became effective spokespersons for their cause (e.g., American Friends Service Committee, 1971; Jackson, 1970; Smith, 1993). Widely publicized, tragic events in several prisons in different parts of the country vividly illustrated how prisoners could be badly mistreated by prison authorities and underscored the potentially serious drawbacks of relying on prisons as the centerpiece in a national strategy of crime control. For example, just a few weeks after the SPE was concluded, prisoners in Attica, New York, held a number of correctional officers hostage in a vain effort to secure more humane treatment. Although national celebrities attempted to peaceably mediate the standoff, an armed assault to retake the prison ended tragically with the deaths of many hostages and prisoners. Subsequent revelations about the use of excessive force and an official cover-up contributed to public skepticism about prisons and doubts about the wisdom and integrity of some of their administrators (e.g., Wicker, 1975).

Legal developments also helped to shape the prevailing national Zeitgeist on crime and punishment. More than a decade before we conducted the SPE, the U.S. Supreme Court had defined the Eighth Amendment's ban on cruel and unusual punishment as one that drew its meaning from what Chief Justice Warren called "the evolving standards of decency that mark the progress of a maturing society" (*Trop v. Dulles*, 1958, p. 101). It is probably fair to say that most academics and other informed citizens anticipated that these standards *were* evolving and in such a way that the institution of prison—as the major organ of state-sanctioned punishment in American society—would be scrutinized carefully and honestly in an effort to apply contemporary humane views, including those that were emerging from the discipline of psychology.

Psychologists Stanley Brodsky, Carl Clements, and Raymond Fowler were engaged in just such a legal effort to reform the Alabama prison system in the early 1970s (*Pugh v. Locke*, 1976; Yackle, 1989). The optimism with which Fowler (1976) wrote about the results of that litigation was characteristic of the time: "The practice of psychology in the nation's correctional systems, long a neglected byway, could gain new significance and visibility as a result [of the court's ruling]" (p. 15). The same sentiments prevailed in a similar effort in which we participated along with psychologist Thomas Hilliard (1976) in litigation that was designed to improve conditions in a special solitary confinement unit at San Quentin (*Spain v. Procunier*, 1976). Along with other psychologists interested in correctional and legal reform, we were confident that psychology and other social scientific disciplines could be put to effective use in the creation and application of evolving standards inside the nation's prisons (see Haney & Zimbardo, 1977).

And then, almost without warning, all of this critical reappraisal and constructive optimism about humane standards and alternatives to incarceration was replaced with something else. The counterrevolution in crime and punishment began slowly and imperceptibly at first and then pushed forward with a consistency of direction and effect that could not be overlooked. It moved so forcefully and seemingly inexorably during the 1980s that it resembled nothing so much as a runaway punishment train, driven by political steam and fueled by media-induced fears of crime. Now, many years after the SPE and that early optimism about psychologically based prison reform, our nation finds itself in the midst of arguably the worst corrections crisis in U.S. history, with every indication that it will get worse before it can possibly get better. For the first time in the 200-year history of imprisonment in the United States, there appear to be no limits on the amount of prison pain the public is willing to inflict in the name of crime control (cf. Haney, 1997b, 1998). Retired judge Lois Forer (1994), in her denunciation of some of these recent trends, warned of the dire consequences of what she called the "rage to punish." But this rage has been indulged so completely that it threatens to override any of the competing concerns for humane justice that once served to make this system more compassionate and fair. The United States has entered what another commentator called the "mean season" of corrections, one in which penal philosophy amounts to little more than devising "creative strategies to make offenders suffer" (Cullen, 1995, p. 340).

The Radical Transformation of 'Corrections'

We briefly recount the series of wrenching transformations that laid the groundwork for the mean season of corrections that the nation has now entered—the some 25 years of correctional policy that have transpired since the SPE was conducted. Whatever the social and political forces that caused these transformations, they collectively altered the correctional landscape of the country. The criminal justice system not only has become increasingly harsh and punitive but also has obscured many of the psychological insights on which the SPE and numerous other empirical studies were based—insights about the power of social situations and contexts to influence and control behavior. Specifically, over a very short period of time, the following series of transformations occurred to radically change the shape and direction of corrections in the United States.

The Death of Rehabilitation

A dramatic shift in correctional philosophy was pivotal to the series of changes that followed. Almost overnight, the concept that had served as the intellectual cornerstone of corrections policy for nearly a century—rehabilitation—was publicly and politically discredited. The country moved abruptly in the mid-1970s from a society that justified putting people in prison on the basis of the belief that their incarceration would somehow facilitate their productive reentry into the free world to one that used imprisonment merely to disable criminal offenders ("incapacitation") or to keep them far away from the rest of society ("containment"). At a more philosophical level, imprisonment was now said to further something called "just deserts"—locking people up for no other reason than they deserved it and for no other purpose than to punish them (e.g., von Hirsch, 1976). In fact, prison punishment soon came to be thought of as its own reward, serving only the goal of inflicting pain.

Determinate Sentencing and the Politicizing of Prison Pain

Almost simultaneously—and, in essence, as a consequence of the abandonment of rehabilitation—many states moved from indeterminate to determinate models of prison sentencing. Because indeterminate sentencing had been devised as a mechanism to allow for the release of prisoners who were rehabilitated early—and the retention of those whose in-prison change took longer—it simply did not fit with the new goals of incarceration. This shift to determinate sentencing did have the intended consequence of removing discretion from the hands of prison administrators and even judges who, studies showed, from time to time abused it (e.g., American Friends Service Committee, 1971). However, it also had the likely unintended consequence of bringing prison sentencing into an openly political arena. Once largely the province of presumably expert judicial decision makers, prison administrators, or parole authorities who operated largely out of the public view, prison sentencing had remained relatively free from at least the most obvious and explicit forms of political influence. They no longer were. Moreover,

determinate sentencing and the use of rigid sentencing guidelines or "grids" undermined the role of situation and context in the allocation of punishment (cf. Freed, 1992).

The Imprisoning of America

The moratorium on new prison construction that was in place at the time of the SPE was ended by the confluence of several separate, powerful forces. For one, legislators continued to vie for the mantle of "toughest on crime" by regularly increasing the lengths of prison sentences. Of course, this meant that prisoners were incarcerated for progressively longer periods of time. In addition, the sentencing discretion of judges was almost completely subjugated to the various aforementioned legislative grids, formulas, and guidelines. Moreover, the advent of determinate sentencing meant that prison administrators had no outlets at the other end of this flow of prisoners to relieve population pressures (which, under indeterminate sentencing, had been discretionary). Finally, federal district court judges began to enter judicial orders that prohibited states from, among other things. cramming two and three or more prisoners into one-person (typically six feet by nine feet) cells (e.g., *Burks v. Walsh*, 1978; *Capps v. Atiyeh*, 1980). Eventually even long-time opponents of new prisons agreed that prisoners could no longer be housed in these shockingly inadequate spaces and reluctantly faced the inevitable: Prison construction began on an unprecedented scale across the country.

Although this rapid prison construction briefly eased the overcrowding problem, prisoner populations continued to grow at unprecedented rates (see Table 16.1). It soon became clear that even dramatic increases in the number of new prisons could not keep pace. In fact, almost continuously over the past 25 years, penologists have described U.S. prisons as "in crisis" and have characterized each new level of overcrowding as "unprecedented." As the decade of the 1980s came to a close, the United States was imprisoning more people for longer periods of time than ever before in our history, far surpassing other industrialized democracies in the use of incarceration as a crime control measure (Mauer, 1992, 1995). As of June 1997, the most recent date for which figures are available, the total number of persons incarcerated in the United States exceeded 1.7 million (Bureau of Justice Statistics, 1998), which continues the upward trend of the previous 11 years, from 1985 to 1996, when the number rose from 744,208 to 1,630,940. Indeed, 10 years ago, long before today's record rates were attained, one scholar concluded, "It is easily demonstrable that America's use of prison is excessive to the point of barbarity, with a prison rate several times higher than that of other similarly developed Western countries" (Newman, 1988, p. 346). A year later, a reviewer wrote in the pages of *Contemporary Psychology*:

> American prison and jail populations have reached historically high levels. . . . It is noteworthy that, although in several recent years the levels of reported crime declined, the prison and jail populations continued to rise. The desire for punishment seems to have taken on a life of its own. (McConville, 1989, p. 928)

The push to higher rates and lengths of incarceration has only intensified since then. Most state and federal prisons now operate well above their rated capacities, with many overcrowded to nearly twice their design limits. At the start of the 1990s, the United States incarcerated more persons per capita than any other modern nation in the world. The international disparities are most striking when the U.S. incarceration rate is contrasted to those of other nations with which the United States is often compared, such as Japan, The Netherlands, Australia, and the United Kingdom; throughout most of the present decade, the U.S. rates have consistently been between four and eight times as high as those of these other nations (e.g., Christie, 1994; Mauer, 1992, 1995). In fact, rates of incarceration have continued to climb in the United States, reaching the unprecedented levels of more than 500 per 100,000 in 1992 and then 600 per 100,000 in 1996. Although in 1990 the United States incarcerated a higher proportion of its population than any other nation on earth (Mauer, 1992), as of 1995, political and economic upheaval in Russia was associated with an abrupt increase in rate of incarceration, and Russia surpassed the United States. . . .

The increase in U.S. prison populations during these years was not produced by a disproportionate increase in the incarceration of violent offenders. In 1995, only one quarter of persons sentenced to state prisons were convicted of a violent offense, whereas three quarters were sent for property or drug offenses or other nonviolent crimes such as receiving stolen property or immigration violations (Bureau of Justice Statistics, 1996). Nor was the increased use of imprisonment related to increased levels of crime. In fact, according to the National Crime Victimization Survey, conducted by the Bureau of the Census, a survey of 94,000 U.S. residents found that many fewer of them were the victims of crime during the calendar year 1995–1996, the year our incarceration rate reached an all-time high (Bureau of Justice Statistics, 1997b).

The Racialization of Prison Pain

The aggregate statistics describing the extraordinary punitiveness of the U.S. criminal justice system mask an important fact: The pains of imprisonment have been inflicted disproportionately on minorities, especially Black men. Indeed, for many years, the rate of incarceration of White men in the United States compared favorably with those in most Western European nations, including countries regarded as the most progressive and least punitive (e.g., Dunbaugh, 1979). Although in recent years the rate of incarceration for Whites in the

United States has also increased and no longer compares favorably with other Western European nations, it still does not begin to approximate the rate for African Americans. Thus, although they represent less than 6 percent of the general U.S. population, African American men constitute 48 percent of those confined to state prisons. Statistics collected at the beginning of this decade indicated that Blacks were more than six times more likely to be imprisoned than their White counterparts (Mauer, 1992). By 1995, that disproportion had grown to seven and one-half times (Bureau of Justice Statistics, 1996). In fact, the United States incarcerates African American men at a rate that is approximately four times the rate of incarceration of Black men in South Africa (King, 1993).

All races and ethnic groups and both sexes are being negatively affected by the increases in the incarcerated population, but the racial comparisons are most telling. The rate of incarceration for White men almost doubled between 1985 and 1995, growing from a rate of 528 per 100,000 in 1985 to a rate of 919 per 100,000 in 1995. The impact of incarceration on African American men, Hispanics, and women of all racial and ethnic groups is greater than that for White men, with African American men being the most profoundly affected. The number of African American men who are incarcerated rose from a rate of 3,544 per 100,000 in 1985 to an astonishing rate of 6,926 per 100,000 in 1995. Also, between 1985 and 1995, the number of Hispanic prisoners rose by an average of 12 percent annually (Mumola & Beck, 1997). . . .

The Overincarceration of Drug Offenders

The increasingly disproportionate number of African American men who are being sent to prison seems to be related to the dramatic increase in the number of persons incarcerated for drug-related offenses, combined with the greater tendency to imprison Black drug offenders as compared with their White counterparts. Thus, although Blacks and Whites use drugs at approximately the same rate (Bureau of Justice Statistics, 1991), African Americans were arrested for drug offenses during the so-called war on drugs at a much higher rate than were Whites (Blumstein, 1993). The most recent data show that between 1985 and 1995, the number of African Americans incarcerated in state prisons due to drug violations (which were their only or their most serious offense) rose 707 percent (see Table 16.1). In contrast, the number of Whites incarcerated in state prisons for drug offenses (as their only or most serious offense) underwent a 306 percent change. In 1986, for example, only 7 percent of Black prison inmates in the United States had been convicted of drug crimes, compared with 8 percent of Whites. By 1991, however, the Black percentage had more than tripled to 25 percent, whereas the percentage of White inmates incarcerated for drug crimes had increased by only half to 12 percent (Tonry, 1995). In the federal prison system, the numbers of African Americans incarcerated for drug violations are shockingly high: Fully 64 percent of male and 71 percent of female Black prisoners incarcerated in federal institutions in 1995 had been sent there for drug offenses (Bureau of Justice Statistics, 1996).

According to a historical report done for the Bureau of Justice Statistics (Cahalan, 1986), the offense distribution of federal and state prisoners—a measure of the types of crimes for which people are incarcerated—remained stable from 1910 to 1984. The classification of some offenses changed. For example, robbery is now included in the category of violent crime rather than being classified with property crimes, as it was in the past. Public order offenses, also called morals charges, used to include vagrancy, liquor law violations, and drug offenses. Drug offenses are no longer classified with public order crimes. Of course, not only have drug offenses been elevated to the status of their own crime category in national statistical compilations and their own especially severe legislated penalties, but there is also a "Drug Czar" in the executive branch and a large federal agency devoted exclusively to enforcing laws against drug-related crimes.

Table 16.1

Change in Estimated Number of Sentenced Prisoners, by Most Serious Offense and Race, Between 1985 and 1995

Most serious offense	Total % change, 1985–1995	White % change, 1985–1995	Black % change, 1985–1995
Total	119	109	132
Violent offenses	86	92	83
Property offenses	69	74	65
Drug offenses	478	306	707
Public-order offenses[a]	187	162	229
Other/unspecified[b]	−6	−72	64

Note. Adapted from *Prisoners in 1996* (Bureau of Justice Statistics Bulletin NCJ 164619, p. 10), by C. J. Mumola and A. J. Beck, 1997, Rockville, MD: Bureau of Justice Statistics. In the public domain.

[a]Includes weapons, drunk driving, escape, court offenses, obstruction, commercialized vice, morals and decency charges, liquor law violations, and other public-order offenses. [b]Includes juvenile offenses and unspecified felonies.

As we noted, the types and proportions of offenses for which people were incarcerated in the United States were highly consistent for the 75 years prior to 1984. For most of the twentieth century, the U.S. prison population consisted of around 60–70 percent offenders against property, 13–24 percent offenders against persons (now called violent crime), around 20 percent public order-morals violations (which included drug offenses), and 10 percent other types of offenders (Cahalan, 1986).

However, these distributions have changed dramatically during the past 10 to 15 years. The federal government is now willing to incarcerate people for a wider range of criminal violations, and both state and federal prisoners remain incarcerated for longer periods of time. The number of violent offenders who are incarcerated has risen but not as steeply as the number of drug offenders who are now sent to prison. In 1995, 23 percent of state prisoners were incarcerated for drug offenses in contrast to 9 percent of drug offenders in state prisons in 1986. In fact, the proportion of drug offenders in the state prison population nearly tripled by 1990, when it reached 21 percent, and has remained at close to that level since then. The proportion of federal prisoners held for drug violations doubled during the past 10 years. In 1985, 34 percent of federal prisoners were incarcerated for drug violations. By 1995, the proportion had risen to 60 percent.

We note in passing that these three interrelated trends—the extraordinary increase in the numbers of persons in prison, the disproportionate incarceration of minorities, and the high percentage of persons incarcerated for drug offenses—reflect a consistent disregard of context and situation in the criminal justice policies of the past 25 years. The unprecedented use of imprisonment per se manifests a policy choice to incarcerate individual lawbreakers instead of targeting the criminogenic social conditions and risk factors that have contributed to their criminality. Sentencing models that ignore situation and context inevitably lead to higher rates of incarceration among groups of citizens who confront race-based poverty and deprivation and other social ills that are related to discrimination. The failure to address the differential opportunity structure that leads young minority group members into certain kinds of drug-related activities and the conscious decision to target those activities for criminal prosecution and incarceration, rather than to attempt to improve the life chances of the urban Black underclass, reflect dispositional and discriminatory views of crime control.

Moreover, excessive and disproportionate use of imprisonment ignores the secondary effects that harsh criminal justice policies eventually will have on the social contexts and communities from which minority citizens come. Remarkably, as the present decade began, there were more young Black men (between the ages of 20 and 29) under the control of the nation's criminal justice system (including probation and parole supervision) than the total number in college (Mauer, 1990). Thus, one scholar has predicted that "imprisonment will become the most significant factor contributing to the dissolution and breakdown of African American families during the decade of the 1990s" (King, 1993, p. 145), and another has concluded that "crime control policies are a major contributor to the disruption of the family, the prevalence of single parent families, and children raised without a father in the ghetto, and the 'inability of people to get the jobs still available'" (Chambliss, 1994, p. 183).

The Rise of the 'Supermax' Prison

In addition to becoming dangerously overcrowded and populated by a disproportionate number of minority citizens and drug offenders over the past 25 years, many U.S. prisons also now lack meaningful work, training, education, treatment, and counseling programs for the prisoners who are confined in them. Plagued by increasingly intolerable living conditions where prisoners serve long sentences that they now have no hope of having reduced through "good time" credits, due to laws imposed by state legislatures, many prison officials have turned to punitive policies of within-prison segregation in the hope of maintaining institutional control (e.g., Christie, 1994; Haney, 1993a; Haney & Lynch, 1997; Perkinson, 1994). Indeed, a penal philosophy of sorts has emerged in which prison systems use long-term solitary confinement in so-called supermax prisons as a proactive policy of inmate management. Criticized as the "Marionization" of U.S. prisons, after the notorious federal penitentiary in Marion, Illinois, where the policy seems to have originated (Amnesty

International, 1987; Olivero & Roberts, 1990), one commentator referred to the "accelerating movement toward housing prisoners officially categorized as violent or disruptive in separate, free-standing facilities where they are locked in their cells approximately 23 hours per day" (Immarigeon, 1992, p. 1). They are ineligible for prison jobs, vocational training programs, and, in many states, education.

Thus, in the 25 years since the SPE was conducted, the country has witnessed the emergence of a genuinely new penal form—supermax prisons that feature state-of-the-art, ultra secure, long-term segregated confinement supposedly reserved for the criminal justice system's most troublesome or incorrigible offenders. Human Rights Watch (1997) described the basic routine imposed in such units: Prisoners "are removed from general population and housed in conditions of extreme social isolation, limited environmental stimulation, reduced privileges and service, scant recreational, vocational or educational opportunities, and extraordinary control over their every movement" (p. 14). (See also Haney, 1993a, 1997d, and Haney and Lynch, 1997, for discussions of the psychological effects of these special conditions of confinement.) By 1991, these prisons imposing extreme segregation and isolation were functioning in some 36 states, with many others in the planning stages (e.g., "Editorial," 1991). A newly opened, highly restrictive, modern "control unit" apparently committed the federal penitentiary system to the use of this penal form for some time to come (Dowker & Good, 1992; Perkinson, 1994). Thus, by 1997 Human Rights Watch expressed concern over what it called "the national trend toward supermaximum security prisons" (p. 13), noting that in addition to the 57 units currently in operation, construction programs already underway "would increase the nationwide supermax capacity by nearly 25 percent" (p. 14).

A constitutional challenge to conditions in California's supermax—one that many legal observers viewed as a test case on the constitutionality of these "prisons of the future"—resulted in a strongly worded opinion in which the federal court condemned certain of its features, suggesting that the prison, in the judge's words, inflicted "stark sterility and unremitting monotony" (*Madrid v. Gomez*, 1995, p. 1229) on prisoners and exposed them to overall conditions that "may press the outer bounds of what most humans can psychologically tolerate" (p. 1267) but left the basic regimen of segregation and isolation largely intact.

Here, too, the importance of context and situation has been ignored. Widespread prison management problems and gang-related infractions are best understood in systematic terms, as at least in large part the products of worsening overall institutional conditions. Viewing them instead as caused exclusively by "problem prisoners" who require nothing more than isolated and segregated confinement ignores the role of compelling situational forces that help to account for their behavior. It also overlooks the capacity of deteriorated prison conditions to continue to generate new replacements who will assume the roles of those prisoners who have been taken to segregation. Finally, the continued use of high levels of punitive isolation, despite evidence of significant psychological trauma and psychiatric risk (e.g., Grassian, 1983; Haney, 1997d; Haney & Lynch, 1997), reflects a legal failure to fully appreciate the costs of these potentially harmful social contexts—both in terms of immediate pain and emotional damage as well as their long-term effects on post-segregation and even post-release behavior.

The Retreat of the Supreme Court

The final component in the transformation of U.S. prison policy during this 25-year period came from the U.S. Supreme Court, as the Justices significantly narrowed their role in examining and correct-

ing unconstitutionally cruel prison conditions as well as drastically redefining the legal standards that they applied in such cases. Ironically, the early constitutional review of conditions of confinement at the start of this historical period had begun on an encouraging note. Indeed, it was one of the things that helped fuel the early optimism about "evolving standards" to which we earlier referred. For example, in 1974, just three years after the SPE, the Supreme Court announced that "there is no iron curtain drawn between the Constitution and the prisons of this country" (*Wolff v. McDonnell*, 1974, pp. 556–567). Given the Warren Court's legacy of protecting powerless persons who confronted potent situations and adverse structural conditions, and the Court's legal realist tendencies to look carefully at the specific circumstances under which abuses occurred (e.g., Haney, 1991), hopes were raised in many quarters that a majority of the Justices would carefully evaluate the nation's worst prison environments, acknowledge their harmful psychological effects, and order badly needed reform.

However, a sharp right turn away from the possibility and promise of the Warren Court's view became evident at the start of the 1980s. The first time the Court fully evaluated the totality of conditions in a particular prison, it reached a very discouraging result. Justice Powell's majority opinion proclaimed that "the Constitution does not mandate comfortable prisons, and prisons . . . which house persons convicted of serious crimes cannot be free of discomfort" (*Rhodes v. Chapman*, 1981, p. 349). None of the Justices attempted to define the degree of acceptable discomfort that could be inflicted under the Constitution. However, Powell used several phrases that were actually taken from death penalty cases to provide a sense of just how painful imprisonment could become before beginning to qualify as "cruel and unusual": Punishment that stopped just short of involving "the *unnecessary* and *wanton* infliction of pain"

(p. 345, citing *Gregg v. Georgia*, 1976, p. 173) would not be prohibited, pains of imprisonment that were not "*grossly* disproportionate to the severity of the crime" (p. 345. citing *Coker v. Georgia*, 1977, p. 592) would be allowed, and harm that was not "*totally* without penological justification" (p. 345, citing *Gregg v. Georgia*, p. 183) also would be acceptable (italics added).

The Supreme Court thus set a largely unsympathetic tone for Eighth Amendment prison cases and established a noninterventionist stance from which it has rarely ever wavered. Often turning a blind eye to the realities of prison life and the potentially debilitating psychological effects on persons housed in badly overcrowded, poorly run, and increasingly dangerous prisons, the Court developed several constitutional doctrines that both limited the liability of prison officials and further undermined the legal relevance of a careful situational analysis of imprisonment. For example, in one pivotal case, the Court decided that the notion that "overall prison conditions" somehow could produce a cruel and unusual living environment—a view that not only was psychologically straightforward but also had guided numerous lower court decisions in which overall conditions of confinement in particular prisons were found unconstitutional was simply "too amorphous" to abide any longer (*Wilson v. Seiter*, 1991, p. 304).

In the same case, the Court decisively shifted its Eighth Amendment inquiry from the conditions themselves to the thought processes of the officials responsible for creating and maintaining them. Justice Scalia wrote for the majority that Eighth Amendment claims concerning conduct that did not purport to be punishment required an inquiry into prison officials' state of mind in this case, their "deliberate indifference" (*Wilson v. Seiter*, 1991). Justice Scalia also had rejected a distinction between short-term deprivations and "continuing" or "systemic" problems of the sort that might have made state of mind less rel-

evant. The argument here had been that evidence of systemic problems would obviate the need to demonstrate state of mind on the part of officials who had presumably known about and tolerated them as part of the correctional status quo. Scalia said instead that although the long duration of a cruel condition might make it easier to establish knowledge and, hence, intent, it would not eliminate the intent requirement.

Prison litigators and legal commentators criticized the decision as having established a constitutional hurdle for conditions of confinement claims that was "virtually insurmountable" and speculated that the impossibly high threshold "reflects recent changes in public attitudes towards crime and allocation of scarce public resources" (Hall, 1993, p. 208). Finally, in 1994, the Court seemed to raise the hurdle to a literally insurmountable level by explicitly embracing the criminal law concept of "subjective recklessness" as the Eighth Amendment test for deliberate indifference (*Farmer v. Brennan*, 1994). In so doing, the Court shunned the federal government's concern that the new standard meant that that triers of fact would first have to find that "prison officials acted like criminals" before finding them liable (*Farmer v. Brennan*, 1994, p. 1980).

This series of most recent cases has prompted commentators to speculate that the Supreme Court is "headed toward a new hands-off doctrine in correctional law" (Robbins, 1993, p. 169) that would require lower courts "to defer to the internal actions and decisions of prison officials" (Hall, 1993, p. 223). Yet, the narrow logic of these opinions suggests that the Justices intend to keep not only their hands off the faltering prison system but their eyes averted from the realities of prison life as well. It is difficult to avoid the conclusion that the Court's refusal to examine the intricacies of day-to-day existence in those maximum security prisons whose deteriorated and potentially harmful conditions are placed at issue is designed to limit the liability of those who create and run them.

Unfortunately, the U.S. Supreme Court was not the only federal governmental agency contributing to this retreat from the meaningful analysis of conditions of confinement inside the nation's prisons and jails. In April 1996, the U.S. Congress passed legislation titled the Prison Litigation Reform Act (PLRA) that significantly limited the ability of the federal courts to monitor and remedy constitutional violations in detention facilities throughout the country. Among other things, it placed substantive and procedural limits on injunctions and consent decrees (where both parties reach binding agreements to fix existing problems in advance of trial) to improve prison conditions. The PLRA also impeded the appointment of "special masters" to oversee prison systems' compliance with court orders and appeared to forbid the filing of legal actions by prisoners for mental or emotional injury without a prior showing of physical injury. Although the full impact of this remarkable legislation cannot yet be measured, it seems to have been designed to prevent many of the problems that have befallen U.S. prisons from ever being effectively addressed. Combined with the Supreme Court's stance concerning prison conditions, the PLRA will likely contribute to the growing tendency to avoid any meaningful contextual analysis of the conditions under which many prisoners are now confined and also to a growing ignorance among the public about the questionable utility of prison as a solution to the nation's crime problem.

Responding to the Current Crisis: Some Lessons From the Stanford Prison Experiment

Where has this series of transformations left the U.S. criminal justice system? With startling speed, national prison policy has become remarkably punitive, and correspondingly, conditions of confinement have dramatically deteriorated in many parts of the country. These transformations have been costly in economic, social, and human terms. At the beginning of the present decade, a stark fact about governmental priorities was reported: "For the first time in history, state and municipal governments are spending more money on criminal justice than education" (Chambliss, 1994, p. 183). In California, the corrections budget alone has now surpassed the state's fiscal outlays for higher education (e.g., Butterfield, 1995; Jordan, 1995). Despite this historic shift in expenditures and the unprecedented prison construction that took place during the past 25 years, many commentators still lament what has been referred to as the "national scandal of living conditions in American prisons" (Gutterman, 1995, p. 373). As we have noted and one reviewer recently observed, "For over a decade, virtually every contemporary commentary on corrections in the United States has reminded us that the system [is] in crisis" (Cullen, 1995, p. 338).

The dimensions of this crisis continue to expand and do not yet reflect what promises to be an even more significant boost in prison numbers—the effects of recently passed, so-called three-strikes legislation that not only mandates a life sentence on a third criminal conviction but, in some states, also doubles the prison sentence for a second criminal conviction and reduces existing good-time provisions for every term (so that all prisoners actually are incarcerated for a longer period of time). This three-strikes legislation was written and rapidly passed into law to capitalize on the public's fear of violent crime (Haney, 1994, 1997b). Despite the fact that the crime rate in the United States has been declining for some time in small but steady increments, many of these bills were written in such a way as to cast the widest possible net—beyond violent career criminals (whom most members of the public had in mind)—to include nonviolent crimes like felony drug convictions and minor property offenses. As a consequence, a disproportionate number of young Black and Hispanic men are likely to be imprisoned for life under scenarios in which they are guilty of little more than a history of untreated addiction and several prior drug-related offenses. The mandate to create lifetime incarceration for so many inmates under circumstances where overcrowding precludes their participation in meaningful programs, treatment, and other activities is likely to raise the overall level of prisoners' frustration, despair, and violence. States will absorb the staggering cost of not only constructing additional prisons to accommodate increasing numbers of prisoners who will never be released but also warehousing them into old age (Zimbardo, 1994).

Remarkably, the radical transformations we have described in the nation's penal policy occurred with almost no input from the discipline of psychology. Correctional administrators, politicians, policymakers, and judicial decision makers not only ignored most of the lessons that emerged from the SPE but also disregarded the insights of a number of psychologists who preceded us and the scores of others who wrote about, extended, and elaborated on the same lessons in empirical studies and theoretical pieces published over the past several decades. Indeed, there is now a vast social science literature that underscores, in various ways, the critical importance of situation and context in influencing social behavior, especially in psychologically powerful situations like prisons. These lessons, insights, and literature deserve to be taken into account as the nation's prison system moves into the next century.

Here then is a series of propositions derived or closely extrapolated from the SPE and the large body of related research that underscores the power of situations and social context to shape and transform

human behavior. Each proposition argues for the creation of a new corrections agenda that would take us in a fundamentally different direction from the one in which we have been moving over the past quarter century.

First, the SPE underscored the degree to which prison environments are themselves powerful, potentially damaging situations whose negative psychological effects must be taken seriously, carefully evaluated, and purposefully regulated and controlled. When appropriate, these environments must be changed or (in extreme cases) eliminated. Of course, the SPE demonstrated the power of situations to overwhelm psychologically normal, healthy people and to elicit from them unexpectedly cruel, yet "situationally appropriate" behavior. In many instances during our study, the participants' behavior (and our own) directly contravened personal value systems and deviated dramatically from past records of conduct. This behavior was elicited by the social context and roles we created, and it had painful, even traumatic consequences for the prisoners against whom it was directed.

The policy implications of these observations seem clear. For one, because of their harmful potential, prisons should be deployed very sparingly in the war on crime. Recognition of the tendency of prison environments to become psychologically damaging also provides a strong argument for increased and more realistic legal and governmental oversight of penal institutions in ways that are sensitive to and designed to limit their potentially destructive impact. In addition, it argues in favor of significantly revising the allocation of criminal justice resources to more seriously explore, create, and evaluate humane alternatives to traditional correctional environments.

Second, the SPE also revealed how easily even a minimalist prison could become painful and powerful. By almost any comparative standard, ours was an extraordinarily benign prison. None of the guards at the "Stanford Prison" were armed, and there were obvious limits to the ways in which they could or would react to prisoners' disobedience, rebellion, or even escape. Yet, even in this minimalist prison setting, all of our "guards" participated in one way or another in the pattern of mistreatment that quickly developed. Indeed, some escalated their definition of "role-appropriate" behavior to become highly feared, sadistic tormentors. Although the prisoners' terms of incarceration were extremely abbreviated (corresponding, really, to very short-term pretrial detention in a county jail), half of our prisoner-participants left before the study was terminated because they could not tolerate the pains of this merely simulated imprisonment. The pains were as much psychological feelings of powerlessness, degradation, frustration, and emotional distress—as physical—sleep deprivation, poor diet, and unhealthy living conditions. Unlike our participants, of course, many experienced prisoners have learned to suppress such outward signs of psychological vulnerability lest they be interpreted as weakness, inviting exploitation by others.

Thus, the SPE and other related studies demonstrating the power of social contexts teach a lesson about the way in which certain situational conditions can interact and work in combination to produce a dehumanizing whole that is more damaging than the sum of its individual institutional parts. Legal doctrines that fail to explicitly take into account and formally consider the totality of these situational conditions miss this psychological point. The effects of situations and social contexts must be assessed from the perspective of those within them. The experiential perspective of prison inmates—the meaning of the prison experience and its effects on them—is the most useful starting point for determining whether a particular set of prison conditions is cruel and unusual. But a macroexperiential perspective does not

allow for the parsing of individual factors or aspects of a situation whose psychological consequences can then be separately assessed. Thus, legal regulators and the psychological experts who assist them also must be sensitive to the ways in which different aspects of a particular situation interact and aggregate in the lives of the persons who inhabit total institutions like prisons as well as their capacity to produce significant effects on the basis of seemingly subtle changes and modifications that build up over time. In contexts such as these, there is much more to the "basic necessities of life" than "single, identifiable human need[s] such as food, warmth or exercise" (*Wilson v. Seiter*, 1991, p. 304). Even if this view is "too amorphous" for members of the current Supreme Court to appreciate or apply, it is the only psychologically defensible approach to assessing the effects of a particular prison and gauging its overall impact on those who live within its walls.

In a related vein, recent research has shown how school children can develop maladjusted, aggressive behavior patterns based on initially marginal deviations from other children that get amplified in classroom interactions and aggregated over time until they become manifested as "problem children" (Caprara & Zimbardo, 1996). Evidence of the same processes at work can be found in the life histories of persons accused and convicted of capital crime (Haney, 1995). In similar ways, initially small behavioral problems and dysfunctional social adaptations by individual prisoners may become amplified and aggravated over time in prison settings that require daily interaction with other prisoners and guards.

Recall also that the SPE was purposely populated with young men who were selected on the basis of their initial mental and physical health and normality, both of which, less than a week later, had badly deteriorated. Real prisons use no such selection procedures. Indeed, one of the casualties of severe overcrowding in many prison systems has been that even rudimentary classification decisions based on the psychological makeup of entering cohorts of prisoners are forgone (see Clements, 1979, 1985). Pathology that is inherent in the structure of the prison situation is likely given a boost by the pathology that some prisoners and guards bring with them into the institutions themselves. Thus, although ours was clearly a study of the power of situational characteristics, we certainly acknowledge the value of interactional models of social and institutional behavior. Prison systems should not ignore individual vulnerabilities in attempting to optimize institutional adjustment, minimize behavioral and psychological problems, understand differences in institutional adaptations and capacities to survive, and intelligently allocate treatment and other resources (e.g., Haney & Specter, in press).

Third, if situations matter and people can be transformed by them when they go into prisons, they matter equally, if not more, when they come out of prison. This suggests very clearly that programs of prisoner change cannot ignore situations and social conditions that prevail after release if they are to have any hope of sustaining whatever positive gains are achieved during periods of imprisonment and lowering distressingly high recidivism rates. Several implications can be drawn from this observation. The first is that prisons must more routinely use transitional or "decompression" programs that gradually reverse the effects of the extreme environments in which convicts have been confined. These programs must be aimed at preparing prisoners for the radically different situations that they will enter in the free world. Otherwise, prisoners who were ill-prepared for job and social situations before they entered prison become more so over time, and the longer they have been imprisoned, the more likely it is that rapid technological and social change will have dramatically transformed the world to which they return.

The SPE and related studies also imply that exclusively individual-centered approaches to crime control (like imprisonment) are self-limiting and doomed to failure in the absence of other approaches that simultaneously and systematically address criminogenic situational and contextual factors. Because traditional models of rehabilitation are person-centered and dispositional in nature (focusing entirely on individual-level change), they typically have ignored the post-release situational factors that help to account for discouraging rates of recidivism. Yet, the recognition that people can be significantly changed and transformed by immediate situational conditions also implies that certain kinds of situations in the free world can override and negate positive prison change. Thus, correctional and parole resources must be shifted to the transformation of certain criminogenic situations in the larger society if ex-convicts are to meaningfully and effectively adapt. Successful post-release adjustment may depend as much on the criminal justice system's ability to change certain components of an ex-convict's situation *after* imprisonment—helping to get housing, employment, and drug or alcohol counseling for starters—as it does on any of the positive rehabilitative changes made by individual prisoners during confinement itself.

This perspective also underscores the way in which long-term legacies of exposure to powerful and destructive situations, contexts, and structures means that prisons themselves can act as criminogenic agents—in both their primary effects on prisoners and secondary effects on the lives of persons connected to them—thereby serving to increase rather than decrease the amount of crime that occurs within a society. Department of corrections data show that about a fourth of those initially imprisoned for nonviolent crimes are sentenced a second time for committing a violent offense. Whatever else it reflects, this pattern highlights the possibility that prison serves to transmit violent habits and values rather than to reduce them. Moreover, like many of these lessons, this one counsels policymakers to take the full range of the social and economic costs of imprisonment into account in calculations that guide long-term crime control strategies. It also argues in favor of incorporating the deleterious effects of prior terms of incarceration into at least certain models of legal responsibility (e.g., Haney, 1995).

Fourth, despite using several valid personality tests in the SPE, we found that we were unable to predict (or even postdict) who would behave in what ways and why (Haney et al., 1973). This kind of failure underscores the possibility that behavioral prediction and explanation in extreme situations like prisons will be successful only if they are approached with more situationally sensitive models than are typically used. For example, most current personality trait measures ask respondents to report on characteristic ways of responding in familiar situations or scenarios. They do not and cannot tap into reactions that might occur in novel, extreme, or especially potent situations—like the SPE or Milgram's (1974) obedience paradigm—and thus have little predictive value when extrapolated to such extreme cases. More situationally sensitive models would attend less to characteristic ways of behaving in typical situations and more to the characteristics of the particular situations in which behavior occurs. In prison, explanations of disciplinary infractions and violence would focus more on the context in which they transpired and less on the prisoners who engaged in them (e.g., Wenk & Emrich, 1972; Wright, 1991). Similarly, the ability to predict the likelihood of reoffending and the probability of repeated violent behavior should be enhanced by conceptualizing persons as embedded in a social context and rich interpersonal environment, rather than as abstract bundles of traits and proclivities (e.g., Monahan & Klassen, 1982).

This perspective has implications for policies of crime control as well as psychological prediction. Virtually all sophisticated, contemporary accounts of social behavior now acknowledge the empirical and theoretical significance of situation, context, and structure (e.g., Bandura, 1978, 1991; Duke, 1987; Ekehammar, 1974; Georgoudi & Rosnow, 1985; Mischel, 1979; Veroff, 1983). In academic circles at least, the problems of crime and violence—formerly viewed in almost exclusively individualistic terms—are now understood through multilevel analyses that grant equal if not primary significance to situational, community, and structural variables (e.g., Hepburn, 1973; McEwan & Knowles, 1984; Sampson & Lauritsen, 1994; Toch, 1985). Yet, little of this knowledge has made its way into prevailing criminal justice policies. Lessons about the power of extreme situations to shape and transform behavior—independent or in spite of preexisting dispositions—can be applied to contemporary strategies of crime control that invest more substantial resources in transforming destructive familial and social contexts rather than concentrating exclusively on reactive policies that target only individual lawbreakers (cf. Masten & Garmezy, 1985; Patterson, DeBaryshe, & Ramsey, 1989).

Fifth, genuine and meaningful prison and criminal justice reform is unlikely to be advanced by persons who are themselves "captives" of powerful correctional environments. We learned this lesson in a modest but direct way when in the span of six short days in the SPE, our own perspectives were radically altered, our sense of ethics, propriety, and humanity temporarily suspended. Our experience with the SPE underscored the degree to which institutional settings can develop a life of their own, independent of the wishes, intentions, and purposes of those who run them (Haney & Zimbardo, 1977). Like all powerful situations, real prisons transform the worldviews of those who inhabit them, on both sides of the bars. Thus, the SPE also contained the seeds of a basic but important message about prison reform—that good people with good intentions are not enough to create good prisons. Institutional structures themselves must be changed to meaningfully improve the quality of prison life (Haney & Pettigrew, 1986).

Indeed, the SPE was an "irrational" prison whose staff had no legal mandate to punish prisoners who, in turn, had done nothing to deserve their mistreatment. Yet, the "psycho-logic" of the environment was more power-ful than the benign intentions or predisposi-tions of the participants. Routines develop; rules are made and applied, altered and fol-lowed without question; policies enacted for short-term convenience become part of the institutional status quo and difficult to alter; and unexpected events and emergencies challenge existing resources and compro-mise treatment in ways that persist long after the crisis has passed. Prisons are espe-cially vulnerable to these common institu-tional dynamics because they are so resistant to external pressures for change and even rebuff outside attempts at scrutinizing their daily operating procedures.

These observations certainly imply that the legal mechanisms supposedly designed to control prison excesses should not focus exclusively on the intentions of the staff and administrators who run the institution but would do well to look instead at the effects of the situation or context itself in shaping their behavior (cf. *Farmer v. Brennan*, 1994). Harmful structures do not require ill-inten-tioned persons to inflict psychological dam-age on those in their charge and can induce good people with the best of intentions to engage in evil deeds (Haney & Zimbardo, 1977; Zimbardo, 1979a). "Mechanisms of moral disengagement" distance people from the ethical ambiguity of their actions and the painful consequences of their deeds, and they may operate with destructive force in many legal and institutional contexts, facili-tating cruel and unusual treatment by other-wise caring and law-abiding persons (e.g., Bandura, 1989; Browning, 1993; Gibson, 1991; Haney, 1997c).

In addition, the SPE and the perspective it advanced also suggest that prison change

will come about only when those who are outside of this powerful situation are empowered to act on it. A society may be forced to presume the categorical expertise of prison officials to run the institutions with which they have been entrusted, but this pre-sumption is a rebuttable one. Moreover, to depend exclusively on those whose perspec-tives have been created and maintained by these powerful situations to, in turn, trans-form or control them is shortsighted and psychologically naive. This task must fall to those with a different logic and point of view, independent of and free from the forces of the situation itself. To be sure, the current legal retreat to hands-off policies in which the courts defer to the presumably greater expertise of correctional officials ignores the potency of prison settings to alter the judg-ments of those charged with the responsibil-ity of running them. The SPE and much other research on these powerful environ-ments teach that this retreat is terribly ill-advised.

Finally, the SPE implicitly argued for a more activist scholarship in which psycholo-gists engage with the important social and policy questions of the day. The implications we have drawn from the SPE argue in favor of more critically and more realistically eval-uating the nature and effect of imprison-ment and developing psychologically informed limits to the amount of prison pain one is willing to inflict in the name of social control (Haney, 1997b, 1998). Yet, this would require the participation of social scientists willing to examine these issues, confront the outmoded models and concepts that guide criminal justice practices, and develop meaningful and effective alternatives. His-torically, psychologists once contributed sig-nificantly to the intellectual framework on which modern corrections was built (Haney, 1982). In the course of the past 25 years, they have relinquished voice and authority in the debates that surround prison policy. Their absence has created an ethical and intellec-tual void that has undermined both the qual-ity and the legitimacy of correctional practices. It has helped compromise the amount of social justice our society now dispenses.

Conclusion

When we conducted the SPE 25 years ago, we were, in a sense, on the cutting edge of new and developing situational and contextual models of behavior. Mischel's (1968) pathbreaking review of the inadequacy of conventional measures of personality traits to predict behavior was only a few years old, Ross and Nisbett (1991) were assistant professors who had not yet written about situational control as perhaps the most important leg in the tripod of social psychology, and no one had yet systematically applied the methods and theories of modern psychology to the task of understanding social contextual origins [of] crime and the psychological pains of imprisonment. Intellectually, much has changed since then. However, without the renewed participation of psychologists in debates over how best to apply the lessons and insights of their discipline to the problems of crime and punishment, the benefits from these important intellectual advances will be self-limiting. It is hard to imagine a more pressing and important task for which psychologists have so much expertise but from which they have been so distanced and uninvolved than the creation of more effective and humane criminal justice policies. Indeed, politicians and policymakers now seem to worship the very kind of institutional power whose adverse effects were so critically evaluated over the past 25 years. They have premised a vast and enormously expensive national policy of crime control on models of human nature that are significantly outmoded. In so doing, they have faced little intellectual challenge, debate, or input from those who should know better.

So, perhaps it is this one last thing that the SPE stood for that will serve the discipline best over the next 25 years. That is, the interrelated notions that psychology can be made relevant to the broad and pressing national problems of crime and justice, that the discipline can assist in stimulating badly needed social and legal change, and that scholars and practitioners can improve these policies with sound data and creative ideas. These notions are as germane now, and needed more, than they were in the days of the SPE. If they can be renewed, in the spirit of those more optimistic times, despite having lost many battles over the past 25 years, the profession still may help win the more important war. There has never been a more critical time at which to begin the intellectual struggle with those who would demean human nature by using prisons exclusively as agencies of social control that punish without attempting to rehabilitate, that isolate and oppress instead of educating and elevating, and that tear down minority communities rather than protecting and strengthening them.

Study Questions

1. Did the Supreme Court's stance change regarding prison policy over the 25-year period covered by this article? If yes, in what ways?

2. What appear to have been the main differences between the Stanford Prison Experiment "prison" and a real prison? In what ways might these differences be beneficial regarding what was revealed by the research?

3. Of all the changes in prison and/or sentencing policy that have occurred over the 25-year period that is covered by this article, which do you think have affected the prison system the most? Why?

4. For what reasons did the prison system see a huge influx of drug offenders?

5. For what reasons do you think the American prison system gave rise to the "supermax" facility? What do you see as the major benefits of the supermax facil-

ity, if any? What do you see as the major detriments of the supermax facility?

Editor's note. Melissa G. Warren served as action editor for this article.

Author's note. Craig Haney, Department of Psychology, University of California, Santa Cruz; Philip Zimbardo, Department of Psychology, Stanford University. We would like to acknowledge our colleague and coinvestigator in the original Stanford Prison Experiment, W. Curtis Banks, who died last year. We also acknowledge the assistance of Marc Mauer and The Sentencing Project . . . [who] helped us locate other sources of information, and Sandy Pisano, librarian at the Arthur W. Melton Library, who helped compile some of the data that appear in the tables and figures.

Correspondence concerning this article should be addressed to Craig Haney, Department of Psychology, University of California, Santa Cruz, CA 95064. Electronic mail may be sent to psylaw@cats.ucsc.edu. Readers interested in the corrections system may contact the American Psychology-Law Society or Psychologists in Public Service, Divisions 41 and 18, respectively, of the American Psychological Association.

References

American Friends Service Committee. (1971). *Struggle for justice: A report on crime and punishment*. New York: Hill & Wang

Amnesty International. (1987). *Allegations of mistreatment in Marion Prison, Illinois, USA*. New York: Author.

Bandura, A. (1978). The self system in reciprocal determinism. *American Psychologist, 33*, 344–358.

Bandura, A. (1989). Mechanisms of moral disengagement. In W. Reich (Ed.), *Origins of terrorism: Psychologies, ideologies, theologies, states of mind* (pp. 161–191). New York: Cambridge University Press.

Bandura, A. (1991). Social cognitive theory of moral thought and action. In W. Kurtines & J. Gewirtz (Eds.), *Handbook of moral behavior and development: Vol. 1. Theory* (pp. 45–102). Hillsdale, NJ: Erlbaum.

Blumstein, A. (1993). Making rationality relevant—The American Society of Criminology 1992 Presidential Address. *Criminology, 31*, 1–16.

Brodt, S., & Zimbardo, P. (1981). Modifying shyness-related social behavior through symptom misattribution. *Journal of Personality and Social Psychology, 41*, 437–449.

Browning, C. (1993). *Ordinary men: Reserve Police Battalion 101 and the final solution in Poland*. New York: Harper Perennial.

Bureau of Justice Statistics. (1991). *Sourcebook of criminal justice statistics*. Washington, DC: U.S. Department of Justice.

Bureau of Justice Statistics. (1996). *Sourcebook of criminal justice statistics, 1996*. Washington, DC: U.S. Department of Justice.

Bureau of Justice Statistics. (1997a, May). *Correctional populations in the United States, 1995* (NCJ 163916). Rockville, MD: Author.

Bureau of Justice Statistics. (1997b, November). *Criminal victimization 1996: Changes 1995–96 with trends 1993–96* (Bureau of Justice Statistics Bulletin NCJ 165812). Rockville, MD: Author.

Bureau of Justice Statistics. (1998, January 18). *Nation's prisons and jails hold more than 1.7 million: Up almost 100,000 in a year* [Press release]. Washington, DC: U.S. Department of Justice.

Burks v. Walsh, 461 F. Supp. 934 (W.D. Missouri 1978).

Butterfield, F. (1995, April 12). New prisons cast shadow over higher education. *The New York Times*, p. A21.

Cahalan, M. W. (1986, December). *Historical corrections statistics in the United States, 1850–1984* (Bureau of Justice Statistics Bulletin NCJ 102529). Rockville, MD: Bureau of Justice Statistics.

Capps v. Atiyeh, 495 F. Supp. 802 (D. Ore. 1980).

Caprara, G., & Zimbardo, P. (1996). Aggregation and amplification of marginal deviations in the social construction of personality and maladjustment. *European Journal of Personality, 10*, 79–110.

Carr, S. (1995). Demystifying the Stanford Prison Study. *The British Psychological Society Social Psychology Section Newsletter, 33*, 31–34.

Chambliss, W. (1994). Policing the ghetto underclass: The politics of law and law enforcement. *Social Problems, 41*, 177–194.

Christie, N. (1994). *Crime control as industry: Towards gulags, Western style?* (2nd ed.). London: Routledge.

Clements, C. (1979). Crowded prisons: A review of psychological and environmental effects. *Law and Human Behavior, 3*, 217–225.

Clements, C. (1985). Towards an objective approach to offender classification. *Law & Psychology Review, 9*, 45–55.

Coker v. Georgia, 433 U.S. 584, 592 (1977).

Cullen, F. (1995). Assessing the penal harm movement. *Journal of Research in Crime and Delinquency 32*, 338–358.

Dowker, F., & Good, G. (1992). From Alcatraz to Marion to Florence. In W. Churchill & J. J. Vander Wall (Eds.) *Cages of steel: The politics of imprisonment in the United, States* (pp. 131–151). Washington, DC: Maisonneuve Press.

Duke, M. (1987). The situational stream hypothesis: A unifying view of behavior with special emphasis on adaptive and maladaptive personality patterns. *Journal of Research in Personality, 21*, 239–263.

Dunbaugh, F. (1979). Racially disproportionate rates of incarceration in the United States. *Prison Law Monitor, 1*, 205–225.

Editorial: Inside the super-maximum prisons. (1991, November 24). *The Washington Post*, p. C6.

Ekehammar, B. (1974). Interactionism in personality from a historical perspective. *Psychological Bulletin, 81*, 1026–1048.

Farmer v. Brennan, 114 S. Ct. 1970 (1994).

Forer, L. (1994). *A rage to punish: The unintended consequences of mandatory sentencing*. New York: Norton.

Fowler, R. (1976). Sweeping reforms ordered in Alabama prisons. *APA Monitor, 7*, pp. 1, 15.

Freed, D. (1992). Federal sentencing in the wake of guidelines: Unacceptable limits on the discretion of sentences. *Yale Law Journal, 101*, 1681–1754.

Georgoudi, M., & Rosnow, R. (1985). Notes toward a contextualist understanding of social psychology. *Personality and Social Psychology Bulletin, 11*, 5–22.

Gibson, J. (1991). Training good people to inflict pain: State terror and social learning. *Journal of Humanistic Psychology, 31*, 72–87.

Grassian, S. (1983). Psychopathological effects of solitary confinement. *American Journal of Psychiatry, 140*, 1450–1454.

Gregg v. Georgia, 428 U.S. 153, 173 (1976) (joint opinion).

Gutterman, M. (1995). The contours of Eighth Amendment prison jurisprudence: Conditions of confinement. *Southern Methodist University Law Review, 48*, 373–407.

Hall, D. (1993). The Eighth Amendment, prison conditions, and social context. *Missouri Law Review, 58*, 207–236.

Haney, C. (1976). The play's the thing: Methodological notes on social simulations. In P. Golden (Ed.), *The research experience* (pp. 177–190). Itasca, IL: Peacock.

Haney, C. (1982). Psychological theory and criminal justice policy: Law and psychology in the "Formative Era." *Law and Human Behavior, 6*, 191–235.

Haney, C. (1983). The good, the bad, and the lawful: An essay on psychological injustice. In W. Laufer & J. Day (Eds.), *Personality theory, moral development, and criminal behavior* (pp. 107–117). Lexington, MA: Lexington Books.

Haney, C. (1991). The Fourteenth Amendment and symbolic legality: Let them eat due process. *Law and Human Behavior, 15*, 183–204.

Haney, C. (1993a). Infamous punishment: The psychological effects of isolation. *National Prison Project Journal, 8*, 3–21.

Haney, C. (1993b). Psychology and legal change: The impact of a decade. *Law and Human Behavior, 17*, 371–398.

Haney, C. (1994, March 3). Three strikes for Ronnie's kids, now Bill's. *Los Angeles Times*, p. B7.

Haney, C. (1995). The social context of capital murder: Social histories and the logic of mitigation. *Santa Clara Law Review, 35*, 547–609.

Haney, C. (1997a). Psychological secrecy and the death penalty: Observations on "the mere extinguishment of life." *Studies in Law, Politics, and Society, 16*, 3–68.

Haney, C. (1997b). Psychology and the limits to prison pain: Confronting the coming crisis in Eighth Amendment law. *Psychology, Public Policy, and Law, 3*, 499–588.

Haney, C. (1997c). Violence and the capital jury: Mechanisms of moral disengagement and the impulse to condemn to death. *Stanford Law Review, 46*, 1447–1486.

Haney, C. (1997d). The worst of the worst: Psychological trauma and psychiatric symptoms in punitive segregation. Unpublished manuscript, University of California, Santa Cruz.

Haney, C. (1998). *Limits to prison pain: Modern psychological theory and rational crime control policy*. Washington, DC: American Psychological Association.

Haney, C., Banks, W., & Zimbardo, P. (1973). Interpersonal dynamics in a simulated prison. *International Journal of Criminology and Penology, 1*, 69–97.

Haney, C., & Lynch, M. (1997). Regulating prisons of the future: A psychological analysis of supermax and solitary confinement. *New York Review of Law and Social Change, 23*, 101–195.

Haney, C., & Pettigrew, T (1986). Civil rights and institutional law: The role of social psychology in judicial implementation. *Journal of Community Psychology, 14*, 267–277.

Haney, C., & Specter, D. (in press). Legal considerations in treating adult and juvenile offenders with special needs. In J. Ashford, B. Sales, & W. Reid (Eds.), *Treating adult and juvenile offenders with special needs*. Washington, DC: American Psychological Association.

Haney, C., & Zimbardo, P. (1977). The socialization into criminality: On becoming a prisoner and a guard. In J. Tapp & F. Levine (Eds.), *Law, justice, and the individual in society: Psychological and legal issues* (pp. 198–223). New York: Holt, Rinehart & Winston.

Hepburn, J. (1973). Violent behavior in interpersonal relationships. *Sociological Quarterly, 14*, 419–429.

Hilliard, T. (1976). The Black psychologist in action: A psychological evaluation of the Adjustment Center environment at San Quentin Prison. *Journal of Black Psychology, 2*, 75–82.

Human Rights Watch. (1997). *Cold storage: Supermaximum security confinement in Indiana*. New York: Author.

Immarigeon, R. (1992). The Marionization of American prisons. *National Prison Project Journal, 7(4)*, 1–5.

Jackson, G. (1970). *Soledad brother: The prison letters of George Jackson*. New York: Coward-McCann.

Jordan, H. (1995, July 8). '96 budget favors prison over college; "3 strikes" to eat into education funds. *San Jose Mercury News*, p. 1A.

King, A. (1993). The impact of incarceration on African American families: Implications for practice. *Families in Society. The Journal of Contemporary Human Services, 74*, 145–153.

Madrid v. Gomez, 889 F. Supp. 1146 (N.D. Cal. 1995).

Maguire, K., & Pastore, A. (Eds.). (1997). *Sourcebook of criminal justice statistics 1996* (NCJ 165361). Washington, DC: U.S. Government Printing Office.

Masten, A., & Garmezy, N. (1985). Risk, vulnerability and protective factors in developmental psychopathology. In F. Lahey & A. Kazdin (Eds.), *Advances in clinical child psychology* (pp. 1–52). New York: Plenum.

Mauer, M. (1990). *More young Black males under correctional control in US than in college*. Washington, DC: The Sentencing Project.

Mauer, M. (1992). Americans behind bars: A comparison of international rates of incarceration. In W. Churchill & J. J. Vander Wall (Eds.), *Cages of steel: The politics of imprisonment in the United States* (pp. 22–37). Washington, DC: Maisonneuve Press.

Mauer, M. (1995). The international use of incarceration. *Prison Journal, 75*, 113–123.

Mauer, M. (1997, June). *Americans behind bars: U.S. and international use of incarceration, 1995*. Washington, DC: The Sentencing Project.

McConville, S. (1989). Prisons held captive. *Contemporary Psychology, 34*, 928–929.

McEwan, A., & Knowles, C. (1984). Delinquent personality types and the situational contexts of their crimes. *Personality & Individual Differences, 5*, 339–344.

Milgram, S. (1974). *Obedience to authority: An experimental view*. New York: Harper & Row.

Miller, G. (1980). Giving psychology away in the '80s. *Psychology Today, 13*, 38ff.

Mischel, W. (1968). *Personality and assessment*. New York: Wiley.

Mischel, W. (1979). On the interface of cognition and personality: Beyond the person-situation debate. *American Psychologist, 34*, 740–754.

Mitford, J. (1973). *Kind and usual punishment: The prison business*. New York: Knopf.

Monahan, J., & Klassen, D. (1982). Situational approaches to understanding and predicting individual violent behavior. In M. Wolfgang & G. Weiner (Eds.), *Criminal violence* (pp. 292–319). Beverly Hills, CA: Sage.

Mumola, C. J., & Beck, A. J. (1997, June). *Prisoners in 1996* (Bureau of Justice Statistics Bulletin NCJ 164619). Rockville, MD: Bureau of Justice Statistics.

National Advisory Commission on Criminal Justice Standards and Goals. (1973). *Task force report on corrections*. Washington, DC: U.S. Government Printing Office.

Newman, G. (1988). Punishment and social practice: On Hughes's The Fatal Shore. *Law and Social Inquiry, 13*, 337–357.

Olivero, M., & Roberts, J. (1990). The United States Federal Penitentiary at Marion, Illinois: Alcatraz revisited. *New England Journal of Criminal and Civil Confinement, 16*, 21–51.

Patterson, G., DeBaryshe, B., & Ramsey, E. (1989). A developmental perspective on antisocial behavior. *American Psychologist, 44*, 329–335.

Perkinson, R. (1994). Shackled justice: Florence Federal Penitentiary and the new politics of punishment. *Social Justice, 21*, 117–132.

Pugh v. Locke, 406 F. Supp. 318 (1976).

Rhodes v. Chapman, 452 U.S. 337 (1981).

Robbins, I. (1993). The prisoners' mail box and the evolution of federal inmate rights. *Federal Rules Decisions, 114*, 127–169.

Ross, L., & Nisbett, R. (1991). *The person and the situation: Perspectives of social psychology*. New York: McGraw-Hill.

Sampson, R., & Lauritsen, J. (1994). Violent victimization and offending: Individual-, situational-, and community-level risk factors. In A. Reiss, Jr. & J. Roth (Eds.), *Understanding and preventing violence: Vol. 3. Social influences* (pp. 1–114). Washington, DC: National Research Council, National Academy Press.

Sandin v. Conner, 115 S. Ct. 2293 (1995).

Scull, A. (1977). *Decarceration: Community treatment and the deviant: A radical view*. Englewood Cliffs, NJ: Prentice Hall.

Smith, C. (1993). Black Muslims and the development of prisoners' rights. *Journal of Black Studies, 24*, 131–143.

Spain v. Procunier, 408 F. Supp. 534 (1976), aff'd in part, rev'd in part, 600 F.2d 189 (9th Cir. 1979).

Toch, H. (1985). The catalytic situation in the violence equation. *Journal of Applied Social Psychology, 15*, 105–123.

Tonry, M. (1995). *Malign neglect: Race, crime, and punishment in America*. New York: Oxford University Press.

Trop v. Dulles, 356 U.S. 86 (1958).

Veroff, J. (1983). Contextual determinants of personality. *Personality and Social Psychology Bulletin, 9*, 331–343.

von Hirsch, A. (1976). *Doing justice: The choice of punishment*. New York: Hill & Wang.

Wenk, E., & Emrich, R. (1972). Assaultive youth: An exploratory study of the assaultive experience and assaultive potential of California Youth Authority wards. *Journal of Research in Crime & Delinquency, 9*, 171–196.

Wicker, T. (1975). *A time to die*. New York: New York Times Books.

Wilson v. Seiter, 501 U.S. 294 (1991).

Wolff v. McDonnell, 418 U.S. 554, 556—557 (1974).

Wright, K. (1991). The violent and victimized in the male prison. *Journal of Offender Rehabilitation, 16*, 1–25.

Yackle, L. (1989). *Reform and regret: The story of federal judicial involvement in the Alabama prison system*. New York: Oxford University Press.

Yee, M. (1973). *The melancholy history of Soledad Prison*. New York: Harper's Magazine Press.

Zimbardo, P. (1973). On the ethics of intervention in human psychological research: With special reference to the Stanford Prison Experiment. *Cognition, 2*, 243–256.

Zimbardo, P. (1975). On transforming experimental research into advocacy for social change. In M. Deutsch & H. Hornstein (Eds.), *Applying social psychology: Implications for research, practice, and training* (pp. 33–66). Hillsdale, NJ: Erlbaum.

Zimbardo, P. G. (1977). *Shyness: What it is and what to do about it*. Reading, MA: Addison-Wesley.

Zimbardo, P. G. (1979a). The psychology of evil: On the perversion of human potential. In T. R. Sarbin (Ed.), *Challenges to the criminal justice system: The perspective of community psychology* (pp. 142–161). New York: Human Sciences Press.

Zimbardo, P. G. (1979b). Testimony of Dr. Philip Zimbardo to U.S. House of Representatives Committee on the Judiciary. In J. J. Bonsignore et al. (Eds.), *Before the law: An introduction to the legal process* (2nd ed., pp. 396-399). Boston: Houghton Mifflin.

Zimbardo, P. G. (1994). *Transforming California's prisons into expensive old age homes for felons: Enormous hidden costs and consequences for California's taxpayers*. San Francisco: Center on Juvenile and Criminal Justice.

Zimbardo, P. G., & Andersen, S. (1993). Understanding mind control: Exotic and mundane mental manipulations. In M. Langone (Ed.), *Recover from cults: Help for victims of psychological and spiritual abuse* (pp. 104–125). New York: Norton.

Zimbardo, P. G., Haney, C., Banks, C., & Jaffe, D. (1974). The psychology of imprisonment: Privation, power, and pathology. In Z. Rubin (Ed.), *Doing unto others: Explorations in social behavior* (pp. 61–73). Englewood Cliffs, NJ: Prentice Hall.

Zimbardo, P. G., Pilkonis, P. A., & Norwood, R. M. (1975, May). The social disease called shyness. *Psychology Today, 72*, 69–70.

Excerpted from "The Past and Future of U.S. Prison Policy: Twenty-Five Years After the Stanford Prison Experiment" by Craig Haney and Philip Zimbardo. *American Psychologist*, 53(7):709–727. Copyright © 1998, American Psychological Association. Reprinted by permission. ✦

17
Torture at Abu Ghraib

Seymour M. Hersh

In April 2004, a series of photographs from the main prisoner detainee facility in Iraq— Abu Ghraib—was obtained by CBS's news show 60 Minutes 2. *The photographs were shocking, as they chronicled what appears to be a series of abusive acts toward Iraqi detainees—many of whom were found to have been unrelated to any insurgency and posed no threat to the coalition forces. The focus of the news stories that surrounded the release of the photographs dealt primarily with the scandal presented to the armed forces. The war was (and remains) highly controversial, and many were questioning the United States' motivation and justification for involving itself in a sovereign nation's affairs. The photographs called into question many aspects of the military involvement in Iraq, and led to a series of highly embarrassing revelations. This chapter by Seymour Hersh, which originally appeared in* The New Yorker *in May 2004, contains relevant information for institutional corrections in the United States. As Hersh documents the numerous sources of potential corruption and abuse of power in Abu Ghraib, the reader should consider ways in which these same conditions could exist in the U.S. prison system, leading to a disruption in the goals of incarceration. For example, consider what happens when different administrative parties— all of whom have dealings with an institution—have conflicting goals. Much like the Stanford Prison Experiment, this "natural experiment" may have much to teach the United States about its own domestic prison system.*

In the era of Saddam Hussein, Abu Ghraib, twenty miles west of Baghdad, was one of the world's most notorious prisons, with torture, weekly executions, and vile living conditions. As many as fifty thousand men and women—no accurate count is possible— were jammed into Abu Ghraib at one time, in twelve-by-twelve-foot cells that were little more than human holding pits.

In the looting that followed the regime's collapse, last April, the huge prison complex, by then deserted, was stripped of everything that could be removed, including doors, windows, and bricks. The coalition authorities had the floors tiled, cells cleaned and repaired, and toilets, showers, and a new medical center added. Abu Ghraib was now a U.S. military prison. Most of the prisoners, however—by the fall there were several thousand, including women and teenagers—were civilians, many of whom had been picked up in random military sweeps and at highway checkpoints. They fell into three loosely defined categories: common criminals; security detainees suspected of "crimes against the coalition"; and a small number of suspected "high-value" leaders of the insurgency against the coalition forces.

Last June, Janis Karpinski, an Army reserve brigadier general, was named commander of the 800th Military Police Brigade and put in charge of military prisons in Iraq. General Karpinski, the only female commander in the war zone, was an experienced operations and intelligence officer who had served with the Special Forces and in the 1991 Gulf War, but she had never run a prison system. Now she was in charge of three large jails, eight battalions, and thirty-four hundred Army reservists, most of whom, like her, had no training in handling prisoners.

General Karpinski, who had wanted to be a soldier since she was five, is a business consultant in civilian life, and was enthusiastic about her new job. In an interview last December with the St. Petersburg *Times*, she said that, for many of the Iraqi inmates at Abu Ghraib, "living conditions now are better in prison than at home. At one point we were concerned that they wouldn't want to leave."

A month later, General Karpinski was formally admonished and quietly suspended, and a major investigation into the Army's prison system, authorized by Lieutenant General Ricardo S. Sanchez, the senior commander in Iraq, was under way. A fifty-three-page report, obtained by *The New Yorker*, written by Major General Antonio M. Taguba and not meant for public release, was completed in late February. Its conclusions about the institutional failures of the Army prison system were devastating. Specifically, Taguba found that between October and December of 2003 there were numerous instances of "sadistic, blatant, and wanton criminal abuses" at Abu Ghraib. This systematic and illegal abuse of detainees, Taguba reported, was perpetrated by soldiers of the 372nd Military Police Company, and also by members of the American intelligence community. (The 372nd was attached to the 320th M.P. Battalion, which reported to Karpinski's brigade headquarters.) Taguba's report listed some of the wrongdoing:

> Breaking chemical lights and pouring the phosphoric liquid on detainees; pouring cold water on naked detainees; beating detainees with a broom handle and a chair; threatening male detainees with rape; allowing a military police guard to stitch the wound of a detainee who was injured after being slammed against the wall in his cell; sodomizing a detainee with a chemical light and perhaps a broom stick, and using military working dogs to frighten and intimidate detainees with threats of attack, and in one instance actually biting a detainee.

There was stunning evidence to support the allegations, Taguba added—"detailed witness statements and the discovery of extremely graphic photographic evidence." Photographs and videos taken by the soldiers as the abuses were happening were not included in his report, Taguba said, because of their "extremely sensitive nature."

The photographs—several of which were broadcast on CBS's *60 Minutes 2* last week—show leering G.I.s taunting naked Iraqi prisoners who are forced to assume humiliating poses. Six suspects—Staff Sergeant Ivan L. Frederick II, known as Chip, who was the senior enlisted man; Specialist Charles A. Graner; Sergeant Javal Davis; Specialist Megan Ambuhl; Specialist Sabrina Harman; and Private Jeremy Sivits—are now facing prosecution in Iraq, on charges that include conspiracy, dereliction of duty, cruelty toward prisoners, maltreatment, assault, and indecent acts. A seventh suspect, Private Lynndie England, was reassigned to Fort Bragg, North Carolina, after becoming pregnant.

The photographs tell it all. In one, Private England, a cigarette dangling from her mouth, is giving a jaunty thumbs-up sign and pointing at the genitals of a young Iraqi, who is naked except for a sandbag over his head, as he masturbates. Three other hooded and naked Iraqi prisoners are shown, hands reflexively crossed over their genitals. A fifth prisoner has his hands at his sides. In another, England stands arm in arm with Specialist Graner; both are grinning and giving the thumbs-up behind a cluster of perhaps seven naked Iraqis, knees bent, piled clumsily on top of each other in a pyramid. There is another photograph of a cluster of naked prisoners, again piled in a pyramid. Near them stands Graner, smiling, his arms crossed; a woman soldier stands in front of him, bending over, and she, too, is smiling. Then, there is another cluster of hooded bodies, with a female soldier standing in front, taking photographs. Yet another photograph shows a kneeling, naked, unhooded male prisoner, head momentarily turned away from the camera, posed to make it appear that he is performing oral sex on another male prisoner, who is naked and hooded.

Such dehumanization is unacceptable in any culture, but it is especially so in the

Arab world. Homosexual acts are against Islamic law and it is humiliating for men to be naked in front of other men, Bernard Haykel, a professor of Middle Eastern studies at New York University, explained. "Being put on top of each other and forced to masturbate, being naked in front of each other—it's all a form of torture," Haykel said.

Two Iraqi faces that do appear in the photographs are those of dead men. There is the battered face of prisoner No. 153399, and the bloodied body of another prisoner, wrapped in cellophane and packed in ice. There is a photograph of an empty room, splattered with blood.

The 372nd's abuse of prisoners seemed almost routine—a fact of Army life that the soldiers felt no need to hide. On April 9th, at an Article 32 hearing (the military equivalent of a grand jury) in the case against Sergeant Frederick, at Camp Victory, near Baghdad, one of the witnesses, Specialist Matthew Wisdom, an M.P., told the courtroom what happened when he and other soldiers delivered seven prisoners, hooded and bound, to the so-called "hard site" at Abu Ghraib—seven tiers of cells where the inmates who were considered the most dangerous were housed. The men had been accused of starting a riot in another section of the prison. Wisdom said:

> SFC Snider grabbed my prisoner and threw him into a pile. . . . I do not think it was right to put them in a pile. I saw SSG Frederick, SGT Davis and CPL Graner walking around the pile hitting the prisoners. I remember SSG Frederick hitting one prisoner in the side of its [sic] ribcage. The prisoner was no danger to SSG Frederick. . . . I left after that.

When he returned later, Wisdom testified:

> I saw two naked detainees, one masturbating to another kneeling with its mouth open. I thought I should just get out of there. I didn't think it was right . . . I saw SSG Frederick walking towards me, and he

said, "Look what these animals do when you leave them alone for two seconds." I heard PFC England shout out, "He's getting hard."

Wisdom testified that he told his superiors what had happened, and assumed that "the issue was taken care of." He said, "I just didn't want to be part of anything that looked criminal."

The abuses became public because of the outrage of Specialist Joseph M. Darby, an M.P. whose role emerged during the Article 32 hearing against Chip Frederick. A government witness, Special Agent Scott Bobeck, who is a member of the Army's Criminal Investigation Division, or C.I.D., told the court, according to an abridged transcript made available to me, "The investigation started after SPC Darby . . . got a CD from CPL Graner. . . . He came across pictures of naked detainees." Bobeck said that Darby had "initially put an anonymous letter under our door, then he later came forward and gave a sworn statement. He felt very bad about it and thought it was very wrong."

Questioned further, the Army investigator said that Frederick and his colleagues had not been given any "training guidelines" that he was aware of. The M.P.s in the 372nd had been assigned to routine traffic and police duties upon their arrival in Iraq, in the spring of 2003. In October of 2003, the 372nd was ordered to prison-guard duty at Abu Ghraib. Frederick, at thirty-seven, was far older than his colleagues, and was a natural leader; he had also worked for six years as a guard for the Virginia Department of Corrections. Bobeck explained:

> What I got is that SSG Frederick and CPL Graner were road M.P.s and were put in charge because they were civilian prison guards and had knowledge of how things were supposed to be run.

Bobeck also testified that witnesses had said that Frederick, on one occasion, "had punched a detainee in the chest so hard that the detainee almost went into cardiac arrest."

At the Article 32 hearing, the Army informed Frederick and his attorneys, Captain Robert Shuck, an Army lawyer, and Gary Myers, a civilian, that two dozen witnesses they had sought, including General Karpinski and all of Frederick's co-defendants, would not appear. Some had been excused after exercising their Fifth Amendment right; others were deemed to be too far away from the courtroom. "The purpose of an Article 32 hearing is for us to engage witnesses and discover facts," Gary Myers told me. "We ended up with a C.I.D. agent and no alleged victims to examine." After the hearing, the presiding investigative officer ruled that there was sufficient evidence to convene a court-martial against Frederick.

Myers, who was one of the military defense attorneys in the My Lai prosecutions of the nineteen-seventies, told me that his client's defense will be that he was carrying out the orders of his superiors and, in particular, the directions of military intelligence. He said, "Do you really think a group of kids from rural Virginia decided to do this on their own? Decided that the best way to embarrass Arabs and make them talk was to have them walk around nude?"

In letters and e-mails to family members, Frederick repeatedly noted that the military-intelligence teams, which included C.I.A. officers and linguists and interrogation specialists from private defense contractors, were the dominant force inside Abu Ghraib. In a letter written in January, he said:

> I questioned some of the things that I saw . . . such things as leaving inmates in their cell with no clothes or in female underpants, handcuffing them to the door of their cell—and the answer I got was, "This is how military intelligence (MI) wants it done.". . . . MI has also instructed us to place a prisoner in an isolation cell with little or no clothes, no toilet or running wa-

ter, no ventilation or window, for as much as three days.

The military-intelligence officers have "encouraged and told us, 'Great job,' they were now getting positive results and information," Frederick wrote. "CID has been present when the military working dogs were used to intimidate prisoners at MI's request." At one point, Frederick told his family, he pulled aside his superior officer, Lieutenant Colonel Jerry Phillabaum, the commander of the 320th M.P. Battalion, and asked about the mistreatment of prisoners. "His reply was 'Don't worry about it.'"

In November, Frederick wrote, an Iraqi prisoner under the control of what the Abu Ghraib guards called "O.G.A.," or other government agencies—that is, the C.I.A. and its paramilitary employees—was brought to his unit for questioning. "They stressed him out so bad that the man passed away. They put his body in a body bag and packed him in ice for approximately twenty-four hours in the shower. . . . The next day the medics came and put his body on a stretcher, placed a fake IV in his arm and took him away." The dead Iraqi was never entered into the prison's inmate-control system, Frederick recounted, "and therefore never had a number."

Frederick's defense is, of course, highly self-serving. But the complaints in his letters and e-mails home were reinforced by two internal Army reports—Taguba's and one by the Army's chief law-enforcement officer, Provost Marshal Donald Ryder, a major general.

Last fall, General Sanchez ordered Ryder to review the prison system in Iraq and recommend ways to improve it. Ryder's report, filed on November 5th, concluded that there were potential human-rights, training, and manpower issues, system-wide, that needed immediate attention. It also discussed serious concerns about the tension between the missions of the military police assigned to guard the prisoners and the intelligence teams who wanted to interrogate them.

Army regulations limit intelligence activity by the M.P.s to passive collection. But something had gone wrong.

There was evidence dating back to the Afghanistan war, the Ryder report said, that M.P.s had worked with intelligence operatives to "set favorable conditions for subsequent interviews"—a euphemism for breaking the will of prisoners. "Such actions generally run counter to the smooth operation of a detention facility, attempting to maintain its population in a compliant and docile state." General Karpinski's brigade, Ryder reported, "has not been directed to change its facility procedures to set the conditions for MI interrogations, nor participate in those interrogations." Ryder called for the establishment of procedures to "define the role of military police soldiers . . . clearly separating the actions of the guards from those of the military intelligence personnel." The officers running the war in Iraq were put on notice.

Ryder undercut his warning, however, by concluding that the situation had not yet reached a crisis point. Though some procedures were flawed, he said, he found "no military police units purposely applying inappropriate confinement practices." His investigation was at best a failure and at worst a coverup.

Taguba, in his report, was polite but direct in refuting his fellow-general. "Unfortunately, many of the systemic problems that surfaced during [Ryder's] assessment are the very same issues that are the subject of this investigation," he wrote. "In fact, many of the abuses suffered by detainees occurred during, or near to, the time of that assessment." The report continued, "Contrary to the findings of MG Ryder's report, I find that personnel assigned to the 372nd MP Company, 800th MP Brigade were directed to change facility procedures to 'set the conditions' for MI interrogations." Army intelligence officers, C.I.A. agents, and private contractors "actively requested that MP guards set physical and mental conditions for favorable interrogation of witnesses."

Taguba backed up his assertion by citing evidence from sworn statements to Army C.I.D. investigators. Specialist Sabrina Harman, one of the accused M.P.s, testified that it was her job to keep detainees awake, including one hooded prisoner who was placed on a box with wires attached to his fingers, toes, and penis. She stated, "MI wanted to get them to talk. It is Graner and Frederick's job to do things for MI and OGA to get these people to talk."

Another witness, Sergeant Javal Davis, who is also one of the accused, told C.I.D. investigators, "I witnessed prisoners in the MI hold section . . . being made to do various things that I would question morally. . . . We were told that they had different rules." Taguba wrote, "Davis also stated that he had heard MI insinuate to the guards to abuse the inmates. When asked what MI said he stated: 'Loosen this guy up for us.' 'Make sure he has a bad night.' 'Make sure he gets the treatment.' " Military intelligence made these comments to Graner and Frederick, Davis said. "The MI staffs to my understanding have been giving Graner compliments . . . statements like, 'Good job, they're breaking down real fast. They answer every question. They're giving out good information.' "

When asked why he did not inform his chain of command about the abuse, Sergeant Davis answered, "Because I assumed that if they were doing things out of the ordinary or outside the guidelines, someone would have said something. Also the wing"—where the abuse took place—"belongs to MI and it appeared MI personnel approved of the abuse."

Another witness, Specialist Jason Kennel, who was not accused of wrongdoing, said, "I saw them nude, but MI would tell us to take away their mattresses, sheets, and clothes." (It was his view, he added, that if M.I. wanted him to do this "they needed to give me paperwork.") Taguba also cited an interview with Adel L. Nakhla, a translator who was an employee of Titan, a civilian contractor. He told of one night when a "bunch of people from MI" watched as a group of handcuffed and shackled inmates were subjected to abuse by Graner and Frederick.

General Taguba saved his harshest words for the military-intelligence officers and private contractors. He recommended that Colonel Thomas Pappas, the commander of one of the M.I. brigades, be reprimanded and receive non-judicial punishment, and that Lieutenant Colonel Steven Jordan, the former director of the Joint Interrogation and Debriefing Center, be relieved of duty and reprimanded. He further urged that a civilian contractor, Steven Stephanowicz, of CACI International, be fired from his Army job, reprimanded, and denied his security clearances for lying to the investigating team and allowing or ordering military policemen "who were not trained in interrogation techniques to facilitate interrogations by 'setting conditions' which were neither authorized" nor in accordance with Army regulations. "He clearly knew his instructions equated to physical abuse," Taguba wrote. He also recommended disciplinary action against a second CACI employee, John Israel. (A spokeswoman for CACI said that the company had "received no formal communication" from the Army about the matter.)

"I suspect," Taguba concluded, that Pappas, Jordan, Stephanowicz, and Israel "were either directly or indirectly responsible for the abuse at Abu Ghraib," and strongly recommended immediate disciplinary action.

The problems inside the Army prison system in Iraq were not hidden from senior commanders. During Karpinski's seven-month tour of duty, Taguba noted, there were at least a dozen officially reported incidents involving escapes, attempted escapes, and other serious security issues that were investigated by officers of the 800th M.P. Brigade. Some of the incidents had led to the killing or wounding of inmates and M.P.s, and resulted in a series of "lessons learned" inquiries within the brigade.

Karpinski invariably approved the reports and signed orders calling for changes in day-to-day procedures. But Taguba found that she did not follow up, doing nothing to insure that the orders were carried out. Had she done so, he added, "cases of abuse may have been prevented."

General Taguba further found that Abu Ghraib was filled beyond capacity, and that the M.P. guard force was significantly undermanned and short of resources. "This imbalance has contributed to the poor living conditions, escapes, and accountability lapses," he wrote. There were gross differences, Taguba said, between the actual number of prisoners on hand and the number officially recorded. A lack of proper screening also meant that many innocent Iraqis were wrongly being detained—indefinitely, it seemed, in some cases. The Taguba study noted that more than sixty percent of the civilian inmates at Abu Ghraib were deemed not to be a threat to society, which should have enabled them to be released. Karpinski's defense, Taguba said, was that her superior officers "routinely" rejected her recommendations regarding the release of such prisoners.

Karpinski was rarely seen at the prisons she was supposed to be running, Taguba wrote. He also found a wide range of administrative problems, including some that he considered "without precedent in my military career." The soldiers, he added, were "poorly prepared and untrained . . . prior to deployment, at the mobilization site, upon arrival in theater, and throughout the mission."

General Taguba spent more than four hours interviewing Karpinski, whom he described as extremely emotional: "What I found particularly disturbing in her testimony was her complete unwillingness to either understand or accept that many of the problems inherent in the 800th MP Brigade were caused or exacerbated by poor leadership and the refusal of her command to both establish and enforce basic standards and principles among its soldiers."

Taguba recommended that Karpinski and seven brigade military-police officers and enlisted men be relieved of command and formally reprimanded. No criminal proceedings were suggested for Karpinski; apparently, the loss of promotion and the indignity of a public rebuke were seen as enough punishment.

After the story broke on CBS last week, the Pentagon announced that Major General Geoffrey Miller, the new head of the Iraqi prison system, had arrived in Baghdad and was on the job. He had been the commander of the Guantánamo Bay detention center. General Sanchez also authorized another investigation into possible wrongdoing by military and civilian interrogators.

As the international furor grew, senior military officers, and President Bush, insisted that the actions of a few did not reflect the conduct of the military as a whole. Taguba's report, however, amounts to an unsparing study of collective wrongdoing and the failure of Amy leadership at the highest levels. The picture he draws of Abu Ghraib is one in which Army regulations and the Geneva conventions were routinely violated, and in which much of the day-to-day management of the prisoners was abdicated to Army military-intelligence units and civilian contract employees. Interrogating prisoners and getting intelligence, including by intimidation and torture, was the priority.

The mistreatment at Abu Ghraib may have done little to further American intelligence, however. Willie J. Rowell, who served for thirty-six years as a C.I.D. agent, told me that the use of force or humiliation with prisoners is invariably counterproductive. "They'll tell you what you want to hear, truth or no truth," Rowell said. " 'You can flog me until I tell you what I know you want me to say.' You don't get righteous information."

Under the fourth Geneva convention, an occupying power can jail civilians who pose an "imperative" security threat, but it must establish a regular procedure for insuring that only civilians who remain a genuine security threat be kept imprisoned. Prisoners have the right to appeal any internment decision and have their cases reviewed. Human Rights Watch complained to Secretary of Defense Donald Rumsfeld that civilians in Iraq remained in custody month after month with no charges brought against them. Abu Ghraib had become, in effect, another Guantánamo.

As the photographs from Abu Ghraib make clear, these detentions have had enormous consequences: for the imprisoned civilian Iraqis, many of whom had nothing to do with the growing insurgency; for the integrity of the Army; and for the United States' reputation in the world.

Captain Robert Shuck, Frederick's military attorney, closed his defense at the Article 32 hearing last month by saying that the Army was "attempting to have these six soldiers atone for its sins." Similarly, Gary Myers, Frederick's civilian attorney, told me that he would argue at the court-martial that culpability in the case extended far beyond his client. "I'm going to drag every involved intelligence officer and civilian contractor I can find into court," he said. "Do you really believe the Army relieved a general officer because of six soldiers? Not a chance."

Study Questions

1. After reading this article, write a brief paragraph summarizing what, in your opinion, were the chief reasons (or primary conditions) that led to the prison abuses at Abu Ghraib.

2. In what ways could the abusive incidents discussed in this chapter have been avoided or prevented?

3. What were the primary goals of the incarceration that occurred at Abu Ghraib? Do any of these goals overlap with the primary goals and philosophies of punishment that characterize the United States' domestic prison system?

4. Aside from the overarching motivation to gather intelligence from the detainees at Abu Ghraib, which of the other conditions described in this chapter do you think could exist in the United States' prison system?

5. How might the issue of "professionalism" (or lack thereof) have played a role in the incidents at Abu Ghraib?

18
The Supreme Court and Prisoners' Rights

Jack E. Call

*The United States' highest court, through the rendering of various decisions (or by choosing not to intervene), has set the tone for many aspects of prison operations. The relationship between the U.S. Supreme Court and the conditions within prisons has been dynamic, particularly over the past 40 years. The author presents a comprehensive summary of numerous landmark cases within prisoner litigation that have been argued before the Supreme Court. Three periods are identified, each of which is characterized by the overall position that the Court appeared to take when confronted with prisoners' rights and the constitutionality of prison conditions. In broad terms, the Supreme Court adhered to a hands-off doctrine prior to the mid-1960s, followed by a prisoners' rights period until 1978, during which a propensity to intervene on several fronts occurred. This prisoners' rights period was followed by a deference period, indicating the Court's desire to place more power and discretion, and the administration of the prisons themselves, into the hands of the lower courts. In addition to detailing these three eras of Supreme Court decision making, the author also highlights many additional cases classified into several areas concerning specific rights. For example, important cases pertaining to access to the court itself, individual rights, due process, and cruel and unusual punishment are reviewed. This chapter offers the reader the opportunity to gain a broad understanding of the most important cases in prisoner litiga-*tion, *as well as a chance to glean a historical perspective.*

As substantive areas of the law go, the law of prisoners' rights is still in its infancy. Until the 1960's, the courts largely stayed out of this area. The movement away from this abstention was led by the lower Federal courts. In the late 1960's, however, the United States Supreme Court began to involve itself as well. Since then, the Supreme Court has decided more than 30 cases dealing with the rights of the incarcerated. Surprisingly, there has been very little scholarly attention paid to the efforts of the Supreme Court *as a whole* in this area. This article attempts to fill in some of this gap in the literature on prisoners' rights. It examines the Supreme Court case law from two perspectives: chronologically and by major subject area.

A Chronological Perspective

Historically, the Supreme Court case law on prisoners' rights can be divided into three periods: (1) the Hands-Off Period (before 1964), (2) the Rights Period (1964–78), and (3) the Deference Period (1979–present).

The Hands-Off Period (Before 1964)

Before the 1960's, courts (including the Supreme Court) did not involve themselves in the issue of prisoners' rights. Initially, this stance was the result of a legal approach that held that prisoners were slaves of the state. Upon conviction, criminals lost virtually all legal rights. Any rights they had were not the rights shared with other citizens, but those rights which the state chose to extend to them.

Ruffin v. Commonwealth[1] illustrates this approach. In rejecting Ruffin's contention that the Virginia Constitution required that he be tried in his home county for a crime

209

he committed while in prison, the Virginia Court of Appeals indicated that

> [t]he bill of rights is a declaration of general principles to govern a society of free men, and not of convicted felons and men civilly dead. Such men have some rights it is true, such as the law in its benignity accords to them, but not the rights of free men. They are the slaves of the State undergoing punishment for heinous crimes committed against the laws of the land.

In time, this convict-as-slave approach gave way to an abstention approach. The courts during this period recognized that prisoners did retain constitutional rights, but it was not the role of the courts to intervene to protect those rights. Instead, courts saw the legislative and executive branches as having responsibility for identifying and honoring the constitutional rights of inmates.

There are several reasons given typically to explain this abstention approach by the courts.[2] First, the courts perceived that to intervene in these matters would be to usurp the proper functions of the legislative and executive branches of government. Second, and somewhat related to the separation of powers concern just mentioned, was a belief by the courts that they lacked the expertise to become involved in these matters. Because of their lack of understanding of the operation of prisons, if courts took steps to protect prisoners' rights, they ran a great risk of interfering with the proper functioning of the institutions.

Third, most prisoners are housed in state prisons. If they sought protection of their rights in Federal courts, these courts felt that their intervention intruded upon the proper functioning of a Federal system of government. And last, most courts, although they seldom said so explicitly, seemed to fear that if they acted to protect prisoners' rights the courts would experience a flood of frivolous lawsuits from prisoners.

As with most of the generalizations that will be made about these historic periods in prisoners' rights, there are exceptions to the generalization that courts declined to intervene on behalf of prisoners during the hands-off period. For example, the Supreme Court held in 1941 that the states could not require inmates to submit formal legal documents to state officials for review and approval before filing those papers with the courts.[3] Nevertheless, such instances of judicial recognition of rights held by prisoners were isolated.

The Rights Period (1964–78)

In the early 1960's, lower Federal courts began moving away from the hands-off approach. They demonstrated an increasing willingness to identify rights of prisoners found in the Constitution and to protect those rights. This change in approach is attributed to several factors.[4]

First, prisoners, perhaps reflecting society as a whole at the time, became more militant and aggressive in asserting their rights. Second, the legal profession developed a cadre of "public interest lawyers" who were willing to take on these cases, either pro bono or with financial support from government and private foundation grants. Third, the judiciary as a whole seemed to become more responsive to the legal arguments advanced by politically disadvantaged groups. Fourth, judges were often presented with cases that involved such horrible conditions of confinement that they cried out for some sort of remedial action.

And last, two developments in Federal law created a more favorable environment for prisoners' rights cases in the Federal courts. The first development involved interpretation of the Civil Rights Statute (42 U.S.C. Section 1983), a post-Civil War law. Lawsuits brought under this statute are commonly referred to as Section 1983 suits. Section 1983 permits a person whose rights under Federal law are violated by a person acting "under color of state law" to sue for damages or some sort of remedial order.

Before 1961, the accepted interpretation of Section 1983 was that a state official who acted in violation of state law was not acting "under color" of state law. In *Monroe v. Pape*,[5] the Supreme Court rejected this prior interpretation as being inconsistent with the desire of Congress to provide relief for persons whose constitutional rights were violated by state and local government officials, even when their actions were not officially approved. This change in the interpretation of Section 1983 enabled prisoners to file their suits complaining of rights violations in Federal courts, where it was generally thought that they would receive a more sympathetic hearing than in state courts.

The second development in Federal law concerned the Supreme Court's interpretation of the Due Process Clause of the 14th amendment, another post-Civil War provision. The Due Process Clause prohibits a *state* from depriving persons of life, liberty, or property without due process of law. Through a long process called Selective Incorporation that began in the 1920's and picked up a full head of steam in the 1960's, the Supreme Court ruled that the Due Process Clause "incorporated" most of the rights contained in the Bill of Rights into the 14th amendment.

This meant that state and local governments had to extend to persons under their jurisdiction most of the rights in the first 10 amendments to the Constitution, such as free speech, freedom of religion, right to counsel, right against self-incrimination, right against unreasonable searches and seizures, and many others. Thus, one's constitutional rights, the violation of which by state and local officials could result in a Section 1983 lawsuit, became more extensive.

In due course, the Supreme Court itself jumped on the prisoners' rights bandwagon, although somewhat inconspicuously at first. In three of its first four prisoners' rights cases, the Court issued per curiam decisions. These are unsigned decisions (i.e., no particular Justice is identified as the opinion's author) usually affirming the decision of the lower court without hearing oral argument and without explaining the Court's reasons for affirming.

In the first of these cases, *Cooper v. Pate*,[6] the Court held unanimously that a state prison inmate could bring a Section 1983 suit alleging that his freedom of religion was violated by the prison's refusal to permit him to purchase certain religious material. Four years later, in *Lee v. Washington*,[7] the Court again unanimously upheld a lower court's order to Alabama to desegregate its prisons and jails, although three Justices concurred in a brief opinion expressing their belief that the Court's decision should not be viewed as prohibiting corrections officials from taking racial tensions into account in their decisionmaking. Then in 1971, in *Younger v. Gilmore*,[8] the Court again unanimously upheld a lower court decision that required a prison to provide inmates an adequate law library.

Sandwiched in between *Lee* and *Younger* in 1969 was the Court's first full opinion venture into prisoners' rights, *Johnson v. Avery*.[9] Johnson was a "writ writer," an inmate who assisted other inmates in preparing legal papers challenging their convictions. He was disciplined by prison authorities for engaging in this activity. The Court held that, "unless and until the State provides some reasonable alternative to assist inmates in the preparation of petitions for post-conviction relief,"[10] it could not constitutionally prohibit inmates from functioning as jailhouse lawyers. This case is important, not only because it was the Court's first prisoners' rights case in over 25 years with a full written opinion, but also because it ruled in favor of the inmate and thereby established the general tone of its cases during the Rights Period.

In two cases the Court upheld the first amendment rights of a prisoner. In *Cruz v. Beto* (1972),[11] the Court held that a prison could not prevent a Buddhist inmate from using the prison chapel, from corresponding with religious advisors, and from distributing religious materials to other inmates, if the prison permitted inmates of other faiths to engage in these same activities.

In *Procunier v. Martinez* (1974),[12] the Court found that prisons could not censor outgoing mail that was viewed by prison authorities as expressing "inflammatory" views, unduly complaining, or "otherwise inappropriate." These standards were too broad and failed to exclude only material that posed a legitimate threat to institutional interests.

If mail was censored (under constitutionally acceptable standards), the inmate sending the mail has to be notified and given an opportunity to object to some official who was not involved in the original censorship decision. Although the Court based this holding on the first amendment rights of the correspondent outside the prison, its effect, of course, was to protect inmates as well.

In a Due Process case, the Court ruled in *Wolff v. McDonnell* (1974)[13] that inmates had a liberty interest in good time credits.[14] Good time credits could not be denied without holding a hearing before which an accused inmate was given notice of the alleged infraction, at which the inmate was given the opportunity to call witnesses and present documentary evidence (unless allowing either would be "unduly hazardous to institutional safety or correctional goals"), and after which the prison would issue a written statement of the reasons for its action and the evidence relied upon in coming to its decision.

The Court issued several rulings upholding the right of inmates to access the courts. The Court ruled in *Wolff* that the *Avery* rule, protecting the status of writ writers when other provisions for legal assistance have not been made, applied to writ writers who were assisting other inmates in the preparation of Section 1983 suits (and was not limited to assisting with habeas corpus petitions).

In *Martinez,* the Court also struck down a prison rule that prohibited visits from employees (other than two licensed investigators) of lawyers who were representing inmates. The clear effect of this rule was to inhibit inmates' ability to access the courts because the rule made it more difficult for attorneys to communicate in person with their clients.

In 1977, in *Bounds v. Smith*,[15] the Court examined the adequacy of the law libraries established by North Carolina for its inmates. Although the Court upheld the adequacy of the libraries, it made it clear that the state was indeed required by the Constitution to establish law libraries to assist inmates in their efforts to petition the courts unless the state provided inmates with adequate assistance from persons trained in the law. And finally, in an eighth amendment case, *Hutto v. Finney* (1978),[16] the Court held that, given the harsh conditions of punitive isolation cells in the Arkansas prison system, inmates could not be placed constitutionally in those cells for more than 30 days.

While these cases demonstrated a willingness by the Court to support the rights of prisoners, there were issues during the Rights Period on which inmates did not receive favorable rulings from the Court. In *Wolff*, the Court refused to extend the rights of counsel, confrontation, and cross-examination to the good time hearings that it required in that case. The Court also indicated that in adopting a rule that mail from attorneys could be opened by the prison in the presence of the inmate receiving the mail, the prison "had done all, and perhaps even more" than the Constitution requires.

In *Pell v. Procunier* (1974),[17] the Court upheld a California prison regulation which prohibited the press from interviewing *individual* inmates. However, it seemed important to the Court's decision that the press was permitted to visit and observe conditions in the prisons and to interview inmates at random.

In *Meachum v. Fano* (1976),[18] the Court held that inmates had no liberty interest under the Due Process Clause in avoiding transfer to another prison where conditions were harsher because such a transfer was "within the normal limits or range of custody" which the conviction authorizes the state to impose. What's more, it makes no difference whether the transfer is simply for administrative reasons, as in *Meachum,* or is for disciplinary reasons, as was the case in *Montanye v. Haymes.*[19]

In *Baxter v. Palmigiano,*[20] decided the same year as *Meachum* and *Montanye,* the Court held that an inmate's right against self-incrimination is not violated if the inmate's refusal to answer questions at a disciplinary hearing is held against him at the hearing. (Note, however, that inmates *do* have a constitutional right not to answer questions at the hearing that would tend to incriminate them, unless they are granted immunity for the statements they are compelled to give.) In *Baxter,* the Court also held that prisons do not have to give reasons for denying an inmate's request to call a witness at the disciplinary hearing, do not have to permit cross-examination of witnesses, and in making their disciplinary decisions may rely upon evidence not presented at the hearing.

Also in 1976, in *Estelle v. Gamble,*[21] the Court held that an inmate cannot prove that inadequate medical care by the prison is cruel and unusual punishment unless he can also prove that prison officials were deliberately indifferent to a serious medical need of the inmate. The next year, in *Jones v. N.C. Prisoners' Labor Union,*[22] the Court concluded that prisons may ban meetings of prisoners' unions, as well as prohibit the unions from soliciting members and from making bulk mailings to members.

It should be clear from a careful consideration of these cases decided during the Rights Period that the Court was not engaged in a prisoners' rights revolution. In many instances it decided that the rights of inmates had to give way to the legitimate needs of the prisons to maintain security, control inmate behavior, and attempt to rehabilitate inmates. Nevertheless, what is most remarkable about the Rights Period is the Court's willingness, first, to recognize that inmates retain constitutional rights and, second, to view those rights as being nearly as important as the legitimate needs of the prisons.

The Deference Period (1979–present)

The year 1979 was chosen to begin the period that I have labeled the Deference Period because that was the year the Supreme Court decided *Bell v. Wolfish.*[23] The Court resolved five issues in that case and ruled against the inmates on all of them. It held that cells of 75 square feet that had been double-bunked were not so overcrowded as to constitute punishment under the Due Process Clause. It also upheld jail rules that: (1) permitted inmates to receive hardback books only if they came directly from the publisher, a bookstore, or a book club (publishers' only rule), (2) prohibited inmates from receiving packages from outside the jail, (3) prohibited inmates from observing shakedown searches of their cells, and (4) subjected inmates to visual body cavity searches after contact visits.

In ruling against the inmates, the Court set the tone for the Deference Period. During this period, inmates would lose on most prisoners' rights issues before the Court, which would stress the need to give deference to the expertise of corrections officials. The Court applauded the judicial trend away from the traditional hands-off approach and the willingness of courts to intervene where institutions were characterized by "deplorable conditions and draconian restrictions." However, the Court followed with this caution:

> But many of these same courts have, in the name of the Constitution, become increasingly enmeshed in the minutiae of prison operations. Judges, after all, are human. They, no less than others in our society, have a natural tendency to believe that their individual solutions to often intracta-

ble problems are better and more workable than those of the persons who are actually charged with and trained in the running of the particular institution under examination. But under the Constitution, the first question to be answered is not whose plan is best, but in what branch of the Government is lodged the authority to initially devise the plan. This does not mean that constitutional rights are not to be scrupulously observed. It does mean, however, that the inquiry of federal courts into prison management must be limited to the issue of whether a particular system violates any prohibition of the Constitution . . . The wide range of "judgment calls" that meet constitutional . . . requirements are confined to officials outside of the Judicial Branch of Government.[24]

In another overcrowding case in 1981, *Rhodes v. Chapman*,[25] the Court held that double-bunking was not unconstitutional per se and that double-bunking of cells of 63 square feet without a showing of specific harmful effects on inmates was not cruel and unusual punishment.[26] As in *Wolfish*, the Court admonished judges that they "cannot assume that state legislatures and prison officials are insensitive to the requirements of the Constitution. . . ."

Several times during this period, the Court held that actions taken against inmates by corrections officials did not affect a liberty interest of inmates and were therefore not subject to the protections of the Due Process Clause. The Court held that an inmate had no liberty interest in: 1) a decision by the Board of Commutation as to whether to commute a life sentence, even though the Board granted 75 percent of all petitions for commutation from lifers and those lifers receiving commutation nearly always were paroled earlier than they would have been otherwise (*Connecticut Board of Pardons v. Dumschat*, 1981[27]); 2) the overturning of an early parole decision, even though the parole board changed its mind because of information it received about dishonesty on the part of the inmate (*Jago v.*

Van Curen, 1981[28]); 3) a decision to transfer an inmate to a prison in another state (*Olim v. Wakinekona*, 1983[29]); and 4) a decision to exclude visitors because of alleged misconduct on their part (*Kentucky v. Thompson*, 1989[30]).

Even in two cases where the Court held that inmates had a liberty interest (*Greenholtz v. Nebraska Penal Inmates*, 1979,[31] and *Hewitt v. Helms*, 1983[32]), it was only because state law had specified conditions under which adverse action could be taken against inmates and provided that this action could be taken only when the specified conditions were found to exist. *Greenholtz* involved the decision whether to grant parole, and *Hewitt* involved whether to place an inmate in administrative segregation. In another important due process decision, the Court ruled in *Superintendent v. Hill* that a decision of a prison administrative body should be upheld when challenged in court if there is "some evidence" in the record to support the decision.[33]

The Court also ruled against inmates in two search cases during this period. In *Hudson v. Palmer*,[34] the Court held that the fourth amendment does not apply to cell searches (even a shakedown search with no reason to think contraband will be found) because inmates have no reasonable expectation of privacy in their cells. The Court also concluded that inmates have no due process right to observe shakedown searches of their cells (*Block v. Rutherford*, 1984[35]).

Inmates also lost several first amendment issues during the Deference Period. In *Block*, the Court rejected an argument that pretrial detainees who were judged by jail officials to be low security risks and who had been in jail more than a month had a constitutional right to *contact* visits. The Court held that it was reasonable for the jail to ban contact visits to prevent contraband from being smuggled in.

In *Turner v. Safley* (1987),[36] the Court held that a prison rule which prohibited inmates from corresponding with inmates in other prisons was constitutional. The Court viewed this regulation as a reasonable way to protect prison security, since the correspondence that was banned could have been used to communicate escape plans or to encourage assaults on other inmates.

O'Lone v. Shabazz (1987)[37] dealt with the right of inmates to practice their religion. Shabazz was a Muslim who was not permitted to observe Jumu'ah services in the prison on Friday afternoons (the only time that Jumu'ah may be observed) because his security classification required him to be on a work detail outside the prison. The Court held that the prison did not have to permit Shabazz to return to the prison for the service because that would have created a security risk. Nor did the prison have to allow Shabazz to stay in the prison all day Friday and then let him make up the work on Saturday because that would require additional prison resources. Thus, the prison's actions in denying Shabazz the opportunity to observe Jumu'ah were reasonable in light of the security and resources needs of the prison.

In *Thornburgh v. Abbott* (1989),[38] the Court dealt with the authority of prisons to exclude publications that are mailed to inmates. The rule at issue permitted wardens in Federal prisons to exclude publications (although only on an issue-by-issue basis) that they deemed to be "detrimental to the security, good order, or discipline of the institution, or . . . [that] might facilitate criminal activity." Publications could not be excluded because they expressed unpopular views or were religious, political, social, or sexual in nature.

The Court found that this regulation was reasonable in light of the prisons' need to maintain security. It distinguished this case from *Procunier v. Martinez,* where the Court had struck down a prison censorship regulation as too broad, on the basis that *Martinez* dealt with incoming mail and this case dealt with outgoing mail. The Court believed that outgoing mail posed greater threats to prison security.

In another case involving an individual right, the Court concluded in *Washington v. Harper* that a mentally ill inmate could, after a hearing, be treated with antipsychotic drugs against his will.[39] Although the Court found that the inmate did have a liberty interest in not being administered the drug, it also found that the policy of involuntary treatment is permissible because it is reasonably related to the prison's interest in controlling the violent behavior of such an inmate.

Inmates also lost three important eighth amendment issues. In *Whitley v. Albers* (1986),[40] an inmate sued a prison guard who had wounded him in the knee during an inmate uprising, alleging that the shooting was cruel and unusual punishment. The inmate alleged that he had not been involved in the uprising, had assured the prison security chief that he would protect from harm a guard that other inmates had taken hostage, and had made no threatening moves just before being shot.

The Court ruled that, in cruel and unusual punishment cases where the government action at issue is not part of the sentence awarded the prisoner, the prisoner must prove that prison officials acted wantonly. In the context of a prison disturbance, that means the inmate must show that officials acted "maliciously and sadistically for the very purpose of causing harm." In this case, according to the Court, the inmate had failed to allege facts from which such a state of mind could be inferred.

In *Wilson v. Seiter* (1991),[41] the Court again addressed the issue of the state of mind necessary to prove a violation of the Cruel and Unusual Punishment Clause in the prison context. This time, rather than dealing with a discreet act against an individual inmate, as had been the case in *Estelle* and *Whitley,* the Court dealt with allegations that the general conditions of confinement in an overcrowded prison were cruel and unusual punishment.

The Court concluded that general conditions of confinement are not part of the sentence awarded a convicted defendant. Therefore, it is necessary to prove that, in permitting overcrowded conditions to persist, prison officials acted wantonly, otherwise officials have not acted with intent to punish inmates. Where general conditions of confinement are at issue, inmates must show that prison officials acted with deliberate [in]difference to some basic human need of the inmates.

The Court also clarified a point that lower courts had dealt with for some [time]. Lower courts had frequently held that the totality of adverse conditions in an institution violated the eighth amendment. The Court rejected this approach. While it conceded that two or more conditions might have a "mutually enforcing effect," the eighth amendment has not been violated unless there is evidence that the effect has been to deprive inmates "of a single, identifiable human need such as food, warmth, or exercise." The Court indicated that interaction of conditions in this way "is a far cry from saying that all prison conditions are a seamless web for Eighth Amendment purposes."

Then in *Farmer v. Brennan* (1994),[42] the Court gave some definition to what it meant by deliberate indifference. After stating the fairly obvious, that deliberate indifference is something more than mere negligence but something less than a specific intent to cause harm to a particular inmate or inmates, the Court concluded that deliberate indifference means recklessness. The Court also recognized that while both civil (tort) law and criminal law utilize the concept of recklessness, their definitions are somewhat different. Tort law usually views recklessness as action "in the face of an unjustifiably high risk of harm that is either known or so obvious that it should be known." This is sometimes referred to as an objective approach to recklessness.

The criminal law, on the other hand, usually takes a subjective approach, requiring that an actor be aware of a disregarded risk. Thus, the difference between the two defini-

tions is that tort law recklessness includes disregard of a risk of which an actor was unaware but should have been aware, while criminal law recklessness does not.

The Court decided that the subjective criminal law approach to recklessness is the one required by the eighth amendment. Although the Court went to some length to explain its reasoning for adopting this approach, in the final analysis it appears that the majority felt that it was simply fairer to hold prison officials responsible only for those risks of which they are actually aware.

In these Deference Period cases discussed so far, the inmates not only lost the case, but often the Court articulated a rule that seems to make it likely that inmates will have a difficult time winning prisoners' rights suits in the future as well.[43] Nevertheless, prisoners experienced a few successes during this period. For example, in the Due Process area, the Court concluded in *Vitek v. Jones* (1980)[44] that inmates have a liberty interest in the decision as to whether to transfer a prisoner to a mental hospital. Even if the state had not used mandatory language that prohibited such a transfer unless there is a finding that the inmate suffers from a mental illness which cannot be treated adequately in the prison, the Court found that the stigmatization of transfer to a mental hospital, coupled with the prospect of subjection to mandatory behavior modification, constitutes the kind of liberty deprivation that is protected by the Due Process Clause itself. We also saw earlier that the Court ruled that mentally ill inmates have a liberty interest in avoiding, involuntary treatment with antipsychotic drugs.[45]

Inmates also won two cases involving eighth amendment issues. In *Hudson v. McMillian* (1992), an inmate sued a guard who had beaten him and caused facial swelling, loosened teeth, a cracked dental plate, and minor bruises, but no permanent injury. The government argued that in order for a harm experienced from the use of excessive force to be sufficient to constitute cruel and unusual punishment, the force had to cause significant injury. The Court rejected this argument, finding that excessive use of force on inmates always violates contemporary standards of decency and therefore violates the eighth amendment.

The Court also concluded that the state of mind standard in all excessive force cases (and not just cases involving prison disturbances, as in *Whitley*) is the malice standard established in *Whitley*. While this can be seen as a loss for inmates, the Court did rule that the guard's use of force in this case was malicious.[46]

In *Helling v. McKinney* (1993),[47] McKinney complained that he had been placed involuntarily in a cell with another inmate who smoked five packs of cigarettes a day. McKinney contended that exposure to this smoke demonstrated deliberate indifference to his health. The prison argued that McKinney failed to meet the objective aspect of his eighth amendment claim because he failed to allege that he had suffered any harm. The Court held that cruel and unusual punishment could be demonstrated by proof of exposure to conditions that "pose an unreasonable risk of serious damage to [plaintiff's] future health." Thus, the harm that must be shown in an eighth amendment case can be either a present harm or an unreasonable risk of a future harm.

The final inmate victory during the Deference Period involved a first amendment issue. We saw earlier that the Court, in applying its rational basis test in *Safley*, upheld a prohibition on inmate correspondence with inmates in other prisons. However, it also concluded in that case that the prison's ban on inmate marriages was not reasonably related to penological interests. It viewed the marriage ban as an exaggerated response to the prison's concern for security and rehabilitation of inmates. This ruling was especially significant in light of the fact that a prison survey taken in 1978 indicated that most prisons did not permit inmate marriages.[48]

The Deference Period witnessed many triumphs for prisons. The common denominator in these cases is the Court's concern that prison officials be permitted to do their difficult jobs without undue interference from the courts. In other words, courts should generally defer to the judgment of corrections officials.

A Substantive Assessment of Supreme Court Law on Prisoners' Rights

How can we assess the current state of this expanding body of Supreme Court case law? The following discussion examines the four major substantive areas that have been addressed most frequently by the Court's cases: (1) right to access the courts, (2) individual rights, (3) due process issues, and (4) cruel and unusual punishment. The overall conclusion is that Supreme Court cases tend to favor inmates with respect to their right to access the courts and tend to favor the prisons in the other three areas.

Right to Access the Courts

It is in this area that the Court has been most protective of prisoners. The Court has made it clear that prisons must either provide inmates with an adequate law library or provide them adequate assistance from persons who have been legally trained.[49] If they opt to provide a law library, they must permit inmates to assist other inmates in the preparation of legal papers.[50] This assistance extends not only to preparation of writs of habeas corpus (attacking the legality of an inmate's conviction), but also includes preparation of civil rights actions (which would typically challenge some aspect of the inmate's conditions of confinement).[51]

If the prison opts to provide legal assistance to inmates rather than a law library, or if an inmate has engaged a lawyer, the institution must have reasonable regulations concerning visitation by employees of the lawyer. A rule that prohibits anyone employed by a lawyer (such as paralegals), other than two licensed investigators, from visiting the prisoner who has engaged the lawyer places an unconstitutional burden on a prisoner's right to access the courts.[52]

Of course, there are many unanswered questions about the right of inmates to access the courts. What restrictions can a prison place on inmates desiring to use a prison law library? What restrictions may be placed on opportunities for a writ writer to consult with the inmate that he is assisting? What is an *adequate* law library? Must institutions provide inmates with paper supplies and notary services?

These unanswered questions and dozens of others like them give the Court ample opportunity to limit the scope of the right of access to the courts. It is worth noting that the Court has not decided an issue in this area since 1977. It may be that the reason why the Court appears to be rather supportive of inmates' rights of access is because it did not address any issues in this area during the present Deference Period.

Individual Rights

The Court's initial efforts in this area suggested that it was going to be rather protective of inmates. In two of its first individual prisoners' rights cases, the Court indicated that members of "minority" religious groups, at least if the number of members is significant, must be permitted to engage in the same kinds of religious activities as members of other, more common religious groups[53] and that rules governing the censorship and withholding of mail from inmates to persons outside the prison would be subjected to close scrutiny by the Court.[54]

It is this latter holding and the Court's subsequent treatment of it that is of greatest significance in this area. Generally, when the Court identifies an individual right as particularly important (or "fundamental"), any actions taken by government which impinge upon that right are subjected to heightened scrutiny by the courts. This means that in deciding whether the government action is constitutional, the government will have to demonstrate that it had a compelling reason for doing what it did, that what it did was necessary in light of this compelling government need, and that government had available to it no means of carrying out its purpose that would have had less impact on the rights of individuals.

It appeared from the Court's opinion in *Procunier v. Martinez* that it intended to take this approach, or one similar to it, in assessing the actions of prisons that adversely affected the individual rights of prisoners. In several later cases involving individual rights of prisoners, the Court ruled against the inmates without a very clear discussion of whether it was using a heightened scrutiny approach.

Then in 1987 in *Turner v. Safley,* the Court made it clear that it was *not* going to use a heightened scrutiny approach in individual rights cases. In its review of prison regulations prohibiting inmate marriages and inmate correspondence with inmates in other prisons, the Court reviewed all its prisoners' rights cases and concluded that these cases had used a rational basis test. The Court stated emphatically that "when a prison regulation impinges on inmates' constitutional rights, the regulation is valid if it is reasonably related to legitimate penological interests."[55]

This approach is usually referred to as the rational basis test. It is a much easier standard for the government to satisfy than the heightened scrutiny approach. Under the rational basis test, the burden is shifted to the party whose rights have allegedly been violated to demonstrate that the government had no rational reason for doing what it did or that, if it did have a rational reason, what it did was not reasonably related to it.

In *Safley,* the Court also established four factors that should be considered in assessing the reasonableness of a prison regulation that impinges upon an individual right of an inmate: (1) whether there is a rational connection between the prison regulation and the legitimate governmental interest put forward to justify it, (2) whether an alternative means of exercising the right exists in spite of what the prison has done, (3) whether striking down the prison's action would have a significant ripple effect on fellow inmates or staff, and (4) whether there are ready alternatives available to the prison or whether the regulation appears instead to be [an] "exaggerated response" to the problem it is intended to address.

The Court has utilized these four factors in determining the constitutionality of the two regulations at issue in *Safley,* the regulation in *Shabazz* that prevented Muslim inmates from participating in Jumu'ah, and the publishers-only regulation in *Thornburgh.* Although the Court did strike down the ban on inmate marriages, it upheld the other three regulations. More importantly, its application of the four *Safley* factors suggests that prisons should not experience great difficulty in satisfying them.

The right of inmates to be free from unreasonable searches and seizures is an individual right that is not affected directly by the rational basis test. However, the Court has engaged in a somewhat similar analysis by comparing the needs of prisons to maintain discipline and security with the interest of prisoners in privacy and finding consistently that the prisoners' interests are outweighed by the prisons' interests. Thus, inmates have no reasonable expectation of privacy in their cells,[56] inmates who have had contact visits may be subjected to visual body cavity inspections even in the absence of any reason to think that the inspections will turn up evidence,[57] and inmates have no right to observe shakedown searches of their cells.[58] It seems apparent that when prisons take actions that adversely affect the individual rights of inmates, those actions will be upheld by the Court unless they are clearly unreasonable.

Due Process Issues

Of the four substantive areas with which Supreme Court prisoners' rights [cases] have dealt most frequently, it is in the area of Due Process rights that the Court has spoken with least clarity. The Due Process Clauses (in the 5th and 14th amendments) raise two basic questions: (1) When is a person entitled to due process of law? (2) When a person is so entitled, what process is due?

In the prison context, the answer to the first question has arisen in the context of actions taken against an inmate. Such actions include (but are certainly not limited to) loss of good time credits, a decision not to grant parole, transfer to a mental hospital, transfer to a less desirable prison, removal to solitary confinement, and denial of a visitor. Since these actions do not deprive an inmate of life or property, the question is whether the inmate has been deprived of a liberty interest in these situations.

The Court has indicated that prisoners acquire liberty interests from one of two sources: (1) the Constitution itself and (2) by creation of state law. The Court has been far from clear as to what kind of interest is a liberty interest protected by the Constitution itself. The Court has indicated that not every "change in the conditions of confinement having a substantial adverse impact on the prisoner involved is sufficient. . . ."[59] Instead, a liberty interest arises when the action taken by the prison is not "within the terms of confinement ordinarily contemplated by a prison sentence."[60]

Unfortunately, this phrase does not carry us very far toward a clear conception of when an inmate has a constitutionally protected liberty interest. What *is* clear is that there are very few such liberty interests. The Court has indicated that denial of a visit from a particular person,[61] granting of parole,[62] commutation of a life sentence,[63] transfer to a prison with less favorable conditions of confinement,[64] transfer to a prison in another state,[65] and transfer to administrative segregation[66] are not such liberty interests. The only liberty interest protected by the Due Process Clause and arising directly under the Constitution which the Court has found that inmates possess is an interest in not being transferred to a mental hospital.[67]

The second source of a liberty interest is by creation of state law. This kind of liberty interest is created when state law provides that a particular action may not be taken against an inmate (what the Court has called "mandatory language") unless certain conditions exist (what the Court has called "specific substantive predicates"). For example, if state law indicates that an inmate may not be placed in administrative segregation unless there is a demonstrated "need for control" or "the threat of a serious disturbance," then it has specified the conditions under which the transfer may occur and prohibited transfer for any other reasons.[68] Consequently, it has created a liberty interest. Determination of the existence of this kind of liberty interest will be very case specific, turning on the particular language used in a particular law or regulation.

In these Due Process cases, the inmate cannot argue that the Due Process Clause prohibits the prison from taking the action it took. Instead, his contention is that in taking this action, the prison failed to extend to him the procedural protections to which he was entitled. Consequently, if it is determined that a prison's action did intrude upon a liberty interest of an inmate, the next question concerns the procedural protections that an inmate is entitled to before this action may be taken. This is a very difficult question to answer because it depends on the severity of the possible consequences to the inmate. Generally, the more severe the action that is being contemplated by the prison, the greater protections that must be extended to the inmate.

The most basic protections are the right to be informed of the alleged basis for the contemplated action (e.g., the prison is considering depriving an inmate of good time credits for allegedly assaulting another inmate in the dining hall) and the right to be heard (i.e., present evidence on one's own behalf). Other possible protections include the rights to an administrative hearing, to be confronted by and cross-examine witnesses for the other side, to a written statement of the reasons for the action decided upon and the evidence relied upon in coming to that decision, and to be represented by counsel.

Limited space here does not permit a thorough treatment of this subject. However, three important generalizations should be noted. First, the Court seems to feel generally that if a liberty interest has been affected, an inmate should have written notice, an opportunity to be heard, and a written statement of the action taken, the reasons for it, and the evidence relied upon.[69] Second, the prison has considerable discretion (in the interests of security) to prohibit confrontation of the witnesses against the inmate.[70] Third, seldom will it be necessary to permit representation by legal counsel. However, the Court has displayed some sensitivity to the fact that many inmates may lack the intellectual and educational tools necessary to ensure that their side of an issue has been presented adequately. Therefore, it sometimes may be necessary to provide an educated, nonlawyer (probably a prison staff member) to assist the inmate in preparing his "case."[71]

The standards established by the Court in Due Process cases are unusually ambiguous and difficult to understand. Nevertheless, the Court has decided enough of these cases to allow a conclusion that the Court does not think inmates should win many of these cases.

Cruel and Unusual Punishment

The eighth amendment prohibits cruel and unusual punishments. The Court has decided three kinds of prisoners' rights cases involving this provision: (1) medical treatment cases, (2) use of force cases, and (3) conditions of confinement cases.

In medical treatment cases, the Court has held that an inmate complaining about inadequate medical treatment must prove that prison officials were deliberately indifferent to a serious medical need of the inmate.[72] This increases the burden on the inmate in that he must prove more than mere negligence, but, as we will see in the next case to be discussed, the Court could have required proof of an even more difficult standard.

In dealing with the use of force issue, the Court decided that in cases where prison officials are dealing with a prison disturbance, they often must make quick, life-or-death decisions and must be concerned not only about the safety of inmates but the safety of their own staff as well. Given the volatility of this kind of situation, the Court concluded that inmates alleging excessive force on the part of prison officials in this situation must prove that officials acted maliciously and sadistically with an intent to cause harm to the inmate.[73] Of course, this is (and was undoubtedly intended by the Court to be) a very difficult standard to meet.

The Court has also decided that this malice standard will apply in *all* use of force cases.[74] However, in also concluding that the malicious infliction of harm violates the eighth amendment regardless of the extent of the harm caused, the Court clearly came down on the side of inmates.[75] Thus, in medical treatment and use of force cases, the Court has straddled the fence between inmate and institutional interests. However, there has been no such equivocation in conditions cases. Here, the Court, with one exception, has developed a body of law that clearly favors prisons.

In two of its earliest conditions cases, the Court took the first important step in favor of prisons by holding that double-bunking cells that were intended to house one inmate is not always unconstitutional.[76] In both cases, it found that double-bunked cells

which provided less square footage per inmate than called for by any of the correctional standards were nevertheless constitutional. Of course, in both cases, the institutions at issue were new, inmates were permitted considerable time out of their cells, and no specific harmful effects were shown to have been caused by the double-bunking.

The Court also decided in a later conditions case that inmates not only had to show that prison conditions had caused inmates to be deprived of some specific necessity of life, but also that prison officials had allowed these conditions to occur through deliberate indifference to their effects on inmates.[77] This case came as a surprise to many students of prisoners' rights law who thought that the requirement that inmates prove a particular state of mind on the part of prison officials in cruel and unusual punishment cases was limited to situations involving a specific act against a particular inmate or group of inmates.

There was also concern on the part of those who generally espoused greater legal protections for inmates that this decision made it virtually impossible for inmates to win most conditions cases because prison officials could argue successfully that they had tried to improve conditions, but the legislature failed to give them the money they needed to do it. Thus, they were not deliberately indifferent to the inmates' needs.[78]

The Court has provided inmates one significant victory in this area. It has held that inmates do not have to wait until they have actually suffered harm before they can prove that they have been subjected to cruel and unusual punishment. It is sufficient if inmates can show that actions or conditions expose them to an unreasonable risk of deprivation of one of life's necessities.[79]

Conclusion

Given the recent trend in the Supreme Court toward resolution of fewer cases each term of court, the Court has provided in the last 25 years a surprisingly large body of case law on prisoners' rights. This may be due to the fact that the legal foundation for such interpretation was not laid before the process of Selective Incorporation of the Bill of Rights, and most of that foundation was not in place until the 1960's. Thus, there is some irony in the fact that the liberal Due Process Revolution of the 1960's may have provided the legal foundation for the conservative prisoners' rights decisions of the 1980's and '90's.

Will this conservative trend continue? Although I tend to think that it will, the evidence in favor of this conclusion is far from conclusive. Justices Scalia and Thomas provide two very consistent votes in favor of prisons. Even though he has not been on the Court long, Justice Thomas has voted very frequently with Justice Scalia on all issues before the Court, and Justice Scalia has never taken a pro-inmate position in a prisoners' rights case. Furthermore, the position taken in the opinions he has written or joined suggest that Justice Thomas is not likely to find a constitutional basis for providing significant protections to prisoners.

Chief Justice Rehnquist's opinion in *Wolfish* provided the rhetorical foundation for the Court's recent emphasis on deference to corrections officials, but he voted with the majority in the pro-inmate decisions in *McMillian* and *Helling*. Nevertheless, he has generally sided with prisons, and there is not much reason to think that this stance will change.

Justice O'Connor authored two of the most important pro-prison opinions, *Whitley* and *Safley,* but she also wrote the pro-inmate *McMillian* opinion. Overall, however, she has rather consistently voted in favor of the prison position. Thus, there appear to be four relatively solid pro-prison Justices on the present Court.

Justice Stevens has established an extensive track record in favor of inmates, but he is the only Justice on the present Court that can be counted on to take a pro-inmate

position regularly. Justices Brennan and Marshall joined him consistently and Justice Blackmun often joined him as well, but they have all retired from the Court.

The remaining Justices—Kennedy, Souter, Ginsburg, and Breyer—have not been on the Court long enough to permit a confident prediction about which side they are likely to support. On criminal justice issues in general, Justice Kennedy has been conservative, and the best bet is that he will vote that way in prisoners' rights cases as well.

Justice Souter, on the other hand, is showing some signs of developing into a moderate, at least, and his few votes in prisoners' rights cases are consistent with that label. If Justices Ginsburg and Breyer live up to most expectations (based on their track record as Federal appellate court judges), they will likely be somewhat supportive of pro-inmate positions.

If all this speculation turns out to be accurate, we can expect to see many 5–4 prisoners' rights decisions decided in favor of prisons in the next several years. The Deference Period may be far from over.

Study Questions

1. In what ways has greater society (i.e., society outside of the prison environment) mirrored the three phases of Supreme Court litigation identified by the author?

2. Which of the issues brought up during the prisoners' rights period was the most important issue, in your opinion? Why did you choose this issue (or case)?

3. Have inmates' rights eroded as a result of the Deference Period? In other words, has the Court's apparent unwillingness to become involved after the rights period caused inmates as a whole to "lose ground" or enjoy fewer rights?

4. From a systemic perspective, what are the pros and cons of allowing inmates easier access to the court system?

5. Of all the individual rights highlighted by the cases reviewed by the author, which do you consider to be the most important? Why did you choose that right?

Notes

1. 62 Va. 790.

2. See generally, Sheldon Krantz and Lynn Branham, *The Law of Sentencing, Corrections, and Prisoners' Rights* (West Publishing, 1991, 4th ed.), pp. 264–66.

3. *Ex Parte Hull*, 61 S.Ct. 640.

4. See generally, Krantz and Branham, pp. 266–69, and Michael Mushlin, *Rights of Prisoners* (Shepard's/McGraw-Hill, 1994, 2nd ed.), pp. 9–11.

5. 365 U.S. 167.

6. 84 S.Ct. 1733.

7. 88 S.Ct. 994.

8. 92 S.Ct. 250.

9. 89 S.Ct. 747.

10. *Id.*, p. 751.

11. 92 S.Ct. 1079.

12. 94 S.Ct. 1800.

13. 94 S.Ct. 2963.

14. The significance of the "liberty interest" issue is that if the Court finds that action taken by corrections authorities impinges upon a liberty interest, then the action must be preceded by a hearing, as well as some other procedural protections related to the hearing. These additional procedural protections vary with the nature of the liberty interest at issue.

15. 97 S.Ct. 1491.

16. 98 S.Ct. 2565.

17. 94 S.Ct. 2800.

18. 96 S.Ct. 2532.

19. 96 S.Ct. 2543 (1976).

20. 96 S.Ct. 1551.

21. 97 S.Ct. 285.

22. 97 S.Ct. 2532.

23. 99 S.Ct. 1861.

24. *Id*, p. 562.

25. 101 S.Ct. 2392.

26. *Wolfish* also involved an overcrowding claim, but there the issue was raised by pretrial detainees. Pretrial detainees are not protected by the Cruel and Unusual Punishment Clause, which extends only to those persons convicted of a crime.

27. 101 S.Ct. 2460.

28. 102 S.Ct. 31.

29. 103 S.Ct. 1741.

30. 109 S.Ct. 1904.

31. 99 S.Ct. 2100.

32. 103 S.Ct. 864.

33. 105 S.Ct. 2768 (1985).

34. 104 S.Ct. 3194 (1984).

35. 104 S.Ct. 3227. The same argument was made and ruled on in *Wolfish*, but the argument had been based on the fourth amendment, not the Due Process Clause.

36. 107 S.Ct. 2254.

37. 107 S.Ct. 2400.

38. 109 S.Ct. 1874.

39. 110 S.Ct. 1028 (1990).

40. 106 S.Ct. 1078.

41. 111 S.Ct. 2821.

42. 55 CrL 2156.

43. Some commentators contend that there are some "victories" for inmates contained within these apparent losses. For example, John Boston, of the ACLU National Prison Project, argues that in *Seiter* the inmates won because the Court rejected the lower appellate court's conclusion that the state of mind required in conditions cases was the malice standard articulated by the Court in *Whitley*. Boston, "Highlights of Most Important Cases," *The National Prison Project Journal*, vol. 6, no. 3, Summer 1991, p. 4 (includes an extensive analysis of *Seiter*).

44. 100 S.Ct. 1254.

45. *Washington v. Harper* (1990).

46. In fact, it would seem that in any case where it is concluded that a guard's use of force was excessive, it would follow logically that the guard acted maliciously as well.

47. 113 S.Ct. 2475.

48. Comment, "Prison Inmate Marriages: A Survey and a Proposal," 12 *University of Richmond Law Review* 443 (1978).

49. *Johnson v. Avery; Bounds v. Smith.*

50. *Johnson v. Avery.*

51. *Wolff v. McDonnell.*

52. *Procunier v. Martinez.*

53. *Cruz v. Beto.*

54. *Procunier v. Martinez.*

55. *Turner v. Safley,* 107 S.Ct. 2254, p. 2261.

56. *Hudson v. Palmer.*

57. *Bell v. Wolfish.*

58. *Block v. Rutherford.*

59. *Meachum v. Fano,* 96 S.Ct. 2632, p. 2538.

60. *Hewitt v. Helms,* 103 S.Ct. 864, p. 869.

61. *Kentucky v. Thompson.*

62. *Greenholtz v. Nebraska Penal Inmates.*

63. *Connecticut Board of Pardons v. Dumschat.*

64. *Meachum v. Fano.*

65. *Olim v. Wakinekona.*

66. *Hewitt v. Helms.*

67. *Vitek v Jones.*

68. *Hewitt v. Helms.*

69. See, for example, *Wolff v. McDonnell, Yitek v. Jones,* and *Hewitt v. Helms.*

70. See, for example, *Wolff v. McDonnell.*

71. *Id.*

72. *Estelle v. Gamble.*

73. *Whitley v. Albers.*

74. *Hudson v. McMillian.*

75. *Id.*

76. *Bell v. Wolfish* and *Rhodes v. Chapman.*

77. *Wilson v. Seiter.*

78. See J. White's concurring opinion in *Wilson,* which for all intents and purposes is really a dissenting opinion.

79. *Helling v. McKinney.*

Excerpted from "The Supreme Court and Prisoners' Rights" by Jack E. Call. Copyright ©1995, *Federal Probation* 59(1):36–46. Reprinted by permission. ✦

Part IV

Institutional Programming and Treatment

With few and isolated exceptions, the rehabilitative efforts that have been reported so far have not had an appreciable effect on recidivism.

— Robert Martinson

After examining more than two decades of correctional research, Martinson's now-famous conclusion had a tremendous impact on the field of corrections. Whatever the limitations of the Martinson study, and there were many, the conclusion drawn by many was that treatment or rehabilitation is not effective. Thus, what became known as the "nothing works" doctrine led to renewed efforts to demonstrate the effectiveness of correctional programs. The effectiveness of correctional programs has been debated and studied for many years. Evaluating the effectiveness of correctional programs is not easy even under the best of circumstances. Political, ethical, and programmatic reasons may not permit the researcher to develop adequate control groups or measures. Furthermore, tracking offenders once they have been released from prison is time consuming, and difficult at best. Despite these constraints, there have been many studies conducted on the effectiveness of correctional programming and treatment.

There are three ways that research is reviewed: the traditional literature review, the ballot-counting approach that Martin-son used, and meta-analysis. The articles in this section illustrate all three approaches. During the past decade, however, it has been meta-analysis that has taken center stage as the best tool for determining effectiveness. Meta-analysis has greatly facilitated our ability to examine the large body of research that exists on correctional effectiveness; this approach uses a quantitative synthesis of research findings in a body of literature. Meta-analysis computes the "effect sizes" between the treatment and outcome. The effect size can be negative (treatment increases recidivism), zero, or positive (treatment reduces recidivism). Meta-analysis also has its limitations. First, like the literature review and ballot-counting approaches, meta-analysis is affected by "what goes into it." In other words, what studies are included in the analysis? Second, how factors are coded can also be an important issue. There are major advantages, however, to the meta-analytic approach. First, it is possible to control for factors that might influence the size of a treatment effect (e.g., size of sample, length of treatment, and quality of research design). Second, it provides a result that can be quantified, replicated, and tested by other researchers. Third, meta-analysis helps build knowledge about a subject such as correctional treatment in a precise and parsimonious way.

The articles in Part IV provide a good overview of how far we have come in learning about the effectiveness of correctional programs. In some ways, they also illustrate the debate over rehabilitation, some of which centers on institutional program-ming. We know that programs are an important part of a correctional institution. What we want is for the most effective programs to be operated and supported. ✦

19
What Works?
Questions and Answers About Prison Reform

Robert Martinson

The tremendous increase of crime during the 1960s heralded a shift in the way Americans would come to view criminals in the next decade, leading to a law-and-order movement in the early 1970s. The Martinson Report, a massive study undertaken at that time to determine the most effective means of rehabilitating prisoners, concluded that, "with few and isolated exceptions, the rehabilitative efforts that have been reported so far have had no appreciable effect on recidivism." These words were interpreted to mean that "nothing works" as far as rehabilitating prisoners was concerned and that a new direction needed to be found. In 1974, a summary of the study's findings was presented by Robert Martinson in The Public Interest. *Other research studies supported Martinson's conclusion and, by the end of the decade, a paradigm shift had occurred in corrections from rehabilitation to deterrence and just deserts. The influence of Martinson's article, the first published account of the above survey, cannot be underestimated—it was "the straw that broke the camel's back." Support for the rehabilitative ideal and the medical model of corrections decreased substantially after its publication.*

In the past several years, American prisons have gone through one of their recurrent periods of strikes, riots, and other disturbances. Simultaneously, and in consequence, the articulate public has entered another one of its sporadic fits of attentiveness to the condition of our prisons and to the perennial questions they pose about the nature of crime and the uses of punishment. The result has been a widespread call for "prison reform," i.e., for "reformed" prisons which will produce "reformed" convicts. Such calls are a familiar feature of American prison history. American prisons, perhaps more than those of any other country, have stood or fallen in public esteem according to their ability to fulfill their promise of rehabilitation.

One of the problems in the constant debate over "prison reform" is that we have been able to draw very little on any systematic empirical knowledge about the success or failure that we have met when we *have* tried to rehabilitate offenders, with various treatments and in various institutional and noninstitutional settings. The field of penology has produced a voluminous research literature on this subject, but until recently there has been no comprehensive review of this literature and no attempt to bring its findings to bear, in a useful way, on the general question of "What works?" My purpose in this [chapter] is to sketch an answer to that question.

The Travails of a Study

In 1966, the New York State Governor's Special Committee on Criminal Offenders recognized their need for such an answer. The Committee was organized on the premise that prisons could rehabilitate, that the prisons of New York were not in fact making a serious effort at rehabilitation, and that New York's prisons should be converted from their existing custodial basis to a new rehabilitative one. The problem for the Committee was that there was no available guidance on the question of what had been shown to be the most effective means of rehabilitation. My colleagues and I were hired by the committee to remedy this defect in our knowledge; our job was to undertake a comprehensive survey of what was known about rehabilitation.

In 1968, in order to qualify for federal funds under the Omnibus Crime Control and Safe Streets Act, the state established a planning organization, which acquired from the Governor's Committee the responsibility for our report. But by 1970, when the project was formally completed, the state had changed its mind about the worth and proper use of the information we had gathered. The Governor's Committee had begun by thinking that such information was a necessary basis for any reforms that might be undertaken; the state planning agency ended by viewing the study as a document whose disturbing conclusions posed a serious threat to the programs which, in the meantime, they had determined to carry forward. By the spring of 1972—fully a year after I had re-edited the study for final publication—the state had not only failed to publish it, but had also refused to give me permission to publish it on my own. The document itself would still not be available to me or to the public today had not Joseph Alan Kaplon, an attorney, subpoenaed it from the state for use as evidence in a case before the Bronx Supreme Court.[1]

During the time of my efforts to get the study released, reports of it began to be widely circulated, and it acquired something of an underground reputation. But this article is the first published account, albeit a brief one, of the findings contained in that 1,400-page manuscript.

What we set out to do in this study was fairly simple, though it turned into a massive task. First we undertook a six-month search of the literature for any available reports published in the English language on attempts at rehabilitation that had been made in our corrections systems and those of other countries from 1945 through 1967. We then picked from that literature all those studies whose findings were interpretable—that is, whose design and execution met the conventional standards of social science research. Our criteria were rigorous but hardly esoteric: A study had to be an evaluation of a treatment method, it had to

employ an independent measure of the improvement secured by that method, and it had to use some control group, some untreated individuals with whom the treated ones could be compared. We excluded studies only for methodological reasons: They presented insufficient data, they were only preliminary, they presented only a summary of findings and did not allow a reader to evaluate those findings, their results were confounded by extraneous factors, they used unreliable measures, one could not understand their descriptions of the treatment in question, they drew spurious conclusions from their data, their samples were undescribed or too small or provided no true comparability between treated and untreated groups, or they had used inappropriate statistical tests and did not provide enough information for the reader to recompute the data. Using these standards, we drew from the total number of studies 231 acceptable ones, which we not only analyzed ourselves but summarized in detail so that a reader of our analysis would be able to compare it with his independent conclusions.

These treatment studies use various measures of offender improvement: recidivism rates (that is, the rates at which offenders return to crime), adjustment to prison life, vocational success, educational achievement, personality and attitude change, and general adjustment to the outside community. We included all of these in our study; but in these pages I will deal only with the effects of rehabilitative treatment on recidivism, the phenomenon which reflects most directly how well our present treatment programs are performing the task of rehabilitation. The use of even this one measure brings with it enough methodological complications to make a clear reporting of the findings most difficult. The groups that are studied, for instance, are exceedingly disparate, so that it is hard to tell whether what "works" for one kind of offender also works for others. In addition, there has been little attempt to replicate studies; therefore one cannot be certain how stable and reliable the various findings are. Just as important, when the various studies use the term "recidivism rate," they may in fact be talking about somewhat different measures of offender behavior—i.e., "failure" measures such as arrest rates or parole violation rates, or "success" measures such as favorable discharge from parole or probation. And not all of these measures correlate very highly with one another. These difficulties will become apparent again and again in the course of this discussion.

With these caveats, it is possible to give a rather bald summary of our findings: *With few and isolated exceptions, the rehabilitative efforts that have been reported so far have had no appreciable effect on recidivism.* Studies that have been done since our survey was completed do not present any major grounds for altering that original conclusion. What follows is an attempt to answer the questions and challenges that might be posed to such an unqualified statement.

Education and Vocational Training

1. *Isn't it true that a correctional facility running a truly rehabilitative program—one that prepares inmates for life on the outside through education and vocational training—will turn out more successful individuals than will a prison which merely leaves its inmates to rot?*

If this *is* true, the fact remains that there is very little empirical evidence to support it. Skill development and education programs are in fact quite common in correctional facilities, and one might begin by examining their effects on young males, those who might be thought most amenable to such efforts. A study by New York State (1964)[2] found that for young males as a whole, the degree of success achieved in the regular prison academic education program, as measured by changes in grade achievement levels, made no significant dif-

ference in recidivism rates. The only exception was the relative improvement, compared with the sample as a whole, that greater progress made in the top 7 percent of the participating population—those who had high I.Q.'s, had made good records in previous schooling, and who also made good records of academic progress in the institution. And a study by Glaser (1964) found that while it was true that, when one controlled for sentence length, more attendance in regular prison academic programs slightly decreased the subsequent chances of parole violation, this improvement was not large enough to outweigh the associated disadvantage for the "long-attenders": Those who attended prison school the longest also turned out to be those who were in prison the longest. Presumably, those getting the most education were also the worst parole risks in the first place.[3]

Studies of special education programs aimed at vocational or social skill development, as opposed to conventional academic education programs, report similarly discouraging results and reveal additional problems in the field of correctional research. Jacobson (1965) studied a program of "skill re-education" for institutionalized young males, consisting of 10 weeks of daily discussions aimed at developing problem-solving skills. The discussions were led by an adult who was thought capable of serving as a role model for the boys, and they were encouraged to follow the example that he set. Jacobson found that over all, the program produced no improvement in recidivism rates. There was only one special subgroup which provided an exception to this pessimistic finding: If boys in the experimental program decided afterwards to go on to take three or more regular prison courses, they did better upon release than "control" boys who had done the same. (Of course, it also seems likely that experimental boys who did *not* take these extra courses did worse than their controls.)

Zivan (1966) also reported negative results from a much more ambitious vocational training program at the Children's Village in Dobbs Ferry, New York. Boys in his special program were prepared for their return to the community in a wide variety of ways. First of all, they were given, in sequence, three types of vocational guidance: "assessment counseling," "development counseling," and "pre-placement counseling." In addition, they participated in an "occupational orientation," consisting of role-playing, presentations via audio-visual aids, field trips, and talks by practitioners in various fields of work. Furthermore, the boys were prepared for work by participating in the Auxiliary Maintenance Corps, which performed various chores in the institution; a boy might be promoted from the Corps to the Work Activity Program, which "hired" him, for a small fee, to perform various artisans' tasks. And finally, after release from Children's Village, a boy in the special program received supportive after-care and job placement aid.

None of this made any difference in recidivism rates. Nevertheless, one must add that it is impossible to tell whether this failure lay in the program itself or in the conditions under which it was administered. For one thing, the education department of the institution itself was hostile to the program; they believed instead in the efficacy of academic education. This staff therefore tended to place in the pool from which experimental subjects were randomly selected mainly "multi-problem" boys. This by itself would not have invalidated the experiment as a test of vocational training for this particular type of youth, but staff hostility did not end there; it exerted subtle pressures of disapproval throughout the life of the program. Moreover, the program's "after-care" phase also ran into difficulties; boys who were sent back to school before getting a job often received advice that conflicted with the program's counseling, and boys actually looking for jobs met with the frustrating fact that the program's personnel, despite con-

certed efforts, simply could not get businesses to hire the boys.

We do not know whether these constraints, so often found in penal institutions, were responsible for the program's failure; it might have failed anyway. All one can say is that this research failed to show the effectiveness of special vocational training for young males.

The only clearly positive report in this area comes from a study by Sullivan (1967) of a program that combined academic education with special training in the use of IBM equipment. Recidivism rates after one year were only 48 percent for experimentals, as compared with 66 percent for controls. But when one examines the data, it appears that this difference emerged only between the controls and those who had successfully *completed* the training. When one compares the control group with all those who had been *enrolled* in the program, the difference disappears. Moreover, during this study the random assignment procedure between experimental and control groups seems to have broken down, so that towards the end, better risks had a greater chance of being assigned to the special program.

In sum, many of these studies of young males are extremely hard to interpret because of flaws in research design. But it can safely be said that they provide us with no clear evidence that education or skill development programs have been successful.

Training Adult Inmates

When one turns to adult male inmates, as opposed to young ones, the results are even more discouraging. There have been six studies of this type; three of them report that their programs, which ranged from academic to prison work experience, produced no significant differences in recidivism rates, and one—by Glaser (1964)—is almost impossible to interpret because of the risk differentials of the prisoners participating in the various programs.

Two studies—by Schnur (1948) and by Saden (1962)—*do* report a positive difference from skill development programs. In one of them, the Saden study, it is questionable whether the experimental and control groups were truly comparable. But what is more interesting is that both these "positive" studies dealt with inmates incarcerated prior to or during World War II. Perhaps the rise in our educational standards as a whole since then has lessened the differences that prison education or training can make. The only other interesting possibility emerges from a study by Gearhart (1967). His study was as one of those that reported vocational education to be nonsignificant in effecting recidivism rates. He did note, however, that when a trainee succeeded in finding a job related to his area of training, he had a slightly higher chance of becoming a successful parolee. It is possible, then, that skill development programs fail because what they teach bears so little relationship to an offender's subsequent life outside the prison.

One other study of adults, this one with fairly clear implications, has been performed with women rather than men. An experimental group of institutionalized women in Milwaukee was given an extremely comprehensive special education program, accompanied by group counseling. Their training was both academic and practical; it included reading, writing, spelling, business filing, child care, and grooming. Kettering (1965) found that the program made no difference in the women's rates of recidivism.

Two things should be noted about these studies. One is the difficulty of interpreting them as a whole. The disparity in the programs that were tried, in the populations that were affected, and in the institutional settings that surrounded these projects make it hard to be sure that one is observing the same category of treatment in each case. But the second point is that despite this difficulty, one can be reasonably sure that, so far, educational and vocational programs have not worked. We don't know why they have failed. We don't know whether the programs themselves are flawed, or whether they are incapable of overcoming the effects of prison life in general. The difficulty may be that they lack applicability to the world the inmate will face outside of prison. Or perhaps the type of educational and skill improvement they produce simply doesn't have very much to do with an individual's propensity to commit a crime. What we do know is that, to date, education and skill development have not reduced recidivism by rehabilitating criminals.

The Effects of Individual Counseling

2. *But when we speak of a rehabilitative prison, aren't we referring to more than education and skill development alone? Isn't what's needed [is] some way of counseling inmates or helping them with the deeper problems that have caused their maladjustment?*

This, too, is a reasonable hypothesis; but when one examines the programs of this type that have been tried, it's hard to find any more grounds for enthusiasm than we found with skill development and education. One method that's been tried—though so far, there have been acceptable reports only of its application to young offenders—has been individual psychotherapy. For young males, we found seven such reported studies. One study, by Guttman (1963) at the Nelles School, found such treatment to be ineffective in reducing recidivism rates; another, by Rudoff (1960), found it unrelated to *institutional* violation rates, which were themselves related to parole success. It must be pointed out that Rudoff used only this indirect measure of association, and the study therefore cannot rule out the possibility of a treatment effect. A third, also by Guttman (1963) but at another institution,

found that such treatment was actually related to a slightly *higher* parole violation
rate; and a study by Adams (1959b and
1961b) also found a lack of improvement in
parole revocation and first suspension
rates.

There were two studies at variance with
this pattern. One by Persons (1966) said
that if a boy was judged to be "successfully"
treated—as opposed to simply being subjected to the treatment experience—he did
tend to do better. And there was one finding
both hopeful and cautionary: At the Deuel
School (Adams, 1961a), the experimental
boys were first divided into two groups,
those rated as "amenable" to treatment and
those rated "non-amenable." Amenable
boys who got the treatment did better than
non-treated boys. On the other hand, "non-
amenable" boys who were treated actually
did worse than they would have done if they
had received no treatment at all. It must be
pointed out that Guttman (1963), dealing
with younger boys in his Nelles School
study, did not find such an "amenability"
effect, either to the detriment of the non-
amenables who were treated *or* to the benefit of the amenables who were treated. But
the Deuel School study (Adams, 1961a) suggests both that there is something to be
hoped for in treating properly selected amenable subjects and that if these subjects are
not properly selected, one may not only
wind up doing no good but may actually
produce harm. There have been two studies
of the effects of individual psychotherapy
on young incarcerated *female* offenders,
and both of them (Adams, 1959a; Adams,
1961b) report no significant effects from the
therapy. But one of the Adams studies
(1959a) does contain a suggestive, although
not clearly interpretable, finding: If this
individual therapy was administered by a
psychiatrist or a psychologist, the resulting
parole suspension rate was almost two-and-
a-half times *higher* than if it was administered by a social worker without this specialized training.

There has also been a much smaller number of studies of two other types of individual therapy: counseling, which is directed
towards a prisoner's gaining new insight
into his own problems, and casework,
which aims at helping a prisoner cope with
his more pragmatic immediate needs.
These types of therapy both rely heavily on
the empathetic relationship that is to be
developed between the professional and the
client. It was noted above that the Adams
study (1961b) of therapy administered to
girls, referred to in the discussion of individual psychotherapy, found that social
workers seemed better at the job than psychologists or psychiatrists. This difference
seems to suggest a favorable outlook for
these alternative forms of individual therapy. But other studies of such therapy have
produced ambiguous results. Bernsten
(1965) reported a Danish experiment that
showed that socio-psychological counseling
combined with comprehensive welfare
measures—job and residence placement,
clothing, union and health insurance membership, and financial aid—produced an
improvement among some short-term male
offenders, though not those in either the
highest-risk or the lowest-risk categories.
On the other hand, Hood, in Britain (1966),
reported generally non-significant results
with a program of counseling for young
males. (Interestingly enough, this experiment *did* point to a mechanism capable of
changing recidivism rates. When boys were
released from institutional care and entered
the army directly, "poor risk" boys among
both experimentals *and* controls did better
than expected. "Good risks" did worse.)

So these foreign data are sparse and not
in agreement; the American data are just as
sparse. The only American study which provides a direct measure of the effects of individual counseling—a study of California's
Intensive Treatment Program (California,
1958a), which was "psychodynamically"
oriented—found no improvement in recidivism rates.

It was this finding of the failure of the Intensive Treatment Program which contributed to the decision in California to de-emphasize individual counseling in its penal system in favor of group methods. And indeed one might suspect that the preceding reports reveal not the inadequacy of counseling as a whole but only the failure of one *type* of counseling, the individual type. Group counseling methods, in which offenders are permitted to aid and compare experiences with one another, might be thought to have a better chance of success. So it is important to ask what results these alternative methods have actually produced.

Group Counseling

Group counseling has indeed been tried in correctional institutions both with and without a specifically psychotherapeutic orientation. There has been one study of "pragmatic," problem-oriented counseling on *young* institutionalized males by Seckel (1965). This type of counseling had no significant effect. For adult males, there have been three such studies of the "pragmatic" and "insight" methods. Two (Kassebaum, 1971; Harrison, 1964) report no long-lasting significant effects. (One of these two did report a real but short-term effect that wore off as the program became institutionalized and as offenders were at liberty longer.) The third study of adults, by Shelley (1961), dealt with a "pragmatic" casework program, directed towards the educational and vocational needs of institutionalized young adult males in a Michigan prison camp. The treatment lasted for six months and at the end of that time Shelley found an improvement in attitudes; the possession of "good" attitudes was independently found by Shelley to correlate with parole success. Unfortunately, though, Shelley was not able to measure the *direct* impact of the counseling on recidivism rates. His two separate correlations are suggestive, but they fall short of

being able to tell us that it really is the counseling that has a direct effect on recidivism.

With regard to more professional group *psychotherapy*, the reports are also conflicting. We have two studies of group psychotherapy on young males. One, by Persons (1966), says that this treatment did in fact reduce recidivism. The improved recidivism rate stems from the improved performance only of those who were clinically judged to have been "successfully" treated; still, the overall result of the treatment was to improve recidivism rates for the experimental group as a whole. On the other hand, a study by Craft (1964) of young males designated "psychopaths," comparing "self-government" group psychotherapy with "authoritarian" individual counseling, found that the "group therapy" boys afterwards committed twice as many new offenses as the individually treated ones. Perhaps some forms of group psychotherapy work for some types of offenders but not others; a reader must draw his own conclusions on the basis of sparse evidence.

With regard to young females, the results are just as equivocal. Adams, in his study of females (1959a), found that there was no improvement to be gained from treating girls by group rather than individual methods. A study by Taylor of borstal (reformatory) girls in New Zealand (1967) found a similar lack of any great improvement for group therapy as opposed to individual therapy or even to no therapy at all. But the Taylor study does offer one real, positive finding: When the "group therapy" girls *did* commit new offenses, these offenses were less serious than the ones for which they had originally been incarcerated.

There is a third study that does report an overall positive finding as opposed to a partial one. Truax (1966) found that girls subjected to group psychotherapy and then released were likely to spend less time reincarcerated in the future. But what is most interesting about this improvement is the very special and important circumstance under which it occurred. The therapists chosen for this program did not merely have to have the proper analytic training; they were specially chosen for their "empathy" and "non-possessive warmth." In other words, it may well have been the therapists' special personal gifts rather than the fact of treatment itself which produced the favorable result. This possibility will emerge again when we examine the effects of other types of rehabilitative treatment later in this article.

As with the question of skill development, it is hard to summarize these results. The programs administered were various; the groups to which they were administered varied not only by sex but by age as well; there were also variations in the length of time for which the programs were carried on, the frequency of contact during that time, and the period for which the subjects were followed up. Still, one must say that the burden of the evidence is not encouraging. These programs seem to work best when they are new, when their subjects are amenable to treatment in the first place, and when the counselors are not only trained people but "good" people as well. Such findings, which would not be much of a surprise to a student of organization or personality, are hardly encouraging for a policy planner, who must adopt measures that are generally applicable, that are capable of being successfully institutionalized, and that must rely for personnel on something other than the exceptional individual.

Transforming the Institutional Environment

3. *But maybe the reason these counseling programs don't seem to work is not that they are ineffective per se, but that the institutional environment outside the program is unwholesome enough to undo any good work that the counseling does. Isn't a truly successful rehabilitative institution the one where the inmate's whole environment is directed towards true cor-rection rather than towards custody or punishment?*

This argument has not only been made, it has been embodied in several institutional programs that go by the name of "milieu therapy." They are designed to make every element of the inmate's environment a part of his treatment, to reduce the distinctions between the custodial staff and the treatment staff, to create a supportive, non-authoritarian, and non-regimented atmosphere, and to enlist peer influence in the formation of constructive values. These programs are especially hard to summarize because of their variety. They differ, for example, in how "supportive" or "permissive" they are designed to be, in the extent to which they are combined with other treatment methods such as individual therapy, group counseling, or skill development, and in how completely the program is able to control all the relevant aspects of the institutional environment.

One might well begin with two studies that have been done of institutionalized adults, in regular prisons, who have been subjected to such treatment; this is the category whose results are the most clearly discouraging. One study of such a program, by Robison (1967), found that the therapy did seem to reduce recidivism after one year. After two years, however, this effect disappeared, and the treated convicts did no better than the untreated. Another study by Kassebaum, Ward, and Wilnet (1971), dealt with a program which had been able to effect an exceptionally extensive and experimentally rigorous transformation of the institutional environment. This sophisticated study had a follow-up period of 36 months, and it found that the program had no significant effect on parole failure or success rates.

The results of the studies of youth are more equivocal. As for young females, one study by Adams (1966) of such a program found that it had no significant effect on recidivism; another study, by Goldberg and

Adams (1964), found that such a program did have a positive effect. This effect declined when the program began to deal with girls who were judged beforehand to be worse risks.

As for young males, the studies may conveniently be divided into those dealing with juveniles (under 18) and those dealing with youths. There have been five studies of milieu therapy administered to juveniles. Two of them—by Lavlicht (1962) and by Jesness (1965)—report clearly that the program in question either had no significant effect or had a short-term effect that wore off with passing time. Jesness does report that when his experimental juveniles did commit new offenses, the offenses were less serious than those committed by controls. A third study of juveniles, by McCord (1953) at the Wiltwyck School, reports mixed results. Using two measures of performance, a "success" rate and a "failure" rate, McCord found that his experimental group achieved both less failure *and* less success than the controls did. There have been two positive reports on milieu therapy programs for male juveniles; both of them have come out of the Highfields program, the milieu therapy experiment which has become the most famous and widely quoted example of "success" via this method. A group of boys was confined for a relatively short time to the unrestrictive, supportive environment of Highfields; and at a follow-up of six months, Freeman (1956) found that the group did indeed show a lower recidivism rate (as measured by parole revocation) than a similar group spending a longer time in the regular reformatory. McCorkle (1958) also reported positive findings from Highfields. But in fact, [as] the McCorkle data show[s], this improvement was not so clear: The Highfields boys had lower recidivism rates at 12 and 36 months in the follow-up period, but not at 24 and 60 months. The length of follow-up, these data remind us, may have large implications for a study's conclusions. But more important were other flaws in the Highfields experiment:

The populations were not fully comparable (they differed according to risk level and time of admission); different organizations—the probation agency for the Highfield boys, the parole agency for the others—were making the revocation decisions for each group; more of the Highfields boys were discharged early from supervision, and thus removed from any risk of revocation. In short, not even from the celebrated Highfields case may we take clear assurance that milieu therapy works.

In the case of male youths, as opposed to male juveniles, the findings are just as equivocal, and hardly more encouraging. One such study by Empey (1966) in a residential context did not produce significant results. A study by Seckel (1967) described California's Fremont Program, in which institutionalized youths participated in a combination of therapy, work projects, field trips, and community meetings. Seckel found that the youths subjected to this treatment committed more violations of law than did their non-treated counterparts. This difference could have occurred by chance; still, there was certainly no evidence of relative improvement. Another study, by Levinson (1962–1964), also found a lack of improvement in recidivism rates—but Levinson noted the encouraging fact that the treated group spent somewhat more time in the community before recidivating, and committed less serious offenses. And a study by the State of California (1967) also shows a partially positive finding. This was a study of the Marshall Program, similar to California's Fremont Program but different in several ways. The Marshall Program was shorter and more tightly organized than its Fremont counterpart. In the Marshall Program, as opposed to the Fremont Program, a youth could be ejected from the group and sent back to regular institutions before the completion of the program. Also, the Marshall Program offered some additional benefits: the teaching of "social survival skills" (i.e., getting and holding a job), group counseling of parents, and an occasional opportunity for boys to visit home. When youthful offenders were released to the Marshall Program, either directly or after spending some time in a regular institution, they did no better than a comparable regularly institutionalized population, though both Marshall youth and youth in regular institutions did better than those who were directly released by the court and given no special treatment.

So the youth in these milieu therapy programs at least do no worse than their counterparts in regular institutions and the special programs may cost less. One may therefore be encouraged—not on grounds of rehabilitation but on grounds of cost effectiveness.

What About Medical Treatment?

4. *Isn't there anything you can do in an institutional setting that will reduce recidivism, for instance, through strictly medical treatment?*

A number of studies deal with the results of efforts to change the behavior of offenders through drugs and surgery. As for surgery, the one experimental study of a plastic surgery program—by Mandell (1967)—had negative results. For non-addicts who received plastic surgery, Mandell purported to find improvement in performance on parole; but when one reanalyzes his data, it appears that surgery alone did not in fact make a significant difference.

One type of surgery does seem to be highly successful in reducing recidivism. A twenty-year Danish study of sex offenders, by Stuerup (1960), found that while those who had been treated with hormones and therapy continued to commit both sex crimes (29.6 percent of them did so) and non-sex crimes (21.0 percent), those who had been castrated had rates of only 3.5 percent (not, interestingly enough, a rate of zero; where there's a will, apparently there's a way) and 9.2 percent. One hopes that the

policy implications of this study will be found to be distinctly limited.

As for drugs, the major report on such a program—involving tranquilization—was made by Adams (1961b). The tranquilizers were administered to male and female institutionalized youths. With boys, there was only a slight improvement in their subsequent behavior; this improvement disappeared within a year. With girls, the tranquilization produced worse results than when the girls were given no treatment at all.

The Effects of Sentencing

5. *Well, at least it may be possible to manipulate certain gross features of the existing, conceptional prison system—such as length of sentence and degree of security—in order to affect these recidivism rates. Isn't this the case?*

At this point, it's still impossible to say that this is the case. As for the degree of security in an institution, Glaser's (1964) work reported that, for both youth and adults, a less restrictive "custody grading" in American federal prisons was related to success on parole; but this is hardly surprising, since those assigned to more restrictive custody are likely to be worse risks in the first place. More to the point, an American study by Fox (1950) discovered that for "older youths" who were deemed to be good risks for the future, a minimum security institution produced better results than a maximum security one. On the other hand, the data we have on youths under 16—from a study by McClintock (1961), done in Great Britain—indicate that so-called Borstals, in which boys are totally confined, are more effective than a less restrictive regime of partial physical custody. In short, we know very little about the recidivism effects of various degrees of security in existing institutions; and our problems in finding out will be compounded by the probability that these effects will vary widely according to the particular *type* of offender that we're dealing with.

The same problems of mixed results and lack of comparable populations have plagued attempts to study the effects of sentence length. A number of studies—by Narloch (1959), by Bernsten (1965), and by the State of California (1956)—suggest that those who are released earlier from institutions than their scheduled parole date, or those who serve short sentences of under three months rather than longer sentences of eight months or more, either do better on parole or at least do no worse.[4] The implication here is quite clear and important: Even if early releases and short sentences produce no improvement in recidivism rates, one could at least maintain the same rates while lowering the cost of maintaining the offender and lessening his own burden of imprisonment. Of course, this implication carries with it its concomitant danger: the danger that though shorter sentences cause no worsening of the recidivism rate, they may increase the total amount of crime in the community by increasing the absolute number of potential recidivists at large.

On the other hand, Glaser's (1964) data show not a consistent linear relationship between the shortness of the sentence and the rate of parole success, but a curvilinear one. Of his subjects, those who served less than a year had a 73 percent success rate, those who served up to two years were only 65 percent successful, and those who served up to three years fell to a rate of 56 percent. But among those who served sentences of *more* than three years, the success rate rose again—to 60 percent. These findings should be viewed with some caution since Glaser did not control for the pre-existing degree of risk associated with each of his categories of offenders. But the data do suggest that the relationship between sentence length and recidivism may not be a simple linear one.

More important, the effect of sentence length seems to vary widely according to type of offender. In a British study (1963),

for instance, Hammond found that for a group of "hard-core recidivists," shortening the sentence caused no improvement in the recidivism rate. In Denmark, Bernsten (1965) discovered a similar phenomenon: That the beneficial effect of three-month sentences as against eight-month ones disappeared in the case of these "hard-core recidivists." Garrity found another such distinction in his 1956 study. He divided his offenders into three categories: "pro-social," "anti-social," and "manipulative." "Pro-social" offenders he found to have low recidivism rates regardless of the length of their sentence; "anti-social" offenders did better with short sentences; the "manipulative" did better with long ones. Two studies from Britain made yet another division of the offender population, and found yet other variations. One (Great Britain, 1964) found that previous offenders—but not first offenders—did better with *longer* sentences, while the other (Cambridge, 1952) found the *reverse* to be true with juveniles.

To add to the problem of interpretation, these studies deal not only with different types and categorizations of offenders but with different types of institutions as well. No more than in the case of institution type can we say that length of sentence has a clear relationship to recidivism.

Decarcerating the Convict

6. *All of this seems to suggest that there's not much we know how to do to rehabilitate an offender when he's in an institution. Doesn't this lead to the clear possibility that the way to rehabilitate offenders is to deal with them outside an institutional setting?*

This is indeed an important possibility, and it is suggested by other pieces of information as well. For instance, Minet (1967) reported on a milieu therapy program in Massachusetts called Outward Bound. It took youths 15½ and over; it was oriented toward the development of skills in the out-of-doors and conducted in a wilderness atmosphere very different from that of most existing institutions. The culmination of the 26-day program was a final 24 hours in which each youth had to survive alone in the wilderness. And Miner found that the program did indeed work in reducing recidivism rates.

But by and large, when one takes the programs that have been administered in institutions and applies them in a non-institutional setting, the results do not grow to encouraging proportions. With casework and individual counseling in the community, for instance, there have been three studies; they dealt with counseling methods from psycho-social and vocational counseling to "operant conditioning," in which an offender was rewarded first simply for coming to counseling sessions and then, gradually, for performing other types of approved sets. Two of them report that the community-counseled offenders did no better than their institutional controls, while the third notes that although community counseling produced fewer arrests per person, it did not ultimately reduce the offender's chance of resuming to a reformatory.

The one study of a non-institutional skill development program, by Kovacs (1967), described the New Start Program in Denver, in which offenders participated in vocational training, role playing, programmed instruction, group counseling, college class attendance, and trips to art galleries and museums. After all this, Kovacs found no significant improvement over incarceration.

There have also been studies of milieu therapy programs conducted with youthful male probationers not in actual physical custody. One of them found no significant improvement at all. One, by Empey (1966), did say that after a follow-up of six months, a boy who was judged to have "successfully" completed the milieu program was less likely to recidivate afterwards than was a "successful," regular probationer. Empey's "successes" came out of an extraordinary program in Provo, Utah, which aimed to rehabilitate by subjecting offenders to a non-supportive milieu. The staff of this program operated on the principle that they were not to go out of their way to interact and be empathetic with the boys. Indeed, a boy who misbehaved was to be met with "role dispossession": He was to be excluded from meetings of his peer group, and he was not to be given answers to his questions as to why he had been excluded or what his ultimate fate might be. This peer group and its meetings were designed to be the major force for reform at Provo; they were intended to develop, and indeed did develop, strong and controlling norms for the behavior of individual members. For one thing, group members were not to associate with delinquent boys outside the program; for another, individuals were to submit to a group review of all their actions and problems; and they were to be completely honest and open with the group about their attitudes, their thinking patterns, their states of mind, and their personal failings. The group was granted quite a few sanctions with which to enforce these norms: They could practice derision or temporary ostracism, or they could lock up an aberrant member for the weekend, refuse to release him from the program, or send him away to the regular reformatory.

One might be tempted to forgive these methods because of the success that Empey reports, except for one thing. If one judges the program not only by its "successful" boys but by all the boys who were subjected to it—those who succeeded and those who, not surprisingly, failed—the totals show *no* significant improvement in recidivism rates compared with boys on regular probation. Empey did find that both the Provo boys and those on regular probation did better than those in regular reformatories—in contradiction, it may be recalled, to the finding from the residential Marshall Program, in which the direct releases given no special treatment did *worse* than boys in regular institutions.

The third such study of non-residential milieu therapy, by McCravy (1967), found not only that there was no significant improvement, but that the longer a boy participated in the treatment, the worse he was likely to do afterwards.

Psychotherapy in Community Settings

There is some indication that individual psychotherapy may "work" in a community setting. Massimo (1963) reported on one such program, using what might be termed a "pragmatic" psychotherapeutic approach, including "insight" therapy and a focus on vocational problems. The program was marked by its small size and by its use of therapists who were personally enthusiastic about the project; Massimo found that there was indeed a decline in recidivism rates. Adamson (1956), on the other hand, found no significant difference produced by another program of individual therapy (though he did note that arrest rates among the experimental boys declined with what he called "intensity of treatment"). And Schwitzgebel (1963, 1964), studying other, different kinds of therapy programs, found that the programs *did* produce improvements in the attitudes of his boys—but, unfortunately, not in their rates of recidivism.

And with *group* therapy administered in the community, we find yet another set of equivocal results. The results from studies of pragmatic group counseling are only mildly optimistic. Adams (1965) did report that a form of group therapy, "guided group interaction," when administered to juvenile gangs, did somewhat reduce the percentage that were to be found in custody six years later. On the other hand, in a study of juveniles, Adams (1964) found that while such a program did reduce the number of contacts that an experimental youth had with police, it made no ultimate difference in the detention rate. And the attitudes of the counseled youth showed no improvement. Finally, when O'Brien (1961) examined a community-based program of group psychotherapy, he found not only that the program produced no improvement in the recidivism rate, but that the experimental boys actually did worse than their controls on a series of psychological tests.

Probation or Parole Versus Prison

But by far the most extensive and important work that has been done on the effect of community-based treatments has been done in the areas of probation and parole. This work sets out to answer the question of whether it makes any difference how you supervise and treat an offender once he has been released from prison or has come under state surveillance in lieu of prison. This is the work that has provided the main basis to date for the claim that we do indeed have the means at our disposal for rehabilitating the offender or at least decarcerating him safely.

One group of these studies has compared the use of probation with other dispositions for offenders; these provide some slight evidence that, at least under some circumstances, probation may make an offender's future chances better than if he had been sent to prison. Or, at least, probation may not worsen those chances.[5] A British study, by Wilkins (1958), reported that when probation was granted more frequently, recidivism rates among probationers did not increase significantly. And another such study by the state of Michigan in 1963 reported that an expansion in the use of probation actually improved recidivism rates—though there are serious problems of comparability in the groups and systems that were studied.

One experiment—by Babst (1965)—compared a group of parolees, drawn from adult male felony offenders in Wisconsin, and excluding murderers and sex criminals, with a similar group that had been put on probation; it found that the probationers committed fewer violations if they had been first offenders, and did no worse if they were recidivists. The problem in interpreting this experiment, though, is that the behavior of those groups was being measured by separate organizations, by probation officers for the probationers, and by parole officers for the parolees; it is not clear that the definition of "violation" was the same in each case, or that other types of uniform standards were being applied. Also, it is not clear what the results would have been if subjects had been released directly to the parole organization without having experienced prison first. Another such study, done in Israel by Shoham (1964), must be interpreted cautiously because his experimental and control groups had slightly different characteristics. But Shoham found that when one compared a suspended sentence plus probation for first offenders with a one-year prison sentence, only first offenders under 20 years of age did better on probation; those from 21 to 45 actually did *worse*. And Shoham's findings also differ from Babst's in another way. Babst had found that parole rather than prison brought no improvement for recidivists, but Shoham reported that for recidivists with four or more prior offenses, a suspended sentence was actually *better*—though the improvement was much less when the recidivist had committed a crime of violence.

But both the Babst and the Shoham studies, even while they suggest the possible value of suspended sentences, probation, or parole for some offenders (though they contradict each other in telling us *which* offenders), also indicate a pessimistic general conclusion concerning the limits of the effectiveness of treatment programs. For they found that the personal characteristics of offenders—"first offender status, or age, or type of offense"—were more important than the form of treatment in determining future recidivism. An offender with a "favorable" prognosis will do better than one without, it seems, no matter how you distribute "good" or "bad," "enlightened" or "regressive" treatments among them.

Quite a large group of studies deals not with probation as compared to other dispositions, but instead with the type of treatment that an offender receives once he is on probation or parole. These are the studies that have provided the most encouraging reports on rehabilitative treatment and that have also raised the most serious questions about the nature of the research that has been going on in the corrections field.

Five of these studies have dealt with youthful probationers from 13 to 18 who were assigned to probation officers with small caseloads or provided with other ways of receiving more intensive supervision (Adams, 1966 [two reports]; Feistman, 1966; Kawaguchi, 1967; Pilnick, 1967). These studies report that, by and large, intensive supervision does work—that the specially treated youngsters do better according to some measure of recidivism. Yet these studies left some important questions unanswered. For instance, was this improved performance a function merely of the number of contacts a youngster had with his probation officer? Did it also depend on the length of time in treatment? Or was it the quality of supervision that was making the difference, rather than the quantity?

Intensive Supervision: The Warren Studies

The widely reported Warren studies (1966a, 1966b, 1967) in California constitute an extremely ambitious attempt to answer these questions. In this project, a control group of youths, drawn from a pool of candidates ready for first admission to a California Youth Authority institution, was assigned to regular detention, usually for eight to nine months, and then released to regular supervision. The experimental group received considerably more elaborate treatment. They were released directly to probation status and assigned to 12-man caseloads. To decide what special treatment was appropriate within these caseloads, the youths were divided according to their "interpersonal maturity level classification," by use of a scale developed by Grant and Grant. And each level dictated its own special type of therapy. For instance, a youth might be judged to occupy the lowest maturity level; this would be a youth, according to the scale, primarily concerned with "demands that the world take care of him. . . . He behaves impulsively, unaware of anything except the grossest effects of his behavior on others." A youth like this would be placed in a supportive environment such as a foster home; the goals of his therapy would be to meet his dependency needs and help him gain more accurate perceptions about his relationship to others. At the other end of the three-tier classification a youth might exhibit high maturity. This would be a youth who had internalized "a set of standards by which he judges his and others' behavior. . . . He shows some ability to understand reasons for behavior, some ability to relate to people emotionally and on a long-term basis." These high-maturity youths could come in several varieties—a "neurotic acting out," for instance, a "neurotic anxious," a "situational emotional reactor," or a "cultural identifier." But the appropriate treatment for these youths was individual psychotherapy, or family or group therapy for the purpose of reducing internal conflicts and increasing the youths' awareness of personal and family dynamics.

"Success" in this experiment was defined as favorable discharge by the Youth Authority; "failure" was unfavorable discharge, revocation, or recommitment by a court. Warren reported an encouraging finding: Among all but one of the "subtypes," the experimentals had a significantly lower failure rate than the controls. The experiment did have certain problems: The experimen-

tals might have been performing better because of the enthusiasm of the staff and the attention lavished on them; none of the controls had been *directly* released to their regular supervision programs instead of being detained first; and it was impossible to separate the effects of the experimentals' small caseloads from their specially designed treatments, since no experimental youths had been assigned to a small caseload with "inappropriate" treatment, or with no treatment at all. Still, none of these problems were serious enough to vitiate the encouraging prospect that this finding presented for successful treatment of probationers.

This encouraging finding was, however, accompanied by a rather more disturbing clue. As has been mentioned before, the experimental subjects, when measured, had a lower *failure* rate than the controls. But the experimentals also had a lower *success* rate. That is, fewer of the experimentals as compared with the controls had been judged to have successfully completed their program of supervision and to be suitable for favorable release. When my colleagues and I undertook a rather laborious reanalysis of the Warren data, it became clear why this discrepancy had appeared. It turned out that fewer experimentals were "successful" because the experimentals were actually committing more offenses than their controls. The reason that the experimentals' relatively large number of offenses was not being reflected in their failure rates was simply that the experimentals' probation officers were using a more lenient revocation policy. In other words, the controls had a higher failure rate because the controls were being revoked for less serious offenses.

So it seems that what Warren was reporting in her "failure" rates was not merely the treatment effect of her small caseloads and special programs. Instead, what Warren was finding was not so much a change in the behavior of the experimental youths as a change in the behavior of the experimental *probation officers*, who knew the "special" status of their charges and who had evidently decided to revoke probation status at a lower than normal rate. The experimentals continued to commit offenses; what was different was that when they committed these offenses, they were permitted to remain on probation.

The experimenters claimed that this low revocation policy, and the greater number of offenses committed by the special treatment youth, were *not* an indication that these youth were behaving specially badly and that policy makers were simply letting them get away with it. Instead it was claimed, the higher reported offense rate was primarily an artifact of the more intense surveillance that the experimental youth received. But the data show that this is not a sufficient explanation of the low failure rate among experimental youth; the difference in "tolerance" of offenses between experimental officials and control officials was much greater than the difference in the rates at which these two systems detected youths committing new offenses. Needless to say, this reinterpretation of the data presents a much bleaker picture of the possibilities of intensive supervision with special treatment.

'Treatment Effect' Versus 'Policy Effects'

This same problem of experimenter bias may also be present in the predecessors of the Warren study, the ones which had also found positive results from intensive supervision on probation; indeed, this disturbing question can be raised about many of the previously discussed reports of positive "treatment effects."

This possibility of a "policy effect" rather than a "treatment effect" applies, for instance, to the previously discussed studies of the effects of intensive supervision on juvenile and youthful probationers. These were the studies, it will be recalled, which

found lower recidivism rates for the intensively supervised.[6]

One opportunity to make a further check on the effects of this problem is provided, in a slightly different context, by Johnson (1962a). Johnson was measuring the effects of intensive supervision on youthful *parolees* (as distinct from probationers). There have been several such studies of the effects on youths of intensive parole supervision plus special counseling and their findings are on the whole less encouraging than the probation studies; they are difficult to interpret because of experimental problems, but studies by Boston University in 1966, and by Van Couvering in 1966, report no significant effects and possibly some bad effects from such special programs. But Johnson's studies were unique for the chance they provide to measure both treatment effects and the effect of agency policy.

Johnson, like Warren, assigned experimental subjects to small caseloads and his experiment had the virtue of being performed with two separate populations and at two different times. But in contrast with the Warren case, the Johnson experiment did not engage in a large continuing attempt to choose the experimental counselors specially, to train them specially, and to keep them informed about the progress and importance of the experiment. The first time the experiment was performed, the experimental youths had a slightly lower revocation rate than the controls at six months. But the second time, the experimentals did *not* do better than their controls; indeed, they did slightly worse. And with the experimentals from the first group—those who *had* shown an improvement after six months—this effect wore off at 18 months. In the Johnson study, my colleagues and I found, "intensive" supervision did not increase the experimental youths' risk of detection. Instead, what was happening in the Johnson experiment was that the first time it had been performed—just as in the Warren study—the experimentals were simply revoked less often per number of offenses committed, and they were revoked for offenses more serious than those which prompted revocation among the controls. The second time around, this "policy" discrepancy disappeared; and when it did, the "improved" performance of the experimentals disappeared as well. The enthusiasm guiding the project had simply worn off in the absence of reinforcement.

One must conclude that the "benefits" of intensive supervision for youthful offenders may stem not so much from a "treatment" effect as from a "policy" effect—that such supervision, so far as we now know, results not in rehabilitation but in a decision to look the other way when an offense is committed. But there is one major modification to be added to this conclusion. Johnson performed a further measurement (1962b) in his parole experiment: He rated all the supervising agents according to the "adequacy" of the supervision they gave. And he found that an "adequate" agent, whether he was working in a small *or* a large caseload produced a relative improvement in his charges. The converse was not true: An inadequate agent was more likely to produce youthful "failures" when he was given a *small* caseload to supervise. One can't much help a "good" agent, it seems, by reducing his caseload size; such reduction can only do further harm to those youths who fall into the hands of "bad" agents.

So with youthful offenders, Johnson found, intensive supervision does not seem to provide the rehabilitative benefits claimed for it; the only such benefits may flow not from intensive supervision itself but from contact with one of the "good people" who are frequently in such short supply.

Intensive Supervision of Adults

The results are similarly ambiguous when one applies this intensive supervision to adult offenders. There have been several studies of the effects of intensive supervision on adult parolees. Some of these are hard to interpret because of problems of comparability between experimental and control groups (general risk ratings, for instance, or distribution of narcotics offenders, or policy changes that took place between various phases of the experiments), but two of them (California, 1966; Stanton, 1964) do not seem to give evidence of the benefits of intensive supervision. By far the most extensive work, though, on the effects of intensive supervision of adult parolees has been a series of studies of California's Special Intensive Parole Unit (SIPU), a 10-year-long experiment designed to test the treatment possibilities of various special parole programs. Three of the four "phases" of this experiment produced "negative results." The first phase tested the effect of a reduced caseload size; no lasting effect was found. The second phase slightly increased the size of the small caseloads and provided for a longer time in treatment; again there was no evidence of a treatment effect. In the fourth phase, caseload sizes and time in treatment were again varied, and treatments were simultaneously varied in a sophisticated way according to personality characteristics of the parolees; once again, significant results did not appear.

The only phase of this experiment for which positive results were reported was Phase Three. Here, it was indeed found that a smaller caseload improved one's chances of parole success. There is, however, an important caveat that attaches to this finding: When my colleagues and I divided the whole population of subjects into two groups—those receiving supervision in the North of the state and those in the South—we found that the "improvement" of the experimentals' success rates was taking place primarily in the North. The North differed from the South in one important aspect: Its agents practiced a policy of resuming both "experimental" and "control" violators to prison at relatively high rates. And it was the North that produced the higher success rate among its experimentals. So this improvement in experimentals' performance was taking place only when accompanied by a "realistic threat" of severe sanctions. It is interesting to compare this situation with that of the Warren studies. In the Warren studies, experimental subjects were being revoked at a relatively *low* rate. These experimentals "failed" less, but they also committed more new offenses than their controls. By contrast, in the Northern region of the SIPU experiment, there was a policy of *high* rate of return to prison for experimentals; and here, the special program *did* seem to produce a real improvement in the behavior of offenders. What this suggests is that when intensive supervision *does* produce an improvement in offenders' behavior, it does so not through the mechanism of "treatment" or "rehabilitation," but instead through a mechanism that our studies have almost totally ignored; the mechanism of *deterrence*. And a similar mechanism is suggested by Lohman's study (1967) of intensive supervision of probationers. In this study intensive supervision led to higher total violation rates. But one also notes that intensive supervision combined the highest rate of technical violations with the lowest rate for *new* offenses.

The Effects of Community Treatment

In sum, even in the case of treatment programs administered outside penal institutions, we simply cannot say that this treatment in itself has an appreciable effect on offender behavior. On the other hand, there is one encouraging set of findings that emerges from these studies. For from many of them there flows the strong suggestion that even if we can't "treat" offenders so as to make them do better, a great many of the programs designed to rehabilitate them at least did not make them do *worse*. And if these programs did not show the advantages of actually rehabilitating, some of them did have the advantage of being less onerous to the offender himself without seeming to pose increased danger to the community. And some of these programs—especially those involving less restrictive custody, minimal supervision, and early release—simply cost fewer dollars to administer. The information on the dollar costs of these programs is just beginning to be developed but the implication is clear: *that if we can't do more for (and to) offenders, at least we can safely do less.*

There is, however, one important caveat even to this note of optimism: In order to calculate the true costs of these programs, one must in each case include not only their administrative cost but also the cost of maintaining in the community an offender population increased in size. This population might well not be committing new offenses at any greater rate; but the offender population might, under some of these plans, be larger in absolute *numbers*. So the total number of offenses committed might rise, and our chances of victimization might therefore rise too. We need to be able to make a judgment about the size and probable duration of this effect; as of now, we simply do not know.

Does Nothing Work?

7. *Do all of these studies lead us irrevocably to the conclusion that nothing works, that we haven't the faintest clue about how to rehabilitate offenders and reduce recidivism? And if so, what shall we do?*

We tried to exclude from our survey those studies which were so poorly done that they simply could not be interpreted. But despite our efforts, a pattern has run through much of this discussion—of studies which "found" effects without making any truly rigorous attempt to exclude competing hypotheses, of extraneous factors permitted to intrude upon the measurements, of recidivism measures which are not all measuring the same thing, of "follow-up" periods which vary enormously and rarely extend beyond the period of legal supervision, of experiments never replicated, of "system effects" not taken into account, of categories drawn up without any theory to guide the enterprise. It is just possible that some of our treatment programs *are* working to some extent, but that our research is so bad that it is incapable of telling.

Having entered this very serious caveat, I am bound to say that these data, involving over two hundred studies and hundreds of thousands of individuals as they do, are the best available and give us very little reason to hope that we have in fact found a sure way of reducing recidivism through rehabilitation. This is not to say that we found no instances of success or partial success; it is only to say that these instances have been isolated, producing no clear pattern to indicate the efficacy of any particular method of treatment. And neither is this to say that factors *outside* the realm of rehabilitation may not be working to reduce recidivism—factors such as the tendency for recidivism to be lower in offenders over the age of 30; it is only to say that such factors seem to have little connection with any of the treatment methods now at our disposal.

From this probability, one may draw any of several conclusions. It may be simply that our programs aren't yet good enough—that the education we provide to inmates is still poor education, that the therapy we administer is not administered skillfully enough, that our intensive supervision and counseling do not yet provide enough personal support for the offenders who are subjected to them. If one wishes to believe this, then what our correctional system needs is simply a more full-hearted commitment to the strategy of treatment.

It may be, on the other hand, that there is a more radical flaw in our present strategies—that education at its best, or that psychotherapy at its best, cannot overcome, or even appreciably reduce, the powerful tendency for offenders to continue in criminal behavior. Our present treatment programs are based on a theory of crime as a "disease"—that is to say, as something foreign and abnormal in the individual which can presumably be cured. This theory may well be flawed, in that it overlooks—indeed, denies—both the normality of crime in society and the personal normality of a very large proportion of offenders, criminals who are merely responding to the facts and conditions of our society.

This opposing theory of "crime as a social phenomenon" directs our attention away from a "rehabilitative" strategy, away from the notion that we may best insure public safety through a series of "treatments" to be imposed forcibly on convicted offenders. These treatments have on occasion become, and have the potential for becoming, so draconian as to offend the moral order of a democratic society; and the theory of crime as a social phenomenon suggests that such treatments may be not only offensive but ineffective as well. This theory points, instead, to decarceration for low-risk offenders—and, presumably, to keeping high-risk offenders in prisons which are nothing more (and aim to be nothing more) than custodial institutions.

But this approach has its own problems. To begin with, there is the moral dimension of crime and punishment. Many low-risk offenders have committed serious crimes (murder, sometimes) and even if one is reasonably sure they will never commit another crime, it violates our sense of justice that they should experience no significant retribution for their actions. A middle-class banker who kills his adulterous wife in a moment of passion is a "low-risk" criminal; a juvenile delinquent in the ghetto who commits armed robbery has, statistically, a much higher probability of committing another crime. Are we going to put the first on probation and sentence the latter to a long term in prison?

Besides, one cannot ignore the fact that the punishment of offenders is the major means we have for *deterring* incipient offenders. We know almost nothing about the "deterrent effect," largely because "treatment" theories have so dominated our research, and "deterrence" theories have been relegated to the status of a historical curiosity. Since we have almost no idea of the deterrent functions that our present system performs or that future strategies might be made to perform, it is possible that there is indeed something that works—that to some extent is working right now in front of our noses, and that might be made to work better—something that deters rather than cures, something that does not so much reform convicted offenders as prevent criminal behavior in the first place. But whether that is the case and, if it is, what strategies will be found to make our deterrence system work better than it does now, are questions we will not be able to answer with data until a new family of studies has been brought into existence. As we begin to learn the facts, we will be in a better position than we are now to judge to what degree the prison has become an anachronism and can be replaced by more effective means of social control.

Study Questions

1. What was the original impetus for Martinson's study of the effectiveness of rehabilitation programs?

2. Discuss the methodology (research design, data collection methods, sample, and measures) used by the author.

3. Many times, authors citing the Martinson Report erroneously state that his conclusion was that "nothing works." What was his actual conclusion? Does this differ from the one stated above?

4. What exactly were the author's conclusions about community treatment programs?

Notes

1. Following this case, the state finally did give its permission to have the work published; it will appear in its complete form in a forthcoming book by Praeger.

2. All studies cited in the text are referenced in the bibliography which appears at the conclusion of the article.

3. The net result was that those who received less prison education—because their sentences were shorter or because they were probably better risks—ended up having better chances than those who received more prison education.

4. A similar phenomenon has been measured indirectly by studies that have dealt with the effect of various parole policies on recidivism rates. Where parole decisions have been liberalized so that an offender could be released with only the "reasonable assurance" of a job rather than with a definite job already developed by a parole officer (Stanton, 1963), this liberal release policy has produced no worsening of recidivism rates.

5. It will be recalled that Empey's report on the Provo program made such a finding.

6. But one of these reports, by Kawaguchi (1967), also found that an intensively supervised juvenile, by the time he finally "failed," had had more previous detentions while under supervision than a control juvenile had experienced.

References

Adams, Stuart. "Effectiveness of the Youth Authority Special Treatment Program: First Interim Report." Research Report No. 5. California Youth Authority, March 6, 1959. (Mimeographed.)

Adams, Stuart. "Assessment of the Psychiatric Treatment Program: Second Interim Report." Research Report No. 15. California Youth Authority, December 13, 1959. (Mimeographed.)

Adams, Stuart. "Effectiveness of Interview Therapy with Older Youth Authority Wards: An Interim Evaluation of the PICO Project." Research Report No. 20. California Youth Authority, January 20, 1961. (Mimeographed.)

Adams, Stuart. "Assessment of the Psychiatric Treatment Program, Phase I: Third Interim Report." Research Report No. 21. California Youth Authority, January 31, 1961. (Mimeographed.)

Adams, Stuart. "An Experimental Assessment of Group Counseling with Juvenile Probationers." Paper presented at the 18th Convention of the California State Psychological Association, Los Angeles, December 12, 1964. (Mimeographed.)

Adams, Stuart, Rice, Rogert E., and Olive, Borden. "A Cost Analysis of the Effectiveness of the Group Guidance Program." Research Memorandum 65-3. Los Angeles County Probation Department, January 1965. (Mimeographed.)

Adams, Stuart. "Development of a Program Research Service in Probation." Research Report No. 27 (Final Report, NIMH Project MH007 18.) Los Angeles County Probation Department, January 1966. (Processed.)

Adamson, LeMay, and Dunham, H. Warren. "Clinical Treatment of Male Delinquents. A Case Study in Effort and Result," *American Sociological Review*, XXI, 3 (1956), 312–320.

Babst, Dean V., and Mannering, John W. "Probation versus Imprisonment for Similar Types of Offenders: A Comparison by Subsequent Violations," *Journal of Research in Crime and Delinquency*, II, 2 (1965), 60–71.

Bernsten, Karen, and Christiansen, Karl O. "A Resocialization Experiment with Short-term Offenders," *Scandinavian Studies in Criminology*, I (1965), 35–54.

California Adult Authority, Division of Adult Paroles. "Special Intensive Parole Unit, Phase I: Fifteen Man Caseload Study." Prepared by Walter I. Stone. Sacramento, CA, November 1956. (Mimeographed.)

California, Department of Corrections. "Intensive Treatment Program: Second Annual Report." Prepared by Harold B. Bradley and Jack D. Williams. Sacramento, CA, December 1, 1958. (Mimeographed.)

California, Department of Corrections. "Special Intensive Parole Unit, Phase II: Thirty Man Caseload Study." Prepared by Ernest Reimer and Martin Warren. Sacramento, CA, December 1958. (Mimeographed.)

California, Department of Corrections. "Parole Work Unit Program: An Evaluative Report." A memorandum to the California Joint Legislative Budget Committee, December 30, 1966. (Mimeographed.)

California, Department of the Youth Authority. "James Marshall Treatment Program: Progress Report." January 1967. (Processed.)

Cambridge University, Department of Criminal Science. *Detention in Remard Homes*. London: Macmillan, 1952.

Craft, Michael, Stephenson, Geoffrey, and Granger, Clive. "A Controlled Trial of Authoritarian and Self-Governing Regimes with Adolescent Psychopaths," *American Journal of Orthopsychiatry*, XXXIV, 3 (1964), 543–554.

Empey, LeMar T. "The Provo Experiment: A Brief Review." Los Angeles: Youth Studies Center, University of Southern California. 1966. (Processed.)

Feistman, Eugene G. "Comparative Analysis of the Willow-Brook-Harbor Intensive Services Program, March 1, 1965 through February 28, 1966." Research Report No. 28. Los Angeles County Probation Department, June 1966. (Processed.)

Forman, B. "The Effects of Differential Treatment on Attitudes, Personality Traits, and Behavior of Adult Parolees." Unpublished Ph.D. dissertation, University of Southern California, 1960.

Fox, Vernon. "Michigan's Experiment in Minimum Security Penology," *Journal of Criminal Law, Criminology, and Police Science*, XLI, 2 (1950), 150–166.

Freeman, Howard E., and Weeks, H. Ashley. "Analysis of a Program of Treatment of Delinquent Boys," *American Journal of Sociology*, LXII, 1 (1956), 56–61.

Garrity, Donald Lee. "The Effects of Length of Incarceration upon Parole Adjustment and Estimation of Optimum Sentence: Washington State Correctional Institutions." Unpublished Ph.D. dissertation, University of Washington, 1956.

Gearhart, J. Walter, Keith, Harold L., and Clemmons, Gloria. "An Analysis of the Vocational Training Program in the Washington State Adult Correctional Institutions." Research Review No. 23. State of Washington, Department of Institutions, May 1967. (Processed.)

Glaser, Daniel. *The Effectiveness of a Prison and Parole System*. New York: Bobbs-Merrill, 1964.

Goldberg, Lisbeth, and Adams, Stuart. "An Experimental Evaluation of the Lathrop Hall Program." Los Angeles County Probation Department, December 1964. (Summarized in Adams, Stuart. "Development of a Program Research Service in Probation," pp. 19–22.)

Great Britain. Home Office. *The Sentence of the Court: A Handbook for Courts on the Treatment of Offenders*. London: Her Majesty's Stationery Office, 1964.

Guttman, Evelyn S. "Effects of Short-Term Psychiatric Treatment on Boys in Two California Youth Authority Institutions." Research Report No. 36. California Youth Authority, December 1963. (Processed.)

Hammond, W.H., and Chayen, E. *Persistent Criminals: A Home Office Research Unit Report*. London: Her Majesty's Stationery Office, 1963.

Harrison, Robert M., and Mueller, Paul F. C. "Clue Hunting About Group Counseling and Parole Outcome." Research Report No. 11. California Department of Corrections, May 1964. (Mimeographed.)

Havel, Joan, and Sulka, Elaine. "Special Intensive Parole Unit: Phase Three." Research Report No. 3. California Department of Corrections, March 1962. (Processed.)

Havel, Joan. "A Synopsis of Research Report No. 10, SIPU Phase IV—The High Base Expectancy Study." Administrative Abstract No. 10. California Department of Corrections, June 1963. (Processed.)

Havel, Joan. "Special Intensive Parole Unit—Phase Four: 'The Parole Outcome Study.'" Research Report No. 13. California Department of Corrections, September 1965. (Processed.)

Hood, Roger. *Homeless Borstal Boys: A Study of Their After-Care and After Conduct.* Occasional Papers on Social Administration No. 18. London: G. Bell & Sons, 1966.

Jacobson, Frank, and McGee, Eugene. "Englewood Project: Re-education: A Radical Correction of Incarcerated Delinquents." Englewood, CO: July 1965. (Mimeographed.)

Jesness, Carl F. "The Fricot Ranch Study: Outcomes with Small versus Large Living Groups in the Rehabilitation of Delinquents." Research Report No. 47. California Youth Authority, October 1, 1965. (Processed.)

Johnson, Bertram. "Parole Performance of the First Year's Releases, Parole Research Project: Evaluation of Reduced Caseloads." Research Report No. 27. California Youth Authority, January 31, 1962. (Mimeographed.)

Johnson, Bertram. "An Analysis of Predictions of Parole Performance and of Judgements of Supervision in the Parole Research Project," Research Report No. 32. California Youth Authority, December 31, 1962. (Mimeographed.)

Kassebaum, Gene, Ward, David, and Wilnet, Daniel. *Prison Treatment and Parole Survival: An Empirical Assessment.* New York: Wiley, 1971.

Kawaguchi, Ray M., and Siff, Leon, M. "An Analysis of Intensive Probation Services—Phase II." Research Report No. 29. Los Angeles County Probation Department, April 1967. (Processed.)

Kettering, Marvin E. "Rehabilitation of Women in the Milwaukee County Jail: An Exploration Experiment." Unpublished Master's Thesis, Colorado State College, 1965.

Kovacs, Frank W. "Evaluation and Final Report of the New Start Demonstration Project." Colorado Department of Employment, October 1967. (Processed.)

Lavlicht, Jerome, et al., in Berkshire Farms Monographs, I, 1 (1962), 11–48.

Levinson, Robert B., and Kitchenet, Howard L. "Demonstration Counseling Project." 2 vols. Washington, DC: National Training School for Boys, 1962–1964. (Mimeographed.)

Lohman, Joseph D., et al., "The Intensive Supervision Caseloads: A Preliminary Evaluation." The San Francisco Project: A Study of Federal Probation and Parole. Research Report No. 11. School of Criminology, University of California, March 1967. (Processed.)

McClintock, F.H. *Attendance Centres.* London. Macmillan, 1961.

McCord, William and Joan. "Two Approaches to the Cure of Delinquents," *Journal of Criminal Law, Criminology and Police Science,* XLIV, 4 (1953), 442–467.

McCorkle, Lloyd W., Elias, Albert, and Bixby, F. Lovell. *The Highfields Story: An Experimental Treatment Project for Youthful Offenders.* New York: Holt, 1958.

McCravy, Newton, Jr., and Delehanty, Dolores S. "Community Rehabilitation of the Younger Delinquent Boy, Parkland Non-Residential Group Center." Final Report, Kentucky Child Welfare Research Foundation, Inc., September 1, 1967. (Mimeographed.)

Mandell, Wallace, et al. "Surgical and Social Rehabilitation of Adult Offenders." Final Report. Montefiore Hospital and Medical Center, With Staten Island Mental Health Society. New York City Department of Correction, 1967. (Processed.)

Massimo, Joseph L., and Shore, Milton F. "The Effectiveness of a Comprehensive Vocationally Oriented Psychotherapeutic Program for Adolescent Delinquent Boys," *American Journal of Orthopsychiatry,* XXXIII, 4 (1963), 634–642.

Minet, Joshua, III, Kelly, Francis J., and Hatch, M. Charles. "Outward Bound, Inc.: Juvenile Delinquency Demonstration Project, Year End Report." Massachusetts Division of Youth Service, May 31, 1967.

Narloch, R. P., Adams, Stuart, and Jenkins, Kendall J. "Characteristics and Parole Performance of California Youth Authority Early Release." Research Report No. 7. California Youth Authority, June 22, 1959. (Mimeographed.)

New York State Division of Parole, Department of Correction. "Parole Adjustment and Prior Educational Achievement of Male Adolescent Offenders, June 1957–June 1961." September 1964. (Mimeographed.)

O'Brien, William J. "Personality Assessment as a Measure of Change Resulting from Group Psychotherapy with Male Juvenile Delinquents." The Institute for the Study of Crime and Delinquency, and the California Youth Authority, December 1961. (Processed.)

Persons, Roy W. "Psychological and Behavioral Change in Delinquents Following Psychotherapy," *Journal of Clinical Psychology*, XXII, 3 (1966), 337–340.

Pilnick, Saul, et al. "Collegefields: From Delinquency to Freedom." A Report . . . on Collegefields Group Educational Center. Laboratory for Applied Behavioral Science, Newark State College, February 1967. (Processed.)

Robison, James, and Kevotkian, Marinette. "Intensive Treatment Project: Phase II. Parole Outcome: Interim Report." Research Report No. 27. California Department of Corrections, Youth and Adult Correctional Agency, January 1967. (Mimeographed.)

Rudoff, Alvin. "The Effect of Treatment on Incarcerated Young Adult Delinquents as Measured by Disciplinary History." Unpublished Master's thesis, University of Southern California, 1960.

Saden, S.J. "Correctional Research at Jackson Prison," *Journal of Correctional Education*, XV (October 1962), 22–26.

Schnur, Alfred C. "The Educational Treatment of Prisoners and Recidivism," *American Journal of Sociology*, LIV, 2 (1948), 142–147.

Schwitzgebel, Robert and Ralph. "Therapeutic Research: A Procedure for the Reduction of Adolescent Crime." Paper presented at meetings of the American Psychological Association, Philadelphia, August 1963.

Schwitzgebel, Robert and Kolb, D.A. "Inducing Behavior Change in Adolescent Delinquents," *Behavior Research Therapy*, I (1964), 297–304.

Seckel, Joachim P. "Experiments in Group Counseling at Two Youth Authority Institutions." Research Report No. 46. California Youth Authority, September 1965. (Processed.)

Seckel, Joachim P. "The Fremont Experiment, Assessment of Residential Treatment at a Youth Authority Reception Center." Research Report No. 50. California Youth Authority, January 1967. (Mimeographed.)

Shelley, Ernest L.V., and Johnson, Walter F., Jr. "Evaluating an Organized Counseling Service for Youthful Offenders," *Journal of Counseling Psychology*, VIII, 4 (1961), 351–354.

Shoham, Shlomo, and Sandberg, Moshe. "Suspended Sentences in Israel: An Evaluation of the Preventive Efficacy of Prospective Imprisonment," *Crime and Delinquency*, X, 1 (1964), 74–83.

Stanton, John M. "Delinquencies and Types of Parole Programs to Which Inmates Are Released." New York State Division of Parole, May 15, 1963. (Mimeographed.)

Stanton, John M. "Board Directed Extensive Supervision." New York State Division of Parole, August 3, 1964. (Mimeographed.)

Stuerup, Georg K. "The Treatment of Sexual Offenders," *Bulletin de la societe internationale de criminologie* (1960), pp. 320–329.

Sullivan, Clyde E., and Mandell, Wallace. "Restoration of Youth Through Training: A Final Report." Staten Island, NY: Wakoff Research Center, April 1967. (Processed.)

Taylor, A.J.W. "An Evaluation of Group Psychotherapy in a Girls Borstal," *International Journal of Group Psychotherapy*, XVII, 2 (1967), 168–177.

Truax, Charles B., Wargo, Donald G., and Silber, Leon D. "Effects of Group Psychotherapy with High Adequate Empathy and Nonpossessive Warmth upon Female Institutionalized Delinquents," *Journal of Abnormal Psychology*, LXXXI, 4 (1966), 267–274.

Warren, Marguerite, et al. "The Community Treatment Project after Five Years." California Youth Authority, 1966. (Processed.)

Warren, Marguerite, et al. "Community Treatment Project, An Evaluation of Community Treatment for Delinquents: A Fifth Progress Report." C.T.P. Research Report No. 7. California Youth Authority, August 1966. (Processed.)

Warren, Margeurite, et al. "Community Treatment Project, An Evaluation of Community Treatment for Delinquents: Sixth Progress Report." C.T.P. Research Report No. 8. California Youth Authority, September 1967. (Processed.)

Wilkins, Leslie T. "A Small Comparative Study of the Results of Probation," *British Journal of Criminology*, VIII, 3 (1958), 201–209.

Zivan, Morton. "Youth in Trouble: A Vocational Approach." Final Report of a Research Demonstration Project, May 31, 1961–August 31, 1966. Dobbs Ferry, NY, Children's Village, 1966. (Processed.)

20
The Principles of Effective Correctional Programs

Don A. Andrews

As we have read, Martinson was actually more cautious in his conclusions than many believe. The message, however, was interpreted as "nothing works." While some have criticized Martinson for his methodology and public pronouncements, the real value of his work comes from others who answered the challenge. Scholars like Don Andrews began focusing on determining "what works" with offenders. Using a relatively new technique, meta-analysis, researchers have been able to demonstrate that correctional treatment can indeed have an appreciable effect on recidivism rates, provided that certain principles are met. The principles of effective intervention identified by Don Andrews include the risk principle (targeting higher-risk offenders), the need principle (targeting crime-producing needs), the responsivity principle (cognitive and behavioral treatment matched with offender need and learning styles), and the fidelity principles (attending to program integrity). These and other important principles are clearly identified and explained in this next chapter.

This chapter provides a brief outline of principles of effective correctional treatment. The principles recognize the importance of individual differences in criminal behaviour. A truly interdisciplinary psychology of criminal conduct (PCC; Andrews &

Bonta, 1998) has matured to the extent that progress has been made with reference to the achievement of two major scientific standards of understanding. In brief, individual differences in criminal activity can be predicted and influenced at levels well above chance and to a practically significant degree. The following principles of effective treatment draw heavily upon that knowledge base. This does not imply that the research base is anywhere near complete with reference to most issues. Rather, all of the following principles are subject to further investigation, including even those principles with relatively strong research support at this time. Also, principles not even hinted at here are expected to be developed and validated in the coming months and years.

To date, PCC has advanced because it is specific about what it attempts to account for, that is, individual differences in criminal behaviour including reoffending on the part of adjudicated offenders. It has advanced also because it recognizes that the risk factors for criminal conduct may be biological, personal, interpersonal, and/or structural, cultural, political and economic; and may reflect immediate circumstances. PCC does not limit its view to the biological, the personal, or to differential levels of privilege and/or victimisation in social origin as may be indexed by age, race, class and gender. This PCC does not purport to be a psychology of criminal justice, a psychology of social justice, a sociology of aggregated crime rates, or a behavioural or social science of social inequality, of poverty, or of a host of other legitimate but different interests.

In applications of PCC, however, these many other legitimate but different interests may not only be of value but may well be paramount. For example, within criminal law and justice systems, principles of retribution and/or restoration may be considered paramount and hence any correctional treatment efforts, if offered at all, must be offered and evaluated within the retributive and/or restorative context. Similarly, the effects of human service efforts may be evaluated within the context of institutional and/or community corrections. Moreover, ideals of justice, ethicality, decency, legality, safety and cost-efficiency are operating in judicial and correctional contexts as they are operating in other contexts of human endeavour. Thus, the principles of effective human service reviewed here are presented in the context of seeking ethical, legal, decent, cost-effective, safe, just and otherwise normative human service efforts aimed at reducing reoffending.

The phrase "otherwise normative" covers a vast area and is included in recognition of the fact that under some political conditions the values and norms of some privileged groups may be dominant no matter how weak the connection between compliance with their norms and the enhancement of peace and security. For example, sentencing according to criminal law and the principle of specific deterrence continues to occur in Canada and other countries even though there is no consistent evidence that reoffending is reduced through increases in the severity of negative sanctioning. Similarly, principles of effective human service in a justice context may be applied even when the sanctions themselves have been handed down with little concern for reducing reoffending (for example, under a pure just desert sanction) or as an attempt to provide restitution for the victim (for example, under a restorative justice disposition).

The following principles have to do with clinically relevant programming and with setting, staff, implementation and integrity issues. The first set of principles, however, restate and underscore the importance of the theoretical and normative issues referred to in the opening paragraphs. The research evidence is appended along with some relevant references to earlier reviews of principles.

Some Principles of Theory, Ideology, Justice and Setting in Seeking Reduced Reoffending

Principle 1

Base your intervention efforts on a psychological theory of criminal behaviour as opposed to a biological, behavioural, psychological, sociological, humanistic, judicial or legal perspective on justice, social equality or aggregated crime rates. When the interest is reduced reoffending at the individual level, theories that focus on some other outcome are of reduced value because they are less likely to identify relevant variables and strategies. The average effects on reduced reoffending of interventions based on alternatives to a psychology of crime have been negative or negligible. . . . In brief, if you are interested in individual differences in criminal activity (for example, reducing reoffending) work from a theory of criminal behaviour.

Principle 2

The recommended psychological perspective is a broad band general personality and social learning approach to understanding variation in criminal behaviour including criminal recidivism. This perspective identifies the [six] following major risk factors for criminal behaviour:

- attitudes, values, beliefs, rationalisations and cognitive emotional states specifically supportive of criminal behaviour;
- immediate interpersonal and social support for antisocial behaviour;
- fundamental personality and temperamental supports such as weak self-control, restless aggressive energy and adventurous pleasure seeking;
- a history of antisocial behaviour including early onset;

- problematic circumstances in the domains of home, school/work, and leisure/recreation;
- substance abuse. (Principles 5–8.)

The general personality and social learning perspectives also identify the major behavioural influence strategies such as modelling, reinforcement and cognitive restructuring in the context of a reasonably high quality interpersonal relationship (Principle 9, 16). The behavioural base of this perspective also suggests that treatment is best offered in the community-based settings in which problematic behaviour occurs (Principle 4). In addition, the behaviour of workers in correctional settings is also under the influence of cognition, social support, behavioural history and fundamental personality predisposition and hence the emphasis placed on the selection, training and supervision of workers (Principle 16, 17).

Principle 3

Introduce human service strategies and do not rely on the principles of retribution or restorative justice and do not rely on principles of deterrence (specific and/or general) and/or on incapacitation. Moreover, seriously consider and introduce but do not rely upon other principles of justice and normative appropriateness such as professional credentials, ethicality, legality, decency, and efficiency. Rather, reductions in reoffending are to be found through the design and delivery of clinically relevant and psychologically appropriate human service under conditions and settings considered just, ethical, legal, decent, efficient, and otherwise normative. In brief, the task assigned by the human service principle of effective service is to design and deliver effective human service in a just and otherwise normative context. The principles of effective human service do not vary greatly with such considerations, although the justice and normative contexts themselves may

vary tremendously. The setting factor of community versus institutional corrections, however, does lead to a separate principle.

Principle 4

Community-based services are preferred over residential/institutional settings but, if justice or other concerns demand a residential or custodial placement, community-oriented services are recommended. Community-oriented services refer to services facilitating return to the community and facilitating appropriate service delivery in the community. The principles of relapse prevention provide guidance for clinically relevant community-oriented services. When services are community-based, a supplementary consideration is to favour home and school-based services rather than agency-based services. For example, the best of the family interventions are not delivered in agency offices but in the natural settings of home and community.

Principles of Risk, Need, Responsivity, Strength, Multimodal Service, and Service Relevant Assessment

Principle 5—*Risk*

More intensive human services are best reserved for higher risk cases. Low risk cases have a low probability of recidivism even in the absence of service. With the lowest risk cases, justice may be served through just dispositions and there is no need to introduce correctional treatment services in order to reduce risk. Indeed, a concern in working with the lowest risk cases is that the pursuit of justice does not inadvertently increase risk through, for example, increased association with offenders and/or the acquisition of pro-criminal attitudes and beliefs. Additionally, recognize that well controlled outcome studies have yet to find reduced reoffending when human service is delivered to the highest risk cases such as very high risk egocentric offenders with extended histories of antisocial behaviour. There is the possibility that psychopaths may put any new skills acquired in treatment to antisocial use (see Principle 10, specific responsivity). At this time, however, there are no well-controlled outcome studies of clinically appropriate treatment with psychopaths.

Principle 6—*Target Criminogenic Need*

Treatment services best attempt to reduce major dynamic risk factors and/or to enhance major protective or strength factors. Criminogenic needs are dynamic risk factors that when reduced are followed by reduced reoffending and/or protective factors that when enhanced are followed by reduced reoffending. Following the major risk factors, the most promising targets include moving antisocial cognition and cognitive emotional states such as resentment in the less antisocial direction, reducing association with antisocial others and enhancing association with anticriminal others, and building self-management, self-regulation and problem solving skills. A history of antisocial behaviour can not be eliminated but new less risky behaviours may be acquired and practised in risky situations (as in relapse prevention programs). Rewards for non-criminal behaviour may be enhanced in the settings of home, school/work and leisure. In the home, the major intermediate targets are enhanced caring, nurturance and mutual respect in combination with monitoring, supervision and appropriate discipline. Similarly, reduced substance abuse may shift the pattern of rewards such that the non-criminal is favoured. The less promising intermediate targets of change include enhancing self-esteem and reducing personal distress without touching personal and interpersonal

supports for crime, increasing fear of official punishment, and a focus on other weak risk factors. In summary, for adherence with the need principle, emphasize the reduction of criminogenic need and do not rely upon or emphasize the reduction of noncriminogenic need.

Principle 7—*Multimodal*

Target a number of criminogenic needs. The meta-analyses now make it clear that a number of the criminogenic needs of high-risk cases are best targeted.

Principle 8—*Assessing Risk and Dynamic Factor*

Adherence to the principles of risk and criminogenic need depend upon the reliable and valid assessment of risk and need. The best instruments sample the major risk factors and can provide evidence of validity with younger and older cases, men and women, and different ethnic groups in a number of justice and correctional contexts. Assessments of risk best sample the eight risk factors as well as very specific indicators when specialized outcomes are sought. The latter specific indicators, for example, would include deviant sexual arousal and cognitive and/or social support for sexual offending when reduced sex offending is the desired outcome. Similarly, attitudinal and social support for battering would be specific risk factors when reduced family violence is the desired outcome. Please do not confuse seriousness of the current offence with risk of reoffending. Seriousness of the offence is an aggravating factor at time of sentencing but not a major risk factor.

Principle 9—*General Responsivity*

Responsivity has to do with matching the style, modes and influence strategies of service with the learning styles, motivation, aptitude and ability of cases. Generally, offenders are human beings and hence the principle suggests use of the most powerful influencing strategies that have been demonstrated with human beings. Consistent with the general personality and social learning perspective, these most powerful approaches are structured behavioural, social learning and cognitive behavioural influence strategies. These fundamentals include reinforcement, modelling, skill acquistion through reinforced practice in the context of role playing and graduated approximations, extinction, and cognitive restructuring. Reinforcement, extinction, modelling effects and the attractiveness of the setting of change are all enhanced by high quality interpersonal relationships characterized as open, warm, non-hostile, non-blaming and engaging. Structuring activities include anticriminal modeling and reinforcement, skill building through structured learning, problem solving, advocacy and brokerage, and the effective use of authority (see Principle 16, staff considerations).

Principle 10—*Specific Responsivity and Strengths*

Specific responsivity factors include personality, ability, motivation, strengths, age, gender, ethnicity/race, language, and various barriers to successful participation in service. The personality set, for example, includes interpersonal anxiety (avoid heavy confrontation), interpersonal and cognitive immaturity (use structured approaches), psychopathy (keep very open communication among all workers) and low verbal intelligence (be concrete). Motivational considerations suggest matching treatment style and goals with level of motivation for change (from not even thinking of change though currently involved in change activities). The relationship principle noted under general responsivity is widely applicable but many feminist scholars stress in particular quality of interpersonal interac-

tions in working with female offenders. Aboriginal writers support the introduction of a spiritual component when working with Aboriginal offenders. When working with reluctant cases the general rule of high quality interpersonal interactions is underscored as is the removal of concrete barriers such as inconvenient timing and location of service. Make use of personal, interpersonal and circumstantial strengths in planning and delivering service. Some of these helpful strengths are problem-solving skills, respect for family, a particularly prosocial friend or being happily employed in delivering effective service.

Principle 11—*Assess Responsivity and Strength Factors*

Sophisticated assessment instruments are available for assessment of some of the personality factors and a new generation of risk/need scales are introducing routine assessment of strength and other responsivity factors. Generally, however, watch for particular strengths and for particular barriers for individual cases and for particular groups such as women and minorities.

Principle 12—*After Care, Structured Follow-up, Continuity of Care, and Relapse Prevention*

This is introduced as a principle on its own because of the need to stress ongoing monitoring of progress and to intervene when circumstances deteriorate or positive opportunities emerge. Generally, and particularly for residential programs, it is important that programming be community oriented and attend to family, associates and other social settings. Going beyond Principle 4, Principle 12 stresses specific and structured after care and follow-up activity and requires co-ordination of applications of all of the previous principles. At a minimum, in the tradition of relapse prevention, high-risk situations and circumstances are identified and low-risk alternative responses are practiced.

Principle 13—*Professional Discretion*

In a few cases, with documented reasons, deviations from the general principles may be introduced. For example, for some young people and their families, it may be recommended that facilitating a move out of a particular apartment building in a particularly high crime area is a priority intermediate goal. Similarly, a major mental disorder such as schizophrenia may move from the minor risk set to the major set when specific symptoms include antisocial thoughts that others are out to get the person and should be "got" first.

Principle 14

Create and record a service plan and any modification of plans through re-assessment of risk/need and progress. The service plan describes how the human service principles of risk, need, general responsivity, specific responsivity, multimodal service, aftercare and professional discretion will be addressed in working with a particular case.

Implementation and Program Integrity

Principle 15—*Integrity in Program Implementation and Delivery*

Integrity has to do with whether the human service activities were introduced and delivered as planned and designed, and indeed whether the delivery of services achieved intermediate objectives. Integrity is enhanced when a highly specific and concrete version of a rational and empirically sound theory is employed. Specificity enhances the opportunity for clarity in who

is being served, what is being targeted, and what style, mode and strategy of service is to be used. Specificity readily yields the production of training and program manuals in printed, taped or other formats. Integrity is enhanced when workers are selected, trained, and clinically supervised with particular reference to the attitudes and skills required for effective service delivery. Integrity is enhanced when the clinical supervisor has been trained and has access to highly relevant consultation services. In addition, specificity implies an understanding of when treatment comes to an appropriate end or an understanding of the appropriate closing of the case. The latter implies that service personnel and researchers know when dosage has been adequate and/or when treatment has been delivered successfully and/or when intermediate targets have been achieved. Thus, integrity may be enhanced through the monitoring of service process and monitoring of the achievement of intermediate objectives. At the highest levels of integrity, when clinical supervision or other styles of monitoring identify problematic circumstances (or unanticipated service opportunities) actions are initiated to modify the service plan and to overcome barriers and build on strengths. Involvement of researchers in the design and/or delivery of service amplifies integrity. In summary and in checklist format, integrity depends upon all of the following:

(a) Specific version of a rational and empirically sound theory

(b) Selection of workers

(c) Training of workers

(d) Clinical supervision of workers

(e) Trained clinical supervisors

(f) Consultation services for clinical supervisors

(g) Printed/taped program manuals

(h) Monitoring of intermediate service process

(i) Monitoring of intermediate change

(j) Action to maximize adherence to service process and enhance appropriate intermediate gain

(k) Adequate dosage/duration/intensity

(l) Involve a researcher in the design, delivery and evaluation of service—in particular, involve a researcher interested in service process, intermediate outcome and ultimate outcome in the design and delivery of service

(m) Other

Implementation and integrity issues involve staff and management issues to such a degree that their importance is underscored through statements of separate principles of staff and management considerations.

Principle 16—*Attend to Staff*

The selection, training and clinical supervision of staff each best reflect the particular attitudes, skills and circumstances that are supportive of the delivery of the service as planned. Reflecting the general social learning and general responsivity principles, staff skill and cognition supportive of effective practice fall into the five general core practice categories of relationship/interaction skills, structuring/contingency skills, personal cognitive supportive of human service, social support for the delivery of clinically appropriate service, and other considerations.

Relationship. Indicators of relationship skills include some combination of the following: being respectful, open, warm (not cold, hostile, indifferent), caring, non-blaming, flexible, reflective, self confident, mature, enthusiastic, understanding, genuine (real), bright and verbal, and other indicators including elements of motivational interviewing strategies (express empathy, avoid argumentation, roll with resistance). Recall from the general responsivity principle that the effectiveness of modelling, reinforcement and even expressions of disapproval are all enhanced in the context of high quality interpersonal relationships.

Structuring. Indicators of structuring skills include some combination of the following social learning/cognitive behavioural strategies reformulated with particular reference to core effective practices. Modelling anticriminal alternatives to procriminal attitudes, values, beliefs, rationalizations, thoughts, feelings and behavioural patterns; anticriminal differential reinforcement; cognitive restructuring; structured learning skills; the practice and training of problem solving skills; core advocacy/brokerage activity; and effective use of authority. More generally expressed, some indicators are being directive, solution focused, contingency based and, from motivational interviewing, developing discrepancy and supporting beliefs that the person can change his or [her] behaviour (supporting prosocial self efficacy).

Personal Cognitive Supports. Some specific indicators including:

- a knowledge base favouring human service activity;
- a belief that offenders can change;
- a belief that core correctional practices work;
- a belief that personally they have the skills to practice at high levels both in terms of relationship and structuring;
- a belief that important others value core practice and value; and
- a belief that reducing recidivism is a worthwhile pursuit.

Social Support for Effective Practice. The two major indicators are association with others who practice and support clinically relevant treatment, and relative isolation from anti-treatment others and from others who promote unstructured, non-directive, client-centered practice and/or isolation from others who promote intensive service for low risk cases and promote the targeting of non-criminogenic needs.

Other. Credentials and other factors will be relevant in so far as they tap into the core practices. Obviously, the area of staff considerations is a major area for future research.

A program scores high on staff considerations when:

(a) staff are selected with reference to high level functioning on the relationship, structuring, cognitive and social support dimension of effective correctional practice;

(b) staff receive preservice and inservice training that supports high levels of core practice;

(c) staff receive on-the-job clinical supervision that is concerned with high level functioning in core practice;

(d) staff are actually observed to be functioning at high levels in their exchanges with offenders.

Principle 17—*Attend to Management*

Effective managers are assumed to be generally good managers with, additionally, the above-noted relationship and structuring skills along with the knowledge base and their own social support system favourable to clinically relevant and psychologically informed human service. It is management that is responsible for implementing the core principles and creating the supports for creating and maintaining integrity. Effective management will take the steps required to develop program champions inside and outside of the agency. Effective management will reward high functioning staff and have programs and sites accredited.

Principle 18—*Attending to Broader Social Arrangements*

The effective prevention and correctional treatment agency in a public manner will locate crime reduction efforts in the context appropriate to local and surrounding conditions. In brief, the correctional agency will be able to clearly locate treatment in locally appropriate contexts of public safety, restorative justice, etc. Similarly, the primary prevention agency will be able to locate their crime prevention efforts in the locally appropriate context of child welfare, family service, mental health, community development, etc. However, if the host agency is preoccupied with punishment, restoration or child welfare etc.—if the host agency is not understanding of or interested in clinically relevant approaches to reduced antisocial behaviour—effectiveness will be reduced.

Study Questions

1. According to the author, why is the psychology of criminal conduct so important in understanding what works?

2. Explain the risk, need, and responsivity principles.

3. Why is program integrity so important?

4. What are the other principles identified by the author?

References

Akers, R. L. (1973). *Deviant behavior: A social learning approach.* Belmont, CA: Wadsworth.

Andrews, D. A. (1979). *The dimensions of correctional counseling and supervision process in probation and parole.* Toronto, ON: Ontario Ministry of Correctional Services.

Andrews, D. A. (1980). Some experimental investigations of the principles of differential association through deliberate manipulations of the structure of service systems. *American Sociological Review, 45,* 448–462.

Andrews, D. A. (1982). *A personal, interpersonal and community-reinforcement perspective on deviant behavior* (PIC-R). Toronto, ON: Ministry of Correctional Services.

Andrews, D. A. (1989). Recidivism is predictable and can be influenced: Using risk assessments to reduce recidivism. *Forum on Corrections Research, 1*(2), 11–18.

Andrews, D. A. (1995a). *Report on an expanded exploration of appropriate correctional treatment.* Paper presented at the American Society of Criminology annual meeting, Boston, MA, 1995.

Andrews, D. A. (1995b). The psychology of criminal conduct and effective treatment. In J. McGuire (Ed.), *What works: Reducing reoffending: Guidelines from research and practice* (pp. 35–62). Chichester, UK: John Wiley & Sons.

Andrews, D. A. (1995c). *Assessing program elements for risk reduction: The Correctional Program Assessment Inventory* (CPAI). Paper presented at "Research to Results," a conference of IARCA (now ICCA), Ottawa, ON. October 11–14th.

Andrews, D. A. (1996). *Behavioral, cognitive behavioral and social learning contributions to criminological theory.* Paper presented at the American Society of Criminology annual meeting, Chicago, Illinois, November.

Andrews, D. A., & Bonta, J. (1998). *The psychology of criminal conduct* (2nd edition). Cincinnati, OH: Anderson.

Andrews, D. A., & Bonta, J. (1994). *The psychology of criminal conduct.* Cincinnati, OH: Anderson.

Andrews, D. A., Bonta, J., & Hoge, R. D. (1990). Classification for effective rehabilitation: Rediscovering psychology. *Criminal Justice and Behavior, 17,* 19–52.

Andrews, D. A., & Carvell, C. (1998). *Core correctional treatment—Core correctional supervision and counseling: Theory, research, assessment and practice.* Ottawa, ON: Carleton University.

Andrews, D. A., & Dowden, C. (under review). *Managing correctional treatment for reduced recidivism: A meta-analytical review of program integrity.* Manuscript submitted for publication.

Andrews, D. A., Dowden, C., & Gendreau, P. (1999). *Clinically relevant and psychologically informed approaches to reduced reoffending: A meta-analytic study of human service, risk, need, responsivity, and other concerns in justice contexts.* Unpublished manuscript, Ottawa, ON: Carleton University.

Andrews, D. A., Gordon, D. A., Hill, J., Kurkowski, K. P., & Hoge, R. D. (1993). *Program integrity, methodology, and treatment characteristics: A metaanalysis of effects of family intervention with young offenders.* A paper based on a presentation at the meetings of the American Society of Criminology, 1992.

Andrews, D. A., Zinger, I., Hoge, R. D., Bonta, J., Gendreau. P., & Cullen, F. T. (1990). Does correctional treatment work? A clinically relevant and psychologically informed meta-analysis. *Criminology, 28,* 369–404.

Antonowicz, D. H., & Ross, R. R. (1994). Essential components of successful rehabilitation programs for offenders. *International Journal of Offender Therapy and Comparative Criminology, 38,* 97–104.

Cleland, C. M., Pearson, F., & Lipton, D. S. (1996). *A meta-analytic approach to the link between needs-targeted treatment and reductions in criminal offending.* American Society of Criminology annual meeting, Chicago, IL, November, 1996.

Dowden, C. (1998). *A meta-analytic examination of the risk, need and responsivity principles and their importance within the rehabilitation debate.* Unpublished master's thesis. Ottawa, ON: Carleton University, Department of Psychology.

Dowden, C., & Andrews, D. A. (1999). What works for female offenders. *Crime and Delinquency, 45,* 438–452.

Garrett, C. J. (1985). Effects of residential treatment of adjudicated delinquents: A meta-analysis. *Journal of Resarch in Crime and Delinquency, 22,* 287–308.

Gendreau, P. (1996). The principles of effective intervention with offenders. In A. Hartland (Ed.), *Choosing correctional options that work.* Newbury Park, CA: Sage.

Gendreau, P., Little, T., & Goggin, C. (1996). A meta-analysis of the predictors of adult offender recidivism: What works! *Criminology, 34*(4), 575–607.

Gendreau, P., & Goggin, C. (1997). Correctional treatment: Accomplishments and realities. In P. Van Voorhis, M. Braswell, & D. L. Lester (Eds.), *Correctional counseling and rehabilitation.* Cincinnati, OH: Anderson.

Gendreau, P., & Ross, R. R. (1979). Effectiveness of correctional treatment: Bibliography for cynics. *Crime and Delinquency, 25,* 463–489.

Gendreau, P., & Ross, R. R. (1987). Revivification of rehabilitation: Evidence from the 1980's. *Justice Quarterly, 4,* 349–408.

Grant, J., & Grant, M. Q. (1959). A group dynamics approach to the treatment of non-conformists in the Navy. *Annals of the American Academy of Political and Social Sciences, 322,* 126–135.

Henggeler, S. W., Schoenwald, S. K., Borduin. C. M., Rowland, M. D., & Cunningham, P. B. (1998). *Multisystemic treatment of antisocial behavior in children and adolescents.* New York, NY: The Guilford Press.

Hill, J. K., Andrews, D. A., & Hoge, R. D. (1991). Meta-analysis of treatment programs for young offenders: The effect of clinically relevant treatment on recidivism, with controls introduced for various methodological variables. *Canadian Journal of Program Evaluation, 6,* 97–109.

Izzo, R., & Ross, R. (1990). A meta-analysis of rehabilitation programs for juvenile delinquents: A brief report. *Criminal Justice and Behavior, 17,* 134–142.

Lipsey, M. W. (1989). *The efficacy of intervention for juvenile delinquency: Results from 400 studies.* Paper presented at the 41st annual meeting of the American Society of Criminology, Reno, Nevada.

Lipsey, M. W. (1992). Juvenile delinquency treatment: A meta-analytic inquiry into the variability of effects. In T. D. Cook, H. Cooper, D. S. Cordray, H. Hartmann, L. V. Hedges, R. J. Light, T. A. Louis, & F. Mosteller (Eds.), *Meta-analysis for explanation: A casebook* (pp. 83–127). New York, NY: Russell Sage Foundation.

Lipsey, M. W. (1995). What do we learn from 400 research studies on the effectiveness of treatment with juvenile delinquents? In J. McGuire (Ed.), *What works: Reducing reoffending: Guidelines from research and practice* (pp. 63–78). Chichester, UK: John Wiley & Sons.

Lipsey, M. W., & Wilson, D. B. (1997). *Effective intervention for serious juvenile offenders: A synthesis of research.* A paper prepared for the OJJDP Study Group on Serious and Violent Juvenile Offenders, Vanderbilt University.

Lösel, F. (1995). The efficacy of correctional treatment: A review and synthesis of meta-evaluations. In J. McGuire (Ed.), *What works: Reducing reoffending: Guidelines from research and practice* (pp. 79–111). Chichester, UK: John Wiley & Sons.

Lösel, F. (1996). Effective correctional programming: What empirical research tells us and what it doesn't. *Forum on Corrections Research, 8*(3), 33–36.

Lösel, F. (1998). *The importance of offender programming: German and international evaluations.* A paper presented at the International Beyond Prisons Symposium, March 15–19, 1998, Donald Gordon Centre, Queen's University, Kingston, ON.

Mayer, J. P., Gensheimer, L. K., Davidson, W. S., & Gottschalk. (1986). Social learning treatment within juvenile justice: A meta-analysis of impact in the natural environment. In S. J. Apter & A. Goldstein (Eds.), *Youth violence: Programs and prospects.* Elmsford, NY: Pergamon.

McGuire, J., & Priestley, P. (1995). Reviewing what works: Past, present and future. In J. McGuire (Ed.), *What works: Reducing reoffending—Guidelines for research and practice* (pp. 3–34). Chichester, UK: John Wiley & Sons.

Palmer, T. (1974, March). The Youth Authority's community treatment project. *Federal Probation,* 3–14.

Palmer, T. (1975). Martinson revisited. *Journal of Research in Crime and Delinquency, 12,* 133–152.

Patterson, G. R. (1982). *Coercive family process.* Eugene, OR: Cascadia.

Trotter, C. (1999). *Working with involuntary clients: A guide to practice.* London, UK: Sage Publications.

Van Voorhis, P., Braswell, M., & Lester, D. L. (1997). *Correctional counseling and rehabilitation.* Cincinnati, OH: Anderson.

Warren, M. (1971). Classification of offenders as an aid to efficient management and effective treatment. *Journal of Crime, Law, Criminology, and Police Science, 62,* 239–258.

21
Substance Abuse Treatment in US Prisons

Roger H. Peters
Marc L. Steinberg

One of the reasons for the increase in the U.S. prison population is an increase in drug-related crimes, combined with current "get tough" policies. Having more inmates with substance abuse problems leads one to easily conclude that substance abuse needs to be addressed if offenders are going to be successfully reintegrated into the community.

Providing treatment in prison has been offered as an important ingredient to successful rehabilitation. Roger H. Peters and Marc L. Steinberg briefly review the history of substance abuse treatment in corrections and provide an overview of efforts in prisons. The authors discuss a number of programs and initiatives from across the country. Perhaps more important, they reiterate that programs meeting certain principles appear to be more effective than those that do not. In summary, these authors conclude that inmates who participate in and complete substance abuse programs in prisons are more likely than others to experience post-release success.

US federal and state prisons have grown dramatically in the last decade, and now include over a million male inmates and 68,000 female inmates (US Department of Justice, 1996a). During the 1980s, state prisoner populations increased by 237 percent and federal prisoner populations increased by 311 percent. Due to prison overcrowding, many states have begun to house prisoners in local jails, including eight states that currently hold more than 10 percent of their prison population in jails. Prison populations are expected to continue growing by 24 percent from 1995 to 2000 (US General Accounting Office, 1996), a figure that does not include more than 500,000 state and federal inmates held in local jails. Rates of prison incarceration (number of prisoners per 100,000 US residents) have also been rising steadily. From 1980 to 1995, incarceration rates increased by 191 percent for state prisoners and 245 percent for federal prisoners. The prison incarceration rate in 1995 was 428 inmates per 100,000 US residents (US General Accounting Office, 1996), and 600 per 100,000 US residents for incarceration in either jails or prisons, which is the highest rate for any developed country in the world.

Several factors contributing to the rapid increase in the US population include changes in law enforcement practices, sentencing law and policy, and in policies regarding release from incarceration. An increase in drug-related crime has also been linked to the surge of cocaine use that began in the mid-1980s and that has continued steadily since that time. Major law enforcement practices that have influenced arrest and incarceration rates include drug 'stings' and 'reverse sting' operations that target street-level users and sellers.

Several legislative changes have also contributed to the rise in US prison populations. The Sentencing Reform Act of 1984 abolished parole for federal offenders and limited time off for good behaviour to 54 days per year. Many state and federal prisoners incarcerated for drug offences (e.g., drug sales) are no longer eligible for parole and must serve mandatory minimum sentences as a result of legislation such as the Anti-Drug Abuse Act passed in 1986. Mandatory minimum sentences have led to increases in time served in federal prisons for drug offences from an average of 22 to 33 months (US Department of Justice, 1995a). Changes in legislation and law enforcement strategies have led to an increase in the proportion of prisoners incarcerated for drug-related charges, from 8 percent in 1980, to 26 percent in 1993. Significantly more federal prisoners are drug offenders than state prisoners (60 percent *vs.* 22 percent; US General Accounting Office, 1996). . . .

Standards and Guidelines for Prison Treatment Services

The following section reviews the legal contours and professional standards that have emerged over the last 20 years to guide the development of substance abuse treatment services in prisons. As described in this section, the courts have been reluctant to prescribe specific aspects of correctional substance abuse treatment services, but have been much more active in identifying required areas of correctional mental health services. As a result, it is the professional rather than legal standards that have provided the most guidance to prison-based substance abuse treatment programmes in the US.

There are currently no legal mandates for providing a broad scope of substance abuse treatment services in jails or prisons (Peters, 1993). In Marshall *vs.* United States (1974), the Supreme Court ruled that a prisoner did not have a constitutional right to drug treatment. In Pace *vs.* Fauver (1979), a district court in New Jersey found that the Eighth Amendment was not violated by failing to provide treatment for alcoholism in a corrections setting. In this case, the court interpreted the Estelle *vs.* Gamble (1976) ruling to mean that the relevant medical condition must be of sufficient seriousness, and must be easily recognisable by a lay person or diagnosed by a physician.

The US Supreme Court has determined that prisons cannot ignore the 'serious medical needs' of an inmate (see the 'deliberate indifference' requirement of Estelle *vs.* Gamble, 1976). The Fourth Circuit Court of Appeals also ruled that there is no distinc-

tion between the right to medical treatment for prisoners and the right to mental health treatment (Bowring *vs.* Godwin, 1977). Another Court of Appeals (McCuckin *vs.* Smith, 1992) determined that a *serious medical need* would exist if non-treatment of the condition could result in further significant injury or unnecessary infliction of pain, impairment in daily activities, or presence of chronic and substantial pain. Substance use disorders would not ordinarily fit these court-described conditions unless there were acute and life-threatening consequences (e.g., acute withdrawal symptoms, suicidal behaviour, or other acute physical conditions related to alcohol or drug toxicity; Cohen, 1993). Thus, constitutionally required substance abuse services for prison inmates appear to be quite circumscribed, and include screening, assessment, and treatment (e.g., crisis intervention, medically supervised detoxification) of acute and life-threatening physical symptoms related to substance use.

In two separate cases, the Court of Appeals of New York (Griffin *vs.* Coughlin, 1996);[1] and the Seventh Circuit Court of Appeals (Kerr *vs.* Farrey, 1996) have recently restricted US prisons from creating special privileges (e.g., family visitation, placement in minimum security facilities, opportunity to earn parole) that are contingent upon participation in self-help programmes such as Alcoholics Anonymous (AA) or Narcotics Anonymous (NA). The courts determined that these programmes contained 'explicit religious content', and that mandatory involvement in such programmes violates constitutional provisions for separation of church and state. As a result of these rulings, and to encourage wider inmate participation in treatment services, many prison systems are exploring the use of alternative self-help programmes, such as Secular Organization for Sobriety (SOS), SMART Recovery, and Rational Recovery (National Commission on Correctional Health Care, 1997).

In the absence of legal standards for providing substance abuse treatment in prisons, several sets of professional standards and guidelines have been developed. However, agencies that have developed these standards do not currently perform regulatory functions to insure that standards related to substance abuse treatment or other health care services have been implemented as intended. The American Correctional Association (ACA; 1990a), in cooperation with the Commission on Accreditation for Corrections has developed several standards for correctional institutions that are relevant to substance abuse treatment services. The ACA recommends written policies and procedures for clinical management of inmates with substance use disorders in the following areas:

- Diagnosis of chemical dependency by a physician.
- Determination by a physician as to whether an individual requires non-pharmacologically or pharmacologically supported care.
- Individualised treatment plans developed and implemented by a multidisciplinary team.
- Referrals to specified community resources upon release when appropriate.

The ACA and NCCHC standards also identify several items related to the substance abuse history that should be included in preliminary screenings.

The Report of the National Task Force of Correctional Substance Abuse Strategies (US Department of Justice, 1991), the National Institute on Corrections (NIC) describes several general guidelines for substance abuse treatment services provided in prison and other correctional settings. In 1993, the Substance Abuse and Mental Health Services Administration, Centre for Substance Abuse Treatment published a set of guidelines for implementing correctional substance abuse treatment programmes,

developed through Project RECOVERY (Wexler, 1993). The guidelines called for the creation of comprehensive state plans for substance abuse treatment services within corrections systems, and planning at the institutional level. Several components of correctional treatment programmes that are recommended by CSAT and NIC include the following:

- Standardised screening and assessment approaches.
- Matching to different levels or types of treatment services.
- Individual treatment plans.
- Case management services.
- Use of cognitive-behavioural/social learning and self-help approaches, including interventions that address criminal beliefs and values.
- Relapse prevention services.
- Self-help groups (e.g., AA, NA).
- Use of therapeutic communities.
- Isolated treatment units.
- Drug testing.
- Continuity of services, including linkages to parole and community-based treatment services.
- Programme evaluation.
- Cross-training of staff.

Overview of the Correctional Treatment Literature

Although Martinson long ago retracted his conclusion that 'nothing works' in correctional treatment (1979), this belief has persisted over time among policymakers and administrators. A significant number of studies conducted since the time of Martinson's work have provided consistent evidence of positive outcomes associated with correctional treatment programmes. Several literature reviews and meta-analyses have reviewed findings from these studies (Andrews, *et al.*, 1990; Gendreau, 1996;

Gendreau and Goggin, 1997; Gendreau and Ross, 1984), and have identified principles of effective correctional treatment programmes. Although these reviews include several programmes that are not dedicated to substance abuse treatment, they are instructive in identifying common principles which are likely to enhance the effectiveness of correctional treatment settings. Across different types of therapeutic programmes developed and tested in correctional settings, those based on social learning, cognitive-behavioural models, skills training, and family systems approaches have proven to be the most effective (Cullen and Gendreau, 1989). Programmes based on non-directive approaches, the medical model, or involving a focus on punishment or deterrence have proven to be 'ineffective'. In reviewing the correctional treatment literature, Gendreau (1996) has identified eight key principles of effective programmes:

1. Intensive services are behavioural in nature. Services should occupy from 40–50 percent of offenders time, and should be of 3–9 months in duration. Programmes should use token economies, modelling, and cognitive-behavioural interventions designed to change offenders' 'cognitions, attitudes, values, and expectations that maintain antisocial behaviour'.

2. Programmes should target the 'criminogenic needs of high-risk offenders' including substance abuse, antisocial attitudes and behaviours, peer associations, and self-control. Risk assessment measures should be provided to identify these 'criminogenic needs'.

3. Treatment programmes should be multimodal, and should match services according to the learning style and personality characteristics of the offender, and to the characteristics of the therapist/counselor.

4. Programmes should include a structured set of incentives and sanctions. This system must be developed and maintained by staff, with ongoing monitoring of antisocial behaviours within treatment units, and positive reinforcers exceeding negative sanctions by an approximate 4:1 ratio.

5. Therapists or counselors should be selected on the basis of effective counseling and interpersonal skills. Staff should have at least an undergraduate degree or equivalent, training in criminal behaviour and offender treatment, and on-the-job training in use of behavioural interventions. Quality of counseling services should be monitored regularly.

6. Programmes should provide a prosocial treatment environment that reduces negative peer influences.

7. Relapse prevention strategies should be provided that provide skills in anticipating and avoiding problem situations, and rehearsing prosocial responses to these situations. Training should be provided to family and friends to reinforce prosocial behaviours, and booster sessions should be provided following release to the community.

8. Linkage and referral to community services should be provided.

These principles of effective correctional treatment reflect several key components of professional standards and guidelines that have been developed by ACA, CSAT, NCCHC, and NIC, including the need for treatment matching, staff training, cognitive-behavioural interventions, relapse prevention services, isolated treatment units, and linkage and referral to community services. However, these principles also point to several new areas that are not incorporated within the standards and guidelines, and/or that have not been implemented widely in prison treatment programmes. These new areas include the following: (1) targeting inmates with significant risk for recidivism and relapse, (2) use of cognitive-behavioural interventions, (3) a focus on criminal thinking, values, behaviours, and impulse control issues, and (4) minimum education requirements for staff of at least a college degree. A major challenge for US prison treatment programmes over the next several decades will be to closely examine principles of effective correctional treatment and to begin to implement these within the context of new or existing substance abuse treatment programmes.

Prison-Based Substance Abuse Treatment Programmes

The following section describes several new substance abuse treatment initiatives developed within US federal and state prison systems during the last 15 years. Several of the programmes described in this section have thrived over a long period of time, while several other programmes have just recently been developed (Chaiken, 1989; Lipton, 1995). Research findings from these programmes demonstrate the effectiveness of correctional substance abuse treatment programmes in reducing substance abuse and criminal recidivism following release from prison (Falkin, Wexler, and Lipton, 1992).

Federal Bureau of Prisons Drug Abuse Programmes

The Federal Bureau of Prisons was one of the first agencies to respond to the recent drug abuse epidemic by developing a comprehensive system of treatment services for prison inmates (Murray, 1992; 1996). The Bureau's Drug Abuse Programmes (DAP's) include four different levels of treatment services (Lipton, 1995; Federal Bureau of Prisons, 1996a,b; 1997). The first level includes a 40-hour drug education programme attended by all prisoners who meet admission criteria. The second level of treatment involves 'non-residential' drug

abuse treatment, in which treatment participants are not isolated from the general prison community. Residential treatment services are provided in the third level, in which participants are isolated from the general inmate population. Thirty four of the Bureau's prisons have a residential treatment programme, which are of varying length (6, 9, or 12 months), and include a minimum of 500 hours of treatment services (Federal Bureau of Prisons, 1996b; Weinman and Lockwood, 1993).

The Bureau's programmes also include transitional services following release from prison. Inmates may be released either to the US Probation Office or to a Community Corrections Centre, which are privately contracted, supervised halfway houses. Transitional treatment services are similar to those obtained in prison, and include ongoing counseling, regular drug testing, and assistance to obtain employment. A comprehensive longitudinal study is underway to examine long-term treatment outcomes for participants in the Bureau of Prisons treatment programmes.

California's Amity Prison Therapeutic Community

California's Amity Prison Therapeutic Community is a 200-bed unit located at the R. J. Donovan Correctional Facility [and] is based on the Stay'n Out programme in New York. The prison treatment programme consists of three phases, including a 2 to 3 month orientation phase. In the second phase, participants assist in daily operations of the therapeutic community and act as role models to newer participants. The third phase of treatment lasts for 1–3 months and involves decision-making skills related to recovery, and developing a plan for re-entry to the community. Following release from the prison, graduates are offered up to one year of aftercare treatment in a therapeutic community programme that serves up to 40 residents.

A recent evaluation of California's Amity prison programme indicated favourable outcomes associated with participation in prison treatment (Lipton, 1995, 1996; Simpson, *et al.*, 1996). Rates of reincarceration during a one year follow-up period after release from prison were 43 percent for those who completed the treatment programme, compared to 63 percent for prisoners not participating in the programme, and 50 percent for those who dropped out of the programme (Lipton, 1995). Only 26 percent of individuals who were placed in an aftercare programme following graduation from the in-prison treatment programme were reincarcerated during the same period. Similar patterns of follow-up outcomes were found in relation to participant drug use.

Delaware's Key-Crest Programme

The 'Key' Programme was established in 1987 by the Delaware Department of Corrections (Hooper, Lockwood, and Inciardi, 1993; Inciardi, 1996; Inciardi *et al.*, 1992; Pan, Scarpiti, Inciardi, and Lockwood, 1993). One year of treatment services are provided for male prisoners in a 140-bed therapeutic community that is modelled after New York's Stay'n Out programme. The Key Programme is unique in that a 6 month transitional phase (Crest Outreach Centre) is provided following completion of the in-prison programme, which includes 'Key' participants and other offenders who are supervised in the community. In the Crest programme, prisoners may hold jobs in the community while residing in the therapeutic community programme (Inciardi, 1996). A six month aftercare component is included as the last phase of the Crest programme.

In a recent evaluation of the Key and Crest programmes, researchers compared four groups who had participated in varying levels of programme services: (1) Key programme only, (2) Crest programme only, (3) combined Key-Crest programmes, and (4) an HIV prevention/education 'control' programme. Six month follow-up results indicated that individuals participating in the Crest programme (only) and the combined Key and Crest programmes were significantly less likely to use drugs or to be arrested than participants in the Key (only) and the control group (Martin, Butzin, and Inciardi, 1995). Positive outcomes associated with the Crest (only) and combined Key/Crest programmes were still evident after controlling for the effects for time spent in treatment.

Florida's Tier Programmes

The Florida Department of Corrections (FDOC) has a long history of supporting innovative prison-based substance abuse treatment. In the early 1970s, with funding through the Law Enforcement Assistance Act (LEAA), FDOC developed several of the first prison therapeutic communities in the country, in addition to specialised treatment programmes for female inmates and youthful offenders (Chaiken, 1989; Florida Department of Corrections, 1995; 1996). Comprehensive Substance Abuse Treatment Programmes are provided in 46 major correctional institutions, 31 community correctional centres, and 7 community facilities.

Inmates are placed in several 'tiers' of treatment services. Tier I services consist of 40 hours of drug education services per week, including an orientation to the importance of substance abuse treatment, and group counseling. Tier II programmes provide treatment for approximately 40 inmates at a time over a period of 4–6 months. Tier III programmes provide 4 months of treatment in an intensive therapeutic community setting and include orientation, treatment, and reentry phases. Tier IV services include 6–12 months of treatment in a residential therapeutic community in 12 institutions, and in seven community based facilities, including a 54-bed treatment programme for inmates placed on work release.

New York's Stay'n Out Programme

One of the longest operating correctional treatment programmes in the US is the Stay'n Out Programme in New York, which provides a highly structured therapeutic community (Wexler and Williams, 1986). In 1989, the New York legislature appropriated $1 billion to augment drug abuse treatment efforts in New York state prisons, which included one 750-bed and seven 200-bed substance abuse treatment facilities (Lipton, 1995).

Outcomes from the Stay'n Out programme were compared to those from milieu treatment, short-term counseling services, a waiting list, and a no-treatment control group (Wexler, Falkin, and Lipton, 1990; Wexler, Falkin, Lipton, and Rosenblum, 1992). Significantly fewer Stay'n Out participants were arrested during follow-up on supervised parole (lasting an average of 3 years) in comparison to other groups (27 percent *vs.* 35 percent in milieu treatment, 40 percent in group or individual counseling, and 41 percent in a no-treatment comparison group). However, there was no evidence that the Stay'n Out programme delayed the time to arrest during follow-up. Positive outcomes were correlated with increasing time in treatment up to one year; but after this duration, positive outcomes began to decline.

Oregon Department of Corrections

Oregon's Cornerstone Programme opened in 1976, and was modelled after the Stay'n Out programme in New York, but with a higher proportion of professionals and trained correction officers (Lipton, 1994; 1995). The Cornerstone programme is housed in a 32-bed residential unit in the Oregon State Hospital. Four phases of treatment are provided over a period of 10–12 months, followed by 6 months of aftercare/transitional services while under parole supervision (Field, 1989).

Several other modified therapeutic community programmes have recently been developed by the Oregon Department of Corrections, including the Turning Point Alcohol and Drug Programme at the Columbia River Correctional Institution, and the Powder River Alcohol and Drug (PRAD) Programme at the Powder River Correctional Facility. The Turning Point programme provides a 50-bed unit for females and a similar unit for males, while the PRAD Programme provides a 50-bed male unit. The Turning Point treatment programme serves as a pre-release institution for female inmates. In 1989, the Parole Transition Release (PTR) Project was initiated by the Oregon Department of Corrections in Washington County, Oregon, with funding from several federal agencies. Treatment services are provided for 35 offenders over a period of approximately 9 months. Treatment begins prior to release from prison, and continues in the community (Field and Karecki, 1992).

An evaluation of the Cornerstone Programme indicates that treatment participants experience significant reductions in re-arrest and recommitment to prison, in comparison to other groups of inmates. Field (1989; 1992) found that rates of re-arrest and reincarceration during follow-up were inversely related to the time spent in the treatment programme. Only 26 percent of Cornerstone Programme graduates were recommitted to prison during a three year follow-up period, as compared to 85 percent of individuals who dropped out of the programme after less than 2 months of participation, 67 percent of nongraduates who completed from 2–5 months of treatment, and 63 percent of non-graduates who completed at least 6 months of treatment.

The Texas Criminal Justice Treatment Initiative

In 1991, under the stewardship of Texas Governor Ann Richards, legislation was enacted to create the Texas Criminal Justice Treatment Initiative, the largest state prison treatment programme in the country at that time. This initiative originally provided $95 million for development of Substance Abuse Felony Punishment (SAFP) programmes and In-Prison Therapeutic Community Treatment (ITC) programmes. The initiative also provided funding for alternatives to incarceration programmes and Transitional Treatment Centres, which are community-based facilities for offenders who have completed a SAFP or ITC programme.

As originally enacted, legislation in Texas authorised the development of 12,000 secure treatment beds within the SAFP programme and corresponding space in community residential and non-residential programmes. The scope of SAFP and ITC programmes have since been substantially reduced by the legislature (Texas Department of Criminal Justice, 1997).

The Substance Abuse Felony (SAFP) System allows those with substance abuse problems who are convicted of non-violent felonies to enter long term (6–12 months) substance abuse treatment as a condition of parole or probation. Programme graduates then participate in 15 months of transitional services. State prisoners are eligible to participate in the In-Prison Therapeutic Community Treatment (ITC) programme, which provides drug treatment services for inmates who are within 9–10 months of parole.

Knight *et al.* (1997) report that ITC graduates are significantly less likely to be involved in criminal activity (7 percent *vs.* 16 percent arrested; 28 percent *vs.* 47 percent reported drug-related offences; and 41 percent *vs.* 55 percent involved in criminal activity as determined by any source), are less likely to have a parole violation 6 months after leaving prison (29 percent *vs.* 48 percent), and were less likely to use alcohol or other drugs, in contrast to an untreated comparison group. ITC graduates who went on to complete the ITC aftercare programme within the 6 month follow-up time frame were found to have lower recidivism rates than non-completers and a comparison group consisting of parolees, and fewer ITC completers used cocaine than the untreated comparison group.

The National Treatment Improvement Evaluation Study

The National Treatment Improvement Evaluation Study (NTIES; Centre for Substance Abuse Treatment, 1997) was conducted by CSAT to determine the long range outcomes of individuals involved in federally funded treatment programmes. Outcome data were obtained for over 4411 individuals, including 709 individuals from the 'correctional' sample, which consisted of 56 percent prison inmates and 44 percent offenders from other criminal justice settings. Participants in correctional treatment experienced the greatest reductions in self-reported criminal behaviour (e.g., 81 percent reduction in selling drugs) and in arrests (66 percent reduction in drug possession arrests, 76 percent reduction in all arrests) among all other types of treatment settings/modalities examined in the NTIES study. Reduced drug use and enhanced mental health and physical health functioning were also observed during follow-up among the correctional sample.

Correctional Treatment of Special Needs Populations

Co-occurring Mental Health and Substance Use Disorders

Rates of both mental health disorders and substance use disorders are significantly higher among offenders than in non-incarcerated populations in the community (Keith, Regier, and Rae, 1991; Weissman, Bruce, Leaf, Florio, and Holzer, 1992; Robins and Regier, 1991). For example, rates of mental health disorders are four times higher among prisoners than in the general population, and rates of substance use are four to seven times higher (Robins and Regier, 1991). In the absence of epidemiological data, it is estimated that 3–11 percent of prison inmates have co-occurring mental health and substance use disorders (Peters and Hills, 1993). Over 600,000 US prison inmates have either a serious mental illness or a substance use disorder, and approximately 130,000 inmates have co-occurring disorders (National GAINS Centre, 1997).

As in community settings, co-occurring disorders are often undetected or untreated in correctional settings. One survey found that many correctional systems had not developed procedures for compiling information regarding the rates of co-occurring disorders in their institutions (Peters and Hills, 1993). Non-detection of co-occurring disorders often leads to misdiagnosis, over-treatment of mental health symptoms with medications, neglect of appropriate interventions, inappropriate treatment planning and referral, and poor treatment outcomes (Drake, Alterman, and Rosenberg, 1993; Hall, Popleis, Stickney, and Gardner, 1978; Teague, Schwab, and Drake, 1990). There are several reasons for the non-detection of mental health and substance use disorders within correctional systems. These include negative consequences perceived by inmates for disclosing symptoms, lack of staff training in diagnosis and management of mental health disorders, and cognitive and perceptual difficulties associated with severe mental illness or toxic effects of recent alcohol or drug use.

Inmates with co-occurring disorders present a number of challenges in correctional settings, and manifest more severe psychosocial problems than other inmates (Peters, Kearns, Murrin, and Dolente, 1992) related to employment, family relationships, and physical health. Offenders with co-occurring disorders are more likely to drop out of treatment or to be terminated from treatment, are more likely to be hospitalised, and are thought to be at greater risk for suicide and criminal recidivism (Peters and Bartoi, 1997). Individuals with co-occurring disorders often do not fit well into existing treatment programmes (Carey, 1991). Once involved in treatment, these individuals do not respond as well as others with single diagnoses (Bowers, Mazure, Nelson, and Jatlow, 1990).

Integrated approaches should be used in screening and assessment of co-occurring disorders among prison inmates (Peters and Bartoi, 1997). Relevant criminal justice, mental health, and substance use information should be reviewed in both screening and assessment of co-occurring disorders. Screening is useful in determining the relationship between co-occurring disorders and prior criminal behaviour, the interaction of these disorders, and motivation for treatment. Because of the high rates of co-occurring disorders in prisons, detection of a single disorder (i.e., either mental health or substance use) should immediately 'trigger' screening for the other type of disorder. Screening and assessment should include an interview, use of self-report and diagnostic instruments as needed, and review of archival records. In the absence of integrated instruments for examining co-occurring disorders, screening and assessment in prisons should include a combination of mental health and substance abuse instruments.

A number of recent initiatives in jails and prisons have been developed to address the treatment needs of this population, including several programmes developed within state prisons in Alabama, Colorado, Delaware, Oregon, and Texas, and one programme in the Federal Bureau of Prisons (*et al.*, 1997). The in-prison dual diagnosis programmes share several features. First, programme staff have experience and training in both mental health and substance abuse treatment. Second, although the disorders were not always addressed simultaneously, both are treated as 'primary' disorders. In addition, each of the programmes utilise psychopharmacological and self-help services, and individual counseling is provided to supplement prisoners' involvement in several standard 'phases' or 'levels' of treatment. Lastly, each of the correctional treatment programmes provide a longterm focus, and recognise the importance of continued treatment following release from prison.

Most programmes for dually diagnosed inmates include a set of structured 'phases' or 'levels' of treatment, which are progressively less intensive over time. Phases of treatment often include an orientation phase focusing on motivation and engagement in treatment, intensive treatment, and relapse prevention and transition services. Aftercare, or linkage to other services is especially important to dually diagnosed prisoners due to their increased vulnerability to relapse (Peters and Hills, 1993). Most existing correctional dual diagnosis programmes provide reentry services to facilitate the transition to aftercare treatment services, work release programmes, or halfway houses (Edens, *et al.*, 1997). Several modifications made to correctional dual diagnosis programmes include smaller client caseloads, use of psycho-educational groups, shorter duration of treatment sessions, and more streamlined content of didactic and process group sessions. These programmes also tend to provide less peer confrontation than in most substance abuse treatment programmes (McLaughlin and Pepper, 1991; Sacks and Sacks, 1995).

Treatment of Female Inmates

From 1986 to 1991, the population of female prisoners increased by 75 percent (Kline, 1993). The growth rate of female prisoners has exceeded that of males, rising at a rate of 12 percent per year since 1980 (Bureau of Justice Statistics, 1994). This growth reflects a substantial influx of individuals arrested for drug-related crimes.

According to the Bureau of Justice Statistics (1994), more than half of incarcerated females committed their crimes under the influence of drugs or alcohol.

Female offenders were found to have higher scores on several scales of the Addiction Severity Index (ASI; McLellan, *et al.*, 1992; Peters, Strozier, Murrin, and Kearns, 1997), reflecting significantly more impairment than males related to drug use, employment, legal status, and psychiatric/psychological functioning (males were more impaired on the scale related to alcohol use). Female offenders were also more likely to report psychiatric problems such as serious depression and anxiety (Peters, *et al.*, 1997).

Fewer than 11 percent of female offenders are involved in substance abuse treatment (Wellisch, Anglin, and Prendergast, 1993a), although a recent survey (American Correctional Association, 1990b) of state prisons indicated that over 40 percent of female inmates needed substance abuse treatment. Specialised and intensive services for female offenders are less likely to be offered in programmes that serve both men and women, in comparison to those serving female inmates exclusively (Wellisch, Prendergast, and Anglin, 1994). Correctional treatment programmes for women are often of limited intensity and duration, do not assess the full range of psychosocial problems among substance abusing female inmates, and do not have sufficient resources to treat the majority of these problems (e.g., sexual abuse, domestic violence; Wellisch, Prendergast, and Anglin, 1994).

Several recommendations for developing correctional substance abuse treatment programmes for women are provided by Wellisch, Anglin, and Prendergast (1993b). These include: (1) developing support for specialised female treatment programmes within the corrections system and in the community, (2) providing a continuum of care, (3) transition planning prior to release from prison, (4) ongoing supervision following release to the community, and (5) procedures for data collection and programme evaluation. Some have called for adoption of a 'co-occurring disorders' treatment model in developing services for substance abusing female inmates, based on the multiple and interrelated psychosocial problems manifested by this population (Peters, *et al.*, 1997). The authors recommend that several key principles in treating co-occurring disorders be considered in developing substance abuse services for female inmates. These principles include the following:

- Mental health services should be a central component of treatment, and not isolated from correctional substance abuse services for women.

- When multiple psychosocial problems are present, each should be treated as equally important as the foci of clinical interventions.

- Co-occurring problems should be treated simultaneously rather than sequentially.

- Integrative assessment and treatment approaches should be used that consider the interactive nature of different problems.

- The sequence of treatment services for female inmates should be determined by areas of more severe functional disturbance. These areas should be addressed earlier in the course of treatment.

- An extended assessment 'baseline' should be provided, reflecting the complexity of psychosocial problems among substance abusing female inmates.

- Correctional and treatment staff should receive training regarding the nature of co-occurring problems/disorders, and their interactive effects.

As with other correctional substance abuse treatment services, programmes for female inmates should be geographically isolated from the general prison population, whenever possible. Roles of correctional officers and treatment staff should be easily distinguishable to reduce conflicts regarding security and treatment issues, and to enhance confidentiality of clinical information shared with staff during treatment. Wellisch, *et al.* (1993b) describe the importance of clearly defining staff roles for dealing with particular rule infractions. Flexibility should be provided in responding to these situations. Correctional treatment programmes should be staffed by females with professional training, and who can serve as role models.

Optimally, correctional treatment programmes for females should include means for participants to maintain contact with their children, since separation from children may greatly influence recovery goals and engagement in treatment (Wellisch, *et al.*, 1993b). Female prisoners often are released to the community as the primary financial provider for their children, yet often do not have adequate job training. Vocational training and job readiness services should be a major component of correctional substance abuse programmes for women. Proper health care is also especially important for female inmates, since many have histories of physical or sexual abuse. They may also have recently given birth, or may be pregnant at the time of incarceration (Wellisch, *et al.*, 1993a, 1993b).

One exemplary substance abuse treatment programme for female inmates is the Passages Programme for Women, developed by the Wisconsin Department of Corrections (Wellisch, *et al.*, 1993b). This programme was created in 1988, through funding by the US Department of Justice. The Passages Programme is a 12 week programme, involving 8 hours of treatment programming per day, 5 days per week in the Women's Correctional Centre (WCC). Programme services are provided for 15 inmates in an isolated treatment unit.

The 12 week Passages Programme includes three phases. The first phase is based on the 12-step approach, but also addresses relapse issues and personal values. The second phase of the programme promotes development of interpersonal skills, while the third phase uses role playing and other techniques to develop coping skills such as assertiveness training, conflict resolution, and communication skills. Programme participants are required to attend at least two AA/NA/CA meetings per week, and receive random drug testing throughout their involvement in the programme. After completion of treatment, inmates are provided re-entry services, or are enrolled in a work/study release programme.

Summary

US prison populations have swelled to over a million inmates since the mid-1980's, due to an ongoing drug epidemic that has been fuelled by decreasing prices of cocaine and availability of relatively cheap synthetic drugs (e.g., 'crystal' methamphetamine), law enforcement efforts targeting street level drug sales, and legislation that has provided more severe penalties for drug-related offences. As traditional punitive approaches have failed to stem the tide of illicit drug use and drug related crime in the community, administrators and policymakers have begun to consider the expansion of treatment and rehabilitative services in prisons. Approximately 55 percent of US prisoners have an alcohol or drug use disorder at the time of incarceration, although only about 10 percent of prisoners currently receive any form of substance abuse treatment. Many of these existing prison treatment programmes are not comprehensive in scope, although several exemplary and intensive initiatives have been developed in recent years.

The history of correctional substance abuse treatment in the US is characterised by significant variability in support and funding. Federal involvement in correctional treatment was encouraged by the Porter Act in 1929 and the Narcotic Addict Rehabilitation Act of 1966, while various state commitment laws enacted in the 1960s encouraged broad use of hospitalisation for narcotic addicts. Although Martinson's bleak review of the correctional treatment literature (1974) summoned a new era of pessimism and decreased funding with regard to prison substance abuse programmes, the 1980s brought a resurgence of interest and support for these programmes. Specialised projects funded by the US Department of Justice and the Substance Abuse and Mental Health Administration have provided significant technical assistance to prison substance abuse treatment programmes, and encouraged dissemination of information regarding effective treatment approaches. Standards and guidelines for implementation of prison treatment programmes have been developed by these and other agencies during the 1980s and 1990s, which provide recommended parameters for screening, assessment, treatment, supervision, evaluation, and other key activities. The courts have not actively defined requirements for correctional substance abuse treatment services, other than providing screening and treatment of acute and life-threatening symptoms such as withdrawal from dependency on alcohol or opiates. The courts recently have enjoined prisons from providing privileges that are contingent on involvement in religious-based treatment (e.g., 12-step programmes).

A number of substance abuse treatment programmes have been developed in US prisons during the past 20 years. These efforts have been supported by federal initiatives such as the CSAT Model Programmes for Correctional Populations, the Byrne Formula Grant Programme, and the more recent Residential Substance Abuse Treatment Formula Grant Program. As described in previous sections, many of the correctional substance abuse treatment programmes share common elements and programme structures. In many cases, programme similarities have emerged as a result of federal initiatives such as Project REFORM and RECOVERY, which encouraged adoption of common elements of treatment through co-ordinated training and consultation activities. Examples of programme similarities include the widespread use of therapeutic communities, that emphasise accountbility to peers and treatment staff, involvement in daily operations and governance of the treatment community, development of prosocial behaviours through a social learning model, and graduated levels of responsibility and privileges.

Each of the US correctional substance abuse treatment programmes that are profiled in this chapter endorse the goal of major lifestyle change, pursuant to abstinence. Most programmes also isolate treatment participants from general population inmates to reduce the potentially disruptive effects to the treatment community. Common admission criteria used by correctional treatment programmes include (1) classification as 'low' to 'medium' security risk, (2) no history of institutional violence, (3) at least moderate substance abuse problems, and (4) sufficient time remaining on the sentence to complete the inprison treatment programme (and in some cases, sufficient time on parole to complete an aftercare programme).

Most of the existing US correctional treatment programmes include different phases of treatment. An orientation phase, followed by an intensive treatment phase and transition phase are common to many of these programmes. Within the various phases of treatment, there are several common types of treatment activities offered, including drug and alcohol education, individual and group counseling, life skills training, job training, and relapse prevention. Several programmes offer cognitive-behavioural interventions and activities

designed to reduce criminal thinking errors. Transition services are also a central component to many correctional treatment programmes, and include development of a re-entry plan, linkages with aftercare treatment providers, parole, and other community services.

Evaluations of correctional substance abuse treatment programmes provide consistent support for the effectiveness of these initiatives. Conclusions from several recent empirical reviews of the correctional treatment literature (Gendreau, 1996; Gendreau and Goggin, 1997) depart significantly from the 'nothing works' doctrine that emerged from Martinson's earlier work. These 'meta-analyses' indicate consistently positive outcomes associated with correctional treatment programmes, with more favourable results obtained from programmes that address criminogenic needs of 'high-risk' offenders, that use cognitive-behavioural techniques, that provide relapse prevention activities, that provide a focus on linkage and referral, and that are intensive, of lengthy duration, and multi-modal in approach.

Findings from the large multi-site NTIES study conducted by the Centre for Substance Abuse Treatment (1997) also support the efficacy of correctional treatment, and indicate that participants in these programmes experience greater post-treatment reductions in criminal behaviour than non-offenders enrolled in several different types of community-based programmes. Controlled treatment outcome studies conducted in five state prison systems surveyed in this chapter all point to significant reductions in post-treatment criminal behaviour and improvements in other areas of psychosocial functioning (e.g., reduced drug use, employment). Length of treatment has also been found to be directly related to treatment outcome in these studies, although there appears to be diminishing effects of treatment beyond one year. Inmates who participate in prison treatment that is followed by an aftercare programme in the community have significantly better outcomes (e.g., lower rates of re-arrest and reincarceration) than inmates who receive only the in-prison treatment. Additional research is needed to examine correctional treatment outcomes among samples that include untreated inmates. Moreover, this research should provide extended follow-up periods, and should examine substance abuse, unreported criminal activity, sanctions received while under community supervision, employment, and use of community services, in addition to more traditional measures of arrest and recommitment to prison.

Study Questions

1. According to Peters and Steinberg, what are three reasons that the prison population has increased?

2. What are the guidelines for prisoners' substance abuse treatment services offered by the Centre for Substance Abuse Treatment and the National Institute of Corrections?

3. According to Gendreau, what are the eight key principles of effective programs?

4. What are co-occurring disorders, and what do the authors recommend with regard to treatment?

Note

1. In Coughlin v. Griffin (1997), the US Supreme Court subsequently denied certiorari, allowing the decision to remain standing.

References

American Correctional Association. (1990a) *Standards for adult correctional institutions, 3rd edition*. Washington, D.C.: St. Mary's Press.

American Correctional Association. (1990b) *The female offender: What does the future hold?* Washington, D.C.: St. Mary's Press.

Andrews, D. A., Zinger, I., Hoge, R. D., Bonta, J., Gendreau, P., and Cullen, F. T. (1990) Does correctional treatment work? A clinically relevant and psychologically informed meta-analysis. *Criminology*, 28, 369–404.

Ball, J. C. (1986) The hyper criminal opiate addict. In B. D. Johnson and F. Wish (Eds.), *Crime rates among drug abusing offenders. Final Report to the National Institute of Justice* (pp. 81–104). New York: Narcotic and Drug Research, Inc.

Ball, J. C., Shaffer, J. W., and Nurco, D. N. (1983) Day-to-day criminality of heroin addicts in Baltimore: A study of the continuity, of offense rates. *Drug and Alcohol Dependence*, 12, 119–142.

Bowers, M. B., Mazure, C. M., Nelson, C. J., and Jatlow, P. I. (1990) Psychotogeme drug use and neuroleptic response. *Schizophrenia Bulletin*, 16, 81–85.

Bowring v. Godwin, 551 F.2d 44 (4th Cir. 1977).

Carey, K. G. (1991) Research with dual diagnosis patients: Challenges and recommendations. *The Behaviour Therapist*, 14, 5–8.

Centre for Substance Abuse Treatment. (1997) *NTIES: The National Treatment Improvement Study-Final Report*. Substance Abuse and Mental Health Services Administration, US Department of Health and Human Services. Rockville, MD.

Chaiken, M. (1986) Crime rates and substance abuse among types of offenders. In B. Johnson and E. Wish (Eds.), *Crime rates among drug-abusing offenders*, 12–54. *Final Report to the National Institute of Justice*. New York: Narcotic and Drug Research, Inc.

Chaiken, M. (1989) *In-prison programmes for drug-involved offenders*. Issues and Practices series, National Institute of Justice. Washington, D.C.: US Department of Justice.

Collins, J. J., Hubbard, R. I., and Rachal, J. V. (1985) Expensive drug use in illegal income: A test of explanatory hypothesis. *Criminology*, 23(4), 743–764.

Cohen, F. (1993) Captives' legal rights to mental health care. *Law and Psychology Review*, 17, 1–39.

Coughlin v. Griffin, 117 US 681 (1997).

Cullen, E. T., and Gendreau, P. (1989) The effectiveness of rehabilitation. In L. Goodstein and D. MacKenzie (Eds.), *The American prison: Issues in research policy* (pp. 23–44). New York: Plenum.

Drake, R. E., Alterman, A. I., and Rosenberg, S. R. (1993) Detection of substance use disorders in severely mentally ill patients. *Community Mental Health*, 29(2), 175–192.

Edens, J. F., Peters, R. H., and Hills, H. A. (1997). Treating prison inmates with co-occuring disorders: An integrative review of existing programmes. *Behavioural Sciences and the Law*, 15, 439–457.

Estelle v. Gamble, 429 US 97 (1976).

Falkin, G. P., Wexler, H. K., and Lipton, D. S. (1992) Drug treatment in state prisons. In D. R. Gerstein and H. J. Harwood (Eds.), *Treating drug problems, volume II* (pp. 89–131). Washington, D.C.: National Academy Press.

Federal Bureau of Prisons. (1996a) [On-line] Federal Beareau of Prisons Quick Facts Available: http://www.bop.gov/facts.html#population.

Federal Bureau of Prisons. (1996b) *Drug abuse programme options in the Federal Bureau of Prisons: Third annual report to Congress.* Washington, D.C.: US Department of Justice.

Federal Bureau of Prisons. (1997) *Federal Bureau of Prisons Drug Abuse Treatment Programmes.* Washington, D.C.: US Department of Justice.

Field, G. (1989) *A study of the effects of intensive treatment on reducing the criminal recidivism of addicted offenders.* Salem, Oregon: Oregon Department of Corrections.

Field, G. (1992) Oregon Prison Drug Treatment programmes. In C. Leukefeld and F. Tims (Eds.), *Drug abuse treatment in prisons and jails* (pp. 142–155). Research Monograph Series, Vol. 118. Rockville, MD: National Institute on Drug Abuse.

Field, G., and Karecki, M. (1992) *Outcome study of the Parole Transition Release project.* Salem, Oregon: Oregon Department of Corrections.

Florida Department of Corrections. (1995) *Substance Abuse Programme Services Office: Comprehensive report. 1995.* Tallahassee, Florida.

Florida Department of Corrections. (1996) *1995–96 annual report: The guidebook to corrections in Florida.* Tallahassee, Florida.

Gendreau, P. (1996) The principles of effective intervention with offenders. In A. Harland (Ed.), *Choosing correctional options that work.* Newbury Park, CA: Sage Publications.

Gendreau, P., and Goggin, C. (1997) Correctional treatment: Accomplishments and realities. In P. VanVourbis, M. Braswell, and D. Lester (Eds.), *Correctional counseling and rehabilitation.* Cincinnati, Ohio: Anderson.

Gendreau, P., and Ross, R. R. (1984) Correctional treatment: Some recommendations for successful intervention. *Juvenile and Family Court Journal,* 34, 31–40.

Griffin v. Coughlin. 88 N.Y. 2d 674 (1996).

Hall, R. C., Popleis, M. K., Stickney, S. K., and Gardner, E. E. (1978) Covert outpatient drug abuse. *Journal of Nervous and Mental Disease,* 166, 343–348.

Henneberg, M. (1994) *Bureau of Justice Statistics Fiscal Year 1994 Progam Plan.* Rockville, MD: National Institute of Justce.

Hooper, R. M., Lockwood, D. L., and Inciardi, J. A. (1993) Treatment techniques in corrections based therapeutic communities. *Prison Journal,* 73, 290–306.

Hubbard, R. L., Marsden, M. E., Rachal, J. V., Harwood, H. J., Cavanaugh, E. R., and Ginzburg, H. M. (1989) *Drug abuse treatment: A national study of effectiveness.* Chapel Hill: University of North Carolina Press.

Inciardi, J. A. (1993) Introduction: A response to the War on Drugs. In J. Inciardi (Ed.), *Drug treatment and criminal justice.* Newbury Park, CA: Sage Publications.

Inciardi, J. A. (1996) The therapeutic community: An effective model for corrections-based drug abuse treatment. In K. Early (Ed.), *Drug treatment behind bars: Prison-based strategies for change.* Westport, CT: Praeger Publishers/Greenwood Publishing Group.

Inciardi, J. A. (1996) *A corrections-based continuum of effective drug abuse treatment.* National Institute of Justice. Research Preview. Washington, D.C.: US Department of Justice.

Inciardi, J. A., Martin, S. S., Lockwood, D. L., Hooper, R. M., and Wald, B. M. (1992) Obstacles to the implementation and evaluation of drug treatment programmes in correctional settings: Reviewing the Delaware KEY experience. In C. Leukefeld and F. Tims (Eds.), *Drug treatment in prisons and jails* (pp. 176–191). Research Monograph Series, Vol. 118. Rockville, MD: National Institute on Drug Abuse.

Johnson, B. D., Lipton, D. S., and Wish, E. D. (1986) *Facts about the criminality about heroin and cocaine abusers and some new alternatives to incarceration.* New York: Narcotic and Drug Research, Inc.

Keith, S. J., Regier, D. A., and Rae, D. S. (1991) Schizophrenic disorders. In D. N. Robins and D. A. Regier (Eds.), *Psychiatric disorders in America.* New York: MacMillan.

Kerr v. Farrey, 95 F.3d 472 (1996).

Kline, S. (1993) A profile of female offenders in state and federal prisons. In M. D. Laurel (Ed.), *Female offenders: Meeting needs of a neglected population.* American Correctional Association.

Knight, K., Simpson, D. D., Chatham, L. R., and Camacho, L. M. (1997) An assessment of prison-based drug treatment: Texas' in-prison therapeutic community programme. *Journal of Offender Rehabilitation,* 2(3/4), 75–100.

Leukefeld, C. G. (1985) The clinical connection: Drugs and crime. *International Journal of the Addictions,* 20(6/7), 1049–1064.

Lipton, D. S. (1994) The correctional opportunity: Pathways to drug treatment for offenders. *The Journal of Drug Issues*, 24(2), 331–348.

Lipton, D. S. (1995) *The effectiveness of treatment for drug abusers under criminal justice supervision*. National Institute of Justice Research Report.

Lipton, D. S. (1996) Prison-based therapeutic communities: Their success with drug abusing offenders. *National Institute of Justice Journal*, 12–20.

Lipton, D. S., Martinson, R., and Wilks, J. (1975) *The effectiveness of correctional treatment*. New York: Praeger Publishers.

Marshall v. United States, 414 US 417 (1974).

Martin, S. S., Butzin, C. A., and Inciardi, J. A. (1995) Assessment of a multistage therapeutic community for drug-involved offenders. *Journal of Psychoactive Drugs*, 27(1), 109–116.

Martinson, R. (1974) What works? Questions and answers about prison reform. *The Public Interest*, 35, 22–54.

Martinson, R. (1979) New findings, new views: A note of caution regarding prison reform. *Hofstra Law Review*, 7, 243–258.

McCuckin v. Smith, 974 F.2d 1050 (9th Cir. 1992).

McLaughlin, P., and Pepper, P. (1991) Modifying the therapeutic community for the mentally ill substance abuser. *New Directions for Mental Health Services*, 50, 85–93.

McLellan, A. T., Kushner, H., Metzger, D., Peters, R., Smith, L., Grissom, G., Pettinati, H., and Argeriou, M. (1992) The fifth edition of the Addiction Severity Index. *Journal of Substance Abuse Treatment*, 9, 199–213.

Murray, D. W. (1992) Drug abuse treatment programmes in the Federal Bureau of Prisons: Initiatives for the 1990's. In C. Leukefeld and F. Tims (Eds.), *Drug treatment in prisons and jails* (pp. 62–83). Research Monograph Series. Vol. 118. Rockville, MD: National Institute on Drug Abuse.

Murray, D. W. (1996) Drug abuse treatment in the Federal Bureau of Prisons: A historical review and assessment of contemporary initiatives. In K. Early (Ed.), *Drug treatment behind bars: Prison-based strategies for change*. Westport, CT: Praeger Publishers/Greenwood Publishing Group.

National Commission on Correctional Health Care. (1997) *CorrectCare*, 11(2), 1–17.

National GAINS Centre. (1997) *The prevalence of co-occuring mental and substance abuse disorders in the criminal justice system. Just the Facts series*. Delmar, New York: The National GAINS Centre.

O'Donnell, J. A., and Ball, J. C. (1966) *Narcotic addiction*. New York: Harper and Row.

Pace v. Fauver, 479 F. Supp. 456 (D. N.J. 1979).

Palmer, I. (1996) Growth-centered intervention: An overview of changes in recent decades. In K. Early (Ed.), *Drug treatment behind bars: Prison-based strategies for change*. Westport, CT: Praeger Publishers/Greenwood Publishing Group.

Pan, H., Scarpiti, F. R., Inciardi, J. A., and Lockwood, D. (1993) Some considerations on therapeutic communities in corrections. In J. Inciardi (Ed.), *Drug treatment and criminal justice*. Newbury Park, CA: Sage Publications.

Peters, R. H. (1993) Substance abuse services in jails and prisons. *Law and Psychology Review*, 17, 86–116.

Peters, R. H., and Bartoi, M. G. (1997) *Screening and assessment of co-occurring disorders in the justice system*. Delmar N.Y.: The National GAINS Centre.

Peters, R. H., Greenbaum, P. E., Edens, J. F., Carter, C. R., and Ortiz, M. M. (1998) Prevalence of DSM-IV substance abuse and dependence disorders among prison inmates. *American Journal of Drug and Alcohol Abuse*, 24(1), 573–587.

Peters, R. H., and Hills, H. A. (1993) Inmates with co-occurring substance abuse and mental health disorders. In H. J. Steadman and J. J. Cocozza (Eds.), *Providing services for offenders with mental illness and related disorders in prisons* (pp. 159–212). Washington, D.C.: The National Coalition for the Mentally Ill in the Criminal Justice System.

Peters, R. H., Kearns, W. D., Murrin, M. R., and Dolente, A. S. (1992) Psychopathology and mental health needs among drug involved inmates. *Journal of Prison and Jail Health*, 11(1), 3–25.

Peters, R. H., Strozier, A. I., Murrin, M. R., and Kearns, W. D. (1997) Treatment of substance-abusing jail inmates: Examination of gender differences. *Journal of Substance Abuse Treatment*, 14(4), 339–349.

Robins, D. N., and Regier, D. A. (1991) *Psychiatric disorders in America: The Epidemiologic Catchment Area Study*. New York: Free Press.

Sacks, S., and Sacks, J. (1995) *Recent advances in theory, prevention, and research for dual disorder*. Paper presented at the Middle Eastern institute on Drug Abuse, Jerusalem, Israel.

Simpson, D. D., Joe, G. W., and Bracy, S. (1982) Six-year follow-up of opioid addicts after admission to treatment. *Archives of General Psychiatry*, 39, 1318–1323.

Simpson, D. D., Knight, K., and Pevoto, C. (1996) *Research summary: Focus on drug treatment in criminal justice settings*. Ft. Worth, TX: Institute of Behavioural Research, Texas Christian University.

Speckart, G., and Anglin, D. M. (1986) Narcotics use and crime: A causal modeling approach. *Journal of Quantitative Criminology,* 2, 3–28.

Teague, G. B., Schwab, B., and Drake, R. E. (1990) *Evaluating services for young adults with severe mental illness and substance use disorders.* Arlington, VA: National Association of State Mental Health Programme Directors.

Texas Department of Criminal Justice (1997) *Department of Criminal Justice.* [On-line]. Available: http://www.lbb.state.tx.us/lbb/members/reports/fiscal/fspscj/FS696.htm. [*sic*]

US Department of Justice. (1988) *Drug use and crime: Special report (NCJ.111940).* Washington, D.C.: Bureau of Justice Statistics.

US Department of Justice. (1991) *Intervening with substance-abusing offenders: A framework for action. Report of the National Task Force on Correctional Substance Abuse Strategies.* Washington, D.C.: National Institute of Corrections.

US Department of Justice. (1992) *A national report: Drugs, crime, and the justice system.* Washington, D.C.: Bureau of Justice Statistics.

US Department of Justice. (1994) *Women in prison.* Washington, D.C.: Bureau of Justice Statistics.

US Department of Justice. (1995a) *Prisoners in 1994.* Washington, D.C.: Bureau of Justice Statistics.

US Department of Justice. (1995b) *Drugs and crime facts, 1994.* Rockville, MD: Bureau of Justice Statistics.

US Department of Justice. (1996a) *Prison and Jail Inmates, 1995.* Washington, D.C.: Bureau of Justice Statistics.

US Department of Justice. (1996b) *Crime in the United States, 1995: Uniform Crime Reports.* Washington, D.C.: Federal Bureau of Investigation.

US Department of Justice. (1997a) *Violent Crime Control and Law Enforcement Act of 1994.* [On-line]. Available: http://gopher.usdoj.gov/crime/crime.html [*sic*]

US Department of Justice. (1997b) *Grant Programmes for 1995.* [On-line]. Available: http://gopher.usdoj.gov/crime/ojp_brf.html [*sic*]

US General Accounting Office. (November, 1996) *Federal and State Prisons: Inmate Populations, Costs, and Projection Models.* Report to the Subcommittee on Crime, Committee on the Judiciary, House of Representatives. Washington, D.C.

Weinman, B. A., and Lockwood, D. (1993) Inmate drug treatment programming in the federal bureau of prisons. In J. Inciardi (Ed.), *Drug treat-*

ment and criminal justice (pp. 194–208). Newbury Park, CA: Sage Publications.

Weissman, M. M., Bruce, M. L., Leaf, P. J., Florio, L. P., and Holzer, C. (1992) Affective disorders. In L. N. Robins and D. A. Regier (Eds.), *Psychiatric disorders in America* (pp. 53–80). New York: Macmillan.

Wellisch, J., Anglin, M. D., and Prendergast, M. I. (1993a) Numbers and characteristics of drug using women in the criminal justice system: Implications for treatment. *Journal of Drug Issues,* 23(1), 7–30.

Wellisch, J., Anglin, M. D., and Prendergast, M. L. (1993b) Treatment strategies for drug-abusing women offenders. In J. Inciardi (Ed.), *Drug treatment and criminal justice* (pp. 5–29). Newbury Park, CA: Sage Publications.

Wellisch, J., Prendergast, M. L., and Anglin, M. D. (1994) *Drug-abusing women offenders: Results of a national survey.* Washington, D.C.: Office of Justice Programmes, National Institute of Justice: Research In Brief, US Department of Justice.

Wexler, H. K. (1993) *Establishing substance abuse treatment programmes in prisons: A practitioner's handbook.* Rockville, MD: Centre for Substance Abuse Treatment.

Wexler, H. K., Falkin, G. P., and Lipton, D. S. (1990) Outcome evaluation of a prison therapeutic community for substance abuse treatment. *Criminal Justice and Behaviour,* 17(1), 71–92.

Wexler, H. K., Falkin, G. P., Lipton, D. S., and Rosenblum, A. B. (1992) Outcome evaluation of a prison therapeutic community for substance abuse treatment. In C. Leukefeld and F. Tims (Eds.), *Drug abuse treatment in prisons and jails* (pp. 156–175). Research Monograph Series, Vol. 118. Rockville, MD: National Institute on Drug Abuse.

Wexler, H. K., and Lipton, D. S. (1993) From reform to recovery: Advances in prison drug treatment. In J. Inciardi (Ed.), *Drug treatment and criminal justice* (pp. 209–227). Newbury Park, CA: Sage Publications.

Wexler, H. K., and Williams, R. (1986) The Stay'n Out therapeutic community: Prison treatment for substance abusers. *Journal of Psychoactive Drugs,* 18, 221–331.

22
Recidivism of
Sex Offenders

Tim Bynum
Madeline Carter
Scott Matson
Charles Onley

With the exception of the violent offender, no type of offender evokes more concern from the public than the sex offender. Recent laws have required sex offender registration and public notification. These strategies are designed to keep better track of sex offenders in the community. While these risk management techniques provide limited assurances that offenders will not recidivate, the more important question is whether or not risk reduction can take place through effective treatment. For many years, it was believed that treatment was ineffective in reducing recidivism among this group of offenders. However, recent studies have demonstrated that treatment can be effective in reducing recidivism for this type of offender. This chapter covers all aspects of this important topic, from defining sex offenders and measuring recidivism to treatment research for both adult and juvenile sex offenders. This chapter ends with a number of implications for sex offender management.

Introduction

The criminal justice system manages most convicted sex offenders with some combination of incarceration, community supervision, and specialized treatment (Knopp,

Freeman-Longo, and Stevenson, 1992). While the likelihood and length of incarceration for sex offenders has increased in recent years,[1] the majority are released at some point on probation or parole (either immediately following sentencing or after a period of incarceration in prison or jail). About 60 percent of all sex offenders managed by the U.S. correctional system are under some form of conditional supervision in the community (Greenfeld, 1997).

While any offender's subsequent reoffending is of public concern, the prevention of sexual violence is particularly important given the irrefutable harm that these offenses cause victims and the fear they generate in the community. With this in mind, practitioners making decisions about how to manage sex offenders must ask themselves the following questions:

- What is the likelihood that a specific offender will commit subsequent sex crimes?

- Under what circumstances is this offender least likely to reoffend?

- What can be done to reduce the likelihood of reoffense?

The study of recidivism—the commission of a subsequent offense—is important to the criminal justice response to sexual offending. If sex offenders commit a wide variety of offenses, responses from both a public policy and treatment perspective may be no different than is appropriate for the general criminal population (Quinsey, 1984). However, a more specialized response is appropriate if sex offenders tend to commit principally sex offenses.

The purpose of this paper is to examine the critical issues in defining recidivism and provide a synthesis of the current research on the reoffense rates of sex offenders. The following sections summarize and discuss research findings on sex offenders, factors and conditions that appear to be associated with reduced sexual offending, and the implications that these findings have for sex offender management. Although studies on juvenile sex offender response to treatment exist, the vast majority of research has concentrated on adult males. Thus, this paper focuses primarily on adult male sex offenders.

Issues in the Measurement of Sex Offender Recidivism

Research on recidivism can be used to inform intervention strategies with sex offenders. However, the way in which recidivism is measured can have a marked difference in study results and applicability to the day-to-day management of this criminal population. The following section explores variables such as the population(s) of sex offenders studied, the criteria used to measure recidivism, the types of offenses studied, and the length of time a study follows a sample. Practitioners must understand how these and other study variables can affect conclusions about sex offender recidivism, as well as decisions regarding individual cases.

Defining the Sex Offender Population Studied

Sex offenders are a highly heterogeneous mixture of individuals who have committed violent sexual assaults on strangers, offenders who have had inappropriate sexual contact with family members, individuals who have molested children, and those who have engaged in a wide range of other inappropriate and criminal sexual behaviors. If we group various types of offenders and offenses into an ostensibly homogenous category of "sex offenders," distinctions in the factors related to recidivism will be masked and differential results obtained from studies of reoffense patterns. Thus, one of the first issues to consider in reviewing any study of sex offender recidivism is how "sex offender" is defined; who is included in this category, and, as important, who is not.

> Sex offenders are a highly heterogeneous mixture of individuals who have committed violent sexual assaults on strangers, offenders who have had inappropriate sexual contact with family members, individuals who have molested children, and those who have engaged in a wide range of other inappropriate and criminal sexual behaviors.

Defining Recidivism

Although there is common acceptance that recidivism is the commission of a subsequent offense, there are many operational definitions for this term. For example, recidivism may occur when there is a new arrest, new conviction, or new commitment to custody. Each of these criteria is a valid measure of recidivism, but each measures something different. While the differences may appear minor, they will lead to widely varied outcomes.

- *Subsequent Arrest*—Using new charges or arrests as the determining criteria for "recidivism" will result in a higher recidivism rate, because many individuals are arrested but for a variety of reasons, are not convicted.

- *Subsequent Conviction*—Measuring new convictions is a more restrictive criterion than new arrests, resulting in a lower recidivism rate. Generally, more confidence is placed in reconviction, since this involves a process through which the individual has been found guilty. However, given the process involved in reporting, prosecution, and conviction in sex offense cases, a number of researchers favor the use of more inclusive criteria (e.g., arrests or charges).

- *Subsequent Incarceration*—Some studies utilize return to prison as the criterion for determining recidivism. There are two ways in which individuals may be returned to a correctional institution. One is through the commission of a new offense and return to prison on a new sentence and the other is through a technical violation of parole. The former is by far the more restrictive criterion, since an offender has to have been found guilty and sentenced to prison. Technical violations typically involve violations of conditions of release, such as being alone with minor children or consuming alcohol. Thus, the use of this definition will result in the inclusion of individuals who may not have committed a subsequent criminal offense as recidivists. When one encounters the use of return to prison as the criterion for recidivism, it is imperative to determine if this includes those with new convictions, technical violations, or both.

Underestimating Recidivism

Reliance on measures of recidivism as reflected through official criminal justice system data obviously omit offenses that are not cleared through an arrest or those that are never reported to the police. This distinction is critical in the measurement of recidivism of sex offenders. For a variety of reasons, sexual assault is a vastly underreported crime. The National Crime Victimization Surveys (Bureau of Justice Statistics) conducted in 1994, 1995, and 1998 indicate that only 32 percent (one out of three) of sexual assaults against persons 12 or older are reported to law enforcement. A three-year longitudinal study (Kilpatrick, Edmunds, and Seymour, 1992) of 4,008 adult women found that 84 percent of respondents who identified themselves as rape victims did not report the crime to authorities. (No current studies indicate the rate of reporting for child sexual assault, although it is generally assumed that these assaults are equally underreported.) Many victims are afraid to report sexual assault to the police. They

may fear that reporting will lead to the following:

- further victimization by the offender;
- other forms of retribution by the offender or by the offender's friends or family;
- arrest, prosecution, and incarceration of an offender who may be a family member or friend and on whom the victim or others may depend;
- others finding out about the sexual assault (including friends, family members, media, and the public);
- not being believed; and
- being traumatized by the criminal justice system response.

> Several studies support the hypothesis that sexual offense recidivism rates are underreported.

These factors are compounded by the shame and guilt experienced by sexual assault victims, and, for many, a desire to put a tragic experience behind them. Incest victims who have experienced criminal justice involvement are particularly reluctant to report new incest crimes because of the disruption caused to their family. This complex of reasons makes it unlikely that reporting figures will change dramatically in the near future and bring recidivism rates closer to actual reoffense rates.

Several studies support the hypothesis that sexual offense recidivism rates are underreported. Marshall and Barbaree (1990) compared official records of a sample of sex offenders with "unofficial" sources of data. They found that the number of subsequent sex offenses revealed through unofficial sources was 2.4 times higher than the number that was recorded in official reports. In addition, research using information generated through polygraph examinations on a sample of imprisoned sex offenders with fewer than two known victims (on average), found that these offenders actually had an average of 110 victims and 318 offenses (Ahlmeyer, Heil, McKee, and English, 2000). Another polygraph study found a sample of imprisoned sex offenders to have extensive criminal histories, committing sex crimes for an average of 16 years before being caught (Ahlmeyer, English, and Simons, 1999).

Offense Type

For the purpose of their studies, researchers must determine what specific behaviors qualify sex offenders as recidivists. They must decide if only sex offenses will be considered, or if the commission of any crime is sufficient to be classified as a recidivating offense. If recidivism is determined only through the commission of a subsequent sex offense, researchers must consider if this includes felonies and misdemeanors. Answers to these fundamental questions will influence the level of observed recidivism in each study.

Length of Follow-Up

Studies often vary in the length of time they "follow-up" on a group of sex offenders in the community. There are two issues of concern with follow-up periods. Ideally, all individuals in any given study should have the same length of time "at risk"—time at large in the community—and, thus, equal opportunity to commit subsequent offenses. In practice, however, this almost never happens. For instance, in a 10-year follow-up study, some subjects will have been in the community for eight, nine, or 10 years while others may have been out for only two years. This problem is addressed by using survival analysis, a methodology that takes into account the amount of time every subject has been in the community, rather than a simple percentage.

Additionally, when researchers compare results across studies, similar time at risk should be used in each of the studies. Obviously, the longer the follow-up period, the more likely reoffense will occur and a higher rate of recidivism will be observed. Many researchers believe that recidivism studies should ideally include a follow-up period of five years or more.

Effect on Recidivism Outcomes

What are we to make of these caveats regarding recidivism—do they render recidivism a meaningless concept? On the contrary, from a public policy perspective, recidivism is an invaluable measure of the performance of various sanctions and interventions with criminal offenders. However, there is often much ambiguity surrounding what appears to be a simple statement of outcomes regarding recidivism. In comparing the results of various recidivism studies, one should not lose sight of the issues of comparable study samples, criteria for recidivism, the length of the follow-up period, information sources utilized to estimate risk of reoffense, and the likelihood that recidivism rates are underestimated.

Factors Associated With Sex Offender Recidivism

In many instances, policies and procedures for the management of sex offenders have been driven by public outcry over highly publicized sex offenses. However, criminal justice practitioners must avoid reactionary responses that are based on public fear of this population. Instead, they must strive to make management decisions that are based on the careful assessment of the likelihood of recidivism. The identification of risk factors that may be associated with recidivism of sex offenders can aid practitioners in devising management strategies that best protect the community and reduce the likelihood of further victimization.

It is crucial to keep in mind, however, that there are no absolutes or "magic bullets" in the process of identifying these risk factors. Rather, this process is an exercise in isolating factors that *tend* to be associated with specific behaviors. While this association reflects a likelihood, it does not indicate that all individuals who possess certain characteristics will behave in a certain manner. Some sex offenders will inevitably commit subsequent sex offenses, in spite of our best efforts to identify risk factors and institute management and treatment processes aimed at minimizing these conditions. Likewise, not all sex offenders who have reoffense risk characteristics will recidivate.

This section explores several important aspects in the study of recidivism and identification of risk factors associated with sex offenders' commission of subsequent crimes.

> The identification of risk factors that may be associated with recidivism of sex offenders can aid practitioners in devising management strategies that best protect the community and reduce the likelihood of further victimization.

Application of Studies of General Criminal Recidivism

The identification of factors associated with criminal recidivism has been an area of significant research over the past 20 years. This work has fueled the development of countless policies and instruments to guide sentencing and release decisions throughout the criminal justice system. If one assumes that sex offenders are similar to other criminal offenders, then the preponderance of research should assist practitioners in identifying risk factors in this population as well. Gottfredson and Hirschi (1990) argued that there is little specialization among criminal offenders. In this view, robbers also commit burglary and those

who commit assaults also may be drug offenders. The extensive research on recidivism among the general criminal population has identified a set of factors that are consistently associated with subsequent criminal behavior. These factors include being young, having an unstable employment history, abusing alcohol and drugs, holding pro-criminal attitudes, and associating with other criminals (Gendreau, Little, and Goggin, 1996).

However, there is some evidence that suggests that sexual offending may differ from other criminal behavior (Hanson and Bussiere, 1998). Although sex offenders may commit other types of offenses, other types of offenders rarely commit sex offenses (Bonta and Hanson, 1995; Hanson, Steffy, and Gauthier, 1993). If this is the case, then a different set of factors may be associated with the recidivism of sex offenders than for the general offender population. This statement is reinforced by the finding that many persistent sex offenders receive low risk scores on instruments designed to predict recidivism among the general offender population (Bonta and Hanson, 1995).

Identification of Static and Dynamic Factors

Characteristics of offenders can be grouped into two general categories. First, there are historical characteristics, such as age, prior offense history, and age at first sex offense arrest or conviction. Because these items typically cannot be altered, they are often referred to as *static* factors. Second are those characteristics, circumstances, and attitudes that can change throughout one's life, generally referred to as *dynamic* factors. Examples of dynamic characteristics include drug or alcohol use, poor attitude (e.g., low remorse and victim blaming), and intimacy problems. The identification of dynamic factors that are associated with reduced recidivism holds particular promise in effectively managing sex offenders because the strengthening of these factors can be encouraged through various supervision and treatment strategies.

Dynamic factors can further be divided into *stable* and *acute* categories (Hanson and Harris, 1998). *Stable dynamic factors* are those characteristics that can change over time, but are relatively lasting qualities. Examples of these characteristics include deviant sexual preferences or alcohol or drug abuse. On the other hand, Hanson and Harris (1998) suggest that *acute dynamic factors* are conditions that can change over a short period of time. Examples include sexual arousal or intoxication that may immediately precede a reoffense.

Understanding Base Rates

Understanding the concept of "base rates" is also essential when studying sex offender recidivism. A base rate is simply the overall rate of recidivism of an entire group of offenders. If the base rate for an entire group is known (e.g., 40 percent), then, without other information, practitioners would predict that any individual in this group has approximately a 40 percent chance of recidivating. If static or dynamic factors related to recidivism are identified, error rates can be improved and this information can be used to make more accurate assessments of the likelihood of rearrest or reconviction. However, if the base rate is at one extreme or the other, additional information may not significantly improve accuracy. For instance, if the base rate were 10 percent, then practitioners would predict that 90 percent of the individuals in this group would not be arrested for a new crime. The error rate would be difficult to improve, regardless of what additional information may be available about individual offenders. In other words, if we simply predicted that no one would be rearrested, we would be wrong only 10 percent of the

time. It is quite difficult to make accurate individual predictions in such extreme situations.

What has come to be termed as "the low base rate problem" has traditionally plagued sex offender recidivism studies (Quinsey, 1980). As noted previously, lack of reporting, or underreporting, is higher in crimes of sexual violence than general criminal violence and may contribute to the low base rate problem. The following studies have found low base rates for sex offender populations:

- Hanson and Bussiere (1998) reported an overall recidivism rate of 13 percent.

- Grunfeld and Noreik (1986) found a 10 percent recidivism rate for rapists.

- Gibbens, Soothill, and Way (1978) reported a 4 percent recidivism rate for incest offenders.

> A base rate is simply the overall rate of recidivism of an entire group of offenders.

Samples of sex offenders used in some studies may have higher base rates of reoffense than other studies. Quinsey (1984) found this to be the case in his summary of sex offender recidivism studies, as have many other authors who have attempted to synthesize this research. There is wide variation in results, in both the amount of measured recidivism and the factors associated with these outcomes. To a large degree, differences can be explained by variations in the sample of sex offenders involved in the studies. Although this is a simple and somewhat obvious point, this basic fact is "responsible for the disagreements and much of the confusion in the literature" on the recidivism of sex offenders (Quinsey, 1984).

Furthermore, results from some studies indicate that there may be higher base rates among certain categories of sex offenders

(Quinsey, Lalumiere, Rice, and Harris, 1995; Quinsey, Rice, and Harris, 1995). For example, in their follow-up study of sex offenders released from a psychiatric facility, Quinsey, Rice, and Harris (1995) found that rapists had a considerably higher rate of rearrest/reconviction than did child molesters.

Conversely, Prentky, Lee, Knight, and Cerce (1997) found that over a 25-year period, child molesters had higher rates of reoffense than rapists. In this study, recidivism was operationalized as a failure rate and calculated as the proportion of individuals who were rearrested using survival analysis (which takes into account the amount of time each offender has been at risk in the community). Results show that over longer periods of time, child molesters have a higher failure rate—thus, a higher rate of rearrest—than rapists (52 percent versus 39 percent over 25 years).

Figure 22.1
New Sex Offenses Charges (Failure Rates)

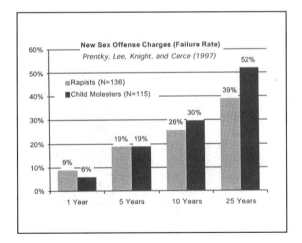

Making Sense of Contradictory Findings

Studies on sex offender recidivism vary widely in the quality and rigor of the research design, the sample of sex offenders and behaviors included in the study, the length of follow-up, and the criteria for suc-

cess or failure. Due to these and other differences, there is often a perceived lack of consistency across studies of sex offender recidivism. For example, there have been varied results regarding whether the age of the offender at the time of institutional release is associated with subsequent criminal sexual behavior. While Beck and Shipley (1989) found that there was no relationship between these variables, Clarke and Crum (1985) and Marshall and Barbaree (1990) suggested that younger offenders were more likely to commit future crimes. However, Grunfeld and Noreik (1986) argued that older sex offenders are more likely to have a more developed fixation and thus are more likely to reoffend. A study by the Delaware Statistical Analysis Center (1984) found that those serving longer periods of incarceration had a lower recidivism rate—while Roundtree, Edwards, and Parker (1984) found just the opposite.

To a large degree, the variation across individual studies can be explained by the differences in study populations. Schwartz and Cellini (1997) indicated that the use of a heterogeneous group of sex offenders in the analysis of recidivism might be responsible for this confusion:

> Mixing an antisocial rapist with a socially skilled fixated pedophile with a developmentally disabled exhibitionist may indeed produce a hodgepodge of results.

Similarly, West, Roy, and Nichols (1978) noted that recidivism rates in studies of sex offenders vary by the characteristics of the offender sample. Such a situation makes the results from follow-up studies of undifferentiated sex offenders difficult to interpret (Quinsey, 1998).

One method of dealing with this problem is to examine recidivism studies of specific types of sex offenders. This approach is warranted, given the established base rate differences across types of sex offenders.[2] Marshall and Barbaree (1990) found in their review of studies that the recidivism rate for specific types of offenders varied:

- Incest offenders ranged between 4 and 10 percent.
- Rapists ranged between 7 and 35 percent.
- Child molesters with female victims ranged between 10 and 29 percent.
- Child molesters with male victims ranged between 13 and 40 percent.
- Exhibitionists ranged between 41 and 71 percent.

In summary, practitioners should recognize several key points related to research studies on sex offender recidivism. First, since sexual offending may differ from other criminal behavior, research specific to sex offender recidivism is needed to inform interventions with sex offenders. Second, researchers seek to identify static and dynamic factors associated with recidivism of sex offenders. In particular, the identification of, and support of, "positive" dynamic factors may help reduce the risk of recidivism. Third, although research studies on recidivism of sex offenders often appear to have contradictory findings, variations in outcomes can typically be explained by the differences in the study populations. Finally, since base rate differences have been identified across types of sex offenses, it makes sense to study recidivism of sex offenders by offense type.

Review of Studies

The following sections present findings from various studies of the recidivism of sex offenders within offense categories of rapists and child molesters.[3] Overall recidivism findings are presented, along with results concerning the factors and characteristics associated with recidivism.

Rapists

There has been considerable research on the recidivism of rapists across various institutional and community-based settings

and with varying periods of follow-up. A follow-up study of sex offenders released from a maximum-security psychiatric institution in California found that 10 of the 57 rapists (19 percent) studied were reconvicted of a rape within five years, most of which occurred during the first year of the follow-up period (Sturgeon and Taylor, 1980). These same authors reported that among 68 sex offenders not found to be mentally disordered who were paroled in 1973, 19 (28 percent) were reconvicted for a sex offense within five years.

In a study of 231 sex offenders placed on probation in Philadelphia between 1966 and 1969, 11 percent were rearrested for a sex offense and 57 percent were rearrested for any offense (Romero and Williams, 1985). Rice, Harris, and Quinsey (1990) conducted a more recent study of 54 rapists who were released from prison before 1983. After four years, 28 percent had a reconviction for a sex offense and 43 percent had a conviction for a violent offense.

Figure 22.2
54 Sex Offenders Released Before 1983

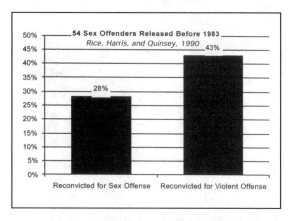

In their summary of the research on the recidivism of rapists, Quinsey, Lalumiere, Rice, and Harris (1995) noted that the significant variation in recidivism across studies of rapists is likely due to differences in the types of offenders involved (e.g., institutionalized offenders, mentally disordered offenders, or probationers) or in the length of the follow-up period. They further noted that throughout these studies, the proportion of offenders who had a prior sex offense was similar to the proportion that had a subsequent sex offense. In addition, the rates of reoffending decreased with the seriousness of the offense. That is, the occurrence of officially recorded recidivism for a nonviolent nonsexual offense was the most likely and the incidence of violent sex offenses was the least likely.

Figure 22.3
A Comparison of Offense Rates for Incest

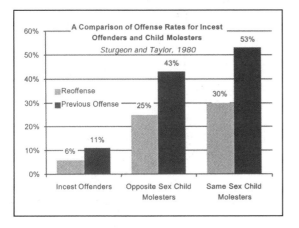

Child Molesters

Studies of the recidivism of child molesters reveal specific patterns of reoffending across victim types and offender characteristics. A study involving mentally disordered sex offenders compared same-sex and opposite-sex child molesters and incest offenders. Results of this five-year follow-up study found that same-sex child molesters had the highest rate of previous sex offenses (53 percent), as well as the highest reconviction rate for sex crimes (30 percent). In comparison, 43 percent of opposite-sex child molesters had prior sex offenses and a reconviction rate for sex crimes of 25 percent, and incest offenders had prior convictions at a rate of 11 percent and a reconviction rate of 6 percent (Stur-

geon and Taylor, 1980). Interestingly, the recidivism rate for same-sex child molesters for other crimes against persons was also quite high, with 26 percent having reconvictions for these offenses. Similarly, a number of other studies have found that child molesters have relatively high rates of nonsexual offenses (Quinsey, 1984).

Several studies have involved follow-up of extra-familial child molesters. One such study (Barbaree and Marshall, 1988) included both official and unofficial measures of recidivism (reconviction, new charge, or unofficial record). Using both types of measures, researchers found that 43 percent of these offenders (convicted of sex offenses involving victims under the age of 16 years) sexually reoffended within a four-year follow-up period. Those who had a subsequent sex offense differed from those who did not by their use of force in the offense, the number of previous sexual assault victims, and their score on a sexual index that included a phallometric assessment.[4] In contrast to other studies of child molesters, this study found no difference in recidivism between opposite-sex and same-sex offenders.

In a more recent study (Rice, Quinsey, and Harris, 1991), extra-familial child molesters were followed for an average of six years. During that time, 31 percent had a reconviction for a second sexual offense. Those who committed subsequent sex offenses were more likely to have been married, have a personality disorder, and have a more serious sex offense history than those who did not recidivate sexually. In addition, recidivists were more likely to have deviant phallometrically measured sexual preferences (Quinsey, Lalumiere, Rice, and Harris, 1995).

Those who committed subsequent sex offenses were more likely to have been married, have a personality disorder, and have a more serious sex offense history than those who did not recidivate sexually.

In a study utilizing a 24-year follow-up period, victim differences (e.g., gender of the victim) were not found to be associated with the recidivism (defined as those charged with a subsequent sexual offense) of child molesters. This study of 111 extra-familial child molesters found that the number of prior sex offenses and sexual pre-occupation with children were related to sex offense recidivism (Prentky, Knight, and Lee, 1997). However, the authors of this study noted that the finding of no victim differences may have been due to the fact that the offenders in this study had an average of three prior sex offenses before their prison release. Thus, this sample may have had a higher base rate of reoffense than child molesters from the general prison population.

Probationers

Research reviewed to this point has almost exclusively focused upon institutional or prison populations and therefore, presumably a more serious offender population. An important recent study concerns recidivism among a group of sex offenders placed on probation (Kruttschnitt, Uggen, and Shelton, 2000). Although the factors that were related to various types of reoffending were somewhat similar with regard to subsequent sex offenses, the only factor associated with reducing reoffending in this study was the combination of stable employment and sex offender treatment. Such findings emphasize the importance of both formal and informal social controls in holding offenders accountable for their criminal behavior. The findings also provide support for treatment services that focus on coping with inappropriate sexual impulses, fantasies, and behaviors through specific sex offender treatment.

Synthesis of Recidivism Studies

There have been several notable efforts at conducting a qualitative or narrative syn-thesis of studies of the recidivism of sex offenders (Quinsey, 1984; Furby, Weinrott, and Blackshaw, 1989; Quinsey, Lalumiere, Rice, and Harris, 1995; Schwartz and Cellini, 1997). Such an approach attempts to summarize findings across various studies by comparing results and searching for patterns or trends. Another technique, known as meta-analysis, relies upon a quantitative approach to synthesizing research results from similar studies. Meta-analysis involves a statistically sophisticated approach to estimating the combined effects of various studies that meet certain methodological criteria and is far from a simple lumping together of disparate studies to obtain average effects.

Meta-analyses have certain advantages over more traditional summaries in that through the inclusion of multiple studies, a reliable estimation of effects can be obtained that is generalizable across studies and samples. As noted earlier, the results obtained from individual studies of sex offenders are heavily influenced by the sample of offenders included in the research. Therefore, there is much to be gained through the use of meta-analysis in summarizing sex offender recidivism (see Quinsey, Harris, Rice, and Lalumiere, 1993).

As has also previously been observed, it is imperative to distinguish between sex offense recidivism and the commission of other subsequent criminal behavior, as well as the type of current sex offense. One of the most widely recognized meta-analyses of sexual offender recidivism (Hanson and Bussiere, 1998) was structured around these dimensions.

Meta-Analysis Studies

In Hanson and Bussiere's meta-analysis, 61 research studies met the criteria for inclusion, with all utilizing a longitudinal design and a comparison group. Across all studies, the average sex offense recidivism rate (as evidenced by rearrest or reconviction) was 18.9 percent for rapists and 12.7

percent for child molesters over a four to five year period. The rate of recidivism for nonsexual violent offenses was 22.1 percent for rapists and 9.9 percent for child molesters, while the recidivism rate for any reoffense for rapists was 46.2 percent and 36.9 percent for child molesters over a four to five year period. However, as has been noted previously and as these authors warn, one should be cautious in the interpretation of the data as these studies involved a range of methods and follow-up periods.

Perhaps the greatest advantage of the meta-analysis approach is in determining the relative importance of various factors across studies. Using this technique, one can estimate how strongly certain offender and offense characteristics are related to recidivism because they show up consistently across different studies.

Figure 22.4

Meta-Analysis of 61 Studies

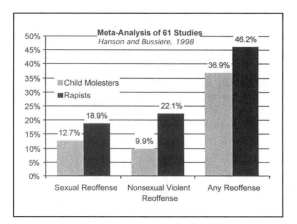

In the 1998 Hanson and Bussiere study, these characteristics were grouped into demographics, criminal lifestyle, sexual criminal history, sexual deviancy, and various clinical characteristics. Regarding demographics, being young and single were consistently found to be related, albeit weakly, to subsequent sexual offending. With regard to sex offense history, sex offenders were more likely to recidivate if

they had prior sex offenses, male victims, victimized strangers or extra-familial victims, begun sexually offending at an early age, and/or engaged in diverse sex crimes.

> Sexual interest in children was the strongest predictor of recidivism across all studies.

The factors that were found through this analysis to have the strongest relationship with sexual offense recidivism were those in the sexual deviance category: sexual interest in children, deviant sexual preferences, and sexual interest in boys. Failure to complete treatment was also found to be a moderate predictor of sexual recidivism. Having general psychological problems was not related to sexual offense recidivism, but having a personality disorder was related. Being sexually abused as a child was not related to repeat sexual offending.

Studies That Focus on Dynamic Factors

As noted earlier, the detection of dynamic factors that are associated with sexual offending behavior is significant, because these characteristics can serve as the focus of intervention. However, many recidivism studies (including most of those previously discussed) have focused almost exclusively on static factors, since they are most readily available from case files. Static, or historical, factors help us to understand etiology and permit predictions of relative likelihood of reoffending. Dynamic factors take into account changes over time that adjust static risk and [inform] us about the types of interventions that are most useful in lowering risk.

In a study focused on dynamic factors, Hanson and Harris (1998) collected data on over 400 sex offenders under community supervision, approximately one-half of whom were recidivists.[5] The recidivists had committed a new sexual offense while on community supervision during a five-year period (1992–1997). A number of significant differences in stable dynamic factors were discovered between recidivists and non-recidivists. Those who committed subsequent sex offenses were more likely to be unemployed (more so for rapists) and have substance abuse problems. The nonrecidivists tended to have positive social influences and were more likely to have intimacy problems. There also were considerable attitudinal differences between the recidivists and non-recidivists. Those who committed subsequent sex offenses were less likely to show remorse or concern for the victim. In addition, recidivists tended to see themselves as being at little risk for committing new offenses, were less likely to avoid high-risk situations and were more likely to report engaging in deviant sexual activities. In general, the recidivists were described as having more chaotic, antisocial lifestyles compared to the non-recidivists (Hanson and Harris, 1998).

The researchers concluded that sex offenders are:

> . . . at most risk of reoffending when they become sexually preoccupied, have access to victims, fail to acknowledge their recidivism risk, and show sharp mood increases, particularly anger.

> These [dynamic] factors will assuredly provide a foundation for developing more effective intervention strategies for sex offenders.

In sum, because meta-analysis findings can be generalized across studies and samples, they offer the most reliable estimation of factors associated with the recidivism of sex offenders. Most meta-analysis studies, however, have focused on static factors. It is critical that more research be conducted to identify dynamic factors associated with sex

offender recidivism. These factors will assuredly provide a foundation for developing more effective intervention strategies for sex offenders.

Characteristics* of recidivists include:

- multiple victims;
- diverse victims;
- stranger victims;
- juvenile sexual offenses;
- multiple paraphilias;
- history of abuse and neglect;
- long-term separations from parents;
- negative relationships with their mothers;
- diagnosed antisocial personality disorder;
- unemployed;
- substance abuse problems; and
- chaotic, antisocial lifestyles.

*It should be noted that these are not necessarily risk factors.

Impact of Interventions on Sex Offender Recidivism

Although not the primary purpose of this document, a few words regarding sex offender treatment and supervision are in order. Factors that are linked to sex offender recidivism are of direct relevance for sex offender management. If the characteristics of offenders most likely to recidivate can be isolated, they can serve to identify those who have the highest likelihood of committing subsequent sex offenses. They can also help identify offender populations that are appropriate for participation in treatment and specialized supervision and what the components of those interventions must include.

Treatment

When assessing the efficacy of sex offender treatment, it is vital to recognize that the delivery of treatment occurs within different settings. Those offenders who receive treatment in a community setting are generally assumed to be a different population than those who are treated in institutions. Thus, base rates of recidivating behavior will differ for these groups prior to treatment participation.

Sex offender treatment typically consists of three principal approaches:

- the *cognitive-behavioral approach,* which emphasizes changing patterns of thinking that are related to sexual offending and changing deviant patterns of arousal;

- the *psycho-educational approach,* which stresses increasing the offender's concern for the victim and recognition of responsibility for their offense; and

- the *pharmacological approach,* which is based upon the use of medication to reduce sexual arousal.

In practice, these approaches are not mutually exclusive and treatment programs are increasingly utilizing a combination of these techniques.

Although there has been a considerable amount of writing on the relative merits of these approaches and about sex offender treatment in general, there is a paucity of evaluative research regarding treatment outcomes. There have been very few studies of sufficient rigor (e.g., employing an experimental or quasi-experimental design) to compare the effects of various treatment approaches or comparing treated to untreated sex offenders (Quinsey, 1998).

Using less rigorous evaluation strategies, several studies have evaluated the outcomes of offenders receiving sex offender treatment, compared to a group of offenders not receiving treatment. The results of these studies are mixed. For example, Barbaree and Marshall (1988) found a substantial difference in the recidivism rates of extra-familial child molesters who participated in a community based cognitive-behavioral

treatment program, compared to a group of similar offenders who did not receive treatment. Those who participated in treatment had a recidivism rate of 18 percent over a four-year follow-up period, compared to a 43 percent recidivism rate for the nonparticipating group of offenders.

However, no positive effect of treatment was found in several other quasi-experiments involving an institutional behavioral program (Rice, Quinsey, and Harris, 1991) or a milieu therapy approach in an institutional setting (Hanson, Steffy, and Gauthier, 1993).

Figure 22.5

Comparison of Recidivism Rates of Treated and Untreated Child Molesters

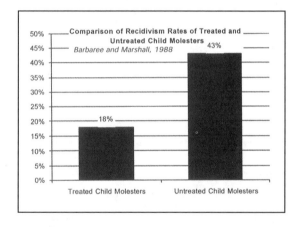

On the other hand, an evaluation of a cognitive-behavioral program that employs an experimental design presented preliminary findings that suggest that participation in this form of treatment may have a modest (though not statistically significant) effect in reducing recidivism. After a follow-up period of 34 months, 8 percent of the offenders in the treatment program had a subsequent sex offense, compared with 13 percent of the control group, who had also volunteered for the program, but were not selected through the random assignment process (Marques, Day, Nelson, and West, 1994).

Some studies present optimistic conclusions about the effectiveness of programs that are empirically based, offense-specific, and comprehensive. A 1995 meta-analysis study on sex offender treatment outcome studies found a small, yet significant, treatment effect (Hall, 1995). This meta-analysis included 12 studies with some form of control group. Despite the small number of subjects (1,313), the results indicated an 8 percent reduction in the recidivism rate for sex offenders in the treatment group.[6]

Recently, Alexander (1999) conducted an analysis of a large group of treatment outcome studies, encompassing nearly 11,000 sex offenders. In this study, data from 79 sex offender treatment studies were combined and reviewed. Results indicated that sex offenders who participated in relapse prevention treatment programs had a combined rearrest rate of 7.2 percent, compared to 17.6 percent for untreated offenders. The overall rearrest rate for treated sex offenders in this analysis was 13.2 percent.[7]

Figure 22.6
Rearrest Rates of Treated and Untreated Sex Offenders

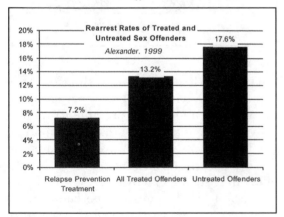

The Association for the Treatment of Sexual Abusers (ATSA) has established a Collaborative Data Research Project with the goals of defining standards for research on treatment, summarizing existing research, and promoting high quality evaluations. As part of this project, researchers are conducting a meta-analysis of treatment studies. Included in the meta-analysis are studies that compare treatment groups with some form of a control group. Preliminary findings indicate that the overall effect of treatment shows reductions in both sexual recidivism, 10 percent of the treatment subjects to 17 percent of the control group subjects, and general recidivism, 32 percent of the treatment subjects to 51 percent of the control group subjects (Hanson, 2000).[8]

Just as it is difficult to arrive at definitive conclusions regarding factors that are related to sex offender recidivism, there are similarly no definitive results regarding the effect of interventions with these offenders. Sex offender treatment programs and the results of treatment outcome studies may vary not only due to their therapeutic approach, but also by the location of the treatment (e.g., community, prison, or psychiatric facility), the seriousness of the offender's criminal and sex offense history, the degree of self-selection (whether they chose to participate in treatment or were placed in a program), and the dropout rate of offenders from treatment.

Juvenile Treatment Research

Research on juvenile sex offender recidivism is particularly lacking. Some studies have examined the effectiveness of treatment in reducing subsequent sexual offending behavior in youth. Key findings from these studies include the following:

- Program evaluation data suggest that the sexual recidivism rate for juveniles treated in specialized programs ranges from approximately 7 to 13 percent over follow-up periods of two to five years (Becker, 1990).

- Juveniles appear to respond well to cognitive-behavioral and/or relapse prevention treatment, with rearrest rates of approximately 7 percent through follow-up periods of more than five years (Alexander, 1999).

- Studies suggest that rates of nonsexual recidivism are generally higher than sexual recidivism rates, ranging from 25 to 50 percent (Becker, 1990; Kahn and Chambers, 1991; Schram, Milloy, and Rowe, 1991).

In a recently conducted study, Hunter and Figueredo (1999) found that as many as 50 percent of youths entering a community-based treatment program were expelled during the first year of their participation. Those who failed the program had higher overall levels of sexual maladjustment, as measured on assessment instruments, and were at greater long-term risk for sexual recidivism.

> More studies measuring the effects of both treatment and supervision are necessary to truly advance efforts in the field of sex offender management.

Supervision

There has been little research on the effectiveness of community supervision programs (exclusively) in reducing reoffense behavior in sex offenders. The majority of supervision programs for sex offenders involve treatment and other interventions to contain offenders' deviant behaviors. Therefore, it is difficult to measure the effects of supervision alone on reoffending behavior—to date, no such studies have been conducted.

Evaluating the Effects of Interventions

Identification of factors associated with recidivism of sex offenders can play an important role in determining intervention strategies with this population. Yet, the effectiveness of interventions themselves on

reducing recidivism must be evaluated if the criminal justice system is to control these offenders and prevent further victimization. However, not only have there been few studies of sufficient rigor on treatment outcomes, less rigorous study results thus far have been mixed. Although one study may find a substantial difference in recidivism rates for offenders who participated in a specific type of treatment, another may find only a modest positive treatment effect, and still other studies may reveal no positive effects. There has been even less research conducted to evaluate the impact of community supervision programs in reducing recidivism. More studies measuring the effects of both treatment and supervision are necessary to truly advance efforts in the field of sex offender management.

Implications for Sex Offender Management

This paper presented a range of issues that are critical in defining the recidivism of sex offenders. Although there are certainly large gaps in criminal justice knowledge regarding the determinants of recidivism and the characteristics of effective interventions, what is known has significant implications for policy and intervention.

The Heterogeneity of Sex Offenders Must Be Acknowledged. Although sex offenders are often referred to as a "type" of offender, there are a wide variety of behaviors and offender backgrounds that fall into this classification of criminals (Knight and Prentky, 1990). As mentioned earlier, many sex offenders have histories of assaulting across sex and age groups—recent research (Ahlmeyer, Heil, McKee, and English, 2000) found that these offenders may be even more heterogeneous than previously believed.

Criminal Justice Professionals Must Continue to Expand Their Understanding of How Sex Offenders Are Different From the General Criminal Population.

Although some sex offenders are unique from the general criminal population (e.g., many extra-familial child molesters), others (e.g., many rapists) possess many of the same characteristics that are associated with recidivism of general criminal behavior. As criminal justice understanding of these offenders and the factors associated with their behavior increases, more refined classification needs to be developed and treatment programs need to be redesigned to accommodate these differences.

Interventions Should Be Based on the Growing Body of Knowledge About Sex Offender and General Criminal Recidivism. Research demonstrates that while sex offenders are much more likely to commit subsequent sexual offenses than the general criminal population, they do not exclusively commit sexual offenses. Therefore, some aspects of intervention with the general criminal population may have implications for effective management of sex offenders. Quinsey (1998) has recommended that in the absence of definitive knowledge about effective sex offender treatment, the best approach would be to structure interventions around what is known about the treatment of offenders in general.

> In the realm of interventions with general criminal offenders, there is a growing body of literature that suggests that the cognitive-behavioral approach holds considerable promise.

In the realm of interventions with general criminal offenders, there is a growing body of literature that suggests that the cognitive-behavioral approach holds considerable promise (Gendreau and Andrews, 1990). Cognitive-behavioral treatment involves a comprehensive, structured approach based on sexual learning theory using cognitive restructuring methods and behavioral techniques. Behavioral methods are primarily directed at reducing arousal and increasing pro-social skills. The cognitive behavioral approach employs peer groups and educational classes, and uses a variety of counseling theories. This approach suggests that interventions are most effective when they address the criminogenic needs of high-risk offenders (Andrews, 1982). The characteristics of programs that are more likely to be effective with this population include skill-based training, modeling of pro-social behaviors and attitudes, a directive but non-punitive orientation, a focus on modification of precursors to criminal behavior, and a supervised community component (Quinsey, 1998).

Although these program characteristics may be instructive in forming the basis for interventions with sex offenders, treatment approaches must incorporate what is known about this particular group of offenders. A number of characteristics that are typically associated with the recidivism of sex offenders were identified in this document, including: victim age, gender, and relationship to the offender; impulsive, antisocial behavior; the seriousness of the offense; and the number of previous sex offenses. Also, an influential factor in sex offender recidivism is the nature of the offender's sexual preferences and sexually deviant interests. The discovery and measurement of these interests can serve as a focus for treatment intervention.

Dynamic Factors Should Influence Individualized Interventions. In addition, dynamic factors associated with recidivism should inform the structure of treatment and supervision, as these are characteristics that can be altered. These factors include the formation of positive relationships with peers, stable employment, avoidance of alcohol and drugs, prevention of depression, reduction of deviant sexual arousal, and increase in appropriate sexual preferences, when they exist.

Interventions that strive to facilitate development of positive dynamic factors in sex offenders are consistent with cognitive-behavioral or social learning approaches to treatment. Such approaches determine interventions based upon an individualized planning process, utilizing standard assessment instruments to determine an appropriate intervention strategy. As Quinsey (1998: 419) noted, "with the exception of antiandrogenic medication or castration, this model is currently the only approach that enjoys any evidence of effectiveness in reducing sexual recidivism."

> . . . dynamic factors associated with recidivism should inform the structure of treatment and supervision. . . .

Conclusion

Although there have been many noteworthy research studies on sex offender recidivism in the last 15 to 20 years, there remains much to be learned about the factors associated with the likelihood of reoffense. Ongoing dialogue between researchers and practitioners supervising and treating sex offenders is essential to identifying research needs, gathering information about offenders and the events leading up to offenses, and ensuring that research activity can be translated into strategies to more effectively manage sex offenders in the community. Ultimately, research on sex offender recidivism must be designed and applied to practice with the goals of preventing further victimization and creating safer communities.

Practitioners must continue to look to the most up-to-date research studies on sex offender recidivism to inform their intervention strategies with individual offenders. Researchers can minimize ambiguity in study results by clearly defining measures of recidivism, comparing distinct categories of sex offenders, considering reoffense rates for both sex crimes and all other offenses, and utilizing consistent follow-up periods (preferably five years of follow-up or more). In order to reduce underestimations of the risk of recidivism, they also must strive to

gather information about offenders' criminal histories from multiple sources, beyond official criminal justice data. In comparing results of various studies, practitioners should not lose sight of how these issues impact research outcomes.

Researchers must also continue to accumulate evidence about the relationship of static and dynamic factors to recidivism—such data can assist practitioners in making more accurate assessments of the likelihood of reoffending. In particular, researchers must strive to identify dynamic characteristics associated with sex offending behavior that can serve as the focus for intervention. This information can be utilized to categorize the level of risk posed by offenders, and help determine whether a particular offender is appropriate for treatment and specialized supervision. However, in order to make objective and empirically based decisions about the type of treatment and conditions of supervision that would best control the offender and protect the public, more rigorous research is needed to study the effects of various treatment approaches and community supervision on recidivism.

Study Questions

1. What are the various ways that *recidivism* can be defined?

2. Why is the length of follow-up important?

3. What is the difference between dynamic and static risk factors?

4. What are some of the contradictory findings from the research on sex offenders?

5. What do we know about the recidivism rates of various types of sex offenders?

6. What do the meta-analytical studies on sex offenders tell us?

7. What is the impact of interventions on sex offender recidivism?

Acknowledgements

Tim Bynum, Ph,D., Michigan State University was the principal author of this paper, with contributions from Madeline Carter, Scott Matson, and Charles Onley.

This project was supported by Grant No. 1997-WT-VX-K007, awarded by the Bureau of Justice Assistance. The Bureau of Justice Assistance is a component of the Office of Justice Programs, which also includes the Bureau of Justice Statistics, the National Institute of Justice, the Office of Juvenile Justice and Delinquency Prevention, and the Office for Victims of Crime. Points of view or opinions in this document are those of the authors and do not represent the official position or policies of the United States Department of Justice.

Notes

1. Since 1980, the number of imprisoned sex offenders has grown by more than 7 percent per year (Greenfeld, 1997). In 1994, nearly one in ten state prisoners were incarcerated for committing a sex offense (Greenfeld, 1997).

2. Recent research suggests that many offenders have histories of assaulting across genders and age groups, rather than against only one specific victim population. Researchers in a 1999 study (Ahlmeyer, English, and Simons) found that, through polygraph examinations, the number [of] offenders who "crossed over" age groups of victims is extremely high. The study revealed that before polygraph examinations, 6 percent of a sample of incarcerated sex offenders had both child and adult victims, compared to 71 percent after polygraph exams. Thus, caution must be taken in placing sex offenders in exclusive categories.

3. The studies included in this paper do not represent a comprehensive overview of the research on sex offender recidivism. The studies included represent a sampling of available research on these populations and are drawn from to highlight key points.

4. Also referred to as plethysmography: a device used to measure sexual arousal (erectile response) to both appropriate (age appropriate and consenting) and deviant sexual stimulus material.

5. For the purposes of this study, recidivism was defined as a conviction or charge for a new sexual offense, a non-sexual criminal charge that appeared to be sexually motivated, a violation of supervision conditions for sexual reasons, and self-disclosure by the offender.

6. For the purposes of this study, recidivism was measured by additional sexually aggressive behavior, including official legal charges as well as, in some studies, unofficial data such as self-report.

7. Length of follow-up in this analysis varied from less than one year to more than five years. Most studies in this analysis indicated a three to five year follow-up period.

8. Average length of follow-up in these studies was four to five years.

References

Ahlmeyer, S., English, K., & Simons, D. (1999). *The impact of polygraphy on admissions of crossover offending behavior in adult sexual offenders.* Presentation at the Association for the Treatment of Sexual Abusers 18th Annual Research and Treatment Conference, Lake Buena Vista, FL.

Ahlmeyer, S., Heil, P., McKee, B., & English, K. (2000). The impact of polygraphy on admissions of victims and offenses in adult sexual offenders. *Sexual Abuse: A Journal of Research and Treatment, 12 (2)*, 123–138.

Alexander, M.A. (1999). Sexual offender treatment efficacy revisited. *Sexual Abuse: A Journal of Research and Treatment, 11 (2)*, 101–117.

Andrews, D.A. (1982). *The supervision of offenders: Identifying and gaining control over the factors which make a difference.* Program Branch User Report. Ottawa: Solicitor General of Canada.

Barbaree, H.E. & Marshall, W.L. (1988). Deviant sexual arousal, offense history, and demographic variables as predictors of reoffense among child molesters. *Behavioral Sciences and the Law, 6 (2)*, 267–280.

Beck, A.J. & Shipley, B.E. (1989). *Recidivism of prisoners released in 1983.* Washington, D.C.: U.S. Department of Justice, Bureau of Justice Statistics.

Becker, J.V. (1990). Treating adolescent sexual offenders. *Professional Psychology: Research, and Practice, 21*, 362–365.

Bonta, J. & Hanson, R.K. (1995). *Violent recidivism of men released from prison.* Paper presented at the 103rd Annual Convention of the American Psychological Association, New York.

Clarke, S.H. & Crum, L. (1985). *Returns to prison in North Carolina.* Chapel Hill, NC: Institute of Government University of North Carolina.

Delaware Statistical Analysis Center. (1984). *Recidivism in Delaware after release from incarceration.* Dover, DE: Author.

English, K., Pullen, S., & Jones, L. (Eds.) (1996). *Managing adult sex offenders: A containment approach.* Lexington, KY: American Probation and Parole Association.

Furby, L., Weinrott, M.R., & Blackshaw, L. (1989). Sex offender recidivism: A review. *Psychological Bulletin, 105 (1)*, 3–30.

Gendreau, P. & Andrews, D.A. (1990). What the meta-analysis of the offender treatment literature tell us about what works. *Canadian Journal of Criminology, 32*, 173–184.

Gendreau, P., Little, T., & Goggin, C. (1996). A meta-analysis of the predictors of adult criminal recidivism: What works. *Criminology, 34*, 575–607.

Gibbens, T.C.N., Soothill, K.L., & Way, C.K. (1978). Sibling and parent-child incest offenders. *British Journal of Criminology, 18*, 40–52.

Gottfredson, M.R. & Hirschi, T. (1990). *A general theory of crime.* Stanford, CA: Stanford University Press.

Greenfeld, L.A. (1997). *Sex offenses and offenders: An analysis of data on rape and sexual assault.* Washington, D.C.: U.S. Department of Justice, Bureau of Justice Statistics.

Grunfeld, B. & Noreik, K. (1986). Recidivism among sex offenders: A follow-up study of 541 Norwegian sex offenders. *International Journal of Law and Psychiatry, 9*, 95–102.

Hall, G.C.N. (1995). Sex offender recidivism revisited: A meta-analysis of recent treatment studies. *Journal of Consulting and Clinical Psychology, 63 (5)*, 802–809.

Hanson, R.K. (2000). *The effectiveness of treatment for sexual offenders: Report of the Association for the Treatment of Sexual Abusers Collaborative Data Research Committee.* Presentation at the Association for the Treatment of Sexual Abusers 19th Annual Research and Treatment Conference, San Diego, CA.

Hanson, R.K. & Bussiere, M. (1998). Predicting relapse: A meta-analysis of sexual offender recidivism studies. *Journal of Consulting and Clinical Psychology, 66 (2)*, 348–362.

Hanson, R.K. & Harris, A. (1998). *Dynamic predictors of sexual recidivism.* Ottawa: Solicitor General of Canada.

Hanson, R.K., Scott, H., & Steffy, R. A. (1995). A comparison of child molesters and nonsexual criminals: Risk predictors and long-term recidivism. *Journal of Research in Crime and Delinquency, 32 (3)*, 325–337.

Hanson, R.K., Steffy, R.A., & Gauthier, R. (1993). Long-term recidivism of child molesters. *Journal of Consulting and Criminal Psychology, 61 (4)*, 646–652.

Hunter, J.A. & Figueredo, A.J. (1999). Factors associated with treatment compliance in a population of juvenile sexual offenders. *Sexual Abuse: A Journal of Research and Treatment, 11*, 49–68.

Kahn, T.J. & Chambers, H.J. (1991). Assessing reoffense risk with juvenile sexual offenders. *Child Welfare, 19*, 333–345.

Kilpatrick, D.G., Edmunds, C.N., & Seymour, A. (1992). *Rape in America: A report to the nation.* Washington, D.C.: National Center for Victims of Crime and Crime Victims Research and Treatment Center.

Knight, R.A. & Prentky, R.A. (1990). Classifying sexual offenders: The development and corroboration of taxonomic models. In W.L. Marshall, D.R. Laws, and H.E. Barbaree (Eds.), *Handbook of sexual assault: Issues, theories, and treatment of the offender* (pp. 23–52). New York: Plenum.

Knopp, F.A., Freeman-Longo, R., & Stevenson, W.F. (1992). *Nationwide survey of juvenile and adult sex offender treatment programs and models.* Orwell, VT: Safer Society Press.

Kruttschnitt, C., Uggen, C., & Shelton, K. (2000). Predictors of desistance among sex offenders: The interactions of formal and informal social controls. *Justice Quarterly, 17 (1)*, 61–87.

Marques, J.K., Day, D.M., Nelson, C., & West, M.A. (1994). Effects of cognitive-behavioral treatment on sex offenders' recidivism: Preliminary results of a longitudinal study. *Criminal Justice and Behavior, 21*, 28–54.

Marshall, W.L. & Barbaree, H.E. (1990). Outcomes of comprehensive cognitive-behavioral treatment programs. In W.L. Marshall, D.R. Laws, and H.E. Barbaree (Eds.), *Handbook of sexual assault: Issues, theories, and treatment of the offender* (pp. 363–385). New York: Plenum.

Prentky, R., Knight, R., & Lee, A. (1997). Risk factors associated with recidivism among extrafamilial child molesters. *Journal of Consulting and Clinical Psychology, 65 (1)*, 141–149.

Prentky, R., Lee, A., Knight, R., & Cerce, D. (1997). Recidivism rates among child molesters and rapists: A methodological analysis. *Law and Human Behavior, 21*, 635–659.

Quinsey, V.L. (1980). The base-rate problem and the prediction of dangerousness: A reappraisal. *Journal of Psychiatry and the Law, 8*, 329–340.

Quinsey, V.L. (1984). Sexual aggression: Studies of offenders against women. In D.N. Weisstub (Ed.), *Law and Mental Health: International Perspectives* (pp. 140–172), Vol. 2. New York: Pergamon.

Quinsey, V.L. (1998). Treatment of sex offenders. In M. Tonry (Ed.), *The handbook of crime and punishment* (pp. 403–425). New York: Oxford University Press.

Quinsey, V.L., Harris, G.T., Rice, M.E., & Lalumiere, M. (1993). Assessing treatment efficacy in outcome studies of sex offenders. *Journal of Interpersonal Violence, 8*, 512–523.

Quinsey, V.L., Lalumiere, M.L., Rice, M.E., & Harris, G.T. (1995). Predicting sexual offenses. In J.C. Campbell (Ed.), *Assessing dangerousness: Violence by sexual offenders, batterers, and child abusers* (pp. 114–137). Thousand Oaks, CA: Sage.

Quinsey, V.L., Rice, M.E., & Harris, G.T. (1995). Actuarial prediction of sexual recidivism. *Journal of Interpersonal Violence, 10 (1)*, 85–105.

Rice, M.E., Harris, G.T., & Quinsey, V.L. (1990). A follow-up of rapists assessed in a maximum security psychiatric facility. *Journal of Interpersonal Violence, 5 (4)*, 435–448.

Rice, M.E., Quinsey, V.L., & Harris, G.T. (1991). Sexual recidivism among child molesters released from a maximum security institution. *Journal of Consulting and Clinical Psychology, 59*, 381–386.

Romero, J. & Williams, L. (1985). Recidivism among convicted sex offenders: A 10-year follow-up study. *Federal Probation, 49*, 58–64.

Roundtree, G.A., Edwards, D.W., & Parker, J.B. (1984). A study of personal characteristics of probationers as related to recidivism. *Journal of Offender Counseling, 8*, 53–61.

Schram, D.D., Milloy, C.D., & Rowe, W.E. (1991). *Juvenile sex offenders: A follow-up study of reoffense behavior.* Olympia, WA: Washington State Institute for Public Policy.

Schwartz, B.K. & Cellini, H.R. (1997). *Sex offender recidivism and risk factors in the involuntary commitment process.* Albuquerque, NM: Training and Research Institute Inc.

Sturgeon, V.H. & Taylor, J. (1980). Report of a five-year follow-up study of mentally disordered sex offenders released from Atascadero State Hospital in 1973. *Criminal Justice Journal, 4*, 31–63.

West, D.J., Roy, C., & Nichols, F.L. (1978). *Understanding sexual attacks: A study based upon a group of rapists undergoing psychotherapy.* London: Heinemann.

23
What Works for Female Offenders
A Meta-Analytic Review

Craig Dowden
Don A. Andrews

Most of the correctional research that exists focuses on male offenders. Over the years crime has been considered a young man's game. However, whereas males compose the largest number of inmates, females are the fastest growing segment of the correctional population. Recent attention has been focused on the neglect that females have experienced, both in terms of research and correctional programming. Some have argued that risk factors for female offenders are different than those for males, and therefore what works for males will not work for females. There has been considerably less research on correctional treatment programs for females, but Craig Dowden and Don Andrews examine the research that is available and conclude that the most effective treatment for females is the same as that for males. Those programs that meet the principles of effective intervention demonstrate the strongest reductions in recidivism. These findings are similar to other research studies that have focused on male offenders.

Considerable debate has occurred regarding the effectiveness of correctional interventions. Although the notion that nothing works (Martinson 1974) predominated in the 1970s, the advent of meta-analytic research has swung the pendulum to a what works perspective (McGuire 1995). Several meta-analytic reviews have been conducted on the rehabilitation literature and, for the most part, have suggested that some types of correctional interventions can effectively reduce recidivism (Andrews, Dowden, and Gendreau forthcoming; Andrews, Zinger, Hoge, Bonta, Gendreau, and Cullen 1990; Dowden 1998; Hill, Andrews, and Hoge 1991; Izzo and Ross 1990; Lipsey 1989, 1995; Losel 1996).

Although the effectiveness of rehabilitation for general offender populations has received widespread attention (Gibbons 1999), research dedicated to female offender populations has been quite limited (Koons, Burrow, Morash, and Bynum 1997). Morash, Bynum, and Koons (1995) identified 67 studies that reported promising intervention strategies for female offenders, but only 12 included an outcome measure, and none linked recidivism to program components.

A qualitative survey study conducted by Koons and her colleagues (1997) also attempted to identify promising intervention strategies for female offenders. In their report, correctional administrators identified treatment needs that they believed were related to successful treatment outcome. These needs included substance abuse education and treatment and the development of parenting and life skills as well as interpersonal and basic education skills. Interestingly, these program targets only partially overlapped with the list of more promising targets for change (i.e., criminogenic needs) outlined by a number of scholars in the correctional treatment literature (Andrews and Bonta 1998; Andrews, Bonta, and Hoge 1990).

Koons and her colleagues (1997) argued that female offenders have several unique needs and concerns such as childcare, pregnancy, and sexual or physical abuse victimization. Nonetheless, their survey results and introductory overview of the what works literature suggested that the principles of effective correctional treatment (i.e., risk, need, and responsivity) may apply regardless of the gender of the treatment population. At the same time, the authors stated that "the question of whether or not these findings (i.e., principles of effective correctional treatment) can be generalized to the female offender population still is very much in need of an answer" (p. 517).

What Are the Principles of Risk, Need, and Responsivity?

Essentially, the risk principle is concerned with identifying those clients who should receive the most intensive allocation of correctional treatment resources and those who require less attention. In other words, this principle states that the amount of intervention that an offender receives must be matched to his or her risk level to reoffend. The highest levels of service should be reserved for the higher risk cases, whereas the minimal levels of service and supervision should be provided for the lower risk cases (Andrews and Bonta 1998; Andrews, Bonta, et al. 1990).

The need principle, on the other hand, is concerned with the targets for change identified within the treatment program. More specifically, theory and some research have demonstrated that when certain risk factors have been altered, reductions in recidivism for offenders have occurred. These more promising targets or dynamic risk factors have been commonly referred to as criminogenic needs (Andrews and Bonta 1998; Andrews, Bonta, et al. 1990), and they are different from other less promising targets that are classified as noncriminogenic needs. Past research has suggested that programs that targeted these latter needs have not led to significant reductions in recidivism (Andrews and Bonta 1998; Andrews, Bonta, et al. 1990). Accordingly, the need principle states that if the primary goal of treatment is reduced recidivism, the criminogenic needs of offenders must be emphasized and targeted.

Although the need principle has received empirical support within a number of meta-

analytic reviews (Cleland, Pearson, and Lipton 1996; Dowden 1998), research has been sorely lacking regarding the applicability of this principle to female offenders. More specifically, research has not focused on whether the criminogenic needs of female offenders are the same as those for general offender populations. For example, one of the promising treatment targets identified within the Koons, Burrow, Morash, and Bynum (1997) study involved focusing on issues of victimization and targeting an offender's level of self-esteem. Traditionally, self-esteem has been classified as a noncriminogenic need (Andrews and Bonta 1998). One of the main goals of the present meta-analytic investigation was to determine whether the list of criminogenic and noncriminogenic needs identified by Andrews and his colleagues (Andrews and Bonta 1998; Andrews, Bonta, et al. 1990) was valid when applied to female offenders.

A third principle of effective correctional treatment is responsivity. This principle is directly concerned with the characteristics of program delivery, and it states that the styles and modes of service used within a treatment program should be matched to the learning styles of offenders. Both general and specific responsivity considerations are encompassed within the responsivity principle. General responsivity states that the most effective types of service are based on cognitive-behavioral and social learning approaches. Specific responsivity focuses on offender characteristics such as interpersonal sensitivity, interpersonal anxiety, and verbal intelligence to name a few. For example, Andrews, Zinger, Hoge, Bonta, Gendreau, and Cullen (1990) stated that "the success of highly verbal, evocative, and relationship-dependent services seems to be limited to clients with high levels of interpersonal, self-reflective, and verbal skill" (p. 376). However, the meta-analytic evidence to date has only examined the effectiveness of the general responsivity principle and has suggested that the most powerful treatment approaches are those that have used concrete social learning and behavioral strategies.

Support for the clinical effectiveness of these three principles was derived from the Andrews, Zinger, Hoge, Bonta, Gendreau, and Cullen (1990) meta-analysis, in which a four-level type-of-treatment variable was used to identify effective correctional treatment programs. This four-level variable consisted of criminal sanctions, inappropriate service, unspecified service, and appropriate service. The results revealed that the appropriate service category (programs that adhered to each of the principles of risk, need, and responsivity) was associated with significantly larger reductions in reoffending when compared to each of the remaining categories. Based on these results, the authors concluded that the most effective correctional interventions were ones that incorporated the principles of effective correctional treatment within their program framework.

Methodology

Sample of Studies

The present study combined two distinct samples of studies. The first was taken directly from Andrews, Zinger, Hoge, Bonta, Gendreau, and Cullen (1990), whereas the second (*n* = 220) was composed of additional studies reported by Andrews (1996), Andrews and Bonta (1998: Resource Note 10.1), and Dowden (1998). Studies selected to be included in the present meta-analysis possessed the following characteristics:

1. The study was composed predominantly or entirely of female offenders.

2. The study included a follow-up period. If several follow-up periods were reported, data from the longest follow-up period were coded to ensure the maximum time at risk in the community.

3. The study compared a group of offenders who received some form of intervention to a control group who did not receive the primary intervention. Individual control groups could have received a diluted form of the treatment program and could even have received alternate services as long as these services could be differentiated from those received by the treatment group.

4. A measure of recidivism was included in the report. Recidivism was defined in several ways. Acceptable definitions included rearrest, reconviction, and parole failures or revocations. The preferred measure of recidivism was reconviction.

Variables Included in the Analysis

Risk. Andrews, Zinger, Hoge, Bonta, Gendreau, and Cullen (1990) directly coded the risk principle only when the primary study reported outcome data for high- and low-risk groups separately. Consequently, an overall examination of the risk principle for their entire sample was not available. For the present meta-analysis, an aggregate approach to coding risk (Lipsey 1989) was introduced. In other words, each study was coded as involving higher or lower risk offenders, depending on whether the majority of those in the study had penetrated the justice system at the time of the study or had a previous criminal offense. The study was coded as involving high-risk cases if either of these characteristics were present. The advantage of this approach over the one originally used by Andrews, Zinger, Hoge, Bonta, Gendreau, and Cullen (1990) was that it allowed a risk score to be entered for each study included in the meta-analysis.

General responsivity. Andrews, Zinger, Hoge, Bonta, Gendreau, and Cullen (1990) only coded for general responsivity within their meta-analysis. To ensure consistency and facilitate comparison of the findings, this method of coding the responsivity principle was maintained. More specifically, social learning or cognitive-behavioral programs that used modeling, role-playing, reinforcement, and graduated practice were considered to be appropriately addressing general responsivity.

Need. Each individual treatment program was examined to determine whether any of the more or less promising targets for intervention outlined by Andrews and Bonta (1998) had been included within it. Once all of the needs within a particular treatment program were identified, an overall need variable was constructed by considering the difference score between the number of criminogenic and noncriminogenic needs targeted within the treatment program of interest. The variable was a binary measure (0 = the difference score was less than or equal to 0 and 1 = the difference score was greater than or equal to 1). This variable was used as the overall test of the need principle. In other words, programs targeting more criminogenic than noncriminogenic needs were considered to be appropriately addressing the need principle; conversely, programs that targeted an equal or greater number of noncriminogenic needs than criminogenic ones were considered to be inappropriately addressing the need principle.

Type of treatment. Because, in the present investigation, the principles of risk, need, and responsivity were examined separately, the next logical step involved the development of a type-of-treatment variable similar to the one used by Andrews, Zinger, Hoge, Bonta, Gendreau, and Cullen (1990). This variable had to do with how well the principles of risk, need, and responsivity were incorporated within a particular treatment program, and it was an objective extension of the original coding procedures used by Andrews, Zinger, Hoge, Bonta, Gendreau, and Cullen (1990). The scoring for the variable was based on the composite risk, need, and responsivity scores, with a simple count to determine the number of principles that the treatment program appropriately addressed. This score determined the type-of-treatment rating received by each particular treatment program.

The possible range of scores for this variable ranged from 0 to 3. Criminal sanctions without the provision of human service were automatically coded 0. The four categories, in order of appropriateness, were *inappropriate service, weak service, promising service,* and *most promising service.* For example, a human service program that incorporated only two of the three principles of risk, need, and responsivity was coded as a promising service.

Procedure

Because the meta-analysis was conducted on a subsample of studies taken from a larger meta-analytic review and the same set of variables was used, we assumed that the interrater agreement ratings would remain the same; therefore, the results for the interrater reliability reported below were based on those presented in the original meta-analysis (Dowden 1998).

The first author coded all of the studies that met the inclusion criteria for the present meta-analysis, using the previously mentioned coding procedures. An honors student in psychology was also trained to use the coding manuals and was given a preliminary sample of five studies to code. Once the student had finished coding these studies, any discrepancies in scoring were discussed with the first author. This procedure ensured that the other rater fully understood the underlying constructs presented within the coding manuals. Once the other coder felt comfortable with the coding manuals, the first author provided him with a random sample of 29 studies, equally drawn from the justice, inappropriate, unspecified, and appropriate categories identified by Andrews, Zinger, Hoge, Bonta, Gendreau, and Cullen (1990).

The interrater reliability ratings were calculated by dividing the total number of correct classifications by the total number of classified variables. The rates of agreement for the core variables were 100 percent (any treatment, $r = 1.00$) and 90 percent for behavioral (r = .79), risk level (r = .79), and criminogenic need (r = .79). The interrater agreement was 76 percent (r = .88) on the four-level type-of-treatment variable.

Calculation of effect sizes. The effect-size measure used in the current study was the phi coefficient. Phi was used as the measure of treatment effect because it provides the magnitude and direction of the association between two binary variables (treatment participation and recidivism) and it is equivalent to the Pearson product-moment correlation coefficient. A valuable characteristic of phi is that it can be translated into the Binomial Effect Size Display (BESD; Rosenthal 1991). The BESD converts this statistic into a value that reflects the difference between the recidivism rates of the treatment group and the control group (assuming a base rate of recidivism of 50 percent and an equal number of cases in each group). For example, using the BESD, a mean correlation coefficient of .20 translates into a recidivism rate of 40 percent for the treatment group (i.e., 50 percent - 20/2) and a corresponding recidivism rate of 60 percent for the control group (50 percent + 20/2).

It should be noted that the analyses were conducted on the unweighted effect-size estimates. Both weighted and unweighted effect-size estimates have been reported in the literature, and we decided to use the unweighted estimates for several reasons. Most importantly, the least-square approaches that can be conducted on the unadjusted estimates allow for a more sophisticated and effective exploration of the hypotheses. For example, several potential moderating variables can be identified, and their independent and joint contributions to effect size can be determined.

Analyses. Two sets of analyses were conducted for each of the major variables. The first set focused on the entire sample of treatment outcome studies in which female offenders predominated to ensure that the maximum number of effect sizes contributed to the analyses. The second set of analyses was conducted on only those studies that were composed entirely of female offender populations. This set of analyses provided an opportunity to examine whether any serious discrepancies existed between the predominantly and entirely female offender studies.

Results and Discussion

What Works: A Focus on Risk, Need, Responsivity, and the Most Promising Service

The present meta-analysis consisted of 45 effect sizes extracted from 26 unique studies that examined the effectiveness of correctional treatment programs for female offenders. Sixteen of the studies were composed entirely of female offenders and contributed 24 effect sizes to the analysis. The small number of studies contributing to the meta-analysis highlighted the relative lack of research that has been conducted on the effectiveness of correctional treatment for female offenders.

A wide range of effect sizes was found within the entire sample of studies. More specifically, these varied from -0.43 to +0.82. The overall, mean effect size for the sample was +0.14 (SD = .24) with a 95 percent confidence interval of +0.07 to +0.21. Using the BESD introduced earlier, this value represented a recidivism rate of 43 percent for the treatment group and 57 percent for the control group. Interestingly, when the analysis focused exclusively on female offenders, the mean effect size was +0.17 (SD = .24).

We hypothesized that human service in a justice context would yield greater reductions in recidivism than criminal sanctioning. Although the mean effect size for criminal sanctions was mildly positive (+0.01; k = 10; SD = .07), analysis of variance revealed that the mean effect size for human service interventions (+0.18; k = 35; SD = .25) was associated with a significantly greater mean

Table 23.1
Mean Effect Size for Each Level of Human Service, Risk, Need, and Responsivity

	Adheres to Principle		
Variable Label	**No (k[a])**	**Yes (k)**	η
Human service			
Predominantly female	.01(10)	.18 (35)	.31*
Solely female	.02 (4)	.20 (20)	.29
Risk			
Predominantly female	−.04 (9)	.19 (36)	.40**
Solely female	−.04 (6)	.24 (18)	.51**
Need			
Predominantly female	.04 (24)	.26 (21)	.49**
Solely female	.09 (11)	.23 (13)	.32
Responsivity			
Predominantly female	.08 (30)	.27 (15)	.38**
Solely female	.12 (16)	.25 (8)	.26

[a] *k* refers to the number of studies that contributed to the mean effect size of interest.
*$p < .05$. **$p < .01$.

reduction in recidivism ($\eta = .31$, $p < .04$). Using the BESD, the mean correlation coefficient for human service studies translated into a recidivism rate of 41 percent for human service programs and 59 percent for the control/companion group. The magnitude of this trend was maintained when the analyses focused exclusively on female offenders (see Table 23.1).

These results suggested that human service programs played an important role in determining the therapeutic potential of a particular intervention. Further analyses were conducted to examine whether the principles of risk, need, and responsivity provided additional information concerning what works for female offenders.

Risk, need, and responsivity principles. Strong support was found for each of the principles of risk, need, and responsivity in the meta-analysis (see Table 23.1). More specifically, stronger treatment effects were revealed in programs that targeted higher versus lower risk cases ($\eta = .31$), predominantly focused upon criminogenic versus noncriminogenic needs ($\eta = .49$), and used

behavioral-social learning versus non-behavioral treatment strategies ($\eta = .38$).

Type of treatment. The mean effect sizes for each level of the type-of-treatment variable are presented in Table 23.2. Using the Scheffe correction, the appropriate treatment category yielded a significantly higher mean effect size compared to the weak and inappropriate programs ($p \leq .05$). These findings replicated the results of Andrews, Zinger, Hoge, Bonta, Gendreau, and Cullen (1990) and suggested that programs that appropriately implemented the principles of risk, need, and responsivity within their framework were associated with reductions in reoffending.

Supplementary analyses of need. The percentage distributions for each of the more and less promising targets for intervention are listed in Tables 23.3 and 23.4, respectively. The mean effect size for each need, when it was and was not targeted, and the magnitude of the association with effect size is presented in these tables.

The categorizations used for each of the criminogenic and noncriminogenic need targets were derived directly from a recent

Table 23.2
Mean Effect Sizes for Each Level of Type of Treatment

Level of Type of Treatment	Predominantly Female (k)[a]	Solely Female (k)
Inappropriate service	.02 (14)	.03 (6)
Weak service	.03 (10)	.10 (5)
Promising service	.17 (9)	.18 (7)
Most promising service	.36 (12)	.34 (6)

[a] *k* refers to the number of studies that contributed to the mean effect size of interest.

Table 23.3
Criminogenic Needs and Their Magnitude of Correlation With Effect Size
Percentage of Tests With Need Targeted, Mean Effect Size When and When Not Targeted,
and Correlation With Effect Size

Need Area Targeted	Percentage	Mean Phi (k)[a]		Correlation With Phi
		Not a Target	Targeted	
Personal criminogenic targets				
Antisocial cognition and skill deficits	18	.11 (37)	.31 (8)	.32*
Antisocial cognition	11	.11 (40)	.38 (5)	.36*
Self-control deficits	11	.13 (40)	.22 (5)	.12
Interpersonal criminogenic targets				
Family and peers	31	.07 (31)	.30 (14)	.45**
Family process	20	.08 (36)	.38 (9)	.51***
Antisocial associates	14	.09 (36)	.35 (9)	.45**
School/work	18	.15 (38)	.10 (7)	−.08
Substance abuse	11	.14 (40)	.14 (5)	−.01

Note: Two targets occurred in less than 5 percent of the studies: Relapse prevention ($k = 1, r = $ N/A) and barriers to treatment ($k = 3, r = .52$***). Components of antisocial cognition include antisocial attitudes ($k = 1, r = $ N/A) and anger ($k = 4, r = .34$*). Components of family process include affection ($k = 9, r = .51$***) and supervision ($k = 4, r = .62$***). Components of antisocial associates include increase contact with prosocial ($k = 8, r = .39$**) and decrease contact with antisocial ($k = 3, r = .08$ n.s.). Components of schoolwork include school ($k = 6, r = -.04$ n.s.) and vocational skills ($k = 1, r = $ N/A). Components of substance abuse include treatment ($k = 4, r = .03$ n.s.) and information ($k = 3, r = .08$ n.s.).

[a] *k* refers to the number of studies that contributed to the mean effect size of interest.

*p < .05. **p < .01. ***p < .001.

meta-analysis of the need principle conducted by Andrews, Dowden, and Gendreau (forthcoming). They combined similar criminogenic and noncriminogenic need factors to create composite need categories. These categories and their subcomponents are presented in Tables 23.3 and 23.4.

Regarding criminogenic needs, Table 23.3 reveals that 31 percent of the treatment programs focused on interpersonal criminogenic need targets, defined as fam-

Table 23.4

Noncriminogenic Needs Rank Ordered by Magnitude of Correlation With Effect Size: Percentage of Tests With Need Targeted, Mean Effect Size When and When Not Targeted, and Correlation With Effect Size

| | | Mean Phi (k)[a] | | |
Need Area Targeted	Percentage	Not a Target	Targeted	Correlation With Phi
Personal noncriminogenic targets	24	.15 (34)	.13 (11)	−.03
Vague emotional/personal problems	20	.14 (36)	.15 (6)	.02
Interpersonal noncriminogenic targets	13	.16 (39)	.01 (6)	−.23
Family (other)	11	.17 (40)	−.06 (5)	−.32*

Note: Low frequency targets include targeting of respect for criminal thinking (k = 1, r = N/A) and cohesive peers (k = 1, r = N/A). Components of personal noncriminogenic targets include fear of official punishment (k = 2, r = -.10) and respect criminal thinking (k = 1, r = 12). Components of interpersonal noncriminogenic targets include increase cohesiveness of antisocial peer groups (k = 1, r = N/A).

[a] k refers to the number of studies that contributed to the mean effect size of interest.

*$p < .05$.

ily process or antisocial associate variables. These need targets yielded the strongest positive association with reduced reoffending (η = .45). The other category of criminogenic needs, personal criminogenic need targets, included focusing on either antisocial cognition or self-control deficits. This category also yielded a significant positive correlation with effect size (η = .37).

An interesting pattern of results emerged when the analyses shifted to the school/work and substance abuse variables and their corresponding relationships with recidivism. More specifically, both school/work (−.08) and substance abuse (−.01) had slightly negative correlations with reduced reoffending.

Personal and interpersonal noncriminogenic need targets were also examined. The results revealed that almost one quarter of the effect sizes targeted personal noncriminogenic needs. Not surprisingly, personal noncriminogenic needs had a slightly negative correlation with effect size (−.03). On the other hand, interpersonal noncriminogenic needs were targeted in only 13 percent of the cases and yielded a moderate negative association with reduced recidivism (−.23). An even more interesting finding appeared when analyses focused on other noncriminogenic forms of family interventions. Although the family-functioning variables classified as criminogenic needs were associated with enhanced reductions in reoffending, vague forms of family intervention (i.e., providing family counseling without specifically identifying the targets for intervention) had a significant negative relationship with effect size (-.32). Clearly, the specific targets of family intervention were important indicators of the therapeutic potential of these particular programs.

Methodological considerations. Several important methodological factors were also considered to determine their relationship with effect size. The majority of these were taken directly from the strongest methodological variables identified by Andrews, Dowden, and Gendreau (forthcoming) in their examination of the strongest potential threats to validity (see Table 23.5). The remaining two variables, age and randomness of design, were included due to their

Table 23.5
The Most Important Methodological and Control Variables
and Their Relationships With Effect Size

Variable	Frequency (percentage)	Simple r	Partial r
CJ[a] sponsor	84	−.29	−.08
CJ[a] referral	87	.34	.21
Nonresidential	71	−.08	.25
Small sample	58	.26	.12
New program	38	.26	−.17
Involved evaluator	18	.64***	.53***
Older (age 18+)	22	.03	.17
Random assignment	31	−.02	−.10

[a] CJ stands for criminal justice.
***$p < .001$.

importance within both meta-analytic and treatment outcome research. The simple and partial correlation coefficients (with type of controlled treatment) for each of these variables are presented in Table 23.5.

Only the involved evaluator variable was significantly correlated with effect size. Although some individuals have claimed that an involved evaluator is a biasing factor in rehabilitation research, we share Lipsey's (1995) view that an involved evaluator may not be a sign of bias but a sign of increased therapeutic integrity. In other words, having an involved evaluator in the implementation and evaluation of the program increases the likelihood that the program will be correctly implemented. Evaluators who are not so involved may not take the same time and consideration in the preliminary stages of program implementation.

Conclusion

The meta-analysis reported here indicated that the principles of risk, need, and general responsivity were important contributors to treatment outcome for female offenders. These results support previous theoretically derived viewpoints (Andrews

and Bonta 1998; Andrews, Bonta, et al. 1990; Andrews, Zinger, et al. 1990).

However, some more specific findings should be emphasized. One of these was that the most promising targets for intervention (i.e., substance abuse and basic education skills) that were identified by a national sample of correctional administrators (Koons et al. 1997) did not emerge as important in our study; rather, the strongest predictors of treatment success were interpersonal criminogenic need targets and, in particular, family process variables. Furthermore, it is clear that personal and interpersonal noncriminogenic needs were not related to treatment outcome; in fact, they were associated with recidivism increases within the treatment group.

Although only a moderate number of effect sizes contributed to the present meta-analysis, it is significant that the principles of risk, need, and responsivity survived all of the strongest threats to validity documented within previous meta-analytic research (Andrews, Dowden, et al. forthcoming). In addition, treatment programs that appropriately addressed these principles were associated with enhanced reductions in recidivism.

The Koons, Burrow, Morash, and Bynum (1997) study suggested that programs that focused on dealing with past victimization issues and targeted self-esteem are promising targets for change for female offenders. Because none of the studies discussed here focused on these treatment targets, it remains unclear as to whether these are criminogenic or noncriminogenic needs for female offenders. These are matters for future study.

Despite these overall findings, one final point should be made. Although the present investigation explored the effectiveness of the principles of risk, need, and responsivity for female offender populations, it did not look at gender as a specific responsivity consideration. More specifically, we did not examine whether making the treatment program more responsive to the specific learning styles of women offenders (i.e., relationship-oriented treatment) had any impact on recidivism. Exploring the effects of gender as a specific responsivity consideration will be the focus of a future meta-analysis.

In conclusion, although promising evidence was uncovered for each of the principles of risk, need, and responsivity, more work needs to be done.

Study Questions

1. Describe the research design, data collection methods, sample, and measures used by the authors in conducting this study.

2. What are the principles of risk, need, and responsivity?

3. Summarize the findings from this study. Why do you think they are important for correctional officials?

Appendix

The following studies were included in the meta-analysis. Studies that were composed predominantly or entirely of female offenders met our inclusion criteria. This standard was adopted to ensure that the maximum number of effect sizes contributed to the meta-analysis. Please note the similarities between the trends for the entire set of studies and those that solely involved female offenders in Table 23.1 and Table 23.2.

Alexander, James F., Cole Barton, R. Steven Schiavo, and Bruce V. Parsons. 1976. "Systems-Behavioral Intervention With Delinquents: Therapist Characteristics, Family Behavior, and Outcome." *Journal of Consulting and Clinical Psychology* 44:556–664.

Borduin, Charles M., Barton J. Mann, Lynn T. Cone, Scott W. Henggeler, Bethany R. Fucci, David M. Blaske, and Robert A. Williams. 1995. "Multisystemic Treatment of Serious Juvenile Offenders: Long-Term Prevention of Criminality and Violence." *Journal of Consulting and Clinical Psychology* 63:569–78.

Buckner, John C. and Meda Chesney-Lind. 1983. "Dramatic Cures for Juvenile Crime: An Evaluation of a Prisoner-Run Delinquency Prevention Program." *Criminal Justice and Behavior* 10:227–47.

Davidson, William S. and Timothy R. Wolfred. 1977. "Evaluation of a Community-Based Behavior Modification Program for Prevention of Delinquency." *Community Mental Health Journal* 13:296–306.

Davies, Jean and Nancy Goodman. 1972. *Girl Offenders Aged 17 to 20 Years*. London, UK: H.M. Stationary Office.

Deng, Xiaogang. 1997. "The Deterrent Effects of Initial Sanction on First-Time Apprehended Shoplifters." *International Journal of Offender Therapy and Comparative Criminology* 41:284–97.

Druckman, Joan M. 1979. "A Family-Oriented Policy and Treatment Program for Female Juvenile Status Offenders." *Journal of Marriage and the Family* 41:627–36.

Gordon, Donald A., Jack Arbuthnot, Kathryn E. Gustafson, and Peter McGreen. 1988. "Home-Based Behavioral Systems Family Therapy With Disadvantaged Juvenile Delinquents." *The American Journal of Family Therapy* 16:243–55.

Gruber, Martin. 1979. "Family Counseling and the Status Offender." *Juvenile and Family Court Journal* 30:23–7.

Johnson, David C., Ronald W. Shearon, and George M. Britton. 1974. "Correctional Education and Recidivism in a Women's Correctional Center." *Adult Education* 24:121–9.

Klein, Nancy C., James F. Alexander, and Bruce V. Parsons. 1977. "Impact of Family Systems Intervention on Recidivism and Sibling Delinquency: A Model of Primary Prevention and Program Evaluation." *Journal of Consulting and Clinical Psychology* 3:469–74.

Meyer, Henry J., Edgar F. Borgotta, and Wyatt C. Jones. 1965. *Girls at Vocational High: An Experiment in Social Work Intervention*. New York: Russell Sage.

Moo, Joy. 1983. "Police Decisions for Dealing With Juvenile Offenders." *British Journal of Criminology* 23:249–62.

O'Donnell, Clifford R., Tony Lydgate, and Walter S. O. Fo. 1979. "The Buddy System: Review and Follow-Up." *Child Behavior Therapy* 1:161–9.

Prendergast, Michael L., Jean Wellisch, and Maimee M. Wong. 1996. "Residential Treatment for Women Parolees Following Prison-Based Drug Treatment: Treatment Experiences, Needs, Services, and Outcomes." *The Prison Journal* 76:253–74.

Rausch, Sharla. 1983. "Court Processing Versus Diversion of Status Offenders: A Test of Deterrence and Labeling Theories." *Journal of Research in Crime and Delinquency* 20:39–54.

Redfering, David L. 1973. "Durability of Effects of Group Counseling With Institutionalized Females." *Journal of Abnormal Psychology* 82:85–6.

Ross, Robert R. and H. Bryan McKay. 1976. "A Study of Institutional Treatment Programs." *International Journal of Offender Therapy and Comparative Criminology* 21:165–73.

Sowles, Richard C. and John H. Gill. 1970. "Institutional and Community Adjustment of Delinquents Following Counseling." *Journal of Consulting and Clinical Psychology* 34:398–402.

Spergel, Irving A., Frederic G. Reamer, and James P. Lynch. 1981. "Deinstitutionalization of Status Offenders: Individual Outcomes and System Effects." *Journal of Research in Crime and Delinquency* 18:4–33.

Stewart, Mary J., Edward L. Vockell, and Rose E. Ray. 1986. "Decreasing Court Appearances of Juvenile Status Offenders." *Social Casework* 67:74–9.

Vito, Gennaro F., Ronald M. Holmes, and Deborah G. Wilson. 1985. "The Effect of Shock and Regular Probation Upon Recidivism: A Comparative Analysis." *American Journal of Criminal Justice* 9:152–62.

Wade, Terry C., Tern L. Morton, Judith E. Lind, and Newton R. Ferris. 1971. "A Family Crisis Intervention Approach to Diversion From the Juvenile Justice System." *Juvenile Justice Journal* 28:43–51.

Wexler, Harry K., Gregory P. Flaken, and Douglas S. Lipton. 1990. "Outcome Evaluation of a Prison Therapeutic Community for Substance Abuse Treatment." *Criminal Justice and Behavior* 17:71–92.

Young, Mark C., John Gartner, Thomas O'Connor, David Larson, and Kevin Wright. 1995. "Long-Term Recidivism Among Federal Inmates Trained as Volunteer Prison Ministers." *Journal of Offender Rehabilitation* 22:97–118.

Zeisel, Hans. 1982. "Disagreement Over the Evaluation of a Controlled Experiment." *American Journal of Sociology* 88:378–89.

References

Andrews, D. A. 1996. "Behavioral, Cognitive Behavioral and Social Learning Contributions to Criminological Theory." Presented at the American Society of Criminology annual meeting, November 20, Chicago, IL.

Andrews, D. A. and James Bonta. 1998. *The Psychology of Criminal Conduct*. 2d ed. Cincinnati, OH: Anderson.

Andrews, D. A., James Bonta, and Robert D. Hoge. 1990. "Classification for Effective Rehabilitation: Rediscovering Psychology." *Criminal Justice and Behavior* 17:19–52.

Andrews, D. A., Craig Dowden, and Paul Gendreau. Forthcoming. "Clinically Relevant and Psychologically Informed Approaches to Reducing Criminal Recidivism: A Meta-Analytic Study of Human Service, Risk, Need, Responsivity and Other Concerns in Justice Contexts." Manuscript submitted for publication.

Andrews, D. A., Ivan Zinger, Robert D. Hoge, James Bonta, Paul Gendreau, and Francis T. Cullen. 1990. "Does Correctional Treatment Work? A Clinically Relevant and Psychologically Informed Meta-Analysis." *Criminology* 28:369–404.

Cleland, Charles M., Frank Pearson, and Douglas S. Lipton. 1996. "A Meta-Analytic Approach to the Link Between Needs-Targeted Treatment and Reductions in Criminal Offending." Presented at the American Society of Criminology annual meeting, November 20, Chicago, IL.

Dowden, Craig. 1998. "A Meta-Analytic Examination of the Risk, Need and Responsivity Principles and Their Importance Within the Rehabilitation Debate." Masters thesis, Department of Psychology, Carleton University, Ottawa, Ontario, Canada.

Gibbons, Don C. 1999. "Review Essay: Changing Lawbreakers—What Have We Learned Since the 1950's?" *Crime & Delinquency* 45:272–93.

Hill, James K., D. A. Andrews, and Robert D. Hoge. 1991. "Meta-Analysis of Treatment Programs for Young Offenders: The Effect of Clinically Relevant Treatment on Recidivism, With Controls Introduced for Various Methodological Variables." *Canadian Journal of Program Evaluation* 6:97–109.

Izzo, Rhena L. and Robert R. Ross. 1990. "Meta-Analysis of Rehabilitation Programs for Juvenile Delinquents." *Criminal Justice and Behavior* 17:134–42.

Koons, Barbara A., John D. Burrow, Merry Morash, and Tim Bynum. 1997. "Expert and Offender Perceptions of Program Elements Linked to Successful Outcomes for Incarcerated Women." *Crime & Delinquency* 43:512–32.

Lipsey, Mark W. 1989. "The Efficacy of Intervention for Juvenile Delinquency: Results from 400 Studies." Presented at the 41st annual meeting of the American Society of Criminology, November, Reno, NV.

——. 1995. "What Do We Learn From 400 Research Studies on the Effectiveness of Treatment with Juvenile Delinquents?" Pp. 63–78 in *What Works: Reducing Reoffending—Guidelines From Research and Practice*, edited by J. McGuire. Winchester, UK: Wiley.

Losel, Friedrich. 1996. "Effective Correctional Programming: What Empirical Research Tells Us and What It Doesn't." *Forum on Corrections Research* 8:33–6.

Martinson, Robert. 1974. "What Works? Questions and Answers About Prison Reform." *The Public Interest* 10:22–54.

McGuire, James, ed. 1995. *What Works: Reducing Reoffending—Guidelines From Research and Practice*. Winchester, UK: Wiley.

Morash, Merry, Tim S. Bynum, and Barbara A. Koons. 1995. *Findings From the National Study of Innovative and Promising Programs for Women Offenders*. East Lansing: Michigan State University, School of Criminal Justice.

Rosenthal, Robert. 1991. *Meta-Analytic Procedures for Social Research*. Rev. ed. Newbury Park, CA: Sage.

24
Identifying and Treating the Mentally Disordered Prison Inmate

Eliot S. Hartstone
Henry J. Steadman
Pamela Clark Robbins
John Monahan

During the 1950s, mental hospitals housed hundreds of thousands of mentally ill Americans. Today, those hospitals have given way to penal institutions. The exact number of mentally ill prisoners is unknown; however, there is little question that the mentally ill pose a significant problem for the correctional system. Providing safe and secure facilities, meeting the needs of special populations, and operating within a budget are all challenges that must be met. Eliot S. Hartstone and his associates offer a glimpse into the scope of mental health problems in prisons. By examining procedures in five states, they provide an overview of how mentally ill prisoners are handled in the United States.

"Mentally disordered offenders" can be considered as an umbrella term embracing four distinct legal categories: defendants who are incompetent to stand trial or not guilty by reason of insanity, persons adjudicated as "mentally disordered sex offenders," and convicted prisoners who are transferred to mental hospitals (Steadman et al., 1982;

Monahan and Steadman, 1983a, 1983b). Public attention has focused on the first three of these categories, perhaps because of a belief that they constitute a form of "beating the system." That is, the offenders in these cases committed what would popularly be considered a crime, yet have escaped criminal conviction. Notorious cases that have raised these issues (although not always successfully), such as John Hinckley, Patricia Hearst, David Berkowitz, and Mark Chapman, no doubt contribute to this public attention.

The media, the public, and legislators, however, have yet to show comparable interest in the fourth category of mentally disordered offenders—persons first convicted of a crime, incarcerated, and later found to be in need of transfer to a mental health facility. It is likely that this lack of interest in mentally disordered inmates reflects the fact that these individuals did not "get away" with their crimes since they have already been convicted and sentenced to prison. Social scientists have also, for the most part, limited their research efforts to "incompetency" (Roesch and Golding, 1980; Mowbrey, 1979; Steadman, 1979) or "insanity" (Rogers and Bloom, 1982; Petrila, 1982; Pasewark et al., 1979; Pasewark and Lanthorn, 1977; Steadman, 1980; Cook and Sigorski, 1974; Morrow and Peterson, 1966) and "mentally disordered sex offender" status (Konecni et al., 1980; Sturgeon and Taylor, 1980). Researchers rarely study the less publicized situation where the prisoner's mental health problems were not manifest, or at least not identified, until after placement in prison (Gearing et al., 1990; Halleck, 1961).

Despite the meager public and research attention garnered by mentally disordered inmates, they constitute the largest category of mentally disordered offenders in the U.S.—54% of all mentally disordered offenders, and 68% of all *male* mentally disordered offenders admitted to mental health facilities in the United States in 1978 (Steadman et al., 1982). In fact, 10,831 inmates were transferred from state prisons into separate mental health units or facilities in 1978 (Steadman et al., 1982). This number does not include those inmates who were experiencing mental health problems but received care (or at least remained) in the general prison population.

It also appears that for at least two reasons, the number of mentally disordered inmates may increase in coming years. First, there is a movement in a number of states to do away with the insanity defense in favor of a "guilty but insane" verdict, which may have the effect of mandating mental health services for specified inmates who previously would have been acquitted by reason of insanity. Second, current trends in criminal sentencing seem likely to result in placing more offenders into state prisons for longer periods. In 1981, the largest annual increase in U.S. history in the number of prison inmates (41,292) was recorded (Gardner, 1982). Thus, even if the proportion of inmates who were mentally disordered remained constant, the absolute number of inmates requiring care would have skyrocketed. Using a low estimate of the proportion (15%) of inmates who are mentally disordered there would have been nearly 6200 more inmates needing mental health services in U.S. prisons in 1982 than in 1981.

The level of management problems that these mentally disordered inmates pose has been demonstrated by Uhlig (1976). Examining a group of 356 offenders throughout New England prisons who had been identified as special management problems, he found that 195 (53%) were diagnosed as having current psychiatric disturbances. Clearly, a major source of conflict in volatile prison settings are mentally disordered inmates. These inmates present problems with which prison officials usually are not prepared or trained to cope. Further, these inmates would appear to create additional management problems for prison officials by generating disruptive behavior among inmates who do not know how to respond

to the unusual and inappropriate behavior displayed by the mentally disordered, and who tend to victimize these more vulnerable inmates. It is also important to note that an additional series of problems results from those inmates who are withdrawn or excessively depressed but who may not be disruptive or create management problems (Hartstone et al., 1982).

Programmatic responses to mentally disordered inmates in the United States have been cyclical: (1) responsibility for mentally disordered prison inmates repeatedly has shifted back and forth from corrections to mental health departments; and (2) the appropriateness of mixing convicted mentally disordered persons in civil mental hospitals has been viewed very differently from one era to another (Steadman and Cocozza, 1974). The experiences in New York illustrate these long-standing issues.

The first move in New York to separate civil mental patients from mentally disordered persons charged with or convicted of crimes occurred in 1782. An "Act Respecting Lunatics" was passed that prevented the overseers of the poor, who were responsible for the mentally disordered, from housing the mentally disordered in jails or "in the same room with any person charged or convicted of an offense" (N.Y. Laws 1827, Ch. 294, Sec. 2). They could be kept only in poorhouses. When the state's first asylum for the mentally disordered was opened in 1842 in Utica, however, the legislative provisions allowed for the mixing of mentally disordered convicts, those confined under indictments or criminal charge, those acquitted by reason of insanity, and patients committed under any civil process. Thus, the mental health system, rather than the more general social welfare system or corrections, came to care for mentally disordered inmates.

By 1855, there was movement again toward separating patients who were convicted or alleged criminals from civil patients. This movement culminated with the 1859 opening of an Asylum for Insane

Convicts at Auburn Penitentiary, the first institution of its kind in the United States. In 1861 the state legislature directed that all mentally disordered male prisoners be transferred from Utica to Auburn. In 1869, Auburn was directed to house those persons acquitted because of insanity as well as defendants charged with murder, attempted murder, or arson who became mentally disordered prior to trial or sentencing. Thus, convicted and unconvicted patients were again confined in the same facility, separate from civil patients, as they had been before Auburn Asylum opened.

A legislative commission established in 1886 located a site in Matteawan to replace the Auburn Asylum, which would be large enough to allow for the separation, within a single facility, of unconvicted patients awaiting trial from mentally disordered convicts. As a *New York Times* article reporting the opening noted, "The two classes of patients differ widely, the criminals giving the officials much anxiety at times. They are frequently dangerous and destructive." As had happened with Auburn soon after its opening, the number of patients at Matteawan quickly increased. While the patient population continued to burgeon at Matteawan, pressure also built for the separation of the "convict insane" from the other criminally insane patients, such as insanity cases. In 1894, the State Lunacy Commission noted that separate institutions were beneficial because the presence of insane convicts "was very objectionable to the ordinary inmates" of state hospitals.

A new facility, Dannemora State Hospital, opened in northern New York in January, 1900, under the auspices of the Department of Corrections. By this time, Matteawan was overcrowded with 719 patients in a building whose capacity was 500. All inmates in the state who were determined to be mentally disordered after a felony conviction would be housed in Dannemora. All other convicted patients and pretrial cases would go to Matteawan. Between 1900 and 1966, the patient population at Matteawan and Danne-

mora climbed steadily, with Matteawan reaching a patient census of over 2000 in the early 1960s. At the same time, Dannemora reached a peak of about 1400 patients. However, in these 66 years little changed in either the statutes or the two facilities.

Throughout the late 1960s and early 1970s, there was a dramatic decrease in the patient census at Matteawan and Dannemora, and a gradual shift for all mental health treatment for all classes of mentally disordered offenders to the Office of Mental Health (OMH). Dannemora was closed in 1972 and Matteawan in 1977, removing the Department of Corrections (DOC) from any direct mental health care responsibilities. Instead, the OMH opened a maximum-security hospital for incompetent defendants and defendants not guilty by reason of insanity in 1972 and one for mentally disordered inmates in 1977. Thus, over this 150-year period, care of mentally disordered inmates in New York shifted from welfare, to mental health, to corrections, and back to mental health.

History appears to be again repeating itself as states continually tinker with their treatment arrangements for mentally disordered inmates, sometimes charging departments of mental health with the responsibility, either by themselves or in concert with departments of corrections, and sometimes mandating treatment by the departments of corrections themselves. Based on our 1978 national survey (Steadman et al., 1982), there appears to be little consensus on the most appropriate arrangements for mentally disordered inmates. This survey revealed that 16 states transferred most (at least 75%) of their mentally disordered inmates into mental health facilities or units administered by the DOC;[1] 28 states transferred the majority into hospitals or units run by the DMH; and six states utilized a combination of DOC and DMH units.

It may be that the lack of consensus across states on how to handle mentally disordered inmates reflects in part a lack of empirical data. There are no data on whether there is a type of arrangement that is optimal for both inmates and facilities, what such an arrangement might look like, and under what circumstances one arrangement is to be preferred over others. As prison populations climb, as the number of beds in state mental hospitals continues to be limited, and as legal rights to minimum health and mental health treatment are confirmed by the courts, more information is needed to facilitate the development of appropriate programs for mentally disordered inmates.

In an effort to provide some empirical data on the needs of these inmates and how the correctional and mental health systems respond to them, this chapter utilizes data from 67 interviews with a wide range of correctional staff in five states. Specifically, these data focus on the placement options available for mentally disordered inmates, the adequacy of procedures used to identify the inmates and transfer them to mental health facilities, and the extent to which the procedures used meet the needs of these inmates.

Methods

Our data are drawn from a national study of the movement of offenders between prisons and mental hospitals funded by the National Institute of Justice. As part of this effort, six states—Arizona, California, Iowa, Massachusetts, New York, and Texas—were identified for an intensive examination of the confinement and criminal careers of inmates and mental patients, and of the practices and processes of transferring prison inmates to mental health facilities. Five of these six states (New York excluded) were found to use Department of Corrections (DOC) mental health settings as the main placement for mentally disordered inmates. It is these five states with their use of *intra*-agency transfers for mentally disordered inmates that are the focus of this chapter.

While approximately two-thirds of the states in the United States transfer most of their mentally disordered inmates to state departments of mental health (DMH), since

the larger states tend to use DOC options, 71% of all prison inmates transferred for mental health services in 1978 were placed in DOC-operated mental health facilities. Any effort to generalize from the data reported here should be limited to those states that transfer the majority of their inmates to DOC mental health settings. The issues discussed here focus only on procedures for dealing with male inmates, since 95.8% of all inmates transferred in our 1978 study were males. Women's programs require specialized study for what are often more haphazard, less formal service arrangements.

Structured interviews were conducted with a wide range of DOC personnel in the five target states between October 1, 1980, and January 31, 1981. The interviews were primarily open-ended, with some Likert-type items, and averaged 90 minutes. A two-person interview team completed interviews with 67 persons employed by the DOC. Interviews were conducted at the DOC central office, the state prison transferring the most inmates, and the mental health setting receiving the most inmate transfers. At the DOC central office, the DOC Commissioner (or Deputy Commissioner) and the mental health treatment director were interviewed. At the prison transferring the most inmates in each state, we interviewed the warden, the treatment director, two direct clinical service providers, and a correctional officer. Hospital or Treatment Center interviews consisted of the facility or unit director, the chief of security, two clinical staff members, and a line staff representative. In instances where there were a number of people in a particular position, we interviewed the person nominated by the facility director. Thus, the information obtained from the interviews reflects a wide range of staff locations and job responsibilities.

Scope of Mental Health Problems in Prisons

The first issue of interest was the perception of the various DOC staff of the scope of the problem and how their estimates compared with prior research. All respondents were asked what percentage of the DOC inmates they believed to be either seriously mentally disordered (that is, psychotic) or suffering from a psychological problem that warranted mental health treatment. The mean responses, separated by staff location, are presented in Table 24.1. It is clear that a sizeable number of state prisoners were suffering from serious mental health problems. As seen in Table 24.1, the respondents in our five target states estimated on average that 5.8% of state DOC inmates were "seriously mentally ill," and that an additional 37.7%, while not psychotic, were suffering from a psychological problem that would significantly benefit from mental health treatment. This table also shows that, when compared to central office administrators, the people actually working in the institutions (that is, prisons and DOC mental hospitals) thought considerably more DOC inmates were psychotic (6.1% versus 4.3%) or experiencing other psychological problems (38.7% versus 30.6%). While the differences may appear at first glance to be small, one must consider that given the size of the total prison populations in these five states, this translates into a difference of 6389 inmates defined as in need of mental health services.[2]

In general, the overall estimates of the respondents are similar to the best estimates of true prevalence of mental disorder that Monahan and Steadman's (1983a) literature review found:

> One is left from these studies with true prevalence rates for serious mental illness (i.e., psychoses) among offenders incarcerated in prison or jails varying from 1 percent (Guze, 1976) to 7 percent (Bolton, 1976). True prevalence rates for less severe forms of mental illness (nonpsychotic mental disorders and personality disorders) vary greatly, ranging up to 15–20 percent (Roth, 1980).

When staff were asked whether they believed there had been any change over the past ten years in the percentage of inmates suffering from a "serious mental illness," 43% of the staff said they believed the percentage of disordered inmates had gone up. In contrast, only 7% of those responding said the number had gone down. Those prison and correctional mental health facility staff persons who felt this problem was becoming increasingly severe offered a variety of explanations. Most respondents cited one of three factors: conditions in the prison, the deinstitutionalization movement in state mental hospitals, and general societal conditions. A prison guard concerned that the prisons themselves were generating the problem stated:

> The environment here in prison is changing for the worse. It is becoming more and more crowded, causing a lot of problems. There are now three to four inmates in one cell; they are in the cell for 12–14 hours at a stretch.

A clinician at a DOC-operated mental hospital blamed the problem there on DMH deinstitutionalization of mental hospitals:

> The main cause [is] deinstitutionalization by (DMH). A lot of these persons are getting criminalized. It is easier for a cop to take John Doe to a lock-up—end up here—than to send him to a state hospital.

A social worker in a state prison stated that she felt there were mental health problems in prison because of general societal conditions:

> There has been an increase in societal population, a breakdown of the families, a pressure packed society. It is a societal problem.

Due to these perceived problems, DOC staff expressed concern that there are sizeable numbers of inmates in the DOC who are experiencing serious psychiatric or psychological problems warranting some form of clinical intervention. The remainder of

Table 24.1

Percentage of Inmates in State Prisons Perceived as Having Mental Health Problems
(by Staff Location)

| | Mental Health Need | | | |
| | Seriously Mentally Ill | | Psychological Problem Warranting Treatment | |
Staff Location	Mean %	(N)	Mean %	(N)
DOC central office	4.3	(9)	30.6	(8)
Mental health facility to which inmates were transferred	6.2	(25)	42.3	(29)
Prison from which inmates were transferred	5.9	(23)	34.4	(24)
Total	5.8	(57)[a]	37.7	(61)[b]

[a] Missing data for 10 cases.

[b] Missing data for 6 cases.

this chapter examines what is happening to those prison inmates who are mentally disordered—where can they receive treatment, and are they identified and placed in the designated mental health settings?

Placement Options and Procedures

While all five state DOCs treated mentally disordered inmates within the agency, these agencies did not all have the same philosophy regarding mental disorder, nor did they establish the same placement options. California had substantially more beds available and transferred more inmates than any of the other states. Within the California Department of Corrections, two major placement options were used for inmates suffering mental health problems. The California Medical Facility at Vacaville (CMF) received those inmates who were most disordered and dangerous, and the California Men's Colony (CMC) utilized one of their prison quadrants usually for less disordered and less violent mentally disordered inmates. Over 3000 inmates are transferred into either the CMF or CMC annually. Prior to 1980, some inmates were transferred to DMH's Atascadero State Hospital, but DOC

staff said that since January 1980 it was practically impossible to get an inmate into Atascadero. As indicated by the number of DOC beds that were available for mental health care, the California DOC approach clearly reflects a philosophy that stresses the importance of recognizing the mentally disordered offender and placing such inmates in a separate facility or unit for treatment.

In three states (Arizona, Iowa, and Massachusetts) there was a single DOC-operated mental hospital. In these three states, the hospitals admitted all categories of "mentally disordered offenders" (transfers, insanity acquittals, and incompetency cases). The hospitals varied considerably in size and transfer admissions. There were 442 beds at Bridgewater State Hospital (Massachusetts), 80 beds at the Iowa Medical Facility, and 40 beds at Alhambra (Arizona). The Massachusetts and Iowa hospitals both admitted approximately 225–275 transfers annually, while the Arizona facility admitted fewer than 15.

The Texas Department of Corrections (TDC) operated with the philosophy that all TDC inmates are TDC's responsibility and should, whenever possible, be maintained in the general population. While a maximum security unit at Rusk State Hospital (operated by DMH) was a potential placement option, the use of this unit decreased from 65 inmates in 1978, to 37 in 1979, to 9 in 1980. Typically, when an inmate's condition caused the TDC to move an inmate out of the general population, the inmate was transferred to the Huntsville Treatment Center (HTC), located within the Huntsville prison. This unit contained 90 beds, an average census of 67, and admitted 20–25 inmates each month. The HTC was used primarily for short-term stabilization and medication, followed by the inmate's immediate transfer back to the general population. On rare and extreme occasions, inmates have been transferred from the HTC to Rusk State Hospital. The number of inmates placed in neither the HTC or Rusk State Hospital seems particularly low given the large number of inmates (approximately 30,000) residing with the Texas Department of Corrections.

In all five study states, the initial identification of the mentally disordered inmate usually resulted from observations made by a correctional officer and a referral to a prison psychologist or psychiatrist. At that point, however, considerable procedural variations occurred in the role of the prison, the mental hospital, the DOC central office, and the courts in determining which inmates were transferred. In only one state (Massachusetts) was judicial approval required. In two states (Arizona, California), transfer decisions were routinely made or approved by representatives of the DOC central office. The mental health receiving facility had an active role in the transfer decisions in two states (Iowa and Arizona), while in Texas the prison psychologist's recommendations were followed without any review. Whatever the means used to review recommendations made by the prison clinician (such as the court or DOC central office), the review appeared to be perfunctory and virtually all inmates recommended for transfer were, in fact, transferred.

An examination of available placement options and transfer procedures implemented in our five study states reveals that, although each of these states transferred most of their inmates into facilities operated within the DOC, variation occurred in the type of placements available, the extent to which they were used, and the procedures implemented for transferring an inmate to one of these facilities.

Adequacy of Identification and Transfer Procedures

Identification

In order to ascertain which inmates were selected for transfer to mental health facilities, we asked all respondents whether transfers occurred primarily for clinical reasons (that is, mental health difficulties) or behavioral reasons (management problems), and what types of inmates were identified for referral to mental hospitals. The majority of our respondents (52.6%) reported that persons were identified for behavioral reasons, 33.3% felt that identification was usually brought about due to clinical reasons, and 14% stated that identification could occur for either reason. In only one state (California) did more respondents attribute identification to clinical reasons (52.6%) more often than to behavioral reasons (36.8%). In each of the other four states, 50% or more of the respondents said inmates were primarily identified for behavioral reasons.

When asked for specific reasons why inmates were identified for referral to mental health facilities, the respondents focused primarily on mental health problems. As presented in Table 24.2, our 67 respondents produced 146 responses: 16.4% of the responses referred to psychosis, 65.1% referred to other mental health reasons, and 15.1% focused solely on violence or management problems. The fact that behavior was felt to be a more important determi-

Table 24.2

Reasons Why Inmates Are Transferred to Mental Health Facility

	Staff Work Location							
	Central Office		**Mental Health Facility**		**Prison**		**Total**	
Reason for Transfer	**%**	**(N)**	**%**	**(N)**	**%**	**(N)**	**%**	**(N)**
Psychotic	25.0	(6)	15.4	(10)	14.0	(8)	16.4	(24)
Other mental illness[a]	45.8	(11)	66.2	(43)	72.0	(41)	65.1	(95)
Management problem/violent	25.0	(6)	15.4	(10)	10.5	(6)	15.1	(22)
Other	4.2	(1)	3.0	(2)	3.5	(2)	3.4	(5)
Total							100.0	(146)

[a] Other mental illness includes (1) DSM II diagnostic classification that does not fall under the heading of psychotic; (2) more general references to mental illness (for example, crazy, flaky, bizarre, mentally ill, unstable); and (3) mentally ill and dangerous.

nant than clinical factors in deciding whether an inmate was identified for transfer would seem to indicate that some inmates who were mentally disordered were not identified because their behavior was not particularly visible or disruptive, and that other inmates may have been identified for transfer due to behaviors which were unacceptable, but not necessarily indicators of real clinical symptomatology. However, given the high percentage of responses citing mental health problems as a reason for transfer, it appears that, while the initial identification may have been precipitated by behavior, the transfer decision typically was based on mental health problems. Thus, while it would seem that there may be some inmates transferred who are only behavior problems (not mentally disordered), the potentially more important problem is the lack of early identification of those mentally disordered inmates whose behavior does not either annoy the DOC staff or disrupt prison operations. It seems likely that there are a number of disordered inmates who go unnoticed and, therefore, untreated.

This interpretation is supported by responses to questions about the appropri-

ateness of the number of inmates transferred and the major weaknesses in the identification of inmates for transfer. Staff were asked how they felt about the number of inmates transferred to a mental health facility or unit. Table 24.3 shows the staff responses by staff location and state. As seen in the table, almost half of the staff members responding felt that "too few" inmates were transferred (47.6%). This compares to the small number of staff (7.9%) who felt that "too many" were transferred. Staff in three states[3] clearly were quite concerned that too few mentally disordered inmates were placed in mental health settings. When examining responses by work location of staff responding, it is interesting to note that while concern over underidentification occurred in all three locations (prisons, 62.5%; mental hospitals, 41.4%; and central office, 30.0%), the percentage of prison staff who felt that not enough inmates were transferred more than doubled the percentage of central office administrators who had that concern. While it is unclear whether this distinction reflects a lack of first-hand knowledge by the administrative staff or the lack of mental health expertise of the prison staff (or

Table 24.3

Staff Perception of the Appropriateness of the Number
of Inmates Transferred (by Staff Location and State)

| | Number of Inmates Transferred | | | | | |
| | Too Few | | Just Right | | Too Many | |
Staff Location	%	(N)	%	(N)	%	(N)
Central office	30.0	(3)	60.0	(6)	10.0	(1)
Mental hospital	41.1	(12)	48.3	(14)	10.3	(3)
Prison	62.5	(15)	33.3	(8)	4.2	(1)
			State			
A	20.0	(2)	70.0	(7)	10.0	(1)
B	62.5	(5)	25.0	(2)	12.5	(1)
C	70.0	(14)	25.0	(5)	5.0	(1)
D	30.8	(4)	69.2	(9)	0.0	(0)
E	41.7	(5)	41.7	(5)	16.7	(2)
Total	47.6	(30)	44.4	(28)	7.9	(5)

both), it is apparent that the prison staff felt they were handling inmates whom they were incapable of treating in the general prison population.

Respondents also were asked to name what they perceived to be the major strengths and weaknesses in the identification of mentally disordered inmates. While most respondents did find some strengths, frequently the strength cited was merely a reiteration of the fact that the system did exist and did identify and place mentally ill inmates. More meaningful strengths that were cited with some regularity by the corrections staff were the quality of the clinical staff, the ability of staff to work together, and the efforts made by prison guards.

Efforts to specify weaknesses in identification were more informative. As seen in Table 24.4, many of the responses dealt directly with the problem of prisons "underidentifying" mentally disordered inmates (miss some mentally disordered inmates, 30%; insufficient number of clinical staff, 17.8%; lack of mental health assessment,

4.5%). Additional responses (such as the lack of clinical training of prison staff) at least indirectly dealt with the same concern. Some examples of responses noting the "underidentification" of mentally disordered inmates were:

There are not enough professional staff; I fear the quietly crazy are not identified. That is what concerns me [prison psychologist].

Problems of spotting someone who needs to be there. We have only 30–40 correctional officers for 2000 inmates. Not enough of us to keep up on what's going on. Inmates usually have to show exceptional behavior before being identified. They could have problems, and not be identified [prison correctional officer].

We primarily have a disturbance identification process rather than a patient need identification [process] [Correctional mental hospital psychiatrist].

Table 24.4

Major Weaknesses in Identifying Inmates for Transfer

Weakness	% of Responses	(N)
Miss some mentally ill inmates	30.0	(27)
Lack of clinical staff in prison	17.8	(16)
Seek to transfer management problems	11.1	(10)
Inadequate training of prison staff	8.9	(8)
Manipulation of staff by inmates	5.6	(5)
Lack of mental health assessment	4.5	(4)
Other	22.1	(20)
Total	100.0	(90)

Procedures

Once an inmate was identified by the prison staff as being mentally disordered, each state had formal procedures for reviewing the transfer of the inmate to a mental health facility. All respondents were asked how well they thought the procedures were working. Almost 85% of those interviewed said the procedures were working either "very well" or "well," and in only one state was there considerable concern over how these procedures were operating (33% said "poorly" or "very poorly"). However, a significant difference was revealed in how staff at different locations (central office, mental hospital, prison) assessed the effectiveness of these procedures. Only one respondent across the five states working either at the central office or the mental health facility said the procedures were operating "poorly" or "very poorly" (2.6%). On the other hand, 36% of the prison staff interviewed viewed the operation of transfer procedures as so problematic as to define them as operating "poorly" or "very poorly." This view was found to be limited to two states. Some of the specific criticisms made by prison staff in these two states were:

> No one's going anywhere. There are a lot of mentally ill people here, but they are not housed as if they're mentally ill. Not treated any differently than other inmates [prison psychologist].

> Bed space problems at (the CMH) and their unwillingness to take our inmates. If they are both psychotic and management problems, they [CMH] keep them only a short period of time and say the inmate is only a management problem and send them back [prison administrator].

> Takes too much time! Courts' fault, always getting involved when they know nothing about it. Afraid we will put people there (the CMH) for punishment. Delay in getting hold of "shrink" and taking care of paper work. Delay is at central office . . . [the mental health facility] sends them back too soon, when they shouldn't be housed here at all. The inmates go back and forth [correctional officer].

While DOC staff from the other three states typically stated that procedures were operating well overall, staff in these states frequently said there were still some major weaknesses in the procedures. In one state the concerns frequently focused around the extent to which the procedures protected inmates from being transferred inappropriately:

> Procedures are not terribly tight, staff could conspire to place a person who is not mentally ill into a mental hospital. Lack of legal safeguards. Not forced to confront

the man and say he is crazy [corrections administrator].

[The Supreme Court] requires there should be an independent review of hospitalization. We don't have this. A good law requires judicial commitment. We don't have this [corrections administrator].

In another state, the issue involved the decision-making process. As seen below, some DOC staff (usually prison staff) felt too much decision-making control was left in the hands of hospital staff. Others (typically hospital staff) felt that too much control was given to the prison and DOC central office.

If _____ [the CMH director] doesn't want someone he doesn't have to take him. He is scared and doesn't want to be bothered by this type of person. He fears they will be disruptive to their program. His power to make this decision is the major weakness in the procedures [correctional officer].

Formal decision is left in the hands of a lay person [central office]. This is a medical facility and he [DOC director] has the ultimate authority. . . . Not a real problem, as long as mental hospital director has right to discharge.

Despite the specific concerns noted above, the respondents were, in general, satisfied with the transfer procedures. The respondents also expressed satisfaction with the receptivity displayed by the DOC mental health facilities to mentally disordered inmates referred by the prison. Almost 90% of the staff interviewed defined the state correctional mental health facility or facilities as either "very" or "somewhat" receptive. The prison staff were considerably more likely to define the mental health facilities as "somewhat" or "very" nonreceptive (22.7%) than the staff at the mental health facilities (3.3%). Almost 75% of the staff responding in each of the five states defined the correctional mental health facility as receptive.

Thus, in general, DOC staff appear to be satisfied with the procedures for inmate transfers from the general prison population into mental health facilities and the receptivity of these facilities to mentally disordered inmates.

One area that generated little concern by the prison staff, DOC central office staff, or mental health staff was the inmate's ability to prevent transfer through procedural safeguards. When asked whether inmates prevented transfer too frequently, as often as they should, or not often enough, 92% of the DOC staff responding said "as often as should be the case." In no state did a sizable percentage of staff express concern that inmates either prevented too many transfers or were unable to prevent transfers often enough. It is not clear whether these responses reflect procedures that gave inmates an optimal amount of input into this decision or whether it more accurately reflects the frequently stated belief of DOC staff that "inmates have no control over these decisions and they shouldn't."

Conclusion

This chapter has used 67 interviews conducted with DOC staff in five states to describe the process of identifying state prisoners suffering from mental disorders and the transferring of these inmates into designated DOC mental health facilities. The major conclusions drawn from these interviews are:

- DOC staff perceive a sizable number of state prisoners to be suffering from a serious psychotic mental disorder (5.8% of all inmates) or psychological problems warranting treatment (37.7%).

- Different states operate with different philosophies on how to handle mentally disordered inmates and therefore identify widely divergent percentages of their inmates as warranting placement in a mental health facility.

- Once the prison psychiatrist or psychologist recommends that an inmate be transferred, it is the rare exception when a review system (prison, DOC, court) reverses that decision.

- Inmates are typically identified in the prison for behavioral management reasons, thereby making it likely that a sizable number of mentally disordered inmates remain in the general population because their behavior is insufficiently visible, annoying, or disruptive.

- A sizable percentage of staff (47.6%) stated they felt "too few" inmates were transferred to mental health settings.

- Staff typically felt that the procedures used to transfer those inmates identified as mentally disordered were working well (84.4%) and that the DOC mental health facilities were receptive to these inmates (85.5%). However, staff working at the prisons were considerably less satisfied with both the procedures and the receptivity of the mental health facilities than were the staff at either the DOC central office or the DOC mental hospitals and treatment centers.

As prison populations continue to burgeon, the problem of mentally disordered inmates will only be exacerbated. Even if the proportion of the inmate population with mental disorders remains constant, the scope of the problem within any given growing prison system will become more acute in terms of absolute human service needs (see Monahan and Steadman, 1983a). While the descriptive work discussed in this chapter is a major first step toward building knowledge in this area, it is essential that more research be devoted to studying mentally disordered inmates. Further research is needed both on inmates themselves and on the system and agencies responsible for their care and treatment.

More information is needed on the prevalence, causes, and correlates of mental disorders within the state prison inmate population. A systematic, multistate study is needed that utilizes an objective instrument across states to assess the extent to which prison inmates suffer from mental disorders. Inmates identified as mentally disordered should be studied for purposes of examining causes and correlates of both the criminal behavior and mental disturbance. Included in this assessment should be an examination of how incarceration and prison conditions contribute to inmate mental health problems and in what ways the prison experience may combine with preprison factors to generate serious inmate symptomatology.

Study Questions

1. What are the two reasons the authors give for the likelihood that the number of mentally ill offenders will increase in coming years?

2. Describe the research design, data collection methods, sample, and measures used by the authors in conducting this study.

3. What is the scope of mental health problems in prisons that the authors describe?

4. What are the conclusions reached by the authors of this study? Why do you think they are important for correctional officials?

Acknowledgments

This work was done under partial support from the National Institute of Justice (79-NI-AX-0126). The assistance of Sharon Kantorowski Davis in the data collection phase of this project is gratefully acknowledged.

Notes

1. According to 1978 admission data, there were 16 states in the country which transferred most (at least 75%) of their mentally disordered inmates to mental health settings within the DOC. They are California, Idaho, Illinois, Iowa, Massachusetts, Michigan, Missouri, Nevada, North Carolina, Oregon, South Carolina, Tennessee, Texas, Utah, and West Virginia. In addition, Arizona changed the agency responsible for the mental hospital treating mentally ill inmates from DMH to DOC at the end of 1978.

2. Information contained in the Bureau of Justice Statistics Bulletin (Department of Justice, 1982) showed that at the end of 1980 the state prison censuses in the five states discussed in this chapter were as follows: Arizona, 4,372; California, 24,569; Iowa, 2,513; Massachusetts, 3,191; Texas, 29,892; total: 64,537.

3. Throughout the remainder of this chapter, we do not identify any of the states by name. We felt that to do so would betray both the confidence and trust the states had in us and risk the anonymity we promised to individual respondents.

References

Cook, G. and C. Sigorski (1974) "Factors affecting length of hospitalization in prisoners adjudicated not guilty by reason of insanity." *Bulletin of the American Academy of Psychiatry and Law* 2: 251–261.

Department of Justice (1982) Bureau of Justice Statistics Bulletin (NCJ 82262). Washington, DC: Author.

Gardner, R. (1982) "Prison population jumps to 369,725." *Corrections Magazine*, 8(4):6–11, 14, 46.

Gearing, M., R. Hecker, and W. Matthey (1990) "The screening and referral of mentally disordered inmates in a state correctional system." *Professional Psychology* 11: 849.

Halleck, S. (1961) "A critique of current psychiatric roles in the legal process." *Wisconsin Law Review* 00: 379–401.

Hartstone, E., H.J. Steadman, and J. Monahan (1982) "*Vitek* and beyond: The empirical context of prison to hospital transfers." *Law and Contemporary Problems* 45, 3.

Konecni, V., E. Mulcahy, and E. Ebbesen (1980) "Prison or mental hospital: Factors affecting the processing of persons suspected of being mentally disordered sex offenders," in P. Lipsitt and B. Sales (eds.) *New Directions in Psychological Research.* New York: Van Nostrand Reinhold.

Monahan, J. and H.J. Steadman (1983a) "Crime and mental disorder: An epidemiological analysis," in N. Morris and M. Tonrey (eds.) *Annual Review of Criminal Justice.* Chicago: University of Chicago Press.

—— [eds.] (1983b) *Mentally Disordered Offenders: Perspectives from Law and Social Science.* New York: Plenum.

Morrow, W.R. and D.B. Peterson (1966) "Follow-up on discharged offenders—'not guilty by reason of insanity' and 'criminal sexual psychopaths.'" *Journal of Criminal Law, Criminology and Police Science* 57: 31–34.

Mowbrey, C.T. (1979) "A study of patients treated as incompetent to stand trial." *Social Psychiatry* 14:31–39.

New York Laws (1827) Chapter 294, Section 2.

New York Times (1892) November 3, p. 9 col. 4.

Pasewark, R.A. and B.W. Lanthorn (1977) "Dispositions of persons utilizing the insanity defense." *Journal of Humanistics* 5:87–98.

——, M.L. Pantle, and H.J. Steadman (1982) "Detention and rearrest rates of persons found not guilty by reason of insanity and convicted felons." *American Journal of Psychiatry* 139, 7: 892–897.

—— (1979) "Characteristics and disposition of persons found not guilty by reason of insanity in New York State, 1971–76." *American Journal of Psychiatry* 136:655–660.

Petrila, J. (1982) "The insanity defense and other mental health dispositions in Missouri." *International Journal of Law and Psychiatry* 5, 1:81–102.

Roesch, R. and S. Golding (1980) *Competency to Stand Trial.* Champaign: University of Illinois Press.

Rogers, J. and J. Bloom (1982) "Characteristics of persons committed to Oregon's Psychiatric Security Review Board." *Bulletin of the American Academy of Psychiatry and the Law* 10, 3:155–164.

Steadman, H.J. (1980) "Insanity acquittals in New York State, 1965–1978." *American Journal of Psychiatry* 137:321–326.

—— (1979) *Beating a Rap: Defendants Found Incompetent to Stand Trial.* Chicago: University of Chicago Press.

—— and J.C. Cocozza (1974) *Careers of the Criminally Insane*. Lexington, MA: D. C. Heath.

Steadman, H.J., J. Monahan, E. Hartstone, S.K. Davis, and P.C. Robbins (1982) "Mentally disordered offenders: A national survey of patients and facilities." *Law and Human Behavior* 6, 1.

Sturgeon, V. and J. Taylor (1980) "Report of a five-year follow-up of mentally disordered sex offenders released from Atascadero State Hospital in 1973." *Criminal Justice Journal of Western State University* 4:31–64.

Uhlig, R.H. (1976) "Hospitilization experience of mentally disturbed and disruptive, incarcerated offenders." *Journal of Psychiatry and Law* 4(1):49–59.

25

A Quantitative Review and Description of Corrections-Based Education, Vocation, and Work Programs

David B. Wilson
Catherine A. Gallagher
Mark B. Coggeshall
Doris L. MacKenzie

Although the very existence of treatment options within correctional institutions has had a varied and controversial past, the fact remains that most institutions of all types have some type of educational, vocational, and/or work program in place. The goals of these work programs are often multifaceted and may offer the institution some type of revenue, or at least reduced expenditure, from the labor of the inmates. Educational, vocational, and/or work programs may also provide the inmates with something constructive to fill their time, thereby making the population as a whole more manageable for line officers and prison administrators.

Prison work programs have also been said to offer rehabilitative skills that inmates may carry with them upon release, thus increasing the likelihood they will "succeed" in the long term. Unfortunately, the effectiveness of these programs has not been explored adequately to determine what precisely works best, if rehabilitation and treatment are at least the pri-

mary goals. The authors of this article provide a meta-analysis of educational, vocational, and work programs that exist inside prisons. Ultimately, they determine that, while the presence of these programs does seem to meet several correctional goals (including reductions in recidivism), more effort is needed to identify the specific components of effective programs.

Educational and vocational programs long have been a part of prisons in the United States.[1] A 1995 survey of all state and federal adult correctional facilities conducted by the Bureau of Justice Statistics[2] showed that 94 percent of all such facilities (1,500 in total) had work programs and 87 percent had education programs. Roughly one third of all facilities employed inmates in a prison industry and about half of the facilities provided vocational training. Basic adult education and secondary education [including general equivalency diploma (GED) programs] were offered by more than 75 percent of the facilities. One third of all facilities provided access to college course work. Overall, almost two-thirds of all inmates participated in a work program and slightly less than one quarter of all inmates participated in an education program. Such programs represent a major financial investment on the part of the criminal justice system. It is critical, therefore, to examine the effectiveness of these programs in achieving the rehabilitative goal of reducing future offending.

Although there is theoretical and empirical evidence that academic underachievement and unemployment are related to criminal offending, evidence of the effectiveness of education, vocation, and work programs is less clear. Reviews of evaluative studies of education programs present an equivocal picture of their effectiveness. Gerber and Fritsch[3] concluded that prison education programs were effective. Similarly, Taylor[4,5] concluded that post-secondary educational programs were able to reduce recidivism and argued that they represent a potentially cost-effective method of crime prevention. Looking more broadly at all education program types, Linden and Perry[1] concluded that while such programs clearly have demonstrated their ability to increase academic achievement, they have not demonstrated their ability to increase post-release employment or to reduce offending. In a review of recent studies of adult basic education (ABE) programs, MacKenzie and Hickman stated that "research in the 1990s has failed to reach a definitive conclusion regarding the effectiveness of correctional education on recidivism."[6]

Reviews of vocational and correctional work programs are similarly equivocal. Gerber and Fritsch[3] interpreted the available evidence as supporting the effectiveness of vocational programs in reducing recidivism. In contrast, MacKenzie and Hickman[6] concluded that while some programs appear effective, others appear detrimental. In general, programs that have multiple components, have follow-up programs, and teach skills relevant to the current job market appear to be the most likely to be successful.[7,8]

Taken together, these reviews highlight the lack of a clear consensus from the empirical literature on the effectiveness of education, vocation, and work programs. A potential source of this ambiguity is the heavy reliance on narrative forms of review. Only two of the above-mentioned research summaries are an exception. Gerber and Fritsch[3] used a vote-counting method of synthesis and MacKenzie and Hickman[6] calculated and reported program effect sizes for each reviewed study. The weaknesses of narrative reviews and vote-counting methods have been well documented.[9] Using current quantitative research synthesis techniques,[10] this study addresses the weakness of prior reviews by conducting a meta-analysis of outcome studies of education, vocation, and work programs for adults involved in the criminal justice systems. The authors address the question of the effectiveness of these programs in reducing post-release criminal involvement. Additionally, the study evaluated the methodological adequacy of this body of empirical work and assessed the relationship between observed effects and both methodological and program features.

Overview of Synthesis Approach

The purpose of this study was to quantitatively synthesize the extant evidence on the effects of education, vocation, and work programs using the method of meta-analysis. The authors defined the research space for this synthesis as those studies that (1) evaluated an education, vocation, or work program for convicted adults or persons identified by the criminal justice system (court) and placed in a diversion program; (2) reported on a post-program measure of recidivism (such as arrest, conviction, self-report, technical violation, or incarceration); (3) included a non-program comparison group, that is, a comparison group that did not receive an education, vocation, or work program; and (4) were published or written after 1975 in the English language. The study did not include nonacademic education programs, such as life-skills training, cognitive or behavioral training, and so forth, as those were judged to represent a distinct form of intervention. Note that these criteria exclude many studies of education, vocation, and work programs that did not examine the effects of these programs relative to a comparison group on a measure of post-release offending.

The veracity of the conclusions drawn from a synthesis is related directly to the adequacy of the search for relevant studies. The study goal was to identify and retrieve all, or nearly all, studies meeting the eligibility criteria stated above. The authors did not restrict this study to published works because there is ample evidence that doing so will produce a biased set of studies.[11,12] The study began by examining the reference lists of review articles.[6] This was augmented by searching the following computerized bibliographic databases in the fall of 1998: *Criminal Justice Periodical Index, Dissertation Abstracts Online, ERIC, NCJRS, Psyc INFO, Social SciSearch, Social Sciences Abstracts,* and *Sociological Abstracts.*

The search terms included correctional education, vocational training, vocational education, ABE, GED, general education diploma, secondary education, correctional industries, and correctional work. This search was restricted by including terms specific to evaluative studies (e.g., evaluation, outcome, comparison, etc.), offender populations (e.g., offender, criminal, convict, prisoner, etc.), and recidivism or reoffense. This search strategy identified 143 potential documents, of which the authors retrieved and examined 133. Ten documents remain elusive to these retrieval efforts and a careful read of their titles and abstracts suggests that they are unlikely to meet the above criteria. Thirty-three unique studies were eligible and included in this synthesis.

From each unique research study, the authors extracted a variety of information describing the research participants, program characteristics, research methodology, and detailed results on post-release measures of offending for each group. Many of these studies reported on multiple programs of interest, such as ABE and post-secondary education, contrasting each with a common comparison group. Therefore, the authors treated each program-comparison as the primary unit of analysis. This resulted in 53 program-comparison contrasts across the 33 studies used in this synthesis.

The initial coding protocol was pilot tested by multiple coders, each coding a small sample of studies. Items with poor agreement and/or items that did not map well onto the characteristics of the studies were modified or dropped. This process was repeated until the authors arrived at a cod-

ing protocol with acceptable inter-rater agreement that was consistent with the characteristics of the eligible studies.

The data extracted from each study were generally in the form of a proportion of program and comparison participants who recidivated. For purposes of this article, the authors examined only one recidivism outcome per program-comparison contrast. When multiple recidivism data were available from a single program-comparison contrast, the authors selected the data representing reincarceration and the data for the longest follow-up period. In the absence of a measure of reincarceration, preference was given to a measure of conviction, then arrest, then other recidivism measures such as composite indicators. A complete coding protocol is available from the authors.

The recidivism data were converted into an index, the odds-ratio, which measured the differential rate of recidivism between the two groups. This measure was selected due to its desirable properties when analyzing dichotomous data.[13] The odds-ratio was interpreted as the odds of a successful outcome in the experimental group relative to the odds of a successful outcome in the control group. An odds is the probability of success divided by the probability of failure. For example, a success rate of 66 percent translates into an odds (not an odds-ratio) of 2 calculated as $0.66/(1 - 0.66)$, whereas a success rate of 50 percent translates into an odds of 1 calculated as $0.50/(1 - 0.50)$. As the name implies, the odds-ratio is the ratio of the respective odds. Using the above two odds produces an odds-ratio of 2. Thus, an experimental group with a success rate of 66 percent has twice the odds of a successful outcome as a comparison group with a success rate of 50 percent. The odds-ratio should not be confused with the risk-ratio. The latter is simply the ratio of the success rate for each group. The success rates of 66 and 50 percent produce a risk-ratio of 1.32 (66/50).

A potential threat to the validity of these findings was the authors' decision to code, when possible, multiple program-comparison contrasts from a single study. This creates statistical dependencies among the effect sizes, potentially biasing the results.[14] The authors concluded that restricting the data set to one program-comparison contrast per study would have obscured valuable data regarding the effectiveness of the programs under consideration. Furthermore, the seriousness of the threat was deemed minimal because the dependencies were across program types (i.e., ABE and vocational training) and the focus of the analyses was on estimating the mean effect size within each program type. The program type mean effect sizes, therefore, were unaffected by these dependencies.

Description of the Research Literature

Table 25.1 presents basic descriptive information for the 33 studies and 53 program-comparison contrasts. Nearly half of these studies were from published sources and nearly one third were local, state, or federal government reports. The remaining documents either were unpublished technical reports or dissertations. Most of the studies were conducted in the United States (31 of the 33). The remaining two studies were conducted in Canada.

The program-comparison contrasts were categorized by the type of program evaluated (see Table 25.1). The most widely examined program types were post-secondary education and vocational education/training programs, with 13 and 17 evaluations of each, respectively. The study's extensive search of the literature identified few evaluations of correctional industries and correctional work programs, greatly reducing the strength of any conclusions that can be drawn about the effects of these programs. Two studies examined multi-component programs: one was a vocational training and correctional industries program and the other combined educational

Table 25.1

Description of Studies

Variable	Frequency	Percent
Document type (N = 33)		
Journal	13	39
Book chapter	1	3
Government report	10	30
Technical report/ dissertation	9	27
Program type (N = 53)		
Adult basic education (ABE)	6	11
General equivalency diploma (GED)	3	6
ABE or GED	5	9
Post-secondary education	13	25
Vocational education/ training	17	32
Correctional industries	2	4
Correctional work	2	4
Multi-component program	2	4
Other	3	6

programming, vocational training, and job placement services. Three program-comparison contrasts could not be classified into this study's scheme. However, other program-comparison contrasts from these studies were categorized into these traditional program types.

The methodological quality of these studies varied but generally was weak, as shown by the data in Table 25.2. The typical research design compared naturally occurring groups of program participants with either nonparticipation in the specific program being evaluated or nonparticipation in any education, vocation, or work program. A few studies contrasted offenders who completed the evaluated program with offenders who dropped out of or were removed from the program. Several studies included a mixture of nonparticipants with unsuccessful or limited program participa-

Table 25.2

Description of Methodology for the Studies and Program-Comparisons

Variable	Study		Program Comparisons	
	Frequency	Percent	Frequency	Percent
Nature of comparison group				
Nonparticipation in program(s) or management as usual	24	72	42	79
Treatment dropouts or unsuccessful participation	4	12	4	8
Mixture of above	4	12	6	11
Cannot tell	1	3	1	2
Used random assignment to conditions	3	9	3	6
Used initial group differences in statistical analyses	7	21	12	23
Used subject level matching	9	27	14	26
Used statistical significance testing	22	67	30	57
Attrition problem, overall	8	24	10	19
Attrition problem, differential	3	9	4	8

tion. More than half made little or no attempt to control for selection bias, that is, differences in the characteristics of offenders who participate in the program relative to those who do not.

Only three studies (six percent of the program-comparison contrasts) used random assignment to conditions. Two-thirds of the studies used statistical significance testing as a basis for inferring differences in post-release offending rates.

Also shown in Table 25.2 is the study's coding of study attrition. Attrition is a potentially serious threat to the validity of inferences from naturalistic field-based evaluative studies.[15] Although the loss of cases due to purely random processes creates no validity threat, it is rare that attrition is of a random nature. Even general attrition across program and comparison groups that is nondifferential, that is, loss of similar cases in both groups, affects the generalizability of the study findings due to the loss of outcome data for that subsample of individuals. Conclusions about the effectiveness of a program can be generalized only to individuals with characteristics comparable to those participants who remained in the study. In the study's coding scheme, the authors referred to this as general attrition and, in the authors' judgment, 19 percent of program-comparison contrasts suffered from this validity threat. Attrition that is differential between a program and a comparison group affects the validity of causal inferences regarding the effectiveness of the program. Differential attrition was judged a potential threat in 8 percent of the program-comparison contrasts. Unfortunately, the ability to make these judgments is highly dependent on the information provided in the written report by the researchers. More studies may have been judged problematic with regard to attrition if additional information had been made available. Considering all of the methodological variables simultaneously, only six program-comparison contrasts were judged to have used a methodology allowing for reasonably strong causal inferences regarding the effects of the program.

Not surprisingly, most of the research participants in these studies were men (see Table 25.3). None of the studies included in

Table 25.3

Description of Study Participants

Variable	Frequency	Percent
All participants male		
Yes	22	42
No	19	36
Cannot tell	12	23
Program participants were:		
Prison inmates	50	94
Probationers	3	6

Table 25.4

Nature of the Recidivism Measure Used in the Odds-Ratio Analysis

Recidivism Measure	Frequency	Percent
Reincarceration	35	66
Arrest	9	17
Conviction	6	11
Parole revocation	2	4
Composite measure	1	2

this synthesis were based solely on a sample of women. Fifteen of the 19 studies known to include women reported sufficient information to determine the actual percentage of men and women. In all 15 studies, women represented 21 percent of the study sample. Thus, the findings from this synthesis cannot be generalized to programs serving women. The vast majority of these studies evaluated programs that were available to the offenders during their period of incarceration. Only three of the program-comparison contrasts evaluated programs for probationers. Slightly less than half (23) of the program-comparison contrasts included offenders from multiple locations within a single system. In general, it appears that the participants in these studies are representative of the general United States and Canadian male prison population.

For purposes of computing the odds-ratio, preference was given to measures of reincarceration rate. More than half of the 53 program-comparison contrasts reported a reincarceration rate (see Table 25.4). For the remaining contrasts, recidivism was measured as arrest rates (17%), conviction rate (11%), parole revocation (4%), and a composite measure that included multiple indicators of recidivism (2%). All studies used official records for determining the outcome status of study participants (for example, no study provided data from a self-report measure of recidivism).

Program-Comparison Contrast Recidivism Outcomes

The vast majority of the findings across the 53 program-comparison contrasts favored the program participants. In 46 of the 53 contrasts, the program group had a lower recidivism rate than the comparison group. In one contrast, the recidivism rate was identical between groups. The mean odds-ratio across these 53 program-comparison contrasts was statistically significant and favored the education, vocation, and work program participants (mean odds-ratio = 1.53, with a 95% confidence interval of 1.36 to 1.72). This mean—and all others reported below—was computed by weighting each odds-ratio by an index of its precision, its inverse variance. This had the result of giving greater weight to studies with larger sample sizes. The authors also assumed that the variance for each odds-ratio had a random effects component.[16–19] This assumption resulted in a more conservative, that is, larger, confidence interval around the mean odds-ratio than under a fixed effects model.

The distribution of odds-ratios was highly heterogeneous, indicating that these effects vary by more than would be expected due to sampling error only, that is, there were real differences in the program effects across studies. These differences may have been due to substantive differences, such as program type, or due to methodological fea-

Figure 25.1

Mean Odds-Ratio and 95 Percent Confidence Interval by Program Type

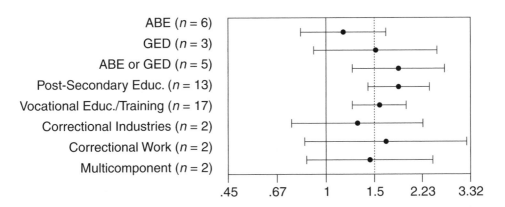

Note: an odds ratio of 1 indicates no difference in recidivism rate, a ratio less than 1 indicates the program increased recidivism, and odds-ratios greater than 1 indicate the program reduced recidivism. The dotted line indicates the overlap between the estimated program effects.

tures, such as methodological quality and nature of the outcome measure.

Figure 25.1 presents the mean odds-ratio and associated confidence interval by major program type. Note that an odds-ratio of one indicates no difference in the recidivism rate between the groups being compared; values between zero and one indicate a negative effect such as higher recidivism for the program group and values greater than one indicate a positive effect such as lower recidivism for the program group. As shown in Figure 25.1, the mean odds-ratio for all program types was greater than one. On average, within each program type, program participants recidivated at a lower rate than nonparticipants. The overlap of the confidence intervals across programs (see dotted line in Figure 25.1) indicates that the data do not provide a basis for drawing conclusions regarding the differential effectiveness of the various program types. This was confirmed with a statistical test analogous to a one-way analysis of variance.[9] Unfortunately, several of the confidence intervals extend below one, suggesting that there currently is insufficient

evidence to rule out sampling error as an explanation for the observed effect. Thus, all of these programs succeed, some more convincingly than others.

The odds-ratio can be difficult to interpret in practical terms. Is a mean odds-ratio of 1.53 something to get excited about? To facilitate interpretation, the authors have translated the mean odds-ratios into recidivism rates for the program groups, fixing the comparison group recidivism rate at 50 percent. These recidivism rates are shown in Figure 25.2 and range from a low of 36 percent to a high of 46 percent.

Thus, the rate of post-release offending for program participants is, on average, 4 to 14 percent lower than for program nonparticipants. This article will now briefly discuss the findings within each program type, highlighting salient study features.

ABE and General Equivalency Diploma

The results for ABE and GED programs appear contradictory. Taken as a whole, the

Figure 25.2
Estimated Percent of Program Participants Recidivating

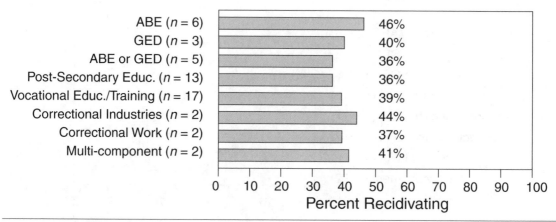

Assuming a 50 Percent Recidivism Rate in the Comparison Group

14 program comparisons contrasts[20–30] evaluating either ABE, GED, or both showed positive and statistically significant effects. The overall effect for the six studies evaluating ABE participation was lower than the overall effect for the five studies examining participation in either an ABE or GED program. Furthermore, the overall effect for ABE programs was not significant. Individually, only one[26] of the ABE effect sizes was statistically significant and it came from a study that used program drop-outs and those released prior to program completion as the comparison group. A negative effect of ABE was observed by one evaluation,[21] although the effect was small and positive findings were found for women and older inmates. All four of the evaluations of GED programs observed positive effects, with two of the four GED programs reporting statistically significant effects and three of the five ABE/GED evaluations reporting statistically significant effects. The large confidence intervals indicate that this difference between ABE, GED, and ABE or GED may be due to sampling error. Furthermore, other methodological differences between these studies are likely to produce instability in the findings. Although the findings across this collection of studies consistently favor the program participants, all of these studies had weak research methodologies, simply comparing either participants with nonparticipants or program noncompleters, with little to no control or adjustment for selection bias. Thus, it is impossible to rule out selection bias as an explanation for the differential recidivism rate.

Post-Secondary Education

Eleven of the 13 studies[21, 22, 24, 31–40] evaluating the effects of post-secondary education programs demonstrated positive effects, seven of which were statistically significant. The overall mean odds-ratio was positive and statistically significant and translates into a recidivism rate of 36 percent relative to 50 percent for the comparison group, a meaningful reduction in recidivism by most standards. The positive effect remains when the analysis is restricted to five higher quality evaluations. A study by Linden et al.[37] used random assignment to conditions, used volunteers from both a maximum and medium security institution in British Columbia, Canada, and required that all participants had at least an eighth-grade education and were approved by the researchers as being capable of completing the course work. This study found a positive effect of involvement in post-secondary course work with 67 percent of the program group recidivating, relative to 77 percent in the comparison group. This translates into an odds-ratio comparable to the mean odds-ratio for this program type. Unfortunately, this effect was not statistically significant given the study's small sample size (33 offenders in each group). The positive finding across this collection of studies is encouraging but the generally weak methodology does not allow for the attribution of the lower rates of recidivism to the post-secondary programs rather than to unique characteristics of inmates who chose to participate in them.

Vocational Education and Training

The largest collection of evaluations was of vocational education/training programs.[20, 21, 24, 28, 41–48] The overall mean odds-ratio for these evaluations was positive and statistically significant (see Figure 25.1). Of the individual effects, 14 were positive and seven of these were statistically significant. As with other program areas, the typical evaluation of vocational programs was methodologically weak. There were, however, two exceptions. Lattimore et al.[45] conducted a randomized evaluation of an integrated vocational training and reentry program with close to 300 participants and found that participants in the integrated program had a lower rate of rearrest than did control group members. Saylor and Gaes,[47] using a high-quality propensity score-based quasi-experimental design, evaluated a vocational training and apprenticeship program, also finding positive program effects. Combining these two high-quality studies yields a statistically significant mean odds-ratio of 1.49 with a 95 percent confidence interval of 1.35 to 1.65.

Although these two evaluations provide strong evidence that vocational programming can reduce post-release offending, both represent better-integrated and more intensive programs than are typically found throughout the criminal justice system. Thus, the generalizability of this finding to typical vocational programs is unwarranted.

Correctional Industries and Correctional Work

Only four studies were identified that evaluated the effects of work programs on recidivism, two evaluating correctional industries programs[47, 49] and two evaluating correctional work.[50, 51] Both types of programs had positive mean odds-ratios roughly comparable in magnitude to the other program types. Unfortunately, neither mean odds-ratio was statistically significant. Analyzing the four studies together, however, the overall mean odds-ratio was significant due to the boost in statistical power. All four of these studies observed lower rates of recidivism in the offenders participating in the work program than the comparison offenders. Two of the observed effects were statistically significant, one for each type of work program.

The sole randomized design examining a correctional work program was conducted by Van Stelle et al.[51] Although the study found small positive effects, the design was compromised severely by a high level of attrition. Furthermore, the generalizability of this finding to other work programs is limited because this program included job placement and community follow-up services in addition to the correctional work.

Although not a randomized design, the study by Saylor and Gaes[47] used the propensity score method to adjust for selection bias and as such, it represents a high-quality quasi-experimental design. This study contrasted participants in a correctional industries program with nonparticipants in either correctional industries or vocational programs. The adjusted effect, controlling for measured group differences, was statistically significant, resulting in an odds-ratio of 1.31, or an estimated recidivism rate for the correctional industries group of 43 percent, relative to a 50 percent rate in the comparison group. Although the propensity score method is unlikely to account for all of the important differences between those offenders participating in work programs and those not participating, the careful attention of this study to the problem of selection bias reduces the likelihood that the finding is an artifact of the participation process rather than an effect of the program. These findings are promising but are insufficient to draw any strong conclusions regarding the effects of correctional work programs on future offending rates for prison inmates.

Multi-Component Programs

Two evaluations examined multi-component programs. Menon et al.[52] studied the impact of Project RIO in Texas, a program incorporating an individualized Employability Development Plan for each inmate, encouraging participation in existing education, vocation, and work programs within the prison system, providing job preparation and job search assistance, and encouraging employers in the community to hire releasees. The participants in this program had higher rates of employment and lower rates of recidivism than nonparticipants, even after adjusting for background characteristics of the offenders.

> These findings are promising but are insufficient to draw any strong conclusions regarding the effects of correctional work programs on future offending rates for prison inmates.

The Saylor and Gaes[47] study discussed above also contrasted offenders who participated in both vocational training and correctional industries programs. The outcomes were positive, favoring program participation, and were highly similar to the outcomes for participation in only vocational training or correctional industries. In other words, there appeared to be no additional advantage to participation in both programs, at least in terms of future recidivism.

Job Placement Services

Three studies evaluated programs that included job placement services.[45, 51, 52] Unfortunately, the authors were unable to identify any study that evaluated the sole effect of job placement services, either by contrasting an education, vocation, or work program with and without job placement services or by examining job placement services as a single program. Although all three of these evaluations had positive findings, no conclusions specific to the important topic of job placement services could be drawn from this collection of studies.

Summary and Conclusions

There is strong support for the claim that participants in corrections-based education, vocation, and work programs recidivate at a lower rate than nonparticipants, with roughly comparable overall effects across the different types of programs. However, the current level of evidence does not allow for conclusions regarding differential effects of these programs.

The typical study included in this meta-analysis was quasi-experimental and compared naturally occurring groups of program participants with nonparticipants. Few studies made any serious attempt, in the authors' opinion, to control for biases produced by this self-selection into programs. Although space restrictions may create some randomness in who participates and who does not in some of the programs evaluated, it seems highly plausible that, as a whole, the comparison individuals differ from the program individuals in ways likely to affect recidivism. For example, the program participants may be more motivated toward positive life changes. It may be this motivation and the engagement in a set of behaviors perceived by the offender as improving their chances at finding satisfactory employment upon release that are critical to success rather than the specific skills learned. Furthermore, the denial of programs to motivated individuals may have detrimental effects, even if it is not the program per se that facilitates positive changes. Unfortunately, the serious potential for self-selection bias in the vast majority of these studies does not allow for a resolution of this issue or the attribution of observed reduction in post-release offending to the activities of the programs.

Focusing specifically on the higher-quality studies revealed promising findings but does not provide sufficient foundation to support a general statement of the effectiveness of these programs. The six program-comparison contrasts that were rated as having a strong methodology came from four studies that consistently found positive effects. Unfortunately, the interventions examined by two of the contrasts were not typical education, vocation, or work programs. The study by Lattimore et al.[45] evaluated a vocational education program that included an individualized plan based on each inmate's vocational interests, aptitudes, and post-release placement. The *Specialized Training and Employment Project* evaluated by Van Stelle et al.[51] included correctional work, job placement services, and community follow-up services. Participants also could receive ABE and/or vocational training services if needed. It is impossible to determine from these studies whether the positive findings were a result of the more enhanced nature of the programming and the findings thus may not generalize to

more typical vocational and work programs found throughout the criminal justice system. These higher-quality studies suggest, however, that at least under certain program configurations, education, vocation, and work programs can lead to reductions in the rate of future offending.

It should be stressed that this review did not examine other potential benefits of education, vocation, and work programs. A common goal of these programs is to increase the employability of offenders, which was not the focus of this analysis. It also can be argued that any effect of these programs on recidivism is mediated by the program's success in increasing both the employment and wage rate for the participants. Furthermore, rehabilitation is not the sole justification for these programs. For example, a nontrivial function of these programs is the reduction of disciplinary problems by providing an incentive for good behavior[53] and reduction of idleness.[47] The large financial investment in these programs and the current public concerns over government spending underscore the need for these programs to demonstrate their effectiveness not only in improving prison life but also in increasing the likelihood that the prisoner will become a productive member of society upon release. As a whole, the current evidentiary base fails to establish a clear causal connection between these programs and future offending. The authors believe, however, that the evidence is encouraging and that it therefore would be unethical to deny motivated inmates the potential benefits of these programs.

Future research that merely compares participants with nonparticipants of these programs is not needed to resolve the questions of the effectiveness of these programs, for it is well established that participants do reoffend at a lower rate than nonparticipants. Rather, the field needs high-quality evaluation studies that can provide a strong basis for establishing a causal connection between the activities of the programs with future positive changes in inmate behavior.

A prison system with demand for these programs that exceeds available resources has a natural opportunity to implement a randomized experiment.[54] Furthermore, the randomization of persons to programs with and without supplemental components, such as job placement or individualized employment planning, is generally both feasible and ethical in these settings. Also, two strong quasi-experimental designs that may be well suited to prison systems include the propensity score method[55] and the regression discontinuity design.[15] Only after the collection and synthesis of several high-quality studies of typical corrections-based education, vocation, and work programs will the issue over the effectiveness of these programs be resolved.

Study Questions

1. What were identified as the primary goals of educational/vocational/work programs within prisons?

2. Of the programs reviewed, which types appeared to have the largest impact on postrelease recidivism?

3. What were some of the primary weaknesses of the study, as cited by the authors?

4. Discuss what new directions may be explored regarding programming in prison, on the basis of findings presented in this study.

Notes

1. R. Linden and L. Perry, "The Effectiveness of Prison Education Programs," *Journal of Offender Counseling Services and Rehabilitation* 6 (1983): 43–57.

2. J.J. Stephan, *Census of State and Federal Correctional Facilities, 1995*. Washington, D.C.: Bureau of Justice Statistics, 1997.

3. J. Gerber and E.J. Fritsch, "Adult Academic and Vocational Correctional Education Programs: A Review of Recent Research," *Journal of Offender Rehabilitation* 22 (1995): 119–142.

4. J.M. Taylor, "Should Prisoners Have Access to Collegiate Education? A Policy Issue," *Educational Policy* 8 (1994): 315–338.

5. J.M. Taylor, "Post-Secondary Correctional Education: An Evaluation of Effectiveness and Efficiency," *Journal of Correctional Education* 43 (1992): 132–141.

6. D.L. MacKenzie and L.J. Hickman, *What Works in Corrections? An Examination of the Effectiveness of the Type of Rehabilitation Programs Offered by Washington State Department of Corrections: Report to the State of Washington Legislature Joint Audit and Review Committee*. College Park, MD: University of Maryland, 1998.

7. S. Bushway and P. Reuter, "Labor Markets and Crime Risk Factors," in *Preventing Crime: What Works, What Doesn't, What's Promising*, eds. L.W. Sherman, et al. Washington, D.C.: Office of Justice Programs, U.S. Department of Justice, 1997.

8. C. Tracy and C. Johnson, *Review of Various Outcome Studies Relating Prison Education to Reduced Recidivism*. Austin, TX: Windham School System, 1994.

9. L.V. Hedges and I. Olkin, *Statistical Methods for Meta-Analysis*. Orlando, FL: Academic Press, 1985.

10. H. Cooper and L.V. Hedges, eds., *The Handbook of Research Synthesis*. New York: Russell Sage Foundation, 1994.

11. H.C. Kraemer, et al., "Advantages of Excluding Underpowered Studies in Meta-Analysis: Inclusionist Versus Exclusionist Viewpoints," *Psychological Methods* 3 (1998): 23–31.

12. M.W. Lipsey and D.B. Wilson, "The Efficacy of Psychological, Educational, and Behavioral Treatment: Confirmation from Meta-Analysis," *American Psychologist* 48 (1993): 1181–1209.

13. J.L. Fleiss, "Measures of Effect Size for Categorical Data," in *The Handbook of Research Synthesis*, ed. H. Cooper and L.V. Hedges. New York: Russell Sage Foundation, 1994.

14. L.J. Glesser and I. Olkin, "Stochastically Dependent Effect Sizes," in *The Handbook of Research Synthesis*, ed. H. Cooper and L.V. Hedges. New York: Russell Sage Foundation, 1994.

15. T.D. Cook and D.T. Campbell, *Quasi-experimentation: Design and Analysis Issues for Field Settings*. Boston: Houghton Mifflin, 1979.

16. L.V. Hedges and J.L. Vevea, "Fixed- and Random-Effect Models in Meta-Analysis," *Psychological Methods* 3 (1998): 486–504.

17. M.W. Lipsey and D.B. Wilson, *Practical Meta-Analysis.* Thousand Oaks, CA: Sage, forthcoming.

18. R.C. Overton, "A Comparison of Fixed-Effects and Mixed (Random-Effects) Models for Meta-Analysis Tests of Moderator Variable Effects," *Psychological Methods* 3 (1998): 354–379.

19. S.W. Raudenbush, "Random Effects Models," in *The Handbook of Research Synthesis*, ed. H. Cooper and L.V. Hedges. New York: Russell Sage Foundation, 1994.

20. K. Adams, et al., "A Large-Scale Multidimensional Test of the Effect of Prison Education Programs on Offenders' Behavior," *The Prison Journal* 74 (1994): 433–449.

21. S.V. Anderson, *Evaluation of the Impact of Correctional Education Programs on Recidivism.* Columbus, OH: Office of Management Information Systems Bureau of Planning and Evaluation, Ohio Department of Rehabilitation and Correction, 1995.

22. M.D. Harer, "Recidivism among Federal Prisoners Released in 1987," *Journal of Correctional Education* 46 (1995): 98–127.

23. K.A. Hull, *Analysis of Recidivism Rates for Participants of the Academic/Vocational/Transition Education Programs Offered by the Virginia Department of Correctional Education.* Richmond, VA: Commonwealth of Virginia Department of Correctional Education, 1995.

24. Z.D. Maciekowich, "Academic Education/Vocational Training and Recidivism of Adult Prisoners," dissertation. Phoenix, AZ: Arizona State University, 1976.

25. A.M. Piehl, *Learning While Doing Time.* Cambridge, MA: John F. Kennedy School of Government, Harvard University, 1995.

26. F.J. Porporino and D. Robinson, *Can Educating Adult Offenders Counteract Recidivism?* Portland, OR: Annual Meeting of the ACA Winter Conference, 1992.

27. C. Ramsey, *The Value of Receiving a General Education Development Certificate While Incarcerated in the South Carolina Department of Corrections on the Rate of Recidivism.* Columbia, SC: South Carolina Department of Corrections, 1988.

28. R.E. Schumacker, et al., "Vocational and Academic Indicators of Parole Success," *Journal of Correctional Education* 41 (1990): 8–12.

29. G.R. Siegel and J. Basta, *The Effect of Literacy and General Education Development Programs on Adult Probationers.* Tucson, AZ: Adult Probation Department of the Superior Court in Pima County, 1997.

30. A. Walsh, "An Evaluation, of the Effects of Adult Basic Education on Rearrest Rates among Probationers," *Journal of Offender Counseling, Services, and Rehabilitation* 9 (1985): 69–76.

31. M.E. Batiuk, et al., "Crime and Rehabilitation: Correctional Education as an Agent of Change," *Justice Quarterly* 14 (1997): 167–180.

32. F.S. Blackburn, *The Relationship between Recidivism and Participation in a Community College Associate of Arts Degree Program for Incarcerated Offenders.* Costa Mesa, CA: Annual Meeting of the Correctional Education Association, 1981.

33. D.D. Clark, *Analysis of Return Rates of the Inmate College Program Participants.* Albany, NY: New York State Department of Correctional Services, 1991.

34. C. Gaither, *An Evaluation of the Texas Department of Corrections' Junior College Program.* Huntsville, TX: Department of Correction Treatment Directorate, Research and Development Division, 1976.

35. J. Holloway and P. Moke, *Post-Secondary Correctional Education: An Evaluation of Parolee Performance.* Wilmington, Ohio: Wilmington College, 1986.

36. M. Langenbach, et al., "Televised Instruction in Oklahoma Prisons: A Study of Recidivism and Disciplinary Actions," *Journal of Correctional Education* 41 (1990): 87–94.

37. R. Linden, et al., "An Evaluation of a Prison Education Program," *Canadian Journal of Criminology* 26 (1984): 65–73.

38. D. Lockwood, "Prison Higher Education and Recidivism: A Program Evaluation," in *Yearbook of Correctional Education.* Burnaby, British Columbia: Institute for the Humanities, Simon Fraser University, 1991.

39. C.J. McGee, *The Positive Impact of Corrections Education on Recidivism and Employment.* Springfield, IL: Illinois Department of Corrections and Illinois Council on Vocational Education, 1997.

40. M. O'Neil, "Correctional Higher Education: Reduced Recidivism?" *Journal of Correctional Education* 41 (1990): 28–31.

41. D. Anderson, "The Relationship between Correctional Education and Parole Success," *Journal of Offender Counseling, Services, and Rehabilitation* 5 (1981): 13–25.

42. B.B. Coffey, "The Effectiveness of Vocational Education in Kentucky's Correctional Institutions as Measured by Employment Status and Recidivism," dissertation. Lexington, KY: University of Kentucky, 1983.

43. S. Davis and B. Chown, *Recidivism among Offenders Incarcerated by the Oklahoma Department of Corrections Who Received Vocational-Technical Training. A Survival Data Analysis of Offenders Released January 1982 through July 1986.* Oklahoma City, OK: Oklahoma State Department of Corrections, 1986.

44. E.A. Downes, et al., "Evaluating the Effects of Vocational Education on Inmates: A Research Model and Preliminary Results," in *The Yearbook of Correctional Education*, ed. S. Duguid. Burnaby, British Columbia: Simon Fraser University, 1989.

45. P.K. Lattimore, et al., "Experimental Assessment of the Effect of Vocational Training on Youthful Property Offenders," *Evaluation Review* 14 (1990): 115–133.

46. J.T. Luftig, "Vocational Education in Prison: An Alternative to Recidivism," *Journal of Studies in Technical Careers* 1 (1978): 31–42.

47. W.G. Saylor and G.G. Gaes, *PREP: Training Inmates through Industrial Work Participation and Vocational and Apprenticeship Instruction.* Washington, D.C.: Federal Bureau of Prisons, 1996.

48. J.L. Winterton, *Transformations: Technology Boot Camp.* Summative Evaluation. Unpublished.

49. K.E. Maguire, et al., "Prison Labor and Recidivism," *Journal of Quantitative Criminology* 4 (1988): 3–18.

50. K.M. Lee, "The Wichita Work Release Center: An Evaluative Study (Kansas)," dissertation. Manhattan, KS: Kansas State University, 1983.

51. K.R. Van Stelle, et al., *Final Evaluation Report: Specialized Training and Employment Project (STEP).* Madison, WI: University of Wisconsin-Madison Medical School, Department of Preventive Medicine, Center for Health Policy and Program Evaluation, 1995.

52. R. Menon, et al., *An Evaluation of Project RIO Outcomes: An Evaluative Report.* College Station, TX: Texas A and M University, Public Policy Resources Laboratory, 1992.

53. J.J. DiIulio, Jr., *No Escape: The Future of American Corrections.* New York: Basic Books, 1991.

54. R.F. Boruch, *Randomized Experiments for Planning and Evaluation: A Practical Guide.* Thousand Oaks, CA: Sage, 1997.

55. P.R. Rosenbaum and D.B. Rubin, "The Central Role of the Propensity Score in Observational Studies for Causal Effects," *Biometrika* 70 (1983): 41–55.

26
Beyond Correctional Quackery

Professionalism and the Possibility of Effective Treatment

Edward J. Latessa
Francis T. Cullen
Paul Gendreau

Despite the widespread advances that have been made in understanding criminal conduct and providing effective interventions, there are many who still practice correctional quackery. In this article, Latessa, Cullen, and Gendreau review four major sources of correctional quackery: failure to use research in designing programs, failure to use appropriate assessment tools, failure to use effective treatment models, and failure to evaluate. Some of the questionable theories they have come across include "treat them as babies and dress them in diapers," "give them a pet," and "put them in touch with their feminine side." They end by reviewing ways that agencies can improve correctional programming for offenders.

Long-time viewers of *Saturday Night Live* will vividly recall Steve Martin's hilarious portrayal of a medieval medical practitioner—the English barber, Theodoric of York. When ill patients are brought before him, he prescribes ludicrous "cures," such as repeated bloodletting, the application of leeches and boar's vomit, gory amputations,

and burying people up to their necks in a marsh. At a point in the skit when a patient dies and Theodoric is accused of "not knowing what he is doing," Martin stops, apparently struck by the transforming insight that medicine might abandon harmful interventions rooted in ignorant customs and follow a more enlightened path. "Perhaps," he says, "I've been wrong to blindly follow the medical traditions and superstitions of past centuries." He then proceeds to wonder whether he should "test these assumptions analytically through experimentation and the scientific method." And perhaps, he says, the scientific method might be applied to other fields of learning. He might even be able to "lead the way to a new age—an age of rebirth, a renaissance." He then pauses and gives the much-awaited and amusing punchline, "Nawwwwwwww!"

The humor, of course, lies in the juxtaposition and final embrace of blatant quackery with the possibility and rejection of a more modern, scientific, and ultimately effective approach to medicine. For those of us who make a living commenting on or doing corrections, however, we must consider whether, in a sense, the joke is on us. We can readily see the humor in Steve Martin's skit and wonder how those in medieval societies "could have been so stupid." But even a cursory survey of *current* correctional practices yields the disquieting conclusion that we are a field in which quackery is tolerated, if not implicitly celebrated. It is not clear whether most of us have ever had that reflective moment in which we question whether, "just maybe," there might be a more enlightened path to pursue. If we have paused to envision a different way of doing things, it is apparent that our reaction, after a moment's contemplation, too often has been, "Nawwwwwwww!"

This appraisal might seem overly harsh, but we are persuaded that it is truthful. When intervening in the lives of offenders—that is, intervening with the expressed intention of reducing recidivism—corrections has resisted becoming a true "profession." Too often, being a "professional" has been debased to mean dressing in a presentable way, having experience in the field, and showing up every day for work. But a profession is defined not by its surface appearance but by its intellectual core. An occupation may lay claim to being a "profession" only to the extent that its practices are based on research knowledge, training, and expertise—a triumvirate that promotes the possibility that what it does can be effective (Cullen, 1978; Starr, 1982). Thus, medicine's professionalization cannot be separated from its embrace of scientific knowledge as the ideal arbiter of how patients should be treated (Starr, 1982). The very concept of "malpractice" connotes that standards of service delivery have been established, are universally transmitted, and are capable of distinguishing acceptable from unacceptable interventions. The concept of liability for "correctional malpractice" would bring snickers from the crowd—a case where humor unintentionally offers a damning indictment of the field's standards of care.

In contrast to professionalism, *quackery* is dismissive of scientific knowledge, training, and expertise. Its posture is strikingly overconfident, if not arrogant. It embraces the notion that interventions are best rooted in "common sense," in personal experiences (or clinical knowledge), in tradition, and in superstition (Gendreau, Goggin, Cullen, and Paparozzi, forthcoming). "What works" is thus held to be "obvious," derived only from years of an individual's experience, and legitimized by an appeal to custom ("the way we have always done things around here has worked just fine"). It celebrates being anti-intellectual. There is never a need to visit a library or consult a study.

Correctional quackery, therefore, is the use of treatment interventions that are based on neither 1) existing knowledge of the causes of crime nor 2) existing knowledge of what programs have been shown to change offender behavior (Cullen and Gendreau, 2000; Gendreau, 2000). The hallmark of correctional quackery is thus igno-

rance. Such ignorance about crime and its cures at times is "understandable"—that is, linked not to the willful rejection of research but to being in a field in which professionalism is not expected or supported. At other times, however, quackery is proudly displayed, as its advocates boldly proclaim that they have nothing to learn from research conducted by academics "who have never worked with a criminal" (a claim that is partially true but ultimately beside the point and a rationalization for continued ignorance).

Need we now point out the numerous programs that have been implemented with much fanfare and with amazing promises of success, only later to turn out to have "no effect" on reoffending? "Boot camps," of course, are just one recent and salient example. Based on a vague, if not unstated, theory of crime and an absurd theory of behavioral change ("offenders need to be broken down"—through a good deal of humiliation and threats—and then "built back up"), boot camps could not possibly have "worked." In fact, we know of no major psychological theory that would logically suggest that such humiliation or threats are components of effective therapeutic interventions (Gendreau et al., forthcoming). Even so, boot camps were put into place across the nation without a shred of empirical evidence as to their effectiveness, and only now has their appeal been tarnished after years of negative evaluation studies (Cullen, Pratt, Miceli, and Moon, 2002; Cullen, Wright, and Applegate, 1996; Gendreau, Goggin, Cullen, and Andrews, 2000; MacKenzie, Wilson, and Kider, 2001). How many millions of dollars have been squandered? How many opportunities to rehabilitate offenders have been forfeited? How many citizens have been needlessly victimized by boot camp graduates? What has been the cost to society of this quackery?

We are not alone in suggesting that advances in our field will be contingent on the conscious rejection of quackery in favor of an *evidence-based corrections* (Cullen and

Table 26.1
Questionable Theories of Crime We Have Encountered in Agency Programs

---

✔ "Been there, done that" theory.

✔ "Offenders lack creativity" theory.

✔ "Offenders need to get back to nature" theory.

✔ "It worked for me" theory.

✔ "Offenders lack discipline" theory.

✔ "Offenders lack organizational skills" theory.

✔ "Offenders have low self-esteem" theory.

✔ "We just want them to be happy" theory.

✔ The "treat offenders as babies and dress them in diapers" theory.

✔ "Offenders need to have a pet in prison" theory.

✔ "Offenders need acupuncture" theory.

✔ "Offenders need to have healing lodges" theory.

✔ "Offenders need drama therapy" theory.

✔ "Offenders need a better diet and haircut" theory.

✔ "Offenders (females) need to learn how to put on makeup and dress better" theory.

✔ "Offenders (males) need to get in touch with their feminine side" theory. ✦

Gendreau, 2000; MacKenzie, 2000; Welsh and Farrington, 2001). Moving beyond correctional quackery when intervening with offenders, however, will be a daunting challenge. It will involve overcoming four central failures now commonplace in correctional treatment. We review these four sources of correctional quackery not simply to show what is lacking in the field but also

in hopes of illuminating what a truly professional approach to corrections must strive to entail.

Four Sources of Correctional Quackery

Failure to Use Research in Designing Programs

Every correctional agency must decide "what to do" with the offenders under its supervision, including selecting which "programs" or "interventions" their charges will be subjected to. But how is this choice made (a choice that is consequential to the offender, the agency, and the community)? Often, no real choice is made, because agencies simply continue with the practices that have been inherited from previous administrations. Other times, programs are added incrementally, such as when concern rises about drug use or drunk driving. And still other times—such as when punishment-oriented intermediate sanctions were the fad from the mid-1980s to the mid-1990s—jurisdictions copy the much-publicized interventions being implemented elsewhere in the state and in the nation.

Notice, however, what is missing in this account: The failure to consider the existing research on program effectiveness. The risk of quackery rises to the level of virtual certainty when nobody in the agency asks, "Is there any evidence supporting what we are intending to do?" The irrationality of not consulting the existing research is seen when we consider again, medicine. Imagine if local physicians and hospitals made no effort to consult "what works" and simply prescribed pharmaceuticals and conducted surgeries based on custom or the latest fad. Such malpractice would be greeted with public condemnation, lawsuits, and a loss of legitimacy by the field of medicine.

It is fair to ask whether research can, in fact, direct us to more effective correctional interventions. Two decades ago, our knowledge was much less developed. But the science of crime and treatment has made important strides in the intervening years. In particular, research has illuminated three bodies of knowledge that are integral to designing effective interventions.

First, we have made increasing strides in determining the *empirically established or known predictors* of offender recidivism (Andrews and Bonta, 1998; Gendreau, Little, and Goggin, 1996; Henggeler, Mihalic, Rone, Thomas, and Timmons-Mitchell, 1998). These include, most importantly: 1) antisocial values, 2) antisocial peers, 3) poor self-control, self-management, and prosocial problem-solving skills, 4) family dysfunction, and 5) past criminality. This information is critical, because interventions that ignore these factors are doomed to fail. Phrased alternatively, successful programs start by recognizing what causes crime and then *specifically design the intervention to target these factors for change* (Alexander, Pugh, and Parsons, 1998; Andrews and Bonta, 1998; Cullen and Gendreau, 2000; Henggeler et al., 1998).

Consider, however, the kinds of "theories" about the causes of crime that underlie many correctional interventions. In many cases, simple ignorance prevails; those working in correctional agencies cannot explain what crime-producing factors the program is allegedly targeting for change. Still worse, many programs have literally invented seemingly ludicrous theories of crime that are put forward with a straight face. From our collective experiences, we have listed in Table 26.1 crime theories that either (1) were implicit in programs we observed or (2) were voiced by agency personnel when asked what crime-causing factors their programs were targeting. These "theories" would be amusing except that they are commonplace and, again, potentially lead to correctional quackery. For example, the theory of "offenders (males) need to get in touch with their feminine side" prompted one agency to have offend-ers dress in female clothes. We cannot resist the temptation to note that you will now know whom to blame if you are mugged by a cross-dresser! But, in the end, this is no laughing matter. This intervention has no chance to be effective, and thus an important chance was forfeited to improve offenders' lives and to protect public safety.

Second, there is now a growing literature that outlines what does *not* work in offender treatment (see, e.g., Cullen, 2002; Cullen and Gendreau, 2000; Cullen et al., 2002; Cullen et al., 1996; Gendreau, 1996; Gendreau et al., 2000; Lipsey and Wilson, 1998; MacKenzie, 2000). These include boot camps, punishment-oriented programs (e.g., "scared straight" programs), control-oriented programs (e.g., intensive supervision programs), wilderness programs, psychological interventions that are non-directive or insight-oriented (e.g., psychoanalytic), and non-intervention (as suggested by labeling theory). Ineffective programs also target for treatment low-risk offenders and target for change weak predictors of criminal behavior (e.g., self-esteem). Given this knowledge, it would be a form of quackery to continue to use or to freshly implement these types of interventions.

Third, conversely, there is now a growing literature that outlines what *does* work in offender treatment (Cullen, 2002; Cullen and Gendreau, 2000). Most importantly, efforts are being made to develop principles of effective intervention (Andrews, 1995; Andrews and Bonta, 1998; Gendreau, 1996). These principles are listed in Table 26.2. Programs that adhere to these principles have been found to achieve meaningful reductions in recidivism (Andrews, Dowden, and Gendreau, 1999; Andrews, Zinger, Hoge, Bonta, Gendreau, and Cullen, 1990; Cullen, 2002). However, programs that are designed without consulting these principles are almost certain to have little or no impact on offender recidivism and may even risk increasing reoffending. That is, if these principles are ignored, quackery is

Table 26.2
Eight Principles of Effective
Correctional Intervention

1. **Organizational Culture**
   Effective organizations have well-defined goals, ethical principles, and a history of efficiently responding to issues that have an impact on the treatment facilities. Staff cohesion, support for service training, self-evaluation, and use of outside resources also characterize the organization.

2. **Program Implementation/Maintenance**
   Programs are based on empirically-defined needs and are consistent with the organization's values. The program is fiscally responsible and congruent with stakeholders' values. Effective programs also are based on thorough reviews of the literature (i.e., meta-analyses), undergo pilot trials, and maintain the staff's professional credentials.

3. **Management/Staff Characteristics**
   The program director and treatment staff are professionally trained and have previous experience working in offender treatment programs. Staff selection is based on their holding beliefs supportive of rehabilitation and relationship styles and therapeutic skill factors typical of effective therapies.

4. **Client Risk/Need Practices**
   Offender risk is assessed by psychometric instruments of proven predictive validity. The risk instrument consists of a wide range of dynamic risk factors or criminogenic needs (e.g., anti-social attitudes and values). The assessment also takes into account the responsivity of offenders to different styles and modes of service. Changes in risk level over time (e.g., 3 to 6 months) are routinely assessed in order to measure intermediate changes in risk/need levels that may occur as a result of planned interventions.

5. **Program Characteristics**
   The program targets for change a wide variety of criminogenic needs (factors that predict recidivism), using empirically valid behavioral/social learning/cognitive behavioral therapies that are directed to higher-risk offenders. The ratio of rewards to punishers is at least 4:1. Relapse prevention strategies are available once offenders complete the formal treatment phase.

6. **Core Correctional Practice**
   Program therapists engage in the following therapeutic practices: anti-criminal modeling, effective reinforcement and disapproval, problem-solving techniques, structured learning procedures for skill-building, effective use of authority, cognitive self-change, relationship practices, and motivational interviewing.

7. **Inter-Agency Communication**
   The agency aggressively makes referrals and advocates for its offenders in order that they receive high quality services in the community.

8. **Evaluation**
   The agency routinely conducts program audits, consumer satisfaction surveys, process evaluations of changes in criminogenic need, and follow-ups of recidivism rates. The effectiveness of the program is evaluated by comparing the respective recidivism rates of risk-control comparison groups of other treatments or those of a minimal treatment group.

Note: Items adapted from the Correctional Program Assessment Inventory—2000, a 131-item Questionnaire that is widely used in assessing the quality of correctional treatment programs (Gendreau and Andrews, 2001).

likely to result. We will return to this issue below.

Failure to Follow Appropriate Assessment and Classification Practices

The steady flow of offenders into correctional agencies not only strains resources but also creates a continuing need to allocate treatment resources efficaciously. This problem is not dissimilar to a hospital that must process a steady flow of patients. In a hospital (or doctor's office), however, it is immediately recognized that the crucial first step to delivering effective treatment is diagnosing or *assessing* the patient's condition and its severity. In the absence of such a diagnosis—which might involve the careful study of symptoms or a battery of tests—the treatment prescribed would have no clear foundation. Medicine would be a lottery in which the ill would hope the doctor assigned the right treatment. In a similar way, effective treatment intervention requires the appropriate assessment of both the risks posed by, and the needs underlying the criminality of, offenders. When such diagnosis is absent and no classification of offenders is possible, offenders in effect enter a treatment lottery in which their access to effective intervention is a chancy proposition.

Strides have been made to develop more effective classification instruments—such as the Level of Supervision Inventory (LSI) (Bonta, 1996), which, among its competitors, has achieved the highest predictive validity with recidivism (Gendreau et al., 1996). The LSI and similar instruments classify offenders by using a combination of "static" factors (such as criminal history) and "dynamic factors" (such as antisocial values, peer associations) shown by previous research to predict recidivism. In this way, it is possible to classify offenders by their level of risk and to discern the types and amount of "criminogenic needs" they

possess that should be targeted for change in their correctional treatment.

At present, however, there are three problems with offender assessment and classification by correctional agencies (Gendreau and Goggin, 1997). First, many agencies simply do not assess offenders, with many claiming they do not have the time. Second, when agencies do assess, they assess poorly. Thus, they often use outdated, poorly designed, and/or empirically unvalidated classification instruments. In particular, they tend to rely on instruments that measure exclusively static predictors of recidivism (which cannot, by definition, be changed) and that provide no information on the criminogenic needs that offenders have. If these "needs" are not identified and addressed—such as possessing antisocial values—the prospects for recidivism will be high. For example, a study of 240 (161 adult and 79 juvenile) programs assessed across 30 states found that 64 percent of the programs did not utilize a standardized and objective assessment tool that could distinguish risk/needs levels for offenders (Matthews, Hubbard, and Latessa, 2001; Latessa, 2002).

Third, even when offenders are assessed using appropriate classification instruments, agencies frequently ignore the information. It is not uncommon, for example, for offenders to be assessed and then for everyone to be given the same treatment. In this instance, assessment becomes an organizational routine in which paperwork is compiled but the information is ignored.

Again, these practices increase the likelihood that offenders will experience correctional quackery. In a way, treatment is delivered blindly, with agency personnel equipped with little knowledge about the risks and needs of the offenders under their supervision. In these circumstances, it is impossible to know which offenders should receive which interventions. Any hopes of individualizing interventions effectively also are forfeited, because the appropriate diagnosis either is unavailable or hidden in the agency's unused files.

Failure to Use Effective Treatment Models

Once offenders are assessed, the next step is to select an appropriate treatment model. As we have suggested, the challenge is to consult the empirical literature on "what works," and to do so with an eye toward programs that conform to the principles of effective intervention. At this stage, it is inexcusable either to ignore this research or to implement programs that have been shown to be ineffective. Yet, as we have argued, the neglect of the existing research on effective treatment models is widespread. In the study of 240 programs noted above, it was reported that two-thirds of adult programs and over half of juvenile programs did not use a treatment model that research had shown to be effective (Matthews et al., 2001; Latessa, 2002). Another study—a meta-analysis of 230 program evaluations (which yielded 374 tests or effect sizes)—categorized the extent to which interventions conformed to the principles of effective intervention. In only 13 percent of the tests were the interventions judged to fall into the "most appropriate" category (Andrews et al., 1999). But this failure to employ an appropriate treatment approach does not have to be the case. Why would an agency—in this information age—risk quackery when the possibility of using an evidence-based program exists? Why not select effective treatment models?

Moving in this direction is perhaps mostly a matter of a change of consciousness—that is, an awareness by agency personnel that quackery must be rejected and programs with a track record of demonstrated success embraced. Fortunately, depending on the offender population, there is a growing number of treatment models that might be learned and implemented (Cullen and Applegate, 1997). Some

of the more prominent models in this regard are the "Functional Family Therapy" model that promotes family cohesion and affection (Alexander et al., 1998; Gordon, Graves, and Arbuthnot, 1995), the teaching youths to think and react responsibly peer-helping ("Equip") program (Gibbs, Potter, and Goldstein, 1995), the "Prepare Curriculum" program (Goldstein, 1999), "Multisystemic Therapy" (Henggeler et al., 1998), and the prison-based "Rideau Integrated Service Delivery Model" that targets criminal thinking, anger, and substance abuse (see Gendreau, Smith, and Goggin, 2001).

Failure to Evaluate What We Do

Quackery has long prevailed in corrections because agencies have traditionally required no systematic evaluation of the effectiveness of their programs (Gendreau, Goggin, and Smith, 2001). Let us admit that many agencies may not have the human or financial capital to conduct ongoing evaluations. Nonetheless, it is not clear that the failure to evaluate has been due to a lack of capacity as much as to a lack of desire. The risk inherent in evaluation, of course, is that practices that are now unquestioned and convenient may be revealed as ineffective. Evaluation, that is, creates accountability and the commitment threat of having to change what is now being done. The cost of change is not to be discounted, but so too is the "high cost of ignoring success" (Van Voorhis, 1987). In the end, a professional must be committed to doing not simply what is in one's self-interest but what is ethical and effective. To scuttle attempts at program evaluation and to persist in using failed interventions is wrong and a key ingredient to continued correctional quackery (more broadly, see Van Voorhis, Cullen, and Applegate, 1995).

Evaluation, moreover, is not an all-or-nothing procedure. Ideally, agencies would conduct experimental studies in which offenders were randomly assigned to a treatment or control group and outcomes, such as recidivism, were measured over a lengthy period of time. But let us assume that, in many settings, conducting this kind of sophisticated evaluation is not feasible. It is possible, however, for virtually all agencies to monitor, to a greater or lesser extent, the *quality* of the programs that they or outside vendors are supplying. Such evaluative monitoring would involve, for example, assessing whether treatment services are being delivered as designed, supervising and giving constructive feedback to treatment staff, and studying whether offenders in the program are making progress on targeted criminogenic factors (e.g., changing antisocial attitudes, manifesting more prosocial behavior). In too many cases, offenders are "dropped off" in intervention programs and then, eight or twelve weeks later, are deemed—without any basis for this conclusion—to have "received treatment." Imagine if medical patients entered and exited hospitals with no one monitoring their treatment or physical recovery. Again, we know what we could call such practices.

Conclusion—Becoming an Evidence-Based Profession

In assigning the label "quackery" to much of what is now being done in corrections, we run the risk of seeming, if not being, preachy and pretentious. This is not our intent. If anything, we mean to be provocative—not for the sake of causing a stir, but for the purpose of prompting correctional leaders and professionals to stop using treatments that cannot possibly be effective. If we make readers think seriously about how to avoid selecting, designing, and using failed correctional interventions, our efforts will have been worthwhile.

We would be remiss, however, if we did not confess that academic criminologists share the blame for the continued use of ineffective programs. For much of the past quarter century, most academic criminolo-

gists have abandoned correctional practitioners. Although some notable exceptions exist, we have spent much of our time claiming that "nothing works" in offender rehabilitation and have not created partnerships with those in corrections so as to build knowledge on "what works" to change offenders (Cullen and Gendreau, 2001). Frequently, what guidance criminologists have offered correctional agencies has constituted *bad* advice—ideologically inspired, not rooted in the research, and likely to foster quackery. Fortunately, there is a growing movement among criminologists to do our part both in discerning the principles of effective intervention and in deciphering what interventions have empirical support (Cullen and Gendreau, 2001; MacKenzie, 2000; Welsh and Farrington, 2001). Accordingly, the field of corrections has more information available to find out what our "best bets" are when intervening with offenders (Rhine, 1998).

We must also admit that our use of medicine as a comparison to corrections has been overly simplistic. We stand firmly behind the central message conveyed—that what is done in corrections would be grounds for malpractice in medicine—but we have glossed over the challenges that the field of medicine faces in its attempt to provide scientifically-based interventions. First, scientific knowledge is not static but evolving. Medical treatments that appear to work now may, after years of study, prove ineffective or less effective than alternative interventions. Second, even when information is available, it is not clear that it is effectively transmitted or that doctors, who may believe in their personal "clinical experience," will be open to revising their treatment strategies (Hunt, 1997). "The gap between research and knowledge," notes Millenson (1997, p. 4), "has real consequences . . . when family practitioners in Washington State were queried about treating a simple urinary tract infection in women, eighty-two physicians came up with an extraordinary 137 different strategies." In response to situations like these, there is a renewed evidence-based movement in medicine to improve the quality of medical treatments (Millenson, 1997; Timmermans and Angell, 2001).

Were corrections to reject quackery in favor of an evidence-based approach, it is likely that agencies would face the same difficulties that medicine encounters in trying base treatments on the best scientific knowledge available. Designing and implementing an effective program is more complicated, we realize, than simply visiting a library in search of research on program effectiveness (although this is often an important first step). Information must be available in a form that can be used by agencies. As in medicine, there must be opportunities for training and the provision of manuals that can be consulted in how *specifically* to carry out an intervention. Much attention has to be paid to implementing programs as they are designed. And, in the long run, an effort must be made to support widespread program evaluation and to use the resulting data both to improve individual programs and to expand our knowledge base on effective programs generally.

To move beyond quackery and accomplish these goals, the field of corrections will have to take seriously what it means to be a *profession*. In this context, individual agencies and individuals within agencies would do well to strive to achieve what Gendreau et al. (forthcoming) refer to as the "3 C's" of effective correctional policies: First, employ *credentialed people;* second, ensure that the *agency is credentialed* in that it is founded on the principles of fairness and the improvement of lives through ethically defensible means; and third, base treatment decisions on *credentialed knowledge* (e.g., research from meta-analyses).

By themselves, however, given individuals and agencies can do only so much to implement effective interventions—although each small step away from quackery and toward an evidence-based practice potentially makes a meaningful difference.

The broader issue is whether the *field* of corrections will embrace the principles that all interventions should be based on the best research evidence, that all practitioners must be sufficiently trained so as to develop expertise in how to achieve offender change, and that an ethical corrections cannot tolerate treatments known to be foolish, if not harmful. In the end, correctional quackery is not an inevitable state of affairs—something we are saddled with for the foreseeable future. Rather, although a formidable foe, it is ultimately rooted in our collective decision to tolerate ignorance and failure. Choosing a different future for corrections—making the field a true profession—will be a daunting challenge, but it is a future that lies within our power to achieve.

Study Questions

1. What are the four sources of correctional quackery identified by the authors?

2. What are the eight principles of effective correctional intervention?

3. What are the three C's identified by the authors?

References

Alexander, James, Christie Pugh, and Bruce Parsons. 1998. *Functional Family Therapy: Book Three in the Blueprints and Violence Prevention Series.* Boulder, CO: Center for the Study and Prevention of Violence, University of Colorado.

Andrews, D. A. 1995. "The Psychology of Criminal Conduct and Effective Treatment." Pp. 35–62 in James McGuire (ed.), *What Works: Reducing Reoffending.* West Sussex, UK: John Wiley.

Andrews, D. A., and James Bonta. 1998. *Psychology of Criminal Conduct,* 2nd ed. Cincinnati: Anderson.

Andrews, D. A., Craig Dowden, and Paul Gendreau. 1999. "Clinically Relevant and Psychologically Informed Approaches to Reduced Re-Offending: A Meta-Analytic Study of Human Service, Risk, Need, Responsivity, and

Other Concerns in Justice Contexts." Unpublished manuscript, Carleton University.

Andrews, D. A., Ivan Zinger, R. D. Hoge, James Bonta, Paul Gendreau, and Francis T. Cullen. 1990. "Does Correctional Treatment Work? A Clinically Relevant and Psychologically Informed Meta-Analysis." *Criminology* 28:369–404.

Bonta, James. 1996. "Risk-Needs Assessment and Treatment." Pp. 18–32 in Alan T. Harland (ed.), *Choosing Correctional Options That Work: Defining the Demand and Evaluating the Supply.* Thousand Oaks, CA: Sage.

Cullen, Francis T. 2002. "Rehabilitation and Treatment Programs." Pp. 253–289 in James Q. Wilson and Joan Petersilia (eds.), *Crime: Public Policies for Crime Control.* Oakland, CA: ICS Press.

Cullen, Francis T. and Brandon K. Applegate, eds. 1997. *Offender Rehabilitation: Effective Correctional Intervention.* Aldershot, UK: Ashgate/Dartmouth.

Cullen, Francis T. and Paul Gendreau. 2000. "Assessing Correctional Rehabilitation: Policy, Practice, and Prospects." Pp. 109–175 in Julie Horney (ed.), *Criminal Justice 2000: Volume 3—Policies, Processes, and Decisions of the Criminal Justice System.* Washington, DC: U.S. Department of Justice, National Institute of Justice.

Cullen, Francis T. and Paul Gendreau. 2001. "From Nothing Works to What Works: Changing Professional Ideology in the 21st Century." *The Prison Journal* 81:313–338.

Cullen, Francis T., Travis C. Pratt, Sharon Levrant Miceli, and Melissa M. Moon. 2002. "Dangerous Liaison? Rational Choice Theory as the Basis for Correctional Intervention." Pp. 279–296 in Alex R. Piquero and Stephen G. Tibbetts (eds.), *Rational Choice and Criminal Behavior: Recent Research and Future Challenges.* New York: Routledge.

Cullen, Francis T., John Paul Wright, and Brandon K. Applegate. 1996. "Control in the Community: The Limits of Reform?" Pp. 69–116 in Alan T. Harland (ed.), *Choosing Correctional Interventions That Work: Defining the Demand and Evaluating the Supply.* Thousand Oaks, CA: Sage.

Cullen, John B. 1978. *The Structure of Professionalism.* Princeton, NJ: Petrocelli Books.

Gendreau, Paul. 1996. "The Principles of Effective Intervention with Offenders." Pp. 117–130 in Alan T. Harland (ed.), *Choosing Correctional Options That Work: Defining the Demand and Evaluating the Supply.* Newbury Park, CA: Sage.

Gendreau, Paul. 2000. "1998 Margaret Mead Award Address: Rational Policies for Reforming Offenders." Pp. 329–338 in Maeve McMahon (ed.), *Assessment to Assistance: Programs for Women in Community Corrections.* Lanham, MD: American Correctional Association.

Gendreau, Paul and D. A. Andrews. 2001. *Correctional Program Assessment Inventory—2000.* Saint John, Canada: Authors.

Gendreau, Paul and Claire Goggin. 1997. "Correctional Treatment: Accomplishments ard Realities." Pp. 271–279 in Patricia Van Voorhis, Michael Braswell, and David Lester (eds.), *Correctional Counseling and Rehabilitation,* 3rd edition. Cincinnati: Anderson.

Gendreau, Paul, Claire Goggin, Francis T. Cullen, and D. A. Andrews. 2000. "The Effects of Community Sanctions and Incarceration on Recidivism." *Forum on Corrections Research* 12 (May): 10–13.

Gendreau, Paul, Claire Goggin, Francis T. Cullen, and Mario Paparozzi. Forthcoming. "The Common Sense Revolution in Correctional Policy." In James McGuire (ed.), *Offender Rehabilitation and Treatment: Effective Programs and Policies to Reduce Re-Offending.* Chichester, UK: John Wiley and Sons.

Gendreau, Paul, Claire Goggin, and Paula Smith. 2001. "Implementing Correctional Interventions in the 'Real' World." Pp. 247–268 in Gary A. Bernfeld, David P. Farrington, and Alan W. Leschied (eds.), *Inside the "Black Box" in Corrections.* Chichester, UK: John Wiley and Sons.

Gendreau, Paul, Tracy Little, and Claire Goggin. 1996. "A Meta-Analysis of the Predictors of Adult Offender Recidivism: What Works?" *Criminology* 34:575–607.

Gendreau, Paul, Paula Smith, and Claire Goggin. 2001. "Treatment Programs in Corrections." Pp. 238–263 in John Winterdyk (ed.), *Corrections in Canada: Social Reaction to Crime.* Toronto, Canada: Prentice-Hall.

Gibbs, John C., Granville Bud Potter, and Arnold P. Goldstein. 1995. *The EQUIP Program: Teaching Youths to Think and Act Responsibly Through a Peer-Helping Approach.* Champaign, IL: Research Press.

Goldstein, Arnold P. 1999. *The Prepare Curriculum: Teaching Prosocial Competencies.* Rev. ed. Champaign, IL: Research Press.

Gordon, Donald A., Karen Graves, and Jack Arbuthnot. 1995. "The Effect of Functional

Family Therapy for Delinquents on Adult Criminal Behavior." *Criminal Justice and Behavior* 22:60–73.

Henggeler, Scott W., with the assistance of Sharon R. Mihalic, Lee Rone, Christopher Thomas, and Jane Timmons-Mitchell. 1998. *Multisystemic Therapy: Book Six in the Blueprints in Violence Prevention Series.* Boulder, CO: Center for the Study and Prevention of Violence, University of Colorado.

Hunt, Morton. 1997. *How Science Takes Stock: The Story of Meta-Analysis.* New York: Russell Sage Foundation.

Latessa, Edward J. 2002. "Using Assessment to Improve Correctional Programming: An Update." Unpublished paper, University of Cincinnati.

Lipsey, Mark W. and David B. Wilson. 1998. "Effective Intervention for Serious Juvenile Offenders." Pp. 313–345 in Rolf Loeber and David P. Farrington (eds.), *Serious and Violent Juvenile Offenders: Risk Factors and Successful Intervention.* Thousand Oaks, CA: Sage.

MacKenzie, Doris Layton. 2000. "Evidence-Based Corrections: Identifying What Works." *Crime and Delinquency* 46:457–471.

MacKenzie, Doris Layton, David B. Wilson, and Suzanne B. Kider. 2001. "The Effects of Correctional Boot Camps on Offending." *Annals of the American Academy of Political and Social Science* 578 (November): 126–143.

Matthews, Betsy, Dana Jones Hubbard, and Edward J. Latessa. 2001. "Making the Next Step: Using Assessment to Improve Correctional Programming." *Prison Journal* 81:454–472.

Millenson, Michael L. 1997. *Demanding Medical Excellence: Doctors and Accountability in the Information Age.* Chicago: University of Chicago Press.

Rhine, Edward E. (ed.). 1998. *Best Practices: Excellence in Corrections.* Lanham, MD: American Correctional Association.

Starr, Paul. 1982. *The Social Transformation of American Medicine: The Rise of a Sovereign Profession and the Making of a Vast Industry.* New York: Basic Books.

Timmermans, Stefan and Alison Angell. 2001. "Evidence-Based Medicine, Clinical Uncertainty, and Learning to Doctor." *Journal of Health and Social Behavior* 42:342–359.

Van Voorhis, Patricia. 1987. "Correctional Effectiveness: The High Cost of Ignoring Success." *Federal Probation* 51 (March): 59–62.

Van Voorhis, Patricia, Francis T. Cullen, and Brandon K. Applegate. 1995. "Evaluating Interventions with Violent Offenders: A Guide for Practitioners and Policymakers." *Federal Probation* 59 (June): 17–28.

Welsh, Brandon C. and David P. Farrington. 2001. "Toward an Evidence-Based Approach to Preventing Crime." *Annals of the American Academy of Political and Social Science* 578 (November): 158–173.

Part V

Release From Prison and Parole

Despite one's opinions about incarceration and punishment, the fact remains that the vast majority of offenders who are incarcerated will be released from prison. Some will complete all of their time and "max" out, while many others will be receiving some conditional release, traditionally called *parole*. Given the large number of offenders incarcerated in the United States, the number of offenders reentering society is staggering. Estimates are that over 600,000 per year will exit prison for the foreseeable future.

Parole from prison, like the prison itself, is primarily an American innovation. It emerged from a philosophical revolution and a resulting tradition of penal reform established in the late eighteenth century in the newly formed United States. As with many other new ideas that emerged in the early United States, parole had its roots in the practices of English and European penal systems. Alexander Maconochie is usually given credit as being the father of parole. In 1840, Captain Maconochie was put in charge of the English penal colony in New South Wales at Norfolk Island, about 1,000 miles off the coast of Australia. To this colony were sent the criminals who were twice condemned. They had been shipped from England to Australia, and then from Australia to Norfolk. Conditions were allegedly horrible, and it was under these conditions that Maconochie devised parole. Although the roots of parole spring from Australia, it was the prison reform movement in the United States that embraced the concept and developed and expanded its use.

Perhaps no aspect of the correctional system came under more attack than parole. Liberals questioned the secretiveness of the process and the arbitrariness of the release decision. Conservatives questioned both the wisdom of releasing offenders after only a portion of their sentence had been served and the effectiveness of parole supervision in protecting the public. Despite these attacks, parole has survived in many states and still remains as a vehicle for release and supervision of offenders in the community.

The failure of prisons to rehabilitate offenders has often been attributed to a lack of support and transitional care and services. One of the ways in which transition from prison to the community is made more effective is through community correctional facilities, often called halfway houses. Halfway houses have a long history in the United States and are considered by many to be essential to the reintegration of offenders back into the community. Substance abuse treatment, housing, employment training, counseling, and family services are some of the programs that community correctional programs such as halfway houses provide. Giving support and assistance to those in need is only one role these programs play. Protecting the community and cost-effectiveness are also critical aspects that need to be factored in when we consider the effectiveness of correctional programs such as halfway houses. ✦

27
Reentry Reconsidered

A New Look at an Old Question

Jeremy Travis
Joan Petersilia

Travis and Petersilia have done a considerable amount of research on the subject of prisoner reentry. As they tell us in this article, offenders reentering society today are less prepared for reintegration than ever before, and the consequences are significant, especially in disadvantaged and lower-income neighborhoods. Travis and Petersilia also point out that linkages between prisoner reentry and health care, family and child welfare, workforce preparation, and other social support systems are important ingredients to enhancing the chances of success for many offenders.

Last year, about 585,000 individuals—nearly 1,600 a day—left state and federal prisons to return home. On one level, this is not particularly noteworthy. Ever since prisons were built, prisoners have faced the challenge of moving from confinement in correctional institutions to liberty on the street. Yet, as we argue in this article, from a number of policy perspectives, the age-old issue of prisoner reintegration has taken on critical importance as we enter the new century. Furthermore, we believe that a renewed research and policy focus on the phenomenon of prisoner reentry can breathe life into old debates about the purposes of punishment, the relationship between offenders and society, and the consequences of the arrest, incarceration, and return of offenders.

We first view the reentry phenomenon through a jurisprudential lens. We argue that a reentry perspective sheds light on three natural experiments in justice policy: namely, the fourfold increase in per capita rates of incarceration, the disintegration of a unified sentencing philosophy, and the weakening of parole as a coherent approach to prisoner reintegration. We then discuss recent changes in the profile of returning prisoners. Third, we examine linkages between the reentry phenomenon and five related social policy domains. Finally, we explore some implications of this reentry perspective for the development of new policies.

Sentencing Policy Through a Reentry Lens

Over the past generation, sentencing policy in the United States has been characterized by three interrelated developments, one well known, two less so: the growth in imprisonment rates, the fragmentation of sentencing philosophy, and the weakening of parole. Taken together, they have had profound consequences on the reintegration of released prisoners.

The Growth of Imprisonment

The per capita rate of imprisonment in America hovered at about 110 per 100,000 from 1925 to 1973, with little variation (Blumstein & Beck, 1999). Starting in 1973, however, the rate of imprisonment has grown steadily, so that our rate is now 476 per 100,000, more than 4 times the 1973 level (Beck, 2000a). State prisons now house 1.2 million people (Beck, 2000a). There are an additional 596,485 people in local jails, a threefold increase since 1980 (Bureau of Justice Statistics, 2000a).

There has been a nearly parallel growth in the size of the population under parole supervision. In 1980, there were 220,000 people on parole, serving the remainder of their prison sentences under community supervision. By 1999, that number had grown to 713,000, more than a threefold increase. Similarly, the probation population increased between 1980 and 1999 from 1.2 million to 3.8 million (Bureau of Justice Statistics, 2000a).

As a natural, predictable consequence of the nation's experiment with increased levels of imprisonment, more people leave prison to return home, typically under some form of criminal justice supervision. As Figure 27.1 shows, the number of people released from state and federal prisons increased from 154,000 in 1980 to about 585,000 in 2000. Because the average length of prison stay has also increased over time, there has been a slight lag between intake levels and release levels in the prison systems. But by 1998 there were similar numbers admitted (615,000) as released (547,000) (Beck, 2000b; Bureau of Justice Statistics, 2000b). Furthermore, now that the nation's prison population is moving toward equilibrium, and even declining in

Figure 27.1

Sentenced Prisoners Released From State and Federal Jurisdictions, 1977–1998

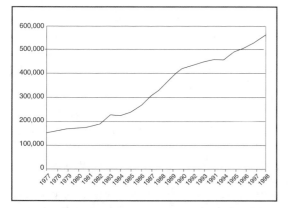

Source: Generated by the Urban Institute based on data from the Bureau of Justice Statistics (2000c).

some states, we can expect that the reentry cohorts may soon peak as well.

In summary, the burden on the formal and informal processes that should work together to support successful reintegration of prisoners has increased enormously. On one level, if the capacity to manage reintegration had kept pace with the flow of released prisoners—as the capacity to incarcerate has basically kept pace with the increase in detained prisoners—then, perhaps, the reentry phenomenon today would be no different than in times past. To borrow the language of the assembly line, the throughput would simply be at a higher level of production. But, as will be shown below, the exponential increase in release cohorts has placed exponentially greater strains on the communities where prisoner removal and return are concentrated. And the philosophical and operational capacity to manage the higher production of released prisoners has not kept pace.

The Fragmentation of Sentencing Philosophy

A second, lesser known development in our sentencing philosophy has been what Michael Tonry (1999, p. 1) called the "fragmentation of American sentencing policy." A generation ago, we had a unifying national sentencing philosophy, what Tonry called "a distinctly American approach to sentencing and corrections, usually referred to as indeterminate sentencing, and it had changed little in the preceding 50 years" (p. 1). Under this approach, all states provided judges with broad ranges of possible sentences, authorized the release of prisoners by parole boards, supervised prisoners after release, and explicitly embraced rehabilitation of offenders as the goal of corrections (Tonry, 1999).

That philosophy came under attack from the left and right ends of the political spectrum. Liberals critiqued indeterminate sentencing by judges and discretionary release decisions by parole boards as presenting opportunities for distortions of justice. Widely disparate sentences for similar offenses and similar offenders were critiqued as violating fundamental principles of fairness. The unreviewable nature of the decisions was seen as presenting opportunities for disparate racial outcomes. And the lingering uncertainty regarding the culmination of a prison term, dependent on the seemingly arbitrary decision of a parole board, was critiqued as adding unnecessary stress to the period of imprisonment (Frankel, 1973).

The criticism from the right was equally fierce. The imposition of indeterminate sentences, with low minimum and high maximum prison terms, was criticized as a fraud on the public. A resurgent belief in "just deserts," the idea that criminal behavior warrants a punishment proportionate to the offense, resonated with a new public belief that the criminal justice system was too lenient (Hirsch, 1976; Wilson, 1975). A review of the literature on the effectiveness of rehabilitation, captured in the famous phrase "nothing works," weakened the intellectual underpinning of the stated purpose of sentencing and correction (Martinson, 1974). Finally, the use of early release as a mechanism to manage burgeoning prison populations strained public confidence in the integrity of the governmental process for managing the severity of punishment (Wright, 1998).

Under attack from left and right, the philosophy of indeterminate sentencing, once embraced by all 50 states and enshrined in the Model Penal Code, lost its intellectual hold on U.S. sentencing policy. Beginning with the abolition of parole in Maine in 1975, "nearly every state has in some way repudiated indeterminate sentencing" and replaced it with a variety of state experiments (Tonry, 1996, p. 4; Tonry, 1999). As of 1998, 17 states had created sentencing commissions, quasi-independent administrative bodies that have designed sentencing grids

that significantly constrain judicial sentencing discretion (Rottman, Flango, Cantrell, Hansen, & LaFountain, 2000). Legislation creating mandatory minimum sentences has been enacted in all 50 states (Austin, Jones, Kramer, & Renninger, 1995). Three-strikes laws have lengthened prison terms for persistent offenders in 24 states (Austin, Clark, Hardyman, & Henry, 1999). Forty states have enacted truth-in-sentencing laws requiring that violent offenders serve at least 50 percent of their sentences in prison; of these 40 states, 27 and the District of Columbia require violent offenders to serve at least 85 percent of their sentences in prison (Ditton & Wilson, 1999).

These developments in U.S. sentencing philosophy can be analyzed from a number of different perspectives. One could analyze their effects on the level of incarceration, the profile of the prison population, plea bargaining practices, or prosecutorial discretion, to name a few. A reentry perspective focuses attention on the impact of these developments on the process of release and reintegration—on the timing of the release decision, the procedures for making the release decision, the preparation of the prisoner for release, the preparation of the prisoner's family and community for his or her release, supervision after release, and the linkages between in-prison and postrelease activities.

For example, as a result of these changes in sentencing philosophy, fewer prisoners are being released because of a parole board decision (see Table 27.1). In 1990, 39 percent were released to supervision by parole board action and 29 percent by mandatory release; by 1998, those figures had been reversed, and 26 percent were released by parole board decision and 40 percent by mandatory release (Beck, 2000b). With widespread adoption of truth-in-sentencing statutes, these trends can be expected to continue, so that release by parole board will become a vestige of a bygone era, retained in some states, but in others

Table 27.1
Inmate Release Decisions, 1990–1998 (in percentages)

| Year | Released to Supervision | | | Expiration of Sentence | Other |
	Parole Board	Mandatory Release	Other Conditional		
1990	39.4	28.8	15.5	12.7	3.6
1995	32.3	39.0	10.1	14.5	4.0
1996	30.4	38.0	10.2	16.7	4.7
1997	28.2	39.7	10.4	16.8	4.9
1998	26.0	40.4	11.2	18.7	3.7

Source: Beck (2000a).

reserved for an aging prison cohort sentenced under the old regime.

The policy and research questions posed by this development have implications for corrections management. Does the absence of a discretionary release process remove an incentive for good behavior? If so, can the loss of that incentive be replaced with another, equally effective incentive? Does the automatic nature of release diminish the prisoner's incentive to find a stable residence or employment on the outside, the factors that traditionally influenced release decisions? Does a mandatory release policy increase or decrease a correctional agency's coordination between life in prison and planning for life outside of prison? Does mandatory release remove the ability of a parole board to revisit the risk posed by the offender, once his prison behavior has been observed? The psychological literature on coping and adaptation in prison concludes that long-term imprisonment may cause depression, anxiety, and mental breakdown (Liebling, 1999). If more inmates are "maxing out," the parole board has no ability to correct for risk-related factors that may have presented themselves during imprisonment. And if parole boards have little authority to extend inmate sentences, what role does that leave for victims? Recent research shows that more than 70 percent of parole boards now invite victims to attend the parole hearing (Petersilia, 1999). As parole boards release fewer prisoners in the future, these victims' rights

become less meaningful (Herman & Wasserman, 2001).

The absence of a dominant sentencing philosophy has also left the current sentencing regime—actually, a national crazy quilt made up of piecemeal sentencing reforms—without a public rationale that would explain the relationship between imprisonment and release. Under the old regime, it was straightforward: When a prison sentence was imposed (under a variety of justifications), the amount of time served would depend on a later determination of release readiness. Release decisions and post-release supervision were part and parcel of the sentencing framework. Under a just-deserts model, for example, the purpose of a period of postrelease supervision is unclear. Under a mandatory minimum sentence, why should an offender serve any more time in the community? If prisons started to look more like jails, with fixed-date releases, what is the rationale for any supervision after release? Why not just show the prisoners the door when they have served their time?

The Weakening of Parole

The increase in incarceration and fragmentation of our sentencing philosophy have created strains on the *raison d'être* and management of parole agencies. Reflecting the notion of a continuous flow from prison to community, with a focus on the endpoint of rehabilitation and reintegration, the word *parole* actually has two operational meanings: it refers both to the agency making a release decision (the parole board) and the agency supervising the offender in the community (typically the "division of parole").

A focus on returning prisoners does not begin with a discussion of parole populations, however, because some prisoners are released without supervision. Returning to Table 27.1, we see that in 1998, 18.7 percent of the released prisoners were released because their sentence had expired, and another 3.7 percent were released without supervision, meaning that 22.4 percent of the 1998 release cohort of 547,000—or about 123,000—left prison with no legal supervision. This form of release is increasing steadily as determinate sentencing reforms take hold—in 1990, only 16.3 percent of the released cohort were released without supervision, meaning that about 69,000 left prison unconditionally that year (Beck, 2000b).

There are two views of this development. On one hand, as discussed below, parole supervision has not been proven effective at reducing new arrests and has been shown to increase technical violations (Petersilia & Turner, 1993). Intensive supervision program clients are subject to much closer surveillance than others under supervision, and more of their violations may come to official attention, resulting in more returns to jail or prison. If noncompliance with technical conditions signaled that offenders were "going bad," then returning them to incarceration might prevent future crime. However, research on the issue has shown no support for the argument that violating offenders on technical conditions suppressed new criminal arrests (Petersilia & Turner, 1993). So, simply increasing parole supervision does not lead to fewer crimes. Therefore, why force more offenders into an ineffective system of supervision? Perhaps, as James Austin (2001) argues, certain offenders who pose low risks should simply be released.

On the other hand, if the transition from prison life to community life is difficult, and if some form of supervision can make that transition more effective, then the loss of a legal connection would appear counterproductive. This view becomes particularly compelling when one considers the stories of prisoners who serve the last years of their sentence in maximum security, then are released to the street without supervision because they reached the end of their sentence. And from a purely a public safety standpoint, the status of parole allows law enforcement greater search and seizure powers and a quick way to remove offenders from the street if they commit a new crime. In this view, both society and ex-offenders stand to benefit from legal supervision.

The increase in prison populations has had the predictable impact on parole caseloads without proportionate increases in resources. As discussed earlier, in 1999 there were 713,000 individuals on parole (or other form of conditional release), more than triple the number on parole in 1980 (Bureau of Justice Statistics, 2000a). Spending has not kept pace with this growth in supervision caseloads. In the 1970s, parole officers handled caseloads averaging 45 offenders; today, most officers are responsible for about 70 parolees (Rottman et al., 2000). At the same time, per capita spending per parolee has decreased from more than $11,000 per year in 1985 to about $9,500 in 1998 (J. P. Lynch & Sabol, 2001).

The nature of parole supervision has shifted over the past two decades as well. The parole field has uneasily accommodated two potentially conflicting objectives, one more akin to social work, one more akin to law enforcement. The introduction of new surveillance technologies, particularly urine testing and electronic monitoring, has provided enhanced capacity to detect parole violations and, thereby, to increase the rate of revocations of liberty (Kleiman, 1999). Signaling a shift in emphasis, recent surveys of parole officers show that more of them prioritize the law enforcement function of parole, rather than its service or rehabilitation functions (M. Lynch, 1998).

For these and other reasons, the rate of parole violations has increased significantly over recent years. In 1985, 70 percent of parolees successfully completed their parole term; by 1997, that number had dropped to 44 percent. Conversely, the percentage of those who fail on parole has increased from less than a third of all parolees in 1985 to 54 percent in 1997 (Petersilia, 1999). Almost 9 percent of all parolees nationally are counted as absconding—meaning their whereabouts are unknown to parole agents (Bonczar & Glaze, 1999).

This rise in rates of parole failures, coupled with an increasing base of parolee populations, has had profound impacts on the nation's prison population. In 1980, parole violators constituted 18 percent of prison admissions; they now constitute 37 percent of prisoners coming in the front door. In 1998, this meant that 207,000 of the 565,000 people admitted to prison were parole violators: individuals who had either been returned to prison on a technical violation or for committing a new offense (Beck, 2000a). The combination of this increase with the leveling off of new prison commitments from new convictions means that parole revocations are now a significant factor in the rising prison populations.

Just as the collapse of a unifying sentencing philosophy has resulted in enormous state variation in punishment regimes, it has also resulted in wide differences in parole practices. For example, in California, 65 percent of the individuals admitted to prisons in 1997 were parole violators; in Florida, parole violators accounted for 12 percent of new admissions; in Pennsylvania, 33 percent (Petersilia, 1999). Nationally, parole violators serve on average another 5 months in prison (Austin, Bruce, Carroll, McCall, & Richards, 2000).

Taken together, these three developments paint a picture of a system that has lost its way. More people are going to prison under differing sentencing philosophies and returning home through a system of reintegration that has diminished capacity to perform that function and now serves more to return reentry failures to prison's front door. One need not engage in illusions about the capacity of this population to obey the law to conclude that the constructs of philosophy, law, policy, and practice are out of alignment. A return to the preexisting arrangement is unlikely; nor is it necessarily desirable in all respects. But, in our view, any sentencing regime should retain a focus on the reintegration goal. No matter what punishment philosophy sends prisoners to prison, no matter how their release is determined, with few exceptions they all come back. It is hard to find a coherent reentry philosophy in the current state of affairs.

The Profile of Reentering Prisoners

The profile of returning prisoners is changing in ways that pose new challenges to successful reentry. The basic demographics have not changed much over the past 20 years. The parole population is mostly male, although the number of incarcerated females has risen steadily over the past decade. Their median age is 34; the median education level is 11th grade. More than half (55 percent) the returning offenders in 1998 were White, whereas 44 percent were African American. Twenty-one percent of offenders on parole in 1998 were Hispanics, who may be of any race (Bonczar & Glaze, 1999).

One characteristic that has changed is the crime for which the offenders were convicted. Reflecting the arrest activities of the "war on drugs," the percentage of released offenders who had been convicted of drug offenses increased significantly during the past 20 years. More than one third (35 percent) of prisoners released to parole in 1997 had been incarcerated for a drug offense, up from 28 percent in 1990 and 12 percent in 1985. Over the same time period, the percentage of parolees who had been convicted of violent offenses declined. In 1997, about a quarter of offenders coming into parole had convictions for violent offenses, down from a third (35 percent) in 1985 (Beck, 2000b).

The profile of returning prisoners is changing in other respects. Due to shifting sentencing policies, including mandatory minimums and truth-in-sentencing laws, the average length of stay in prison is increasing. Those released to parole in 1997 served an average of 27 months in prison—5 months longer than those released in 1990 (Beck, 2000b). This longer time in prison translates into a longer period of detachment from family and other social networks, posing new challenges to the process of reintegration.

More sobering is the decrease in the preparation of these prisoners for their release. As shown in Figure 27.2, in 1997 approximately a third of the inmates about to be released participated in vocational (27 percent) or educational (35 percent) programs—down from 31 percent and 43 percent, respectively, in 1991. The level of participation in pre-

Figure 27.2
Offenders to Be Released in the Next 12 Months: Percentage Participating in Prison Programs, 1991 and 1997

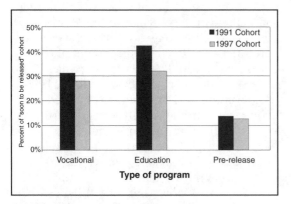

SOURCE: J. P. Lynch and Sabol (2001).

release planning did not decline, but only 12 percent of prisoners about to be released participated in prerelease planning at all. Of the entire prison population, an estimated 7 percent report participation in prison industries, whereas 24 percent are altogether idle (Austin et al., 2000).

The inescapable conclusion is that we have paid a price for prison expansion, namely a decline in preparation for the return to community. There is less treatment, fewer skills, less exposure to the world of work, and less focused attention on planning for a smooth transition to the outside world.

Another important perspective is that the growing numbers of returning offenders are increasingly concentrated in neighborhoods already facing enormous disadvantage. A majority of prisoners are released into counties that contain the central cities of metropolitan areas. In 1996, an estimated two thirds of the 489,000 state prison releases were released into these counties. Fewer than 50 percent of 220,000 prisoners were released into these counties in 1984 (J. P. Lynch & Sabol, 2001). Presumably, the releases are more highly concentrated within the central cities of these core counties than they are in nearby suburbs. And the central cities typically are less wealthy than neighboring areas, and they face other challenges such as loss of labor market share to suburban regions (J. P. Lynch & Sabol, 2001).

Research also suggests that there are high concentrations of prisoners in a relatively small number of neighborhoods within the central cities of the core counties. For example, J. P. Lynch and Sabol (2001) have conducted analyses using data on Ohio State prisoners from Cuyahoga County, which includes the city of Cleveland. More than two thirds of the county's prisoners and most of the block groups with high rates of incarceration come from Cleveland. Concentrations are such that three tenths of 1 percent of the block groups in the county account for approximately 20 percent of the county's prisoners. In such "high-rate" block groups, somewhere between 8 percent and 15 percent of the young Black males are incarcerated on a given day.

High rates of removal and return of offenders may further destabilize disadvantaged neighborhoods. Recent research by Todd Clear and Dina Rose indicates that high incarceration and return rates may disrupt a community's social network, affecting family formation, reducing informal control of children and income to families, and lessening ties among residents. Clear, Rose, and Ryder (2001) also argue that when removal and return rates hit a certain tipping point, they may actually result in higher crime rates, as the neighborhood becomes increasingly unstable and less coercive means of social control are undermined.

However, the question of whether incarceration policies of the past 15 years have had a beneficial or detrimental effect on the social capital of communities is far from settled (J. P. Lynch & Sabol, 2000b). Alternative theories suggest that this tipping point may differ across communities and that, in some cases—particularly in very high-poverty, high-crime areas—incarceration may be an effective tool for controlling crime. Research shows that residents in these communities want a greater police presence and more attention to the chronic crime problems surrounding them. We do not yet know the relative benefits of removal and returns in various types of communities—there are clearly incapacitation benefits to crime control in many communities, but those may erode without a focus on reentry and reintegration.

In sum, the prisoners moving through the high-volume, poorly designed assembly line that has, in many respects, lost a focus on reintegration, are less well prepared individually for their return to the community and are returning to communities that are not well prepared to accept them.

Social Policy Dimensions of Reentry

A focus on reentry highlights connections between criminal justice policy and other social policy domains that are provocative and suggest new directions for research and policy. In this section, we set aside issues of criminal justice policy—for example, the purposes of punishment—and examine, instead, the overlapping considerations with other policy domains.

Health Policy

The population moving through correctional facilities in the United States presents serious health problems; the question is how to coordinate criminal justice and health policies in ways that improve health outcomes and, secondarily, justice outcomes. Interestingly, a period of incarceration often has positive consequences for the health status of a prisoner—in part because adequate health care is constitutionally required, but also because the food and living environment are more conducive to better health outcomes than many situations in the community. Yet the consequences for a prisoner's mental health may be adverse, and for substance abusers the effects of incarceration depend heavily on the management of the risk of relapse.

The overlap between the public health population and the criminal justice population is striking. For example, as Hammett (2001) shows, nearly one quarter of all people living with HIV or AIDS, one third living with Hepatitis C, and one third with tuberculosis in the United States in 1997 were released from a correctional facility (prison or jail) that year. These data suggest that correctional facilities could provide efficient access to large numbers of people posing serious public health risks, but embracing this challenge would require reconfiguration of the health and justice professions. For criminal justice policy makers, attention would need to be paid to diagnostic screening and treatment capabilities in all prisons and jails. From a reentry perspective, the two professions would need careful collaboration to ensure a smooth transition of care from prison or jail to community health care. Whether this capacity exists, and whether criminal justice supervision could increase the likelihood of healthy outcomes, are open questions.

Some 80 percent of the state prison population report a history of drug and/or alcohol use, including 74 percent of the "soon-to-be-released" prisoners (Beck, 2000b; Mumola, 1999). However, in-prison treatment is not readily available to those who need it. Despite a significant infusion of federal monies to fund treatment in state prisons, only 10 percent of state inmates reported participating in professional substance abuse treatment since admission, down from 25 percent in 1991 (Bureau of Justice Statistics, 1999). (When one includes participation in drug abuse programs such as self-help groups and educational programs, the participation rates increase to 24 percent of the 1997 prison population, down from 30 percent in 1991 [Bureau of Justice Statistics, 1999].) Of the soon-to-be-released group who were using drugs in the month prior to incarceration, only 18 percent had participated in treatment since prison admission. And only 22 percent of the alcohol abusers had participated (Beck, 2000b).

The concern about the connections between criminal justice policy and drug treatment policy is brought into sharp focus by two distinct research findings. First, there is a significant body of evaluation literature demonstrating that in-prison drug treatment in the period leading up to release can, if combined with treatment in the postrelease period, significantly reduce both drug use and recidivism (Harrison, 2001). So, careful planning of treatment programs, along with supervision during reentry, will enhance health and safety. The second research finding comes from

research on the brain. This research concludes "addiction is a brain disease" (Leshner, 1998, p. 2). Consequently, the return of a former addict to his old neighborhood places him at high risk of relapse, in part because the old haunts act as a trigger to his brain mechanisms and heighten the cravings. So, the criminal justice policy of requiring a parolee to return to his community may merely be placing a recovering addict at the crossroads of greatest risk.

Inmates with mental illness are also increasingly being imprisoned—and ultimately being released. In 1998, the Bureau of Justice Statistics estimated that 16 percent of jail or prison inmates reported either a mental condition or an overnight stay in a mental hospital (Ditton, 1999). There are relatively few public mental health services available, and studies show that even when they are available, mentally ill individuals fail to access available treatment because they fear institutionalization, deny that they are mentally ill, or distrust the mental health system (Lurigio, 2001). Untreated mentally ill individuals may engage in criminal behaviors that eventually lead to arrest and conviction.

Family and Child Welfare Policy

One of the undeniable aspects of imprisonment is that relationships with family are strained. Not surprisingly, then, the increase in incarceration has significant consequences for family and child welfare policy. Most prisoners are parents—about one half of the men and two thirds of the women. According to the Bureau of Justice Statistics, in 1999 more than 1.5 million minor children in the United States had a parent who was incarcerated, an increase of more than half a million since 1991. About 7 percent of all African American children currently have a parent in prison (Mumola, 2000).

Incarceration has consequences for child rearing. When fathers are imprisoned, about 90 percent of their children remain in the custody of their mothers. When mothers are incarcerated, however, fewer than a third of their children stay with their fathers, placing new demands on the extended family, peer networks, and child welfare systems (Hagan & Dinovitzer, 1999).

The high rates of incarceration in poor neighborhoods create a high level of ongoing disruption in family relationships. Sometimes, the removal of a family member is a good outcome—someone who has been violent in the home, draining resources to support a drug habit, or otherwise posing negative consequences for the family's well-being. But the removal of large numbers of mostly male young adults also drains the community of a key ingredient of social capital—community men. These complex relationships, combined with the great distance between many prisons and prisoners' communities, require creative management on the part of the families and the private and governmental support systems that could minimize the harm to children and families.

The reentry perspective focuses policy attention on the moment of release. How is the family prepared for this moment? How is the prisoner prepared? If there is a history of dysfunction, whose responsibility is it to minimize the harm? Particularly in the instance of domestic violence or child abuse, what is the role of the state and the police in managing the reentry safely?

Workforce Participation

The current strong economy presents unusual opportunities for linkages between ex-offenders and the world of work. Approximately two thirds of prisoners had a job just prior to their incarceration (J. P. Lynch & Sabol, 2000a). However, released offenders have very low employment rates, suggesting that incarceration may reduce the employability and future earnings of young men (Western, Kling, & Weiman, 2001). The stigma of incarceration makes ex-inmates unattractive for entry-level or union jobs, civil disabilities limit ex-felons access to skilled trades or the public sector, and incarceration undermines the social networks that are often necessary to obtain legitimate employment. Moreover, Nagin and Waldfogel (1998) found that the effect of imprisonment on employment and future earnings is particularly pronounced for inmates older than 30, suggesting that as the prison and parole population ages, employment prospects become bleaker.

Civic Participation

In many ways, prisoners leave prison with only part of their debt to society paid. Much more is owed, and it may never be paid off. For example, one of the traditional consequences of a felony conviction has been the loss of voting rights. The laws of 46 states and the District of Columbia contain such stipulations. Fourteen states permanently deny convicted felons the right to vote. Eighteen states suspend the right to vote until the offender has completed the sentence and paid all fines. As a result, some 4 million Americans, 1.4 million of whom are African American (equaling 13 percent of the Black male adult population), are disenfranchised in this way (Fellner & Mauer, 1998).

In a spate of laws beginning in the late 1980s, a number of states now require that sex offenders be registered with the police upon release from prison and/or that the community be notified in some way that a sex offender is living in the neighborhood. Today, every state requires convicted sex offenders to register with law enforcement on release (so-called "Megan's laws").

These kinds of disqualifications and burdens (for a review, see Petersilia, 1999) constitute a very real component of the punishment—taken together, they reflect a philosophy akin to internal exile under which ex-offenders are cut off from civic participation, banned from certain employment opportunities, and required to display their status as ex-offender when required.

Racial Disparities

No discussion of imprisonment would be complete without a focus on the impact of incarceration on different racial groups. Bonczar and Beck (1997) calculated that in 1991, an African American male had a 29 percent chance of being incarcerated at least once in his lifetime, 6 times higher than that for White males. In fact, the Bureau of Justice Statistics estimated that 9 percent of Black males in their late 20s and 3 percent of Hispanic males in their late 20s were in prison at the end of 1999 (Beck, 2000a). Looked at differently, more than one third of Black male high school dropouts were in prison or jail in the late 1990s; a higher percentage of this group were imprisoned than employed (Western & Pettit, 2000).

The consequences of imprisonment on minority communities—and our democracy—are profound. Just the impact on voting rights and civic participation generally is very disturbing. Denying large segments of the minority population the right to vote will likely alienate them further and spawn beliefs about the state that are contentious (Clear, Rose, & Ryder, 2001). Greater alienation and disillusionment with the political process also erodes residents' feelings of commitment and makes them less willing to participate in local activities. This is important because our most effective crime fighting tools require community collaboration and active engagement (Sherman et al., 1997). An increase in alienation between the community and the agencies of justice will make it more difficult for those agencies to turn back to communities and ask for assistance in neighborhood-based approaches (Petersilia, 2000).

It strikes us that this abbreviated summary of some of the data presented at the Reentry Roundtable that we cohosted in October 2000 (most of which are found in [Volume 47 of *Crime & Delinquencey*]) argue strongly for strategic engagement between these varied policy sectors and criminal justice policy using the moment of reentry as the focal planning point. For example, the high degree of public health concerns presented by the criminal justice population is a compelling case for coordination of health care in the prison and in the community. Similarly, the creation of seamless treatment systems for returning prisoners with histories of substance abuse would keep a significant number of offenders from returning to prison. The linkage between prison-based work and community-based work also seems manageable, particularly in a low-unemployment economy. Furthermore, we applaud the work under way in a number of states to reconsider the reach of the current voter disqualification laws. Finally, we hope that the new community focus on reentry with geocoded data and analysis of the impact of imprisonment and reentry on poor, minority communities can provide a new dimension to the ongoing debate about the impact of criminal justice on our pursuit of racial justice.

Implications of the Reentry Perspective

We find the reentry perspective helpful in shining light into the dusty corners of some old debates about criminal justice policy. We have three particular corners in mind: the logic of parole, the mission of corrections, and the allocation of public and private responsibilities for the reintegration of offenders. Our overarching conclusion resembles the rallying cry of welfare reformers—we think we should abolish the system of parole as we know it and replace it with a new system focused squarely on the goal of reintegration.

The Logic of Parole

Parole has both operational and jurisprudential meanings for criminal justice policy. At an operational level, it refers both to a method of making release decisions and a form of community supervision. As this article has demonstrated, we have concluded that both operational meanings of the word have lost political ground in recent years. We think a reentry analysis makes a compelling case for a reconsideration of the jurisprudential logic of parole as well. The central tenet of our parole system is the idea that a prisoner is expected to serve a portion of his sentence in the community, and he risks return to prison—often for the remainder of his sentence—if he fails to meet certain conditions.

We would substitute a new, two-part jurisprudential logic, namely that (a) completion of a prison sentence represents payment of a debt to society, and (b) every substantial period of incarceration should be followed by a period of managed reentry. In other words, we think it is important to decouple the rationale for the imposition of a sentence to imprison for a period of time from the rationale for community supervision for a period of time. The former should be justified in terms of deterrence, retribution, rehabilitation, or incapacitation, the traditional underpinnings of a criminal sentence; the latter should be justified in terms of reintegration. In this view, if a criminal sentence requires imprisonment, the sentence would be served when the prison phase is completed. After completion of the prison sentence, the reentry phase would begin. For released prisoners who pose little risk and can accomplish reintegration easily, the reentry phase could be quite short, perhaps as short as a month. For those who pose greater risks and face greater difficulty reestablishing themselves, the reentry phase would be longer, but upper bounds would be established proportionate to both the risk and the original offense.

Supervision during this period would be the responsibility of a new, community-based entity. The expectations placed on the returning prisoner would be related to successful reintegration—for example, getting a job, staying sober, attending mental health counseling, or making restitution to the victim. Failure to meet expectations during this period of managed reentry would not result in return to prison, as in traditional parole jurisprudence, because the sentence would have been served with the completion of the prison term. Rather, as with drug courts, failure could result in graduated sanctions, up to a short deprivation of liberty, if those sanctions are demonstrably effective at changing behavior. In this system, if the released prisoner commits a new crime, it would be treated as a new crime to be prosecuted in a traditional manner, not as a violation of a condition of release as often happens now.

There are important and interesting experiments in this new approach to the task of reintegration. The Wisconsin Sentencing Commission articulated this risk-based philosophy in its final report, and Wisconsin has launched pilot projects to test these ideas (Smith & Dickey, 1999). Washington state has embraced a risk-based approach to postprison supervision (Lehman, in press). The new concept of a reentry court reflects these principles as well (Travis, 2000). As originally proposed, reentry courts would have the authority to impose sanctions for failure to meet conditions associated with a reintegration plan, but not on the theory that the original sentence remains in effect. These courts would also provide a public forum that would underscore the importance of the work of reintegration for the offender and the community alike. We recognize that some sentencing reforms, such as the federal system's, have implemented a new status of "supervised release" to replace parole, but we prefer a new conceptualization of the connection between the reintegration mandate and our sentencing jurisprudence, not a reinstatement of parole under a different name.

For our proposal to take full shape, two revisions to a state's sentencing framework would be required. First, the duration of the criminal sentence would be defined as coinciding with completion of the prison term. The truth-in-sentencing philosophy reflects this idea somewhat, but with an emphasis on creating a fixed prison term. In our proposal, by contrast, we would still allow for early completion of a prison term (and thereby early completion of the criminal sentence) upon a showing of good conduct in prison to create incentives for conforming behavior in prison life. Second, a new legal status of reentry supervision would be created, with upper time limits and incentives for early completion. During this period following prison release, the power of the state to revoke liberty would be statutorily limited to a system of graduated, parsimonious sanctions related to failures to meet reentry conditions. We believe these statutory clarifications would reflect a public recognition of the need to reintegrate returning prisoners into our society.

The Mission of Corrections

We think that the department of corrections should also embrace the new mission of reintegrating returning prisoners. To do this, corrections agencies would be expected (and funded) to create a seamless set of systems that span the boundaries of prison and community. For example, corrections agencies would create linkages between in-prison job training and community-based employment and job training and between in-prison health care and community-based health care. They would be expected to link mental health services on both sides of the wall or to work with community-based domestic violence services when a prisoner with a history of spousal abuse is released. They would be expected to give a prisoner the tools to succeed—for example, identification, driver's license,

access to social security or other benefits, or housing, upon release. Where necessary, the department of corrections would be authorized to purchase services to ensure a smooth transfer of responsibility, for example, the first few months' rent if no private housing is available or transitional mental health counseling to help cushion the shock of return if community-based care is not available.

Just as welfare reform forced welfare agencies to shift from a dependency model to a model of transition to independence, so too a reentry perspective should force corrections agencies to take practical steps to move prisoners toward independence. In the case of welfare reform, this shift meant that welfare agencies invested in child care, job training, and employee assistance programs—whatever it took to move the client from welfare to work. Similarly, we would expect corrections agencies to make strategic investments in transitional services to move prisoners toward independence. The necessary step here is that corrections agencies must embrace reintegration as a goal, and we note with interest that the Ohio Department of Rehabilitation and Corrections, under the leadership of Reginald Wilkinson, has officially adopted this new mandate (Wilkinson, in press).

Allocation of Responsibilities for Reintegration

Who is responsible for successful reintegration? Clearly, the released prisoner has an important role to play, a role that we think is enhanced if made visible and explicit, as in a reentry court. We have also argued that a corrections agency has a role to play, creating a seamless linkage between in-prison programs and community programs to increase the chances of successful reintegration. Yet, our reentry analysis suggests that many of the key activities are distinctly local. For example, this discussion implies that the health, child welfare, job placement, drug treatment, and other service entities need to be mobilized to support prisoner reintegration. Most of these are city- or county-level functions and therefore require the leadership of the mayor or other executive. In our traditional configuration of responsibilities, we have oddly placed responsibility for "reentry management" in a state agency, typically a parole division or a corrections agency. Yet, we have also created community supervision functions in probation or pretrial release agencies, which are often county or city based. These artificial distinctions are barriers to reentry management.

We think it important to move these activities as close to the community as possible. This is where the problems and assets can be found—the risks to relapse can be identified here; the positive power of social networks can be found here. Ultimately, reentry management should be community based, with a focus on marshalling community resources to assist in successful reintegration. The legal status of the individual—whether on parole, probation, or pretrial release, whether adult or juvenile—matters somewhat, but we could envision a community supervision system that embraced all types of individuals, in all types of legal relationships with the criminal justice system. We are impressed by the idea of a community justice development organization now being developed by the Center for Alternative Sentencing and Employment Services (CASES) in New York City. This idea borrows from the successes of community development corporations over the past 20 years that have managed the creation of housing, employment opportunities, and economic growth as intermediaries between federal, state, and local governments responsible for those functions and community institutions that are sometimes better at carrying them out. The researchers and planners at CASES have analyzed the probation and parole caseloads of certain neighborhoods and have asked a simple question: Why can't supervision of those individuals be organized along neighborhood lines, with much of the supervisory responsibility devolved to a community-based entity?

The creation of a community-based intermediary working on criminal justice issues could conceivably win the trust of the community and coalesce community capacity such as churches, small businesses, service providers, schools, and civic institutions to support the work of reintegration of returning prisoners. This new entity could broker the relationship between those institutions and the formal agencies of the justice system. The state system could then devolve the supervision functions of reentry management to the community justice development corporation and retain responsibility for the imposition of sanctions to a reentry court or other backstop system. The function of the government employees now called parole officers would be redefined in this new paradigm. Some of those functions would be performed by community justice corporation employees; other functions more related to enforcement of conditions of reentry would be performed under the auspices of the reentry court or other governmental entity. As with drug courts, it would be important that "carrots and sticks" be used in concert to produce the desired behavioral outcomes.

In sum, we find this reentry perspective suggests new ways of thinking about the underpinnings of our concept of parole, a new mandate for corrections, and a new mission at the local level to coalesce public and private capabilities to increase positive outcomes of the reentry process. This realignment of philosophy and operational capacity is not just about crime policy; it is ultimately about community well-being. And maybe good crime policy results will follow.

Study Questions

1. How has sentencing policy affected the reentry issue?

2. What changes have occurred in parole, and how does this affect prisoner reentry?

3. What is the profile of prisoners reentering society today?

4. What are the social policy dimensions of reentry, and why are they so important?

5. What are some of the solutions that are offered by the authors?

References

Austin, J. (2001). Prisoner reentry: Current trends, practices, and issues. *Crime & Delinquency, 47,* 314–334.

Austin, J., Bruce, M. A., Carroll, L., McCall, P. L., & Richards, S. C. (2000, November). *The use of incarceration in the United States.* Paper prepared for the annual meeting of the American Society of Criminology, San Francisco.

Austin, J., Clark, J., Hardyman, P., & Henry, D. A. (1999). Impact of "three strikes and you're out." *Punishment & Society, 1,* 131–162.

Austin, J., Jones, C., Kramer, J., & Renninger, P. (1995). *National assessment of structured sentencing, final report* (Bureau of Justice Statistics Publication No. NJS 167557). Washington, DC: U.S. Department of Justice, Bureau of Justice Assistance.

Beck, A. (2000a). Prisoners in 1999. *Bureau of Justice Statistics, bulletin* (Bureau of Justice Statistics Publication No. NCJ 183476). Washington, DC: U.S. Department of Justice, Bureau of Justice Statistics.

Beck, A. (2000b, April 13). *State and federal prisoners returning to the community: Findings from the Bureau of Justice Statistics.* Paper presented at the First Reentry Courts Initiative Cluster Meeting, Washington, DC. For more information, see http://www.ojp.usdoj.gov/bjs/pub/pdf/sfprc.pdf

Blumstein, A., & Beck, A. (1999). Population growth in U.S. prisons, 1980–1996. In M. Tonry & J. Petersilia (Eds.), *Prisons.* Chicago: University of Chicago Press.

Bonczar, T. P., & Beck, A. (1997). Lifetime likelihood of going to state or federal prison. In *Bureau of Justice Statistics, special report* (Bureau of Justice Statistics Publication No. NCJ 160092). Washington, DC: U.S. Department of Justice, Bureau of Justice Statistics.

Bonczar, T. P., & Glaze, L. E. (1999). Probation and parole in the United States, 1998. In *Bureau of Justice Statistics, bulletin* (Bureau of Justice Statistics Publication No. NCJ 178234). Washington, DC: U.S. Department of Justice, Bureau of Justice Statistics.

Bureau of Justice Statistics. (1999). *Correctional populations in the United States, 1997* (Bureau of Justice Statistics Publication No. NCJ 177613). Washington, DC: U.S. Department of Justice, Bureau of Justice Statistics.

Bureau of Justice Statistics. (2000a, June 23). *Correctional population trends.* Washington, DC: U.S. Department of Justice, Bureau of Justice Statistics. Retrieved February 22, 2001, from the World Wide Web: http://www.ojp.usdoj.gov/bjs/keytabs.htm

Bureau of Justice Statistics. (2000b, August 2). *Sentenced prisoners admitted to state or federal jurisdiction.* Washington, DC: U.S. Department of Justice, Bureau of Justice Statistics. Retrieved February 22, 2001, from the World Wide Web: http://www.ojp.usdoj.gov/bjs/dtdata.htm#justice

Bureau of Justice Statistics. (2000c, June 9). *Total sentenced prisoners released from state or federal jurisdiction.* Available: http://www.ojp.usdof.gov/bjs/dtdata.htm#justice

Clear, T. R., Rose, D. R., & Ryder, J. A. (2001). Incarceration and the community: The problem of removing and returning offenders. *Crime & Delinquency, 47,* 335–367.

Ditton, P. M. (1999). Mental health and treatment of inmates and probationers. In *Bureau of Justice Statistics, special report* (Bureau of Justice Statistics Publication No. NCJ 174463). Washington, DC: U.S. Department of Justice, Bureau of Justice Statistics.

Ditton, P. M., & Wilson, D. (1999). Truth and sentencing in state prisons. In *Bureau of Justice Statistics, special report* (Bureau of Justice Statistics Publication No. NCJ 170032). Washington, DC: U.S. Department of Justice, Bureau of Justice Statistics.

Fellner, J., & Mauer, M. (1998). Losing the vote: The impact of felony disenfranchisement laws in the United States (Criminal Justice Briefing Sheet No. 1046). Washington, DC: The Sentencing Project. Available: http://www.sentencingproject.org/pubs_05.ctm

Frankel, M. (1973). *Criminal sentences: Law without order.* New York: Hill and Wang.

Hagan, J., & Dinovitzer, R. (1999). Collateral consequences of imprisonment for children, communities, and prisoners. In M. Tonry & J. Petersilia (Eds.), *Prisons*. Chicago: University of Chicago Press.

Hammett, T. M. (2001). Health-related issues in prisoner reentry. *Crime & Delinquency, 47,* 390–409.

Harrison, L. D. (2001). The revolving prison door for drug-involved offenders: Challenges and opportunities. *Crime & Delinquency, 47,* 462–484.

Herman, S., & Wasserman, C. (2001). A role for victims in offender reentry. *Crime & Delinquency, 47,* 428–445.

Hirsch, A. von. (1976). *Doing justice: The choice of punishments* (Rep. of the Committee for the Study of Incarceration). New York: Hill and Wang.

Kleiman, M. (1999). Getting deterrence right: Applying tipping models and behavioral economics to the problems of crime control. *Perspectives on Crime and Justice: 1998–1999 Lecture Series, 3* (Bureau of Justice Statistics Publication No. NCJ 178244). Washington, DC: National Institute of Justice.

Lehman, J. D. (in press). Re-inventing community corrections in Washington state. *Corrections Management Quarterly, 5(3).*

Leshner, A. I. (1998). Addiction is a brain disease—And it matters. *National Institute of Justice Journal,* No. 237, 2–6.

Liebling, A. (1999). Prison suicide and prisoner coping. In M. Tonry & J. Petersilia (Eds.), *Prisons*. Chicago: University of Chicago Press.

Lurigio, A. J. (2001). Effective services for parolees with mental illnesses. *Crime & Delinquency, 47,* 446–461.

Lynch, J. P., & Sabol, W. J. (2000a, December 5). *Analysis of Bureau of Justice Statistics data: Survey of inmates of state correctional facilities, 1991 and 1997.* Urban Institute First Tuesdays Presentation, Washington, DC.

Lynch, J. P., & Sabol, W. J. (2000b). Prison use and social control. In *Policies, processes and decisions of the criminal justice system.* Washington, DC: U.S. Department of Justice.

Lynch, J. P., & Sabol, W. J. (2001). *Prisoner reentry in perspective* (Urban Institute Crime Policy Report). In *Crime policy report*. Washington, DC: Urban Institute Press.

Lynch, M. (1998). Waste managers? New penology, crime fighting, and the parole agent identity. *Law and Society Review, 32,* 839–869.

Martinson, R. (1974). What works? Questions and answers about prison reform. *Public Interest, 35,* 22–45.

Mumola, C. J. (1999). Substance abuse and treatment, state and federal prisoners, 1997. In *Bureau of Justice Statistics, special report* (Bureau of Justice Statistics Publication No. NCJ 172871). Washington, DC: U.S. Department of Justice, Bureau of Justice Statistics.

Mumola, C. J. (2000). Incarcerated parents and their children. In *Bureau of Justice Statistics, special report* (Bureau of Justice Statistics Publication No. NCJ 182335). Washington, DC: U.S. Department of Justice, Bureau of Justice Statistics.

Nagin, D., & Waldfogel, J. (1998). The effects of conviction on income through the life cycle. *International Review of Law and Economics, 18,* 25–40.

Petersilia, J. (1999). Parole and prisoner reentry in the United States. In M. Tonry & J. Petersilia (Eds.), *Prisons*. Chicago: University of Chicago Press.

Petersilia, J. (2000). When prisoners return to the community: Political, economic, and social consequences. In *Sentencing & Corrections, Issues for the 21st Century, 9* (Bureau of Justice Statistics Publication No. NCJ 184253). Washington, DC: National Institute of Justice.

Petersilia, J., & Turner, S. (1993). Intensive probation and parole. In M. Tonry (Ed.), *Crime and justice: A review of research* (Vol. 17). Chicago: University of Chicago Press.

Rottman, D. B., Flango, C. R., Cantrell, M. T., Hansen, R., & LaFountain, N. (2000). *State court organization 1998* (Bureau of Justice Statistics Publication No. NCJ 178932). Washington, DC: U.S. Department of Justice, Bureau of Justice Statistics.

Sherman, L., Gottfredson, D., MacKenzie, D., Eck, J., Reuter, P., & Bushway, S. (1997). *Preventing crime: What works, what doesn't, what's promising.* College Park: University of Maryland Press.

Smith, M. E., & Dickey, W. J. (1999). Reforming sentencing and corrections for just punishment and public safety. In *Sentencing & Corrections, Issues for the 21st Century, 4* (Bureau of Justice Statistics Publication No. NCJ 175724). Washington, DC: National Institute of Justice.

Tonry, M. (1996). *Sentencing matters.* New York: Oxford University Press.

Tonry, M. (1999). The fragmentation of sentencing and corrections in America. In *Sentencing & Corrections, Issues for the 21st Century, 1*

(Bureau of Justice Statistics Publication No. NCJ 175721). Washington, DC: National Institute of Justice.

Travis, J. (2000). But they all come back: Rethinking prisoner reentry. In *Sentencing & Corrections, Issues for the 21st Century,* 7 (Bureau of Justice Statistics Publication No. NCJ 181413). Washington, DC: National Institute of Justice.

Western, B., Kling, J. R., & Weiman, D. F. (2001). The labor market consequences of incarceration. *Crime & Delinquency, 47,* 410–427.

Western, B., & Pettit, R. (2000). Incarceration and racial inequality in men's employment. *Industrial and Labor Relations Review, 54,* 3–16.

Wilkinson, R. A. (in press). Offender reentry: A storm overdue. *Corrections Management Quarterly, 5* (3).

Wilson, J. Q. (1975). *Thinking about crime.* New York: Vintage.

Wright, R. F. (1998). Managing prison growth in North Carolina through structured sentencing. *National Institute of Justice, Program Focus* (Bureau of Justice Statistics Publication No. NCJ 168944). Washington, DC: National Institute of Justice.

28
Halfway Houses (Updated)*

Edward J. Latessa
Lawrence F. Travis III
Christopher T. Lowenkamp

There are many who believe that providing offenders who are released from prison with support and assistance can mean the difference between them remaining out or returning to prison. No correctional program offers more reintegrative opportunities than community residential programs, often called halfway houses. Some halfway houses provide minimal services and support, such as a warm meal and a place to sleep, while others offer a wide range of services and treatment. Whether the program is considered "three hots and a cot" or a full-service facility, halfway houses play an important role in the supervision and rehabilitative efforts of the correctional system. For many years, proponents of halfway houses have argued that they were effective in reducing recidivism for offenders. Unfortunately, there was not much empirical evidence to support that contention, at least until recently. In the following article, Latessa, Travis, and Lowenkamp present the results from a major study of halfway houses that was conducted in Ohio. This study demonstrates that halfway houses can indeed reduce recidivism, provided that services and treatment are consistent with the principles of effective intervention.

What's in a Name?

Until recently, community corrections residential programs were subsumed under the general title of halfway houses. This label, however, has proven to be inadequate as a description of the variety of residential programs used with correctional populations today. The International Halfway House Association, founded in 1964, has itself changed its name to reflect more accurately the variety of purposes and persons served by residential programs.

The contemporary name given to such programs, community corrections residential facilities, is a broader title that reflects the role expansion of the traditional halfway house that has occurred in recent years. Rush (1991) defines a residential facility as "a correctional facility from which residents are regularly permitted to depart, unaccompanied by any official, for the purposes of using community resources, such as schools or treatment programs, and seeking or holding employment" (p. 265).

This definition is free of any reference to incarceration that was implicit in the term *halfway*. Further, it does not necessitate the direct provision of any services to residents within the facility, and clearly identifies the program with a correctional mission. Thus, unlike the traditional halfway house, the community residential facility serves a more diverse population and plays a broader correctional role. Traditional halfway houses are included within the category of residential facilities, but their ranks are swelled by newer adaptations, such as community corrections centers, prerelease centers, and restitution centers.

The Development of Community Residential Programs

Halfway houses as transitional programming for inmates released from prisons are not a new phenomenon (Latessa & Allen, 1982). Their origins can be traced at least as far back as the early nineteenth century in England and Ireland (Keller & Alper, 1970).

In the United States, the exact origin of halfway houses is not clear, but one such program was started in New York City in 1845, the Isaac T. Hooper Home (Rush, 1991, p. 143). A halfway house for released female prisoners was opened in Boston, Massachusetts, in 1864. For nearly 100 years, halfway houses tended to be operated by charitable organizations for the benefit of released inmates. Halfway house programs did not begin a period of expansion until after World War II (Beha, 1977).

In the 1950s, specialized residential programs designed to deal with substance-abusing offenders were added to the traditional halfway house programs. Residential programs for alcoholic or drug addicted offenders opened and spread throughout this period, and into the 1960s. For typical criminal offenders, however, halfway house placements were rare.

In the middle 1960s, the President's Commission on [Law Enforcement] and Administration of Justice (1967) signaled a change in correctional philosophy toward the goal of reintegration. Reintegration placed increased emphasis on the role of the community in corrections, and on the value of keeping offenders in the community, rather than in prison, whenever possible. This ideology of community corrections supported the notion of residential placements for convicted offenders, and halfway houses began a period of unprecedented expansion, supported by federal funds from programs as diverse as the Office of Economic Opportunity and the Law Enforcement Assistance Administration (Hicks, 1987, p. 6).

During the early 1980s, however, support for halfway house programs dwindled. The effects of recession, demise of LEAA, and a general hardening of public attitudes toward offenders worked against the continued growth and development of halfway houses or other residential programs. This period of retrenchment was, however, short-lived. The same forces that temporarily halted the growth of residential programs soon added their weight to continued development.

In the last decade, community corrections residential facilities have grown in response to the crisis of prison crowding. Allen et al. (1978, p. 1) attribute an increased use of halfway houses with parole populations to three factors: the philosophy of reintegration, success with such programs in the mental health field, and the lower costs of halfway houses compared with prisons. To these was added the need to respond to prison crowding in the 1980s.

The lack of prison capacity, coupled with an increasing emphasis on risk control and retributive sentencing, spurred a search for intermediate sanctions. Over the last several years, a number of observers have called for the creation of penal sanctions that range in severity between incarceration and traditional probation supervision (McCarthy, 1987). They suggest that such sanctions will allow the correctional system to meet the punitive and risk-control goals of sentencing, especially with those persons diverted from prison or jail because of crowding.

The list of intermediate sanctions includes house arrest, electronic monitoring, and intensive supervision (*Federal Probation*, 1986; Petersilia, 1987). DuPont (1985) explicitly identifies a role for community residential facilities as an adjunct to traditional probation or parole supervision. Such facilities would serve to increase both the punitive severity and public safety of traditional community-based corrections.

In an era when both correctional costs and populations grow yearly, planners, practitioners, and policymakers have supported a wide range of correctional alternatives. As Guynes (1988) has observed, one effect of prison and jail crowding has been a dramatic increase in probation and parole populations. Further, Petersilia (1985), among others, suggests that these larger supervision populations are increasingly made up of more serious and more dangerous offenders. Community residential facilities have come to be seen as an important option for the management and control of these growing and more dangerous offender populations.

A result has been the redefinition of the role of community residential facilities. The traditional role of transitional placement for offenders, or as a response to special needs populations such as substance abusers, has been expanded. Residential placement has emerged as a correctional alternative in its own right.

Hicks (1987) observes that the use of residential placement as an alternative to incarceration or traditional community supervision has engendered some changes in operations and philosophy. She terms this a movement "toward supervision rather than treatment." Thus in many cases residential facilities provide little more than a place to live and access to community resources. The emphasis in these programs is upon custody and control rather than counseling and correction.

Prison on the Cheap?

Unable or unwilling to underwrite the costs of prison for large numbers of convicted offenders, several jurisdictions have supported community residential facilities. As Hicks (1987) notes, "Budget weary legislators often view halfway houses as an inexpensive lunch" (p. 7). Residential programs, they hope, will provide public safety as well as incarceration, but at a fraction of the cost. As substitute prisons, however, the atmosphere of these programs has changed. Traditional halfway houses, where staff and programs are designed for the provision of direct services to residents, still continue.

These programs provide counseling, substance abuse treatment, educational and vocational training, and a variety of social services. In other, newer programs, especially those operated by corrections departments, the atmosphere is closer to that of a minimum-security prison than a rehabilitative community.

This addition of residential programs as "bed space" to the traditional use of such programs as treatment modalities has led to a schizophrenic field of practice. In most facilities, rules and regulations are stricter, and enforcement more rigid, than in earlier days. Additionally, a number of "large" facilities, housing hundreds of residents, have been added. Typically "pre-release" centers, these larger facilities house prison inmates eligible for parole, or in the final months before their release.

The recent growth in community residential facilities has complicated the picture. These facilities serve a variety of clients, ranging from as-yet-unconvicted offenders diverted from court through prison inmates. Facility sizes range from those housing fewer than 10 residents to those with populations in the hundreds. Treatment services range from programs providing full services to those in which few, if any, direct services are available to residents. The one constant is that residents live in the facilities for a period of time, and are generally free to leave the facilities during approved hours, for approved purposes, without escort.

Residential Facilities in Contemporary Corrections

As the foregoing discussion illustrates, it is not possible to describe the average residential facility. Diversity in population, program, size, and structure is the rule. It is, unfortunately, also not possible to know for certain how many such facilities are in operation today, or the number of offenders served by them. As Hicks (1987) observes, "There are no national figures, only educated guesses" (p. 1).

The International Halfway House Association published a directory of residential facilities in 1981 that lists almost 2,300 facilities with a combined capacity of nearly

100,000 beds (Gatz & Murray, 1981). Not all of these facilities, however, serve correctional populations. Five years earlier, Seiter et al. (1977) estimated that approximately 400 facilities existed that served correctional populations, with a capacity of about 10,000 beds. In 1978, a survey of parole authorities revealed the existence of nearly 800 facilities, with almost 15,000 inmates being paroled to halfway house placements. More recently, the National Institute of Corrections supported a survey that identified 641 community corrections residential facilities. The identification was based on the characteristics of residents as under correctional supervision, among other criteria.

While the methods and definitions employed in these different studies varied considerably, the results are fairly consistent. Given these admittedly incomplete data, it is possible to estimate that there are in excess of 600 residential facilities in operation today. Further, it appears that the number of facilities has grown as much as 50 percent in the last decade.

It is not possible to estimate the number of offenders served by these facilities with any certainty. Length of residence is typically short, on the order of three to four months, meaning that a facility with 50 beds may serve 150 to 200 individuals annually. Based on the probability that a halfway house would serve three to four times as many residents as it has beds in each year, Allen and his colleagues (1978, p. 2) estimate that roughly 10,000 beds equals 30,000 to 40,000 residents each year. Further, many of those in residential facilities are included in the totals of other correctional population counts, such as the number of prison inmates or persons under parole supervision. Still, it is clear that the total number of residents in these facilities each year is substantial.[1]

Types of Facilities

The large number of facilities and their differing traditions, populations, and services render it difficult to assess the impact of residential programs. Beyond noting that these programs have played an important role in the provision of services to convicted offenders, and that their importance as alternatives to imprisonment has increased, the variety of facilities means that questions of effectiveness must be narrowly drawn.

Allen and his colleagues (1978), for example, have developed a four-class typology of halfway houses, using two dimensions to yield four possible types of facilities. Halfway houses can be either public or private, and they can be either interventive or supportive in program. Public or private, of course, relates to the organization of the facility as either a government entity or not. Program types are based on whether the services of the facility are designed to intervene in problem areas of the residents' lives, such as substance abuse counseling, or to provide a supportive environment in which residents use community resources.

This simple typology indicates that different facilities must be assessed differently. For example, a residential facility designed to provide supportive services would not be well evaluated on the basis of direct service provision. Similarly, a program aimed at intervention would not be well understood solely in terms of resident length of stay. Rather, the type of program offered in a facility must form an important base of any assessment effort.

What Do We Know About the Effectiveness Question?

Despite the long tradition of residential community correctional programs, until recently the research literature concerned with them was sparse and inconclusive. In 2002 however, the largest study of community correctional facilities was conducted

(Lowenkamp & Latessa, 2002). This study included an examination of 38 halfway houses and over 6,400 offenders (3,200 each in the treatment and comparison groups). While results from this study showed that overall halfway houses did indeed reduce recidivism, not all programs were effective. Furthermore, programs had a much more pronounced effect on higher risk offenders, and higher quality programs performed better than low quality. Figure 28.1 shows the overall reductions in recidivism for the programs under study. These data indicate

that most of the programs reduced recidivism. Figures 28.2 through 28.5 show the results based on the risk level of the offenders. These data indicate that while few programs were effective with lower risk offenders (those with a relatively low probability to recidivate in the first place), as the risk increased, so did the effects. For higher risk offenders, the vast majority of halfway houses showed substantial reductions in recidivism.

Figure 28.1
Change in Recidivism Rates for All Offenders

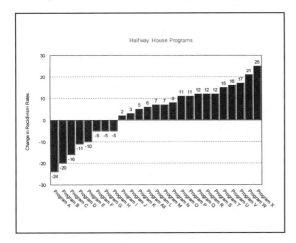

Figure 28.3
Change in Recidivism Rates for Low/Moderate-Risk Offenders

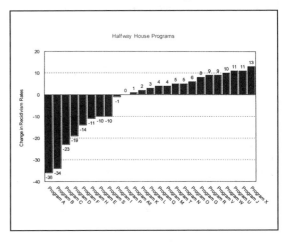

Figure 28.2
Change in Recidivism Rates for Low-Risk Offenders

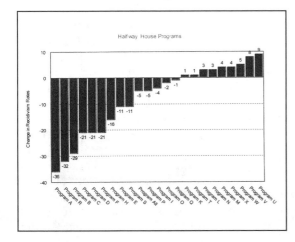

Figure 28.4
Change in Recidivism Rates for Moderate-Risk Offenders

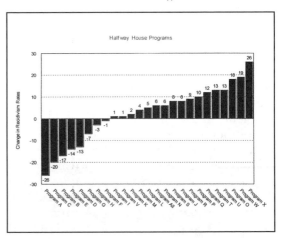

Figure 28.5
Change in Recidivism Rates for
High-Risk Offenders

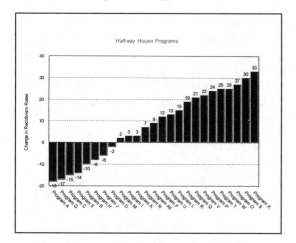

The Future of Residential Facilities

What does the future hold for residential community correctional facilities? Residential facilities that evolved from traditional halfway houses are now becoming multiservice agencies.

Second, residential community correctional facilities will continue to grow and develop new programs. In large part this will be a response to the crowding of local and state correctional institutions. Many traditional residential facilities will seize the opportunity and will diversify and offer a wider range of programs and services, such as victim assistance programs, family and drug counseling, drunk driver programs, work release centers, and house arrest, electronic monitoring, and day programs for offenders.

Finally, while there has been an increase in public sector operation of residential facilities, particularly prerelease and reintegration centers, it will be the private sector that will continue to play a dominant role in the development and operation of residential correctional programs. A number of arguments support private provision of community-based correctional services. Principal among these is cost-effectiveness. Proponents argue that the private sector will contain costs and thus, for the same dollar amount, provide more, or at least better, service. Government agencies, it is suggested, cannot achieve the same level of cost-efficient operation as can private, especially for-profit, companies.

As Clear, Hairs, and Record (1982) succinctly summarize: "Due to 'domestication' (characterized by a lack of competition and critical self-assessment), corrections officials often are inadvertently rewarded by taking a budget-administration approach rather than a cost-management stance." The attraction of private involvement in community corrections is the promise of a free market, or, as Greenwood (1981) put it, "They would be free to innovate, to use the latest technology and management techniques as in any profit service industry."

Another, perhaps more compelling, reason for the continued development of private community residential programs is that they can offer what Gendreau and Ross (1987) call "therapeutic integrity." That is, because of their accountability to the contractor and the possibility of competition, privately operated programs may provide more intensive and higher-quality service provision than might government agencies. Indeed, many who have studied public community correctional agencies have lamented the increasingly bureaucratic role of the change agent (Clear & Latessa, 1989), noting the large number of staff who are simply "putting in time" for retirement or who are encumbered by paperwork and red tape. It often seems that organizational goals outweigh concerns about effective treatment and service delivery.

Of course, this is really an issue of accountability that involves some nonmonetary value questions. This is one of the fundamental differences between the private and public sectors. Private enterprise often measures outcome in terms of profit, while the public sector measures it in terms of social value and benefits. While there is no empirical evidence that the private sector is "better" at providing services, reducing recidivism, and so forth, there is a growing sentiment that it ought to at least be given a chance. Privately run facilities may also be in a better position to lobby for more services, staff, and programs. One need only look at the typical adult probation department, where caseloads range from 150 to 300, to see how ineffective they have been in garnering additional resources. Private providers may, because of contractual agreements, be better able to advocate for additional support.

Of more importance than the simple dichotomy between public and private operation is the future evolution of the mission of community corrections residential facilities. The traditional halfway house had a charitable, quasi-volunteer, and service-oriented mission (Wilson, 1985). The contemporary multiservice community agency or department of corrections-operated facility is more formal, legalistic, and control oriented. As correctional agencies contract with both new private sector vendors and older, charitable programs, the emphasis in residential facilities may change from treatment to custody. Further, as the importance of correctional contracts for the support and spread of residential facilities grows, the "community" nature of these programs may increasingly be replaced by a more formal, governmental administrative style. That is, the forces that currently support the development of programs may ultimately change them in fundamental ways.

The traditional halfway house operated by a civic-minded reform group for the purpose of assisting offenders may be replaced by for-profit or nonprofit contractors working for the government. Thus, rather than a focus on the needs and interests of the community and the offender, the emphasis may be placed on the needs of the correctional system for bed space.

Of course, it is also entirely likely that the current confusion in residential programs will continue. There will continue to be traditional halfway houses focused on the needs of residents, with deep roots in the community. There will also be a variety of custody and crowding-control facilities designed to provide minimal direct services. Only time will tell what the future of community corrections residential facilities will be. The one thing that is clear is that some form of such facilities will exist in the future.

Study Questions

1. What are some of the possible reasons that halfway houses were more effective with higher risk offenders?

2. Trace the historical development of halfway houses.

3. What are the different types and models of halfway houses?

4. What are some of the differences between traditional halfway houses and more contemporary community residential centers?

5. What does the future hold for halfway houses?

Authors' Note

*This is an updated version of "Residential Community Correctional Programs" first published in *Smart Sentencing: The Emergence of Intermediate Sanctions,* James M. Byrne, Arthur L. Lurigio, and Joan Petersilia (eds.). Copyright © 1992 by Sage Publications. New material on the effectiveness of halfway houses has been added to the original article.

Endnote

1. Estimating the size of the community corrections residential facility population is hazardous at best. In her 1987 article, however, Hicks reported interviews with representatives of California, Texas, and the Federal Bureau of Prisons. These officials estimated that by 1988, the combined total of offenders served in residential facilities for these three

jurisdictions would exceed 7,000. Given that these numbers do not include probationers or misdemeanants in all three jurisdictions, a conservative extrapolation yields an estimated 70,000 offenders in residential facilities during 1988. This represents about 10 percent of the prison population for that year.

References

Allen, H. E., Carlson, E. W., Parks, E. C., & Seiter, R. P. (1978). *Program models: Halfway houses*. Washington, DC: U.S. Department of Justice.

Beha, J. A. (1977). Testing the functions and effects of the parole halfway house: One case study. *Journal of Criminal Law and Criminology*, 67, 335–350.

Clear, T., Hairs, P. M., & Record, A. L. (1982). Managing the cost of corrections. *Prison Journal*, 53, 1–63.

Clear, T., & Latessa, E. J. (1989, March). Intensive surveillance versus treatment. Paper presented at the annual meeting of the Academy of Criminal Justice Sciences, Washington, DC.

DuPont, P. (1985). *Expanding sentencing options: A governor's perspective*. Washington, DC. National Institute of Justice.

Federal Probation. (1986). *Intensive probation supervision* [Special issue]. Vol. 50, No. 2.

Gatz, N., & Murray, C. (1981). An administrative overview of halfway houses. *Corrections Today*, 43, 52–54.

Gendreau, P., & Ross, R. R. (1987). Revivification of rehabilitation: Evidence from the 1980's. *Justice Quarterly*, 4, 349–407.

Greenwood, P. (1981). *Private enterprise prisons? Why not?* Santa Monica, CA: RAND Corporation.

Guynes, R. (1988). *Difficult clients, large caseloads plague probation, parole agencies*. Washington, DC: U.S. Department of Justice.

Hicks, N. (1987). A new relationship: Halfway houses and corrections. *Corrections Compendium*, 12(4), 1, 5–7.

Keller, O. J., & Alper, G. (1970). *Halfway houses: Community centered correction and treatment*. Lexington, MA: D. C. Heath.

Latessa, E. J., & Allen, H. E. (1982). Halfway houses and parole: A national assessment. *Journal of Criminal Justice*, 10(2), 153–163.

Latessa, E. J., & Travis, L. F. (1986, October). Halfway houses versus probation: A three year follow-up of offenders. Paper presented at the annual meeting of the Midwestern Criminal Justice Association, Chicago.

Lowenkamp, C. T., & Latessa, E. J. (2002). *Evaluation of Ohio's halfway houses and community-based correctional facilities*. University of Cincinnati.

McCarthy, B. R. (Ed.). (1987). *Intermediate punishments: Intensive supervision, home confinement, and electronic surveillance*. Monsey, NY: Criminal Justice Press.

Petersilia, J. (1985). *Probation and felon offenders*. Washington, DC: U.S. Department of Justice.

Petersilia, J. (1987). *Expanding options for criminal sentencing* (Publication No. R-3544-EMC). Santa Monica, CA: RAND Corporation.

President's Commission on Law Enforcement and Administration of Justice. (1967). *Taskforce report: Corrections*. Washington, DC: Government Printing Office.

Rush, G. E. (1991). *The dictionary of criminal justice* (3rd ed.). Guilford, CT: Dushkin.

Seiter, R. P., Carlson, E. W., Bowman, H., Grandfield, H., Beran, N. J., & Allen, H. E. (1977). *Halfway houses*. Washington, DC: Government Printing Office.

Wilson, G. P. (1985). Halfway house programs for offenders. In L. F. Travis (Ed.), *Probation, parole, and community corrections* (pp. 151–164). Prospect Heights, IL: Waveland.

Excerpts from and revisions to "Smart Sentencing: The Emergence of Intermediate Sections" by Edward J. Latessa and Lawrence F. Travis III. Revisions (2005) by Edward J. Latessa, Lawrence F. Travis III, and Christopher T. Lowencamp. Copyright © 1992 by Sage Publishing, Inc. Reprinted by permission.   ✦

29
Welcome Home?

Examining the 'Reentry Court' Concept from a Strengths-Based Perspective

Shadd Maruna
Thomas P. LeBel

A*s we have learned, the number of offenders returning to the community is at an all-time high and the numbers will only continue to grow. One of the new concepts for more effectively assisting these offenders is the reentry court. This innovation draws some of its elements from drug and mental health courts that have sprung up around the country. Reentry courts hold out the promise for bringing together various components of the community in an effort to reduce risk, address needs, and provide the support and supervision necessary to reintegrate offenders back into the community.*

I*n the book *After Prison—What?* Maud Booth writes, "When one thinks that this prejudice and marking of discharged prisoners robs them of any chance of gaining a living, and in many instances forces them back against their will into a dishonest career, one can realize how truly tragic the situation is" (119). That was written in 1903. According to Verne McArthur, in his book *Coming Out Cold: Community Reentry from a State Reformatory*, "The released offender confronts a situation at release that virtually ensures his failure" (1). That was written in 1974.

Unfortunately, the conditions faced by ex-convicts today have not improved much and may have even deteriorated since these conclusions were reached. Fast forwarding to the present, Jeremy Travis and Joan Petersilia (2001:301) write, "Prisoners moving through the high-volume, poorly designed assembly line (of corrections) . . . are less well prepared individually for their return to the community and are returning to communities that are not well prepared to accept them." Additionally, there has been a radical change in the scale of the reentry problem over the last 100 years. Nearly 600,000 individuals will be released from US prisons this year (that is over 1,600 per day) compared to 170,000 in 1980 and only a few thousand at the turn of the century when Booth was writing.

In addition, largely due to new "tough on crime" approaches in paroling practice, reentering society has been made a more difficult and precarious transition than ever before. Of the 459,000 US parolees who were discharged from community supervision in 2000, 42 percent were returned to incarceration—11 percent with a new sentence and 31 percent in some other way (Bureau of Justice Statistics 2001). In a recent study of 272,111 prisoners released in 15 states in 1994, 67.5 percent were rearrested within three years, as compared to an estimated 62.5 percent in a similar study of 1983 releases (Langan and Levin 2002). Because of the enormous growth of the prison population since the early 1980s, this small change translates into huge numbers. In 1980, 27,177 paroled ex-convicts were returned to state prisons. In 1999, this number was 197,606. As a percentage of all admissions to state prisons, parole violators more than doubled from 17 percent in 1980 to 35 percent in 1999. In California, a staggering 67 percent of prison admissions were parole failures (Hughes, Wilson, and Beck 2001). These figures indicate that the reentry problem is not only a product of the 1990's incarceration boom, but is actually a leading cause of the boom as well. It is no wonder then that former Attorney General Janet Reno (2000:1) referred to ex-convict reentry as "one of the most pressing problems we face as a nation."

As such, the broad new proposals for revamping reentry policy through a "jurisprudential lens" (Travis and Petersilia 2001: 291) that have emerged in recent years (e.g., Office of Justice Programs 1999; Travis 2000) could not be more welcome or better timed. Before leaving office, the Clinton Administration developed a series of relatively large-scale initiatives intended to address the reentry crisis through a scattering of experimental pilot programs. The Clinton Administration's reentry proposals (OJP 2001) were never fully implemented, but the Bush Administration has developed its own reentry project (OJP 2002), which borrows much of the content of its predecessor's plan.

Among the most significant of the new proposals[1] is the "reentry court" experiment, based on the drug court model, which would cast judges as "reentry managers" (Travis 2000:8). Whereas, the role of the judiciary typically ends after sentencing, the reentry court model would move the court system into a "sentence management" role, overseeing the convicted person's eventual return to the community.

A reentry court is a court that manages the return to the community of individuals being released from prison, using the authority of the court to apply graduated sanctions and positive reinforcement and to marshal resources to support the prisoner's reintegration, much as drug courts do, to promote positive behavior by the returning prisoner (OJP 1999:2).

The concept of the reentry court is very much still under development, and the pilot sites in California, Colorado, Delaware, Florida, Iowa, Kentucky, New York, Ohio, and West Virginia all differ significantly in their emphases and approaches. Still, the underlying premises are largely borrowed from drug treatment courts and other problem-solving courts. According to the Office of Justice Programs (1999:79), these core elements include:

- *Assessment and strategic reentry planning* involving the ex-offender, the judiciary, and other key partners—this sometimes involves the development of a contract or treatment plan.

- *Regular status assessment meetings* involving both the ex-offender and his circle of supporters or representatives from his family and community.

- *Coordination of multiple support services* including substance abuse treatment, job training programs, faith institutions, and housing services.

- *Accountability to community* through the involvement of citizen advisory boards, crime victims' organizations, and neighborhood groups.

- *Graduated and parsimonious sanctions* for violations of the conditions of release that can be swiftly, predictably, and universally applied.

- *Rewards for success*, especially by negotiating early release from parole after established goals are achieved or by conducting graduation ceremonies similar to those used in drug courts.

The working assumption is that "offenders respond positively to the fact that a judge is taking an interest in their success" (OJP 1999:6). In addition, "The frequent appearances before the court with the offer of assistance, coupled with the knowledge of predictable and parsimonious consequences for failure, assist the offender in taking the steps necessary to get his life back on track" (6). With the explicit intention of reducing recidivism and assisting ex-offenders, reentry courts clearly have the potential to embody the principles of therapeutic jurisprudence (Wexler 2001) in the same way that drug treatment courts often do (see Hora, Schma, and Rosenthal 1999). Reentry court advocates also hope that these courts will achieve the level of popular and political support that drug courts have enjoyed.

As with any transplantation of a model from one context to the next, however, one must be cautious about applying the drug court model to the reentry process. After all, the success of the drug court movement in many ways might be attributable to features unique to addiction recovery or to the population of clients participating in the programs (i.e., non-violent, drug-involved offenders). Pioneering drug court judge, Hon. Richard Gebelein (2000), makes a case to this effect in trying to explain the popularity of drug courts in an era in which there is allegedly little support for the rehabilitative ideal. Gebelein argues that drug courts have succeeded because, unlike previous failed rehabilitative efforts, the drug court movement has been able to provide a clear narrative of what is causing the criminal behavior of the drug court clients and what they need to get better. Drug court's "advantage over 'plain old' rehabilitation," Gebelein (2000:3) suggests, is "the focus on one problem (addiction) that is causally related to crime committed by one group of offenders (addicts)." He argues that the narrative that addiction is a disease and, as such, needs to be treated by professionals, is one that makes sense to the public and to policy makers at this point in history.

The critical question, then, is: *Is there a similar narrative for how and why reentry should work?* In this paper, we will argue that a new narrative, which we refer to as a strengths-based or "restorative" narrative, is emerging in multiple fields that would fit nicely with the reentry court concept. Unfortunately, the current reentry proposals do not seem to reflect an explicitly restorative agenda and therefore may suffer the same fate as previous efforts to improve offender reentry processes.

Reentry: An Initiative in Need of a Narrative

Bullets kill and bars constrain, but the practice of supervision inevitably involves the construction of a set of narratives which allows the kept, the keepers, and the public to believe in a capacity to control (crime) that cannot afford to be tested too frequently.

— Jonathan Simon (1993) *Poor Discipline: Parole and the Social Control of the Underclass*

In his tremendous history of parole in the United States, Simon (1993:9) writes, "One of the primary tasks of an institution that exercises the power to punish is to provide a plausible account of what it does and how it does what it does." This might be particularly important for community corrections, which, as Fogel (1984:85) notes, lacks the "forceful imagery that other occupations in criminal justice can claim: police catch criminals, prosecutors try to get them locked up, judges put them in prisons, wardens keep them locked up, but what do probation officers do?" Simon argues that a good correctional narrative needs some rather obvious components. It needs, first, a plausible theory of criminogenesis (what causes people to commit crime?) and, second, a set of practices that appear capable of reversing this process.

Unlike the drug court model described by Gebelein, today's reentry system seems to have no such compelling narrative for what it does or how it works. In fact, Rhine (1997: 74) concludes that the lack of a "plausible narrative of community-based supervision" is "the most pressing and vexing problem facing probation and parole administrators today." The "growing conviction that the system no longer represents a credible response to the problem of crime" (Rhine 1997:71) has led to several new proposals to severely curtail or even abandon parole supervision[2] entirely (e.g., Austin 2001). One of the participants at a recent expert panel on the future of community corrections stated this matter quite bluntly: "Public regard for probation is dangerously low, and for the most part in most places, what passes for probation supervision is a joke. It's conceptually bankrupt and it's politically not viable. . . . We have to realize that we don't have broad public legitimacy" (Dickey and Smith 1998:3). Another participant described the public mood toward community corrections as a "malaise." He continued, "Even more importantly, there is a malaise in our own house [among probation professionals]" (Dickey and Smith 1998:5).

It is in this climate that the reentry court initiative has emerged with the promise of breathing new life into a much-maligned system of parole and community supervision. If instituted on a broad scale, the reentry court would represent a significant change in the structure of how the process of prison release works. It is not clear, however, that this important new policy initiative is being accompanied by a new policy *narrative*. In fact, the discourse around these new reentry initiatives may sound eerily familiar to those who have followed the history of parole in the US. According to Reno (2000:3):

> The reentry court is modeled on the . . . theory of a carrot and stick approach, in using the strength of the court and the wisdom of the court to really push the issue. . . . The message works with us: stay clean, stay out of trouble, and we'll help you get a job, we'll help you prepare in terms of a skill. But if you come back testing positive for drugs, if you commit a further crime, if you violate the conditions of your release, you're going to pay.

This description unfortunately makes the new reentry court initiative sound suspiciously like "simply another word for parole supervision, which many have tried to discredit and dismantle" (Austin 2001:314).

Indeed, Reno's stick and carrot are key symbols of the two reigning paradigms in parole practice over the last 100 years, which can be broken down into the familiar dichotomy of punishment and welfare (Garland 1985), monitor and mentor, or cop and social worker. We refer to these as "risk-based" and "need-based" narratives, respectively. Both are deficit models—that is, they emphasize convicts' problems—but they

require very different technologies and connote different meanings.

Below, we briefly outline both narratives, discussing their plausibility as explanatory accounts and their internal coherence. In addition, using a therapeutic jurisprudence lens, we will also evaluate each narrative in terms of its fit with established psychological principles regarding sustained behavior change (see Wexler 2001), and the empirical evaluation research referred to as "what works" (Gendreau, Cullen, and Bonta 1994). Finally, whenever possible, we will try to present the convicted person's own interpretation of these narratives, as these subjective perceptions are also crucial in understanding the success or failure of correctional practice.

Control Narratives (Risk-Based)

The February 2000 press release from U.S. Senator Joseph Biden's office announcing the "first-ever" reentry court in Delaware began with the macho headline "Biden Introduces Tough New Court Program for Released Inmates." Getting "tough" on those who have already "paid their debt" to society has become a standard, if not always coherent reentry narrative. The basic story, here, seems to be that ex-prisoners are dangerous, and they need to be watched carefully at all times. Indeed, this implication is clear in the new name given to the Reentry Initiative in the United States. Originally titled "Young Offender Reentry Initiative" (OJP 2001) under the Clinton Administration, the Bush Administration transformed the project into the "Serious and Violent Offender Reentry Initiative" (OJP 2002) and have toughened up the language of control substantially in their version of the proposal. Whereas the Clinton Administration's call for proposals emphasized the problems of substance abuse, mental illness, and stigmatization, the Bush Administration's reworking focuses on minimizing the risks posed by the "most predatory" ex-convicts.

This points out another important difference between drug courts and the reentry courts. Whereas drug courts explicitly exclude violent offenders, the reentry court plan would focus almost exclusively on persons thought to be at risk for violence. Peyton and Gossweiler (2001) found that of 212 reporting drug courts in their study, only seven of them include persons with violence in their criminal histories. Indeed, drug courts that receive federal funding are prohibited from admitting offenders with current violent charges or with prior convictions of violent felony crimes. Because of the different public and professional assumptions about the differences between persons convicted of violent versus nonviolent crime (and in particular, drug-related nonviolent crime), treatment of these two populations probably require different narratives.

Underlying the "risk management" approach to violence is the assumption that returning ex-convicts will respond best to the constant threat of sanctions (or, at any rate, if they do not, then they are too dangerous to be out of prison). In terms of policy prescriptions, this narrative suggests the need for an "electronic panopticon" (Gordon 1991) or "pee 'em and see 'em" (Cullen 2002) approach to reentry involving electronic monitoring, intensive supervision (i.e., additional home and office visits), random drug testing, home confinement, extensive behavior restrictions, strict curfews, and expanded lengths of supervision. The basic idea is that these forms of tough community controls can reduce recidivism by thwarting an offender's criminal instincts.

Empirically, these prototypically "tough" community sanctions—intensive community supervision in particular—have failed to live up to the promise of the control narrative. Petersilia and Turner's (1993) nine-state random-assignment evaluation found no evidence that the increased surveillance in the community deterred offenders from committing crimes. At the same time, their research quite conclusively showed that this additional control increased the probability that technical violations would be detected, leading to greater use of incarceration (and hence much higher costs).

Further, the control narrative has little support from the psychological literature on behavioral change. Specific deterrence in general has long been pronounced "dead" as a social scientific concept (see esp. McGuire 1995), and the literature is especially critical of the notion that prisons could serve as an effective deterrent. For instance, psychological research on effective punishment suggests that, to be effective, punishing stimuli must be immediate, predictable, and as intense as possible—none of which is possible in even the most Draconian correctional intervention (Gendreau, Goggin, and Cullen 1999).

Research on effective planned change similarly suggests that power-coercive strategies are the least likely to promote internalization and long-term change (Chin and Benne 1976). Kelman (1958), for instance, discusses three means of changing behavior: change via compliance, change via identification, and change via internalization. The first strategy, utilizing power-coercive means, may achieve instrumental compliance, Kelman says, but is the least likely of the three to promote "normative re-education" and long-term transformation once the "change agent" has been removed (see also Bottoms 2000). This hypothesis is empirically supported in MacKenzie and De Li's (2002) rigorous study of intensive supervision probation. They write:

> The disappointing factor is the possibility that the offenders may be influenced only as long as they are being supervised. . . . When probation is over, these offenders may return to their previous levels of criminal activity because the deterrent effect of arrest may wear off when they are no longer under supervision (37–38).

Heavy-handed control tactics can undermine the perceived legitimacy in paroling authorities among clients (see Tyler, Boeckmann, Smith, and Huo 1997). For instance, parole conditions that include prohibitions against associating with fellow ex-convicts or entering drinking establishments (both of which are nearly impossible to enforce) are often viewed as evidence that the entire parole process is a joke. Persons returning from the trauma of prison with few resources and little hope are likely to become "defiant" (Sherman 1993) at the "piling up of sanctions" (Blomberg and Lucken 1994) involved in such risk-based supervision. And constant threats that are not backed up can lead to a form of psychological inoculation. Colvin, Cullen, and Vander Ven (2002:22) write:

> Coercive interpersonal relations constitute the most aversive and negative forces individuals encounter. These are most likely to produce a strong sense of anger. The anger is only intensified if the individual perceives the coercive treatment as unjust or arbitrary. Instead of producing conformity, such coercive treatment creates greater defiance of authority.

Ex-convicts often feel they have paid their debt to society already and should therefore be left alone after release. Far from endorsing a "seamless" transition from prison control to community control, ex-convict academics Alan Mobley and Chuck Terry (2002) write, "No one wants the separation of prison and parole more urgently than do prisoners. When people 'get out,' they want to *be out*. Any compromise or half-measure, any 'hoops' or hassles placed in their path, breeds resentment." The extent of this resentment is apparent in the fascinating, and apparently somewhat widespread, phenomenon of convicts choosing to "max out" their sentences inside a prison rather than be released early and face high levels of supervision (see also Petersilia and Deschenes 1994).

Most importantly, however, the control narrative suffers from the "deeply entrenched view" that "equates punishment and control with incarceration, and that accepts alternatives as suitable only in cases where neither punishment nor control is thought necessary" (Smith 1984:171). Essentially, if parolees are such dangerous men and need so much supervision, then why aren't they still in prison? The average US parole officer—who has a caseload of 69 parolees each averaging 1.6 face-to-face contacts per month (Camp and Camp 1997)—simply cannot compete with the iron bars, high walls and razor wire of the prison when it comes to securing constraint-based compliance (see Bottoms 2000:92–93). Colvin and his colleagues (2002:23) write, "Although in theory consistent coercion can prevent crime, it is highly difficult to maintain consistent coercion in interpersonal relations, which requires nearly constant monitoring to detect noncompliance." As a result, of course, those who truly support a risk-centered narrative traditionally oppose parole release altogether, supporting instead maximum use of incapacitation.

Support Narratives (Need-Based)

The traditional counter to a risk-based parole system is a program of aftercare based on needs. Here the story is that ex-convicts are people with multiple deficits: some resulting from their incarceration (e.g., post-traumatic stress, disconnection from family, unfamiliarity with the world of work); some existing prior to incarceration (e.g., poor educational history, psychological problems, anger issues); and some attributable to societal forces outside of their control (e.g., discrimination, abuse, poverty, isolation). The most significant of these deficits, in the support narrative, are those deemed "criminogenic needs" or those problems that seem to be empirically related to offending (cognitive deficits are especially important here). In order to reduce crime, these needs must be "met" or at least "addressed." Specifically, released prisoners are thought to need access to programs in addiction counseling, cognitive therapy, life skills training, anger management, and the like.

Like the control narrative, this account has intuitive appeal. Yet, unlike in the case of coercive strategies of control, there is a well-known body of research (the so-called "What Works" literature) that supports the notion that rehabilitative interventions can marginally reduce recidivism rates when treatment is correctly matched to a client's criminogenic needs (see Gendreau et al. 1994). Moreover, in the few studies that ask returning prisoners themselves what would help to keep them "straight," basic "survival" needs (i.e., concerns like housing and employment) are almost always mentioned prominently (e.g., Erickson, Crow, Zurcher, and Connet 1973).

The support narrative, however, is a difficult sell politically. As everyone has needs, can it make sense for the state to prioritize the needs of persons who have recently been punished by the criminal justice system? As Bazemore (forthcoming) argues, "The notion of someone who has hurt another citizen . . . getting help or service without making amends for what has been damaged flies in the face of virtually universal norms of fairness." This was recently illustrated vividly in New York State, where gubernatorial candidate Carl McCall suggested that ex-convicts should receive help getting into college programs. During a discussion with homeless shelter residents who complained of difficulties receiving federal assistance for education because of their criminal records, McCall stated, "Just because you're an ex-offender, you should not be denied education aid. In fact, if you're an ex-offender I think you ought to get a preference." This simple statement of the support position set off an eruption of protest from his gubernatorial opponents, both Democratic and Republican, one of whom said, "Now he wants ex-convicts to get preference over hard-working students. No wonder Carl McCall was such a failure as president of the N.Y.C. Board of Education" (Nagourney 2002:B1).

Indeed, if the State ever really tried to meet all of the needs of ex-convicts (including financial, esteem, and self-actualization needs) and not just those needs deemed "criminogenic," the outpouring of generosity would surely contradict all principles of justice—let alone the controversial notion of "less eligibility." Who would not want to go to prison if the reward awaiting them upon release was that all their needs would be met? Of course, the needs of ex-convicts are rarely met in the 1.6 monthly meetings with a parole officer, referral or placement orders, and social service access that are at the heart of the casework model. "Needs" in correctional terms have come to connote something quite different than the way the word was defined by Maslow (1970), who left "procriminal attitudes" or "criminal associates" off his hierarchy. In their powerful essay contrasting criminogenic needs to human needs, Tony Ward and Claire Stewart (forthcoming:4) point out: "Even when the focus has been on offenders' needs, policy makers tend to be concerned with reducing further crimes or the incidence of disruptive behavior within prisons rather than the enhancement of their well being[3] and capabilities." In fact, needs have become synonymous with risk factors, and "meeting needs" can often equate to expanding the net of social control. So, for example, random mandatory drug testing for marijuana use gets framed as meeting a person's need to stop risky behaviors. It is unclear what is meant to represent the carrot in such treatment.

Combining Carrots and Sticks: An Odd Couple?

The traditional, middle-ground position, which appeals to Reno and many of the contemporary reentry reformers is to resolve the pendulous mentor-monitor debate by trying to do both. Basically, the idea is that if one combines a control approach (which does not really work, but is assumed to have public support) with a treatment approach (that works a little, but is thought to lack widespread support), the end result will be a program that is both popular and effective.

Instead, more often than not, the result of mixing such disparate goals is a "muddle" (Dickey and Smith 1998). David Fogel (1978:10–11) once quipped, "A parole officer can be seen going off to his/her appointed rounds with Freud in one hand and a .38 Smith and Wesson in the other. . . . Is Freud a backup to the .38? Or is the .38 carried to 'support' Freud?" The history of crime control in the 20th Century suggests that when both tools (the therapeutic and the punitive) are available, the latter will almost always win out or at least undermine the former (Garland 1985). Although parents and parental guardians are comfortable combining a disciplinary role with a social support role, this cop-and-counselor combination may not be possible in the much more limited relationship between the reentry court judge and the ex-convict or the parole officer and parolee. Indeed, more often than not, interventions premised on a combination-deficit model end up becoming "almost all stick and no carrot" (Prison Reform Trust 1999).

Theoretically, control strategies are intended to encourage instrumental compliance during the supervisory period, while the treatment strategies are designed to help participants internalize new, moral values. That is, the therapy or the job training is what is really going to work, but without the heavy coercion, the ex-prisoners will not show up for the treatment. And this hypothesis has some empirical support (MacKenzie and Brame 2001; Petersilia and Turner 1993). In particular, it has been well established that persons coerced into drug treatment programs fare equally as well as those who enter voluntarily (Farabee, Prendergast, and Anglin 1998).

Nonetheless, coercing compliance is one thing, but coercing good behavior is quite another. Consistent coercion may produce minimal levels of criminal behavior but it also produces very low levels of prosocial behavior (Colvin, Cullen, and Vander Ven 2002:28). Paul Gendreau and his colleagues (1999:89) argue this forcefully:

> Punishment only trains a person what not to do. If one punishes a behaviour what is left to replace it? In the case of high-risk offenders, simply other antisocial skills! This is why punishment scholars state that the most effective way to produce behavioural change is not to suppress "bad" behaviour, but to shape "good" behavior.

Carrot and stick models of reentry assign a largely passive role to the ex-prisoner and hence are unlikely to inspire intrinsically motivated self-initiative (Bazemore 1999). As such, critics argue that the operant conditioning implied in the carrot and stick metaphor confounds blind conformity with responsible behavior. Clark (2000:42) writes: "Compliance makes a poor final goal for drug courts. Obedience is not a lofty goal. We can teach animals to obey."

Moreover, coerced treatment is often resented by correctional consumers, who prefer self-help groups to state-sponsored reform programs (Irwin 1974; Mobley and Terry 2002). The eminent social psychologist George H. Mead (1918) explained the reason why combination control-support efforts are doomed to failure, almost a century ago:

> The two attitudes, that of control of crime by the hostile procedure of the law and that of control through comprehension of social and psychological conditions, cannot be combined. To understand is to forgive, and the social procedure seems to deny the very responsibility which the law affirms. On the other hand the pursuit by criminal justice inevitably awakens the hostile attitude in the offender and renders the attitude of mutual comprehension practically impossible (592).

In a process evaluation of the experimental Reentry Partnership Initiative, Faye Taxman and colleagues (2002:8) found telling evidence in support for this view. They write: "Program designers assumed offenders would be willing to be under additional community supervision in exchange for access to free community-based services on demand. They were surprised when almost no one took them up on the offer." The authors conclude that the offenders' past experiences with law enforcement, supervision agencies, and treatment providers had "left them dubious about the real intention of these agencies and staff." Therefore, the authors decide that any further "efforts to find fault, increase revocations, or speed a return to the justice system will only undermine the reentry goals" (8; see also Tyler et al. 1997).

Finally, the carrot and stick model of reentry fails to assign a meaningful role to the community. Although the process of reintegration has always had as much to do with the community as it has with the individual, carrot and stick reintegration models focus almost exclusively on the individual ex-prisoner. If reentry is to be a meaningful concept, presumably it implies more than physically reentering society, but also includes some sort of "relational reintegration" back into the moral community. Braithwaite and Braithwaite (2001:49) list four facets of what they call "reintegration":

- *Approval of the person—praise*

- *Respectfulness*

- *Rituals to terminate disapproval with forgiveness*

- *Sustaining pride in having the offender included as a member of communities of care (families, the school, the law abiding community at large).*

Reintegration, then, means full inclusion in and *of* a wider moral community. Social dependency and intensive supervision (or so-called carrots and sticks) seem to be the opposite of this sort of moral and social inclusion.

Strengths-Based Reentry: An Emerging Narrative?

Nobody makes the critical point: We need these people. The country is missing something because a huge bulk of its population is not a part of it. They have talents we need.

— Mimi Silbert, co-founder of Delancey Street (cited in Mieszkowski 1998).

An alternative paradigm is emerging (actually reemerging) in social service areas related to corrections that may be useful in re-imagining reentry. For the sake of consistency (and not just to invent another new term), we will refer to this as a "strengths-based" paradigm[4] (see also Bazemore 1999; Nissen and Clark forthcoming; van Wormer 2001)—or else "restorative reentry."[5] Strengths-based or restorative approaches ask not what a person's deficits are, but rather what positive contribution the person can make. Nissen and Clark (forthcoming) caution that strengths (of youths, families, and communities) are believed to be the most commonly wasted resources in the justice system. Strengths need to be assessed and "targeted" in the same way that risks and needs traditionally have been. To do so, one simply asks "How can this person make a useful and purposeful contribution to society?" In Jeremy Travis's (2000:7) words: "Offenders are seen as assets to be managed rather than merely liabilities to be supervised." This shift represents a move away from the notion of entitlement to the principle of "social exchange" (Levrant, Cullen, Fulton, and Wozniak 1999:22) or to what Bazemore (1999) calls "earned redemption."

Importantly, we make no pretension to "discovering" (and most certainly not inventing) this paradigm. Strengths-based themes have been a staple of progressive criminal justice reforms at least since the time of Maconochie's Mark System. After a recent rejuvenation in the 1960's and 1970's under the guise of the "New Careers Movement" (Cressey 1965; Grant 1968), however, this theme largely disappeared from correctional practice and rhetoric. The case being made in this section is only that there are signs that a strengths narrative seems to be coming back in multiple guises in the social services, and that this theme may be an appropriate one to introduce into the reentry debate.

In the reentry context, the strengths *narrative* begins with the assumption that ex-convicts are stigmatized persons, and implicitly that this stigma (and not some internal dangerousness or deficit) is at the core of what makes ex-convicts likely to reoffend. The "narrative of criminogenesis" that Simon (1993) calls for, then, is clearly based on a labeling/social exclusion story— on which, of course, the very idea of "reintegration" is also premised (Duffee and McGarrell 1990). Johnson (2002:319) writes, "released prisoners find themselves 'in' but not 'of' the larger society" and "suffer from a presumption of moral contamination." To combat this social exclusion, the strengths paradigm calls for opportunities for ex-convicts to make amends, demonstrate their value and potential, and make positive contributions to their communities. In the language of the New Careers movement, the goal is to "devise ways of creating more helpers" (Pearl and Riessman 1965:88). Strengths-based practice, like the New Careers movement before it, would seek "to transform receivers of help (such as welfare recipients) into dispensers of help; to structure the situation so that receivers of help will be placed in roles requiring the giving of assistance" (Pearl and Riessman 1965: 88–89).

These accomplishments are thought to lead to "a sense of hope, an orientation toward the future, and the willingness to take responsibility" (Richie 2001:385). Moreover, such demonstrations send a message to the community that the offender is worthy of further support and investment in their reintegration (Bazemore 1999). Ideally, these contributions can be recognized and publicly "certified" in order to symbolically "de-label" the stigmatized person (see Maruna 2001:chapter eight). Although this sort of reentry is always a challenge, it is far more likely to occur in a reciprocal situation: one needs "to do something to get something" (Toch 1994:71). A participant in the Rethinking Probation conference discussed the intuitive appeal of such a narrative:

> Let me put it this way, if the public knew that when you commit some wrongdoing, you're held accountable in constructive ways and you've got to earn your way back through these kinds of good works, . . . (probation) wouldn't be in the rut we're in right now with the public (Dickey and Smith 1998:36).

This symbolic appeal of transforming the probationer into a "giver rather than a consumer of help" is also evidenced by the enthusiasm around community service as a sanction in the 1970s, especially in Europe.

Strengths-Based Practices: A Growing Trend

Indeed, the narrative seems to have become somewhat contagious, at least among academics, over the last half-decade or so. Variations of strengths-based practice can now be found in every form of social work practice in the United States (Saleebey 1997) and are slowly making their way into traditional criminal justice practice (Clark 2000, 2001; Nissen and Clark forthcoming; van Wormer 2001). Identical paradigm shifts seem to be taking place across a variety of other disciplines including the focus on "positive psychology," developmental resilience, appreciative inquiry, wellness research, solution-focused therapy, assets-based community development, and narrative therapy. All of these new paradigms share an anti-pathologizing approach that focuses on building on strengths rather than correcting deficits.

In a criminal justice framework, strength approaches would ask not what needs to be done to a person in response to an offence, but rather what the person can accomplish to make amends for his or her actions (e.g., in the form of community service contributions). In the last 30 years, virtually every US probation department has had some experience with community service as a sanction, and it has been widely viewed as a rare penal success story. Yet despite its origins as a rehabilitative panacea, community service is no longer uniformly justified using a strengths narrative. According to Bazemore and Maloney (1994:24), "punishment now appears to have become the dominant objective of service sanctions in many jurisdictions." Indeed, in the United Kingdom this shift has been made explicit by the relabeling of community service as a "community punishment order." When it is strengths-based, community service work is voluntarily agreed upon and involves challenging tasks that could utilize the talents of the offender in useful, visible roles (McIvor 1998).

Probation and parole projects in which offenders visibly and directly produce things the larger community wants, such as gardens, graffiti-free neighborhoods, less dangerous alleys, habitable housing for the homeless . . . have also helped build stronger communities, and have carved channels into the labor market for the offenders engaged in them (Dickey and Smith 1998:35).

These volunteer activities could take place both inside as well as outside the prison. In a partnership program with Habitat for Humanity, convicts from 75 prisons (working alongside volunteers from the community) built over 250 homes for low income Americans in 1999 (Ta 2000). Prisoners in New York State have been involved in the crucial work of providing respite care to fellow inmates dying of AIDS and other illnesses in the prison system. In the year 2000, as part of a service learning curricula focused on "personal responsibility and rep-

aration," prisoners in the state of Ohio performed more than 5 million hours of community service work, including rehabbing low-income homes, training pilot and companion dogs, and repairing computers to be donated to schools (Wilkinson 2001). Perhaps most impressive among the contributions made by prisoners is the little publicized but essential work that teams of prisoners have voluntarily undertaken in fighting the forest fires ravaging America's national parks. Prisoners are routinely sent into areas struck by flooding or other natural disasters to provide support to relief efforts.

Prisoners also have initiated parenting programs—like the Eastern Fathers' Group (EFG) that was created "by" and "for" incarcerated fathers at a maximum-security New York State prison (Lanier and Fisher 1990). Consisting of mutual support meetings, monthly educational seminars, and a certified parenting education course, the EFG served to heighten participants' sense of accomplishment and responsibility. At the same time it helped fathers work through the grief they experienced over the loss or deterioration of family bonds. Surveys of prisoners in the United States show that 55 percent of State and 63 percent of Federal prisoners have children under the age of eighteen, and almost half of those parents were living with their children at the time they were incarcerated (Bureau of Justice Statistics 2000). Active engagement in parenting while incarcerated is thought to provide a "stability zone" for offenders that "softens the psychological impact of confinement" (Toch 1975) and may help reduce recidivism and "transmit prosocial attitudes to a future generation" (Lanier and Fisher 1990:164).

Another characteristically strengths-based role is that of the "wounded healer" or "professional ex-" (Brown 1991:219), defined as a person who desists from a "deviant career" by "replacing it" with an occupation as a paraprofessional,[6] lay therapist, or counselor. Although it is impossible to measure the true extent of the "professional ex-" phenomenon, Brown (1991:219) estimated that around three-quarters of the counselors working in the over ten thousand substance abuse treatment centers in the United States are former substance abusers themselves. Describing female "wounded healers," Richie (2001:385) writes:

> Most services that are successful in helping women reintegrate into the community have hired (or are otherwise influenced by) women who have been similarly situated. The extent to which women have a peer and/or mentoring relationship with someone whom they perceive is "like them" is critical.

In addition to such professional work, thousands of former prisoners and addicts freely volunteer their time helping others in mutual aid groups like Bill Sands' Seventh Step organization. Indeed, the "twelve steps" of Alcoholics Anonymous (AA) and Narcotics Anonymous (NA) are premised around an explicit service orientation, codified in the Twelfth Step and the Fifth Tradition, which encourages those who find sobriety to assist others in taking this journey. According to O'Reilly (1997:128), "next to avoiding intoxicants," the therapeutic power of *helping* is "the major premise upon which (AA) is built." AA and NA members who have been sober for many years often remain with the organization, not so much because they need to *receive* any more counseling, but because the act of counseling *others* can itself be empowering and therapeutic. Members who stay connected to the program eventually take on the role of sponsors and become the mentors and teachers of the next generation of recovering addicts. AA's co-founder Bill Wilson said that he felt that his own sobriety was dependent upon his acting as a mentor in this way.

With little doubt, the best existing model for a strengths-based, mutual aid society for ex-convicts outside prison is the Delancey Street program based in San Francisco. Founded in 1971 by Mimi Silbert and ex-convict John Maher, Delancey Street has grown from an organization consisting of ten recovering addicts (and one criminal psychologist) living in an apartment to a thriving organization with 1,500 full-time residents in five self-run facilities, more than 20 businesses that double as training schools, and an annual operating budget of close to $24 million (Boschee and Jones 2000; Mieszkowski 1998). The program is self-supporting and has no professional staff. Instead, taking an "each one teach one" approach, older residents teach and train newer arrivals [who] then utilize these new skills to sustain the organization once the more senior residents "graduate" into private housing and independent careers. Silbert says residents "learn a fundamental lesson . . . that they have something to offer. These are people who have always been passive. . . . But strength and power come from being on the giving end" (Boschee and Jones 2000:11).

Finally, in recent years there have been several attempts to coordinate the efforts and energies of a variety of such mutual aid groups in the name of creating lasting social change. In what is being called the "New Recovery Movement" (White 2001:16), wounded healers are also beginning to become "recovery activists," turning their "personal stories into social action" (19), and turning "recovery outwards" (19). Instead of working solely on their own addiction problems, recovering persons and their supporters would mobilize their strengths in order to change "the ecology of addiction and recovery" (White 2001:19). These and other mutual aid efforts are thought to help transform individuals from being part of the problem into being part of the solution as they give their time in the service of helping others.

Theoretical and Empirical Support for the 'Helper Principle'

Although these activities can be justified on many grounds, one of the central theoretical premises all of these strengths-based practices share is some faith in the "helper principle" (Pearl and Riessman 1965). Promoted in the 1960's New Careers Movement, the helper principle simply says that it may be better (that is, more reintegrative) to give help than to receive it (see also Cullen 1994:543–544). The alleged benefits of assuming the role of helper include a sense of accomplishment, grounded increments in self-esteem, meaningful purposiveness, and a cognitive restructuring toward responsibility (Toch 2000). Rather than coercing obedience, strengths-based practices are thought to develop intrinsic motivations toward helping behaviors—what Nissen and Clark (forthcoming:70) call the "difference between compliance and growth." Clients are supposedly "turned on" to prosocial behavior through involvement with activities that utilize their strengths. In the words of Alexis de Tocqueville (1835/1956: 197), "By dint of working for one's fellow-citizens, the habit and the taste for serving them is at length acquired." In addition, as part of a helping collective, the "wounded healer" or community volunteer is thought to obtain "a sense of belonging and an esprit de corps" (Pearl and Riessman 1965: 83). According to the helper principle, all these experiences should be related to successful reintegration and social inclusion.

Recent research on desistance from crime might provide some indirect empirical support for this claim. For instance, as is well known, Sampson and Laub (1993) found that one-time offenders who were employed and took responsibility for providing for their spouses and children were significantly more likely to desist from crime than those who made no such bonds. A less well known finding of their research was that desistance was strongly correlated with assuming financial responsibility for one's aging parents or siblings in need as well (Sampson and Laub 1993:219–220). One way to interpret these findings might be to hypothesize that nurturing behaviors may be inconsistent with a criminal life-

style. Indeed, Lynne Goodstein speculates that women's traditional responsibility for other family and community members may be one reason that females are so dramatically underrepresented in criminal statistics (cited in Cullen 1994).

Moreover, quasi-experimental evaluations of community service sentencing consistently show that it outperforms standard probation and other sanctions in reducing recidivism (Rex 2001; Schneider 1986). Further, McIvor (1998) found that people who viewed their experience of community service as "rewarding" had lower rates of recidivism than those who found it a chore, indicating that this impact is less about deterrence and more likely something to do with prosocial modeling or moral development (Van Voorhis 1985). McIvor (1998) writes, "In many instances, it seems, contact with the beneficiaries gave offenders an insight into other people, and an increased insight into themselves; . . . greater confidence and self-esteem; . . . (and) the confidence and appreciation of other people" (McIvor 1998:55–56; cited in Rex 2001).

More recently, longitudinal studies have tried to assess the long-term impact of volunteer work on life course trajectories. Uggen and Janikula (1999) investigated the question of whether involvement in volunteer work can induce a change in a person's likelihood of antisocial conduct. They found a robust negative relationship between volunteer work and arrest even after statistically controlling for the effects of antisocial propensities, prosocial attitudes, and commitments to conventional behavior. Uggen and Janikula (1999:355) conclude:

> What is it about the volunteer experience that inhibits antisocial behavior? We suggest that the informal social controls emphasized in social bond, social learning, and reintegrative theories are the mechanism linking volunteer work and antisocial behavior. Informal social controls are con-

sonant with Tocquevillian conceptions of "self-interest, rightly understood," in which volunteers are gradually socialized or "disciplined by habit rather than will."

Finally, Maruna's (2001) research on the psychology of desistance from crime offers further evidence of a link between a "generative" identity and criminal reform. In a clinical comparison of successfully and unsuccessfully reformed ex-convicts, Maruna found that those who were able to "go straight" were significantly more care-oriented, other-centered and focused on promoting the next generation. They tried to find some meaning in their shameful life histories by turning their experiences into cautionary or hopeful stories of redemption, which they shared with younger offenders in similar situations. Whereas active offenders characterized themselves as being doomed or predestined to failure, reformed offenders had an almost overly optimistic sense of control over their future and strong internal beliefs about their own self-worth. In short, their personal narratives (the stories they told about how they were able to "go straight") resembled "strength narratives" far more than control or support narratives. Indeed, the latter seemed to characterize the narratives of active offenders.

None of this research is firm evidence in favor of the "helper principle." In particular, although these studies may suggest a basic incompatibility between helping activities and criminal lifestyles, they tell us little about how to "create more helpers." Indeed, the lack of research on mutual aid organizations, self-help groups, and informal mentoring and parenting among convicts and exconvicts is rather startling considering how much research is funded each year to examine the impact of greater controls and, less frequently, treatment programming (see Uggen and Piliavin 1998:1421–1422). Still, as a narrative—that is, a theoretical premise—the restorative idea of "earned redemption" seems to have at least

some plausibility from the limited research that exists.

A Strengths-Based Reentry Court

Become future focused: the past, and the focus on past failures, can open the door to demoralization and resignation—hope is future based.
            —Michael D. Clark (2001:23)

Strengths-based practices and principles may be uniquely suited to the new reentry court idea. First, unlike traditional jurisprudence, reentry courts would presumably be future-oriented rather than focused on the past. Determining guilt and devising a fair response to a criminal act are responsibilities that belong to other courts. The reentry court's role might more reasonably be understood as dispensing "reintegration"—not release from prison or supervision (as is the traditional role of the parole board), but rather a release from the stigma of the original conviction. The work of reentry, then, would be the facilitation of opportunities to make amends for what one has done and the recognition of these contributions and accomplishments. True to its name, then, the reentry court could become a "court of redemption," through which a stigmatized person has the opportunity to formally "make good."

Rewarding positive achievements, rather than punishing violations, is an unusual role for the courts. Parole as it is currently practiced focuses almost entirely on detecting and punishing failure—even though the "what works" principles suggest that positive reinforcement should outweigh punishment by a 4:1 ratio (Gendreau et al. 1994). As conformity is all that is required of deficit-based parole, it makes little sense to commend or acknowledge persons simply for doing what they are supposed to and following the rules. Indeed, the primary "reward" available in parole today is to "get off" parole early, a particularly strange and unceremonious process.[7]

Alternatively, a strengths-based reentry court might be modeled on Braithwaite's (2001:11) notion of "active responsibility": "Passive responsibility means holding someone responsible for something they have done in the past. Active responsibility means the virtue of taking responsibility for putting things right for the future." The court would not be concerned with past offenses, misbehavior in prison or even violations of parole. All of these crimes and misdemeanors are properly punished by other authorities. The focus, instead, would be on monitoring, recording, and judging what the individual has done to redeem him or herself through victim reparation, community service, volunteer work, mentoring, and parenting.[8] Witnesses would be called, testimony would be offered, tangible evidence would be produced—not in the name of establishing guilt or innocence, but rather in order to assess the contribution being made by the returning prisoner both in prison and afterwards. The reentry court could then be the setting for a "public recognition ceremony" acknowledging these contributions and accomplishments as "a milestone in repaying (one's) debt to society" (Travis 2000:9).

With no powers to punish, a strengths court, then, would be more a challenge to returning ex-convicts than a threat. That is, the ex-offender would be given an opportunity to be publicly and formally reintegrated if they were willing to pay a debt to society in terms of their service and contribution. Winick (1991:246) refers to this as "harnessing the power of the bet":

> Many people do not respond well when told to do so. Unless they themselves see merit in achieving the goal, sometimes even when the costs of noncompliance are high, they may well resent pressure imposed by others and refuse to comply or may act perversely in ways calculated to frustrate achievement of the goal. By con-

trast, the offer to wager can be accepted or rejected. The choice is up to the individual. The law strongly favors allowing such choice, rather than attempting to achieve public or private goals through compulsion.

Winick (1991:247) argues that, unlike coerced compliance, this challenge model is likely to mobilize "the self-evaluative and self-reinforcing mechanisms of intrinsic motivation" and effect "lasting attitudinal and behavioral change in the individual."

The notion of rewarding success, of course, is a key component of the reentry court idea. In drug treatment courts,[9] "applause is common" and "even judicial hugs are by no means a rare occurrence" (Wexler 2001:21). Travis (1999:133) asserts that "the court should use positive judicial reinforcement by serving as a public forum for encouraging pro-social behavior and for affirming the value of individual effort in earning the privilege of successful reintegration." In the experimental Reentry Partnership Initiatives, successful "reentry graduates" may eventually move from being "recipients of services" to acting as role models and "guardians" for newly released offenders just entering the structured reentry phase of the process (Taxman et al. 2002: 18; similar recommendations were proposed by Erickson et al. 1973:103–105). Among other program requirements, each participant in Richland County, Ohio's new reentry court is required to complete 300 hours of community service work that commences upon incarceration (Wilkinson 2001). Finally, all reentry courts are required to outline milestones in the reentry process (such as the completion of this sort of volunteer work) that would trigger recognition and an appropriate reward (Office of Justice Programs 1999).

A strengths approach would probably take this further, and following Johnson (2002: 328) would recast the reentry court process as "a mutual effort at reconciliation, where offender and society work together to make amends—for hurtful crimes and hurtful punishments—and move forward."

Braithwaite and Braithwaite (2001:16) have argued that praise may work in the exact opposite form that shaming does. That is, while it is better to shame an individual act and not the whole person, it may be better to praise the whole person than the specific act.

> So when a child shows a kindness to his sister, better to say 'you are a kind brother' than 'that was a kind thing you did'. . . . (P)raise that is tied to specific acts risks counter productivity if it is seen as an extrinsic reward, if it nurtures a calculative approach to performances that cannot be constantly monitored. . . . Praising virtues of the person rather than just their acts . . . nourishes a positive identity (Braithwaite and Braithwaite 2001:16).

According to Makkai and Braithwaite (1993:74), such praise can have "cognitive effects on individuals through nurturing law-abiding identities, building cognitive commitments to try harder, encouraging individuals who face adversity not to give up . . . and nurturing belief in oneself."

As such, the strengths-based reentry court would need to go beyond the occasional rewarding of specific acts of service and instead build gradually to a more holistic "earned redemption" of the participant's character and reputation. This might take the shape of a "status elevation ceremony" that could "serve publicly and formally to announce, sell, and spread the fact of the Actor's new kind of being" (Lofland 1969: 227). In such rituals, "Some recognized member(s) of the conventional community must publicly announce and certify that the offender has changed and that he is now to be considered essentially noncriminal" (Meisenhelder 1977:329). These need not be once-off occasions. Just as Braithwaite and Braithwaite (2001) propose that reintegration ceremonies may need to occur more than once, multiple certification rituals may be needed in multiple domains in order to counteract the stigma faced by former prisoners. If endorsed and supported by the same social control establishment involved in the "status degradation" process of conviction and sentencing, this public redemption might carry considerable social and psychological weight for participants and observers (Maruna 2001:chapter eight).

Most importantly, the reward would also involve the "expiration" of the individual's criminal history—allowing the person freedom from having to declare previous convictions to potential employers, licensing bodies, or other authorities and to resume full citizenship rights and responsibilities.[10] The ultimate prize, then, for (proactive) "good behavior" would be permission to legally move on from the past and wipe the slate clean. This, it seems, may better represent the definition of "reintegration."

Study Questions

1. What are the core elements of problem-solving courts such as reentry courts?

2. Briefly describe the risk- and needs-based approaches outlined in the article.

3. What are some of the "carrots and sticks" referred to in the article?

4. What is a strengths-based approach to reentry courts? Give some examples.

Notes

1. The original Clinton agenda also involved a substantial new project referred to as the Reentry Partnership Initiative (RPI), which is beyond the scope of this paper, although similar in many ways to the reentry court. For instance, the stated goal of the RPI initiative is to "improve risk management of released offenders . . . by enhancing surveillance, risk and needs assessments, and pre-release planning" (RPI Report 2000:1; see also Taxman, Young, Byrne, Holsinger, and Anspach 2002).

2. These should be seen as distinct from previous efforts to abolish parole release structures, which largely left post-incarceration supervision intact.

3. Even in the most progressive versions of the support narrative, this level of need-fulfillment is difficult to achieve. For instance, Sullivan and Tifft (2001) point out that although there is much talk in restorative justice circles about "meeting the needs" of offenders as well as victims, the two are seen as significantly different. While crime victims are thought to need understanding, support and love from those around them, offenders are said to need a job, clothing, and shelter. Sullivan and Tifft (2001:83) write, "By focusing on this level of needs alone, we do not show the same level of concern for them as we do for those who have been harmed."

4. This of course is an umbrella term that encompasses approaches that go by many other names (most notably Restorative Justice, the New Careers movement, relational rehabilitation, and the New Recovery Movement).

5. "Restorative Reentry" is the preferred phrase of the Open Society Institute's remarkable array of strengths-based, advocacy projects sponsored as part of the After Prison Initiative (see <http://www.soros.org/crime/CJIGuidelines.htm#tapi>).

6. Interestingly, the Clinton Administration's original Young Offender Initiative (OJP 2001: 12) stated: "Applicants are encouraged to use ex-offenders as staff and those with a history of substance abuse or mental illness. Having some staff with these backgrounds helps the therapeutic process and builds the community's capacity to continue services after the grant ends." There is no mention of utilizing the strengths of ex-offenders in this way in the Bush Administration's initiative.

7. When one of this paper's authors earned his freedom after 56 months of parole supervision, he was offered not so much as a "congratulations" or a "good luck" from the officer who had such power over his life. In fact, he only found out that he had been released from parole supervision when he called his PO to get a travel pass to visit family out of state. The memorable dialog proceeded something as follows: "So, does that mean I'm free?" "Yes, you don't need to report anymore." "Do I have all of my rights back?" "I don't know anything about that." "Thanks."

8. Research in the substance abuse field by Petry, Tedford, and Martin (2001:34) suggests that prosocial activity reinforcement (that is, rewarding positive behaviors) is more effective than reinforcement that is purely directed toward the absence of negative behaviors (e.g., drug abstinence). For instance, they found that prosocial activity reinforcement may result in improvements in psychosocial functioning (employment, medical, family problems) that are not apparent when drug abstinence alone is reinforced.

9. At their best, drug courts can epitomize the ideals of therapeutic jurisprudence, a clearly strengths based approach (see Hora, Schma, and Rosenthal 1999). Still, these ideals are not always realized in practice and one should be careful about exaggerating the role of praise in the actual practice of problem-solving courts. Ethnographers report that participants who successfully complete one large-scale drug court program, for instance, receive only "a congratulatory remark from the judge along with a T-shirt and key chain, claiming they are now '2 smart 4 drugs'" (Miethe, Lu, and Reese 2000:536). Burdon and colleagues (2001:78) write: "Descriptions of actual drug court operations reveal that most drug courts emphasize sanctions for noncompliance and few routinely use reinforcement of positive, desired behavior. (When used) rewards tend to be intermittent and, in contrast to sanctions, less specific, not immediately experienced, and based on a subjective evaluation of a defendant's progress in treatment."

10. Like many other observers, we would argue that ex-convicts should retain their full civil rights (voting, jury membership, etc.) regardless of reentry court participation. These rights are entitlements and should not be used as "rewards" even in a reciprocity based reentry program.

References

Austin, James. 2001. "Prisoner Reentry: Current Trends, Practices, and Issues." *Crime and Delinquency* 47:314–334.

Bazemore, Gordon. 1999. "After Shaming, Whither Reintegration: Restorative Justice and Relational Rehabilitation." Pp. 155–194 in *Restorative Juvenile Justice: Repairing the Harm of Youth Crime*, edited by G. Bazemore and L. Walgrave. Monsey, NY: Criminal Justice Press.

Bazemore, Gordon. Forthcoming. "Reintegration and Restorative Justice: Toward a Theory and Practice of Informal Social Control and Support." In *Ex-Offender Reintegration: Desistance from Crime After Prison,* edited by S. Maruna and R. Immarigeon. Albany, NY: SUNY Press.

Bazemore, Gordon and Dennis Maloney. 1994. "Rehabilitating Community Service: Toward Restorative Service Sanctions in a Balanced Justice System." *Federal Probation* 58:24–35.

Blomberg, Thomas and Karol Lucken. 1994. "Stacking the Deck by Piling Up Sanctions: Is Intermediate Punishment Destined to Fail?" *The Howard Journal* 33(1):62–80.

Booth, Maud B. 1903. *After Prison—What?* New York: Fleming H. Revell Company.

Boschee, Jerr and Syl Jones. 2000. "Recycling Excons, Addicts and Prostitutes: The Mimi Silbert Story." [Online]. Available: www.socialent.org/pdfs/MimiSilbertStory.pdf

Bottoms, Anthony E. 2000. "Compliance and Community Penalties." Pp. 87–116 in *Community Penalties: Change and Challenges,* edited by A. Bottoms, L. Gelsthorpe, and S. Rex. Cullompton: Willan.

Braithwaite, John. 2001. "Intention Versus Reactive Fault." Pp. 345–357 in *Intention in Law and Philosophy,* edited by N. Naffine, R. Owens, and John Williams. Aldershot, UK: Ashgate.

Braithwaite, John and Valerie Braithwaite. 2001. "Part One." Pp. 3–69 in *Shame Management Through Reintegration,* edited by E. Ahmed, N. Harris, J. Braithwaite, and V. Braithwaite. Cambridge: University of Cambridge Press.

Brown, David J. 1991. "The Professional Ex-: An Alternative for Exiting the Deviant Career." *The Sociological Quarterly* 32:219–230.

Burdon, William M., John M. Roll, Michael L. Prendergast, and Richard A. Rawson. 2001. "Drug Courts and Contingency Management." *Journal of Drug Issues* 31:73–90.

Bureau of Justice Statistics. 2000. *Incarcerated Parents and Their Children* (NCJ 182335). Washington, DC: U.S. Department of Justice.

Bureau of Justice Statistics. 2001, August 28. *Probation and Parole in the United States, 2000— Press Release* (NCJ 188208). Washington, DC: U.S. Department of Justice.

Camp, Camille G. and George M. Camp. 1997. *The Corrections Yearbook.* South Salem, NY: Criminal Justice Institute, Inc.

Chin, Robert and Kenneth D. Benne. 1976. "General Strategies for Effecting Changes in Human Systems." Pp. 22–44 in *The Planning of Change,* 3rd ed., edited by W. G. Bennis, K. D. Benne, R. Chin, and K. Corey. New York: Holt, Rinehart and Winston.

Clark, Michael D. 2000. "The Juvenile Drug Court Judge and Lawyer: Four Common Mistakes in Treating Drug Court Adolescents." *Juvenile and Family Court Journal* 51(4):37–46.

Clark, Michael D. 2001. "Influencing Positive Behavior Change: Increasing the Therapeutic Approach of Juvenile Courts." *Federal Probation* 65(1):18–27.

Colvin, Mark, Francis T. Cullen, and Thomas M. Vander Ven. 2002. "Coercion, Social Support, and Crime: An Emerging Theoretical Consensus." *Criminology* 40:19–42.

Cressey, Donald R. 1965. "Social Psychological Foundations for Using Criminals in the Rehabilitation of Criminals." *Journal of Research in Crime and Delinquency* 2:49–59.

Cullen, Francis T. 1994. "Social Support as an Organizing Concept in Criminology: Presidential Address to the Academy of Criminal Justice Sciences." *Justice Quarterly* 11:527–559.

Cullen, Francis T. 2002. "Rehabilitation and Treatment Programs." Pp. 253–289 in *Crime: Public Policies for Crime Control,* edited by J. Q. Wilson and J. Petersilia. Oakland, CA: Institute for Contemporary Studies.

Dickey, Walter J. and Michael E. Smith. 1998. *Dangerous Opportunity: Five Futures for Community Corrections: The Report from the Focus Group.* Washington, DC: U.S. Department of Justice, Office of Justice Programs.

Duffee, David E. and Edmund F. McGarrell. 1990. *Community Corrections: A Community Field Approach.* Cincinnati, Ohio: Anderson.

Erickson, Rosemary J., Wayman J. Crow, Louis A. Zurcher, and Archie V. Connet. 1973. *Paroled But Not Free.* New York: Human Sciences Press.

Farabee, David, Michael Prendergast, and M. Douglas Anglin. 1998. "The Effectiveness of Coerced Treatment for Drug-abusing Offenders." *Federal Probation* 62(1):3–10.

Fogel, David. 1978. "Foreword." Pp. 7–15 in *Dangerous Men: The Sociology of Parole* by Richard McCleary. Beverly Hills, CA: Sage Publications.

Fogel, David. 1984. "The Emergence of Probation as a Profession in the Service of Public Safety: The Next Ten Years." Pp. 65–99 in *Probation and Justice: Reconsideration of Mission,* edited by P. D. McAnany, D. Thompson, and D. Fogel. Cambridge, MA: Oelgeschlager, Gunn, and Hain.

Garland, David. 1985. *Punishment and Welfare: A History of Penal Strategies*. Brookfield, VT: Gower Publishing Company.

Gebelein, Richard S. 2000. *The Rebirth of Rehabilitation: Promise and Perils of Drug Courts*. Papers from the Executive Sessions on Sentencing and Corrections (NCJ 181412). Washington, DC: U.S. Department of Justice, National Institute of Justice.

Gendreau, Paul, Francis T. Cullen, and James Bonta. 1994. "Intensive Rehabilitation Supervision: The Next Generation in Community Corrections?" *Federal Probation* 58:173–84.

Gendreau, Paul, Claire Goggin, and Francis T. Cullen. 1999. *The Effects of Prison Sentences on Recidivism*. A Report to the Corrections Research and Development and Aboriginal Policy Branch, Solicitor General of Canada, Ottawa.

Gordon, Diana. 1991. *The Justice Juggernaut: Fighting Street Crime, Controlling Citizens*. New Brunswick, NJ: Rutgers University Press.

Grant, J. Douglas. 1968. "The Offender as a Correctional Manpower Resource." Pp. 226–234 in *Up from Poverty: New Career Ladders for Nonprofessionals*, edited by F. Riessman and H.L. Popper. New York: Harper and Row.

Hora, Peggy F., William G. Schma, and John T. A. Rosenthal. 1999. "Therapeutic Jurisprudence and the Drug Treatment Court Movement: Revolutionizing the Criminal Justice System's Response to Drug Abuse and Crime in America." *Notre Dame Law Review* 74:439–537.

Hughes, Timothy A., Doris. J. Wilson, and Allen J. Beck. 2001. *Trends in State Parole, 1990–2000*. Washington, D.C.: U.S. Department of Justice, Bureau of Justice Statistics: Special Report.

Irwin, John. 1974. "The Trouble with Rehabilitation." *Criminal Justice and Behavior* 1(2):139–149.

Johnson, Robert. 2002. *Hard Time*, 3rd ed. Belmont, CA: Wadsworth.

Kelman, Herbert C. 1958. "Compliance, Identification and Internalization: Three Processes of Opinion Change." *Journal of Conflict Resolution* 2:51–60.

Langan, Patrick A. and David J. Levin. 2002. *Recidivism of Prisoners Released in 1994* (NCJ 193427). Washington, D.C.: U.S. Department of Justice, Bureau of Justice Statistics.

Lanier, Charles S. and Glenn Fisher. 1990. "A Prisoners' Parenting Center (PPC): A Promising Resource Strategy for Incarcerated Fathers." *Journal of Correctional Education* 41:158–165.

Levrant, Sharon, Francis T. Cullen, Betsy Fulton, and John F. Wozniak. 1999. "Reconsidering Restorative Justice: The Corruption of Benevolence Revisited?" *Crime and Delinquency* 45:3–27.

Lofland, John. 1969. *Deviance and Identity*. Englewood Cliffs, NJ : Prentice-Hall.

MacKenzie, Doris L. and Robert Brame. 2001. "Community Supervision, Prosocial Activities, and Recidivism." *Justice Quarterly* 18(2):429–448.

MacKenzie, Doris L. and Spencer De Li. 2002. "The Impact of Formal and Informal Social Controls on the Criminal Activities of Probationers." *Journal of Research in Crime and Delinquency* 39:243–276.

Makkai, Toni and John Braithwaite. 1993. "Praise, Pride and Corporate Compliance." *International Journal of the Sociology of Law* 21: 73–91.

Maruna, Shadd. 2001. *Making Good: How Exconvicts Reform and Rebuild Their Lives*. Washington, D.C.: American Psychological Association Books.

Maslow, Abraham H. 1970. *Motivation and Personality*, 2nd ed. New York: Harper and Row.

McArthur, Verne A. 1974. *Coming Out Cold: Community Reentry from a State Reformatory*. Lexington, MA: Lexington Books.

McGuire, James. 1995. "The Death of Deterrence." In *Does Punishment Work? Proceedings of a Conference Held at Westminster Central Hall*, London, UK, edited by J. McGuire and B. Rowson. London: ISTD.

McIvor, Gillian. 1998. "Pro-social Modelling and Legitimacy: Lessons from a Study of Community Service." In *Pro-social Modelling and Legitimacy: The Clarke Hall Day Conference*, edited by S. Rex and A. Matravers. Cambridge: Institute of Criminology, University of Cambridge.

Mead, George H. 1918. "The Psychology of Punitive Justice." *American Journal of Sociology* 23: 577–602.

Meisenhelder, Thomas. 1977. "An Exploratory Study of Exiting from Criminal Careers." *Criminology* 15:319–334.

Mieszkowski, Katherine. 1998. "She Helps Them Help Themselves." *Fast Company* 15:54–56.

Miethe, Terrance D., Hong Lu, and Erin Reese. 2000. "Reintegrative Shaming and Recidivism Risks in Drug Court: Explanations for Some Unexpected Findings." *Crime and Delinquency* 46:522–541.

Mobley, Alan and Charles Terry. 2002. *Dignity, Resistance and Re-Entry: A Convict Perspective.* Unpublished manuscript.

Nagourney, Adam. 2002, June 20. "McCall Urges Giving Help on Tuition to Ex-convicts." *New York Times,* B1.

Nissen, Laura B. and Michael D. Clark. Forthcoming. *Power of the Strengths Approach in the Juvenile Drug Court—Practice Monograph.* Washington, D.C.: U.S. Department of Justice, Office of Justice Programs, Juvenile Drug Court Programs Office.

O'Reilly, Edmund B. 1997. *Sobering Tales: Narratives of Alcoholism and Recovery.* Amherst, MA: University of Massachusetts Press.

Office of Justice Programs. 1999. *Reentry Courts: Managing the Transition from Prison to Community, A Call for Concept Papers.* Washington, D.C.: U.S. Department of Justice, Office of Justice Programs.

Office of Justice Programs. 2001. *Young Offender Initiative: Reentry Grant Program.* Washington, D.C.: U.S. Department of Justice, Office of Justice Programs.

Office of Justice Programs. 2002. *Serious and Violent Offender Reentry Initiative—Going Home.* Washington, D.C.: U.S. Department of Justice, Office of Justice Programs.

Pearl, Arthur and Frank Riessman. 1965. *New Careers for the Poor: The Nonprofessional in Human Service.* New York: The Free Press.

Petersilia, Joan and Elizabeth P. Deschenes. 1994. "What Punishes? Inmates Rank the Severity of Prison vs. Intermediate Sanctions." *Federal Probation* 58:38.

Petersilia, Joan and Susan Turner. 1993. "Intensive Probation and Parole." Pp. 281–335 in *Crime and Justice: An Annual Review of Research, Vol. 19,* edited by M. Tonry. Chicago, IL: University of Chicago Press.

Petry, Nancy M., Jacqueline Tedford, and Bonnie Martin. 2001. "Reinforcing Compliance with Nondrug-related Activities." *Journal of Substance Abuse Treatment* 20:33–44.

Peyton, Elizabeth A. and Robert Gossweiler. 2001. *Treatment Services in Adult Drug Courts: Report on the 1999 National Drug Court Treatment Survey* (NCJ 188085). Washington, D.C.: U.S. Department of Justice, Office of Justice Programs.

Prison Reform Trust. 1999. *Prison Incentives Scheme.* London: Prison Reform Trust.

Reentry Partnerships Initiative Report 2000. "Reducing the Threat of Recidivism." *RPI Report: Newsletter of the Reentry Partnerships Initiative* 1:12.

Reno, Janet. 2000. *Remarks of the Honorable Janet Reno on Reentry Court Initiative,* John Jay College of Criminal Justice, New York, February 10, 2000.

Rex, Sue. 2001. "Beyond Cognitive-Behaviouralism? Reflections on the Effectiveness Literature." In *Community Penalties: Change and Challenges,* edited by A. E. Bottoms, L. Gelsthorpe, and S. Rex. Cullompton, UK: Willan.

Rhine, Edward E. 1997. "Probation and Parole Supervision: In Need of a New Narrative." *Corrections Management Quarterly* 1(2):71–75.

Richie, Beth 2001. "Challenges Incarcerated Women Face as They Return to Their Communities: Findings from Life History Interviews." *Crime and Delinquency* 47:368–389.

Saleebey, Dennis. 1997. The *Strengths Perspective in Social Work Practice,* 2nd ed. New York: Longman.

Sampson, Robert J. and John Laub. 1993. *Crime in the Making: Pathways and Turning Points Through Life.* Cambridge, MA: Harvard University Press.

Schneider, Anne L. 1986. "Restitution and Recidivism Rates of Juvenile Offenders: Results from Four Experimental Studies." *Criminology* 24: 533–552.

Sherman, Lawrence W. 1993. "Defiance, Deterrence, and Irrelevance: A Theory of the Criminal Sanction." *Journal of Research in Crime and Delinquency* 30:445–473.

Simon, Jonathan. 1993. *Poor Discipline: Parole and the Social Control of the Underclass, 1890–1990.* Chicago: The University of Chicago Press.

Smith. Micheael E. 1984. "Will the Real Alternatives Please Stand Up?" *New York University Review of Law and Social Change* 12:171–97.

Sullivan, Dennis and Larry Tifft. 2001. *Restorative Justice: Healing the Foundations of Our Everyday Lives.* Monsey, NY: Willow Free Press.

Ta, Christine. 2000, October. "Prison Partnership: It's About People." *Corrections Today* 62(6): 114–123.

Taxman, Faye S., Douglas Young, James M. Byrne, Alexander Holsinger, and Donald Anspach. 2002. *From Prison Safety to Public Safety: Innovations in Offender Reentry.* University of Maryland, College Park, Bureau of Government Research.

Toch, Hans. 1975. *Men in Crisis: Human Breakdowns in Prisons.* Chicago: Aldine.

Toch, Hans. 1994. "Democratizing Prisons." *Prison Journal* 73:62–72.

Toch, Hans. 2000. "Altruistic Activity as Correctional Treatment." *International Journal of Offender Therapy and Comparative Criminology* 44:270–278.

Tocqueville, Alexis. 1835/1956. *Democracy in America.* New York: Knopf. (Original work published in 1835).

Travis, Jeremy. 1999. "Prisons, Work and Re-entry." *Corrections Today* 61(6):102–33.

Travis, Jeremy. 2000. *But They All Come Back: Rethinking Prisoner Reentry, Research in Brief—Sentencing and Corrections: Issues for the 21st Century* (NCJ 181413). Washington, D.C.: U.S. Department of Justice, National Institute of Justice.

Travis, Jeremy and Joan Petersilia. 2001. "Reentry Reconsidered: A New Look at an Old Question." *Crime and Delinquency* 47:291–313.

Tyler, Tom R., Robert J. Boeckmann, Heather J. Smith, and Yuen J. Huo. 1997. *Social Justice in a Diverse Society.* Denver, CO: Westview Press.

Uggen, Christopher and Jennifer Janikula. 1999. "Volunteerism and Arrest in the Transition to Adulthood." *Social Forces* 78:331–362.

Uggen, Christopher and Irving Piliavin. 1998. "Asymmetrical Causation and Criminal Desistance." *Journal of Criminal Law and Criminology* 88:1399–1422.

Van Voorhis, Patricia. 1985. "Restitution Outcome and Probationers' Assessments of Restitution: The Effects of Moral Development." *Criminal Justice and Behavior* 12:259–287.

van Wormer, Katherine. 2001. *Counseling Female Offenders and Victims: A Strengths-Restorative Approach.* New York: Springer.

Ward, Tony and Claire Stewart. Forthcoming. "Criminogenic Needs and Human Needs: A Theoretical Model." *Psychology, Crime and Law.*

Wexler, David, B. 2001. "Robes and Rehabilitation: How Judges Can Help Offenders 'Make Good.'" *Court Review* 38:18–23.

White, William L. 2001. *The Rhetoric of Recovery Advocacy: An Essay on the Power of Language.* [Online]. Available: http://www.bhrm.org/advocacy/recovadvocacy.htm

Wilkinson, Reginald A. 2001. "Offender Reentry: A Storm Overdue." *Corrections Management Quarterly* 5(3):46–51.

Winick, Bruce J. 1991. "Harnessing the Power of the Bet: Wagering with the Government as a Mechanism for Social and Individual Change." Pp. 219–290 in *Essays in Therapeutic Jurisprudence,* edited by David B. Wexler and Bruce J. Winick. Durham, NC: Carolina Academic Press.

30
Effective Services for Parolees With Mental Illnesses

Arthur J. Lurigio

In the 1950s, there were many more mentally ill persons in mental hospitals than there were offenders incarcerated in prison. Today just the opposite is true. Unfortunately, many of our citizens with mental illness end up housed in our prisons and jails. Lurigio's article explores a number of important issues. First, the factors that have led to increased numbers of mentally ill individuals being incarcerated are explored. Second, he discusses how parole has changed and the implications for the mentally ill offender. Third, he gives us some idea of the prevalence of mental illness among the parole population. Fourth, he discusses the programs and care that are often provided mentally ill offenders. Finally, suggestions are made for improving parole practices to meet the needs of the mentally ill offender.

In the current article, I examine the mental health services needs of persons with serious mental illnesses (PSMIs) in the correctional system. Persons with schizophrenia, bipolar disorder, or major depression are among the most severely disabled mentally ill with respect to their inability to function and the chronicity of their illnesses. Thus, for the purposes of this article, I use the term *PSMIs* to refer primarily to individuals who are afflicted with one or more of those three disorders and who also can have co-occurring substance abuse and dependence disorders.

The article is divided into four major sections. In the first section, I describe factors that have resulted in PSMIs' becoming a growing segment of the correctional population. In the second section, I explore the changing face of parole supervision and the implications of those changes for the care of PSMIs who are released from prison and into the community. Because of the paucity of data on mentally ill parolees, I discuss in section three the prevalence of mental illnesses among adult prisoners and probationers and attempt to draw inferences from those data to the parolee population. I also explore in the third section mental health care for prison inmates and special programs for PSMIs on probation and parole. I conclude the article with several suggestions for improving parole practices to meet the needs of PSMIs.

PSMIs in the Criminal Justice System

More than 25 years ago, Abramson (1972) noted that the mentally ill were becoming criminalized (i.e., they were being processed increasingly through the criminal justice system instead of the mental health system). Since that time, data have suggested that PSMIs are arrested and incarcerated at levels that exceed their representation in the general population and their tendencies to commit serious crimes. Based on these data, numerous mental health advocates and researchers have asserted that persons traditionally treated in mental health agencies and psychiatric hospitals were being shunted more frequently into jails and prisons (e.g., Gibbs, 1983; Guy, Platt, Zwerling, & Bullock, 1985; Laberge & Morin, 1995; Lamb & Grant, 1982; Lurigio & Lewis, 1987; Morgan, 1981; Teplin, 1983, 1984a, 1984b; Whitmer, 1980). The criminalization of PSMIs can be attributed to the declining populations of state hospitals, the passage of restrictive commitment laws, the splintering of treatment systems, and the war on drugs (Lurigio & Swartz, 2000; Teplin, 1984a).

A fundamental change in mental health policy, known as *deinstitutionalization*, shifted the focus of care for PSMIs from psychiatric hospitals to local community mental health centers, and this is the first major factor contributing to the criminalization of the mentally ill (Borzecki & Wormith, 1985; Grob, 1991; Lurigio & Swartz, 2000; Whitmer, 1980). After World War II, state mental hospitals began to release thousands of PSMIs to community based facilities designated to provide follow-up psychiatric treatment and services.

The policy of deinstitutionalization substantially reduced the state mental hospitals census, which fell from 559,000 patients in 1955 to 72,000 patients in 1994 (Center for Mental Health Services, 1994). The length of stay in psychiatric hospitals and the number of beds available for care also declined sharply (Kiesler, 1982). The deinstitutionalization movement was greatly fueled by journalistic exposures of patient abuse, effective medications to treat severe mental illnesses, federal entitlement programs that paid for community-based mental health services, and insurance coverage for inpatient psychiatric care in general hospitals (Sharfstein, 2000).

The policy of deinstitutionalization was never properly implemented, however. Although it achieved its goal of reducing the use of state hospitals, it never succeeded in providing adequate, appropriate, or well-coordinated outpatient treatment for large percentages of PSMIs, especially those with the most severe and chronic mental disorders (Shadish, 1989). In other words, the unsuccessful transition to community mental health care had the most tragic effects on patients least able to handle the basic tasks of daily life. Many became unbidden charges of the criminal justice system because of the dearth of treatment and other services in the community (Grob, 1991; Torrey et al., 1992).

Mental health law reform has made it difficult to commit PSMIs to psychiatric hospitals and is the second major factor contributing to the criminalization of the mentally ill (Torrey, 1997). Serious restrictions on the procedures and criteria for involuntary commitment sorely limit the use of psychiatric hospitalizations for PSMIs.

Most state mental health codes require psychiatric hospital staff to produce clear and convincing evidence that patients being committed involuntarily are either a danger to themselves or others or are so gravely disabled by their illnesses that they are unable to care for themselves. Moreover, mental health codes strengthened patients' rights to due process, according patients many of the constitutional protections granted to defendants in criminal court proceedings (e.g., due process). Thus, only the most dangerous or profoundly mentally ill are hospitalized, resulting "in greatly increased numbers of mentally ill persons in the community who may commit criminal acts and enter the criminal justice system" (Lamb & Weinberger, 1998, p. 487).

The third major factor that fostered the criminalization of the mentally ill is the compartmentalized nature of the mental health system and other treatment systems (Laberge & Morin, 1995). The mental health system consists of fragmented services for predetermined subsets of patients. The bulk of psychiatric programs, for example, are designed to treat "pure types" of clients, either mentally ill or developmentally disabled, alcoholic or chemically dependent. By the same token, a vast majority of drug treatment staff are unwilling or unable to serve persons with mental disorders and frequently refuse to accept such clients. Hence, individuals with multiple afflictions (i.e., dual diagnoses or comorbidity), who constitute large percentages of PSMIs in the criminal justice system, might be deprived entirely of services because they fail to meet stringent admission criteria (Abram & Teplin, 1991). When dually diagnosed persons—most of them with serious mental ill-nesses and substance abuse and dependence disorders—come to the attention of the police, officers are left with arrest as the only feasible response given the lack of available referrals within narrowly defined treatment systems (Brown, Ridgely, Pepper, Levine, & Ryglewicz, 1989).

The fourth major factor associated with the criminalization of PSMIs is the incarceration of large numbers of persons for violations of drug laws. Offenders convicted of drug possessions and sales (who also have high rates of drug use) constitute one of the fastest growing subpopulations in the nation's prisons (Bureau of Justice Statistics, 1999). A fairly large proportion of these incarcerees have co-occurring mental illnesses (Swartz & Lurigio, 1999), accounting partially for the growth in the prevalence of imprisoned PSMIs, most of whom are eventually placed on parole supervision (Lurigio & Swartz, 2000).

Parole Supervision in the United States

Parole release and supervision strategies have changed significantly in the past decade. Public support for parole dwindled as parole became increasingly synonymous with "leniency" for serious criminals. In continuing efforts to promote more punitive and restrictive sentencing policies and truth-in-sentencing laws, several politicians called for the abolishment of parole (Petersilia, 1999).

Such proclamations were made seemingly to assure the public that by keeping more serious offenders behind bars for longer periods of time, criminals would be receiving their "just deserts" (i.e., "bad guys would stop being let out of prison early") and communities would be safer. This message resonated with citizens and lawmakers alike. At the end of 1998, 14 states abolished early prison release by parole board authority, and several others drastically restricted

the use of parole (Ditton & Wilson 1999; Fabelo, 1999). A number of states also eliminated or greatly curtailed parole supervision but later reinstated discretionary release mechanisms and monitoring services "after data suggested that the length of prison sentence served had actually decreased following the elimination of parole and the ability to provide surveillance or treatment of high-risk offenders had significantly declined" (Petersilia, 1999, p. 482). Despite parole's many detractors, the size of the parole population grew ineluctably with the explosion of the nation's prison population. From 1981 to 1999, the rate of persons on parole in the United States climbed steadily from 136 to 352 per 100,000 adult residents, an increase of 159%. At the end of 1999, the adult parole population was 712,713, the highest number of parolees in history (Bureau of Justice Statistics, 2000a).

Contemporary parole supervision, known as "mandatory supervised release," "controlled release," and "community control," has become more surveillance oriented and punitive, shedding its traditional identity as a vehicle for offender rehabilitation and reintegration (Petersilia, 1998). Today's parole agents are more likely than their predecessors to come from law enforcement backgrounds and embrace a control model of parole supervision that focuses more on surveillance and detection and less on treatment and rehabilitation (Irwin & Austin, 1994; Parent, 1993).

The abandonment or transformation of parole had detrimental effects, overall, on correctional practices (Petersilia, 1999). Without the prospect of early parole release, inmates have fewer incentives for engaging in good behavior or participating in rehabilitative programs, and prison administrators have fewer mechanisms for relieving institutional crowding. Parole boards have lost their ability to keep more violent inmates in prison and identify the services needs of releasees, including psychiatric and drug treatments, employment and job training, and educational remediation.

Clear, Byrne, and Dvoskin (1993) argued that changes in parole release mechanisms have adversely affected mentally ill parolees, pointing to preliminary evidence that PSMIs seldom qualify for early release options and therefore remain incarcerated longer than non-PSMIs. Segregated from the general population because of their symptoms, which are frequently misconstrued as disciplinary problems, inmates with serious mental illnesses are often precluded from participating in programs that would earn them good time credits (Jemelka, Trupin, & Chiles, 1989; Kupers, 1999).

In the past few years, parole agents have had access to relatively scarce resources for offender services and have been responsible for managing large caseloads of releasees under more onerous conditions of supervision. In a survey of parole agencies, Camp and Camp (1997), for example, found that 64% assisted parolees with job training and development, 32% had drug detoxification services, 59% had drug treatment programs, but none provided specialized mental health services.

As a result of burgeoning caseloads, more stringent conditions of release, and fewer services, an unprecedented number of persons fail on parole and return to prison. In 1997, nearly 80% of California's 104,000 parolees, for example, returned to prison for violations; that year, 65% of all California prison admissions were parole violators (Austin & Lawson, 1998). As Petersilia (1999) observed, "Revocation to prison is becoming a predictable (and increasingly short) transition on the prison-to-parole and back-to-prison revolving door cycle" (p. 484).

PSMIs in Prison and on Parole

To date, no studies have directly measured the numbers of PSMIs on parole.

Nonetheless, some inferences can be drawn about the prevalence of serious mental illnesses among parolees from prison and probation statistics and from surveys of offenders and parole agency administrators. Each of these sources of data is limited, but together they provide a useful starting point for gauging the nature and extent of parolees' mental health problems.

Data on the prevalence of mental disorders among the adult prison population are often difficult to interpret and have dubious utility for prison mental health services planning, research, and policy (Pinta, 2000). Epidemiological studies of PSMIs in prisons have produced widely varying results because of differences in defining serious mental illnesses and in using diagnostic criteria and assessment tools for research purposes (Clear et al., 1993). For example, prevalence estimates in prisons for the schizophrenic disorders range from 1.5% to 4.4%; for major depression, from 3.5% to 11.4%; and for bipolar disorder, from 0.7% to 3.9% (Jemelka, Rahman, & Trupin, 1993). These rates are many times higher than those found in the general population for the same psychiatric illnesses (e.g., Robins & Regier, 1991).

According to Jemelka et al. (1993), the best methodological studies of the prevalence of PSMIs in prisons indicate that "at any given time, 10% to 15% of state prison populations are suffering from a major mental disorder and are in need of the kinds of psychiatric services associated with these illnesses" (p. 11). Pinta (1999) also reviewed studies of current mental illnesses among prisoners and found an average prevalence rate of approximately 15%.

With a state prison population in the United States of 1,366,721 at the end of 1999 (Bureau of Justice Statistics, 2000b), the preceding estimates suggest that prisons house between approximately 137,000 and 195,000 PSMIs. A majority of imprisoned PSMIs will ultimately be placed on parole or other types of conditional release and require mental health and adjunctive supportive services (Petersilia, 1999). However, in a national survey, parole agency administrators estimated that only 5% of parolees are PSMIs (Boone, 1995). If this estimate is accurate, then a total of 36,000 PSMIs were on parole at the end of 1999 (see Bureau of Justice Statistics' [2000b] estimate of number of year-end parolees).

Prisoners' and probationers' self-reports have also been used to examine rates of serious mental illnesses among these populations. A Bureau of Justice Statistics survey found that in midyear 1998, 283,800 mentally ill persons were incarcerated in prisons and jails (Ditton, 1999). More than 16% of the jail detainees and 16% of the state prison iiunates reported in a personal interview an emotional illness or an overnight stay in mental hospitals or mental health facilities (Ditton, 1999).

Mentally ill prison inmates were less likely than non–mentally ill inmates to be incarcerated for drug crimes, but they were more likely than non–mentally ill inmates to be incarcerated for violent crimes and to report that they were under the influence of alcohol and drugs at the time of their current offenses. Compared with non–mentally ill inmates, they were also more likely to report being homeless or living in a shelter during the 12 months prior to the arrests that led to their prison convictions. The percentages of mentally ill incarcerees who reported that they had obtained mental health treatment during their recent incarcerations in prisons and jails were 61% and 41%, respectively.

In the Bureau of Justice Statistics' annual survey of adult probationers, nearly 548,000 offenders were identified as mentally ill at the end of 1998 (Ditton, 1999). Probationers identified as mentally ill reported that they had experienced an "emotional condition" or had been admitted overnight in a mental hospital or mental health facility. A majority of mentally ill probationers were sentenced for public order or property crimes. Compared with nonmentally ill probationers, a higher percentage of mentally ill pro-

bationers were sentenced for violent crimes (18% vs. 28%, respectively), and a lower percentage of them were sentenced for drug crimes (23% vs. 16%, respectively) (Ditton, 1999).

In summary, data suggest that at least 5% to 10% of parolees have serious mental illnesses. To serve the needs of PSMIs effectively, more and better prevalence data must be collected. National surveys containing questions on psychiatric treatment histories should be implemented in prisons and parole agencies. Furthermore, prison and parole staff should employ standardized assessment tools at intake to determine the prevalence of serious mental illnesses and send these data to a clearinghouse that would compile the information for national prevalence estimates. In addition, standardized screening for severe mental illnesses should be done at admission to prison- and parole-based drug treatment programs to identify persons with comorbid disorders (Lurigio & Swartz, 2000).

Mental Health Care for Prisoners and Parolees

Several court cases have established the right of PSMIs to receive mental health treatment and services in prisons. In 1976, *Estelle v. Gamble* accorded prisoners the right to treatment for physical illnesses. One year later, *Bowring v. Godwin* declared that the right to treatment for physical ailments extends to psychiatric conditions. In 1980, *Vitek v. Jones* stated that mentally ill prisoners have a right to an administrative hearing, similar to a civil commitment procedure, before being transferred to a mental health care facility. Also in 1980, the landmark case of *Ruiz v. Estelle* established minimal standards of mental health care for prison inmates.

Comprehensive prison mental health care includes several key elements (Althouse, 2000; American Association for Correctional Psychology, 2000; Nieto, 1999;

Steadman & Cocozza, 1993). At intake, evaluation procedures should be employed, such as preliminary screenings, mental status examinations, and psychiatric histories, to identify inmate mental health problems that require different levels of care. Crisis intervention services should provide short-term emergency care for inmates who are an immediate danger to themselves or others.

Longer term care should involve structured treatment and rehabilitative services that consist of pharmacotherapy; life skills training; employment readiness interventions; recreational activities; and special programs for mentally ill sex offenders, inmates with codisorders, and PSMIs with HIV. Segregated facilities must be available for the care of the most severely and chronically disturbed inmates. Individualized case plans and managers should track the progress of PSMIs to ensure that current treatment and services needs are being satisfied. In addition, mechanical restraints, tasers, and other inmate management tools that exert strenuous force must be used more sparingly and judiciously with incarcerated PSMIs (Kupers, 1999). Transitional and aftercare programs help PSMIs move successfully from more to less restrictive environments in the prison, from prison to parole supervision, and from parole supervision to community reintegration (Jemelka et al., 1993; Rice & Harris, 1993). As Nieto (1999) noted, "the goal of reducing the number of parolees with mental health needs who commit new crimes or violate their parole, depends in part on the availability of aftercare services" (p. 16). Similarly, Althouse (2000) underscored the importance of community-based mental health care as a condition of parole for PSMIs. Unfortunately, the quality of correctional aftercare programs for PSMIs has been woefully inadequate (Lurigio & Swartz, 2000).

Mental disorders in parolee populations are likely to be ignored unless offenders' psychiatric symptoms are an explicit part of their offenses, are specified in their release plans, or are florid at the time of discharge (Carroll & Lurigio, 1984). Mentally ill parolees with less outwardly expressed symptoms usually receive scant attention from community corrections staff. Parole officers generally lack the experience and background necessary to deal effectively with emotionally troubled clients. Moreover, parole officers—particularly those who work in large urban jurisdictions—have large caseloads that prohibit them from focusing a lot of attention on highly troubled clients (Lurigio, 1996b). Overall, PSMIs on parole are an underidentified and underserved population, and most parole officers are unable to handle the problems of these offenders successfully (Veysey, 1994).

With additional resources and training for parole officers, parole can be an effective supervision mechanism for PSMIs (Lurigio, 1996a). By using parole as a platform for services, mandated mental health treatment and other related interventions can become conditions of supervision. However, fewer than 25% of the parole administrators responding to a national survey reported that they operated special programs for mentally ill clients (Boone, 1995). Nonetheless, some probation and parole agencies have created exclusive caseloads for PSMIs in which intensive case evaluation and management are combined with counseling, crisis stabilization, and supervised referrals for services (Veysey, 1996).

Special Programs for PSMIs

Cook County, Illinois. Several special programs in community corrections have been implemented to more effectively and humanely supervise PSMIs. The Cook County (Chicago) Adult Probation Department's Mental Health Unit (MHU), for example, has been recognized by the American Probation and Parole Association as an example of "best practices" in community corrections (Lurigio & Martin, 1998). The unit consists of five probation officers and one supervisor, each with a background in mental health. Officers spend the majority of their time monitoring their caseloads, which are significantly smaller than standard probation caseloads. Potential MHU clients can be referred to the unit by judges or other probation officers working in Chicago and in surrounding suburban court locations.

MHU officers initially screen probationers to determine offenders' eligibility for the unit. Officers base their decisions mostly on probationers' previous psychiatric histories and hospitalizations. The multiple problems of PSMIs complicate case assessments and require MHU officers to proceed with caution when they attempt to build relationships and trust with PSMIs. Rapport between officers and clients develops very slowly, and MHU's clients take longer to adjust to their probations than do clients in regular caseloads (Lurigio, Thomas, & Jones, 1996). MHU officers refer probationers for mental health services, matching them with treatment facilities and changing services if a different treatment regimen is warranted. MHU officers engage in several activities to assist clients in fulfilling their treatment mandates. They counsel probationers, help them budget their time and resources, and support them with any difficulties they experience in treatment. Officers also help clients access disability benefits, get Supplemental Security Income, and obtain medical cards. Through MHU's efforts, the Cook County Adult Probation Department was approved as a site for Medicaid reimbursements.

California. The California Department of Corrections provides specialized services for mentally ill parolees through five Parolee Outpatient Clinics (POCs) and a Conditional Release Program known as CONREP (Nieto, 1999). POCs are located in San Diego, Los Angeles, San Francisco, Sacramento, and Fresno. The clinics serve mentally ill parolees exclusively and are staffed by licensed psychiatrists and psychologists. Although POCs served nearly 9,000 mentally ill parolees in 1998, estimates suggest that 70% of the inmates who received mental health care in prison "do not receive the same level of care while on parole" and that 50% of them live outside the catchment area of the five POCs (Nieto, 1999).

CONREP is a small but successful community-based program for PSMIs who are transferred from prisons to state hospitals and to outpatient psychiatric programs as a condition of parole. Eligible participants must have been in mental health treatment in prison for 90 days or more during the past year and must be assessed as a substantial risk to public safety. After completing treatment in a secured hospital facility, CONREP parolees are held to stringent conditions of release and receive mental health care in the community. Studies show that CONREP participants are 4 times less likely to reoffend than are unconditional release offenders, a success rate that is comparable to the performance of parolees in similar programs in New York and Oregon (California Department of Mental Health, 1998).

Baltimore. The U.S. Parole Office in Baltimore developed a specialized mental health program in 1996 for mentally ill offenders on federal probation, parole, supervised release, or conditional release in the community (Roskes & Feldman, 1999, 2000). The program involves the close coordination of a probation officer with community-based treatment providers, including a psychiatrist and two master's-level therapists. Services consist of psychiatric and medical interventions, drug treatment, assertive case management, urine toxicology screening, and integrated programs for PSMIs with substance abuse and dependence disorders. When necessary, the program's clinical staff places clients in intensive outpatient, inpatient, or residential remedial services.

The program's mental health professionals and probation officer routinely exchange information about clients' progress. Staff coordinate their responses to participants' failures to adhere to treatment or other conditions of release, and they typically employ therapeutic interventions before they resort to punitive sanctions in response to those failures.

A preliminary study of the program found that clients' violation rates fell from 56% before they were in the program to 19% after they participated in the program (Roskes & Feldman, 1999). In Roskes and Feldman's (2000) view, the success of the program depends on several factors, such as individualized treatment plans and services, guaranteed payment to providers for underinsured or uninsured clients, a contract between the program and a pharmacy to ensure the continual flow of medications, and a staff philosophy that views rule infractions and setbacks as treatment deficits instead of grounds for violations.

Improving Parole Practices for PSMIs

As my preceding discussion suggests, services for mentally ill parolees should be provided through special programs that are staffed by officers with educational backgrounds and experiences in the mental health domain. Specialized units can monitor smaller caseloads, which is crucial because parolees with severe mental illnesses require a lot of time and attention (Nieto, 1999). In general, this population has multiple problems: comorbidity with substance abuse disorders and developmental disabilities, poor physical health, housing and financial difficulties, homelessness, joblessness, and a lack of social support (Veysey, 1996). These clients need habilitation as much as rehabilitation. As Veysey (1996) has written,

For [parole] services to be successful in the supervision of persons with mental illness, they must address the broad range of offender needs. This does not mean that [parole agencies] must provide all of these services. They must, however, collaborate closely with the community services agencies that provide mental health, substance abuse, health care, and other human services. (p. 156)

A special program's target population of PSMIs and its criteria for client eligibility must be clearly defined and communicated to the corrections staff who transfer or refer PSMIs to specialized mental health units after their release from prison. Without this communication, there is a danger of inappropriate clients' (e.g., persons with substance abuse problems only or difficult clients with no mental illnesses or psychiatric histories) being "dumped" into the program, increasing the difficulty of keeping case loads down to a reasonable size. Moreover, repeated rejection of inappropriate placements might make prison discharge staff less willing to refer suitable candidates to the program. When everyone involved in referring clients to the program understands client admission requirements, such problems can be minimized from the outset.

Mental health agencies are sometimes reluctant to accept mentally ill parolees because of their criminal backgrounds and the stigmatization of imprisonment; other agencies reject PSMIs because of their dual diagnoses or lack of insurance (Lurigio & Martin, 1998). According to Roskes and Feldman (1999), mental health practitioners often refuse to treat PSMIs with criminal histories because they fear that such clients will victimize them or that they will be forced to testify in court about violations of treatment conditions or other rule-breaking behaviors.

Parole administrators should sign contractual agreements with local mental health agencies to ensure that clients will be accepted for services. Absent these agreements, placements into treatment will be haphazard. Forging formal agreements will also give program staff an opportunity to tout their efforts and to cultivate long-term professional relationships with mental health practitioners.

The collaboration and coordination of parole and mental health staff are essential to the success of any special programming for PSMIs on parole (Roskes & Feldman, 1999). As Boone (1995) noted, however, "turf issues and boundaries [between the mental health and criminal justice systems] seem to present a monumental impediment to serving the mentally ill probationer or parolee" (p. 18). Along similar lines, efforts should be made to link criminal justice and mental health databases. Such linkages would ensure the expeditious exchange of information about parolees who are receiving or have received psychiatric services (Nieto, 1999).

Cross-training for mental health and correctional staff goes a long way toward increasing their mutual understanding and respect. In addition, cross-training greatly improves the working relationships between the two groups. Most important, cross-training encourages a team approach to working with clients.

Parole agents should find alternative strategies for handling the technical violations of releasees with mental illnesses. In Veysey's (1996) words, "if community supervision staff adhere to rigid sanctions for technical violations with regard to treatment compliance, special-needs clients—particularly those with mental illness—are likely to fail" (p. 158).

Violations are often a function of clients' symptoms or their difficulties in following directions. A failure to report, for example, might result from cognitive impairment, delusions, confusion, or side effects of psychotropic medications. As a rule, incarceration or other harsh penalties should be avoided when responding to such instances. More effective options include relapse prevention techniques and systems of progressive sanctions. Parole officers can view technical violations as opportunities to build closer alliances with PSMIs and assist them in avoiding future, and more serious, problems including subsequent criminal activity. As Nieto (1999) recommended,

> Mentally disordered parolees who violate the terms of their parole, or who fail to maintain a required treatment regime and aftercare program, need to be committed to either a locked psychiatric facility for treatment or a less restrictive mental health treatment program that meets the parolee's treatment needs. (p. 21)

Clinical consultations with psychiatrists and psychologists can be vital in helping parole agents manage case loads with PSMIs. Mental health specialists, for example, can lend their expertise in diagnosing and managing difficult clients, and these specialists can help sharpen staffs' diagnostic and clinical skills during case conferences. If funding is available, psychiatrists should be hired to dispense medications on-site, a tremendous asset to programs given clients' typically poor compliance with medication regimens. Mental health professionals can also support and encourage program staff and help relieve the stress and discouragement that inevitably arises when dealing with PSMIs.

The National Coalition for Mental and Substance Abuse Health Care in the Justice System stated that any comprehensive vision of care for PSMIs on probation and parole must

- build lasting bridges between the mental health and criminal justice systems, leading to coordinated and continual health care for clients of both systems;

- involve clients in treatment decisions;

- ensure public safety as well as the safety of offenders;

- facilitate the successful integration of offenders into the community;

- promote offender responsibility and self-sufficiency;

- permit equal access to all health care services, including medical, psychiatric, substance abuse, and psychological interventions;

- avoid discriminating against or stigmatizing PSMIs;

- accommodate clients with multiple needs and problems;

- be sensitive and responsive to the special needs of mentally ill women and people of color by developing diverse, culturally sensitive programs;

- require families to be involved in treatment and supervision plans of PSMIs;

- match services and treatments to clients' specific problems and needs;

- and raise public awareness about PSMIs in the criminal justice system. (Lurigio, 1996b, p. 168)

In conclusion, the multifarious problems of parolees will always necessitate a team approach for interventions to be effective. Entire communities should assume responsibility for the care of mentally ill parolees by implementing neighborhood-based, integrated, and accountable networks of treatment, services, and support. These networks should be designed by all stakeholders involved in identifying and treating PSMIs on community corrections supervision: prison discharge staff, parole agents, mental health and drug treatment practitioners, and habilitation specialists who provide the mentally ill with housing and life skills training.

Study Questions

1. What are some of the reasons that the number of mentally ill offenders has grown?

2. How have parole supervision strategies changed over the years?

3. What are some of the estimates of the number of mentally ill parolees?

4. What are the elements of comprehensive prison mental health care?

5. Describe some of the special programs for mentally ill parolees.

6. How does the author suggest we improve the care of mentally ill parolees?

References

Abram, K. M., & Teplin, L. A. (1991). Co-occurring disorders among mentally ill jail detainees. *American Psychologist, 46,* 1036–1045.

Abramson, M. F. (1972). The criminalization of mentally disordered behavior: Possible side effect of a new mental health law. *Hospital and Community Psychiatry, 23,* 101–107.

Althouse, R. (2000). AACP standards: A historical overview (1978–1980). *Criminal Justice and Behavior, 27,* 430–433.

American Association for Correctional Psychology. (2000). Standards for psychology services in jails, prisons, correctional facilities, and agencies. *Criminal Justice and Behavior, 27,* 433–494.

Austin, J., & Lawson, R. (1998). *Assessment of California parole violations and recommended intermediate programs and polices.* San Francisco: National Council on Crime and Delinquency.

Boone, H. B. (1995). Mental illness in probation and parole populations: Results from a national survey. *Perspectives, 19,* 14–26.

Borzecki, M., & Worrnith, J. S. (1985). The criminalization of the psychiatrically ill: A review of the Canadian perspective. *Psychiatric Journal of the University of Ottawa, 10,* 241–247.

Brown, V. B., Ridgely, M. S., Pepper, B., Levine, I. S., & Ryglewicz, H. (1989). The dual crisis: Mental illness and substance abuse. *American Psychologist, 44,* 565–569.

Bureau of Justice Statistics. (1999). *Prison statistics.* Washington, DC: Author.

Bureau of Justice Statistics. (2000a). *Prison statistics.* Washington, DC: Author.

Bureau of Justice Statistics. (2000b). *Probation and parole statistics.* Washington, DC: Author.

California Department of Mental Health. (1998). *Questions and answers about the effectiveness of CONREP.* Sacramento, CA: Author.

Camp, C., & Camp, G. (1997). *The corrections yearbook.* South Salem, NY: Criminal Justice Institute.

Carroll, J. S., & Lurigio, A. J. (1984). Conditional release on probation and parole: Diagnosis, prediction, and treatment. In L. Teplin (Ed.), *Mental health and criminal justice* (pp. 247–351). Beverly Hills, CA: Sage.

Center for Mental Health Services, Survey and Analysis Branch. (1994). *Resident patients in state and county mental hospitals.* Rockville, MD: Author.

Clear, T. R., Byrne, J. M., & Dvoskin, J. A. (1993). The transition from being an inmate: Discharge planning, parole, and community-based services for mentally ill offenders. In H. J. Steadman & J. J. Cocozza (Eds.), *Mental illness in America's prisons* (pp. 131–158). Seattle, WA: The National Coalition for the Mentally Ill in the Criminal Justice System.

Ditton, P. P. (1999). *Mental health and treatment of inmates and probationers.* Washington, DC: U.S. Department of Justice, Bureau of Justice Statistics.

Ditton, P. P., & Wilson, D. J. (1999). *Truth in sentencing in state prisons.* Washington, DC: U.S. Department of Justice, Bureau of Justice Statistics.

Fabelo, T. (1999). *Biennial report to the 76th Texas legislature.* Austin, TX: Criminal Justice Policy Council.

Gibbs, J. J. (1983). Problems and priorities: Perceptions of jail custodians and social service providers. *Journal of Criminal Justice, 11,* 327–349.

Grob, G. N. (1991). *From asylum to community: Mental health policy in modern America.* Princeton, NJ: Princeton University Press.

Guy, E., Platt, J. J., Zwerling, I., & Bullock. S. (1985). Mental health status of prisoners in an urban jail. *Criminal Justice and Behavior, 12,* 29–53.

Irwin, J., & Austin, J. (1994). *It's about time: America's imprisonment binge.* Belmont, CA: Wadsworth.

Jemelka, R., Trupin, E. W., & Chiles, J. A. (1989). The mentally ill in prison: A review. *Hospital and Community Psychiatry, 40,* 481–490.

Jemelka, R.P., Rahman, S., & Trupin, E. W. (1993). Prison mental health: An overview. In H. J. Steadman and J. J. Cocozza (Eds.), *Mental illness in America's prisons* (pp. 9–24). Seattle, WA: National Coalition for the Mentally Ill in the Criminal Justice System.

Kiesler, C.A. (1982). Public and professional myths about mental hospitalization: An empir-ical reassessment of policy-related beliefs. *American Psychologist, 37,* 1323–1339.

Kupers, T. (1999). *Prison madness: The mental health crisis behind bars and what we must do about it.* San Francisco: Jossey-Bass.

Laberge, D., & Morin, D. (1995). The overuse of criminal justice dispositions: Failure of diversionary policies in the management of mental health problems. *International Journal of Law and Psychiatry, 18,* 389–414.

Lamb, H. R., & Grant, R. W. (1982). The mentally ill in an urban county jail. *Archives of General Psychiatry, 39,* 17–22.

Lamb, H. R., & Weinberger, L. E. (1998). Persons with severe mental illness in jails and prisons: A review. *Psychiatric Services, 49,* 483–492.

Lurigio, A. J. (1996a). Responding to the mentally ill on probation and parole: Recommendations and action plans. In A. J. Lurigio (Ed.), *Community corrections in America: New directions and sounder investments for persons with mental illness and codisorders* (pp. 166–171). Seattle, WA: National Coalition for Mental and Substance Abuse Health Care in the Justice System.

Lurigio, A. J. (Ed.). (1996b). *Community corrections in America: New directions and sounder investments for persons with mental illness and codisorders.* Seattle, WA: National Coalition for Mental and Substance Abuse Health Care in the Justice System.

Lurigio, A. J., & Lewis, D. A. (1987). *Toward a taxonomy of the criminal mental patient.* Unpublished manuscript, Northwestern University, Center for Urban Affairs and Policy Research, Evanston, IL.

Lurigio, A. J., & Martin, N. (1998). Casework practice with mentally ill probationers. In R. A. Wilkinson (Ed.), *Best practices: Excellence in corrections* (pp. 280–284). Lanham, MD: American Correctional Association.

Lurigio, A. J., & Swartz, J. A. (2000). Changing the contours of the criminal justice system to meet the needs of persons with serious mental illness. In J. Horney (Ed.), *Policies, processes, and decisions of the criminal justice system* (pp. 45–108). Washington, DC: U.S. Department of Justice, National Institute of Justice.

Lurigio, A. J., Thomas, J., & Jones, M. E. (1996). *A study of the Mental Health Unit operations.* Chicago: Cook County Adult Probation Department.

Morgan, C. (1981). Developing mental health services for local jails. *Criminal Justice and Behavior, 8,* 259–273.

Nieto, M. (1999). *Mentally ill offenders in California's criminal justice system.* Sacramento, CA: California Research Bureau.

Parent, D. (1993). Structuring policies to address sanctions for absconders and violators. In E. Rhine (Ed.), *Reclaiming offender accountability: Intermediate sanctions for probation and parole violators* (pp. 43–58). Laurel, MD: American Correctional Association.

Petersilia, J. M. (1998). Probation and parole. In M. Tonry (Ed.), *The handbook of crime and punishment* (pp. 563–588). New York: Oxford University Press.

Petersilia, J. M. (1999). Parole and prisoner reentry in the United States. In M. Tonry & J. M. Petersilia (Eds.), *Prisons* (pp. 479–529). Chicago: University of Chicago Press.

Pinta, E. R. (1999). The prevalence of serious mental disorders among U.S. prisoners. *Correctional Mental Health Report, 1,* 34, 44–47.

Pinta, E. R. (2000). Prison mental disorder rates—What do they mean? *Correctional Mental Health Report, 1,* 81, 91–92.

Rice, M., & Harris, G. T. (1993). Treatment for prisoners with mental disorders. In H. J. Steadman & J. J. Cocozza (Eds.), *Mental illness in America's prisons* (pp. 91–130). Seattle, WA: National Coalition for the Mentally Ill in the Criminal Justice System.

Robins, L. N., & Regier, D. A. (Eds.). (1991). *Psychiatric disorders of America: The epidemiologic catchment area study.* New York: Free Press.

Roskes, E., & Feldman, R. (1999). A collaborative community-based treatment program for offenders with mental illness. *Psychiatric Services, 50,* 1614–1619.

Roskes, E., & Feldman, R. (2000). Treater or monitor? Collaboration betWeen mental health providers and probation officers. *Correctional Mental Health Report, 1,* 69–70.

Shadish, W. R. (1989). Private sector care for chronically mentally ill individuals: The more things change, the more they stay the same. *American Psychologist, 44,* 1142–1147.

Sharfstein, S. S. (2000). Whatever happened to community mental health? *Psychiatric Services, 51,* 616–626.

Steadman, H. J., & Cocozza. J. J. (Eds.). (1993). *Mental illness in America's prisons.* Seattle, WA: National Coalition for the Mentally Ill in the Criminal Justice System.

Steadman, H. J., McCarty, D. W., & Morrissey, J. P. (1989). *The mentally ill in jail: Planning for essential services.* New York: Guilford.

Swartz, J. A., & Lurigio, A. J. (1999). Psychiatric illness and comorbidity among adult male jail detainees in drug treatment. *Psychiatric Services, 50,* 1628–1630.

Teplin, L. A. (1983). The criminalization of the mentally ill: Speculation in search of data. *Psychological Bulletin, 94,* 54–67.

Teplin, L. A. (1984a). Criminalizing mental disorder. *American Psychologist, 39,* 794–803.

Teplin, L. A. (1984b). Managing disorder: Police handling of the mentally ill. In L. A. Teplin (Ed.), *Mental health and criminal justice* (pp. 157–176). Beverly Hills, CA: Sage.

Teplin, L. A. (1991). Police handling of the mentally ill: Styles, strategies, and implications. In H. J. Steadman (Ed.), *Effectively addressing the mental health needs of jail detainees* (pp. 10–14). Seattle, WA: National Coalition for the Mentally Ill in the Criminal Justice System.

Torrey, E. E. (1997). *Out of the shadows: Confronting America's mental illness crisis.* New York: John Wiley.

Torrey, E. E., Steiber, J., Ezekiel, J., Wolfe, S. M., Sharfstein, J., Noble, J. H., & Rynn, L. M. (1992). *Criminalizing the seriously mentally ill.* Washington, DC: Public Citizen's Health Research Group and the National Alliance for the Mentally Ill.

Veysey, B. (1994). Challenges for the future. In *Topics in community corrections* (pp. 3–10). Longmont, CO: U.S. Department of Justice, National Institute of Corrections.

Veysey, B. M. (1996). Effective strategies for providing mental health services to probationers with mental illness. In A. J. Lurigio (Ed.), *Community corrections in America: New directions and sounder investments for persons with mental illness and codisorders* (pp. 151–165). Seattle, WA: National Coalition for Mental and Substance Abuse Health Care in the Justice System.

Whitmer, G. (1980). From hospitals to jails: The fate of California's deinstitutionalized mentally ill. *American Journal of Orthopsychiatry, 50,* 65–75.

Part VI

New Directions

The final section of this book examines several topics, including the United States' obsession with "getting tough" on offenders, the movement toward restorative justice, and a consideration of the costs associated with punishment. We begin by looking at "three strikes and you're out," the increased use of incarceration and the death penalty, and the disturbing consequences of how these policies make it difficult to be optimistic about the direction of corrections. Although public policy has led to increased use of incarceration, some have advocated a more humane approach to dealing with crime through the process of restorative justice. Whether this approach is feasible is discussed in the Levrant et al. article. Finally, faced with budget cuts and financial downturns, many legislators are questioning the wisdom of continued prison population growth. The question for the future is how corrections will respond to the challenge of maintaining public safety while reducing recidivism rates of the offenders it serves at a price we can afford. Ultimately, public safety is best served when offenders leave the correctional system and lead crime-free, prosocial lives. ✦

31
Three Strikes and You're Out
The Political Sentencing Game

Peter J. Benekos
Alida V. Merlo

*"Three strikes and you're out." This phrase is
now being used throughout the country in
reference to particular criminal sanctions.
The analogy to baseball is not accidental; it
has appeal as an all-American slogan. But, as
this selection by Peter J. Benekos and Alida V.
Merlo shows, the new three-strikes laws are
just that: slogans. The only benefit of these
laws is in political rhetoric. Unlike most
other topics in corrections, there is little debate about the utility of the three-strikes laws.
Nearly all penologists agree that such laws
are ineffective. The authors here clearly demonstrate how the politicalization of crime
control translates into poor public policy.*

The "WAR on crime" has added another
weapon to the arsenal of getting tough on
crime: "three strikes and you're out." From
the slogans of "just say no" to "if you can't do
the time, don't do the crime," it is ironic that
the latest metaphor for crime policy parallels the baseball players' strike of 1994. The
recent initiatives to mandate life sentences
for three-time convicted felons are responses to the public's fear of crime and
frustration with the criminal justice system
and indicate the continuation of politicized
crime policy.

In the 30 states that have introduced
"three-strikes" legislation and in the 10 that

have passed tougher sentencing for repeat
offenders (*Criminal Justice Newsletter*,
1994c, p. 1), politicians have demonstrated
quick-fix responses to the complex and difficult issues of crime, violence, and public
anxiety over the disorder and decline in
America. The United States Congress also
finally overcame differences to legislate a
new get-tough crime bill that not only
includes a provision of life imprisonment
for a third felony conviction but also authorizes the death penalty "for dozens of existing or newly created federal crimes"
(Idelson, 1994, p. 2138).

Notwithstanding the critics of these sentencing policies (Currie, 1994; Gangi, 1994;
Gladwell, 1994; Kramer, 1994; Lewis, 1994;
Raspberry, 1993) politicians have rushed to
embrace the "get even tougher" sentencing
proposals because they have learned that
"politically, it still works" (Schneider, 1993,
p. 24). "Crime used to be the Republicans'
issue, just as the economy was the Democrats'. No more" (Schneider, 1993, p. 24). In
his commentary on how the "misbegotten"
three-strikes piece of legislation became
part of the crime bill, Lewis writes that "the
answer is simple: politics. Democrats
wanted to take the crime issue away from
Republicans. Republicans responded by
sounding 'tougher' " . . . and "President
Clinton wanted something—anything—
labeled 'crime bill' " (Lewis, 1994, p. A13).

This [chapter] reviews the ideological
and political context of these sentencing
reforms, examines get-tough legislation in
three states and on the Federal level, and
considers the consequences of increasing
sentencing severity. The review suggests
that baseball sentencing will further distort
the distribution of punishments and will
contribute to an escalation of political posturing on crime policies.

Politicalization of Crime

In a sense, this is what baseball sentencing is about: using the fear factor as a politi-

cal issue; relying on what Broder calls "bumper sticker simplicity" to formulate crime policy (1994b, p. 6), and taking a tough stance on sentencing criminals as symbolic of doing something about crime. The politicizing of crime as a national issue can be traced to the 1964 Presidential election when Barry Goldwater promoted the theme of "law and order" and challenged Lyndon Johnson's "war on poverty" as a soft-headed response to crime and disorder (Cronin, Cronin, & Milakovich, 1981).

Thirty years ago the voters chose "social reform, civil rights, and increased education and employment opportunities" over a "get-tough response to crime that included expanding police powers and legislating tougher laws" (Merlo & Benekos, 1992a, p. x). Today's election results reflect a reversal of policy and the expansion of the Federal role in crime control (*Congressional Digest*, 1994).

Even though Johnson won the 1964 election, the "nationalization" of the crime issue was established and the Federal Government began "a new era of involvement in crime control" (*Congressional Digest*, 1994, p. 162): "the law and order issue just wouldn't go away" (Cronin et al., 1981, p. 22) and it became embedded in the public's mind and on the national agenda (Merlo and Benekos, 1992a, p. x).

In his 1965 address to Congress, President Johnson "called for the establishment of a blue ribbon panel to probe 'fully and deeply into the problems of crime in our Nation'" (*Congressional Digest*, 1994, p. 162). This led to the Law Enforcement Assistance Act of 1965, the Omnibus Crime Control and Safe Streets Act of 1968, and more recently to the Comprehensive Crime Control Act of 1984, the Anti-Drug Abuse Act of 1986, the Anti-Drug Abuse Act of 1988, the Crime Control Act of 1990, and finally, the Violent Crime Control and Law Enforcement Act of 1994 (*Congressional Digest*, 1994, pp. 163, 192), which was signed by President Clinton on September 13, 1994. Since 1965 to 1992, the Federal spending for the "administration of justice" has "risen from $535 million to an estimated $11.7 billion" (*Congressional Digest*, 1994, p. 162).

From Horton to Davis and McFadden

The lessons of crime and politics were learned again in the Presidential election of 1988 when the then Vice President George Bush invoked the get-tough issue when he challenged Massachusetts Governor Michael Dukakis on his state's correctional policies that allowed a convicted murderer serving a life sentence to participate in the furlough program (Merlo & Benekos, 1992a, p. x).

Willie Horton became the poster child of Republicans and reminded Democrats (as well as doubting Republicans) that appearing to be soft on crime (and criminals) was politically incorrect. The Willie Horton incident "effectively crystalized a complex problem by presenting it as a dramatic case history of one individual" (The Sentencing Project, 1989, p. 3). Ironically, even without the Willie Horton incident, the 1980s were a period of conservative crime policy in which get-tough sentencing reforms were implemented throughout the country (Merlo & Benekos, 1992b). As part of these get-tough, get-fair, just deserts, determinate sentencing reforms, penalties were increased, mandatory sentences were legislated, and prisons became overcrowded (Shover & Einstadter, 1988, p. 51).

Similar to the Willie Horton situation, in 1993 another tragic case also became a "condensation symbol" for the public's perception that crime was increasing, that violent criminals were getting away with murder, that sentences were too lenient, and that offenders were getting out of prison after serving only small portions of their sentences. The California case which outraged the public was the October 1, 1993, abduction and murder of 12-year-old Polly Klaas by a parolee who had been released after serving 8 years of a 16-year sentence for a 1984 kidnapping (*New York Times,* 1993, p. A22).

Richard Allen Davis, who was arrested November 30, 1993, had convictions for two kidnappings, assault, and robbery and had spent "a good part of his adult life in jail" (*New York Times,* 1993, p. A22). At the time of his arrest, he was in violation of a pass from the halfway house that he was released to and therefore was also charged as a parole violator.

This type of crime fuels public fear and outrage and becomes fodder for politicians who respond by calling for tougher sentences to curb the perceived increases in crime and violence. Coincidentally to Davis' arrest, the FBI released its semiannual tabulation of crime which "showed that the rate of crime as a whole declined 5 percent in the first six months of 1993 from the same period the year before and that the rate of violent crime dropped 3 percent" (Lewis, 1993, p. B6).

These data, however, are not comforting to a public which sees the Klaas incident as evidence of the horrific and violent crimes which grip the nation in fear. "The public doesn't rely on statistics to generate their perception of the level of crime. People's perceptions are based on what they see and hear going on around them" (Michael Rand of the Justice Department, cited in Lewis, 1993, p. B6). In reviewing 1994 state political campaigns, Kurtz observed that "although other traditional hot-button issues—welfare, taxes, immigration, personal ethics—also are prominent, crime remains the 30-second weapon of choice, and the charge most often is that an incumbent is responsible for turning dangerous inmates loose" (1994, p. 12).

Recent 'Baseball Sentencing' Legislation

In order to provide a clearer picture of the legislation that is designed to impose mandatory life sentences (without possibility of parole or early release), we examined the recently enacted Violent Crime Control and Law Enforcement Act of 1994 and similar statutes in the states of Washington, California, and Georgia. The Violent Crime Control and Law Enforcement Act of 1994, signed by President Clinton on September 13, 1994, authorizes mandatory life imprisonment for persons convicted on two previous separate occasions of two serious violent felonies or one or more serious violent felonies and one or more serious drug offenses. According to the new Federal code, a "serious violent felony" includes offenses ranging from murder and aggravated sexual abuse to arson, aircraft piracy, car-jacking, and extortion (U.S. Government Printing Office, 1994, pp. 194–195).

In the State of Washington, the "Persistent Offender Accountability Law" was approved by the voters in November 1993 by a 3 to 1 victory and became effective in December 1993 (*Corrections Digest,* 1994a). Under the revised statute, an offender who is categorized as a "persistent offender" must be sentenced to life imprisonment without any hope of parole if he or she has been convicted of a "most serious offense" and has two prior separate convictions for crimes that meet the "most serious offense" definition (*Washington Laws,* 1994, p. 1). Included in the definition of "most serious offense" are crimes ranging from "manslaughter in the second degree" to "promoting prostitution in the first degree" or any felony defined under any law as a Class A felony or criminal solicitation of or criminal conspiracy to commit a Class A felony (*Washington Laws,* 1994, p. 13).

In March 1994, Governor Pete Wilson signed California Assembly Bill 971 into law. Its most publicized provision is the requirement that judges impose ". . . an indeterminate sentence of a minimum of 25 years to life, or triple the normal sentence, whichever is greater, on offenders convicted of certain serious or violent felonies if they have two previous convictions for any felony" (Tucker, 1994, p. 7). The offenses included in the category of serious or violent felony range from murder and rape to burglary, any felony using a firearm, and selling or giving drugs such as heroin, cocaine, and PCP to a minor (California Penal Code, §1192.7).

In Georgia the voters approved "The Sentence Reform Act of 1994" which authorizes life imprisonment without possibility of parole, pardon, early release, leave, or any other measure designed to reduce the sentence for any person convicted of a second "serious violent felony." Under Georgia law, a serious violent felony is defined as ". . . murder or felony murder, armed robbery, kidnapping, rape, aggravated child molestation, aggravated sodomy and aggravated sexual battery" (Georgia Statutes, 17-10-6.1).

Despite the fact that this law became effective January 1, 1995, any felony committed before that date in Georgia or in another jurisdiction, which meets the Georgia definition of a "serious violent felony," would count as one of the "strikes." The Federal code and the Washington and California laws contain similar language. The offender's criminal record in the state where the most recent conviction occurs as well as his or her record in other states or on the Federal level determine the number of "strikes." In short, an offender may already have the requisite number of convictions even as the mandatory sentencing provisions first become effective.

When the Federal criminal code and the three-strikes laws are compared, it appears that the Georgia law is the most restrictive. Unlike the others, it contains a "two-strikes" versus a "three-strikes" provision. However, upon closer inspection, Georgia's law is the only one of the four reviewed here that requires mandatory life imprisonment for crimes that can be strictly identified as violent. By contrast, the Federal law and the Washington and California laws include a variety of nonviolent crimes such as burglary, prostitution, and drug trafficking that

can result in a mandatory life sentence in prison. In California, for example, a criminal twice convicted of the property crime of burglary may be sentenced to life in prison for a third burglary conviction.

In order to clarify the intent of the legislation—that these offenders serve lengthy prison sentences—some states such as Washington stipulate that the Governor is "urged to refrain from pardoning or granting clemency" to offenders sentenced until the offender has reached the age of 60 (*Final Legislative Report* 1994, p. 1). In order to discourage the Governor's use of pardons as a way to minimize the effects of the legislation, Washington law mandates that the Governor provide reports twice each year on the status of these "persistent offenders" he or she has released during his or her term of office and that the reports continue to be made for as long as the offender lives or at least 10 years after his or her release from prison (*Final Legislative Report*, 1994, p. 1).

Effects of Baseball Legislation

Thermodynamic Effects of Baseball Punishment

While the get-tough rhetoric continues to capture the public's support, the consequences of increased sentencing penalties are having an unintended but not unanticipated impact on the criminal justice system. In California where the mandatory statute "makes no distinction between 'violent' and 'serious' felonies . . . a superior court judge, Lawrence Antolini, declared the three-strikes law unconstitutional" because it "metes out 'cruel and unusual' jail terms" for nonviolent criminals and "robs justices of the power to evaluate the nuances of individual cases" (Peyser, 1994, p. 63). In an article about the tough California sentencing law, a *New York Times* report indicated that "judges in many California jurisdictions have been indicating their reluctance to follow the new law . . . by changing some felony charges to misdemeanors" (1994c, p. A9). In addition, Supreme Court Justice Anthony Kennedy has also criticized the "increasing use of mandatory minimum sentences, saying the practice was unwise and often unfair" (*New York Times*, 1994a, p. A14).

And, as some judges find fault with the harsher sentencing laws, prosecutors are also raising doubts about the ability of the courts to handle the number of cases which fall under the baseball sentencing provisions. In California, where the District Attorney's Association opposed the three-strikes law, Los Angeles County District Attorney Gil Garcetti voiced concerns that the broad nature of California's sentencing law would expand the number of felons subject to life in prison (*Criminal Justice Newsletter*, 1994a, p. 6). In an interview with National Public Radio, Garcetti stated that Los Angeles County alone would need 40 more prosecutors to handle the increase in the number of cases (National Public Radio, 1994). What Garcetti was referring to is the potential increase in the number of accused offenders who refuse to plea-bargain and would rather take their chances on a trial (Peyser, 1994, p. 63). For example, a convicted murderer in California, Henry Diaz, originally entered guilty pleas to three counts of child molestation. When he learned that "one of the incidents occurred after the 'three-strikes' law went into effect on March 7 (1994), making (him) eligible for sentencing under the new law," he withdrew his guilty plea and requested a trial (*New York Times*, 1994d, p. A19). Responses such as this give the California Judicial Council reason to "estimate that the new law will require an additional $25 million per year to try more felony cases" (*Criminal Justice Newsletter*, 1994a, p. 7).

These types of judicial responses illustrate a hydraulic, thermodynamic effect where getting tough may in fact result in being softer. For example, "the law allows prosecutors to move to dismiss criminals'

prior convictions 'in the furtherance of justice'—namely, if they believe the law mandates an elephantine sentence for a puny offense" (Peyser, 1994, p. 63). Another avenue to circumvent the law is a "wiggle" factor where district attorneys can "classify certain crimes that straddle the felony-misdemeanor line as misdemeanors" (Peyser, 1994, p. 63).

In addition, some district attorneys have reported "instances in which crime victims had told prosecutors they would not testify if a conviction meant the defendant would fall under the requirements of the new law" (*New York Times*, 1994c, p. A9). As Griset observed in her study of determinate sentence reforms, legislators fail to "recognize the inevitability of the exercise of discretion at all points in the criminal justice system" and as a result develop policies which are incongruent and inconsistent with the reality of the criminal justice system (1991, p. 181). The above examples illustrate her conclusions and also suggest an inverse relationship between the severity of sanctions and the likelihood that those sanctions will be applied (Black, 1976). Police officers are also experiencing the effects of these baseball "swings" at offenders: "suspects who are more prone to use violence when cornered" (Egan, 1994, p. A11). In one case in Seattle, a suspect threatened to shoot police after he was cornered. "After the suspect was taken into custody, the police were told by his acquaintances that he thought he was facing a three-strikes charge. Rather than face life in prison, he decided to confront officers" (Egan, 1994, p. A11).

Prisons and Prisoners: Economic and Social Impact

With crime uppermost in votes' minds, the new Federal crime bill was frequently featured in the 1994 election campaigns. Incumbent members of Congress informed their constituents of the immediate effects of the legislation on their home state. For example, New Jersey has been promised $77 million for new prisons and 3,800 police officers. Pennsylvania is slated for $110 million for prisons and 4,200 new police officers (*The Vindicator*, 1994, p. A5). These tangible results of the crime bill are intended to provide voters with a sense of security and satisfaction. However, the public has not yet focused on the long-term costs of these new initiatives.

There is little doubt that an immediate effect of the legislation will be to increase the already enormous prison population in the United States. According to The Sentencing Project research, there are currently 1.3 million Americans incarcerated (Mauer, 1994a, p. 1). The incarceration rate is 519 per 100,000, making the United States' rate second only to Russia's (Mauer, 1994a, p. 1). In the United States, the incarceration rate of African-Americans (1,947 per 100,000) as compared to the incarceration rate of whites (306 per 100,000) is even more striking; Mauer's analysis illustrates that there are currently more African-American males in prisons and jails in the United States than enrolled in institutions of higher education (Mauer, 1994a, pp. 1–2). In terms of future projections, the National Council on Crime and Delinquency (NCCD) contends that if the remainder of the states follow in the footsteps of the Federal Government and of those states such as Washington and California, the inmate population in American prisons will rise to a minimum of 2.26 million within the next 10 years (*Corrections Digest*, 1994b, p. 1).

An increase of over a million inmates will mandate an increase in the level of funding necessary to accommodate such a large population. According to NCCD estimates, the Federal Government and the states will need an additional $351 billion during the next 10 years (*Corrections Digest*, 1994b, p. 1). In California, the effects of the three-strikes provision are estimated to increase the costs of operating the state prisons by $75 million for fiscal year 1994–1995 (Tucker, 1994, p. 7). The requisite prison construction that will be necessary to fulfill the legislative provisions is estimated to cost California residents $21 billion (Mauer, 1994a, p. 22). The Federal grants that the states are hoping to receive from the Federal Government will fall far short of these costs.

In addition, there are also the costs associated with providing health care and security for inmates over the age of 50. Based upon demographic data obtained from the California Department of Corrections, NCCD projects that the number of inmates who are 50 years of age or older will increase by 15,300 from 1994 to 1999. Although these older inmates comprised only 4 percent of California's prison population in 1994, it is estimated that they will represent 12 percent of the prison population in 2005 (NCCD, 1994, p. 3). State officials in California expect that the full impact of this legislation will be realized in the year 2020 at which time over 125,000 inmates or 20 percent of the prison population will be 50 years of age or older (NCCD, 1994, p. 3).

The New Jersey Department of Corrections has estimated that a new baseball sentencing bill would have a substantial financial impact on prison costs. In a financial impact statement, the Office of Legislative Services reported that "for every inmate who is not paroled as a result of this bill, an additional $80,000 in construction costs and $1 million in operating costs would be incurred over the lifetime of that inmate . . . that accounting breaks down to $25,000 per year per inmate for operating costs or an additional $3.75 million each year for 30 years, or $1.7 billion" (Gray, 1994, p. B9). In other words, Todd Clear estimates it would cost "$1 million to lock up a 30-year [old] criminal for life" (Clear cited in Levinson, 1994, p. B2).

In his review of the costs of crime and punishment, Thomas not only finds that "the fastest growing segment of state budgets in fiscal 1994 is corrections" but he considers that as more funds are put into public safety and crime control, there are fewer funds for other public and social programs (Thomas, 1994, p. 31). For example, Geiger reports that "70 percent of all the prison space in use today was built since 1985. Only 11 percent of our nation's classrooms were built during the 1980s" (1994, p. 22).

In an assessment of the consequences of baseball sentencing laws on prison costs, The Sentencing Project cautioned that "the most significant impact of these proposals, though, will begin to take place 10–20 years after their implementation, since the prisoners affected by these proposals would generally be locked up for at least that period of time under current practices" (1989, p. 2).

Confronted with the fact that an older inmate population will have a higher incidence of circulatory, respiratory, dietary, and ambulatory difficulties than younger inmates, prison officials need to anticipate and plan for geriatric services and programs now. Another realization is that these inmates pose the least risk in terms of criminal behavior. As a group, they are not a threat to society since crime is primarily an activity of young males. As a result, while the United States will be spending millions of dollars on the incarceration of these older prisoners, this is unlikely to reduce the incidence of crime.

Mauer (1994a) contends that these sentencing policies will have several lasting effects. First, the money spent to build new prisons will represent a commitment to maintain them for at least 50 years. Once the public has invested the requisite capital for construction, the courts will continue to fill the beds. Second, the funds that will be allocated to the increased costs of corrections will not be able to be used for other crime prevention measures. There will be little money available to improve the effectiveness of other components of the system such as juvenile justice, and diversion or early intervention programs will receive only limited funding and support. Third, the

incarceration rate of African American males will continue to increase. As a result, there is little reason to believe that the status of young African American males will improve when their representation in American prisons and jails exceeds their representation in college classrooms. Fourth, there will be little opportunity to fully examine and discuss crime in the political arena because prevailing policies will be so dependent upon a limited range of sentencing initiatives (Mauer, 1994a, p. 23). Once the "quick fix" mentality to crime has been adopted, it is less likely to expect a divergence from the "punitive-reactive" response to crime.

Assessing the Effectiveness of Baseball Sentences

While some legislatures and policy wonks would disagree, "there is no reason to believe that continuing to increase the severity of penalties will have any significant impact on crime" (The Sentencing Project, 1989, p. 2). In their critique of incarceration trends, Irwin and Austin observed that political rhetoric has distorted rational sentencing policies and resulted in large increases in the number of prisoners, many of whom are nonviolent, without any corresponding reductions in crime (1994).

In a study of California's get-tough-on-crime strategy, "which quadrupled the prison population between 1980 and 1992," Joan Petersilia concluded "that the much higher imprisonment rates in California had no appreciable effect on violent crime and only slight effects on property crime" (Petersilia, cited in Broder, 1994a, p. 4). Despite such findings that these measures may be ineffective in reducing crime, and notwithstanding the spiraling costs of baseball sentencing, the punishment model continues to prevail.

In her review of retributive justice and determinate sentencing reforms, Griset (1991, p. 186) concludes that the determinate ideal arose as a reaction, a backlash against the perceived evil of the reigning paradigm. While the theoretical underpinnings of determinacy attracted a large following, in practice the determinate ideal has not lived up to the dreams or the promises of its creators.

With a similar argument, Robert Gangi, executive director of the Correctional Association of New York, writes that "three strikes and you're out represents extension of a policy that has proven a failure" (1994, p. A14).

With a strong momentum toward tougher sentences and the success of get-tough political posturing on crime issues, it is unlikely that baseball metaphors will fall into disuse. For example, a proposal in Oregon would offer voters a "grand slam" package for crime. This package would require prisoners to work or study, prohibit sentence reductions without a two-thirds legislative vote, make sentencing alternatives to prison more difficult, and impose mandatory minimum sentences for all violent offenders older than 15 (Rohter, 1994, p. A12).

Conclusion

In this review of the recently enacted Federal crime bill and the Washington, California, and Georgia statutes, and in the assessment of the anticipated consequences of recent sentencing statutes, baseball punishment is characterized as the latest episode in the search for the "quick fix" to a complicated and disturbing social problem. These attempts to prevent crime, however, are misguided and will prove to be far more costly and ineffective than their proponents and the public could have anticipated. In the rush to enact "three-strikes legislation," elected officials and the electorate appear to have given little thought to the long-term effects of these provisions.

In terms of additional systemic costs, these laws will have a considerable effect on an already over-burdened court system. The process of justice relies extensively on an offender entering into a plea agreement. Once these laws become enacted, there will be little incentive for an offender to plead guilty to any charges which could result in longer periods of incarceration. If offenders know that pleading guilty will constitute a first or second strike let alone a third, there is a greater likelihood that they will demand a trial. As a result, such legislation will necessitate additional funding for more prosecutors, judges, and court administrative and support staff.

One of the distressing aspects of these sentencing proposals is that they seem to have far-reaching effects on other offender populations. Included in the newly enacted Federal code is a provision to try as adults those juveniles who are 13 years of age and charged with certain violent crimes. It will be possible for the first strike to have been committed at age 13. This tendency to treat juvenile offenders more harshly is but one manifestation of a trend in juvenile justice mandating waiver into the adult court and sentencing younger juveniles to prison. Efforts to confront the crime problem would be more effective if society addressed the tough issues of gun availability, family violence, and drug prevention (Mauer, 1994c).

The "three-strikes" legislation has also raised public expectations far beyond the likelihood of success. A *Wall Street Journal* NBC News poll found that 75 percent of Americans interviewed believed that enacting such legislation would make a "major difference" in the crime rate (*Criminal Justice Newsletter*, 1994d, p. 1). Apparently, elected officials and the media have succeeded in pandering to the American penchant for oversimplifying the causes of crime.

Despite legislative sentencing changes, the *crime* problem has not been addressed. Absent a commitment to do more than get tough on criminals, the "three-strikes" legislation is just one more costly slogan which will have no appreciable benefit for society. Research and commentary on the consequences of baseball punishment suggest that prison populations will continue to grow, corrections expenditures will consume larger percentages of government budgets, and sentence severity will have "no discernible effect on the crime rate" (Currie, 1994, p. 120). As the rhetoric pushes punitive policies to the margin, baseball metaphors and politicalization of sentencing will continue to divert attention from addressing the antecedents and correlates of crime. It is not surprising that the emotionalizing of policy results in "feel-good bromides, like 'three-strikes' . . . that create the illusion of problem solving" (Kramer, 1994, p. 29).

Study Questions

1. How does the politicalization of crime influence legislation?

2. What are some of the negative effects of "three-strikes laws"?

3. If criminal justice experts agree that this type of legislation is ineffective and politicians know that, then why do you suppose that such legislation continues to be enacted?

References

Allen, Harry. (1994). Personal Communication. (September 17).

Balz, Dan. (1994). "Pete Wilson: Practicing the Politics of Survival." *The Washington Post National Weekly Edition.* (August 29–September 4): 14.

Black, Donald. (1976). *The Behavior of Law.* New York: Academic Press.

Booth, William. (1994). "Florida Turns Up the Heat on Crime." *The Washington Post National Weekly Edition*. (February 21–27): 37.

Broder, David. (1994a). "Population Explosion." *The Washington Post National Weekly Edition.* (April 25–May 1): 4.

———. (1994b). "When Tough Isn't Smart." *The Criminologist.* (July/August) 19: 4, 6.

California Legislative Service. (1994). Chapter 12 (A–B. No. 971) (West) 1994 Portion of 1993–94 Regular Session. "An Act to Amend Section 667 of the Penal Code."

California Penal Code Section 1192.7

Congressional Digest. (1994). "The Federal Role in Crime Control." Washington, DC (June–July).

Corrections Digest. (1994a). "Experts Doubt '3 Strikes You're Out' Laws Will Effectively Curb Crime." (February 9): 7–9.

———. (1994b). "Senate Crime Bill Will More Than Double American Prison Population by Year 2005." (March 9): 1–4.

Crime Control Digest. (1994). " 'Three-time Loser' Bill to be Introduced in House." (January 24): 5–6.

Criminal Justice Newsletter. (1994a). "California Passes a Tough Three-Strikes-You're-Out Law." (April 4): 6–7.

———. (1994b). "Texas Comptroller Warns of 'Prison-Industrial Complex.'" (May 2): 2–3.

———. (1994c). "State Legislators Moving Toward Tougher Sentencing." (June 15): 1–2.

———. (1994d). "State Chief Justices Oppose Senate Crime Bill Provisions." (February 15): 1–3.

Cronin, Thomas, Tania Cronin, and Michael Milakovich. (1981). *U.S. v. Crime in the Streets.* Bloomington, IN: Indiana University Press.

Currie, Elliot. (1994). "What's Wrong with the Crime Bill." *The Nation.* (January 31) 258: 4, 118–121.

Egan, Timothy. (1994). "A 3-Strike Penal Law Shows It's Not as Simple as It Seems." *New York Times.* (February 15): A1, A11.

Final Legislative Report. (1994). Fifty-Third Washington State Legislature. 1994 Regular Session and First Special Session.

Gangi, Robert. (1994). "Where Three-Strikes Plan Takes Us in 20 Years." *New York Times.* (February 7): A14.

Geiger, Keith. (1994). "Upgrading School Buildings." *The Washington Post National Weekly Edition.* (September 26–October 2): 22.

Georgia Statutes 17-10-6.1 Code of Georgia, Title 17. Criminal Procedure, Chapter 10 Sentence and Punishment, Article 1. Procedure for Sentencing and Imposition of Punishment.

Gladwell, Malcolm. (1994). "The Crime Bill May Not Be the Cure." *The Washington Post National Weekly Edition.* (June 6–12): 33.

Gleason, Bucky. (1994). "Anti-Crime Packages Don't Work." *Erie Times News.* (October 9): A1, A12.

Gray, Jerry. (1994). "New Jersey Senate Approves Bill to Jail 3-Time Criminals for Life." *New York Times.* (May 13): A1, B9.

Griset, Pamala. (1991). *Determinate Sentencing: The Promise and the Reality of Retributive Justice.* Albany, NY: State University of New York Press.

Idelson, Holly. (1994). "Crime Bill's Final Version." *Congressional Quarterly.* (July 30) 52: 30, 2138.

Irwin, John, and James Austin. (1994). *It's About Time: America's Imprisonment Binge.* Belmont, CA: Wadsworth.

Kramer, Michael. (1994). "Tough. But Smart?" *Time.* (February 7): 29.

Kurtz, Howard. (1994). "The Campaign Weapon of Choice." *The Washington Post National Weekly Edition.* (September 19–25): 12.

Levinson, Arlene. (1994). "Three Strikes and You're Out." *Erie Morning News.* (January 25): B2.

Lewis, Anthony. (1994). "Crime and Politics." *New York Times.* (September 16): A13.

Lewis, Neil. (1993). "Crime Rates Decline; Outrage Hasn't." *New York Times.* (December 3): B6.

Mauer, Marc. (1994a). "Americans Behind Bars: The International Use of Incarceration, 1992–1993." The Sentencing Project. Washington, DC.

——. (1994b). "An Assessment of Sentencing Issues and the Death Penalty in the 1990s." The Sentencing Project. Washington, DC.

——. (1994c). "Testimony of Marc Mauer Before the House Judiciary Committee, Subcommittee on Crime and Criminal Justice on 'Three Strikes and You're Out.'" (March 1): 1–13.

Merlo, Alida, and Peter Benekos. (1992a). "Introduction: The Politics of Corrections" in Peter Benekos and Alida Merlo (eds.) *Corrections: Dilemmas and Directions.* Cincinnati, OH: Anderson Publishing.

——. (1992b). "Adapting Conservative Correctional Policies to the Economic Realities of the 1990s." *Criminal Justice Policy Review.* (March) 6: 1, 1–16.

National Council on Crime and Delinquency. (1994). "The Aging of California's Prison Population: An Assessment of Three Strikes Legislation." 1–6.

National Public Radio. (1994). Broadcast on "All Things Considered" (September 30).

Neri, Albert. (1994a). "With Candidates in Dead Heat, Ridge Uses Casey in Ad." *Erie Morning News.* (October 6): A14.

——. (1994b). "Singel Faces Up to His Worst Nightmare." *Erie Times News.* (October 9): B3.

New York Times. (1993). "Hunt for Kidnapped Girl, 12, Is Narrowed to Small Woods." (December 3): A22.

——. (1994a). "Mandatory Sentencing Is Criticized by Justice." (March 10): A14.

——. (1994b). "Georgia Voters to Consider '2-Strikes' Law." (March 16): A10.

——. (1994c). "California Judge Refuses to Apply a Tough New Sentencing Law." (September 20): A9.

——. (1994d). "Killer Withdraws Plea in a '3 Strikes' Case." (September 28): A19.

Peyser, Marc. (1994). "Strike Three and You're Not Out." *Newsweek.* (August 29): 63.

Raspberry, William. (1993). "Digging In Deeper." *The Washington Post National Weekly Edition.* (November 1–7): 29.

Reno, Janet. (1994). "Memorandum from the Attorney General: The Violent Crime Control and Law Enforcement Act of 1994." (September 15): 1–5.

Rohter, Larry. (1994). "States Embracing Tougher Measures for Fighting Crime." *New York Times.* (May 10): A1, A12.

Schneider, William. (1993). "Crime and Politics: Incumbents Got Mugged by Fear in Our Streets." *The Washington Post National Weekly Edition.* (November 15–21): 24.

The Sentencing Project. (1989). "The Lessons of Willie Horton." Washington, DC.

Shover, Neal and Werner Einstadter. (1988). *Analyzing American Corrections.* Belmont, CA: Wadsworth.

——. (1994). "Why '3 Strikes and You're Out' Won't Reduce Crime." Washington, DC.

Thomas, Pierre. (1994). "Getting to the Bottom Line on Crime." *The Washington Post National Weekly Edition.* (July 18–24): 31.

Tucker, Beverly. (1994). "Can California Afford 3 Strikes?" *California Teachers Association Action* (May): 7; 17.

U.S. Government Printing Office. (1994). "The Violent Crime Control and Law Enforcement Act of 1994." Conference Report. Washington, DC.

The Vindicator. (1994). "Law Will Star in Fall Campaigns." (August 28): A5.

Walker, Samuel. (1994). *Sense and Nonsense About Crime and Drugs: A Policy Guide,* 3rd ed. Belmont, CA: Wadsworth.

Washington Laws. (1994). *1994 Pamphlet Edition Session Laws* Fifty-Third Legislature 1994 Regular Session. Chapter 1 "Persistent Offenders—Life Sentence on Third Conviction." (Statute Law Committee) Olympia, WA.

32
'Infamous Punishment'
The Psychological Consequences of Isolation
Craig Haney

Another new trend that nearly equals the "three-strikes" legislation, but is not as politicized, is the use of ultramaximum security prisons. Recalcitrant inmates are often placed into these types of institutions after causing trouble in the general prison population. An extreme example of such a prison is Pelican Bay, as described by Craig Haney in the following selection. It is little more than a dungeon with bare floors, in which there is no chance of seeing the outside world nor any opportunity for meaningful human contact. The results of such an experiment were already determined when New York devoted one wing of its prison to total isolation. Complete isolation can have devastating psychological consequences for inmates, many of whom serve time under horrific conditions because they are mentally disturbed. Although this arrangement makes the job of administering corrections easier, it spells disaster for everyone else involved, including the community into which most of these inmates will ultimately be released.

Since the discovery of the asylum, prisons have been used to isolate inmates from the outside world, and often from each other. As most students of the American penitentiary know, the first real prisons in the United States were characterized by the regimen of extreme isolation that they imposed upon their prisoners. Although both the Auburn and Pennsylvania models (which varied only in the degree of isolation they imposed) eventually were abandoned, in part because of their harmful effects upon prisoners,[1] most prison systems have retained and employed—however sparingly—some form of punitive solitary confinement. Yet, because of the technological spin that they put on institutional design and procedure, the new super-maximum security prisons are unique in the modern history of American corrections. These prisons represent the application of sophisticated, modern technology dedicated entirely to the task of social control, and they isolate, regulate, and surveil more effectively than anything that has preceded them.

The Pelican Bay SHU

The Security Housing Unit at California's Pelican Bay State Prison is the prototype for this marriage of technology and total control.[2] The design of the Security Housing Unit—where well over a thousand prisoners are confined for periods of six months to several years—is starkly austere. Indeed, Pelican Bay's low, windowless, slate-gray exterior gives no hint to outsiders that this is a place where human beings live. But the barrenness of the prison's interior is what is most startling. On each visit to this prison I have been struck by the harsh, visual sameness and monotony of the physical design and the layout of these units. Architects and corrections officials have created living environments that are devoid of social stimulation. The atmosphere is antiseptic and sterile; you search in vain for humanizing touches or physical traces that human activity takes place here. The "pods" where prisoners live are virtually identical; there is little inside to mark location or give prisoners a sense of place.

Prisoners who are housed inside these units are completely isolated from the natural environment and from most of the natural rhythms of life. SHU prisoners, whose housing units have no windows, get only a glimpse of natural light. One prisoner captured the feeling created here when he told me, "When I first got here I felt like I was underground." Prisoners at Pelican Bay are not even permitted to see grass, trees or shrubbery. Indeed, little or none exists within the perimeters of the prison grounds, which are covered instead by gray gravel stones. This is no small accomplishment since the prison sits adjacent to the Redwood National Forest and the surrounding landscape is lush enough to support some of the oldest living things on earth. Yet here is where the California Department of Corrections has chosen to create the most lifeless environment in its—or any—correctional system.

When prisoners do get out of their cells for "yard," they are released into a barren concrete encasement that contains no exercise equipment, not even a ball. They cannot see any of the surrounding landscape because of the solid concrete walls that extend up some 20 feet around them. Overhead, an opaque roof covers half the yard; the other half, although covered with a wire screen, provides prisoners with their only view of the open sky. When outside conditions are not intolerably inclement (the weather at Pelican Bay often brings harsh cold and driving rain), prisoners may exercise in this concrete cage for approximately an hour-and-a-half a day. Their movements are monitored by video camera, watched by control officers on overhead television screens. In the control booth, the televised images of several inmates, each in separate exercise cages, show them walking around and around the perimeter of their concrete yards, like laboratory animals engaged in mindless and repetitive activity.

Prisoners in these units endure an unprecedented degree of involuntary, enforced idleness. Put simply: prisoners here have virtually nothing to *do*. Although prisoners who can afford them are permit-

ted to have radios and small, regulation size televisions in their cells, there is no *activity* in which they may engage. Except for the limited exercise I have described and showers (three times a week), there are no prison routines that regularly take them out of their cells. All prisoners are "cell fed"—twice a day meals are placed on tray slots in the cell doors to be eaten by the prisoners inside. (Indeed, on my first tour of the institution one guard told me that this was the only flaw in the design of the prison—that they had not figured out a way to feed the prisoners "automatically," thus eliminating the need for any contact with them.) Prisoners are not permitted to do work of any kind, and they have no opportunities for educational or vocational training. They are never permitted out on their tiers unless they are moving to and from showers or yard, or being escorted—in chains and accompanied by two baton-wielding correctional officers per inmate—to the law library or infirmary outside the unit. Thus, with minor and insignificant exceptions, a prisoner's entire life is lived within the parameters of his 80-square-foot cell, a space that is typically shared with another prisoner whose life is similarly circumscribed.

All movement within these units is tightly regulated and controlled, and takes place under constant surveillance. Prisoners are permitted to initiate little or no meaningful behavior of their own. When they go to shower or "yard," they do so at prescribed times and in a prescribed manner and the procedure is elaborate. Guards must first unlock the padlocks on the steel doors to their cells. Once the guards have left the tier (they are never permitted on the tier when an unchained prisoner is out of his cell), the control officer opens the cell door by remote control. The prisoner must appear naked at the front of the control booth and submit to a routinized visual strip search before going to yard and, afterwards, before returning to his cell. Some prisoners are embarrassed by this public display of nudity (which takes place not only in front of control officers and other prisoners, but whomever else happens to be in the open area around the outside of the control booth). As might be expected, many inmates forego the privilege of taking "yard" because of the humiliating procedures to which they must submit and the draconian conditions under which they are required to exercise. Whenever prisoners are in the presence of another human being (except for those who have cellmates), they are placed in chains, at both their waist and ankles. Indeed, they are chained even *before* they are permitted to exit their cells. There are also special holding cages in which prisoners are often left when they are being moved from one place to another. Prisoners are kept chained even during their classification hearings. I witnessed one prisoner, who was apparently new to the process, stumble as he attempted to sit down at the start of his hearing. Because he was chained with his hands behind his back, the correctional counselor had to instruct him to "sit on the chair like it was a horse"—unstable, with the back of the chair flush against his chest.

The cells themselves are designed so that a perforated metal screen, instead of a door, covers the entrance to the cells. This permits open, around-the-clock surveillance whenever guards enter the tiers. In addition, television cameras have been placed at strategic locations inside the cellblocks and elsewhere within the prison.

Because the individual "pods" are small (four cells on each of two floors), both visual and auditory surveillance are facilitated. Speakers and microphones have been placed in each cell to permit contact with control booth officers. Many prisoners believe that the microphones are used to monitor their conversations. There is little or no personal privacy that prisoners may maintain in these units.

Psychological Consequences

The overall level of long-term social deprivation within these units is nearly total

and, in many ways, represents the destructive essence of this kind of confinement. Men in these units are deprived of human contact, touch and affection for years on end. They are denied the opportunity for contact visits of any kind; even attorneys and experts must interview them in visiting cells that prohibit contact. They cannot embrace or shake hands, even with visitors who have traveled long distances to see them. Many of these prisoners have not had visits from the outside world in years. They are not permitted to make phone calls except for emergencies or other extraordinary circumstances. As one prisoner told me: "Family and friends, after the years, they just start dropping off. Plus, the mail here is real irregular. We can't even take pictures of ourselves" to send to loved ones.[3] Their isolation from the social world, a world to which most of them will return, could hardly be more complete.

The operational procedures employed within the units themselves insure that even interactions with correctional staff occur infrequently and on highly distorted, unnatural terms. The institutional routines are structured so that prisoners are within close proximity of staff only when they are being fed, visually searched through the window of the control booth before going to "yard," [or] being placed in chains and escorted elsewhere within the institution. There is always a physical barrier or mechanical restraint between them and other human beings.

The only exceptions occur for prisoners who are double-celled. Yet double-celling under these conditions hardly constitutes normal social contact. In fact, it is difficult to conceptualize a more strained and perverse form of intense and intrusive social interaction. For many prisoners, this kind of forced, invasive contact becomes a source of conflict and pain. They are thrust into intimate, constant co-living with another person—typically a total stranger—whose entire existence is similarly and unavoidably co-mingled with their own.

Such pressurized contact can become the occasion for explosive violence. It also fails to provide any semblance of social "reality testing" that is intrinsic to human social existence.[4]

The psychological significance of this level of long-term social deprivation cannot be overstated. The destructive consequences can only be understood in terms of the profound importance of social contact and social context in providing an interpretive framework for all human experience, no matter how personal and seemingly private. Human identity formation occurs by virtue of social contact with others. As one SHU prisoner explained: "I liked to be around people. I'm happy and I enjoy people. They take that away from you [here]. It's like we're dead. As the Catholics say, in purgatory. They've taken away everything that might give a little purpose to your life." Moreover, when our reality is not grounded in social context, the internal stimuli and beliefs that we generate are impossible to test against the reactions of others. For this reason, the first step in any program of extreme social influence—ranging from police interrogation to indoctrination and "brainwashing"—is to isolate the intended targets from others, and to create a context in which social reality testing is controlled by those who would shape their thoughts, beliefs, emotions, and behavior. Most people are so disoriented by the loss of social context that they become highly malleable, unnaturally sensitive, and vulnerable to the influence of those who control the environment around them. Indeed, this may be its very purpose. As one SHU prisoner told me: "You're going to be what the place wants you to be or you're going to be nothing."

Long-term confinement under these conditions has several predictable psychological consequences. Although not everyone will manifest negative psychological effects to the same degree, and it is difficult to specify the point in time at which the destructive consequences will manifest themselves, few escape unscathed. The

norms of prison life require prisoners to struggle to conceal weakness, to minimize admissions of psychic damage or pain. It is part of a prisoner ethic in which preserving dignity and autonomy, and minimizing vulnerability, is highly valued. Thus, the early stages of these destructive processes are often effectively concealed. They will not be apparent to untrained or casual observers, nor will they be revealed to persons whom the prisoners do not trust. But over time, the more damaging parts of adaptation to this kind of environment begin to emerge and become more obvious.[5]

The first adaptation derives from the totality of control that is created inside a place like Pelican Bay. Incarceration itself makes prisoners dependent to some degree upon institutional routines to guide and organize their behavior. However, the totality of control imposed in a place like Pelican Bay is extreme enough to produce a qualitatively different adaptation. Eventually, many prisoners become entirely dependent upon the structure and routines of the institution for the control of their behavior. There are two related components to this adaptation. Some prisoners become dependent upon the institution to *limit* their behavior. That is, because their behavior is so carefully and completely circumscribed during their confinement in lockup, they begin to lose the ability to set limits for themselves. Some report becoming uncomfortable with even small amounts of freedom because they have lost the sense of how to behave without the constantly enforced restrictions, tight external structure, and totality of behavioral restraints.

Other prisoners suffer an opposite but related reaction, caused by the same set of circumstances. These prisoners lose the ability to *initiate* behavior of any kind—to organize their own lives around activity and purpose—because they have been stripped of any opportunity to do so for such prolonged periods of time. Apathy and lethargy set in. They report being tired all the time, despite the fact that they have been allowed to do nothing. They find it difficult to focus their attention, their minds wander, they cannot concentrate or organize thoughts or actions in a coherent way. In extreme cases, a sense of profound despair and hopelessness is created.

The experience of total social isolation can lead, paradoxically, to social withdrawal. That is, some prisoners in isolation draw further into themselves as a way of adjusting to the deprivation of meaningful social contact imposed upon them. They become uncomfortable in the course of the little social contact they are permitted. They take steps to avoid even that—by refusing to go to "yard," refraining from conversation with staff, discouraging any visits from family members or friends, and ceasing correspondence with the outside world. They move from being starved for social contact to being frightened by it. Of course, as they become increasingly unfamiliar and uncomfortable with social interaction, they are further alienated from others and disoriented in their presence.

The absence of social contact and social context creates an air of unreality to one's existence in these units. Some prisoners act out as a way of getting a reaction from their environment, proving to themselves that they still exist, that they are still alive and capable of eliciting a human response—however hostile—from other human beings. This is the context in which seemingly irrational refusals of prisoners to "cuff up" take place—which occur in the Pelican Bay SHU with some regularity, in spite of the knowledge that such refusals invariably result in brutal "cell extractions" in which they are physically subdued, struck with a large shield and special cell extraction baton, and likely to be shot with a taser gun or wooden or rubber bullets before being placed in leg irons and handcuffs.[6]

In some cases, another pattern emerges. The line between their own thought processes and the bizarre reality around them becomes increasingly tenuous. Social contact grounds and anchors us; when it is

gone, there is nothing to take its place. Moreover, for some, the environment around them is so painful and so painfully impossible to make sense of, that they create their own reality, one seemingly "crazy" but easier for them to tolerate and make sense of. Thus, they live in a world of fantasy instead of the world of control, surveillance, and inhumanity that has been imposed upon them by the explicit and conscious policies of the correctional authorities.

For others, the deprivations, the restrictions, and the totality of control fills them with intolerable levels of frustration. Combined with the complete absence of activity or meaningful outlets through which they can vent this frustration, it can lead to outright anger and then to rage. This rage is a reaction against, not a justification for, their oppressive confinement. Such anger cannot be abated by intensifying the very deprivations that have produced it. They will fight against the system that they perceive only as having surrounded and oppressed them. Some will lash out violently against the people whom they hold responsible for the frustration and deprivation that fills their lives. Ultimately, the outward expression of this violent frustration is marked by its irrationality, primarily because of the way in which it leads prisoners into courses of action that further insure their continued mistreatment. But the levels of deprivation are so profound, and the resulting frustration so immediate and overwhelming, that for some this lesson is unlikely ever to be learned. The pattern can only be broken through drastic changes in the nature of the environment, changes that produce more habitable and less painful conditions of confinement.

The magnitude and extremity of oppressive control that exists in these units helps to explain another feature of confinement in the Pelican Bay SHU that, in my experience, is unique in modern American corrections. Prisoners there have repeatedly voiced fears of physical mistreatment and brutality on a widespread and frequent basis. They speak of physical intimidation and the fear of violence at the hands of correctional officers. These concerns extend beyond the physical intimidation that is structured into the design of the units themselves—the totality of restraint, the presence of guards who are all clad in heavy flak jackets inside the units, the use of chains to move prisoners out of their cells, and the constant presence of control officers armed with assault rifles slung across their chests as they monitor prisoners within their housing units. Beyond this, prisoners speak of the frequency of "cell extractions" which they describe in frightening terms. Most have witnessed extractions in which groups of correctional officers (the previously described "cell extraction team") have entered prisoners' cells, fired wooden or rubber bullets and electrical tasers at prisoners, forcibly chained and removed them from their cells, sometimes for the slightest provocation (such as the failure to return food trays on command). And many note that this mistreatment may be precipitated by prisoners whose obvious psychiatric problems preclude them from conforming to SHU rules or responding to commands issued by correctional officers.[7] One prisoner reported being constantly frightened that guards were going to hurt him. The day I interviewed him, he told me that he had been sure the correctional staff was "going to come get him." He stuck his toothbrush in the door of his cell so they couldn't come inside. He vowed "to hang myself or stop eating [and] starve to death" in order to get out of the SHU.

I believe that the existence of such brutality can be attributed in part to the psychology of oppression that has been created in and around this prison. Correctional staff, themselves isolated from more diverse and conflicting points of view that they might encounter in more urban or cosmopolitan environments, have been encouraged to create their own unique worldview at Pelican Bay. Nothing counters the prefabricated ideology into which they step at Pelican Bay, a prison that was designated as a place for the "worst of the worst" even before the first prisoners ever arrived. They work daily in an environment whose very structure powerfully conveys the message that these prisoners are not human beings. There is no reciprocity to their perverse and limited interactions with prisoners—who are always in cages or chains, seen through screens or windows or television cameras or protective helmets—and who are given no opportunities to act like human beings. Pelican Bay has become a massive self-fulfilling prophecy. Violence is one mechanism with which to accommodate to the fear inevitably generated on both sides of the bars.

Psychiatric Disorders

The psychological consequences of living in these units for long periods of time are predictably destructive, and the potential for these psychic stressors to precipitate various forms of psychopathology is clear-cut. When prisoners who are deprived of meaningful social contact begin to shun all forms of interaction, withdraw more deeply into themselves and cease initiating social interaction, they are in pain and require psychiatric attention. They get little or none.[8] Prisoners who have become uncomfortable in the presence of others will be unable to adjust to housing in a mainline prison population, not to mention free society. They are also at risk of developing disabling, clinical psychiatric symptoms. Thus, numerous studies have underscored the role of social isolation as a correlate of mental illness. Similarly, when prisoners become profoundly lethargic in the face of their monotonous, empty existence, the potential exists for this lethargy to shade into despondency and, finally, to clinical depression. For others who feel the frustration of the totality of control more acutely, their frustration may become increasingly difficult to control and manage. Long-term problems of impulse control may develop that are psychiatric in nature.

This kind of environment is capable of creating clinical syndromes in even healthy personalities, and can be psychologically destructive for anyone who enters and endures it for significant periods of time. However, prisoners who enter these places with *pre-existing* psychiatric disorders suffer more acutely. The psychic pain and vulnerability that they bring into the lockup unit may grow and fester if unattended to. In the absence of psychiatric help, there is nothing to keep many of these prisoners from entering the abyss of psychosis.

Indeed, in the course of my interviews at Pelican Bay, numerous prisoners spoke to me about their inability to handle the stress of SHU confinement. Some who entered the unit with pre-existing problems could perceive that they had gotten worse. Others had decompensated so badly that they had no memory of ever having functioned well, or had little awareness that their present level of functioning was tenuous, fragile, and psychotic. More than a few expressed concerns about what they would do when released—either from the SHU into mainline housing, or directly into free society (as a number are). One prisoner who was housed in the unit that is reserved for those who are maintained on psychotropic medication told me that he was sure that the guards in this unit were putting poison in his food. He was concerned because when released (this year), he told me "I know I won't be able to work or be normal."

Many SHU prisoners also reported being suicidal or self-mutilating. A number of them showed me scars on their arms and necks where they had attempted to cut themselves. One prisoner told me matter-of-factly, "I've been slicing on my arms for years, sometimes four times a day, just to see the blood flow." One suicidal prisoner who is also deaf reported being cell extracted because he was unable to hear the correctional officers call count (or "show skin"—a procedure used so that staff knows a prisoner is in his cell). He now sleeps on the floor of his cell "so that the officers can see my skin." Another prisoner, who has reported hearing voices in the past and seeing "little furry things," has slashed his wrists on more than one occasion. Instead of being transferred to a facility where he could receive mental health treatment—since obviously none is available at Pelican Bay—he has been moved back and forth between the VCU and SHU units. While in the VCU, he saw a demon who knew his name and frequently spoke to him. As I interviewed him, he told me that the voices were cursing at him for talking to me. In the course of our discussion, he was clearly distracted by these voices and, periodically, he laughed inappropriately. One psychotic SHU prisoner announced to me at the start of our interview that he was a "super power man" who could not only fly, but see through steel and hear things that were being said about him from great distances. He had lived in a board-and-care home and been maintained on Thorazine before his incarceration. Although he had attempted suicide three times while at Pelican Bay, he was confident that when he was placed back in the mainline he would not have to attempt to kill himself again—because he thought he could convince his cellmate to do it for him. Another flagrantly psychotic SHU prisoner talked about a miniature implant that the Department of Corrections had placed inside his head, connected to their "main computer," which they were using to control him electronically, by programming him to say and do things that would continually get him into trouble. When I asked him whether or not he had seen any of the mental health staff, he became agitated and earnestly explained to me that his problem was medical—the computer implant inserted into his brain—not psychiatric. He offered to show me the paperwork from a lawsuit he had filed protesting this unauthorized medical procedure.

When prison systems become seriously overcrowded—as California's is (operating now at more than 180 percent of capacity)—psychiatric resources become increasingly scarce and disturbed prisoners are handled poorly, if at all. Often, behavior that is caused primarily by psychiatric disfunction results in placement in punitive solitary confinement, where little or no psychiatric precautions are taken to protect or treat them. They are transferred from one such punitive isolation unit to another, in what has been derisively labeled "bus therapy."[9] In fact, I have come to the conclusion that the Pelican Bay SHU has become a kind of "dumping ground" of last resort for many psychiatrically disturbed prisoners who were inappropriately housed and poorly treated—because of their psychiatric disorders—in other SHU units. Because such prisoners were unable to manage their disorders in these other units—in the face of psychologically destructive conditions of confinement and in the absence of appropriate treatment—their continued rules violations, which in many cases were the direct product of their psychiatric disorders, have resulted in their transfer to Pelican Bay. Thus, their placement in the Pelican Bay SHU is all the more inappropriate because of the process by which they got there. Their inability to adjust to the harsh conditions that prevailed at these other units should disqualify them for placement in this most harsh and destructive environment, yet, the opposite appears to be the case.

Conclusions

Although I have seen conditions elsewhere that approximate those at the Pelican Bay SHU, and have testified about their harmful psychological effects, I have never seen long-term social deprivation so totally and completely enforced. Neither have I seen prisoner movements so completely regimented and controlled. Never have I seen the technology of social control used to this degree to deprive captive human beings of the opportunity to initiate meaningful activity, nor have I seen such an array of deliberate practices designed for the sole purpose of preventing prisoners from engaging in any semblance of normal social intercourse. The technological structure of this environment adds to its impersonality and anonymity. Prisoners interact with their captors over microphones, in chains or through thick windows, peering into the shields that hide the faces of cell extraction teams as they move in coordinated violence. It is axiomatic among those who study human behavior that social connectedness and social support are the prerequisites to long-term social adjustment. Yet, persons who have been wrenched from a human community of any kind risk profound and chronic alienation and asociality.

A century and a half ago, social commentators like Dickens and de Tocqueville marveled at the willingness of American society to incarcerate its least favored citizens in "despotic" places of solitary confinement.[10] De Tocqueville understood that complete isolation from others "produces a deeper effect on the soul of the convict," an effect that he worried might prove disabling when the convict was released into free society. Although he admired the power that American penitentiaries wielded over prisoners, he did not have the tools to measure their long-term effects nor the benefit of more than a hundred years of experience and humane intelligence that has led us away from these destructive interventions. Ignoring all of this, places like Pelican Bay appear to have brought us full circle. And then some.

Study Questions

1. Describe the physical environment and social interactions in the SHU at Pelican Bay.

2. How do such brutalizing conditions affect the human psyche?

3. What is the relationship between psychologically disturbed prisoners and treatment of prisoners at SHU?.

4. Compare this system of punishment to the early experiments with solitary confinement.

Notes

1. In words it appears to have long since forgotten, the United States Supreme Court more than a century ago, characterized solitary confinement as an "infamous punishment" and provided this explanation for its abandonment: "Experience demonstrated that there were serious objections to it. A considerable number of the prisoners fell, after even a short confinement into a semi-fatuous condition, from which it was next to impossible to arouse them, and others became violently insane; others still, committed suicide; while those who stood the ordeal better were not generally reformed, and in most cases did not recover sufficient mental activity to be of any subsequent service . . . [I]t is within the memory of many persons interested in prison discipline that some 30 or 40 years ago the whole subject attracted the general public attention, and its main feature of solitary confinement was found to be too severe." *In re Medley*, 134 U.S. 160, 168 (1890).

2. Its predecessor, the federal prison at Marion, Illinois, is now more than 25 years old and a technological generation behind Pelican Bay. Although many of the same oppressive conditions and restrictive procedures are approximated at Marion, these comments are focused on Pelican Bay, where my observations and interviews are more recent and where conditions are more severe and extreme. In addition to some of the descriptive comments that follow, conditions at the Pelican Bay SHU have been described in Elvin, J. "Isolation, Excessive Force Under Attack at California's Supermax," *NPP JOURNAL*, Vol. 7, No. 4, (1992), and White, L. "Inside the Alcatraz of the '90s," *California Lawyer* 42–48 (1992). The unique nature of this environment has also generated some media attention. E.g., Hentoff, N., "Buried Alive in American Prisons," *The Washington Post*, January 9, 1993; Mintz, H., "Is Pelican Bay Too Tough?" 182 *The Recorder*, p. 1, September

19, 1991; Roemer, J. "High-Tech Deprivation," *San Jose Mercury News*, June 7, 1992; Ross, J. "High-tech dungeon," *The Bay Guardian* 15–17, (1992). The creation of such a unit in California is particularly unfortunate in light of fully 20 years of federal litigation over conditions of confinement in the "lockup" units in four of the state's maximum security prisons (Deuel Vocational institution, Folsom, San Quentin, and Soledad). E.g., *Wright v. Enomoto*, 462 F. Supp. 397 (N.D. Cal. 1976). In a lengthy evidentiary hearing conducted before judge Stanley Weigel, the state's attorneys and corrections officials were present during expert testimony from numerous witnesses concerning the harmful effects of the punitive solitary confinement they were imposing upon prisoners in these units. Except for some disagreement offered up by Department of Corrections employees, this testimony went unanswered and unrebutted. *Toussaint v. Rusben*, 553 F. Supp. 1365 (N.D. Cal. 1983), *aff'd in part Toussaint v. Yockey*, 722 F.2d 1490 (9th Cir. 1984). Only a few years after this hearing, and while a federal monitor was still in place to oversee the conditions in these other units, the Department of Corrections began construction of Pelican Bay. In apparent deliberate indifference to this extensive record, and seemingly without seeking any outside opinions on the psychological consequences of housing prisoners in a unit like the one they intended to create or engaging in public debate over the wisdom of such a project, they proceeded to commit over $200 million in state funds to construct a prison whose conditions were in many ways worse than those at the other prisons, whose harmful effect had been litigated over the preceding decade.

3. Most corrections experts understand the significance of maintaining social connectedness and social ties for long-term adjustment in and out of prison. See, e.g., Schafer, N. "Prison Visiting: Is It Time to Review the Rules?" *Federal Probation* 25–30 (1989). This simple lesson has been completely ignored at Pelican Bay.

4. Indeed, in my opinion, double-celling in Security Housing Units like those at Pelican Bay constitutes a clear form of overcrowding. As such, it can be expected to produce its own, independently harmful effects, as

the literature on the negative consequences of overcrowding attests.

5. Although not extensive, the literature on the negative psychological effects of solitary confinement and related situations is useful in interpreting contemporary observations and interview data from prisoners placed in punitive isolation like Pelican Bay. See, e.g., Heron, W. "The Pathology of Boredom," *Scientific American*, 196 (1957); Burney, C. *"Solitary Confinement,"* London: Macmillan (1961); Cormier, B., & Williams, P. "Excessive Deprivation of Liberty," *Canadian Psychiatric Association Journal* 470–484 (1966); Scott, G., & Gendreau, P. "Psychiatric Implications of Sensory Deprivation in a Maximum Security Prison," 12 *Canadian Psychiatric Association Journal* 337–341 (1969); Cohen, S., & Taylor, L., *Psychological Survival*, Harmondsworth: Penguin (1972); Grassian, S., "Psychopathological Effects of Solitary Confinement," 140 *American Journal of Psychiatry* 1450–1454 (1983); Jackson, M. *Prisoners of Isolation: Solitary Confinement in Canada*, Toronto: University of Toronto Press (1983); Grassian, S., & Friedman, N., "Effects of Sensory Deprivation in Psychiatric Seclusion and Solitary Confinement," 8 *International Journal of Law and Psychiatry* 49–65 (1986); Slater, R. "Psychiatric Intervention in an Atmosphere of Terror," 7 *American Journal of Forensic Psychiatry* 6–12 (1986); Brodsky, S., & Scogin, F., "Inmates in Protective Custody: First Data on Emotional Effects," 1 *Forensic Reports* 267–280 (1988); and Cooke, D. "Containing Violent Prisoners: An Analysis of the Barlinnie Special Unit," 29 *British Journal of Criminology* 129–143 (1989).

6. This description of cell extraction practices is corroborated not only by numerous prisoner accounts of the process but also by explicit Department of Corrections procedures. Once a decision has been made to "extract" a prisoner from his cell, this is how the five-man cell extraction team proceeds: the first member of the team is to enter the cell carrying a large shield, which is used to push the prisoner back into a corner of the cell; the second member follows closely, wielding a special cell extraction baton, which is used to strike the inmate on the upper part of his body so that he will raise his arms in self-protection; thus unsteadied, the inmate is pulled off balance by another member of the team whose job is to place leg irons around his ankles; once downed, a fourth member of the team places him in handcuffs; the fifth member stands ready to fire a taser gun or rifle that shoots wooden or rubber bullets at the resistant inmate.

7. One of the basic principles of any unit premised on domination and punitive control—as the Pelican Bay Security Housing Unit is—is that a worse, more punitive and degrading place always must be created in order to punish those prisoners who still commit rule infractions. At Pelican Bay, that place is termed the "Violence Control Unit" (which the prisoners refer to as "Bedrock"). From my observations and interviews, some of the most psychiatrically disturbed prisoners are kept in the VCU. Prisoners in this unit are not permitted televisions or radios, and they are the only ones chained and escorted to the door of the outside exercise cage (despite the fact that no prisoner is more than four cells away from this door). In addition, there are plexiglass coverings on the entire outside facing of the VCU cells, which results in a significant distortion of vision into and out of the cell itself. Indeed, because of the bright light reflected off this Plexiglas covering, I found it difficult to see clearly into any of the upper-level VCU cells I observed, or even to look clearly into the faces of prisoners who were standing right in front of me on the other side of this plexiglass shield. Inside, the perception of confinement is intensified because of this added barrier placed on the front of each cell.

8. In the first several years of its operation, Pelican Bay State Prison had *one* full-time mental health staff member, and not a single PhD psychologist or psychiatrist, to administer to the needs of the entire prison population, which included over 1,000 SHU prisoners, as well as over 2,000 prisoners in the general population of the prison. Although the size of the mental health staff has been increased somewhat in recent years, it is still the case that no advance screening is done by mental health staff on prisoners admitted to the SHUs to determine pre-existing psychiatric disorders or suicide risk, and no regular monitoring is performed by mental health staff to assess the negative psychological consequences of exposure to this toxic environment.

9. Cf. Toch, H., "The Disturbed Disruptive Inmate: Where Does the Bus Stop?" *10 Journal of Psychiatry and Law* 327–350, (1982).

10. Dickens, C., *American Notes for General Circulation*. London: Chapman and Hall (1842); Beaumont, G., & de Tocqueville, A., *On the Penitentiary System in the United States and Its Application in France*, Montclair, NJ (1833, 1976).

33

'This Man Has Expired'

Witness to an Execution

Robert Johnson

Capital punishment is another long-touted solution to the problem of violent crime. After a decade-long moratorium that ended with the execution of Gary Gilmore in 1977, capital punishment moved into full swing in the 1980s and 1990s. However, a period of readjustment followed the moratorium, in which most death-sentenced cases during and shortly thereafter resulted in life sentences. At that time, the process of review was very slow, but in recent years the likelihood of a death sentence actually being carried out has increased. Reversals are less frequent and cases are moving along at a more rapid pace. There are currently over 3,000 inmates awaiting execution on death rows across the United States. In the following article, the work of the execution team described by Robert Johnson has just begun.

The death penalty has made a comeback in recent years. In the late sixties and through most of the seventies, such a thing seemed impossible. There was a moratorium on executions in the U.S., backed by the authority of the Supreme Court. The hiatus lasted roughly a decade. Coming on the heels of a gradual but persistent decline in the use of the death penalty in the Western world, it appeared to some that executions would pass from the American scene [cf Commonweal, January 15, 1988]. Nothing could have been further from the truth.

Beginning with the execution of Gary Gilmore in 1977, over 100 people have been put to death, most of them in the last few years. Some 2,200 prisoners are presently confined on death rows across the nation. The majority of these prisoners have lived under sentence of death for years, in some cases a decade or more, and are running out of legal appeals. It is fair to say that the death penalty is alive and well in America, and that executions will be with us for the foreseeable future.

Gilmore's execution marked the resurrection of the modern death penalty and was big news. It was commemorated in a best-selling tome by Norman Mailer, *The Executioner's Song*. The title was deceptive. Like others who have examined the death penalty, Mailer told us a great deal about the condemned but very little about the executioners. Indeed, if we dwell on Mailer's account, the executioner's story is not only unsung; it is distorted.

Gilmore's execution was quite atypical. His was an instance of state-assisted suicide accompanied by an element of romance and played out against a backdrop of media fanfare. Unrepentant and unafraid, Gilmore refused to appeal his conviction. He dared the state of Utah to take his life, and the media repeated the challenge until it became a taunt that may well have goaded officials to action. A failed suicide pact with his lover staged only days before the execution, using drugs she delivered to him in a visit marked by unusual intimacy, added a hint of melodrama to the proceedings. Gilmore's final words, "Let's do it," seemed to invite the lethal hail of bullets from the firing squad. The nonchalant phrase, at once fatalistic and brazenly rebellious, became Gilmore's epitaph. It clinched his outlaw-hero image, and found its way onto tee shirts that confirmed his celebrity status.

Befitting a celebrity, Gilmore was treated with unusual leniency by prison officials during his confinement on death row. He was, for example, allowed to hold a party the night before his execution, during which he was free to eat, drink, and make merry with his guests until the early morning hours. This is not entirely unprecedented. Notorious English convicts of centuries past would throw farewell balls in prison on the eve of their executions. News accounts of such affairs sometimes included a commentary on the richness of the table and the quality of the dancing. For the record, Gilmore served Tang, Kool-Aid, cookies and coffee, later supplemented by contraband pizza and an unidentified liquor. Periodically, he gobbled drugs obligingly provided by the prison pharmacy. He played a modest arrangement of rock music albums but refrained from dancing.

Gilmore's execution generally, like his parting fete, was decidedly out of step with the tenor of the modern death penalty. Most condemned prisoners fight to save their lives, not to have them taken. They do not see their fate in romantic terms; there are no farewell parties. Nor are they given medication to ease their anxiety or win their compliance. The subjects of typical executions remain anonymous to the public and even to their keepers. They are very much alone at the end.

In contrast to Mailer's account, the focus of the research I have conducted is on the executioners themselves as they carry out typical executions. In my experience executioners—not unlike Mailer himself—can be quite voluble, and sometimes quite moving, in expressing themselves. I shall draw upon their words to describe the death work they carry out in our name.

Death Work and Death Workers

Executioners are not a popular subject of social research, let alone conversation at the dinner table or cocktail party. We simply don't give the subject much thought. When we think of executioners at all, the imagery runs to individual men of disreputable, or at least questionable, character who work stealthily behind the scenes to carry out their grim labors. We picture hooded men hiding in the shadow of the gallows, or anonymous figures lurking out of sight behind electric chairs, gas chambers, firing blinds, or, more recently, hospital gurneys. We wonder who would do such grisly work and how they sleep at night.

This image of the executioner as a sinister and often solitary character is today misleading. To be sure, a few states hire freelance executioners and traffic in macabre theatrics. Executioners may be picked up under cover of darkness and some may still wear black hoods. But today, executions are generally the work of a highly disciplined and efficient team of correctional officers.

Broadly speaking, the execution process as it is now practiced starts with the prisoner's confinement on death row, an oppressive prison-within-a-prison where the condemned are housed, sometimes for years, awaiting execution. Death work gains momentum when an execution date draws near and the prisoner is moved to the death house, a short walk from the death chamber. Finally, the process culminates in the death watch, a twenty-four-hour period that ends when the prisoner has been executed.

This final period, the death watch, is generally undertaken by correctional officers who work as a team and report directly to the prison warden. The warden or his representative, in turn, must by law preside over the execution. In many states, it is a member of the death watch or execution team, acting under the warden's authority, who in fact plays the formal role of executioner. Though this officer may technically work alone, his teammates view the execution as a shared responsibility. As one officer on the death watch told me in no uncertain terms: "We all take part in it; we all play 100 percent in it, too. That takes the load off this one individual [who pulls the switch]." The formal executioner concurred. "Everyone on the team can do it, and nobody will tell you I did it. I know my team." I found nothing in my research to dispute these claims.

The officers of these death watch teams are our modern executioners. As part of a larger study of the death work process, I studied one such group. This team, comprised of nine seasoned officers of varying ranks, had carried out five electrocutions at the time I began my research. I interviewed each officer on the team after the fifth execution, then served as an official witness at a sixth electrocution. Later, I served as a behind-the-scenes observer during their seventh execution. The results of this phase of my research form the substance of this [chapter].

The Death Watch Team

The death watch or execution team members refer to themselves, with evident pride, as simply "the team." This pride is shared by other correctional officials. The warden at the institution I was observing praised members of the team as solid citizens—in his words, country boys. These country boys, he assured me, could be counted on to do the job and do it well. As a fellow administrator put it, "an execution is something [that] needs to be done and good people, dedicated people who believe in the American system, should do it. And there's a certain amount of feeling, probably one to another, that they're part of that—that when they have to hang tough, they can do it, and they can do it right. And that it's just the right thing to do."

The official view is that an execution is a job that has to be done, and done right. The death penalty is, after all, the law of the land. In this context, the phrase "done right" means that an execution should be a proper, professional, dignified undertaking. In the words of a prison administrator, "We had to be sure that we did it properly, professionally, and [that] we gave as much dignity to the person as we possibly could in the process. . . . If you've gotta do it, it might

just as well be done the way it's supposed to be done—without any sensation."

In the language of the prison officials, "proper" refers to procedures that go off smoothly, "professional" means without personal feelings that intrude on the procedures in any way. The desire for executions that take place "without any sensation" no doubt refers to the absence of media sensationalism, particularly if there should be an embarrassing and undignified hitch in the procedures, for example, a prisoner who breaks down or becomes violent and must be forcibly placed in the electric chair as witnesses, some from the media, look on in horror. Still, I can't help but note that this may be a revealing slip of the tongue. For executions are indeed meant to go off without any human feeling, without any sensation. A profound absence of feeling would seem to capture the bureaucratic ideal embodied in the modern execution.

The view of executions held by the execution team members parallels that of correctional administrators but is somewhat more restrained. The officers of the team are closer to the killing and dying, and are less apt to wax abstract or eloquent in describing the process. Listen to one man's observations:

> It's a job. I don't take it personally. You know, I don't take it like I'm having a grudge against this person and this person has done something to me. I'm just carrying out a job, doing what I was asked to do. . . . This man has been sentenced to death in the courts. This is the law and he broke this law, and he has to suffer the consequences. And one of the consequences is to put him to death.

I found that few members of the execution team support the death penalty outright or without reservation. Having seen executions close up, many of them have lingering doubts about the justice or wisdom of this sanction. As one officer put it:

I'm not sure the death penalty is the right way. I don't know if there is a right answer. So I look at it like this: if it's gotta be done, at least it can be done in a humane way, if there is such a word for it. . . . The only way it should be done, I feel, is the way we do it. It's done professionally, it's not no horseplaying. Everything is done by documentation. On time. By the book.

Arranging executions that occur "without any sensation" and that go "by the book" is no mean task, but it is a task that is undertaken in earnest by the execution team. The tone of the enterprise is set by the team leader, a man who takes a hard-boiled, nononsense approach to correctional work in general and death work in particular. "My style," he says, "is this: if it's a job to do, get it done. Do it and that's it." He seeks out kindred spirits, men who see killing condemned prisoners as a job—a dirty job one does reluctantly, perhaps, but above all a job one carries out dispassionately and in the line of duty.

To make sure that line of duty is a straight and accurate one, the death watch team has been carefully drilled by the team leader in the mechanics of execution. The process has been broken down into simple, discrete tasks and practiced repeatedly. The team leader describes the division of labor in the following exchange:

The execution team is a nine-officer team and each one has certain things to do. When I would train you, maybe you'd buckle a belt, that might be all you'd have to do. . . . And you'd be expected to do one thing and that's all you'd be expected to do. And if everybody does what they were taught, or what they were trained to do, at the end the man would be put in the chair and everything would be complete. It's all come together now.

So it's broken down into very small steps. . . .

Very small, yes. Each person has *one* thing to do.

I see. What's the purpose of breaking it down into such small steps?

So people won't get confused. I've learned it's kind of a tense time. When you're executin' a person, killing a person—you call it killin', executin', whatever you want—the man dies anyway. I find the less you got on your mind, why, the better you'll carry it out. So it's just very simple things. And so far, you know, it's all come together, we haven't had any problems.

This division of labor allows each man on the execution team to become a specialist, a technician with a sense of pride in his work. Said one man,

My assignment is the leg piece. Right leg. I roll his pants' leg up, place a piece [electrode] on his leg, strap his leg in . . . I've got all the moves down pat. We train from different posts; I can do any of them. But that's my main post.

The implication is not that the officers are incapable of performing multiple or complex tasks, but simply that it is more efficient to focus each officer's efforts on one easy task.

An essential part of the training is practice. Practice is meant to produce a confident group, capable of fast and accurate performance under pressure. The rewards of practice are reaped in improved performance. Executions take place with increasing efficiency, and eventually occur with precision. "The first one was grisly," a team member confided to me. He explained that there was a certain amount of fumbling, which made the execution seem interminable. There were technical problems as well: The generator was set too high so the body was badly burned. But that is the past, the officer assured me. "The ones now, we know what we're doing. It's just like clockwork."

The Death Watch

The death-watch team is deployed during the last twenty-four hours before an execution. In the state under study, the death watch starts at 11 o'clock the night before the execution and ends at 11 o'clock the next night when the execution takes place. At least two officers would be with the prisoner at any given time during that period. Their objective is to keep the prisoner alive and "on schedule." That is, to move him through a series of critical and cumulatively demoralizing junctures that begin with his last meal and end with his last walk. When the time comes, they must deliver the prisoner up for execution as quickly and unobtrusively as possible.

Broadly speaking, the job of the death watch officer, as one man put it, "is to sit and keep the inmate calm for the last twenty-four hours—and get the man ready to go." Keeping a condemned prisoner calm means, in part, serving his immediate needs. It seems paradoxical to think of the death watch officers as providing services to the condemned, but the logistics of the job make service a central obligation of the officers. Here's how one officer made this point:

> Well, you can't help but be involved with many of the things that he's involved with. Because if he wants to make a call to his family, well, you'll have to dial the number. And you keep records of whatever calls he makes. If he wants a cigarette, well, he's not allowed to keep matches so you light it for him. You've got to pour his coffee, too. So you're aware what he's doing. It's not like you can just ignore him. You've gotta just be with him whether he wants it or not, and cater to his needs.

Officers cater to the condemned because contented inmates are easier to keep under control. To a man, the officers say this is so. But one can never trust even a contented, condemned prisoner.

The death-watch officers see condemned prisoners as men with explosive personalities. "You don't know what, what a man's gonna do," noted one officer. "He's liable to snap, he's liable to pass out. We watch him all the time to prevent him from committing suicide. You've got to be ready—he's liable to do anything." The prisoner is never out of at least one officer's sight. Thus surveillance is constant, and control, for all intents and purposes, is total.

Relations between the officers and their charges during the death watch can be quite intense. Watching and being watched are central to this enterprise, and these are always engaging activities, particularly when the stakes are life and death. These relations are, nevertheless, utterly impersonal; there are no grudges but neither is there compassion or fellow-feeling. Officers are civil but cool; they keep an emotional distance from the men they are about to kill. To do otherwise, they maintain, would make it harder to execute condemned prisoners. The attitude of the officers is that the prisoners arrive as strangers and are easier to kill if they stay that way.

During the last five or six hours, two specific team officers are assigned to guard the prisoner. Unlike their more taciturn and aloof colleagues on earlier shifts, these officers make a conscious effort to talk with the prisoner. In one officer's words, "We just keep them right there and keep talking to them—about anything except the chair." The point of these conversations is not merely to pass time; it is to keep tabs on the prisoner's state of mind, and to steer him away from subjects that might depress, anger, or otherwise upset him. Sociability, in other words, quite explicitly serves as a source of social control. Relationships, such as they are, serve purely manipulative ends. This is impersonality at its worst, masquerading as concern for the strangers one hopes to execute with as little trouble as possible.

Generally speaking, as the execution moves closer, the mood becomes more somber and subdued. There is a last meal. Prisoners can order pretty much what they want, but most eat little or nothing at all. At this point, the prisoners may steadfastly maintain that their executions will be stayed. Such bravado is belied by their loss of appetite. "You can see them going down," said one officer. "Food is the last thing they got on their minds."

Next the prisoners must box their meager worldly goods. These are inventoried by the staff, recorded on a one-page checklist form, and marked for disposition to family or friends. Prisoners are visibly saddened, even moved to tears, by this procedure, which at once summarizes their lives and highlights the imminence of death. At this point, said one of the officers, "I really get into him; I watch him real close." The execution schedule, the officer pointed out, is "picking up momentum and we don't want to lose control of the situation."

This momentum is not lost on the condemned prisoner. Critical milestones have been passed. The prisoner moves in a limbo existence devoid of food or possessions; he has seen the last of such things, unless he receives a stay of execution and rejoins the living. His identity is expropriated as well. The critical juncture in this regard is the shaving of the man's head (including facial hair) and right leg. Hair is shaved to facilitate the electrocution; it reduces physical resistance to electricity and minimizes singeing and burning. But the process has obvious psychological significance as well, adding greatly to the momentum of the execution.

The shaving procedure is quite public and intimidating. The condemned man is taken from his cell and seated in the middle of the tier. His hands and feet are cuffed, and he is dressed only in undershorts. The entire death watch team is assembled around him. They stay at a discrete distance, but it is obvious that they are there to maintain control should he resist in any way or make any untoward move. As a rule, the man is overwhelmed. As one officer told me in blunt terms, "Come eight o'clock, we've got a dead man. Eight o'clock is when we shave the man. We take his identity; it goes with the hair." This taking of identity is indeed a collective process—the team makes a forceful "we," the prisoner their

helpless object. The staff is confident that the prisoner's capacity to resist is now compromised. What is left of the man erodes gradually and, according to the officers, perceptibly over the remaining three hours before the execution.

After the prisoner has been shaved, he is then made to shower and don a fresh set of clothes for the execution. The clothes are unremarkable in appearance, except that velcro replaces buttons and zippers, to reduce the chance of burning the body. The main significance of the clothes is symbolic: they mark the prisoner as a man who is ready for execution. Now physically "prepped," to quote one team member, the prisoner is placed in an empty tomblike cell, the death cell. All that is left is the wait. During this fateful period, the prisoner is more like an object "without any sensation" than like a flesh-and-blood person on the threshold of death.

For condemned prisoners, like Gilmore, who come to accept and even to relish their impending deaths, a genuine calm seems to prevail. It is as if they can transcend the dehumanizing forces at work around them and go to their deaths in peace. For most condemned prisoners, however, numb resignation rather than peaceful acceptance is the norm. By the accounts of the death-watch officers, these more typical prisoners are beaten men. Listen to the officers' accounts:

> A lot of 'em die in their minds before they go to that chair. I've never known of one or heard of one putting up a fight. . . . By the time they walk to the chair, they've completely faced it. Such a reality most people can't understand. Cause they don't fight it. They don't seem to have anything to say. It's just something like "Get it over with." They may be numb, sort of in a trance.

> They go through stages. And, at this stage, they're real humble. Humblest bunch of people I ever seen. Most all of 'em is real, real weak. Most of the time you'd only need

one or two people to carry out an execution, as weak and as humble as they are.

These men seem barely human and alive to their keepers. They wait meekly to be escorted to their deaths. The people who come for them are the warden and the remainder of the death watch team, flanked by high-ranking correctional officials. The warden reads the court order, known popularly as a death warrant. This is, as one officer said, "the real deal," and nobody misses its significance. The condemned prisoners then go to their deaths compliantly, captives of the inexorable, irresistible momentum of the situation. As one officer put it, "There's no struggle. . . . They just walk right on in there." So too, do the staff "just walk right on in there," following a routine they have come to know well. Both the condemned and the executioners, it would seem, find a relief of sorts in mindless mechanical conformity to the modern execution drill.

Witness to an Execution

As the team and administrators prepare to commence the good fight, as they might say, another group, the official witnesses, are also preparing themselves for their role in the execution. Numbering between six and twelve for any given execution, the official witnesses are disinterested citizens in good standing drawn from a cross-section of the state's population. If you will, they are every good or decent person, called upon to represent the community and use their good offices to testify to the propriety of the execution. I served as an official witness at the execution of an inmate.

At eight in the evening, about the time the prisoner is shaved in preparation for the execution, the witnesses are assembled. Eleven in all, we included three newspaper and two television reporters, a state trooper, two police officers, a magistrate, a businessman, and myself. We were picked up in the parking lot behind the main office of the corrections department. There was nothing unusual or even memorable about any of this. Gothic touches were notable by their absence. It wasn't a dark and stormy night; no one emerged from the shadows to lead us to the prison gates.

Mundane considerations prevailed. The van sent for us was missing a few rows of seats so there wasn't enough room for all of us. Obliging prison officials volunteered their cars. Our rather ordinary cavalcade reached the prison but only after getting lost. Once within the prison's walls, we were sequestered for some two hours in a bare and almost shabby administrative conference room. A public information officer was assigned to accompany us and answer our questions. We grilled this official about the prisoner and the execution procedure he would undergo shortly, but little information was to be had. The man confessed ignorance on the most basic points. Disgruntled at this and increasingly anxious, we made small talk and drank coffee.

At 10:40 P.M., roughly two-and-a-half hours after we were assembled and only twenty minutes before the execution was scheduled to occur, the witnesses were taken to the basement of the prison's administrative building, frisked, then led down an alleyway that ran along the exterior of the building. We entered a neighboring cell block and were admitted to a vestibule adjoining the death chamber. Each of us signed a log, and was then led off to the witness area. To our left, around a corner some thirty feet away, the prisoner sat in the condemned cell. He couldn't see us, but I'm quite certain he could hear us. It occurred to me that our arrival was a fateful reminder for the prisoner. The next group would be led by the warden, and it would be coming for him.

We entered the witness area, a room within the death chamber, and took our seats. A picture window covering the front wall of the witness room offered a clear view of the electric chair, which was about twelve feet away from us and well-illuminated. The chair, a large, high-back solid oak structure with imposing black straps, dominated the death chamber. Behind it, on the back wall, was an open panel full of coils and lights. Peeling paint hung from the ceiling and walls; water stains from persistent leaks were everywhere in evidence.

Two officers, one a hulking figure weighing some 400 pounds, stood alongside the electric chair. Each had his hands crossed at the lap and wore a forbidding, blank expression on his face. The witnesses gazed at them and the chair, most of us scribbling notes furiously. We did this, I suppose, as much to record the experience as to have a distraction from the growing tension. A correctional officer entered the witness room and announced that a trial run of the machinery would be undertaken. Seconds later, lights flashed on the control panel behind the chair indicating that the chair was in working order. A white curtain, opened for the test, separated the chair and the witness area. After the test, the curtain was drawn. More tests were performed behind the curtain. Afterwards, the curtain was reopened, and would be left open until the execution was over. Then it would be closed to allow the officers to remove the body.

A handful of high-level correctional officials were present in the death chamber, standing just outside the witness area. There were two regional administrators, the director of the Department of Corrections, and the prison warden. The prisoner's chaplain and lawyer were also present. Other than the chaplain's black religious garb, subdued grey pinstripes and bland correctional uniforms prevailed. All parties were quite solemn.

At 10:58 the prisoner entered the death chamber. He was, I knew from my research, a man with a checkered, tragic past. He had been grossly abused as a child, and went on to become grossly abusive of others. I was told he could not describe his life, from childhood on, without talking about confrontations in defense of a precarious sense of self—at home, in school, on the streets, in the prison yard. Belittled by life and choking with rage, he was hungry to be noticed. Paradoxically, he had found his moment in the spotlight, but it was a dim and unflattering light cast before a small and unappreciative audience. "He'd pose for cameras in the chair—for the attention," his counselor had told me earlier in the day. But the truth was that the prisoner wasn't smiling, and there were no cameras. The prisoner walked quickly and silently toward the chair, an escort of officers in tow. His eyes were turned downward, his expression a bit glazed. Like many before him, the prisoner had threatened to stage a last stand. But that was lifetimes ago, on death row. In the death house, he joined the humble bunch and kept to the executioner's schedule. He appeared to have given up on life before he died in the chair.

En route to the chair, the prisoner stumbled slightly, as if the momentum of the event had overtaken him. Were he not held securely by two officers, one at each elbow, he might have fallen. Were the routine to be broken in this or indeed any other way, the officers believe, the prisoner might faint or panic or become violent, and have to be forcibly placed in the chair. Perhaps as a precaution, when the prisoner reached the chair he did not turn on his own but rather was turned, firmly but without malice, by the officers in his escort. These included the two men at his elbows, and four others who followed behind him. Once the prisoner was seated, again with help, the officers strapped him into the chair.

The execution team worked with machine precision. Like a disciplined swarm, they enveloped him. Arms, legs, stomach, chest, and head were secured in a matter of seconds. Electrodes were attached to the cap holding his head and to the strap holding his exposed right leg. A leather mask was placed over his face. The last officer mopped the prisoner's brow, then touched his hand in a gesture of farewell.

During the brief procession to the electric chair, the prisoner was attended by a chaplain. As the execution team worked feverishly to secure the condemned man's body, the chaplain, who appeared to be upset, leaned over him and placed his forehead in contact with the prisoner's, whispering urgently. The priest might have been praying, but I had the impression he was consoling the man, perhaps assuring him that a forgiving God awaited him in the next life. If he heard the chaplain, I doubt the man comprehended his message. He didn't seem comforted. Rather, he looked stricken and appeared to be in shock. Perhaps the priest's urgent ministrations betrayed his doubts that the prisoner could hold himself together. The chaplain then withdrew at the warden's request, allowing the officers to affix the death mask.

The strapped and masked figure sat before us utterly alone, waiting to be killed. The cap and mask dominated his face. The cap was nothing more than a sponge encased in a leather shell with a metal piece at the top to accept an electrode. It looked decrepit and resembled a cheap, ill-fitting toupee. The mask, made entirely of leather, appeared soiled and worn. It had two parts. The bottom part covered the chin and mouth, the top the eyes and lower forehead. Only the nose was exposed. The effect of a rigidly restrained body, together with the bizarre cap and the protruding nose, was nothing short of grotesque. A faceless man breathed before us in a tragicomic trance, waiting for a blast of electricity that would extinguish his life. Endless seconds passed. His last act was to swallow, nervously, pathetically, with his Adam's apple bobbing. I was struck by that simple movement then, and can't forget it even now. It told me, as nothing else did, that in the prisoner's restrained body, behind that mask, lurked a fellow human being who, at some level, however primitive, knew or sensed himself to be moments from death. The condemned man sat perfectly still for what seemed an eternity but was in fact no more than thirty seconds. Finally the electricity hit him. His body stiffened spasmodically, though only

briefly. A thin swirl of smoke trailed away from his head and then dissipated quickly. The body remained taut, with the right foot raised slightly at the heel, seemingly frozen there. A brief pause, then another minute of shock. When it was over, the body was flaccid and inert.

Three minutes passed while the officials let the body cool. (Immediately after the execution, I'm told, the body would be too hot to touch and would blister anyone who did.) All eyes were riveted to the chair; I felt trapped in my witness seat, at once transfixed and yet eager for release. I can't recall any clear thoughts from that moment. One of the death watch officers later volunteered that he shared this experience of staring blankly at the execution scene. Had the prisoner's mind been mercifully blank before the end? I hoped so.

An officer walked up to the body, opened the shirt at chest level, then continued on to get the physician from an adjoining room. The physician listened for a heartbeat. Hearing none, he turned to the warden and said, "This man has expired." The warden, speaking to the director, solemnly intoned: "Mr. Director, the court order has been fulfilled." The curtain was then drawn and the witnesses filed out.

The Morning After

As the team prepared the body for the morgue, the witnesses were led to the front door of the prison. On the way, we passed a number of cell blocks. We could hear the normal sounds of prison life, including the occasional catcall and lewd comment hurled at uninvited guests like ourselves. But no trouble came in the wake of the execution. Small protests were going on outside the walls, we were told, but we could not hear them. Soon the media would be gone; the protestors would disperse and head for their homes. The prisoners, already home, had been indifferent to the proceedings, as they always are unless the condemned prisoner had been a figure of some consequence in the convict community. Then there might be tension and maybe even a modest disturbance on a prison tier or two. But few convict luminaries are executed, and the dead man had not been one of them. Our escort officer offered a sad tribute to the prisoner: "The inmates, they didn't care about this guy."

I couldn't help but think they weren't alone in this. The executioners went home and set about their lives. Having taken life, they would savor a bit of life themselves. They showered, ate, made love, slept, then took a day or two off. For some, the prisoner's image would linger for that night. The men who strapped him in remembered what it was like to touch him; they showered as soon as they got home to wash off the feel and smell of death. One official sat up picturing how the prisoner looked at the end. (I had a few drinks myself that night with that same image for company.) There was some talk about delayed reactions to the stress of carrying out executions. Though such concerns seemed remote that evening, I learned later that problems would surface for some of the officers. But

no one on the team, then or later, was haunted by the executed man's memory, nor would anyone grieve for him. "When I go home after one of these things," said one man, "I sleep like a rock." His may or may not be the sleep of the just, but one can only marvel at such a thing, and perhaps envy such a man.

Study Questions

1. Describe the execution process, including the work of the death watch team.

2. What functions are served by the elaborate and impersonal procedures used, and how are they carried out?

3. Do you believe that this impersonal process is more civilized than previous forms of executions (e.g., stoning or hanging)? Would you expect this type of execution to be more or less effective as a form of retribution and deterrence than previous methods?

Excerpts from " 'This Man Has Expired': Witness to an Execution" by Robert Johnson. *Commonweal Foundation, 66* (1): 9–15. Copyright © 1989 by Commonweal Foundation. Reprinted by permission. ✦

34
It's About Time
America's Imprisonment Binge

John Irwin
James Austin

Over the past 30 years, the prison population in the United States has been on an upward spiral. Despite unprecedented growth in prison construction during this period, we have not been able to build ourselves out of the dilemma of too many prisoners for too few prison beds. In this article, Irwin and Austin begin by discussing costs, crime reduction, shifts in crime, and forms of punishments, then provide a grim interpretation of the prison situation. They end, however, by offering some solutions and a glimmer of hope for the future.

Our study of the American prison system revealed that most of the unprecedented numbers of people we are sending to prison are guilty of petty property and drug crimes or violations of their conditions of probation or parole. Their crimes or violations lack any of the elements that the public believes are serious or associates with dangerous criminals. Even offenders who commit frequent felonies and who define themselves as "outlaws," "dope fiends," crack dealers, or "gang bangers" commit mostly petty felonies. These "high-rate" offenders, as they have been labeled by policy makers and criminologists, are, for the most part, uneducated, unskilled (at crime as well as conventional pursuits), and highly disorganized persons who have no access to any form of rewarding, meaningful conventional life.

They usually turn to dangerous, mostly unrewarding, petty criminal pursuits as one of the few options they have to earn money, win some respect, and avoid monotonous lives on the streets. Frequently, they spend most of their young lives behind bars.

What may be more surprising is that a majority of all persons sent to prison, even the high-rate offenders, aspire to a relatively modest conventional life and hope to prepare for that while serving their prison sentences. This should be considered particularly important because very little in the way of equipping prisoners for a conventional life on the outside is occurring in our prisons. In preceding decades, particularly the 1950s and 1960s, a much greater effort was made to "rehabilitate" prisoners. Whatever the outcome of these efforts (as this is a matter of some dispute), rehabilitation has been all but abandoned. Prisons have been redefined as places of punishment. In addition, rapid expansion has crowded prisoners into physically inadequate institutions and siphoned off most available funds from all services other than those required to maintain control. Prisons have become true human warehouses—often highly crowded, violent, and cruel.

The Financial Cost

We must consider the costs and benefits of increased imprisonment rates. The financial cost is the easiest to estimate. Most people are aware that prisons are expensive to build and operate. Few, however, understand just how expensive. Indeed, previous estimates routinely cited by public officials have dramatically underestimated the amounts of money spent on housing prisoners and building new prisons.

Prison and jail administrators typically calculate operating costs by dividing their annual budget by the average daily prison population. However, this accounting practice is misleading and produces patently low estimates of the true costs of imprisonment. For example, agency budgets often exclude contracted services for food, medical care, legal services, and transportation provided by other government agencies. According to two studies conducted in New York, these additional expenses increased the official operating costs by 20 to 25 percent. An independent audit of the Indiana prison system found that actual expenditures were one-third higher than those reported by the agency. Besides these "hidden" direct expenditures, there are other costs that are rarely included in such calculations. To name only a few, the state loses taxes that could be paid by many of the imprisoned, pays more welfare to their families, and maintains spacious prison grounds that are exempt from state and local real estate taxation. In the New York study conducted by Coopers and Lybrand in 1977, these costs amounted to over $21,000 per prisoner.

Although there is considerable variation among the states, on the average prison officials claim that it costs about $20,000 per year to house, feed, clothe, and supervise a prisoner. Because this estimate does not include indirect costs, the true annual expenditure probably exceeds $30,000 per prisoner.

The other enormous cost is prison construction. Prisons are enclosed, "total" institutions in which prisoners are not only housed, but guarded, fed, clothed, and worked. They also receive some schooling and medical and psychological treatment. These needs require—in addition to cellblocks or dormitories—infirmaries, classrooms, laundries, offices, maintenance shops, boiler rooms, and kitchens. Dividing the total construction costs of one of these institutions by the number of prisoners it houses produces a cost per "bed" of as low as $7,000 for a minimum-security prison to $155,000 for a maximum-security prison.

Instead of using current tax revenues to pay directly for this construction, however, the state does what most citizens do when they buy a house—that is, borrow the money, which must be paid back over several decades. The borrowing is done by selling bonds or using other financing instruments that may triple the original figure. The costs of prison construction are further increased by errors in original bids by contractors and cost overruns caused by delays in construction, which seem to be the rule rather than the exception. A recent survey of 15 states with construction projects revealed that cost overruns averaged *40 percent* of the original budget projections.

Consequently, when a state builds and finances a typical medium security prison, it will spend approximately $268,000 per bed for construction alone. So in the states that have expanded their prison populations, the cost per additional prisoner will be $39,000 a year. This includes the cost of building the new cell amortized 30 years. In other words, the 30-year cost of adding space for one prisoner is more than $1 million.

These enormous increases in the cost of imprisonment are just beginning to be felt by the states. Budgetary battles in which important state services for children, the elderly, the sick, and the poor are gutted to pay for prisons have already begun. In coming years, great cutbacks in funds for public education, medical services for the poor, highway construction, and other state services will occur.

Crime Reduction

Those who are largely responsible for this state of affairs—elected officials who have harangued on the street crime issue and passed laws resulting in more punitive sentencing policies, judges who deliver more and longer prison terms, and government criminal justice functionaries who have supported the punitive trend in criminal justice policies—promised that the great expansion of prison populations would reduce crime in our society. A key U.S. Department of Justice official recently summarized the government's scientific basis for supporting incarceration as the best means for reducing crime as follows: "Statisticians and criminal justice researchers have consistently found that falling crime rates are associated with rising imprisonment rates, and rising crime rates are associated with falling imprisonment rates." Former Attorney General William Barr more recently restated this position, arguing that the country had a "clear choice" of either building more prisons or tolerating higher violent crime rates. This view implies that increasing the government's capacity to imprison is the single most effective strategy for reducing crime. . . .

Demographic Shifts and Crime Rates

There are several reasons to question the interpretation that reductions for NCVS property crimes validate the "imprisonment reduces crime" perspective. First is the failure to incorporate the influence of shifting demographics on crime rates. Most crimes are committed by males between the ages of 15 and 24. As that population grows or subsides, one can expect associated fluctuations in the crime rates. Before changes in crime rates can be attributed to changes in imprisonment rates, the influence of demographic changes must be taken into consideration.

Beginning in the early 1960s, the size of this age group began to grow and continued to grow through the 1970s—the exact period of the rise in crime rates. By the late 1970s, this age group as a percentage of the population began to decline and the crime rate began to ebb by 1980. A recent article by two criminologists found that most of the decline in crime rates observed since 1979–1985 was a direct result of a declining "at-risk" population. When we take into account the influence of this demographic shift, reductions in the NCVS from 1980 to 1988 are largely attributable (60 percent of

the crime reduction explained) to reductions in the ages 15–24 high-crime-rate population. The same analysis, when applied to the UCR data, actually shows an increase in UCR during the same time period.

The NCVS rates are also influenced by significant changes that have occurred over the past two decades in the number, characteristics, and location of U.S. households. In the most recent publication on NCVS, the Justice Department acknowledged that, since 1973, the size of the American household has (1) declined, (2) shifted from urban areas to suburban locations, and (3) shifted from the Northeast and Midwest to the South and the West.

The first two conditions automatically reduce crime rate estimates because smaller households located in suburban areas are less likely than larger and urban households to experience crime. The third condition, relocation to the West where crime rates are highest, increases the likelihood of households being victimized. These trends in the NCVS must be more carefully analyzed before conclusions can be made that a tripling of the imprisonment rate is solely responsible for declines in personal and household theft.

Drug Trafficking and Property Crime

A second reason to question the drop in NCVS and UCR property crimes since 1980 is related to the dramatic increase in drug trafficking that began in 1980. It is very possible that the decline in burglary and theft reflected a change in criminal activity from these crimes to the more lucrative and less difficult drug trade business. It is difficult to prove with statistics that this shift has indeed occurred because drug dealing is not reported by the NCVS. But for those criminologists who spend time observing America's deteriorating inner cities, it is obvious that street crime has shifted from household burglaries to drug trafficking.

Prison Versus Other Forms of Punishment

Even if the NCVS figures reflect a true drop in property crime, it cannot be concluded that imprisonment was the cause of the decline. . . . [O]ther and less punitive forms of correctional supervision (probation, parole, and jail populations) grew just as fast as the prison population. Statistically and substantively, it could be argued that NCVS crime rate reductions were related to greater use of probation and short jail terms since they are applied to a far larger number of offenders than prison.

State-by-State Comparisons

The *best* test of the proposition that increasing prison populations has reduced crime is a comparison between the 50 states and the District of Columbia, which serve as experiments on this issue. This is because they not only differ in their crime and imprisonment rates, but they have also undergone dramatically different changes in these over the last fifteen years.

The period 1980 to 1991 is ideal for this comparison. The national crime rate peaked in 1980, as it did individually in all but 13 states. (These peaked in 1981 or 1982.) Also, after increasing slowly for several years, the national rate of incarceration began to rise steeply. . . . All the states increased their prison populations in that 12-year period, but they did so by very different amounts, from 26 to 742 per 100,000. The states and D.C., in a sense, are 51 different "petri dishes" (used in biological experiments), each with its unique array of factors that could be related to changes in crime rates, into which the experimental variable—increases in imprisonment—is introduced. If a causal relationship existed, we would see a consistent pattern—namely,

states that increased their imprisonment rates the most would show the largest reductions in crime rates. Conversely, states that increased their imprisonment rates more slowly would show higher increases in crime rates.

Actually, there is no pattern. . . . Most states (34) experienced decline in crime rates. However, there is no tendency for those that increased their prison populations the most to have greater decreases in crime. In fact, the opposite is true. The states that increased their prison populations by less than 100 per 100,000 were more likely to have experienced a decrease in crime than those that increased imprisonment rates by more than 200. . . .

We analyzed this distribution by regression analysis, which establishes the line from which the points deviate the least (whether or not the distribution calls for a line) and measures to what extent the points deviate from it. This is indicated in a coefficient of correlation—R. When R is 1.0, the points all lie on the line. In our case, R was .08179 in the positive direction. This suggests that in the 12-year period, there was a very slight tendency for more incarceration to be related to *increases* in crime. It would be simple minded to conclude that this is a causal relationship. But it is very reasonable to recognize that this state by state comparison strongly indicates that the massive increases in incarceration failed to produce *any* reduction in crime rates.

The California Imprisonment Experiment

If we were to pick a state to test the imprisonment theory, California would be the obvious choice, for this state's prison population has increased from 19,623 in 1977 to over 110,000 by 1992. Former Attorney General William Barr believes California should serve as the model for the rest of the country. California, he states, "quadrupled its prison population during the 1980s and various forms of violent crimes fell by as much as 37 percent. But in Texas, which did not increase prison space, crime increased 29 percent in the decade."

A closer examination of the California data presents a very different picture than that cited by Barr. . . . During this period, the size of the prison population increased by 237 percent (from 29,202 to 97,309) and the jail population increased by 118 percent (34,064 to 74,312). Prison operating costs increased by 400 percent, and jail operating costs increased by 265 percent. As of 1990, Californians were paying nearly $3 billion per year to operate the state's prisons and jails.

What has been the impact of this substantial investment in violent crime? Contrary to the claim that the violent crime rate (homicide, rape, robbery, and assault) has dropped, the rate actually *increased* by 21 percent. Substantial declines did occur, but only for burglary and larceny theft—a phenomenon that, as we noted earlier, was at least partially attributable to growth in illegal drug trafficking and shifts in the at-risk population. More interesting is the fact that after 1984 the overall crime rate, and especially violent crimes and auto theft, have grown despite a continued escalation of imprisonment. . . .

California is now so strapped for funds that it must dramatically reduce the number of its parole officers and has been unable to open two brand new prisons, capable of holding 12,000 inmates. The state now has the most overcrowded prison system in the nation (183 percent of rated capacity) and spends millions of dollars each year on court cases challenging the crowded prison conditions. Despite the billions of dollars now being spent each year in locking up offenders, the public is as fearful of crime as it was a decade ago. Clearly, the grand California imprisonment experiment has done little to reduce crime or the public's fear of crime.

The Costs of Further Escalating the Imprisonment Binge

Many argue that crime has not been reduced in California or nationally simply because we have not incarcerated enough persons. They suggest that if we were willing to imprison many times more people for much longer periods of time, significant reductions in crime would occur, that is, "street crime." (The pervasive and more expensive other forms of crime, e.g., white collar crime, are not and would not be affected by imprisonment.)

This viewpoint is not mere speculation but one that is being regularly advocated by many politicians. Former Attorney General William Barr listed 24 steps the government should take to reduce violent crime including "truth in sentencing" that requires inmates to serve the full amount of their sentences, increased use of mandatory minimum prison sentences, relaxation of evidentiary rules to increase conviction rates, greater use of the death penalty, and increased numbers of police officers. President Clinton campaigned on adding 100,000 police officers to the streets to increase arrests. And, both political parties have formally advocated the need to get even tougher with criminals.

. . .The major components of such a program would be as follows:

Policy 1: Add 100,000 police officers;

Result: Increases the number of felony arrests from 3.6 million to 4.2 million;

Policy 2: Increase the conviction rate from 65 percent to 75 percent;

Result: Increases the number of convictions from 2.3 million to 3.4 million;

Policy 3: Increase the proportion of convictions resulting in a prison sentence from 19 percent to 40 percent;

Result: Increases the number of prison admissions from 475,000 to 1.5 million;

Policy 4: Adopt a "truth in sentencing" policy that would require offenders to serve 80 percent of their prison terms;

Result: Length of stay in prison would increase from 1.6 years to 5 years.

The net result of these reforms would be to create a prison population of 7.5 million. Such a massive expansion of the prison population would undoubtedly have a profound impact on the crime rate. But there would be a heavy price to pay. An additional 6.7 million prison beds would have to be constructed at a cost of at least $376 billion. Annual operating costs would escalate from $15.1 billion to $133 billion.

To do this constitutionally while preserving a semblance of our civil rights would require an expansion of the other parts of the criminal justice system—the jails, courts, and police departments. Assuming that the use of probation and parole would be reduced there would be limited savings on the least expensive components of the correctional system.

The annual price of all this escalation, less the prison construction costs, would probably exceed $220 billion as opposed to the $74 billion now being spent, with most of these costs being borne by state governments to operate large scale prison systems. States now spend only $14 billion on corrections alone (which includes probation and parole services). Total state general fund expenditures in 1990 totaled $300 billion. Consequently, to operate such a massive prison system at the state level would require over one third of all state revenues to be dedicated to prison operations. And these costs would not include the nearly $376 billion in capital construction funds or increases to local government to expand and operate its law enforcement, court systems, and local jails.

Unless we wanted to strip down or abandon many other government enterprises—education, welfare, transportation, medical services—we would have to greatly increase state taxes to pay for this massive experiment in imprisonment. In many ways—the financial costs, the social disruptions, the removal of a very large percent of young males—this policy would be like World War II, prolonged for decades.

Of course there would be other consequences. The nation's incarceration rate would increase from 310 per 100,000 to over 3,000 per 100,000. Since 47 percent of the current prison population is black, it would mean that most of the nation's 5.5 million black males age 18–39 would be incarcerated and we would look a lot like South Africa of the 1950s and 1960s.

It is still not clear what this would do to overall crime rates. Certainly, the removal of such a large portion of young males would reduce the forms of street crime we are presently experiencing. However, it is impossible to anticipate what new forms of social problems, crime, and upheavals this punitive experiment would cause. The massive social disruptions—such as the removal of most young, black males—might result in unanticipated new types of violent, criminal activities. In a few years, millions of parolees, who probably will be considerably socially crippled and embittered by their long prison terms, will be returning to society. They will at least be an enormous nuisance and burden, but also may engage in a lot of crime. Even if we assume that crime would eventually decline, how long would we have to maintain such a large prison system to continually deter and incapacitate each successive generation of potential criminals?

Since we do not believe Americans are ready for this costly solution to the crime problem through imprisonment, we are left with its failure. . . .

Voodoo Criminology

The failure of the massive expansion of prison populations to accomplish its most important objective—the reduction of crime—should come as no surprise because the idea that increased penalties will reduce crime is based on a simplistic and fallacious theory of criminal behavior. It starts with the idea that every person is an isolated, willful actor who makes completely rational decisions to maximize his or her pleasure and to minimize his or her pain. Consequently, individuals only commit crimes when they believe it will lead to more pleasure, gain, or satisfaction and with minimal risk for pain or punishment. If penalties for being caught are small or nonexistent, then many persons who are not restrained by other factors (e.g., strong conventional morals or the disapproval of close friends or family) will commit crimes—indeed, a *lot* of crimes. Only by increasing the certainty and severity of punishment, this thinking goes, will people "think twice" and be deterred.

The punishment/incapacitation/deterrence theory assumes that all individuals have access to the same conventional lifestyles for living out a law-abiding life. This is not true for most of the individuals who are caught up in our criminal justice system. For many, particularly young members of the inner-city underclass, the choice is not between conventional and illegal paths to the good life, but between illegal and risky paths or no satisfaction at all. They are faced with a limited and depressing choice between a menial, dull, impoverished, undignified life at the bottom of the conventional heap or a life with some excitement, some monetary return, and a slim chance of larger financial rewards, albeit with great risks of being imprisoned, maimed, or even killed. Consequently, many "choose" crime despite the threat of imprisonment.

For many young males, especially African Americans and Hispanics, the threat of going to prison or jail is no threat at all but rather an expected or accepted part of life. Most minority males will be punished by the criminal justice system during their lifetime. Deterrence and punishment are effective only when the act of punishment actually worsens a person's lifestyle. For millions of males, imprisonment poses no

such threat. As a young black convict put it when Claude Brown told him that his preprison life meant that there was a "60 percent chance he will be killed, permanently maimed, or end up doing a long bit in jail":

> "I see where you comin' from, Mr. Brown," he replied, "but you got things kind of turned around the wrong way. You see, all the things that you say could happen to me is dead on the money and that is why I can't lose. Look at it from my point of view for a minute. Let's say I go and get wiped [killed]. Then I ain't got no more needs, right? All my problems are solved. I don't need no more money, no more nothing, right? Okay, supposin' I get popped, shot in the spine and paralyzed for the rest of my life—that could happen playing football, you know. Then I won't need a whole lot of money because I won't be able to go no place and do nothin', right?"

> "So, I'll be on welfare, and the welfare check is all the money I'll need, right? Now if I get busted and end up in the joint [prison] pullin' a dime and a nickel, like I am, then I don't have to worry about no bucks, no clothes. I get free rent and three squares a day. So you see, Mr. Brown, I really can't lose."

America's Farm System for Criminals

Most people who engage in crime do so not as isolated individuals, but—like we all are—as participants in various social organizations, groups, or "social systems," each of which has its own rules and values. Some groups in our society (often because of subjection to reduced circumstances such as poverty, idleness, and incarceration over an extended period of time) develop preferences for deviant lifestyles. For example, young males who were abused as children, dropped out of school, lived in poverty, abused drugs, and served many juvenile jail and prison sentences have become immersed in deviant values and are distanced from any set of conventional values. They are most satisfied when engaging in specialized deviant practices related to their unique culture—wild partying involving drug use and sex along with extremely risky behavior involving extreme displays of machismo.

Since crime is not the sole product of individual motives, efforts, especially by the state, to punish the individual without addressing the social forces that produced that individual will fail. Individuals do not decide to sell drugs, purchase drugs, and set up single-proprietor operations on their own. Most street crime involves groups, organizations, and networks. Drug dealers are persons who have been involved in groups and networks of people who use drugs, have connections, know or are dealers. The same is true of gang bangers, hustlers, and thieves.

In effect, America has created a lower-class culture designed to produce new cohorts of street criminals each generation. Similar to organized sports, most of these criminal operations have major leagues, minors leagues, and a bench. Children come up through the ranks, learn the game, and finally move into the starting lineup once they reach their adolescent years. When they are temporarily or permanently removed (that is, arrested, imprisoned, or killed), they are replaced by others from the bench to continue the game. When the bench is depleted, someone comes up from the minors. Much as in professional and college sports, the span of their career is short, with their most active crime years taking place between the ages of 15 and 24.

Our impoverished inner-city neighborhoods (or what is left of them as neighborhoods) have almost unlimited reserves milling about who are kept out of the starting lineup by managers and first-string players. As soon as the police arrest the "kingpin" drug dealer, the leaders of a gang, some of the top pimps or hustlers, new recruits move in to take over these positions.

This characterization of criminal operations also explains why the War on Drugs, which has been going on for at least a decade, has failed. During the 1980s, the government spent billions of tax dollars and arrested millions for drug possession or drug trafficking. Regularly, the media reported that a new large-scale drug operation and some kingpin drug dealers [had] been caught. Drugs continue to be at least as available as they were before the new arrests, however, as "new" kingpins quickly and often violently replace the recently departed leaders.

Even if a particular type of criminal operation dies out, new crime games appear. In the late 1980s, the news media and government officials were blaming crack cocaine dealing for unprecedented numbers of homicides in Los Angeles inner city neighborhoods. However, sociologist Jack Katz discovered that, contrary to the media's reports, homicide rates in the crack neighborhoods had not changed over the last decade. Earlier in the 1980s, rival gangs were killing each other over territory. It seems, using the sport analogy, that the number of players available for crime games is related to broader social conditions, such as the existence of a large under-employed population of young males who have the ordinary youthful desires for respect, excitement, and gratification but are confronted with extremely limited access to legitimate means of acquiring them. Thus, the number of potential players remains constant over an extended period. Only the types of games being played change from season to season.

Cutting Our Losses on the Prison Solution

The past decade has witnessed the uncritical adoption of a national policy to reduce crime by increasing the use of imprisonment. That policy has failed. Despite a more than doubling of the correctional industrial complex and a tripling of criminal justice system costs, crime in general has not been reduced. Though there is evidence that property crimes committed against households have declined, all measures of crime are increasing. Moreover, it appears that crime is likely to increase in the near future. This is not news to the American public, which is increasingly apprehensive about personal safety even as their taxes are increased to pay for the failed imprisonment policy.

For these reasons, the grand imprisonment experiment, which has dominated America's crime reduction policy for the past 15 years, should not only be severely questioned but abandoned. It has simply failed to produce its primary objective—reduced crime. This is not to say that certain offenders should not be imprisoned and, in some cases, for lengthy periods; a few individuals are truly dangerous and need to receive long sentences. But to argue that all offenders should be so treated is misguided and ineffective.

Reducing crime means addressing those factors that are more directly related to crime. This means reducing teenage pregnancies, high school dropout rates, unemployment, drug abuse, and lack of meaningful job opportunities. Although many will differ on how best to address these factors, the first step is to acknowledge that these forces have far more to do with reducing crime than escalating the use of imprisonment.

The "prison reduces crime" theory has not worked. Crime, especially violent crime, is not declining. We need to cut our losses and try crime prevention policies that will work. It may well take a decade before the fruits of such an effort are realized, but we can no longer afford to keep investing in a widespread crime reduction policy that has failed so ubiquitously.

The Social Costs of Imprisonment

The full range and depth of the social costs, which are tremendous, are much more difficult to identify and measure accurately. Though most of the persons in our sample were not contributing significantly to the support of a family, some were. About 40 percent indicated that they were employed at the time of arrest and 25 percent stated that they had been employed most of the time in the period before arrest. Many prisoners sent to prison are married and have children. Moreover, all of them have mothers, fathers, brothers, sisters, uncles, aunts, or cousins. Though it is sometimes true that a prisoner was causing family and friends a great deal of difficulty, usually relatives experience some disruption and pain when persons are sent to prison. The removal of an individual from his social contexts does some harm to his family, friends, and employer, though the amount of this harm is hard to calculate.

Perhaps the highest cost of our careless extension of the use of imprisonment is the damage to thousands of people, most of whom have no prior prison record and who are convicted of petty crimes, and the future consequences of this damage to the society. These persons are being packed into dangerous, crowded prisons with minimal access to job training, education, or other services that will prepare them for life after prison. Some marginally involved petty criminals are converted into hard-core "outlaws"—mean, violence-prone convicts who dominate crowded prison wards.

Making matters worse, a growing number of prisoners are being subjected to extremely long sentences. These long-termers are not only stacking up in prisons and filling all available space, but their long terms, much of which they serve in maximum-security prisons that impose severe deprivation on them, result in more loss of social and vocational skills, more estrangement, and more alienation.

It must be kept in mind that virtually all of these profoundly damaged individuals will be released from prison and will try to pick up life on the outside. For the most part, their chances of pursuing a merely viable, much less satisfying, conventional life after prison are small. The contemporary prison experience has converted them into social misfits and cripples, and there is a growing likelihood that they will return to crime, violence, and other forms of disapproved deviance.

This ultimate cost of imprisonment—that which society must suffer when prisoners are released—continues to be confirmed by research. The Rand Corporation study cited earlier found that convicted felons sent to prison or granted probation had significantly higher rates of rearrest after release than those on probation. In California, which has by far the nation's most overcrowded prison system, the recidivism rate (the rate of reimprisonment of prisoners released on parole), has doubled in the last five years.

Even more tragically, imprisonment is increasingly falling on blacks, Hispanics, and other people of color. Sixty years ago, almost one-fourth of all prison admissions were nonwhite. Today, nearly half of all prison admissions are nonwhite. Nationally, the imprisonment rate of blacks is at least ten times higher than for whites. Hispanics are incarcerated at a rate three times higher than whites. Studies show that a black male American has a 50 percent chance of being arrested once by age 29.

Our Vindictive Society

Crime has incurred another profound cost: the increase of general vindictiveness in our society. Historically, Americans (as compared to Europeans and Japanese, for example) have been highly individualistic, which means, for one thing, that they are prone to blaming individuals for their actions. In America, according to the dominant ideology, everyone is responsible for his or her acts and every act is accomplished by a willful actor. Consequently, every undesirable, harmful, "bad" act is the work of a blameful actor. This belief has resulted in our being the most litigious people in the world and has given us the world's largest legal profession. It has also led us to criminalize more and more behavior and to demand more and more legal action against those who break laws. Today many Americans want someone blamed and punished for every transgression and inconvenience they experience.

Social science should have taught us that all human behavior is only partially a matter of free will and that persons are only partially responsible for their deeds. Everyone's actions are always somewhat influenced or dominated by factors not of one's own making and beyond personal control (with economic situation being the most influential and obvious).

Moreover, seeking vengeance is a pursuit that brings more frustration than satisfaction. It has not only been an obstacle in solving many social problems and in developing cooperative, communal attitudes (the lack of which are one of the important causes of the crime problem), but it is in itself a producer of excessive amounts of anxiety and frustration. Ultimately, vindictiveness erects barriers between people, isolates them, and prevents them from constructing the cooperative, communal social organizations that are so necessary for meaningful, satisfying human existence. Ironically, it is just these social structures that contain the true solution to our crime problem.

The Crime Problem as a Diversion

Our tendency toward vindictiveness is greatly nurtured by the media, politicians, and other public figures who have persistently harangued on the crime issue. They do this largely because the crime issue is seductive. It is seductive to politicians because they can divert attention away from larger and more pressing problems, such as the economy and pollution, whose solution would require unpopular sacrifices, particularly for them and other more affluent segments of the society. Street crime is seductive to the media because it fits their preferred "sound bite" format of small bits of sensational material. Likewise, it is deeply seductive to the public, who, though they fear crime, possess at the same time deep fascination for it.

It's About Time

We *must* turn away from the excessive use of prisons. The current incarceration binge will eventually consume large amounts of tax money, which will be diverted from essential public services such as education, child care, mental health, and medical services—the very same services that will have a far greater impact on reducing crime than building more prisons. We will continue to imprison millions of people under intolerably cruel and dangerous conditions. We will accumulate a growing number of ex-convicts who are more or less psychologically and socially crippled and excluded from conventional society, posing a continuing nuisance and threat to others. We will severely damage some of our more cherished humanitarian values, which are corroded by our excessive focus on blame and vengeance. And we will further divide our society into the white affluent classes and a poor nonwhite underclass, many of them convicts and ex-convicts. In effect, we are gradually putting our own apartheid into place.

We believe that these trends can be reversed without jeopardizing public safety. But how should we accomplish a turnaround of this magnitude? First, we must recognize that crime can, at best, be marginally reduced by escalating the use of imprisonment. If we are to truly reduce crime rates, we as a society must embark on a decade-long strategy that reverses the social and economic trends of the previous decade. In particular, we must jettison the overly expensive and ineffective criminal justice approach and redirect our energies on the next generation of youth, who already are at risk for becoming the generation of criminals.

The "crime reduction" reforms we have in mind have little to do with criminal justice reform. Rather, these reforms would serve to reduce poverty, single-parent families headed by females, teenage pregnancies and abortions, welfare dependency, unemployment, high dropout rates, drug abuse, and inadequate health care. These, and not "slack" imprisonment policies, are the social indicators that have proven to be predictive of high crime rates.

The programs and policies that will work, such as better prenatal health care for pregnant mothers, better health care for children to protect them against life-threatening illnesses, Head Start, Job Corps, and Enterprise Zones, have been well-documented. We will also need a level of commitment from our major corporate leaders to reduce the flight of jobs, especially the so-called blue-collar and industrial jobs, from this country to Third World nations where cheap labor can be exploited for profits but at tremendous cost to this country. Given the current fiscal crisis facing most states and the federal government, however, it will be extremely difficult to continue a traditional and increasingly expensive war against crime and at the same time launch new social and economic policies that will reduce crime rates in the long term.

So how do we go about cutting our losses? We begin by reducing, or at least reducing the rate of growth in, the prison population and reallocating those "savings" to prevention programs target[ing] at-risk youth and their families. But is it realistic to assume that prison populations and their associated costs can be lowered without increasing crime? How, exactly, should we proceed?

Many methods of reducing prison populations have been advocated. Some argue that certain classes of felony crimes should be reclassified as misdemeanors or decriminalized completely. In the late 1960s, there was a great deal of support to do this for many minor drug offenses. Others claim that a significant number of those convicted of felonies could be diverted from prison to probation and new forms of alternatives to prison, including intensive probation, house arrest, electronic surveillance, and greater use of fines and restitution.

We are persuaded, however, that these "front-end" reforms would not substantially reduce prison crowding. Historically, well-intentioned alternatives have had marginal impact on reducing prison populations. Instead, they have had the unintended consequence of widening the net of criminal justice by imposing more severe sanctions on people who otherwise would not be sentenced to prison. Moreover, they have little support with public officials, who, like the public, are increasingly disenchanted with probation and other forms of community sanctions.

For alternatives to work, legislators, prosecutors, police, judges, and correctional agencies would all have to agree on new laws and policies to implement them. Such a consensus is unlikely to occur in the near future, since these measures are replete with controversy and disagreement. Even if the forces that are presently driving the punitive response to crime abated considerably, it would take several years to work through these disagreements and effect changes in the laws and policies that would slowly produce an easing of prison population growth. Such a slow pace of reform would not allow states to avoid the catastrophe that is rapidly developing in our prisons.

Even diversion of a substantial number of offenders from prison would not have a major impact on prison population growth. "Front-end" diversion reforms are targeted for those few offenders who are already serving the shortest prison terms (usually less than a year). The recent flood of tougher sentencing laws has greatly lengthened prison terms for offenders charged with more serious crimes and repeat property or drug offenders. Consequently, it is this segment of the prison population that is piling up in the prisons. The problem is that inmates with long sentences are unlikely to be candidates for diversion from prison.

For these reasons, we believe the single most direct solution that would have an immediate and dramatic impact on prison crowding and would not affect public safety is to *shorten prison terms*. This can be done swiftly and fairly through a number of existing mechanisms, such as greater use of existing good-time credit statutes and/or accelerating parole eligibility.

Indeed, many states have launched such programs with no impact on crime rates. Between 1980 and 1983, the Illinois Director of Corrections released more than 21,000 prisoners an average of 90 days early because of severe prison crowding. The impact on the state's crime rate was insignificant, yet the program saved almost $50 million in tax dollars. A study of the program found that the amount of crime that could be attributed to early release was less than 1 percent of the total crime of the state. In fact, the state's crime rate actually *declined* while the early release program was in effect. Based on these findings, the state expanded its use of "good time" by another 90 days. A recent study of that expanded program found that the state was now saving over $90 million per year in state funds, even taking into account the costs of early release crimes (which represented less than 1 percent of all crimes committed in Illinois) to crime victims. The governor has declared that no more new prisons will be built in Illinois.

An earlier demonstration of how swiftly and easily prison populations can be reduced occurred in California from 1967 to 1970. When Ronald Reagan became governor, he instructed the parole board to reduce the prison population. The board began shortening sentences, which it had the power to do within the indeterminate sentence system, and in two years lowered the prison population from 28,000 to less than 18,000.

Many other states are following these examples. A recent study of the Oklahoma preparole program found that inmates could be released earlier by three to six months without influencing the state's crime rate and at considerable savings to the state. Specifically, that study found that for each inmate released early, the state saved over $9,000 per inmate, even when taking into account the costs of crimes committed by these offenders had they remained in prison. Texas, Tennessee, and Florida are just a few states that have been required by the federal courts to reduce overcrowded prison systems by shortening prison terms.

For such a policy to work, prison terms would have to be shortened across the board, including inmates serving lengthy sentences for crimes of violence who, because of their age, no longer pose a threat to public safety. Since the average prison stay in the United States is approximately two years, even marginal reductions in the length of stay for large categories of inmates would have substantial effects on population size. Using the 1990 figure of approximately 325,000 new prison sentences, and assuming that 80 percent of those inmates (representing those who are nonviolent and have satisfactory prison conduct records) had their prison terms reduced by 30 days, the nation's prison population would have declined by 27,000 inmates. A 90-day reduction would result in 80,000 fewer prisoners; a six-month reduction, 160,000 fewer prisoners. Assuming a conservative average cost of $25,000 per inmate, the nation would avert as much as $4 billion a year in operating costs and reduce the need to construct new prisons.

Unless such a reform is adopted, prison populations as well as crime rates will continue to rise indefinitely into the twenty-first century. Reducing prison terms by the amounts advocated may only slow the rate of expansion. But it can be done with no cost to public safety and with enormous dollar savings. Most important, these averted costs can be redirected to more promising social reforms targeted at high-risk and disadvantaged youth and their families. Only by cutting our losses on our failed policy of unchecked punishment and imprisonment can we adequately address those social and economic forces that feed America's crime problem.

Study Questions

1. How do the authors determine that crime rates are not reduced by a policy of increased incarceration?

2. What are some of the negative ramifications of a policy of further incarceration?

3. What policies do the authors suggest in place of incarceration?

Excerpts from *It's About Time: America's Imprisonment Binge*, 1st Edition, by John Irwin and James Austin. Copyright © 1994. Reprinted with permission of Wadsworth, an imprint of the Wadsworth Group, a division of Thomson Learning. ✦

35
Reconsidering Restorative Justice

The Corruption of Benevolence Revisited?

Sharon Levrant
Francis T. Cullen
Betsy Fulton
John F. Wozniak

Restorative justice is being embraced across the country as a progressive way to deal with offenders, victims, and the communities in which they reside. Advocates point to the restoration and involvement of victims in the correctional process, and believe that by bringing offenders and victims together many benefits can accrue, including reductions in recidivism. Can a system designed around an adversarial and oftentimes punitive approach become truly restorative? Will restorative programs do more harm than good by widening the net? Are victims willing and able to participate in a meaningful way? And why would we expect restorative programs to have an effect on recidivism? These questions are addressed in this article by Levrant and her colleagues. As we shall learn, the promise of restorative justice may be difficult to achieve.

Three decades have passed since the rehabilitative agenda was pushed aside for crime control policies rooted in a "get tough" philosophy. This orientation has led to harsh forms of punishment, including a dramatic increase in incarceration, the passage of "three strikes and you're out" laws, the reinstatement of the death penalty, and a return to chain gangs. Even community-based sanctions are "unabashedly fierce," emphasizing rigorous surveillance and the enforcement of increasingly stringent conditions of supervision (Clear and Hardyman 1990, p. 46). Clear (1994, p. 3) characterizes this growth in these levels of punishment as a "penal harm" movement justified by both a retributive philosophy of inflicting deserved pain on offenders and the utilitarian arguments of deterrence and incapacitation.

It is tempting to portray the penal harm movement as having achieved complete hegemony over correctional policies. To be sure, it is a powerful way of thinking with which few policy makers publicly take issue. Still, penal harm ideology has undermined but not stamped out alternative perspectives. Surveys of the public, for example, reveal that citizens favor early intervention programs over prisons as a solution to crime (Cullen, Wright, Brown, Moon, Blankenship, and Applegate 1998), are willing to use community sanctions as an option instead of incarceration (Turner, Cullen, Sundt, and Applegate 1997), and continue to support rehabilitation as an important goal of corrections (Applegate, Cullen, and Fisher 1997). In accordance, the space still exists for progressive policies to be put forth that challenge the idea that harming offenders is the only, or the best, means of controlling crime.

In this context, restorative justice is emerging as an increasingly popular alternative to penal harm or getting tough. The primary focus of restorative justice is on the ways in which crime disrupts relationships between people within a community (Center for Restorative Justice and Mediation 1996). In its purest form, it is an informal approach to the criminal law that focuses on ways to repair these social relationships (Wilmerding 1997). Thus, it attempts to hold offenders accountable through both shaming and reintegration processes (Braithwaite 1989) in hopes of strengthen-

455

ing community bonds and providing crime victims with an opportunity to regain their personal power (Center for Restorative Justice and Mediation 1996).

Restorative justice is often contrasted with retributive justice. Within a retributive justice framework, sanctions are imposed for the purposes of inflicting pain on the offender that is proportionate to the pain that his or her offense caused to victims and communities (Newman 1978). Within a restorative justice framework, this goal of punishment for its own sake is replaced with the goal of restoration—of repairing harm and rebuilding relationships (Center for Restorative Justice and Mediation 1996). According to restorative justice advocates, the goal of restoration can only be achieved through programs and practices that extend beyond a singular focus on the offender and that are designed to meet the needs of a variety of criminal justice system clientele, including offenders, victims, and the community (Maloney and Umbreit 1995; Van Ness 1986; Wilmerding 1997).

Notably, restorative justice is not merely a theoretical paradigm but also is now influencing criminal justice policy. A 1997 statutory change in Maryland's Juvenile Causes Act, for example, called for a balanced and restorative approach to juvenile justice (State of Maryland Department of Juvenile Justice 1997). This approach is based on the belief that, in addition to offenders, clients of the juvenile justice system include the victims and communities injured by offenders. Thus, juvenile justice reform in Maryland is aimed at building a comprehensive system that balances three important goals: (1) public safety and community protection, (2) offender accountability, and (3) offender competency and character development. Maryland's vision for the future includes enhanced prevention and early intervention opportunities for at-risk youth and families, a continuum of sanctions for delinquent youth, and an active role for victims and community members in the juvenile justice process.

Similarly, the Vermont Department of Corrections has been restructured to include two primary service tracks: The risk management service track is designed to provide intensive treatment and supervision to high-risk felony offenders and the reparative service track requires low-risk, nonviolent offenders to make reparation to the victim and the community (Dooley 1996). Reparative probation boards have been instituted in the reparative service track as a means of actively involving community members in the justice process (Dooley 1996). These boards consist of five citizen-volunteers from the offender's respective community who are responsible for meeting with the offender to develop a reparative agreement that requires the offender to (1) restore and make whole the victim(s) of his or her crime, (2) make amends to the community, (3) learn about the impact of the crime, and (4) learn ways to avoid reoffending (Walther and Perry 1997).

Maryland's balanced and restorative approach to juvenile justice and Vermont's reparative service boards are just two examples of a robust restorative justice movement. By the end of 1995, 24 states had adopted or were considering juvenile statutes and procedures that reflected the restorative justice concept (Freivalds 1996). Furthermore, there has been a proliferation of programs designed to address victims' needs, including victim notification, restitution, and victim-offender mediation (VOM) programs. VOM programs have been implemented in more than 1,000 communities in North America and Europe (Umbreit, Coates, and Roberts 1997). VOMs bring victims and offenders together in the presence of a trained mediator to negotiate an agreement for the payment of restitution or for other methods of repairing the harm caused by the crime (Umbreit 1994). Although these programs are narrow in scope, they reflect the general principles of restorative justice, which hold offenders accountable for repairing harm to victims and value victims' perspectives as to how the harm is best repaired (Center for Restorative Justice and Mediation 1996).

According to Bazemore (1994), this widespread acceptance of restorative justice can be attributed to its underlying values, which provide common ground for parties who have historically disagreed about criminal justice policy. Conservatives and liberals alike support the emphasis on addressing the needs of crime victims and holding offenders accountable for the harm they cause (Clear 1994; Zehr 1990). Liberals, however, are most attracted to restorative justice because of its potentially humanistic and balanced approach to justice. Restorative justice moves away from a state-centered definition of crime to a definition that accounts for the injuries suffered by victims and communities (Van Ness 1986). Thus, rather than blaming or punishing the offender through incarceration, it focuses on repairing the harm done to victims and communities through a process of negotiation, mediation, victim empowerment, and reparation (Bazemore and Maloney 1994). In its ideal form, restorative justice balances the need to hold offenders accountable for their wrongdoing with the need for their acceptance and reintegration into the community (Braithwaite 1989; Zehr 1990). It broadens the focus of justice from offender-oriented penal harm to community-oriented peacemaking and only considers justice to be achieved when the suffering of offenders, victims, and communities has ended and crime has been reduced (Pepinsky and Quinney 1991). For all of these reasons, progressives are casting skepticism aside and readily accepting restorative justice as a viable alternative to the get tough policies now in place.

Restorative justice appeals to conservatives for different reasons. Conservatives see restorative justice as an extension of the victims' rights movement that seeks to involve victims in the criminal justice process and to compensate victims for the losses incurred from crime (Schafer 1976; Van Ness and Strong 1997). Rather than the balanced approach to justice advocated by liberal proponents, conservatives endorse restorative justice as a means of securing more justice for victims. In so doing, they often attempt to increase the punishment of offenders at the expense of restoration.

In the middle of these conflicting perspectives, restorative justice is trying to find a place in correctional policy. The question remains whether, as liberal advocates believe, restorative justice ultimately will prove to be a truly progressive reform. This article addresses this question through a critical analysis of the restorative justice movement. Two central issues are explored. First, commentators have pointed out that correctional reforms implemented with good intentions often have been corrupted to serve less admirable goals and interests (see, e.g., Cullen and Gilbert 1982; Rothman 1980). Thus, despite its benevolent possibilities, will restorative justice programs be corrupted and have untoward, unanticipated consequences? Second, given the current knowledge about changing offender behavior, there is little reason to conclude that restorative justice can have a meaningful effect on recidivism. This latter issue is critical given that a perceived failure to reduce recidivism contributed to the decline of rehabilitation and boosted the legitimacy of punitive correctional policies in recent years (Cullen and Gilbert 1982; Hahn 1998). Although not fully dismissing the potential of restorative justice, we believe that there is danger in the impetuous adoption of this model without further examination of these issues and more rigorous research on restorative justice outcomes.

The Corruption of Benevolence?

In the 1970s, many liberals joined with conservatives in rejecting rehabilitation and in endorsing reforms, especially determinate sentencing, that constrained the dis-

cretion exercised by criminal justice officials. Believing that these reforms would
result in increased justice (e.g., equity in
sentencing decisions), liberals largely overlooked the possibility that their strange bed-
fellows—conservatives—would use the
rejection of the rehabilitative ideal as a
means to achieve their goal of getting tough
on offenders. In hindsight, it now appears
that the liberals' benevolent hopes of doing
justice were corrupted by conservatives
who succeeded in passing harsh laws that
ultimately increased the punishment of and
harm done to offenders (Cullen and Gilbert
1982; Griset 1991).

In endorsing restorative justice, liberals
once again are embracing a reform also
being trumpeted by conservatives. In doing
so, it seems prudent to consider the lesson
of the antirehabilitation movement: Progressive sentiments are no guarantee that
reforms will not be corrupted and serve
punitive ends. In this context, this section
explores four potential unanticipated consequences of restorative justice: (1) it will
serve as a means of getting tough on offenders; (2) it will not be restorative for victims,
offenders, or communities; (3) it will be
more of a symbolic than a substantive
reform; and (4) it will reinforce existing
race and class biases besetting the criminal
justice system.

Getting Tough Through Restorative Justice

According to progressive advocates,
restorative justice policies offer potential
benefits to offenders, including the opportunity to reconcile with their victims, a
more lenient sentence, and the chance for
reintegration into society. It remains to be
seen, however, whether conservatives will
endorse these goals and work with liberals
to create a balanced reform or whether they
will use restorative justice as yet another
opportunity to impose more punishment on
offenders. Six considerations suggest that

the restorative justice movement may not
achieve its progressive goals and, in fact,
may increase the extent and harshness of
criminal sanctions.

First, Brown (1994) notes that restorative
justice systems lack the due process
protections and procedural safeguards that
are awarded to offenders in the more formal
adversarial system. Although programs
vary, counsel are generally discouraged
from attending mediation hearings because
they create barriers for a smooth mediation
process. Furthermore, the informality of
the system contributes to more lenient rules
of evidence. Information presented at conferences also can be used in a formal trial if
the offender fails to reach an agreement
with the victim during mediation. Restorative justice advocates believe that the cost
of diminished offender rights is outweighed
by the benefits of accountability (Berzins
and Prashaw 1997; Van Ness 1986). Brown
(1994) argues, however, that the loss of
rights can result in an offender receiving
more severe punishment than he or she
would receive through the adversarial process.

Second, despite the progressive rhetoric
of restoration, offenders may be coerced
into participating in the mediation process
because of perceived threats of a harsher
punishment if they refuse to do so (Brown
1994; Van Ness and Strong 1997). According to Brown (1994), in certain jurisdictions, prosecutors and judges can consider
offenders' refusal to participate in VOM
conferences in their charging and sentencing decisions. The problem of coercion can
be exacerbated if people who normally
would not be subjected to state controls
through the formal criminal justice process
are coerced into participating in restorative
justice programming.

Third and relatedly, restorative justice
programs can potentially widen the net of
social control (Bazemore and Umbreit
1995; Umbreit and Zehr 1996; Van Ness and
Strong 1997). The increased influence that
the community has in sanctioning can lead

restorative justice programs to target offenders who commit minor offenses and are at a low risk of reoffending. For example, market research in Vermont revealed that citizens wanted the criminal justice system to take minor offenses more seriously (Walther and Perry 1997). Thus, instead of diverting offenders from intrusive forms of punishment (e.g., electronic monitoring, intensive supervision probation, incarceration), restorative justice may place more control over the lives of nonserious offenders who may have otherwise received no formal supervision.

Fourth, Bazemore and Umbreit (1995) contend that if broad changes do not take place to make the system restorative, then restorative justice sanctions will likely increase the supervisory requirements that offenders must satisfy. A survey of offenders participating in Vermont's Reparative Probation Program revealed that offenders perceived the program to be much more demanding than regular probation (Walther and Perry 1997). Furthermore, it was discovered that contrary to the program's design, offenders were subjected to both reparative conditions and traditional probation supervision. Until a complete paradigm shift has occurred, restorative justice policies will potentially inflict additional punishment on offenders.

Fifth, as conditions of probation expand through restorative justice programs, the potential that offenders will not meet these conditions also increases. This higher level of noncompliance, combined with heightened public scrutiny and a demand for offender accountability, will likely result in the revocation of more offenders. Other community corrections reforms have experienced a similar phenomenon. For example, the closer surveillance of offenders in intensive supervision programs has led to the increased detection of technical violations (Cullen, Wright, and Applegate 1996). Because of an emphasis on stringent responses to noncompliance, detected violations in these programs have often been

followed by the revocation of probation and incarceration (Petersilia and Turner 1993). Thus, restorative justice programs may not only increase social control within the community but may also result in more offenders being sent to prison because they fail to comply with the additional sanctions imposed within the restorative justice framework.

According to Braithwaite and Mugford (1994), one strategy to circumvent this problem is to provide offenders with the opportunity to have multiple conferences when they fail to fulfill the requirements of their mediation agreements. Still, if the victim-offender agreements reached at conferences are to be meaningful, limits will have to be placed on how many repeated conferences there can be before an offender must be held accountable in criminal court and risk incarceration. Even if offenders are not incarcerated for failing to comply with the mediation agreement, they will face an escalating number of conditions. Net-widening and revocation for technical violations are the likely result.

Sixth, restorative justice may increase punishment if reforms fail to develop policies and programs that are able to reintegrate offenders into society. Karp (1998) notes, however, that shaming penalties are gaining popularity because they can fulfill the retributive aims of the public. Lawrence (1991) also sees a danger in advocating shaming activities. He suggests that they may be wrongly interpreted as a revival of support for public shaming practices, such as the ducking stool and the scarlet letter, without an emphasis on the reintegrative element of community acceptance and support.

In summary, although restorative justice policies are being advocated as a benevolent means of addressing the crime problem, they may increase the punitiveness of the social control imposed on offenders in several ways: offenders may lose certain rights and privileges that are granted through the current adversarial process, offenders may be coerced into participating in restorative justice programs because of formal pressures from practitioners within the criminal justice system, restorative justice may widen the net of social control by targeting low risk offenders, offenders may be subjected to greater levels of supervision, offenders may have a greater likelihood of incarceration for technical violations because of the increased probation conditions and scrutiny they face, and, finally, restorative justice programs may not achieve their goal of offender reintegration and therefore fail to restore fully the harmed relationships that result from the crime. This propensity for getting tough with restorative justice creates doubt about the restorative capacities of current practices.

Restoration extends far beyond the popular conception of repaying victims for their monetary losses. It involves making victims whole again, reintegrating offenders back into the community, and strengthening community bonds (Center for Restorative Justice and Mediation 1996; Van Ness and Strong 1997; Zehr 1990). Several methods have been developed to accomplish the goal of restoration. The following sections of this article will analyze the potential of these methods for restoring victims, offenders, and communities.

Are Programs Restorative for Victims?

Making victims whole again involves redressing their monetary losses, giving them a voice in the justice process, and reducing their fears regarding future victimization (Center for Restorative Justice and Mediation 1996). Several methods have been developed to restore the victims of crime. Restitution is the oldest and most familiar method of victim restoration (American Probation and Parole Association [APPA] 1994). In addition to redressing victims' monetary losses, restitution offers a means of restoring the relationship between the victim and the offender (Galaway 1977). It provides one of the few tangible ways to compensate crime victims.

Other popular methods of victim restoration include VOM programs, family-group conferences, and various forms of community-sentencing panels—all of which bring offenders, victims, and/or communities together to resolve the conflict created by crime. Research suggests that these programs have some restorative value. Evaluations of VOMs have revealed high rates of victim and offender satisfaction with resulting reparative agreements (Marshall 1992; Niemeyer and Shichor 1996; Umbreit 1994; Umbreit et al. 1997), perceptions of fair treatment (Umbreit et al. 1997), reduced fear and anxiety among crime victims, and an increased likelihood of offenders completing the restitution agreement (Umbreit 1994). Victims participating in family-group conferences have stated that the conferences provided them with a voice in the justice process, an improved understanding as to why the crime occurred, and a chance to assess the likelihood of recidivism (Maxwell and Morris 1997). Clearly, the potential exists for achieving victim restoration. Several considerations, however, may limit the restorative capacities of current victim-oriented programs.

The limits of restitution. Although restitution provides a concrete method to compensate crime victims, there are limits on the extent to which victims are fully restored. First, according to Ferns (1994), it is the victim's perspective regarding the extent of losses that must be considered when assessing whether restitution occurs. Because the financial losses experienced by a victim may exceed those stipulated for by court orders, full monetary restoration may not be achieved (APPA 1994). Even if the victim receives financial satisfaction, if the offender remains hostile toward the victim, the latter may remain emotionally dissatisfied and not be restored (Brookes 1998). Second, although all states have made some type of provisions for victim restitution, much of the restitution ordered by the court is never collected (Seymour 1996). Third, the common practice of using an intermediary to collect restitution from offenders and disburse it to crime victims (APPA 1994) would appear to limit the degree to which a relationship between the two parties is either understood or repaired.

Limits to victim-offender conferencing. Marshall (1992) suggests that the effectiveness of mediation programs depends on the involved parties being open and active during the resolution process, using the mediation to solve problems rather than to assign blame, and ensuring that the needs of all parties are heard. This implies, first and foremost, that the parties must be present and, second, that the mediator, victim, and offender possess the competencies needed for a successful mediation.

Research indicates that the rate at which offenders and victims participate in victim-offender conferences is influenced by several factors. One factor is the type of crime involved: Studies have found that victims and offenders are most likely to appear at mediations for minor personal and property crimes and least likely to appear for serious personal crimes (Niemeyer and Shichor 1996; Umbreit 1994). Another factor is the nature of the victim-offender relationship; absent a continuing relationship with the offender, the victim may be less inclined to participate (Lindner 1996). Finally, according to Maxwell and Morris (1997), many victims do not attend family-group conferences because they are not invited or are not given adequate notice. Seymour (1996) suggests that regardless of the reason, victims too often are left out of the restorative justice equation, which limits the extent to which restoration can be achieved.

Even if victims and offenders do make it to the "restorative justice table" (Seymour 1996), what evidence would indicate that community members, offenders, and victims possess the requisite skills for an effective mediation? Often, community volunteers are responsible for facilitating mediations (Dooley 1996; Ruddell 1996). Although careful screening and training are important safeguards, it is questionable whether citizen volunteers have the capacity to effectively mediate conflict between a potentially emotional victim and a resistant offender. Walther and Perry (1997) found that Vermont's reparative board members were reluctant to involve victims in the mediation process. They speculated that this reluctance stemmed from a lack of knowledge about how to deal with victims' emotions or from a fear that victims will view the board meetings as a forum for seeking retribution.

Victims and offenders may be equally unprepared for mediation. Lindner (1996) has suggested that a face-to-face meeting with the offender could be traumatic for the victim rather than restorative. Furthermore, Maxwell and Morris (1997) found that about 25 percent of the victims participating in family-group conferences reported feeling worse after attending a conference because of their personal inability to express themselves adequately, the offender's lack of sincerity, and the family's inability to make reparation. Given these findings, it appears that inadequate attention to the competencies required for effective mediation can potentially undermine the goal of victim restoration.

Are Programs Restorative for Offenders?

As indicated previously, restorative justice practices emphasize the importance of holding offenders responsible for restoring victims of crime. Another commonly stated objective, however, is to ensure that offenders entering the criminal justice system exit the system more capable of being responsible and productive citizens (Center for Restorative Justice and Mediation 1996; Maloney, Romig, and Armstrong 1998; Zehr 1990). This objective is achieved, it is argued, by teaching offenders right from wrong through various corrective techniques and through their reintegration into the community.

Corrective techniques. Restorative justice advocates suggest that, when rooted in a restorative justice philosophy, restitution and community service can serve corrective purposes for offenders by helping them to recognize the harm that they caused to victims (Bazemore and Maloney 1994; Galaway 1977; Lawrence 1991). Berzins and Prashaw (1997), however, question the degree to which this corrective aspect of restorative justice programs can be achieved within the existing adversarial justice system. For example, the majority of criminal cases are resolved through a guilty plea process that lessens the severity of the charge and encourages the offender to evade responsibility for the real damage done to victims and communities (Center for Restorative Justice and Mediation 1996). The goal of offender correction also may be undermined by the retributive nature of many restitution and community service programs (Shapiro 1990). Within a retributive model, the goal of offender correction is likely to be displaced by the goal of offender compliance. If so, offenders may identify themselves as "victims of the justice system" and identify the victims as "privileged avengers" (Brookes 1998).

Reintegration. Restorative justice recognizes the need to ensure that offenders are given the opportunity for forgiveness after they have been held responsible for their actions (Van Ness 1986). According to Braithwaite (1989), effective "reintegrative shaming" requires the expression of disapproval for the purpose of invoking remorse, followed by gestures of forgiveness designed to accept the offender back into the community. Absent community acceptance and opportunities for change, offenders may be stigmatized, encouraged to participate in criminal subcultures, and become reinvolved in criminal activity (Braithwaite 1989). Thus, successful reinte-

gration requires changes in the offender and in the community. Consistent with this view, Byrne (1986) suggests that a primary role for probation and parole officers should be to work with communities in an effort to increase acceptance, support, and opportunities for offenders. Similarly, Clear (1996) argues for a movement toward a "corrections of place" that broadens the role of corrections beyond the supervision of offenders to organizing community groups and developing crime prevention strategies.

This community focus, however, is potentially problematic. Similar to attempts to implement community policing, this revised focus would alter the contemporary roles and responsibilities of corrections personnel and thus would require major changes in agency operations, including the decentralization of activities and facilities, new training, and revised schedules (Community Policing Consortium 1994). Given the resource constraints currently experienced by community corrections, these changes would be difficult to achieve. Although community corrections agencies are responsible for supervising 75 percent of the correctional population, they only receive one tenth of every dollar spent on corrections (Petersilia 1996). Officers typically are burdened with unmanageable caseloads and struggle to keep up with current supervisory responsibilities. Facing these realities, how can probation officers be expected to expand their role to include community mobilization?

Aside from various corrective techniques and reintegration, the role of rehabilitation in offender restoration is seldom discussed by restorative justice proponents. If rehabilitative programming is incorporated into reparative agreements, it is often done so as an afterthought rather than as a carefully conceived plan for addressing the factors that contribute to an offender's criminal behavior. This shortcoming will ultimately affect the degree to which communities can be restored through restorative justice practices.

Are Programs Restorative for Communities?

Community restoration involves strengthening community bonds in a way that minimizes fear of crime and fortifies informal social controls (Center for Restorative Justice and Mediation 1996; Pranis 1996). Practices designed to restore communities range from community service projects by offenders to grassroots approaches that engage citizens in collective action against crime (Pranis 1996).

Community service by offenders provides the community with the tangible benefit of work and offers much needed resources to the government and to other nonprofit service organizations (Maloney and Umbreit 1995; Van Ness 1986). Engaging offenders in community service also may improve public safety by limiting offenders' opportunities for crime (Maloney and Umbreit 1995) and by developing skills and attitudes conducive to prosocial behaviors. Although a worthy starting point, a simple program of community service cannot begin to achieve true community restoration. Putney (1997) thus argues for a broader grassroots approach to restorative justice that engages communities in owning and resolving problems that reintegrates offenders and that establishes lines of mutual accountability.

The effectiveness of both narrow and broad restorative methods is bounded, however, by two factors: the degree of community interest in participating in restorative justice initiatives and the range of opportunities available to offenders (e.g., social programs, employment, education). Organizing and maintaining community involvement has been cited as one of the most perplexing implementation problems faced by community policing programs (Grinc 1994). Studies of crime prevention programs suggest that neighborhood organizations are difficult to sustain in disadvantaged communities (Garafalo and McLeod 1986; Silloway and McPherson 1985; Skogan 1990, 1996). Skogan (1996)

contends that in these communities, crime and fear stimulate withdrawal from community life and limit the ability to collectively respond to local problems. Furthermore, Currie (1985, 1998) argues that without government policies that invest in poverty-stricken communities by providing support in the form of welfare, health care, and early childhood intervention programs, piecemeal restorative justice practices are not likely to reverse the structural inequality that contributes to crime. Based on the difficulties associated with changing community characteristics, community restoration appears to be a utopian goal within the restorative justice framework.

Substantive or Symbolic Reform?

Zehr (1990) contends that a paradigm shift occurs when reformers are frustrated by an existing model's inability to solve a problem. He argues that the retributive justice system is failing to solve the crime problem and needs to be replaced by programs that are better able to address issues of crime. The question remains whether the reforms that are being put forth as restorative are part of a true paradigm shift that is redefining the crime problem and responses to it or whether they are symbolic reforms that simply rename components of the current retributive justice paradigm. Three key issues are integral to determining whether an agency will achieve substantive or symbolic reform.

First, the substance of restorative justice reforms depends on the degree of staff commitment to a new philosophy of justice. Dooley (1996) recognized that the success of Vermont's Reparative Probation Boards was hindered by staff resistance to philosophical changes and subsequent changes in operations. Second, even if the staff is committed to restorative justice goals, to move toward these goals, staff members must be willing to change their roles from that of service provider to community justice facilitator (Bazemore and Day 1996).

This alteration in job orientations has been difficult to achieve (Bazemore and Day 1996). For example, most community corrections agencies have had difficulty getting staff to focus on restoring victims of crime (Bazemore 1994). Immarigeon and Daly (1997) caution "that it is naive to suppose that restorative justice processes and outcomes will entirely replace those of traditional criminal justice in the foreseeable future" (p. 16). Third, organizations must secure sufficient human and financial resources to operate quality programs that are capable of achieving restoration.

The resource and organizational obstacles faced by agencies may create incentives to abandon substantive reform and merely to label current sanctioning schemes as restorative while retaining their retributive focus. The appeal of resorting to such a euphemism may be heightened because programs with restorative aims are better able to gain public support (Colson and Van Ness 1989). In the end, symbolic reform may accrue the desired organizational benefits without having to tackle the challenges of substantive reform.

Race and Class Effects

Despite their progressive underpinnings, restorative justice programs may have unintended class and racial biases that work to the disadvantage of poor and minority offenders. First, advocates have given little thought to how the quality and harshness of restorative justice will vary by the economic status of communities. Although speculative at this point, it is likely that affluent communities will have the resources to develop programs that are more integrative because they offer a greater number of quality services to offenders.

Second, within the restorative justice process, might affluent offenders be treated more favorably? In victim-offender mediation conferences, for example, it is possible that offenders who are more educated, better dressed, and more skilled verbally will negotiate more favorable sanctions. It is instructive that mediators in VOM programs tend to be White, male, and better educated—traits that may converge with those of more affluent offenders (Walther and Perry 1997). More generally, the informal, individualized nature of restorative justice provides few guarantees that racial and class inequities will be easily detected.

Third, there may be class and thus racial differences in the ability of offenders to meet the conditions of restorative sanctions and therefore to avoid harsher penalties, including the revocation of probation. The most obvious example is the requirement of providing victims with restitution—a common feature of restorative sanctions—which may be difficult for disadvantaged offenders to fulfill (Hahn 1998). On a broader level, however, it seems likely that affluent offenders will be more able to draw on family supports (e.g., private drug treatment, parental monitoring) to meet the conditions imposed by restorative sanctions. If so, then larger inequalities in society are likely to be reproduced within the framework of restorative justice.

In summary, restorative justice remains an unproved movement that risks failure and perhaps does more harm than good. Its attractiveness lies more in its humanistic sentiments than in any empirical evidence of its effectiveness. Evaluating restorative justice becomes further complicated when the issue of recidivism is considered. Bazemore and Day (1996) argue that a true assessment of restorative justice programs must involve more than examining how well they reduce recidivism. Although this may be so, the survival of a correctional philosophy is influenced by its ostensible ability to control crime (as the popularity of the get tough movement amply shows). Thus, the next section of this article will evaluate the capacity for restorative justice policies to decrease offender recidivism based on the growing body of literature about what works to change offender behaviors.

Changing the Offender Behavior: The Utilitarian Challenge

Many correctional reforms over the past 20 years have developed in response to correctional crises and political pressures rather than from a careful evaluation of policy options and empirical evidence of effectiveness (Cochran 1992). In fact, the very argument that contributed to the demise of rehabilitation—that it failed to reduce recidivism and protect public safety—has been all but ignored in recent progressive reforms. Instead, liberals have tried to promote reforms that promised to reduce the use of incarceration and to advance the legal rights granted to offenders. Whatever the value of these reforms, the result has been that correctional policy has largely been forfeited to conservatives who boldly claim that crime can be reduced by locking up more offenders (Cullen, Van Voorhis, and Sundt 1996). By failing to critically evaluate the capacity for restorative justice practices to lower crime, liberal advocates are in danger of experiencing another setback in their quest for a more progressive system of justice.

Restorative justice proponents, either explicitly or implicitly, argue that crime can be lessened through restorative practices. Pranis (1996) asserts that programs rooted in a restorative justice philosophy decrease crime by strengthening community bonds and enhancing informal mechanisms of social control. Braithwaite (1989) argues that the reintegrative aspect of restorative justice policies reduces recidivism by allowing an offender to remain a part of society and to avoid the criminal subcultures and the labeling process that perpetuate delinquency. Still others claim that specific restorative justice programs have the capacity to change offender behavior. For example, it is argued that victim-offender mediation can facilitate changes in offenders' behavior by forcing them to recognize the harm that their criminal behavior causes to victims and communities (Ruddell 1996; Umbreit 1994). Bazemore and Maloney (1994) suggest that community service would be more rehabilitative in nature if it was guided by a restorative justice philosophy.

These claims, however, seem more based on wishful thinking than on a systematic understanding of how to change the conduct of offenders. Although programs with a restorative orientation may occasionally reduce recidivism (see, e.g., Umbreit 1994), the current knowledge base on offender change would suggest that restorative interventions are likely to have effects on recidivism that are modest, if not inconsequential. In the following section, we elaborate this point by assessing the extent to which restorative programs have features that coincide with the principles of effective treatment.

Effective Correctional Interventions

Since 1975, an abundance of literature reviews and meta-analyses have examined the effectiveness of various correctional interventions (Palmer 1992). There is an increasing consensus that programs that achieve a reduction in recidivism share common features (Andrews, Zinger, Hoge, Bonta, Gendreau, and Cullen 1990; Gendreau and Andrews 1990; Izzo and Ross 1990; Lipsey and Wilson 1998). These characteristics, often referred to as "the principles of effective intervention," are summarized briefly below (Andrews, Zinger, et al. 1990; Gendreau 1996; Gendreau and Andrews 1990).

Three principles of effective intervention address the importance of matching offenders to services based on their risk, need, and personal characteristics (Andrews and Bonta 1994; Andrews, Bonta, and Hoge 1990). The risk principle suggests that levels of service should be matched to the risk level of the offender (Andrews and Bonta 1994). This principle is based on several studies that have found that intensive services are necessary to achieve a significant reduction in recidivism among high-risk offenders, but that when applied to low-risk offenders, intensive services have a minimal or positive effect on recidivism (Andrews, Bonta, et al. 1990). This latter phenomenon has been called an interaction effect in which additional efforts to intervene with low-risk offenders actually increase recidivism (Clear and Hardyman 1990; Neithercutt and Gottfredson 1974).

The need principle suggests that changes in recidivism are dependent on changes in the criminogenic needs of offenders (Andrews and Bonta 1994). Criminogenic needs are dynamic factors that are potentially changeable and that are associated with recidivism, such as antisocial attitudes, substance abuse, poor family communication, and antisocial peer associations (Andrews and Bonta 1990). Thus, when these factors are reduced, there is a decreased likelihood of recidivism. The responsivity principle suggests that in addition to matching services with an offender's risks and needs, the learning styles and personality characteristics of offenders can influence treatment effectiveness (Andrews and Bonta 1990; Van Voorhis 1997). For example, high anxiety offenders do not generally respond well to confrontation (Warren 1983), whereas offenders with below-average intellectual abilities do not respond to cognitive skills programs as well as do offenders with above average intellectual abilities (Fabiano, Porporino, and Robinson 1991).

In addition to the above-mentioned principles relevant to offender treatment matching, effective interventions are rooted in behavioral or cognitive-behavioral models of treatment (Clements 1988; Gendreau 1996; Izzo and Ross 1990; Palmer 1996). According to Gendreau (1996), well designed behavioral programs combine a system of reinforcement with modeling by the treatment provider to teach and motivate offenders to perform prosocial behaviors. Cognitive-behavioral models are designed to enhance perspective taking, interpersonal problem solving, and self-control techniques so as to improve offenders' responses to their environments and stressful situations (Clements 1988).

The most effective interventions possess other similar characteristics. First, they occupy 40 percent to 70 percent of high-risk offenders' time (Gendreau 1996). Second, they last at least 23 weeks (Lipsey and Wilson 1998). Third, they employ service providers who relate to offenders in interpersonally sensitive and constructive ways and who are trained and supervised appropriately. Fourth, they use relapse prevention techniques to monitor and to anticipate problem situations and to train offenders to rehearse alternative behaviors. Last, effective interventions link offenders to other services in the community that are relevant to their needs.

Meta-analyses of correctional interventions have found that programs that meet these principles are achieving, on average, a recidivism reduction of 50 percent (Andrews, Zinger, et al. 1990). Interventions that depart from these principles have a dismal success rate. For example, a meta-analysis of studies on punishment and deterrence-based programs, such as intensive supervision, boot camp, Scared Straight programs, and electronic monitoring programs, revealed that these strategies produced slight increases in recidivism (Gendreau, Fulton, and Goggin forthcoming; Gendreau and Little 1993; see also Lipsey and Wilson 1998). Given the increasing knowledge base on what works to change offender behavior, to what extent can we expect restorative justice programs to reduce recidivism? In addressing this question, the next section will examine the degree to which restorative justice programs reflect these principles.

Assessing Restorative Justice Programs

As currently implemented, most restorative justice programs fail to incorporate the principles of effective intervention, particularly as they relate to the risk, need, and responsivity principles. In restorative justice, the primary criterion for matching sanctions to offenders is the nature and extent of the harm caused by the crime. The seriousness of the offense, however, is not consistently related to an offender's risk of recidivism (Correctional Service Canada 1989; Goldkamp and Gottfredson 1985). Thus, restorative justice programs run the dual risks of producing an interaction effect in low-risk offenders and of underservicing high-risk offenders.

Traditionally, restorative justice programs have targeted low-risk nonviolent offenders for participation (Dooley 1996; Ruddell 1996). These offenders typically are unlikely to recidivate. If subjected to unnecessary sanctions and services, however, their chances for noncompliance, and hence revocation, are increased (Clear and Hardyman 1990). The opposite problems exist for high-risk offenders who increasingly are being included in restorative justice programs. Given research findings that suggest that intensive services are required to reduce recidivism among high-risk offenders, it is unlikely that, for example, a one-hour victim-offender mediation session will lessen criminal propensities among these offenders. Thus, the restorative approach runs the risk of becoming the progressives' equivalent of conservative Scared Straight programs, which attempt to shock youth into positive behavior by subjecting them to an afternoon in prison (Finckenauer 1982).

It is also highly unlikely that restorative justice programs will, as currently implemented, produce lasting changes in an offender's criminogenic needs. As discussed previously, restorative justice programs are currently implemented in a piecemeal fashion and are focused primarily on victim restoration. The only criminogenic need that is even remotely targeted by these practices is lack of empathy or sensitivity to others—a part of many offenders' antisocial values system (Gendreau, Andrews, Goggin, and Chanteloupe 1992). Victim-offender mediation and victim-impact panels are common approaches to developing an offender's empathy toward victims of crime. However,

they lack the behavioral framework and relapse-prevention component needed to reinforce improved attitudes in a manner that leads to internalization and continued improvements. Instead, they provide only short-term confrontations with victims that may result in more punishment for the offender. Furthermore, these victim-oriented programs fail to help offenders make generalizations about how their behavior influences others over the long term or fail to teach offenders alternative ways of behaving.

Findings from a study of a restitution program demonstrate the limitations of restorative justice programs that do not abide by the responsivity principle. Van Voorhis (1985) found that low-maturity offenders, as measured by Kohlberg's stages of moral development, were more likely than high-maturity offenders to view restitution as a means of obtaining a lenient sentence and were significantly less likely to provide restitution to their victims. Thus, restitution does not appear to be a viable mechanism for changing the antisocial attitudes of low-maturity offenders and, more important, for reducing the likelihood of their future criminal behavior.

More generally, meta-analyses conclude that restitution programs have modest, if not weak, effects on recidivism. In a meta-analysis of 10 restitution interventions with serious, noninstitutionalized juvenile offenders, Lipsey and Wilson (1998) found that the mean effect of restitution on recidivism across the studies was .17. Although not inconsequential, this result is modest when compared with behaviorally oriented and individual counseling programs that had an effect size in Lipsey and Wilson's analysis of .43. Even less promising results were found in Gendreau et al.'s (forthcoming) meta-analysis of 16 studies of restitution programs. They found that the mean size of the effect of restitution on recidivism was only .04.

Community service programs also have failed to incorporate the principles of effective intervention. Bazemore and Maloney

(1994) suggest that to achieve the full potential of community service, the assigned activity should "bring the offender and conventional adults together" and "provide for a sense of accomplishment, closure, and community recognition" (p. 30). Programs designed in this manner would provide offenders with the modeling and positive reinforcement that are needed to motivate prosocial behavior. However, because community service has historically been imposed as an additional punishment or condition of probation supervision, little attention has been paid to such treatment goals and related practices. In fact, the image of offenders in bright orange jumpsuits picking up trash on the side of the road suggests that some community service assignments may be stigmatizing. In these instances, the extent to which offenders learn attitudes and skills conducive to prosocial behavior is likely to be limited.

In contrast, victim-impact classes conducted by the California Youth Authority may prove more effective. The primary goal of these classes is to make offenders understand the devastating effects of crime (Seymour 1996). Youth participate in a six-week course that teaches alternative ways to resolve conflict. According to Seymour (1996), the curriculum is an educational model that is culturally sensitive and appropriate for the offenders' age and cognitive development. Although too brief in duration for high-risk offenders, this curriculum appears to include the behavioral and cognitive components required to change offender behavior.

Until more programs operating within the restorative justice framework incorporate the principles of effective intervention, the likelihood of producing reductions in recidivism is limited. This, in turn, will compromise the extent to which other restorative goals can be achieved because victims and communities will continue to suffer from the criminal behavior of these repeat offenders. A truly restorative program will be rooted in empirical evidence on what works in changing offender behavior.

Conclusion: Restorative Justice and Rehabilitation

Restorative justice is increasingly embraced—by criminologists and by policy makers—as an alternative correctional paradigm to the prevailing view that penal harm is the solution to crime. By offering something to everyone—victims, offenders, and the community—restorative justice is, at first glance, seemingly deserving of the excitement that it is generating. Our essay, however, is a cautionary reminder that jumping on this bandwagon may be premature, if not risky. Regardless of the benevolent rhetoric that is often used to describe the goals of restorative justice (e.g., peacemaking, communitarian), there is reason to believe that this paradigm will be corrupted and may do more harm than good.

Our goal, however, is not simply nay-saying. By illuminating potential problem areas, we hope that those implementing restorative justice programs will not oversell the intervention or be blind to its dangers. We also recognize that restorative justice potentially avoids a crucial weakness in other progressive policy agendas: the charge that the intervention is a form of entitlement to offenders. This problem is readily seen in the traditionally progressive approach of rehabilitation. Given the principle of less eligibility, any provision of treatment services to offenders is open to attack because such social welfare is undeserved. In contrast, restorative justice demands a certain level of accountability from offenders. Their reintegration depends on their willingness to make efforts to restore victims and the community. Accordingly, the paradigm moves away from entitlement to the principle of social exchange.

As noted, however, a fundamental weakness of restorative justice is its failure to provide a plausible blueprint for how to control crime. This failure is critical because the substantial hegemony of the penal harm or get tough movement has been due to the compelling promise that this strategy will protect society by locking up as many wicked people as possible. In contrast, restorative justice provides few answers for how to deal with serious and persistent offenders. It is especially disturbing that advocates of restorative justice have ignored the research on the behavioral change of offenders in favor of the hope—based on a new and unproved criminological theory—that brief interludes of public shaming will change deeply rooted criminal predispositions. No progressive policy agenda will take hold, we argue, unless citizens are convinced that it will not jeopardize their safety. The failure to control crime inevitably will lead to a new round of penal harm.

Although a marriage may prove uneasy, an alternative approach is to explore bringing together the ideals of restorative justice and rehabilitation. If rehabilitation were seen as part of a process that held offenders accountable and tried to restore victims (e.g., through public service, working to pay victim restitution), then it would be less vulnerable to the criticism that it is only concerned with the welfare of offenders. Alternatively, if restorative justice embraced the logic and knowledge of the rehabilitative ideal, it would have a scientifically informed approach of how to change offenders' behavior. In short, restorative justice transforms rehabilitation from an entitlement or welfare paradigm to an accountability paradigm, whereas rehabilitation transforms restorative justice from a paradigm that speculates in questionable ways about changing offenders to one that can be the conduit through which effective services can be transmitted.

Merging these two correctional paradigms undoubtedly would be a daunting task and would not obviate the need to address other problems relating to these two paradigms. Even so, the dual concepts of restoration and rehabilitation are powerful ideas that can challenge the view that harming offenders is the only and best solution to crime. It is instructive that the public continues to support rehabilitation as an important goal of corrections (Applegate et al. 1997), and it seems likely that this support would increase if offenders, as part of their correctional service, were working to restore victims and the community. In short, beyond pure altruism or benevolent sentiments, why should citizens want to invest in or do good for offenders? One potentially compelling and progressive answer is that doing so will allow offenders to restore those that they have harmed and will make them less likely to harm again.

Study Questions

1. What is *restorative justice*, and why is it being advocated by so many?

2. In what ways can restorative justice be another way to "get tough" with offenders?

3. According to Levrant et al., what are some of the limitations to restorative justice programs?

4. How can we evaluate the effectiveness of restorative justice programs?

5. According to Levrant and her colleagues, why will it be difficult to implement a restorative justice model in the current correctional system?

References

American Probation and Parole Association (APPA). 1994. *A Guide to Enhancing Victim Services Within Probation and Parole*. Lexington, KY: American Probation and Parole Association.

Andrews, D. A. and James Bonta. 1994. *The Psychology of Criminal Conduct*. Cincinnati, OH: Anderson.

Andrews, D. A., James Bonta, and Robert D. Hoge. 1990. "Classification for Effective Rehabilitation: Rediscovering Psychology." *Criminal Justice and Behavior* 17:19–52.

Andrews, D. A., Ivan Zinger, Robert D. Hoge, James Bonta, Paul Gendreau, and Francis T. Cullen. 1990. "Does Correctional Treatment Work? Clinically Relevant and Psychologically Informed Meta-Analysis." *Criminology* 28:369–404.

Applegate, Brandon K., Francis T. Cullen, and Bonnie S. Fisher. 1997. "Public Support for Correctional Treatment: The Continuing Appeal of the Rehabilitative Ideal." *The Prison Journal* 77:237–258.

Bazemore, Gordon. 1994. "Developing a Victim Orientation for Community Corrections: A Restorative Justice Paradigm and a Balanced Mission." *Perspectives* Special Issue:19–25.

Bazemore, Gordon and Susan E. Day. 1996. "Restoring the Balance: Juvenile and Community Justice." *Juvenile Justice* 3:3–14.

Bazemore, Gordon and Dennis Maloney. 1994. "Rehabilitating Community Service: Toward Restorative Service Sanctions in a Balanced Justice System." *Federal Probation* 58 (1):24–35.

Bazemore, Gordon and Mark Umbreit. 1995. "Rethinking the Sanctioning Function in Juvenile Court: Retributive or Restorative Responses to Youth Crime." *Crime & Delinquency* 41:296–316.

Berzins, Lorraine and Rick Prashaw. 1997. "A New Imagination for Justice and Corrections." *The ICCA Journal of Community Corrections* 8 (2):22–25.

Braithwaite, John. 1989. *Crime, Shame and Reintegration*. New York: Cambridge University Press.

Braithwaite, John and Stephen Mugford. 1994. "Conditions of Successful Reintegration Ceremonies: Dealing With Juvenile Offenders." *British Journal of Criminology* 2034:139–171.

Brookes, Derek R. 1998. "Evaluating Restorative Justice Programs." *Humanity and Society* 22: 23–37.

Brown, Jennifer G. 1994. "The Use of Mediation to Resolve Criminal Cases: A Procedural Critique." *Emory Law Journal* 43:1247–1309.

Byrne, James M. 1986. "Reintegrating the Concept of Community Into Community-Based Corrections." *Crime & Delinquency* 35:471–499.

Center for Restorative Justice and Mediation. 1996. *Restorative Justice: For Victims, Communities, and Offenders*. Minneapolis: University of Minnesota, Center for Restorative Justice and Mediation.

Clear, Todd R. 1994. *Harm in American Penology: Offenders, Victims, and Their Communities*. Albany: State University of New York Press.

——. 1996. "Toward a Corrections of 'Place': The Challenge of 'Community' in Corrections." *National Institute of Justice Journal* (August):52–56.

Clear, Todd R. and Patricia Hardyman. 1990. "The New Intensive Supervision Movement." *Crime & Delinquency* 36:42–60.

Clements, Carl. 1988. "Delinquency Prevention and Treatment: A Community-Centered Perspective." *Criminal Justice and Behavior* 15: 286–305.

Cochran, Donald. 1992. "The Long Road From Policy Development to Real Change in Sanctioning Practice." Pp. 307–318 in *Smart Sentencing: The Emergence of Intermediate Sanctions*, edited by J. Byre, A. Lurigio, and J. Petersilia. Newbury Park, CA: Sage.

Colson, Charles W. and Daniel W. Van Ness. 1989. *Convicted New Hope for Ending America's Crime Crisis*. Westchester, IL: Crossway.

Community Policing Consortium. 1994. *Understanding Community Policing: A Framework for Action*. Washington, DC: U.S. Department of Justice, Bureau of Justice Assistance.

Correctional Service Canada. 1989. "What Does Type of Offense Tell Us About Recidivism?" *Forum on Corrections Research* 1(2):3–4.

Cullen, Francis T. and Karen E. Gilbert. 1982. *Reaffirming Rehabilitation*. Cincinnati, OH: Anderson.

Cullen, Francis T., Patricia Van Voorhis, and Jodie L. Sundt. 1996. "Prisons in Crisis: The American Experience." Pp. 21–52 in *Prisons 2000: An International Perspective on the Current State and Future of Imprisonment*, edited by R. Matthews and P. Francis. New York: St. Martin's.

Cullen, Francis T., John P. Wright, and Brandon K. Applegate. 1996. "Control in the Community: The Limits of Reform?" Pp. 69–116 in *Choosing Correctional Interventions That Work: Defining the Demand and Evaluating the Supply*, edited by A. T. Harland. Newbury Park, CA: Sage.

Cullen, Francis T., John P. Wright, Shayna Brown, Melissa Moon, Michael B. Blankenship, and Brandon K. Applegate. 1998. "Public Support for Early Intervention Programs: Implications for a Progressive Policy Agenda." *Crime & Delinquency* 44:187–204.

Currie, Elliott. 1985. *Confronting Crime: An American Challenge*. New York: Pantheon.

——. 1998. *Crime and Punishment in America*. New York: Metropolitan.

Dooley, Michael J. 1996. "Reparative Probation Boards." Pp. 185–192 in *Restoring Hope Through Community Partnerships: The Real Deal in Crime Control*, edited by B. Fulton. Lexington, KY: American Probation and Parole Association.

Fabiano, Elizabeth, Frank Porporino, and Dave Robinson. 1991. "Canada's Cognitive Skills Program Corrects Offenders' Faulty Thinking." *Corrections Today* 53 (August): 102–108.

Ferns, Ray. 1994. "Restorative Case Management: The Evolution of Correctional Case Management." *Perspectives* 18 (Summer):36–41.

Finckenauer, James O. 1982. *Scared Straight! and the Panacea Phenomenon*. Englewood Cliffs, NJ: Prentice Hall.

Freivalds, Peter. 1996. "Balanced and Restorative Justice Project." Office of Juvenile Justice and Delinquency Prevention Fact Sheet (July).

Galaway, Burt. 1977. "Restitution as an Integrative Punishment." Pp. 341–347 in *Assessing the Criminal: Restitution, Retribution, and the Legal Process*, edited by R. E. Barnett and H. Hagel III. Cambridge, MA: Ballinger.

Garafalo, James and Maureen McLeod. 1986. "Improving the Effectiveness and Utilization of Neighborhood Watch Programs." Presented to the National Institute of Justice from the Hindelang Criminal Justice Research Center, State University of New York at Albany.

Gendreau, Paul. 1996. "The Principles of Effective Intervention With Offenders." Pp. 117–130 in *Choosing Correctional Options That Work*, edited by A. T. Harland. Thousand Oaks, CA: Sage.

Gendreau, Paul and D. A. Andrews. 1990. "Tertiary Prevention: What the Meta-Analyses of the Offender Treatment Literature Tell Us About What Works." *Canadian Journal of Criminology* 32:173–184.

Gendreau, Paul, D. A. Andrews, Claire Goggin, and Francoise Chanteloupe. 1992. "The Development of Clinical and Policy Guidelines for the Prediction of Criminal Behavior in Criminal Justice Settings." Department of Psychology, University of New Brunswick, St. John. Unpublished manuscript.

Gendreau, Paul, Betsy Fulton, and Claire Goggin. Forthcoming. "Intensive Supervision in Probation and Parole Settings." In *Handbook of Offender Assessment and Treatment*, edited by C. R. Hollin. Chichester, UK: Wiley.

Gendreau, Paul and Tracy Little. 1993. "A Meta-Analysis of the Effectiveness of Sanctions on Offender Recidivism." Department of Psychology, University of New Brunswick, St. John. Unpublished manuscript.

Goldkamp, John and Michael Gottfredson. 1985. *Policy Guidelines for Bail: An Experiment in Court Reform*. Philadelphia: Temple University.

Grinc, Randolph M. 1994. " 'Angels in Marble': Problems in Stimulating Community Involvement in Community Policing." *Crime & Delinquency* 40:442.

Griset, Pamala L. 1991. *Determinate Sentencing: The Promise and the Reality of Retributive Justice*. Albany: State University of New York Press.

Hahn, Paul H. 1998. *Emerging Criminal Justice: Three Pillars for a Proactive Justice System*. Thousand Oaks, CA: Sage.

Immarigeon, Russ and Kathleen Daly. 1997. "Restorative Justice: Origins, Practices, Contexts, and Challenges." *The ICCA Journal on Community Corrections* 8 (2):13–19.

Izzo, Rhena and Robert Ross. 1990. "Meta-Analysis of Rehabilitation Programs for Juvenile Delinquents: A Brief Report." *Criminal Justice and Behavior* 17:134–142.

Karp, David R. 1998. "The Judicial and Judicious Use of Shame Penalties." *Crime & Delinquency* 44:277–294.

Lawrence, Richard. 1991. "Reexamining Community Corrections Models." *Crime & Delinquency* 37:449–464.

Lindner, Charles. 1996. "VORP: An Unproven Fringe Movement." *Perspectives* 20 (Winter): 15–17.

Lipsey, Mark and David Wilson. 1998. "Effective Intervention for Serious Juvenile Offenders: A Synthesis of Research." Pp. 313–345 in *Serious and Violent Juvenile Offenders: Risk Factors and Successful Interventions*, edited by R. Loeber and D. P Farrington. Thousand Oaks, CA: Sage.

Maloney, Dennis, Dennis Romig, and Troy Armstrong. 1998. *Juvenile Probation: The Balanced Approach*. Reno, NV: National Council of Juvenile and Family Court Judges.

Maloney, Dennis and Mark Umbreit. 1995. "Managing Change: Toward a Balanced and Restorative Justice Model." *Perspectives* 19 (2):43–46.

Marshall, Tony F. 1992. "Restorative Justice on Trial in Britain." Pp. 15–28 in *Restorative Justice on Trial: Pitfalls and Potentials of Victim-Offender Mediation—Internatinal Research Perspectives*, edited by H. Messmer and H. U. Otto. Boston: Kluwer.

Maxwell, Gabrielle and Allison Morris. 1997. "Family Group Conferences and Restorative Justice." *The ICCA Journal on Community Corrections* 8 (2):37–40.

Neithercutt, Michael G. and Don M. Gottfredson. 1974. *Caseload Size Variation and Differences in Probation/Parole Performance*. Washington, DC: National Center for Juvenile Justice.

Newman, Graeme. 1978. *The Punishment Response*. Philadelphia: J. B. Lippincott.

Niemeyer, Mark and David Shichor. 1996. "A Preliminary Study of a Large Victim/Offender Reconciliation Program." *Federal Probation* 60 (3):30–34.

Palmer, Ted. 1992. *The Re-Emergence of Correctional Intervention*. Newbury Park, CA: Sage.

——. 1996. "Programmatic and Nonprogrammatic Aspects of Successful Intervention." Pp. 131–182 in *Choosing Correctional Options That Work*, edited by A. T. Harland. Thousand Oaks, CA: Sage.

Pepinsky, Harold and Richard Quinney, eds. 1991. *Criminology as Peacemaking*. Bloomington: Indiana University Press.

Petersilia, Joan. 1996. "A Crime Control Rationale for Reinvesting in Community Corrections." *Perspectives* 20 (2):21–29.

Petersilia, Joan and Susan Turner. 1993. "Evaluating Intensive Supervision Probation/Parole: Results of Nationwide Experiment." *Research in Brief*, National Institute of Justice, Washington, DC.

Pranis, Kay. 1996. "A Hometown Approach to Restorative Justice." *State Government News* 39 (9):14–16.

Putney, Bart. 1997. "A Grassroots Approach to Restorative Justice." *The ICCA Journal on Community Corrections* 8 (2):20–21.

Rothman, David J. 1980. *Conscience and Convenience: The Asylum and Its Alternatives in Progressive America*. Boston: Little, Brown.

Ruddell, Regina. 1996. "Victim Offender Reconciliation Program." Pp. 171–172 in *Restoring Hope Through Community Partnerships: The Real Deal in Crime Control*, edited by B. Fulton.

Lexington, KY: American Probation and Parole Association.

Schafer, Stephen. 1976. "The Victim and Correctional Theory: Integrating Victim Reparation With Offender Rehabilitation." Pp. 227–236 in *Criminal Justice and the Victim*, edited by W. F. McDonald. Beverly Hills, CA: Sage.

Seymour, Anne. 1996. "Putting Victims First." *State Government News* 39 (9):24–25.

Shapiro, Carol. 1990. "Is Restitution Legislation the Chameleon of the Victims' Movement." Pp. 73–80 in *Criminal Justice, Restitution, and Reconciliation*, edited by B. Galaway and J. Hudson. Money, NJ: Willow Tree Press.

Silloway, Glenn and Marlys McPherson. 1985. "The Limits to Citizen Participation in a Government Sponsored Community Crime Prevention Program." Presented at the annual meeting of the American Society of Criminology, San Diego, CA.

Skogan, Wesley G. 1990. *Disorder and Decline: Crime and the Spiral of Decay in Urban Neighborhoods*. Berkeley: University of California Press.

——. 1996. "The Community's Role in Community Policing." *National Institute of Justice Journal* (August):31–34.

State of Maryland Department of Juvenile Justice. 1997. *A Comprehensive Strategy for Balanced and Restorative Justice*. Baltimore: State of Maryland Department of Juvenile Justice.

Turner, Michael G., Francis T. Cullen, Jodie L. Sundt, and Brandon K. Applegate. 1997. "Public Tolerance for Community-Based Sanctions." *The Prison Journal* 77:6–26.

Umbreit, Mark S. 1994. "Victim Empowerment Through Mediation: The Impact of Victim Offender Mediation in Four Cities." *Perspectives* Special Issue:25–30.

Umbreit, Mark S., Robert Coates, and Ann W. Roberts. 1997. "Cross-National Impact of Restorative Justice Through Mediation and Dialogue." *The ICCA Journal on Community Corrections* 8 (2):46–50.

Umbreit, Mark and Howard Zehr. 1996. "Restorative Family Group Conferences: Differing Models and Guidelines for Practice." *Federal Probation* 60 (3):24–29.

Van Ness, Daniel W. 1986. *Crime and Its Victims*. Downers Grove, IL: InterVarsity Press.

Van Ness, Daniel W. and Karen H. Strong. 1997. *Restoring Justice*. Cincinnati, OH: Anderson.

Van Voorhis, Patricia. 1985. "Restitution Outcome and Probationer's Assessments of Restitution: The Effects of Moral Development." *Criminal Justice and Behavior* 12:259–287.

——. 1997. "Correctional Classification and the 'Responivity Principle'." *Forum on Corrections Research* 209 (1):46–50.

Walther, Lynne and John Perry. 1997. "The Vermont Reparative Probation Program." *The ICCA Journal on Community Corrections* 8 (2): 26–34.

Warren, Marguerite. 1983. "Application of Interpersonal Maturity Theory to Offender Populations." Pp. 23–49 in *Personality Theory, Moral Development, and Criminal Behavior*, edited by W. Laufer and J. Day. Lexington, MA: Lexington Books.

Wilmerding, John. 1997. "Healing Lives, Mending Society." *Quaker Abolitionist* 3 (2):4–5.

Zehr, Howard. 1990. *Changing Lenses*. Scottdale, PA: Herald Press.

36
Dollars and Sentences

Legislators' Views on Prisons, Punishments, and the Budget Crisis

Vera Institute of Justice

For more than 30 years, correctional policy in the United States has centered on "getting tough" with offenders. Many policy makers and legislators enacted punitive practices at a time when budgets were flush and funding competing programs was relatively easy. As the prison population has soared, however, so have the costs. Many states, now faced with tough decisions about what programs to fund, are often finding themselves reexamining some of the sentencing laws that have led to record incarceration rates. In this article, nine legislators from around the country come together to discuss their views, how their states are responding, and the sometimes different ways they are dealing with the choices that have to be made.

Introduction

On the final day of February 2003, nine state legislators from around the country sat down around a table at the Denver offices of the National Conference of State Legislatures with a common agenda. These men and women—representatives and senators; Republicans and Democrats; Midwesterners, Easterners, Southerners, and Westerners had been carefully selected by NCSL and the Vera Institute of Justice not only for

their manifest diversity but also for what they shared. As legislative leaders responsible for criminal justice, all had an abiding interest in the future of corrections within the severe budgetary storms that were raging across their home states and the nation.

By any measure, the conditions that prompted the meeting were critical. For the second year in a row, a faltering economy and declining stock markets were shrinking state revenues. At the same time, new homeland security costs, increases in health spending, and unfunded federal mandates such as the No Child Left Behind Act were increasing expenditures. And the problems seemed to be getting worse by the day. Only a month earlier, in January, an NCSL survey showed that even though an aggregate $49.1 billion shortfall had been addressed at the outset of the fiscal year, two-thirds of the 50 states would need to find an additional $26 billion in savings by June.[1] Worse, for fiscal year 2004, beginning in July in most states, forecasters envisioned an even larger budgetary shortfall of at least $68.5 billion (by April, that figure would be boosted to $78.4 billion).[2] With the third straight year of budget shortfalls looming and most of the easy cuts already enacted, services once considered untouchable were falling prey to legislators desperate for additional savings.

Criminal justice spending—and in particular the costs associated with corrections—presented one of the most difficult dilemmas in almost every state. The last decade of the twentieth century and the first years of the new millennium had been a period of significant growth for most state prison systems. From 1990 to 1999, aggregate state spending on corrections rose from $17.2 billion to almost $35 billion.[3] During roughly the same period, from 1990 to mid-year 2002, state prison populations almost doubled from nearly 685,000 to more than 1.2 million.[4] This unprecedented period of growth had been fueled by "tough on crime" policies, including abolition of parole, lengthier sentences for violent crimes, and mandatory minimum sentences for many drug offenses. These policies had been enacted in response to public concerns about crime and largely paid for by the longest uninterrupted expansion of the U.S. economy in post-War history. But by 2000 many of the conditions that made the growth possible had begun to change: crime rates had been in decline for several years; fears about public safety had diminished, and the clouds of economic recession had begun to form over statehouses.

The legislators gathered in Denver—four judiciary chairs, one corrections chair, and four others with substantial experience on judiciary, appropriations, or criminal justice committees—knew that the budgets of corrections agencies were facing severe cuts. Stop-gap measures such as reducing staff through furloughs and hiring freezes, closing or delaying construction of prisons, or eliminating educational, vocational, and substance abuse programs had already yielded some savings. But with the system stretched to its limit—at the end of 2001, most state prisons were operating anywhere from 1 percent to 16 percent above capacity—the next wave of reductions would be especially painful.[5]

"Your first reaction is just sheer blind panic as you realize the magnitude of what you've got to do," said Texas Representative Ray Allen, who was facing a state deficit perhaps as large as $14 billion and a mandate to find $172 million in corrections savings by June as well as an additional $525 million (12 percent of the corrections budget) for the coming biennium. Although none of the other participants confronted a deficit the size of Texas', they all were grappling with similar problems. For their mutual benefit—as well as for the benefit of other legislators facing the same challenges—the nine were asked to share their experience and their expectations in a roundtable discussion about the ongoing financial maelstrom, their own states' response, and the likely impact on the future of corrections.

A Catalyst for Change

The roundtable members were selected in part because their diverse perspectives promised a wide-ranging discussion. It soon became evident, however, that as a result of the crisis, many were either in unfamiliar circumstances or reconsidering long-standing positions. Some, like Nebraska Senator Dwite Pedersen, whose advocacy of work-release options in lieu of prison used to leave him at odds with what he called the "punitive good old boy club," reported suddenly finding a warmer reception for their ideas. "The budget shortfall brought great credibility to what I've been trying to do since I've been in the legislature," he said. Idaho Senator Denton Darrington, who described himself as one of those "good old boys" was on the other end of the spectrum. While determined to stand by his record— "Good time will not be on the table as long as I'm chairman of the Judiciary and Rules Committee"—Darrington acknowledged that he was likely to make some concessions in the area of substance abuse treatment for offenders, even at the risk of being labeled "soft on crime." "I can stand it because I haven't had that label much," he noted.

These comments suggested an across-the-board trend toward rehabilitative policies, but the details of the conversation revealed a far more complex situation. For while many of the proposals that arose emphasized the provision of services to reduce offender recidivism, they often shared another characteristic that had its own distinct appeal: over time these programs can cost less money. As an illustration of this confluence, consider Connecticut's decision in 2001 to lift mandatory minimum sentences for drug-related offenses. According to Representative Michael Lawlor, crime maps drawn up during the debate showed that state laws requiring mandatory minimums for drug offenses committed within 1,500 feet of schools, day care centers, or public housing projects effectively blanketed the entire metropolitan areas of the largest cities. In New Haven, only the Yale University Golf Course, a marsh and landfill, and a city park surrounding a sewage treatment facility were exempt. "When people saw that, we began to understand how we weren't really targeting serious offenders, we were basically targeting everybody in an urban area," Lawlor recalled. The laws were ultimately reformed because many people wanted to correct this unintended consequence and be fairer toward urban offenders. Lawlor noted, however, that some victims' rights advocates also supported the change because they recognized that keeping small-time urban drug offenders in jail longer diverted money that might be spent incarcerating violent criminals.

Most of the roundtable participants agreed that the budget crisis—aided by the waning politicization of corrections policies—had created a unique climate in which rehabilitative and fiscal agendas appeared to be coalescing within the same proposals. The result was a window of opportunity that Rep. Allen called the "silver lining" in the budget cloud. "In Texas we've had 100 years of a very deeply held mindset that is punitive in nature," he explained. "Nothing short of a 10 to 15 billion dollar crisis would even get people to discuss any alternatives, because we've always done it this way and we've done it bigger, and tougher, and meaner than anybody else in the country." Senator Donald Cravins of Louisiana, who began arguing for change well before the budget crisis hit, also saw a "bright side" to the crisis. "It will cause us to do better with what we've got."

Doing better with incarceration policy, according to the legislators, came in two basic forms. The first included relatively minor adjustments to practices or procedures. These were designed to eke out whatever savings or cost avoidances had been missed by earlier reductions in corrections budgets. The second included more ambitious attempts to change fundamental structures—and, in some cases, tenets—of

sentencing and incarceration policy to build what some saw as new efficiencies, as well as what others considered new rationality, into state criminal justice systems.

Modest Suggestions

Within the first group, there was plenty of discussion of initiatives that, if enacted, would amount to little more than tinkering around the edges of the problem. These proposals are worth noting because they illustrate how far states are willing to look to find savings. A conspicuous example came from Texas, where extreme necessity was proving the mother of invention. This large border state was eyeing ways to shift costs associated with re-arrested Mexican nationals to the federal government, contending that such detentions are necessary only because federal agents fail to patrol the borders effectively. "If they're going to be incarcerated and held, they ought to be held in a federal prison, not a state one," said Rep. Allen.

Many of these minor suggestions represent attempts to correct unintended consequences of existing legislation or policies. Connecticut statutes that prohibit former felons from doing many kinds of work caught the attention of Rep. Lawlor. "You can't work in a nursing home, you can't drive a school bus, you can't work in any kind of school system, you can't have any kind of public safety-related job. And the list gets longer all the time," he said. By making it harder to find employment, Lawlor said, these restrictions increase the risk of recidivism—which adds to corrections costs. "I'm not saying we should encourage convicted felons to be working in hospitals. I'm just saying that maybe that rule needs a little bit more flexibility." Representative Jari Askins of Oklahoma described a similar dysfunction in her state's prisons. A Department of Corrections official had recently complained to her that a single infraction as minor as smoking a cigarette could demote inmates from the least-restrictive of four levels of confinement to the most-restrictive level and decrease the likelihood of an earlier release. "We need to implement an intermediate sanction there," she said.

Substantive Changes

The second group—farther-reaching substantive changes—generated the most provocative discussion among the legislators. This is partially because even though the participants often focused on the details of policy, the conversation was really about how states are beginning to redefine their structural and philosophical approaches to corrections policy. The risks and rewards of this enterprise—implicating issues of economics, politics, fairness, and public safety—appeared never to be far from their minds.

The proposals that emerged from this conversation could themselves be divided into subgroups. The first were ideas that were important strictly because they would affect lots of people and save substantial amounts of money. Others were noteworthy for how far they departed from the dominant priorities of the past 20 years. Both categories, however, were distinguished by their ambition and interest in fundamental structural change.

Texas provided an example of an initiative that was significant according to the first subcategory. Noting that privatizing prison operations was "one of the few things we can do that actually saves money," Rep. Allen announced that his state was contemplating "a considerable—perhaps even shocking—amount of privatization." Should this come to pass, it would represent a dramatic expansion of an existing policy. During the first six months of 2002, the number of Texas inmates in private facilities actually dropped from 16,331, to 10,764, leaving the proportion of the state's inmate population in private prisons at 6.8 percent, only slightly ahead of the national rate for state and federal inmates, 6.1 percent.[6]

Two other proposals, from Texas and Louisiana, dealing with the emerging issue of geriatric and compassionate release, illustrate the latter subgroup. Because several states already operate release programs for elderly or ill inmates, Texas' proposal to parole offenders in a coma does not represent a conspicuously new direction of thought. (Because the state had only two such inmates at the time of the roundtable, it didn't promise great savings either.) But a similar initiative from Louisiana to make parole available to approximately 250 inmates who have completed 40 to 50 years of a life sentence for heroin possession is significant. For even though it, too, promises a modest overall financial impact, the Louisiana proposal marks a dramatic change from the past decade's insistence on "truth in sentencing," where offenders whose crimes are seen as serious are understood to serve a certain amount of the sentence imposed—often 85 percent—without possibility of early release.

Most of the ideas that legislators thought could best help states weather the budgetary storm were high scorers in both categories: they promised to affect many people, and they substantially departed from the popular trends of the previous two decades, when mandatory minimum sentences, three-strikes legislation, and truth-in-sentencing laws yielded a 281 percent increase in the nation's incarcerated populations and a 601 percent increase in expenditures for state and local corrections.[7]

Reducing Prison Time. One structural change the participants debated was the effort by some states to reduce offenders' lengths of stay in prison by adjusting sentencing mechanisms. Michigan, for example, was among the many states that enacted mandatory minimum sentencing laws during the latter half of the twentieth century, beginning with its 1978 legislation requiring life in prison without parole for offenders found guilty of delivering more than 650 grams of heroin or cocaine. These laws satisfied public clamor for harsher consequences, but they also increased prison populations—and attendant costs. Representative Bill McConico pointed out that on the day after the roundtable, the state would relax these mandatory minimum laws substantially when three bills he introduced went into effect. The new statutes replaced many of the state's harshest minimum sentences with sentencing guidelines and substituted a standard five-year probation for obligatory lifetime probation for the lowest-level drug offenders. The *Detroit News* estimated that these changes could save the state $41 million in 2003 alone.[8] Louisiana offered a dramatic example of mandatory minimum sentencing reform too. According to Sen. Cravins, the state began dismantling mandatory minimum sentences before the budget crisis even hit, when he helped to pass legislation that granted judges greater sentencing discretion for about 30 nonviolent, mostly drug, offenses.

Oregon, on the other hand, was unlikely to address minimum sentence requirements, according to Representative Floyd Prozanski. Since 1994, when voters approved a stiff mandatory minimum sentencing initiative known as Measure II, prison populations had grown from about 8,500 to 12,000 inmates. While Prozanski thought legislators would be reluctant to contradict the electorate's will, he said he believed they might try to reduce population pressure by focusing on non-Measure II offenses. "Because of the budget situation, I predict that we will make an attempt to give good time at least for those individuals," he said.

Senator Don Redfern said Iowa was likely to address its financial problems by wrestling with truth-in-sentencing laws, which were enacted to allay fears that good time, early release, and parole were excusing offenders from serving much of their stated sentences. At the time of the roundtable, these laws required offenders to fulfill at least 85 percent of their sentences before becoming eligible for parole. However, a legislative panel that had been specially appointed to investigate cost-cutting options for the coming budget had recommended reducing that percentage, making offenders eligible for parole or work release after serving as little as 50 percent of their sentences.[9] The spirit of the recommendation, if not quite the scale, appealed to Sen. Redfern because it could yield savings without requiring dramatic changes. "Even shortening a term two, three, or four months is going to have a pretty significant impact over at least a couple of year period," he noted. There was very little enthusiasm for early release—often used as a stop-gap measure to free inmates before their sentences are up, frequently without ongoing supervision. Roundtable participants expressed fears of a political backlash should any such former inmate commit a headline-making offense. In contrast, increases in the rate of parole, a procedure that benefits from established, deliberative processes and the promise of supervision after release, garnered cautious support. "I don't think you'll see any mass paroling," said Sen. Cravins, "but I think you will see an escalation of the number of people who will be leaving the system through parole." Indeed, this trend had already begun. Rep. Askins reported that from a low of 8 percent not long ago, the rate of parole granted to eligible offenders in Oklahoma is now closer to 25 percent. In Texas, said Rep. Allen, the rate hovered around 16 percent until "we finally pumped it way up to 25 percent this year." In Michigan, Rep. McConico noted, "our parole board really just refused to let anyone go in the '90s." Now, he says, the rate is close to 40 percent. These increases did not result from statutory changes alone. Political pressure was also a factor. A term-limited governor operating under fewer political constraints facilitated the increase in Oklahoma. In Iowa, parole counselors were explicitly told to "be more aggressive in seeking out and considering people that might be good options for parole," said Sen. Redfern.

Community-Based Responses. Along with their willingness to reduce prison time for certain offenders, the nine legislators expressed—to varying degrees—a complementary interest in developing a continuum of community-based alternatives to prison. Community corrections initiatives that both supervise offenders and require programming in key areas such as education, job training, and alcohol and chemical dependency reflect a growing awareness that one sanction may not fit all offenders, and that money can be saved—and, as some participants noted, perhaps lives improved—by tailoring consequences to fit individual circumstances.

"When most people talk about inmates, they see the word 'inmates' as being a homogenous mass of interchangeable parts," said Rep. Allen. "But there are really many, many sub-populations with many, many different needs." He contended that corrections systems can make meaningful distinctions among such groups as drug addicts, the mentally ill, and young people from dysfunctional families. Allen said he hoped Texas would begin applying this logic to a cohort of 5,400 inmates, many of whom were serving as many as 10 years for offenses involving less than one ounce of cocaine. For 3,700, it is their first offense. "We think they're worth a try in drug court and local sanctions. And if that doesn't work, I'll build a prison bed and put them in it," he said. The Texan justified replacing prison time with up to 180 days in a treatment program followed by dose supervision in aftercare saying, "It is no longer fiscally possible, no matter how conservative you are, to incarcerate people and spend $150,000 each on them when a fraction of that money would probably get them free of their habit and in productive society." Moreover, he added, "Every 19-year-old first-time offender who sleeps in a prison bed in a prison that's full denies me an opportunity to put an armed robber in a bed."

Many of the participants were likewise betting that carefully applying intermediate sanctions to probationers and parolees could reduce the number of technical violators who swell prison rolls. A broader, more nuanced array of responses to choose from whenever an offender breaks the conditions of release—such as curfews, additional check-ins, drug tests, or even the right to send someone to jail for a few days as Oregon's Community Correction Act allows—would reduce the likelihood that the offender will be remanded to prison for minor infractions.

Advocates of these initiatives often characterized them as shifting resources from incarceration to community-based or noncustodial sanctions. As several participants observed, developing such efforts may forestall someone going to prison, such as when a first-time offender is sentenced to drug rehabilitation or a probationer who fails a drug test is remanded to county jail for three days. Sen. Cravins, however, pushed the concept even further, pointing out that a disproportionate amount of crime in Louisiana occurs in a handful of communities. "There are some blocks in New Orleans that cost us $10 million [a year]," he said, referring to the criminal justice costs incurred for offenders who live in these specific areas. Cravins suggested that a truly comprehensive system to reduce criminal justice spending ought to consider investing an equivalent amount in those communities to preempt crime before it happens. "How do we redirect those dollars to try to turn the tide?" he asked.

A Question of Funding

While the idea of creating a coherent graduated system of sanctions that could save money over time had wide appeal, the level of enthusiasm for these measures was tempered by several specific reservations. The most salient of these was whether or not such programs were viable in the current fiscal climate. Just a week before coming to Denver, Rep. McConico had been in a corrections subcommittee meeting discussing new programs when word came that Michigan's governor had just announced across-the-board cuts in education spending. Suddenly, no one had the stomach to pursue new corrections initiatives and the meeting adjourned. "On one hand all these creative ideas are coming at the right time," McConico lamented. "But when you have no money, you have to take from somewhere to do it."

Even existing programs are at risk in the current budget conditions. Sen. Redfern noted, for example, that although Iowa has a strong history in community corrections, most of this programming had already been cut back. "We figure that eight years from now we'd be saving money if we had all these programs, but we just don't have the money [to fund them] today," he said. And, as Sen. Cravins noted, the credibility and effectiveness of programs that are not completely eliminated may be critically compromised if their funding is severely curtailed. "What judge is going to put someone in probation if the caseloads have gone to 150 to 1?" he asked. "What parole officer will not revoke parole if an inmate is on a caseload of 130 to 1?"

A handful of proposals involved schemes to allow programs to pay for themselves. Rep. Allen said that Texas' Prison Industry Enhancement program, which puts inmates to work at prevailing wages, could generate tens of millions of dollars in prison labor. Sen. Pedersen suggested that Nebraska may be able to pay for new programming with money from fees on probation and parole services. In most cases, however, money for existing or new programs must be found in already-tight state resources. Given this grim reality, Rep. Allen observed that the primary challenge for most states is not so much to build new programs but rather "to protect the pieces from the current emergency until we can come back and start putting them together into an orderly whole that we think will have an impact that is greater than we're receiving from just the sum of the parts."

Guaranteeing Results

The other principal reservation raised during the roundtable concerned the effectiveness of these programs. Legislators and citizens want to be sure that initiatives they fund will realize their goals—whether those are reducing drug dependence, say, or preparing inmates for work—without jeopardizing public safety. The question of what programs achieve this balance elicited considerable discussion.

"The thing that changes these people is work," said Sen. Pedersen, who argued that inmates who work are more likely to return to productive life after prison. According to Rep. Allen, work can also be used to improve inmate conduct. "Twenty-five jobs can change the character of a whole institution," he said, referring to a facility in Lockhart, Texas, which he said reported only one major disciplinary case since 1991. "If you have to abide by the rules to be eligible to apply to get hired, 1,000 inmates will change their behavior," he said.

Programs designed to rehabilitate offenders with drug problems inspired the most hope and the most skepticism. Yet despite their ambivalence, many of the legislators felt they had no choice but to pursue this option. "I'm as frustrated as anybody about the ineffectiveness of drug treatment programs," said Rep. Lawlor. "But isn't it fair to ask, what's the effectiveness of all this incarceration? If the goal was to reduce the number of people using or selling drugs, I'm not sure that the incarceration option has been a success either." Rep. Allen defended drug programs on a purely fiscal level. "If you deploy that drug treatment in prison as an added cost, then there may not be a justification for it. But if you deploy that drug treatment on the front end as a treatment program which stops the recidivism of some—even if it's only 20 percent—but serves as a short-term diversion from long-term incarceration, then you have gained something."

Sen. Darrington expressed support for most of these efforts, but he was also an outspoken advocate of effectiveness of a different kind. "With all the treatment that we do," he reminded the others, "with all the diversion we do on the front end, and all the help that we give them on the tail end to get out and get jobs, there has to be a sanction at the end of the day if they violate."

Is the Budget Crisis the Only Thing Driving These Changes?

Rep. McConico recalled that when he introduced his bills to reduce mandatory minimum sentences in Michigan, both the governor and the chair of the senate judiciary committee told reporters they had "no interest in McConico's get-out-of-jail-free bills." Then, after the first conference to estimate the state budget, he was "called into the governor's office to see how we can make these bills happen." The first time Rep. Allen approached corrections administrators for new policy ideas, they were reluctant to talk for fear of losing their jobs. "Then when the director of the corrections system put his cuts on the table, all their jobs were cut anyway," he said. "And so folks started talking about a new vision."

These anecdotes illustrate how the budget crisis has spurred states to rethink their corrections policies. But legislators' willingness to respond to the crisis has been buttressed by a concurrent development in the political climate. Rep. Askins noticed the change in the last elections: for the first time since she was elected to the Oklahoma Legislature in 1994, she said, her polls showed that education and health care were more important issues than crime. A similar shift occurred in Iowa, leading Sen. Redfern to venture that crime was no longer the electoral "wedge issue" it was in the 1980s and 1990s, when Republicans and Democrats tried to outmaneuver each other on public safety. In the current atmosphere, said Idaho's Sen. Darrington, criminal jus-

tice issues were "more partisan from a personal philosophical point of view than Democrat versus Republican."

Several factors contribute to this change. First is a growing awareness among the general public that increases in corrections spending come at the cost of other government spending and services. "Every community, not just the inner cities, is realizing that everything is being cut and they're seeing corrections increasing or staying constant," noted Rep. McConico. Elected officials are taking note. "Whether or not you think everybody in jail deserves to be there, it's another issue when you're weighing that against the stuff that makes you popular, like roads and schools," observed Rep. Lawlor.

While many elected officials are readjusting their positions in response to the new prevailing wind, the roundtable participants noted that many others came into office with it. Michigan, according to Rep. McConico, experienced a "massive turnover" in legislators during the last election. "A lot of the people who were impediments to some of the initiatives that people have been offering for the last 8 to 10 years are no longer there," he said.

Term limits have played a part in this process, of course. In many cases, they helped replace a generation of lawmakers who came of age in the get-tough 1980s and 1990s. But Rep. Prozanski observed a similar effect after the repeal of term limits in Oregon in 2002. Under term limits, he said, individual legislators often took extreme positions and had little incentive to cooperate with others. Now that the limits have been overturned, many Oregon legislators are rediscovering the value of compromise. "We're in a rebirth of long-term relationships," he said. "Partisanship is still there to some point, but I believe its going to continue to get better."

The maturing of victims' rights advocacy groups is also an important development. There are now several crime victims rights organizations in Prozanski's state, split between those seeking more severe punishments and those who are willing to weigh reform initiatives. As noted earlier, Rep. Lawlor was able to ally himself with victims' rights activists in reducing Connecticut's minimum sentences for low-level nonviolent offenders. They "actually supported these changes because they wanted more emphasis on violent crimes against innocent victims," he said.

The spread of illegal drug use has also been a factor in the new political environment. In the 1980s, the public perceived the worst illegal drug problems to be limited to urban areas where crack cocaine was endemic. In contrast, today the growing demand for methamphetamine is, in Sen. Redfern's words, "more in the rural areas than the urban areas." The extent of this problem was illustrated by Sen. Darrington's admission, "In any rural community in my part of the country everybody will know somebody who has had their life destroyed by drugs." As Idaho's case illustrates, illegal drugs have clearly become a local issue all across the nation, compelling many legislators to reconsider their fixed positions on how to respond. "We would not have had this discussion 10 years ago because I don't think there was enough interest," said Sen. Cravins. "The drug epidemic now crosses all lines, which forces us to sit down and talk."

Yet as severe as the drug problem is, Rep. Askins reminded the group that money remains the most fundamental factor in the current reassessment of corrections policy. Oklahomans are angry about drugs, she said, and most of the people she has spoken with about the problem were calling for more of the same—tougher sentences. It is the cash shortage, many noted, that makes such a course impossible and that is forcing the conversation. Faced with an enormous budget deficit, policymakers have little choice but to work together. "We have a Republican governor and a Democratic legislature, and we are definitely on the same page when it comes to figuring out a way to

bring these costs under control without affecting public safety," noted Rep. Lawlor. Rep. Allen said much the same thing when he admitted, "I'm a hardcore conservative back home and I sound like the liberals that I came in to displace."

Looking to the Future

Just as the roundtable participants' views of the current crisis are shaped by their attitudes toward corrections and the situation within their respective states, so too are their visions of the future. Some, like Sen. Darrington of Idaho, expect to "continue along the road" with no substantial changes in corrections policy. "My view is that we will continue to work toward diversion on the front end for your low-level criminal. We'll continue to become more professional with hearing officers and our Commission of Pardons and Parole. We'll continue to try to do more work programs. And I would suggest that what we ought to be doing with treatment is being really quite selective." Others, especially Rep. Allen, anticipated dramatic changes. Texas is "moving pretty rapidly toward a different model," said Allen, predicting a substantially remodeled system in the next decade. "We're still going to have a tough system. It probably will be the toughest of all the 50 states. But we hope that it will at least be tough, plus smart, and perhaps considerably more efficient than it is today."

The roundtable participants recognized that they face a double challenge as they make policy and face elections. If they are to develop smarter sentencing, corrections, and prison policies, they must provide the leadership needed to persuade important constituencies that they know what they are doing.

Much discussion focused on the need to build public support for such changes, particularly after decades of conditioning voters to think about crime policies as either "soft" or "tough." "A lot of us created the mania that exists today because we're the ones who go before the cameras in an election, with a jail door swinging in the background, saying, 'I'll be tough on crime,'" observed Sen. Cravins. "Well, now we have the job of going back to our constituents and saying, 'Yeah, we're going to be tough on crime. But by the same token, let's try to use resources wisely.'" Sen. Redfern concurred: "We're going to have to convince them that the kinds of things we're doing are not going to jeopardize public safety, but make cost-effective sense—plus prepare someone, because most of our prisoners eventually get out."

To build this support, many participants observed, several related issues need to be addressed. Policymakers must overcome public anger about drug abuse that too often precludes rational responses to the problem. They must correct false or exaggerated impressions, such as the idea in Idaho that judges are too soft when, according to Sen. Darrington, they're really quite forceful. Ignorance about the true fiscal costs of corrections policies will also have to be confronted. And advocates of change must parry what Sen. Redfern described as the "degree of cynicism" that looks at reform initiatives and says, "You're only doing that because you're running out of money."

Some of this is already happening, of course. "I make it a big part of my job to go out there and educate the public," said Nebraska's Sen. Pedersen—an assertion any of the others might have made as well. But, as Rep. Askins reminded the others, it's easier to talk about the fine points of corrections policy outside a campaign season. "I'd much rather have the conversation in a coffee shop than try to deal with it in a bullet point in a campaign ad," she said, "because I can at least have the discussion in the coffee shop."

Legislators interested in negotiating changes will also have to educate their colleagues and corrections administrators. Rep. Allen described his own change of mind on these issues, saying, "As I learned about the

reality of the system, I realized that calling for a tougher system was going to be less productive than I had thought." Rep. McConico was able to win public support for his proposals by developing influential support elsewhere. "I went to the people who in the public's mind had the credibility from the starting point," he explained. To combat any impression that his was a partisan initiative, he included Republican colleagues with a background in law enforcement, such as former state troopers and prosecutors. He also courted professional groups like the prosecutors association whose members' inside knowledge and credentials allowed them to see beyond the reductionist dichotomy of tough and soft. "Once the prosecutors and the judges were on board with it, that lent instant credibility. People said, 'Okay, prosecutors are not going to try to put [dangerous] people back on the streets,'" McConico said.

Educating constituents in order to change policies need not be the only kind of outreach, however. Several participants felt that as leaders they also were called on to remind the public that it, too, has a role in alleviating the prison situation. As Sen. Darrington said, "I don't think we're doing a very good job as policymakers of standing up in our respective bodies and going into our communities to say, 'Look, there's a way to avoid the bad food in prison. There's a way to avoid the hard bed. There's a way to avoid the parole board. Don't do the crime.'" Sen. Cravins agreed: "We don't use the bully pulpit at our disposal to tell people about those fundamental things that they have to do as a community. I think at some point in this discussion and debate, whether it's in our respective statehouses or our respective districts, that's going to have to be one of the key roles we play."

Updates

The states represented at the roundtable continue to confront the budget crisis and related criminal justice issues. Following are highlights of actions taken between the date of the roundtable and the publication of this report.

Connecticut

- Approved plans to transfer up to 1,000 inmates to Virginia under an existing contract
- Cut its budget through layoffs, early retirement, and a $6.2 million reduction in alternative programs
- Authorized opening a new 600-bed correctional facility which had been delayed to avoid $3.5 million in costs
- Legislation pending to authorize diversionary programs for technical probation and parole violators, with savings to be invested in community

Idaho

- Imposed a 2 percent surcharge on liquor sales in order to provide a permanent source of funding for drug courts
- Rejected efforts to repeal the state's mandatory minimum sentences for drug offenders and legislation to make more offenders eligible for "good time" release

Iowa

- Lowered from 85 percent to 70 percent the amount of their maximum sentences that inmates must serve under truth-in-sentencing laws before they are eligible for parole
- Aligned penalties for crack and powder cocaine

Louisiana

- Closed the Swanson Correctional Center for Youth–Madison-Parish Unit

- Rejected a plan to create diversionary programming for technical probation and parole violators and reinvest the savings in the community

Michigan

- Approved expansion of the drug court program to create more sites and to include some technical parole violators
- Continued release of prisoners under rollback of most of the state's mandatory minimum requirements for drug offenses

Nebraska

- Established a Community Corrections Council to develop and implement enhanced community corrections, felony sentencing guidelines, and improved data collection and analysis
- Authorized October 2004 closure of one of nine state prisons

Oklahoma

- State Board of Corrections erased a multimillion-dollar budget deficit with $9 million emergency funding, six days of employee furloughs, and $3.9 million in internal cuts, including a hiring freeze
- Rejected a bill to make marijuana possession a misdemeanor rather than a felony

Oregon

- Began releasing jail inmates early after voters rejected a temporary income tax hike that would have provided additional funds
- Legislature passed a $1 billion corrections budget, restoring funding to house low-level felony offenders and open a new 400-bed minimum security facility

Texas

- Legislature approved a budget calling for more than $230 million in corrections cuts
- Passed a bill mandating probation and treatment for certain first-time drug possession offenders
- Legislature defeated a bill for a new agency to oversee the bidding process for running prisons with authority to contract with private companies

Activity in Other States

A number of other jurisdictions have also made changes to their sentencing and incarceration policies to avoid costs and produce better outcomes. As of July 1, these include:

Alabama

- Enacted three bills authorizing voluntary sentencing guidelines, expanding community corrections, and raising the felony theft threshold
- $3 million in new state general funds expected to go to community corrections

Arizona

- Reduced sentences for some drug offenses and channeled the savings to transitional drug treatment services

Colorado

- Created community supervision options for some nonviolent technical parole violators and allowed judges to send some low-level drug offenders to probation, county jail, or community corrections instead of prison

Delaware

- Legislature approved a bill increasing penalties for some violent offenses, reducing mandatory minimum sentences for many drug trafficking and manufacturing crimes, and allowing many drug offenders to be incarcerated at lower levels of supervision
- Legislature shortened probations in an effort to reduce the percentage of technical parole violators returning to prison

Indiana

- Created—but did not fund—a "forensic diversion" program allowing judges to suspend sentences of nonviolent offenders and divert them to treatment when substance abuse or mental illness was a contributing factor in the crime

Kansas

- Authorized diverting first- and second-time nonviolent drug possessors from prison to mandatory treatment
- $6.6 million in state general funds earmarked for building treatment capacity

Missouri

- Reduced the maximum prison sentence for the lowest category of felonies
- Granted nonviolent felons the opportunity to seek release after 120 days in prison and serve the balance of their sentence on probation, parole, or in another court-approved program
- Gave judges discretion to order treatment in lieu of certain prescribed penalties

Washington

- Accelerated implementation of a new sentencing guideline grid for drug offenses that reduces sentences and encourages treatment
- Ended post-release supervision for some nonviolent offenders
- Directed corrections savings to a Criminal Justice Treatment Account to fund treatment

In Addition

- Several states, including Arizona, Indiana, New Mexico, and Wisconsin, authorized or established sentencing commissions or study groups to examine their sentencing and incarceration policies
- Arkansas, Kentucky, Montana, North Dakota, Oklahoma, and Washington all released prisoners before their expected release date in late 2002 or in 2003

Study Questions

1. What is driving this discussion of prison costs, and why now?
2. What are some of the substantive changes that were being discussed?
3. Is the budget the only thing driving these changes?
4. What are some states doing to solve this problem? What is your state doing?

Endnotes

1. National Conference of State Legislatures. *State Budget Gaps Growing at Alarming Rate According to New NCSL National Fiscal Report*, NCSL News (February 4, 2003).
2. Ibid. and National Conference of State Legislatures. *Three Years Later, State Budget Gaps Linger*, NCSL News (April 24, 2003).
3. Sidra Lea Gifford, *Justice Expenditure and Employment Extracts, 1999* (Bureau of Justice Statistics, U.S. Department of Justice, January 8, 2002).
4. Paige M. Harrison and Jennifer Karberg, *Prison and Jail Inmates at Midyear 2002* (Bureau of Justice Statistics, U.S. Department of Justice, April 2003, NCJ 198877).
5. Ibid.
6. Ibid.
7. See *Justice Expenditure and Employment Extracts, 1999* and Sidra Lea Gifford, *Justice Expenditures and Employment in the United States* (Bureau of Justice Statistics, U.S. Department of Justice, 1999 1–4, February 2002).
8. Sinclair, Norman, "Dad of 4, 1,249 other drug prisoners see freedom," *The Detroit News* 1/30/03.
9. Obradovich, Kathie, "Budget-cutting panel advises earlier parole," *Quad City Times* 12/10/02.

Index